ONE GOD, ONE PEOPLE

RESOURCES FOR BIBLICAL STUDY

Editor
Davina C. Lopez, New Testament

Number 104

ONE GOD, ONE PEOPLE

Oneness and Unity in Early Christianity

Edited by
Stephen C. Barton and Andrew J. Byers

Atlanta

Copyright © 2023 by SBL Press

All rights reserved. No part of this work may be reproduced or transmitted in any form or by any means, electronic or mechanical, including photocopying and recording, or by means of any information storage or retrieval system, except as may be expressly permitted by the 1976 Copyright Act or in writing from the publisher. Requests for permission should be addressed in writing to the Rights and Permissions Office, SBL Press, 825 Houston Mill Road, Atlanta, GA 30329 USA.

Library of Congress Control Number: 2023944606

Contents

Abbreviations ix

Introduction: Oneness and Unity in Worlds
Contemporary and Ancient
Andrew J. Byers... 1

Part 1. Oneness and Unity in the Scriptures of Israel

1. One God, One People: Reflections on a Reconciled and
Reconciling Pentateuch
Walter J. Houston 13

2. Is YHWH the God of the Nations as Well? Jonah's Universal
Conception of the Oneness of God
Anna Sieges-Beal...33

Part 2. Oneness and Unity in the Classical World

3. The Politics of Oneness among the Greeks
Lynette Mitchell..51

4. The Politics of Oneness among the Romans
James R. Harrison 75

Part 3. Oneness and Unity in Early Judaism

5. The Qumran *yaḥad*: Aspects of Oneness, Unity, and
Separation in the Dead Sea Scrolls
Carsten Claussen 101

vi   Contents

6. The Number One: Oneness, Unity, and the One God
in Philo of Alexandria
Jutta Leonhardt-Balzer 127

7. Oneness, Unity, and Josephus's Theological Politics
Kylie Crabbe...145

Part 4. Oneness and Unity in the
New Testament and Early Christianity

8. Jesus, the Shema, and Oneness in the Synoptic Gospels:
The Formation of Early Christian Identity
Elizabeth E. Shively and Max Botner..171

9. One Flock, One Shepherd, One God: The Oneness
Motif of John's Gospel
Andrew J. Byers 195

10. One Lord, One People: Kingship and Oneness in Acts
Alan J. Thompson..217

11. Paul on Oneness and Unity in 1 Corinthians
Stephen C. Barton 237

12. One Seed and One God: Divine Oneness and Ecclesial
Unity in Galatians and Romans
Robbie Griggs 259

13. Unity in Christ: Virtue and the Reign of the Good
King in Ephesians and Colossians
Julien C. H. Smith 283

14. Oneness and the Once for All in the Catholic Epistles
and Hebrews
Nicholas J. Moore..301

15. Social Surds and the Crisis of Ecclesial Oneness in 1 Clement
T. J. Lang...321

Contents   vii

16. "I Was Doing My Part, Therefore, as a Man Set on Unity":
Ignatius of Antioch and Unity and Concord in the Church
John-Paul Lotz 341

Contributors 363
Ancient Sources Index 365
Modern Authors Index 394

Abbreviations

Primary Sources

Ab urbe cond.	Livy, *Ab urbe condita*
Abr.	Philo, *De Abrahamo*
Adv. Jud.	Tertullian, *Adversus Judaeos*
Adul. amic.	Plutarch, *Quomodo adulator ab amico internoscatur*
Aen.	Vergil, *Aeneid*
Aet.	Philo, *De aeternitate mundi*/*On the Eternity of the World*
Agr.	Cicero, *De Lege agraria*; Philo, *De agricultura*; Tacitus, *Agricola*
A.J.	Josephus, *Antiquitates judaicae*
Alex.	Plutarch, *Alexander*
Alex. fort.	Plutarch, *De Alexandri magni fortuna aut virtute*
Anab.	Arrian, *Anabasis*
Ann.	Tacitus, *Annales*
Ant. rom.	Dionysius of Halicarnassus, *Antiquitates romanae*
Antid.	Isocrates, *Antidosis* (*Or.* 15)
Apoc.	Seneca, *Apocalyntosis Claudii*/*The Pumpkinification of Claudius*
Apol.	Justin, *Apologia*/*Apology*; Tertullian, *Apologeticus*/*Apology*
Ath. pol.	Aristotle, *Athēnaīn politeia*/*Constitution of Athens*
Att.	Cicero, *Epistulae ad Atticum*
Aug.	Seutonius, *Augustus*
b.	Babylonian Talmud
Bell civ.	Appian, *Bella civilia*
Bell. gall.	Caesar, *Bellum gallicum*/*Gallic War*
Ber.	Berakot

-ix-

B.J.	Josephus, *Bellum judaicum*/*Jewish War*
Cam.	Plutarch, *Camillus*
C. Ap.	Josephus, *Contra Apionem*/*Against Apion*
Carm.	Horace, *Carmina*/*Odes*
Cat.	Cicero, *In Catalinam*/*Against Cataline*
CD	Cairo Genizah copy of the Damascus Document
Cher.	Philo, *De cherubim*/*On the Cherubim*
Civ.	Augustine, *De civitate Dei*/*City of God*
Clem.	Seneca, *De clementia*
Clu.	Cicero, *Pro Cluentio*
Comm. Jo.	Origen, *Commentarii in evangelium Joannis*
Conf.	Philo, *De confusione linguarum*/*On the Confusion of Tongues*
Contempl.	Philo, *De vita contemplativa*/*On the Contemplative Life*
Cor.	Demosthenes, *De corona*/*On the Crown*
Cyr.	Xenophon, *Cyropaedia*
De arch.	Vitruvius, *De architectura*
Decal.	Philo, *De decalogo*/*On the Decalogue*
Demosth.	Dinarchus, *In Demosthenem*/*Against Demosthenes*
Deo	Philo, *De Deo*/*On God*
Did.	Didache
Diatr.	Epictetus, *Diatribai* (*Dissertationes*)
Ebr.	Philo, *De ebrietate*/*On Drunkenness*
Ecl.	Calpurnius Siculus, *Eclogae*; Vergil, *Eclogae*
Ep.	Seneca, *Epistulae morales*
Eph.	Ignatius, *To the Ephesians*
Epigr.	Marital, *Epigramma*/*Epigrams*
Epod.	Horace, *Epodi*/*Epodes*
Eth. nic.	Aristotle, *Ethica nicomachea*/*Nicomachian Ethics*
Evag.	Isocrates, *Evagoras* (*Or. 9*)
Exc.	Clement of Alexandria, *Excerpta ex Theodoto*/*Excerpts from Theodotus*
Fast.	Ovid, *Fasti*
Flacc.	Philo, *In Flaccum*/*Agains Flaccus*
Fug.	Philo, *De fuga et inventione*/*On Flight and Finding*
Geogr.	Strabo, *Geographica*/*Geography*
Georg.	Vergil, *Georgica*
Gig.	Philo, *De gigantibus*/*On Giants*

Abbreviations

Haer.	Irenaeus, *Adversus haereses* (*Elenchos*)/*Against Heresies*
Har. resp.	Cicero, *De haruspicum responso*
Her.	Philo, *Quis rerum divinarum heres sit*/*Who Is the Heir?*
Herm. Vis.	Shepherd of Hermas, Vision(s)
Hist.	Diodorus Siculus, *Historiae*; Herodotus, *Historiae*; Polybius, *Historiae*; Tacitus, *Historiae*
Hist. eccl.	Eusebius, *Historia ecclesiastica*/*Ecclesiastical History*
Hist. rom.	Dio Cassius, *Historiae romanae*
Il.	Homer, *Iliad*
Inv.	Cicero, *De inventione rhetorica*
Ios.	Philo, *De Iosepho*/*On the Life of Joseph*
LAB	Liber antiquitatum biblicarum
Leg.	Cicero, *De legibus*; Philo, *Legum allegoriae*/*Allegorical Interpretation*; Plato, *Leges*/*Laws*
Leg. man.	Cicero, *Pro Lege manilia*
Legat.	Philo, *Legation ad Gaium*/*Embassy to Gaius*
Let. Aris.	Letter of Aristeas
Lysis.	Plutarch, *Lysistrata*
m.	Mishnah
Magn.	Ignatius, *To the Magnesians*
Med.	Marcus Aurelius, *Meditations*
Mem.	Xenophon, *Memorabilia*
Metam.	Ovid, *Metamorphoses*
Mos.	Philo, *De vita Mosis*/*On the Life of Moses*
Mur.	Cicero, *Pro Murena*
Mut.	Philo, *De mutatione nominum*/*On the Change of Names*
Nat.	Pliny the Elder, *Naturalis historia*
Nem.	Pindar, *Nemeonikai*/*Neman Odes*
Nic.	Isocrates, *Nicocles* (*Or.* 3)
Num. Rab.	Numbers Rabbah
Od.	Homer, *Odyssey*
Off.	Cicero, *De officiis*
Ol.	Pindar, *Olympionikai*/*Olympian Odes*
Op.	Hesiod, *Opera et dies*/*Works and Days*
Opif.	Philo, *De opificio mundi*/*On the Creation of the World*
Or.	Aelius Aristides, *Orationes*; Dio Chrysostom, *Orationes*

xii Abbreviations

Pan.	Pliny, *Panegyricus*
Panath.	Isocrates, *Panathanaicus* (*Or.* 12)
Paneg.	Isocrates, *Panegyricus* (*Or.* 4)
Phaedr.	Plato, *Phaedrus*
Phil.	Cicero, *Orationes philippicae*
Phld.	Ignatius, *To the Philadelphians*
Phys.	Aristotle, *Physica/Physics*
Plant.	Philo, *De plantitione/On Planting*
Pol.	Aristotle, *Politica/Politics*
Post.	Philo, *De posteritate Caini/On the Posterity of Cain*
Praec. ger. rei publ.	Plutarch, *Praecepta gerendae rei publicae*
Praem.	Philo, *De praemiis et poenis/On Rewards and Punishments*
Princ. iner.	Plutarch, *Ad principem ineruditum*
Prob.	Philo, *Quod omnis probus liber sit/That Every Good Person Is Free*
Prom.	Aeschylus, *Prometheus vinctus/Prometheus Bound*
Prot.	Plato, *Protagoras*
P.W.	Thucydides, *Peloponnesian War*
QE	Philo, *Questiones et solutiones in Exodum/Questions and Answers on Exodus*
QG	Philo, *Quaestiones et solutiones in Genesin/Questions and Answers on Genesis*
Quint. fratr.	Cicero, *Epistulae ad Quintum fratrem*
Ran.	Aristophanes, *Ranae/Frogs*
Rep.	Cicero, *De republica*
Res gest. divi Aug.	Res Gestae divi Augusti
Resp.	Plato, *Respublica*
Rom.	Ignatius, *To the Romans*
Sacr.	Philo, *De sacrificiis Abelis et Caini/On the Sacrifices of Cain and Abel*
Saec.	Horace, *Carmen saeculare*
Sat.	Petronius, *Satyrica*
Shabb.	Shabbat
Sib. Or.	Sibylline Oracles
Silv.	Statius, *Silvae*
Smyrn.	Ignatius, *To the Smyrnaeans*
Somn.	Philo, *De somniis/On Dreams*
Spec.	Philo, *De specialibus legibus/On the Special Laws*

Abbreviations

Strom.	Clement of Alexandria, *Stromateis/Miscellanies*
Suppl.	Aeschylus, *Supplices/Suppliant Women*
T. Benj.	Testament of Benjamin
T. Dan	Testament of Dan
T. Gad	Testament of Gad
T. Iss.	Testament of Issachar
T. Lev.	Testament of Levi
T. Naph.	Testament of Naphtali
Theaet.	Plato, *Theaetetus*
Theb.	Statius, *Thebais/Thebaid*
Theog.	Hesiod, *Theogonia/Theogony*
Ti. C. Gracch.	Plutarch, *Tiberius et Caius Gracchus*
Tib.	Suetonius, *Tiberius*
Tr.	Ovid, *Tristia*
Trall.	Ignatius, *To the Trallians*
Vesp.	Suetonius, *Vespasianus*
Virt.	Philo, *De virtutibus/On the Virtues*

Secondary Resources

AB	Anchor (Yale) Bible
ABRL	Anchor (Yale) Bible Reference Library
ABR	*Australian Biblical Review*
AGJU	Arbeiten zur Geschichte des antiken Judentums und des Urchristentums
AJEC	Ancient Judaism and Early Christianity
ANRW	Temporini, Hildegard, and Wolfgang Haase, eds. *Aufstieg und Niedergang der römischen Welt: Geschichte und Kultur Roms im Spiegel der neueren Forschung.* Part 2, *Principat.* Berlin: de Gruyter, 1972–.
ATANT	Abhandlungen zur Theologie des Alten und Neuen Testaments
ATD	Das Alte Testament Deutsch
BBET	Beiträge zur biblischen Exegese und Theologie
BCAW	Blackwell Companions to the Ancient World
BCILL	Bibliothèque des cahiers de l'Institute Linguistique de Louvain
BEATAJ	Beiträge zur Erforschung des Alten Testaments und des antiken Judentums

BETL	Bibliotheca Ephemeridum Theologicarum Lovaniensium
BHAW	Blackwell History of the Ancient World
BHQ	Biblia Hebraica Quinta
BHT	Beiträge zur historischen Theologie
Bib	*Biblica*
BibInt	Biblical Interpretation Series
BibSem	Biblical Seminar
BJS	Brown Judaic Studies
BMC	Head, Barclay V., and Reginal Stuart Poole. *Catalogue of the Greek Coins of Ionia*. London: Trustees of the British Museum, 1892.
BMSEC	Baylor-Mohr Siebeck Studies in Early Christianity
BN	*Biblische Notizen*
BNTC	Black's New Testament Commentaries
BTB	*Biblical Theology Bulletin*
BurH	*Buried History*
BWANT	Beiträge zur Wissenschaft vom Alten und Neuen Testament
BZAW	Beihefte zur Zeitschrift für die alttestamentliche Wissenschaft
BZNW	Beihefte zur Zeitschrift für die neutestamentliche Wissenschaft
CBQ	*Catholic Biblical Quarterly*
CC	Continental Commentaries
CIL	*Corpus Inscriptionum Latinarum*. Berlin, 1862–.
CJ	*Classical Journal*
ClQ	*Classical Quarterly*
CRBS	*Currents in Research, Biblical Studies*
CSCO	Corpus Scriptorum Christianorum Orientalium
DK	Diels, Hermann, and Walther Kranz, eds. *Die Fragmente der Vorsokratiker*. 7th ed. Berlin: Weidmann, 1954.
ECL	Early Christianity and Its Literature
EDNT	Balz, Horst, and Gerhard Schneider, eds. *Exegetical Dictionary of the New Testament*. 3 vols. Grand Rapids: Eerdmans, 1990–1993.
EGF	Davies, Malcolm, ed. *Epicorum Graecorum Fragmenta*. Göttingen: Vandenhoeck & Ruprecht, 1988.

	Abbreviations	xv

EGGNT	Exegetical Guide to the Greek New Testament
EKKNT	Evangelisch-katholischer Kommentar zum Neuen Testament
FAT	Forschungen zum Alten Testament
FGrHist	Jacoby, Felix, ed. *Die Fragmente der griechischen Historiker*. 3 vols. Leiden: Brill, 1954–1964.
FJTC	Flavius Josephus: Translation and Commentary
frag(s).	fragment(s)
FRLANT	Forschungen zur Religion und Literatur des Alten und Neuen Testaments
GIBM	Newton, C. T., Edward Lee Hicks, and Gustav Hirschfield, eds. *The Collection of Greek Inscriptions in the British Museum*. 4 vols. Oxford: Clarendon: 1874–1916.
GRBS	*Greek, Roman, and Byzantine Studies*
HBT	*Horizons in Biblical Theology*
HCS	Hellenistic Culture and Society
HDR	Harvard Dissertations in Religion
HNT	Handbuch zum Neuen Testament
HTKNT	Herders theologischer Kommentar zum Neuen Testament
HTR	*Harvard Theological Review*
IBC	Interpretation: A Bible Commentary for Teaching and Preaching
ICC	International Critical Commentary
IG	*Inscriptiones Graecae*. Editio Minor. Berlin: de Gruyter, 1924–.
InvM	Kern, Otto, ed. *Die Inschriften von Magnesia am Maeander*. Berlin: Spemann, 1900.
JAJ	*Journal of Ancient Judaism*
JBL	*Journal of Biblical Literature*
JBLMS	Journal of Biblical Literature Monograph Series
JHebS	*Journal of Hebrew Scriptures*
JHI	*Journal of the History of Ideas*
JHS	*Journal of Hellenic Studies*
JPTSup	Journal of Pentecostal Theology Supplement Series
JQR	*Jewish Quarterly Review*
JR	*Journal of Religion*
JRS	*Journal of Roman Studies*

JSJSup	Journal for the Study of Judaism Supplement
JSNTSup	Journal for the Study of the New Testament Supplement Series
JSOT	*Journal for the Study of the Old Testament*
JSOTSup	Journal for the Study of the Old Testament Supplement Series
JSPSup	Journal for the Study of the Pseudepigrapha Supplement Series
JTI	*Journal of Theological Interpretation*
JTS	*Journal of Theological Studies*
KAV	Kommentar zu den Apostolischen Vätern
KEK	Kritisch-exegetischer Kommentar über das Neue Testament
LCL	Loeb Classical Library
LCM	*Liverpool Classical Monthly*
LIMC	Ackerman, H. Christoph, and Jean-Robert Gisler, eds. *Lexicon Iconographicum Mythologiae Classicae*. 8 vols. Zurich: Artemis, 1981–1997.
LNTS	Library of New Testament Studies
MH	*Museum Helveticum*
Mionnet *Suppl.* 6	Mionnet, Téodore Edme. *Description de médailles antiques, grecques et romaines, avec leur degré de rarite et leur estimation*. Supplement 6. Paris: Testu, 1833.
MnemosyneSup	Mnemosyne Supplements
NIB	Keck, Leander, ed. *New Interpreter's Bible*. 12 vols. Nashville: Abingdon, 1994–2004.
NICNT	New International Commentary on the New Testament
NICOT	New International Commentary on the Old Testament
NovT	*Novum Testamentum*
NovTSup	Supplements to Novum Testamentum
NRTh	*Nouvelle Revue Théologique*
NSBT	New Studies in Biblical Theology
NTL	New Testament Library
NTS	*New Testament Studies*
ÖBS	Österreichische biblische Studien
OGIS	Dittenberger, Wilhelm. *Orientis graeci inscriptiones selectae*. 2 vols. Lipzig: Hirzel, 1903.

Abbreviations xvii

OTP	Charlesworth, James H., ed. *The Old Testament Pseudepigrapha*. 2 vols. ABRL. Garden City, NY: Doubleday, 1983–1985.
par(r).	parallel(s)
PNTC	Pillar New Testament Commentary
PRSt	*Perspectives in Religious Studies*
PTMS	Pittsburgh Theological Monograph Series
PTSDSSP	Princeton Theological Seminary Dead Sea Scrolls Project
QD	Quaestiones disputatae
RB	*Revue biblique*
RBS	Resources for Biblical Study
RelSoc	Religion and Society
RevExp	*Review and Expositor*
RevQ	*Revue de Qumrân*
RIC	Mattingly, Harold, et al. *Roman Imperial Coinage*. London: Spink, 1923–1967, 1984.
SBLDS	Society of Biblical Literature Dissertation Series
SBLMS	Society of Biblical Literature Monograph Series
ScrHier	Scripta Hierosolymitana
SCS	Septuagint and Cognate Studies
SDSS	Studies in the Dead Sea Scrolls and Related Literature
SEG	Supplementum epigraphicum graecum
SIMA	Studies in Mediterranean Archaeology
SJ	Studia Judaica
SJLA	Studies in Judaism in Late Antiquity
SNTSMS	Society for New Testament Studies Monograph Series
SNTSU	Studien zum Neuen Testament und seiner Umwelt
SNTW	Studies of the New Testament and Its World
SP	Sacra Pagina
SPhA	Studies in Philo of Alexandria
SPhiloM	Studia Philonica Monograph Series
STAC	Studien und Texte zu Antike und Christentum/Studies and Texts in Antiquity and Christianity
STDJ	Studies on the Texts of the Desert of Judah
StHell	Studia Hellenistica
SVTG	Septuaginta: Vetus Testamentum Graecum
SVTP	Studia in Veteris Testamenti Pseudepigrapha
SymS	Symposium Series

xviii   Abbreviations

TDNT   Kittel, Gerhard, and Gerhard Friedrich, eds. *Theological Dictionary of the New Testament*. Translated by Geoffrey W. Bromiley. 10 vols. Grand Rapids: Eerdmans, 1964–1976.
TDOT   Botterweck, G. Johannes, Helmer Ringgren, and Heinz-Josef Fabry, eds. *Theological Dictionary of the Old Testament*. Translated by John T. Willis et al. 17 vols. Grand Rapids: Eerdmans, 1974–2021.
TLZ   *Theologische Literaturzeitung*
TPAPA   *Transactions and Proceedings of the American Philological Association*
TSAJ   Texts and Studies in Ancient Judaism
TynBul   *Tyndale Bulletin*
UTB   Uni-Taschenbücher
VC   *Vigiliae Christianae*
VCSup   Supplements to Vigiliae Christianae
VT   *Vetus Testamentum*
VTSup   Supplements to Vetus Testamentum
WBC   Word Biblical Commentary
Weimarer Ausgabe Hermann, Rudolf, Gerhard Ebeling, et al., eds. *D. Martin Luthers Werke*. 120 vols. Weimar, 1883–2009.
WTJ   *Westminster Theological Journal*
WUNT   Wissenschaftliche Unterssuchungen zum Neuen Testament
YCS   *Yale Classical Studies*
ZAC   *Zeitschrift für Antikes Christentum/Journal of Ancient Christianity*
ZBK   Zürcher Bibelkommentare
ZNW   *Zeitschrift für die neutestamentliche Wissenschaft*

Introduction:
Oneness and Unity in
Worlds Contemporary and Ancient

Andrew J. Byers

While pondering how to introduce this volume on oneness and unity in early Christianity and its wider historical contexts, I took time over a lunch break to watch the first debate of the 2020 US presidential election. As an American living in the United Kingdom, the painful longing to be engaged in the political crises of this cultural moment tussled with the relief over my distance from the virulent fray. Yet I was awaiting news on an application for Indefinite Leave to Remain, the right to reside permanently in my host country. Given the anti-immigrant sentiment that gave shape to so many of the policies and guidelines, the waiting was fraught with anxiety. The entire process seems designed to remind applicants that they are outsiders viewed with suspicion. As many immigrants know, to join another society formally requires the negotiation of serious bureaucratic and financial obstacles.

That presidential debate was so disturbing not only because the candidates were slinging ad hominem remarks and persistently interlocked in rhetorical fisticuffs; the most troublesome part of the debate was the reminder of the larger-scale reality that behind the sparring was a society at bitter odds with itself. The candidates openly embraced representative roles, emblematizing a nation coming apart and ostensibly unwilling to seek reconciliation. Further, I was watching the polemics unfold while living in another country that openly criticizes American plans for a border wall yet continues to raise the height of its own walls figuratively through increased immigrations controls. One country has claimed to be "one nation, under God," and the other is hailed as a kingdom "united." The latter had just voted to leave a much larger union, and the one nation

-1-

of "united" states appeared more divided than ever, with the political maps streaked in defiant hues of red and blue.

Maintaining a union, shoring up unity, and defining oneness are not, of course, projects limited to contemporary societies. My reading during the week I watched the presidential debate included Plutarch's *bioi* of Lycurgus and Solon, two ancient Greek leaders who established core institutional and cultural norms for Sparta and Athens, respectively. I also read Augustine's profile of the character and duties of a Christian emperor reflecting the values and aims of a different city, the city of God (*Civ.* 5.24). In my leisure reading, I came across the foreboding remarks of John Adams, the first US vice president, that "there is nothing I dread so much as a division of the Republic into two great parties, each arranged under its leader and converting measures in opposition to each other."[1] I was also reading through the final drafts of the essays included in this book. The coinciding of the 2020 US presidential debate, my anxious waiting to hear about my immigration status, and the reading of historical and contemporary writers accentuated the significance of studying ancient texts for the sake of understanding our own times.

Oneness and unity, variously defined by disparate writers and groups over the centuries, are not only political and sociological ideas. For most ancient thinkers and for many today, they are also *theological* ideas. In the tradition of the Abrahamic faiths, so influential on the emergence of later Western empires and on the development of the modern nation-state, the oneness and unity of a people correspond in some fashion with the oneness and unity of God. This collection of essays examines the connections between divine and social oneness and unity throughout a range of texts from a wide spectrum of cultural milieus. Though the sharper focus falls on early Christianity, those early Christian writers were shaped by the scriptures of Israel, the moral treatises and political propaganda of the Greeks and Romans, and the theological reflections on social identity in early Jewish literature. Exploring these important texts from antiquity, and especially from the period of early Christianity, holds promise for resourcing the ongoing quest in human societies to generate unity in a world divided.

---

1. Found in a letter to William Smith (May 20, 1790); cited in David McCullough, *John Adams* (New York: Simon & Schuster, 2001), 422.

Introduction 3

An increased interest in the connections between social unity and theological oneness has taken root in the study of biblical texts and early Christianity. Though earlier studies viewed New Testament oneness theologies as deriving from Greco-Roman sources, there is a growing consensus that the early Christian writers were drawing primarily on the Jewish confession that "God is one."[2] An increasing number of scholars relate this classic formula from the Shema (see Deut 6:4) to key New Testament texts that envision allegiance to Christ (who somehow participates in divine oneness, see, e.g., 1 Cor 8:6 and John 10:30) as the basis for social harmony and group solidarity.[3] The Jewish theological conviction that "God is one" features significantly in many of the essays in this volume, but prior interpreters were right to explore potential connections between the New Testament's language of unity and oneness with other instances in the wider cultural streams. Our volume's range of focus honors the complexity of ideas about divine and social oneness and the inevitable interchange of those ideas across the cultures of antiquity.

---

2. See, e.g, Erik Peterson, *Heis Theos: Epigraphische, formgeschichtliche und religionsgeschichtliche Untersuchungen zur Antiken "Ein Gott"-Akklamation*, Ausgewählte Schrifen 8 (Würzburg: Echter, 2012); and Mark L. Appold, *The Oneness Motif in the Fourth Gospel: Motif Analysis and Exegetical Probe into the Theology of John* (Eugene, OR: Wipf & Stock, 2011).

3. Some of these studies will appear in the footnotes of the relevant chapters, but for now, see by way of example John J. R. Lee, *Christological Rereading of the Shema (Deut 6.4) in Mark's Gospel*, WUNT 2/533 (Tübingen: Mohr Siebeck, 2020); Alan J. Thompson, *One Lord, One People: The Unity of the Church in Acts in Its Literary Setting*, LNTS 359 (London: T&T Clark/Bloomsbury, 2013); Christopher R. Bruno, *"God Is One": The Function of Eis Ho Theos as a Ground for Gentile Inclusion in Paul's Letters*, LNTS 497 (London: Bloomsbury, 2013); Kim Huat Tan, "Jesus and the Shema," in *Handbook for the Study of the Historical Jesus*, ed. Tom Holmén and Stanley E. Porter, 4 vols. (Leiden: Brill, 2011), 3:2677–2707; Tan, "The Shema and Early Christianity," *TynBul* 59 (2008): 181–206; Erik Waaler, *The Shema and the First Commandment in First Corinthians: An Intertextual Approach to Paul's Re-reading of Deuteronomy*, WUNT 2/253 (Tübingen: Mohr Siebeck, 2008). Earlier studies include Birger Gerhardsson, *The Shema in the New Testament: Deut 6:4–5 in Significant Passages* (Lund: Novapress, 1996); Joel Marcus, "Authority to Forgive Sins upon the Earth: The Shema in the Gospel of Mark," in *The Gospels and the Scriptures of Israel*, ed. W. Richard Stegner and Craig A. Evans, JSNTSup 104 (Sheffield: Sheffield Academic, 1994), 196–211; N. T. Wright, "Monotheism, Christology, and Ethics: 1 Corinthians 8," in *The Climax of the Covenant: Christ and the Law in Pauline Theology* (Minneapolis: Fortress, 1991), 120–36; Johannes Beutler, "Das Hauptgebot im Johannesevangelium," in *Das Gesetz im neuen Testament*, ed. Karl Kertelge, QD 108 (Freiburg im Breisgau: Herder, 1986), 226–29.

4   Andrew J. Byers

Summary of Chapters

The book is divided into four parts. In part 1, "Oneness and Unity in the Scriptures of Israel," Walter J. Houston offers a fitting opening chapter by studying the fundamental ideas of divine and social oneness in the Pentateuch. He shows that the claim "God is one" is both inclusive and exclusive. The former dimension is demonstrated throughout the creation and patriarchal narratives in the generic name Elohim by which this divine being appropriates identities and functions of other gods and thus engages with broader humanity; exclusive oneness is demonstrated in the Moses narrative through Israel's unique vocation of binding itself to this Lord whose name is revealed as YHWH. Houston claims that both the inclusive and exclusive components of God's oneness are stitched into the Pentateuch to address disunity among God's people.

Anna Sieges-Beal explores the tension between inclusivity and exclusivity as social corollaries of divine oneness in the postexilic prophetic literature. As monotheistic faith developed in the crucible of exile, a question that rose to prominence concerned the relationship of Israel's one God to the nations. The particularity of this God could be used to justify the exclusiveness of Israel's election, as in Joel and in later portions of Isaiah. If God is one, the descendants of Abraham alone constitute a corresponding one nation. The particularity of YHWH, however, was also deployed to resource a more universalistic vision in which any and all nations may offer worship and thereby share in the benefits of Israel. Sieges-Beale features Jonah as the ironic exemplar of this view in which the one God of Israel is for all people spanning all places.

In part 2, "Oneness and Unity in the Classical World," Lynette Mitchell challenges recent trends that perceive a rigid dichotomy between ancient Greeks and the Other. After the collapse of the Mycenaean civilization, disparate Greek communities throughout the Mediterranean world adopted practices of identity formation that forged boundary lines that were permeable and even inclusive. The hosting of shared cultic events at recognized sanctuaries established unifying regional networks. The telling of foundation stories and the crafting (or discovery) of common genealogies reinforced the idea of one Hellenic identity comprising diverse strands and encompassing vast geographical space. Greek ideas of oneness and unity thus accommodated a broad range of diversity over several centuries.

This inclusive kind of social oneness, however, could be exploited for imperial agendas. James R. Harrison's essay picks up where Mitchell's ends with Alexander the Great imposing a unity of humankind for the purpose of establishing autocratic power. Roman ideas of unity and oneness are varied, but they provided a rhetoric for asserting authority over barbarians and other people groups on the borderlands. Though Cicero called for a more magnanimous oneness, the Greek idea of οἰχουμένη became synonymous with the Roman idea of *imperium*. In the agonistic politics and civil wars leading up to the *pax* of Augustus, seeking unity among the vying ancestral houses and interest groups was political folly. But the unity of Rome eventually provided in the Julio-Claudian dynasty was enacted through oppression and domination, however grandly portrayed in the writings and iconography of the day.

The chapters in part 3, "Oneness and Unity in Early Judaism," focus on Qumran, Philo, and Josephus. Studies on the Essene community behind the Dead Sea Scrolls often focus on the sectarian social features that reinforced their sense of separation from the world around them. In his chapter on this early Jewish group, Carsten Claussen focuses on those exercises and ideas that bound them together in a *yaḥad*, a self-identification connoting unity and togetherness. Their theological convictions underwrote a carefully organized social life. Requirements for admission, purity practices, property sharing, torah study, table etiquette, regular meetings, and calendar observance all served the consolidation of group identity while enforcing intergroup boundaries.

Jutta Leonhardt-Balzer makes a unique contribution in her analysis of Philo's carefully reasoned and often surprising understanding of oneness. While he draws on a range of philosophical traditions, Philo's rationale is chiefly grounded in an arithmological theology in which "one" signifies God. Like the Creator, "one" is the independent, unmixed, and ungenerated generator of the other numbers. It is only when human beings are unified in their worship of the one God that their collective oneness is welcome, and this unity can include not only faithful Jews but proselytes from other ethnicities. Oneness is therefore sourced in the one God and finds proper social expression as humans orient their lives and worship around him.

Kylie Crabbe shows that, in the works of Josephus, unity is extolled as a virtue and linked to the singularity of the Jewish God whose oneness is signified by the one temple and distilled socially through the practice of Jewish law. In his portraitures of various Jewish groups, evaluations align with the degree of internal concord (as among the Pharisees and Essenes) or discord (as among the Sadducees). Since Roman rule is divinely sanc-

6   Andrew J. Byers

tioned, Josephus decries the Jewish revolutionaries for inciting στάσις and posits that the disunity that plagued their ranks assured their defeat. In spite of his pro-Roman rhetoric, however, Crabbe discerns a continuity across Josephus's treatment of unity and social concord in which Jewish particularism is celebrated and the eventual reign of God is anticipated.

The largest section of the book is part 4, "Oneness and Unity in the New Testament and Early Christianity." Elizabeth E. Shively and Max Botner open this arena of study by examining the synoptic evangelists' positioning of the Shema's command to love God with all of one's being alongside the command to love one's neighbor in Lev 19:17–18. Such a collocation is a christological reconfiguration of the scriptural and early Jewish coordination of piety and worship (εὐσεβεία) alongside just and honorable treatment of others (διακιοσύνη). In order to practice εὐσεβεία, one must recognize Jesus's identification with the one God; in order to practice διακιοσύνη, one must honor one's neighbor (Mark), even one's enemy (Matthew) and the Other (Luke) within the ethical model Christ commands and embodies. Such a Christocentric anchoring of love for the one God with love for others gives shape to the Christian community envisioned by each evangelist, erecting confessional social boundaries while demolishing others.

My own essay explores the significance of oneness for the Fourth Evangelist. In John's Gospel, Jesus's prayer at the end of the farewell discourse "that they may be one, as we are one" follows a sophisticated sequence of development. Two sets of oneness texts from scripture, the Shema (Deut 6:4–9) and Ezek 34 and 37, imbue Johannine oneness with connotations that are theological, christological, and ecclesiological. In John 17, Jesus is not just praying for unity or social harmony (for an allegedly fragmented Johannine community); instead, he is praying that his disciples might be incorporated into the one people of the one Davidic Shepherd who shares in the divine identity of Israel's one God. Moreover, the name that Jesus prays his followers will share with him and with the Father is the circumlocution "one." I close the essay arguing that Deut 6:4–9 serves as a subtext underlying the entire gospel. Just as Israel's inception was premised on love for the one God expressed in the honoring of his words, a Johannine Israel is formed through the reception of the Word who is one with God.

Alan J. Thompson's essay on Acts argues that Luke's thematic pairing of early Christian unity alongside Jesus's universal lordship is premised on a widely recognized link in political discourse between kingship and concord. Since a unified populace was symptomatic of a praiseworthy reign, Roman emperors were keen to preserve and enforce social cohesion. Luke's narrative portraits of Christian community and his attention to conflict resolution highlight the reign of Christ, the true royal lord whose unifying forces of forgiveness, love, and the Holy Spirit are more effective than the unifying forces of military threat or harsh governance. Unity in Acts thus articulates a political reality revelatory of the divine.

Stephen C. Barton offers a comprehensive account of oneness and unity in 1 Corinthians. Paul's most divided community was so heavily moored to the agonistic and competitive social systems of the dominant culture that he has to persuade them toward a reconfiguration of values and a reaffirmation of their mutual participation in the one body of Christ. The language of oneness and a diverse range of unitive terms and ideas are strategically deployed not simply to beckon a fractured social group back into cohesion, but to align their new eschatological existence with the "one God" of Israel, the "one Lord" of Christian faith, and the "one and the same Spirit" of their baptism.

For Robbie Griggs, the leitmotif of oneness in Galatians sheds light on some of the knottiest conundrums in Pauline theology. The antithesis between Christ and the law is not ultimately grounded in a human inability to comply with its demands, or in Israel's failure to live by its commands, or in a dogmatic preference for the Christ-event, or even in a new eschatological moment in redemptive history. For Paul, there is one God with one soteriological plan announced by a singular gospel that generates one people who are neither Jew nor gentile per se. The role of torah is thus temporally fixed and enduring until the definitive work of Jesus. For Paul, it is only within the church—a culturally diverse people who are nonetheless one—that the law's moral vision can find its intended teleology in a corporate embodiment of the "one word" of neighbor-love.

With some parallels to Thompson's chapter, Julien C. H. Smith understands the theme of unity in Ephesians and Colossians as grounded in the vision of the ideal king in biblical, early Jewish, and Greco-Roman political ideology. Smith identifies and explores a tension in this ecclesial unity: If the oneness is enabled by divine and royal decree, how can it be maintained by the community? Smith demonstrates that Christ not only establishes a cosmic unity in which the church participates, but also distributes gifts as a benefactor of virtue by which social barriers are dissolved. By putting on the moral character of Christ the king, Christian communities distinguish themselves from others within their Mediterranean milieu. This distinctiveness is not antagonistic but winsome in its social manifestation of concord and peace.

Nicholas J. Moore provides a wide-ranging analysis of several themes throughout the Catholic Epistles and Hebrews collectively treated under the rubric of "on(c)eness." His essay opens with a discussion of divine oneness in James and the letters of John that have direct social and ethical consequences. Since God is one, Christian devotion to this singular God must also be singular and wholehearted as expected of Israel in the Shema of Deut 6:4–9. Within James's polemical sights are divided loyalty, disrupted community, and double-mindedness, expressed with the use of the δι- prefix, that fall short in honoring the one God. Though the Shema is not directly referred to in the Johannine Epistles, Moore makes the case that divine oneness underlies the double love commands to love God and one another. Turning to Jude, 1 Peter, and Hebrews, attention is drawn to the theologically significant "onceness." In related but varying ways, these writers deployed the term ἅπαξ (and its cognates) to express the singularity of a divine event (whether a revelation, Christ's death, or Christ's entrance into heaven) that bears implications for the life of Christian communities.

Oneness is sometimes preserved by expedient acts of exclusion. T. J. Lang considers Clement of Rome's exhortation to the disruptive party in Corinth to remove themselves in a noble act of self-imposed exile. Using the imagery of a "social surd," Lang argues that there were some social scenarios in early Christianity that evaded established tactics for securing unity. The Corinthian situation addressed in 1 Clement required a creative solution that went beyond Pauline practice. Rather than shunning, ostracizing, or excommunicating those who were disrupting ecclesial harmony, Clement offered an alternative option that gave honor and fame to the disturbers of peace and assured them that they would be welcome elsewhere.

The most ardent proponent of Christian unity in the eastern part of the empire was surely Ignatius of Antioch. John-Paul Lotz's study on the sociopolitical dimensions of Ignatius's theologically ordered ideas of oneness and unity forms a suitable capstone chapter, closing the volume with reflections on a highly developed idea of Christian unity that prompts questions for ongoing studies. To situate Ignatius within the intellectual and political climate of the Second Sophistic, Lotz opens with an overview of the term ὁμόνοια/*concordia* and then compares the Syrian bishop with the writings of a contemporary. Dio Chrysostom's *Orations* shed light on Ignatius's *Epistles*, where the bishop-in-bonds creatively deploys the language and images of his cultural milieu to consolidate ecclesial unity in the person and office of the bishop and in a shared commitment to orthodox doctrine.

We offer these studies in the hope that they will contribute rich resources from the worlds of the scriptures, Greco-Roman and Jewish antiquity, and early Christianity to ongoing reflection on ideas and practices conducive of the unity of humankind. In a dangerously divided world, what is needed more than ever are imaginations able to conceive what it will take to build bridges rather than walls. Fresh readings from our cultural, political, and religious forebears are a good place to start.

Bibliography

Appold, Mark L. *The Oneness Motif in the Fourth Gospel: Motif Analysis and Exegetical Probe into the Theology of John.* Eugene, OR: Wipf & Stock, 2011.

Beutler, Johannes. "Das Hauptgebot im Johannesevangelium." Pages 226–36 in *Das Gesetz im Neuen Testament.* Edited by Karl Kertelge. QD 108. Freiburg im Breisgau: Herder, 1986.

Bruno, Christopher R. *"God Is One": The Function of Eis Ho Theos as a Ground for Gentile Inclusion in Paul's Letters.* LNTS 497. London: Bloomsbury, 2013.

Gerhardsson, Birger. *The Shema in the New Testament: Deut 6:4–5 in Significant Passages.* Lund: Novapress, 1996.

Lee, John J. R. *Christological Rereading of the Shema (Deut 6.4) in Mark's Gospel.* WUNT 2/533. Tübingen: Mohr Siebeck, 2020.

Marcus, Joel. "Authority to Forgive Sins upon the Earth: The Shema in the Gospel of Mark." Pages 196–211 in *The Gospels and the Scriptures of Israel.* Edited by W. Richard Stegner and Craig A. Evans. JSNTSup 104. Sheffield: Sheffield Academic, 1994.

McCullough, David. *John Adams.* New York: Simon & Schuster, 2001.

Peterson, Erik. *Heis Theos: Epigraphische, formgeschichtliche und religionsgeschichtliche Untersuchungen zur Antiken "Ein Gott"-Akklamation.* Ausgewählte Schrifen 8. Würzburg: Echter, 2012.

Tan, Kim Huat. "Jesus and the Shema." Pages 2677–2707 in vol. 3 of *Handbook for the Study of the Historical Jesus.* Edited by Tom Holmén and Stanley E. Porter. 4 vols. Leiden: Brill, 2011.

———. "The Shema and Early Christianity." *TynBul* 59 (2008): 181–206.

Thompson, Alan J. *One Lord, One People: The Unity of the Church in Acts in Its Literary Setting*. LNTS 359. London: T&T Clark/Bloomsbury, 2013.

Waaler, Erik. *The Shema and the First Commandment in First Corinthians: An Intertextual Approach to Paul's Re-reading of Deuteronomy*. WUNT 2/253. Tübingen: Mohr Siebeck, 2008.

Wright, N. T. "Monotheism, Christology, and Ethics: 1 Corinthians 8." Pages 120–36 in *The Climax of the Covenant: Christ and the Law in Pauline Theology*. Minneapolis: Fortress, 1991.

Part 1
Oneness and Unity in the Scriptures of Israel

1
One God, One People:
Reflections on a Reconciled and Reconciling Pentateuch

Walter J. Houston

It is appropriate for this collection of essays to begin with the Pentateuch. From a literary point of view, that is according to the texts as they appear in the canons of the Hebrew and Christian Bibles, the Pentateuch is the point of origin of the doctrine of one God, and alone in the canon is taken as Scripture by *all* those who claim the name of Israel and worship that one God.

Two matters will be discussed in this essay. The first is in what way, or rather in what ways, the oneness of God is conceived in the Pentateuch. The other is how the Pentateuch displays the unity of Israel as God's people, and at a deeper level the unity of humanity under God their creator. As will be seen, these questions are closely linked.

1.1. One God?

Everyone knows that the Old Testament teaches monotheism. But as with other things that everyone knows, the idea needs examining. Generally speaking, the question the scholarly literature discusses is not whether or in what sense there is monotheism in the Hebrew Bible, but when it began to be either implicitly accepted or explicitly stated.[1] A theological question thus becomes a question in the history of religion.

Further, the trouble with the usual scholarly approach is that the concept of monotheism is unexamined: it is taken for granted that everyone

---

1. See Nathan MacDonald, *Deuteronomy and the Meaning of "Monotheism,"* FAT 2/1 (Tübingen: Mohr Siebeck, 2003), 21–52.

-13-

14 Walter J. Houston

knows what it means. Consider for example the way in which Gerhard von Rad speaks of the Hebrew Bible's monotheism in his *Old Testament Theology*. It occupies exactly two pages.[2] He quite correctly, and in contrast to some others, observes that monotheism as such has a limited profile in the Old Testament, which gives weight rather to the commandment to have no other gods by the side of YHWH. But even he assumes his readers know what he means by monotheism.

> At what time were the gods of the Canaanite pantheon, into whose company the stranger Jahweh had made his entrance (Ps. LXXXII), demoted to be a body of Elohim-beings with the function of singing praises? Where, and where not, is the term "gods" simply rhetorical embellishment?... His [Isaiah's] view of history leaves no place whatsoever for the gods of other nations or any functions they might exercise.[3]

But if the Canaanite gods are Elohim-beings, what are they but gods, since *elohim* means gods? Further, if Isaiah views YHWH as the Lord of history, how does that preclude other gods from existing or exercising functions in nature, for example? Such incoherence could be avoided by being clear from the start about the terms used. If monotheism means believing in the existence of only one god, its precise sense must depend on what one means by a god and therefore what it would mean for there to be only one such being.

The question of what may be meant by a god in the Hebrew Bible is discussed by Jaco Gericke under the heading "the concept of generic godhood."[4] He shows that in the Hebrew Bible there are texts that assume that a god is a being with certain properties, "knowing good and evil," for example (Gen 3:5, 22), or knowledge of the past and the future (Isa 41:21–24), or great wisdom (Ezek 28:3–4), or immortality (Gen 3:22; Ezek

---

2. Gerhard Von Rad, *Old Testament Theology*, trans. D. M. G. Stalker, 2 vols. (London: SCM, 1975), 1:210–12.

3. Von Rad, *Old Testament Theology*, 1:211–12. A footnote (212 n. 49) refers to Pss 95:3, 97:7: אלילים, literally "nothings," does not deny the foreign gods' existence, but is "a way of rendering them contemptible."

4. Gericke, *The Hebrew Bible and Philosophy of Religion*, RBS 70 (Atlanta: Society of Biblical Literature, 2012), 259–92. Strangely, Gericke does not discuss the concept of monotheism itself; on occasion he uses the expression casually like other Hebrew Bible scholars.

1. One God, One People 15

28:9).[5] Although these texts are addressed to beings that are assumed not to possess such properties, they assume that if they did, they would be at least "like" gods (Gen 3:5), and the בני אלוהים in Deut 32:8 4Q37 (4QDeutʲ; cf. LXX) and such beings elsewhere must indeed be gods.[6] But all of these properties together would not add up to the definition of God in classical theism, and using that definition such gods as those in Deut 32 or those addressed in Pss 96 and 97 are no gods. Whether we call a text monotheistic may thus depend on whether we understand it using the text's idea of what a god is or our own.

The consequence for this chapter is that we will try to avoid the term monotheism and will ask of any text alleged to be monotheistic what *precise* idea of God's oneness makes sense in its context. We shall find that there are two quite different, and even in certain respects opposed, concepts of oneness, or monotheism, in the Pentateuch. Classically expressed in the Shema, Deut 6:4–5, and in Deuteronomy generally is an *exclusive* and *relational* concept. YHWH is one *for Israel*, the one God in that YHWH is the one God Israel is to worship or have any relationship with, and YHWH's oneness *excludes* all other gods, without denying their existence.[7]

Turning to Genesis, we find, in distinction from Deuteronomy, an *inclusive* concept of God's oneness. It is inclusive in that God is first introduced (in Gen 1:1) under the generalizing name "God," אלהים in Hebrew, rather than specifically as YHWH, and is portrayed as in relationship with the whole human race through their ancestors. Later God is identified with YHWH, but not only YHWH. In the story of the ancestors of Israel, God is also called by them by other names, mostly based on El, the ancient name in Ugarit and Canaan of the high god and creator.

But as we follow the story through from Genesis into Exodus, we find that this inclusive God's exclusive name YHWH is revealed to Israel, and only Israel, in his deliverance of them from Egypt. Thus, the two conceptions are *reconciled*.

---

5. Gericke, *Hebrew Bible and Philosophy of Religion*, 279–81.

6. Carmel McCarthy, ed., *Deuteronomy*, BHQ 5 (Stuttgart: Deutsche Bibelgesellschaft, 2007), 93.

7. To MacDonald (*Deuteronomy*) belongs the distinction of having demonstrated beyond dispute that this is the sense of Deuteronomy's monotheism.

1.1.1. YHWH's Exclusive Oneness

"Hear, O Israel" (Deut 6:4).[8] What is Israel to hear? There exist almost as many versions in English of the following four words in the Hebrew, יהוה אלהינו יהוה אחד, as there are versions of the Old Testament as a whole. The uncertainty lies in the ambiguity of the syntax, even having regard to the context. Literally, "YHWH our-God YHWH one." This is a Hebrew verbless clause (aka nominal sentence), or possibly two, which in English would require "is" to link subject and predicate. But which is the subject and which the predicate? (In Hebrew an indefinite predicate will often precede the subject.[9]) Another question is the precise meaning of "one." Is it the numeral one, implying either singleness or uniqueness, or does it perhaps mean "alone"?

There is no space here to examine all the possibilities.[10] I will take a few shortcuts. The first is to exclude any construal that makes YHWH the subject and "our God" the predicate: for everywhere else these are in apposition, "YHWH our God."[11] The second is to say that אחד, "one," is unlikely to mean "alone," as there is a word, לבדו, that properly means "alone." And the third is that "one" cannot be qualifying YHWH, "one YHWH," because a proper name cannot be a count noun.[12] That leaves us with virtually only one possible translation: "YHWH our God, YHWH is one."[13] But this does not mean that the verse cannot be saying that YHWH *alone* is Israel's God; for "one" may well be used to mean "unique," unique, that is, as Israel's God, Israel's one and only: Nathan MacDonald compares Song 6:9, "My dove, my perfect one *is one*."[14] Moreover, this sense is virtually demanded by the context, Deut 6:5, "and you shall love YHWH your God with all your heart and with all your soul and with all your might." The whole

---

8. Unless otherwise noted, all translations are mine.

9. Francis I. Andersen, *The Hebrew Verbless Clause in the Pentateuch*, JBLMS 14 (Nashville: Abingdon for the Society of Biblical Literature, 1970), 37–38.

10. See Andersen, *Hebrew Verbless Clause*, 47; MacDonald, *Deuteronomy*, 62–75; Moshe Weinfeld, *Deuteronomy 1–11: A New Translation with Introduction and Commentary*, AB 5 (New York: Doubleday, 1991), 332, 337–38, 349–51.

11. Weinfeld, *Deuteronomy 1–11*, 337.

12. "One YHWH" as in, e.g., KJV, NRSV margin; for the prohibition on count nouns, see Andersen, *Hebrew Verbless Clause*, 47.

13. NIV, NRSV margin. MacDonald appears to favor this (*Deuteronomy*, 62–70).

14. MacDonald, *Deuteronomy*, 74; R. W. L. Moberly, *Old Testament Theology: Reading the Bible as Christian Scripture* (Grand Rapids: Baker Academic, 2015), 20.

1. One God, One People 17

broader context (Deut 6–11) is devoted to instilling the message that Israel must be devoted to YHWH, to the exclusion of all other gods. But as MacDonald has shown, Deuteronomy does not teach monotheism if that is taken to mean that no other gods exist, in the text's own understanding of that word. On the contrary, if other gods are a temptation for Israel (strongly implied by, e.g., Deut 7:1–6), they must be thought of as real.[15]

MacDonald takes much of Deuteronomy, excluding the law code (12–26), into his argument. He notes the scholarly consensus that while the Shema and other early parts of the book do not in themselves imply monotheism, "these verses are now read in a monotheistic sense" because of the editorial framework in which they have been placed, including such statements as Deut 4:35, "YHWH is God [האלהים, with the article]; there is none beside, apart from him [אין עוד מלבדו]," or 4:39, "YHWH is God in heaven above and on the earth beneath, there is none beside [אין עוד]."[16] MacDonald suggests that the Hebrew האלהים, with the article, "can … be best rendered into English with 'God,'" capitalized, "making a claim about YHWH's uniqueness" but not denying the existence of other deities.[17] But, he says, the phrase אין עוד, which I have translated "none beside," should not be translated "no other": its usage elsewhere refers to the possible presence of the item "in a person's immediate domain," not to its absolute nonexistence.[18] The sense is that because of YHWH's uniqueness, there is no other god that Israel need take into account. At 7:9 it is YHWH's faithfulness to Israel that marks him out as God (האלהים). MacDonald argues that the recognition of YHWH as God is consistently bound up with his relation to Israel.

But here one aspect of MacDonald's argument may be questioned: Deut 4:39 implies not just that YHWH is the only God for Israel but is God without rival "in heaven above and on earth beneath," hardly Israel's "immediate domain." Despite the impression given by the sentence (4:34) beginning "Has a god ever tried to go and take a people for himself," the passage effectively denies that it is possible to find any gods, other than YHWH, in heaven or earth. It surely goes beyond the thematic of the

---

15. MacDonald, *Deuteronomy*, 72.

16. For the editorial framework, see MacDonald, *Deuteronomy*, 78.

17. MacDonald, *Deuteronomy*, 80. I would compare this with the use in the United Kingdom of "the King," meaning our own king, without denying the existence of other kings.

18. MacDonald, *Deuteronomy*, 84

18   Walter J. Houston

exclusive oneness of YHWH; and this is not surprising, for in 4:32 there is
a clear allusion to the Priestly account of creation in Gen 1, including the
use of אלהים without the article to refer to the Creator.[19] In other words,
the chapter, or 4:32–40 at the least, has been influenced by the inclusive
understanding of God's oneness found in Gen 1.[20]

But certainly the exclusive understanding dominates Deuteronomy,
and it also emerges repeatedly in the narrative and laws of Exodus and
Numbers, and in the Holiness Code in Leviticus. It is especially formative in the Sinai narrative of Exod 19–24; 32–34. Highlights here include
the first commandment of the Decalogue, "You shall have no other gods
before me."[21] The covenant concluded in Exod 24 commits Israel to the
observance of all the commandments, but this one above all.

What are the social and historical roots of this doctrine of exclusivity,
of one God for one people? YHWH as far back as our historical knowledge
goes had been the god of the nation of Israel and the official supreme god
of the states of Israel and Judah. But in the ancient Near East there were
always a range of deities who were available for worship without challenging the right of the supreme god to his official position and functions.
Israel was no exception. It is the authority of the Pentateuch itself that
ultimately constrained them to acknowledge YHWH as their one and only
exclusive God.

Various hypotheses have been offered to explain this. Most convincing, in my opinion, is the view that the seeds of the transformation
had already been sown in the monarchic period. Morton Smith,
seconded by Bernhard Lang, developed the hypothesis of the "Yahweh-
alone party" in monarchic Israel and Judah, a movement demanding
the abandonment of all other gods, and in sociological terms probably nurtured among the Levites (see Exod 32:26) and prophetic circles
stemming from Elijah and Elisha.[22] It is represented by the prophetic
books of Hosea and Jeremiah, as well as Deuteronomy and the writ-

---

19. Timo Veijola, *Das 5. Buch Mose Deuteronomium, Kapitel 1,1–16–17*, ATD 8.1
(Göttingen: Vandenhoeck & Ruprecht, 2004), 115.

20. Veijola, *Deuteronomium*, 115.

21. The precise meaning of על־פני is a relatively insignificant question.

22. Smith, *Palestinian Parties and Politics That Shaped the Old Testament* (London:
SCM, 1971); Lang, "The Yahweh-Alone Movement and the Making of Jewish Mono-
theism," in *Monotheism and the Prophetic Minority: An Essay in Biblical History and
Sociology* (Sheffield: Almond Press, 1983), 13–59.

1. One God, One People 19

ings it influenced. The collapse of the kingdoms gave them the chance to influence the nation in the direction of their own beliefs—but not without some compromise, as we will see.

1.1.2. God's Inclusive Oneness

R. W. L. Moberly observes that Israel's ancestors are presented in Gen 12–50 as YHWH-worshipers but with a type of religion very different from any later Yahwism, especially Mosaic Yahwism as represented by Exodus to Deuteronomy.[23] There is an "absence of a sense of urgent religious choice … a lack of conflict between patriarchal and Canaanite religion."[24] The idea of holiness is not found. In other words, the idea of exclusive oneness is absent.

But this does not mean that there are any competing gods. Rather, the same God is referred to under various names. Elohim is identical with YHWH. So also is El with whatever sobriquets. At specific points, often when there is a theophany, the god seen or heard or worshiped by one of the ancestors is given a name by him, usually one compounded with El (אל), although the context makes it clear that it is YHWH/Elohim who is present. Although El is often used in the Hebrew Bible as a word for God or a god, and so translated in English versions, it is in origin the name of the Canaanite high god, *'Ilu* in the Ugaritic texts. Thus in Gen 14:18–20 Abram accepts a blessing from, and gives tithes to, Melchizedek, "king of Salem … priest of 'El 'Elyon ['God most high']." At 21:33 he plants a tamarisk at Beersheba and "called on YHWH, 'El 'Olam ['God eternal' or 'God of ages']." At 33:20 Jacob sets up an altar at Shechem "and called it 'El the God of Israel."[25] At 35:7, similarly, he builds an altar at Bethel, "and called the place 'El of Bethel."

This does not mean that at every site the deity was necessarily, in historical fact, acknowledged with the name in the text. But place names can sometimes confirm it, such as Beth-el itself, "house of El," not Beth-yahu; even the very name of the nation, Israel, not Isra-yahu, suggests its original god was El rather than YHWH.[26]

---

23. Moberly, *The Old Testament of the Old Testament: Patriarchal Narratives and Mosaic Yahwism* (Minneapolis: Fortress, 1992), 79–104.

24. Moberly, *Old Testament of the Old Testament*, 99. Genesis 35:2–4 is a rare exception in these chapters.

25. Or "El *is* the God of Israel" (John Van Seters, "The Religion of the Patriarchs in Genesis," *Bib* 61 [1980]: 223).

26. Walter J. Houston, *The Pentateuch*, SCM Core Text (London: SCM, 2013), 151.

But from a theological point of view, the names themselves are less significant than the fact that at important sites of the worship of YHWH, the text shows YHWH as being pleased to accept prayer under different names before the true name was known. YHWH has taken over the identity of the gods of the old sacred sites. YHWH is one God, but *inclusively* absorbs their identity.

As the text stands, therefore, Genesis presents the ancestors as worshipers of the one God YHWH, but under other names. If the oldest forms of their stories sprang from a polytheistic worldview (consider, e.g., Abraham's three visitors in Gen 18, or Jacob's mysterious assailant at the ford of Jabbok in Gen 32:22–32), it has been assimilated to an inclusive monotheism by the work of successive editors.

It is usually assumed that the reason why the ancestors do not address God as YHWH is because the ancestors lived before Moses and could not have known it.[27] Konrad Schmid, on the other hand, mounts an extensively supported argument that the stories of the ancestors originally had no relationship to the story of the exodus and constituted an alternative, even competing, origin legend for Israel.[28] The argument is carefully assessed by David Carr, who concludes that the ancestral narrative as a whole (according to the earlier sources, and setting aside its Priestly framework [P]) cannot be read as completely independent of the Moses story, but that its older parts, and particularly the Jacob stories, bear "the fewest marks of being originally linked to" it.[29] Notably, these largely use Elohim. They may thus be a legend of Israel's origins cultivated in circles distinct from those that acknowledged the revelation to Moses and the exodus as the origin of the nation.

Thus the story of Jacob at Bethel (Gen 28:10–22) preserves an old foundation legend of the temple of Bethel (28:10–12, 17–19): see David M. Carr, *Reading the Fractures of Genesis: Historical and Literary Approaches* (Louisville: Westminster John Knox, 1996), 205–8; and cf. Claus Westermann, *Genesis 12–36: A Commentary* (London: SPCK, 1985), 453–55.

27. So Moberly, *Old Testament of the Old Testament*, 45: "The regular usage of Elohim is because the writers take seriously the pre-Yahwistic context of the patriarchal stories."

28. Schmid, *Genesis and the Moses Story*, Siphrut 3 (Winona Lake, IN: Eisenbrauns, 2010).

29. Carr, "Genesis in Relation to the Moses Story: Diachronic and Synchronic Perspectives," in *Studies in the Book of Genesis: Literature, Redaction and History*, ed. André Wénin, BETL 155 (Leuven: Leuven University Press; Peeters, 2001), 294.

1. One God, One People

Albert de Pury refers for evidence to Hos 12.[30] Every episode in the life of Jacob found in Genesis is mentioned in the chapter: he is presented as an appropriate ancestor for the unreliable and deceitful Ephraim; and according to de Pury he is contrasted throughout with Moses, a contrast that reaches its climax in Hos 12:12–13 (13–14 MT): "Jacob fled to the countryside of Aram, and Israel slaved for a woman; for a woman he kept flocks. But by a prophet YHWH brought Israel up from Egypt, and by a prophet he was kept." "Hosea does not oppose two personalities of Israel's past but two conceptions of Israel's identity, genealogical and vocational."[31] Should Israel identify themselves as the *descendants* of Jacob or the *followers* of Moses?

There are as many interpretations of the enigmatic poem of Hos 12 as there are commentators.[32] But if in eighth-century (northern) Israel the stories of both Jacob and Moses were known, were they cultivated in different circles, with not only opposed "conceptions of Israel's identity," but opposed conceptions of the identity of God? The God of the genealogical Israel would be the inclusive Elohim, while the God of the vocational Israel, the Israel defined by its obedience to prophecy, would be the exclusive YHWH.

We can only speculate as to the circles in which the story of Jacob may have been cultivated and an inclusive God acknowledged. Carr's suggestion that they have "perhaps some link to ancestral worship [*sic*; he may mean 'ancestor worship'] in ancient Israelite households and villages" is perhaps as good as any.[33]

1.1.3. Reconciling the Stories

Exclusive and inclusive conceptions of God's oneness may have existed simultaneously in tribal and monarchic Israel, but in the Pentateuch they stand side by side as the religious character of two successive phases in the

---

30. Albert de Pury, "The Jacob Story and the Beginning of the Formation of the Pentateuch," in *A Farewell to the Yahwist: The Composition of the Pentateuch in Recent European Interpretation*, ed. Thomas B. Dozeman and Konrad Schmid, SymS 34 (Atlanta: Society of Biblical Literature, 2006), 59–62.

31. De Pury, "Jacob Story," 60.

32. See, e.g., A. A. Macintosh, *Hosea*, ICC (Edinburgh: T&T Clark, 1997), who translates the key verse 12:13 quite differently.

33. Carr, "Genesis," 294.

22 Walter J. Houston

prehistory of Israel. A few non-P passages in Genesis and Exodus make the link between them, such as Gen 15:12–16 and Exod 3:1–15, probably anticipating the Priestly narrative.[34] It is the latter that develops this conception of history systematically, with a clear, if sparse, narrative thread and a theory of revelation.[35] It functions to bring together or reconcile the divergent foundation myths of Israel and with them the divergent conceptions of God's oneness, and it does this by a combination of historical and theological moves.

Historically, it places the ancestors chronologically before Moses, which was of course the only way of fitting them into a single history. This involves presenting the divine promises to them of blessing and land as fulfilled only after the sojourn in Egypt and the exodus. It also arranges the notices of the three ancestors, which were probably separate legends from different parts of the country, in three successive generations.

Theologically, it conceives of God as revealed in different ways at different stages of history and to different groups. The narrative begins not with Abraham, but with creation, and it is significant that God is initially introduced to the reader simply as "God," Elohim, אלהים *without* the article. To us this way of referring to the deity is to be taken for granted. Anciently, gods had names by which they were addressed by their worshipers. To use the simple "God" as a *name* for a god whose true name will only be revealed later requires explanation. De Pury argues that in Gen 1 the usage is intended to signify the one supreme, universal, and eternal Creator and Lord of the world, by whatever name that God may be known: YHWH, Ahura Mazda, Marduk, and whatever other names of the Creator may be acknowledged by other nations are identical.[36] If this daring thesis is correct, the P narrative, which goes on to embrace the stories of both the ancestors and the exodus, offers at its outset the most inclusive conception of God of all, and at the same time it is truly monotheistic: there is no place for any other god.

It can certainly be agreed that P's God is the Creator God of the entire cosmos, who is accessible as God to all people. At key points in the primeval

---

34. Houston, *Pentateuch*, 108; Schmid makes them later; *Genesis*, 236–37.

35. Schmid, *Genesis*, 238–48.

36. Albert de Pury, "Gottesname, Gottesbezeichnung und Gottesbegriff: *Elohim* als Indiz zur Entstehungsgeschichte des Pentateuch," in *Die Patriarchen und die Priesterschrift/Les Patriarches et le document sacerdotal*, ATANT 99 (Zurich: TVZ, 2010), 185.

1. One God, One People   23

history God speaks to persons who represent the whole of humanity (Gen 1:28–30; 6:13–21, etc.), and even Abraham is the ancestor of a wider group than Israel alone. He is revealed to the ancestors by a name, El Shaddai, modeled on the El names of the older sources. P thus identifies the god of the ancestors with the universal God of the primeval narrative.

But at the same time it is made clear that Israel is to have a unique relationship with God, through a covenant "between me and you [Abraham] and your seed after you, to be God for you and your seed after you" (Gen 17:7). The true and most intimate name of this God is revealed exclusively to Israel, through Moses: "I am YHWH. I appeared to Abraham, to Isaac, and to Jacob as El Shaddai, but by my name YHWH I was not known to them" (Exod 6:2–3). And at 6:7 we read "I take you [the Israelites] as my people, and I shall be your God." Their function in the divine economy is to prepare the dwelling for YHWH's gracious presence on earth with YHWH's people (Exod 29:45–46). In this way the universal God of Gen 1, who speaks to the first humans and to Noah, establishes an exclusive and binding relationship with Israel alone.

The redactors of the Pentateuch take the P narrative as the backbone of the story and fit the non-P material around it. The broad cosmic and international dimensions of the text, as well as its linking of distinct national traditions, suggest an attempt to assure a traumatized and disoriented people of their place in the new international order under Persian rule. But can we speak of *a* people or merely of disparate groups?

1.2. The Oneness of the People of God

We have seen that the oneness of God is intimately bound up in the Pentateuch with the oneness of God's people. The exclusive God of Deuteronomy is known as God (האלהים) only through relationship with the one people of Israel; and the inclusive God of Genesis, though the God of the whole human race, only becomes eventually known in history by acting on behalf of Israel: the drumbeat refrain "they shall know that I am YHWH" sounds through the story of the exodus.

But two mortal dangers threatened the unity of Israel and may be said in one way or another to have become reality, while being firmly opposed by the Pentateuch.

For the first, we recall the contrast between the zealous Yahwists of Deuteronomy promoting the exclusivity of YHWH as Israel's God and the identity of Israel as YHWH's holy people and those, probably the great

24   Walter J. Houston

majority under the monarchy, who found their identity in being descendants of Abraham or of Jacob, whose tale is told in Genesis. There was a potential conflict here, which could be suppressed as long as the kingdoms survived, but that could burst into the open after their fall.

The other had existed from very early in the people's existence, the tension between different geographically based groups, between Israel and Judah, or at a later stage between Samaria and Yehud, and still later Samaritans and Jews, a still unhealed division that only seems insignificant because of the numerical insignificance today of the Samaritans.

1.2.1. Conflict over the Identity of Israel: The Issue, and the Pentateuch's Answer

A challenge lay before the people after the fall of the two kingdoms: Do you wish to define yourselves simply as the children of Jacob/Israel, or (also) as the disciples of Moses? But such challenges can easily lead to schism between those who accept the challenge and those who refuse it.

That this was not avoided in ancient Israel is evident from a couple of texts in Ezekiel: 11:14–21 and 33:23–29. The deportees are assured in 11:20: "they shall be my people, and I shall be their God." The covenant formula is granted to a *section* of the people, those who have been in exile, with the implication that those who have not have forfeited their status as YHWH's people by their "abominations" (11:18).

In Ezek 33:23–29, an oracle given to Ezekiel immediately after the fall of the city in 587 (33:21), the survivors appear as congratulating themselves on having the opportunity to take over the land, in that Abraham, though only one man, "took over the land" [וייִרש את-הארץ] (33:24)—in the person of his descendants, it is implied—whereas there are many of them. The reference to Abraham is clearly not a mere comparison: they refer to Abraham because he is their revered ancestor, and they are members of his clan, which expanded to take over the whole of Judah. They derive their identity from Abraham, and probably ignore or reject the whole of the exodus and covenant tradition. YHWH's response in a series of uncompromising rhetorical questions (33:25–26) is that a people who commit such crimes as they—eating "on the blood," idolatry, bloodshed, reliance on violence, abomination, and adultery—will never take over the land. This is not a random list of crimes, but (apart from "relying on your swords") a list of sins characteristic of the Holiness tradition. They will not survive (33:27–29), and it is implied that it is the exiles, who are ready to

1. One God, One People

accept the Mosaic view of YHWH and his requirements, who will survive and take over the land, as in 11:17, and at length in chapters 36–37.

It is widely held that a clash between an exclusivist community of returned exiles and those Judeans who had survived in the land took place in the early Persian period.[37] From the evidence in Ezekiel, and the general likelihood that the remainers clung to the polytheism of the monarchic period, this seems probable, and it is not unlikely that an aspect of the conflict concerned land rights, as in Ezekiel, as the exiles had belonged to the elite and would have had extensive landholdings. But it is difficult to extract any evidence for this from contemporary sources. The book of Ezra is certainly not contemporary, and holds to the ideology of the empty land: there were in Persian-period Judah no genuine Israelites who did not belong to the *golah*, the returned exile community—hence logically excluding any such clash.[38] Those conflicts in the book that concern identity, and they are frequent, are invariably represented as being with foreigners, as in Ezra 4:2 or 9:1–2. But many scholars presume that the adversaries and the excluded women in chapter 10 are actually Judeans subject to Othering, ideologically painted as foreign.[39]

A recent view is that the adversaries under attack in the book, not only in 4:2, are primarily Samarians, at a point well into the Hellenistic period when relations between Jerusalem and Samaria had broken down, and hence that the conflict belongs to the other complex discussed here, in §1.2.2.[40]

Whatever the reality, the torah's attitude to such potential schism is clear. It takes no account of it. The sins of the people of Israel—disbelief, murmuring, idolatry, outright refusal of their duty—are the sins of the

---

37. E.g., Lester L. Grabbe, *Ezra-Nehemiah*, Old Testament Readings (London: Routledge, 1998), 136–38.

38. For the date of Ezra, see, e.g., H. G. M. Williamson, *Ezra, Nehemiah*, WBC 16 (Waco, TX: Word, 1985), xxxvi: "say around 300 B.C." Most commentators give a similar date.

39. E.g., Yonina Dor, "The Rite of Separation of the Foreign Wives in Ezra-Nehemiah," in *Judah and the Judeans in the Achaemenid Period*, ed. Oded Lipschits, Gary N. Knoppers, and Manfred Oeming (Winona Lake, IN: Eisenbrauns, 2011), 173–74.

40. Benedikt Hensel, *Juda und Samaria: Zum Verhältnis zweier nach-exilischer Jahwismen*, FAT 110 (Tübingen: Mohr Siebeck, 2016), 313–14: "Die Texte der Mischehenproblematik zielen … vornehmlich auf eine Disqualifizierung der Garizim-Gemeinde" (314).

people as a whole. It is never divided between an apostate mass and a faithful minority. Apparent exceptions prove the rule. If the Levites, after the episode of the golden calf, are commanded to strike people down (Exod 32:26–29), they strike at random. The whole people have sinned; the whole people cannot be killed, but the three thousand who are killed are no worse than the rest. Similarly, with the plagues that rage through the people and are stayed after the deaths of thousands (Num 16:46–50 [17:11–15 MT]; 25:8–9).

The structure of the Pentateuch's reconciled narrative is entirely against the kind of division suggested in Ezek 33. Genesis and Exodus, ancestors and Moses, stand side by side in a single narrative that is as continuous as the material allows: the generation of the exodus are the descendants of Abraham, Isaac, and Jacob. All Israelites taking the torah as the token of their identity must acknowledge both their descent from Abraham, Isaac, and Jacob and their commitment to the covenant accepted at Exod 24:7. Finally, Deuteronomy proclaims disaster on the entire people if they are unfaithful to YHWH and disobey the commandments (Deut 28), and the restoration of the entire people in the mercy of YHWH (30); summarily, 30:15–20.

1.2.2. Geographical Division and the Pentateuch on the Unity of the People

Throughout most of their history, the people of Israel have not possessed political unity. For most of the monarchic period, they lived in two kingdoms, Israel and Judah, that were separate and sometimes hostile to each other. As the two kingdoms were picked off separately by the great powers, they were formed into separate provinces. During the Persian period, there continued to be two distinct provinces, each with its own often native governor, and each with its own temple of YHWH. This distinction continued through the Hellenistic period (Samaria and Judaea) up to the time of the Hasmonean kingdom, when Samaria was conquered by John Hyrcanus (128 BCE) and the temple on Mt. Gerizim destroyed (112–111 BCE). The kingdom was thus unified down to the end of the reign of Herod the Great (died 4 BCE). But the Romans again frequently treated the two areas differently.

However, no ethnic distinction corresponded to this political disunity. The peoples of both areas regarded themselves as Israelites and have generally been so treated in scholarship. They had the same supreme God,

1. One God, One People

spoke the same language, and had a closely similar culture. It is true that some recent scholars have argued that Judah was a quite separate people that only claimed to represent Israel after the kingdom of Israel had fallen, or even later.[41] But Avraham Faust examines the archaeological evidence for distinctive marks of ethnicity in (mainly) the monarchic period, and finds that they point unanimously to Israel and Judah being ethnically identical: such major marks as the so-called four-room house, lack of painted decoration on pottery, rarity of imported pottery, and avoidance of pork are widely distributed through both kingdoms (except for Canaanite enclaves in the northern valleys), and generally absent in neighboring areas.[42] Theoretically there could be other marks of ethnicity, not archaeologically detectable, that were not shared, but all that we have point to shared ethnicity.

Despite the importation of foreign settlers to the former territory of the kingdom of Israel after 720, most evidence suggests that the general population of at least the central hill country continued to be ethnically Israelite.[43] The peoples of Samaria and Judaea continued to accept each other as Israelite at least up to the early Hellenistic period.[44] But the destruction of the temple on Gerizim, as might have been expected, led to bitter hostility between them. It was possibly only from this point on that they regarded each other as distinct peoples.[45] In the Persian period there is evidence for cordial relations between Samaria and the priestly leadership in Jerusalem (Neh 13:28). Nehemiah was hostile, but this attitude does not seem to have been shared by the Judean leadership generally.[46] Thus, the situation is similar to that during the monarchy: there was politi-

---

41. Philip R. Davies, *In Search of "Ancient Israel": A Study in Biblical Origins*, JSOTSup (Sheffield: JSOT Press, 1992), 73; Israel Finkelstein and Neal Asher Silberman, *The Bible Unearthed: Archaeology's New Vision of Ancient Israel and its Sacred Texts* (New York: Simon & Schuster, 2001), 150.

42. Faust, "An All-Israelite Identity: Historical Reality or Biblical Myth?," in *The Wide Lens in Archaeology: Honoring Brian Hesse's Contributions to Anthropological Archaeology*, ed. Justin Lev-Tov, Paula Hesse, and Allan Gilbert, Archaeobiology 2 (Atlanta: Lockwood, 2017), 169–90.

43. Gary N. Knoppers, *Jews and Samaritans: The Origins and History of Their Early Relations* (New York: Oxford University Press, 2013), 18–44.

44. Hensel, *Juda und Samaria*, 194.

45. Cf. Knoppers, *Jews and Samaritans*, 217–39, who shows that the breach was not absolute.

46. Knoppers, *Jews and Samaritans*, 158–59.

cal difference and hostility, but the peoples were friendly. We have already seen that the book of Ezra cannot be trusted as evidence for this period: the impression given in Ezra 4:1–2 that the people, or at least the leaders, of Samaria, were foreigners brought there by the Assyrians (similarly in 2 Kgs 17:24–34) is misleading. The Assyrians did settle people in the area from elsewhere in the empire, but they did not displace the native population, other than the upper classes who had been deported.[47] Thus the book rather represents the conditions of a later period when suspicions had developed between the peoples. This would have been when the story in 2 Kgs 17 developed. The earliest contemporary evidence of hostility seems to be Ben Sira's dismissive comment at Sir 50:25–26 (ca. 180 BCE), but doubtless it had been growing before then.

The Pentateuch, on the other hand, is rooted in the earlier sense of unity between north and south, reflects it and celebrates it. It remains the one canonical corpus that is recognized as scripture by both Jews and Samaritans. There is some evidence that its redaction was a collaborative effort between the scribal and priestly elites of Yehud and Samaria.[48] Certainly there was nothing in the text pointing unequivocally to an origin on one side or the other before the Samaritan revisions in (probably) the first century BCE that created what we know as the Samaritan Pentateuch.[49] Its contents strongly support the unity of the divided people.

The stories of both ancestors and exodus involve both sections of the people. In the full development of the narrative, linking the ancestral story with that of the exodus, the sons who are born to Jacob (Gen 29:31–30:24; 35:16–20; 49:1–28), and are thus great-grandsons of Abraham, become the ancestors of all the tribes of Israel. Jacob goes down into Egypt with his entire family, except of course for Joseph and his sons, who were already there (Gen 46:8–27; Exod 1:1–5). In Egypt the family flourishes and greatly multiplies (Exod 1:7), so that Jacob's sons become the eponymous ancestors of the tribes. It is clearly intended that these tribes are the entire people of Israel in the broader application of the name. The people are the בני־ישראל (the "children of Israel"), as repeatedly referred to in the subsequent narrative ("the Israelites" in most modern transla-

---

47. Knoppers, *Jews and Samaritans*, 43–44.

48. Walter J. Houston, "Between Salem and Mount Gerizim: The Context of the Formation of the Torah Reconsidered," *JAJ* 5 (2014): 311–34; Hensel, *Juda und Samaria*, 170–94.

49. Houston, "Salem and Mount Gerizim," 323–31.

1. One God, One People

29

tions, which fails to register the strong familial sense of national identity in this usage). And it is these children of Israel as a whole who leave Egypt under the leadership of Moses (Exod 12:40–42; note "*all* the children of Israel" in the last sentence).

There are a number of places in subsequent parts of the Pentateuch where further enumerations of the tribes are made. Their precise enumeration varies somewhat, but the number twelve is always maintained: it is symbolic of totality.[50] Thus the list of leaders at Num 1:5–16 and the list of tribes numbered that follows (1:20–42) exclude Levi, who is given special treatment (1:47–48), but the tale of twelve is made up by dividing Joseph between Ephraim and Manasseh. The same occurs in Num 26. All the lists include Judah, as well as Joseph as one tribe or two, and other tribes that were reckoned to the kingdom of Israel.

It is always this whole people that is addressed by YHWH or by Moses in the giving of the law and the making of the covenant. It is always this whole people that acts in concert in Exodus and Numbers. The only case where some tribes threaten to act independently is in Num 32, where the Reubenites and Gadites want to stay where they are rather than take part in the invasion of the land, whose borders are defined in Num 34 in a way that excludes their territory.

Moreover, the unity thus maintained by the people in their time in the wilderness is ordained for them when they enter the promised land. In the first law given to them by Moses, in Deut 12, they are told that they must offer their sacrifices not at any place they see but at "the place that YHWH will choose in one of your tribes" (Deut 12:14): one place of sacrifice for one people to one God. [51] The place is not identified. The usual scholarly view is that Jerusalem is meant, while in the dramatic situation Moses is supposed to have no precise knowledge of the topography of the land, which he had never seen. But this depends on the supposition that both the writing of Deuteronomy and the composition of the Pentateuch as a whole took place in Jerusalem and were addressed to a Judean public. As I have mentioned, there is evidence, not least the mere fact that the Torah is recognized as scripture by the Samaritans, that Samaria was also

---

50. The blessing of Moses in Deut 33 is an exception: Simeon is omitted and not compensated for.

51. The SP has "that YHWH has chosen" (בחר as against יבחר) in all twenty places where the phrase occurs. Whatever the precise significance of this variant, it still does not identify the place.

30 Walter J. Houston

involved in the composition; and some of the material in Deuteronomy itself bears marks of a northern origin, notably chapter 27, with its references to Mounts Gerizim and Ebal (27:4, 13–14), which stand on either side of Shechem.

It is more probable, therefore, that the "place that YHWH will choose/ has chosen" is left deliberately unidentified so that the text may be neutral between the claims of Mt. Gerizim and Jerusalem.[52] There remain clear references at other points to both places: Jerusalem (Salem) in Gen 14:18 and Gerizim in Deut 27:13 (also in 27:4, according to the Samaritan text). By a tragic irony, this diplomatic vagueness intended to avoid conflict became in the end the trigger for the descent of the relationship into open warfare and sacrilegious destruction. John Hyrcanus felt himself authorized to destroy the Samaritan sanctuary because the text demanded that the place for the worship of YHWH should be in just "one of your tribes," and that could only be "the tribe of Judah, Mount Zion, which he loves" (Ps 78:68).

The text, however, survives, and continues to challenge the people of God to make real the unity that it asserts.

1.3. Conclusion:
The Unity of the Human Race under the Universal God

It is possible to define this unity in a quite different and more comprehensive way, still on the basis of the Pentateuch. We have seen that YHWH/ God is first introduced in Genesis as the universal creator God who creates and deals with the entire human race. After its near-destruction in the flood, God speaks to Noah to grant a covenant to his descendants and all creatures on earth (Gen 9:8–16), promising never to destroy them in a flood again. In the following chapter, the nations of the known world are listed according to their supposed descent from the sons of Noah. This makes it clear that all the nations of the earth belong to a single line of descent (so Acts 17:26): there are no races, only the human race. One nation is chosen for the privilege and responsibility of maintaining the dwelling for God on earth; that is all. God is the God of all peoples, of one human race. To acknowledge God is to acknowledge our responsibility to love all our fellow humans and to live and act as the one family that we are.

---

52. Cf. Knoppers, *Jews and Samaritans*, 194–212.

Bibliography

Andersen, Francis I. *The Hebrew Verbless Clause in the Pentateuch*. JBLMS 14. Nashville: Abingdon for the Society of Biblical Literature, 1970.

Carr, David M. "Genesis in Relation to the Moses Story: Diachronic and Synchronic Perspectives." Pages 273–95 in *Studies in the Book of Genesis: Literature, Redaction and History*. Edited by André Wénin. BETL 155. Leuven: Leuven University Press; Peeters, 2001.

———. *Reading the Fractures of Genesis: Historical and Literary Approaches*. Louisville: Westminster John Knox, 1996.

Davies, Philip R. *In Search of "Ancient Israel": A Study in Biblical Origins*. JSOTSup 148. Sheffield: JSOT Press, 1992.

Dor, Yonina. "The Rite of Separation of the Foreign Wives in Ezra-Nehemiah." Pages 173–88 in *Judah and the Judeans in the Achaemenid Period*. Edited by Oded Lipschits, Gary N. Knoppers, and Manfred Oeming. Winona Lake, IN: Eisenbrauns, 2011.

Faust, Avraham. "An All-Israelite Identity: Historical Reality or Biblical Myth?" Pages 169–90 in *The Wide Lens in Archaeology: Honoring Brian Hesse's Contributions to Anthropological Archaeology*. Edited by Justin Lev-Tov, Paula Hesse, and Allan Gilbert. Archaebiology 2. Atlanta: Lockwood, 2017.

Finkelstein, Israel, and Neal Asher Silberman. *The Bible Unearthed: Archaeology's New Vision of Ancient Israel and Its Sacred Texts*. New York: Simon & Schuster, 2001.

Gericke, Jaco. *The Hebrew Bible and Philosophy of Religion*. RBS 70. Atlanta: Society of Biblical Literature, 2012.

Grabbe, Lester L. *Ezra-Nehemiah*. Old Testament Readings. London: Routledge, 1998.

Hensel, Benedikt. *Juda und Samaria: Zum Verhältnis zweier nach-exilischer Jahwismen*. FAT 110. Tübingen: Mohr Siebeck, 2016.

Houston, Walter J. "Between Salem and Mount Gerizim: The Context of the Formation of the Torah Reconsidered." *JAJ* 5 (2014): 311–34.

———. *The Pentateuch*. SCM Core Text. London: SCM, 2013.

Knoppers, Gary N. *Jews and Samaritans: The Origins and History of Their Early Relations*. New York: Oxford University Press, 2013.

Lang, Bernhard. "The Yahweh-Alone Movement and the Making of Jewish Monotheism." Pages 13–59 in *Monotheism and the Prophetic Minority: An Essay in Biblical History and Sociology*. Sheffield: Almond Press, 1983.

MacDonald, Nathan. *Deuteronomy and the Meaning of "Monotheism."* FAT 2/1. Tübingen: Mohr Siebeck, 2003.

Macintosh, A. A. *Hosea.* ICC. Edinburgh: T&T Clark, 1997.

McCarthy, Carmel, ed. *Deuteronomy.* BHQ 5. Stuttgart: Deutsche Bibelgesellschaft, 2007.

Moberly, R. W. L. *The Old Testament of the Old Testament: Patriarchal Narratives and Mosaic Yahwism.* Minneapolis: Fortress, 1992.

———. *Old Testament Theology: Reading the Bible as Christian Scripture.* Grand Rapids: Baker Academic, 2015.

Pury, Albert de. "Gottesname, Gottesbezeichnung und Gottesbegriff: *Elohim* als Indiz zur Entstehungsgeschichte des Pentateuch." Pages 173–94 in *Die Patriarchen und die Priesterschrift/Les Patriarches et le document sacerdotal.* ATANT 99. Zurich: TVZ, 2010.

———. "The Jacob Story and the Beginning of the Formation of the Pentateuch." Pages 51–72 in *A Farewell to the Yahwist: The Composition of the Pentateuch in Recent European Interpretation.* Edited by Thomas B. Dozeman and Konrad Schmid. SymS 34. Atlanta: Society of Biblical Literature, 2006.

Rad, Gerhard von. *Old Testament Theology.* Translated by D. M. G. Stalker. 2 vols. London: SCM, 1975.

Schmid, Konrad. *Genesis and the Moses Story.* Siphrut 3. Winona Lake, IN: Eisenbrauns, 2010.

Smith, Morton. *Palestinian Parties and Politics That Shaped the Old Testament.* London: SCM, 1971.

Van Seters, John. "The Religion of the Patriarchs in Genesis." *Bib* 61 (1980): 220–33.

Veijola, Timo. *Das 5. Buch Mose Deuteronomium, Kapitel 1,1–16–17.* ATD 8.1. Göttingen: Vandenhoeck & Ruprecht, 2004.

Weinfeld, Moshe. *Deuteronomy 1–11: A New Translation with Introduction and Commentary.* AB 5. New York: Doubleday, 1991.

Westermann, Claus. *Genesis 12–36: A Commentary.* London: SPCK, 1985.

Williamson, H. G. L. *Ezra, Nehemiah.* WBC 16. Waco, TX: Word, 1985.

2

Is YHWH the God of the Nations as Well?
Jonah's Universal Conception of the Oneness of God

Anna Sieges-Beal

2.1. Introduction

Within the prophetic literature of the Hebrew Bible, the oneness of God comes into stark focus in the writings of the scribal prophets of the postexilic period. Primary among the concerns of these created prophetic personalities is the God of Abraham's relationship to the nations. If the God of the descendants of Abraham is the only god, how should people envision the one God's relationship to a wide variety of people? Under the rule of two great empires, first Persia and then Greece, the covenant people of the one God, YHWH, not only had to reckon with how their own relationships with these nations should play out but also, more importantly, with how the one God would interact with the nations.

This essay will examine the rise of monotheism within the consciousness of the covenant people in the postexilic period. It will spotlight the universalistic ideology in the book of Jonah as a counterpoint to the ideology found in other prophetic writings of the period, specifically that of Joel and postexilic Isaiah. Broadly speaking, these three prophetic voices (Jonah, Joel, and Isaiah) constitute the primary configurations for the one God's relationship to the nations within prophetic literature. These three views exist on a continuum. The first view, exemplified by the prophet Joel and typified throughout prophetic literature, suggests that YHWH will, one day, destroy the nations in judgment. In this view, YHWH is the one God of one people, the descendants of Abraham. This perspective is typified in the oracles against the nations of the Major Prophets (Isa 13–23; Jer

-33-

34 Anna Sieges-Beal

46–51; and Ezek 25–32). Similarly, in the Minor Prophets, Obadiah and Zech 9:1–8 mirror the particularistic ideology of Joel.

Portions of Isaiah, Jeremiah, and the Book of the Twelve promote an ideology of YHWH's acceptance of the nations if they travel to Jerusalem to worship. For example, the vision that closes Isaiah (66:18–24) includes every nation in worship at the temple. The delineation for those who are welcome and those who are not is not an ethnic line but the standard of righteousness versus wickedness. Similarly, Jer 4:17; Micah 4; and Zech 8 suggest that the nations will come to Jerusalem to worship YHWH.

The book of Jonah represents the final view on this spectrum from particularism to universalism. In contrast to the other traditions found within prophetic literature, Jonah asserts that YHWH could be worshiped among the nations, apart from the temple in Jerusalem. The book of Jonah uniquely challenges the other prophetic visions by suggesting that YHWH's compassion extends to the nations and by incorporating vignettes of foreigners worshiping YHWH outside of Jerusalem.

2.2. The Rise of Monotheism

These three prophetic approaches to the nations are uniquely situated in the postexilic world. Though divine oneness had been a growing and shifting ideology during the monarchy, it took on new dimensions as a result of the crisis of the exile. Rather than agreeing that the covenant God had been defeated by a foreign god (as was the common mode of thought in the ancient Near East when one nation defeated another), YHWH worshipers suggested quite the opposite. YHWH had not been defeated by a foreign god because those gods do not exist. YHWH was in control of the foreigners as well and could use such foreigners to chastise Israel. This monistic ideology did not arise overnight for the covenant people. Rather, a long history of elevating YHWH for the degradation of other divine beings made such a move possible.[1]

In his volume, *The Memoirs of God*, Mark S. Smith lays out a hypothesis (based on his other more scholarly works) for the degradation of other members of the pantheon within Israel and Judah.[2] Based on

---

1. Mark S. Smith, *The Memoirs of God: History, Memory, and the Experience of the Divine in Ancient Israel* (Minneapolis: Fortress, 2004), 107–23.

2. See Mark S. Smith, *The Origins of Biblical Monotheism: Israel's Polytheistic Background and the Ugaritic Texts*, new ed. (New York: Oxford University Press, 2003); and

texts such as Deut 32:8–9; Gen 49:25; and Ps 82, Smith surmises that Israel's original pantheon went through a series of rearrangements.[3] Deified figures that had once functioned as a part of the divine family (e.g., בני האלהים, Gen 6:4) were demoted to messengers of the divine realm or angels. Smith links the decline of the divine family to the decline of patrilineal ties within Judah.[4] As more families were displaced from the land, the patrilineal ties weakened. Such a change is likely reflected in Ezek 18:4 in which the divine voice declares that children will no longer be held accountable for the sins of their parent. The weakening of the family made it more likely for the divine family to fade away. Thus, while the Judahite divinity may have once had a wife and children, the family structure deteriorated, and family members were demoted to lesser divine being such as angels.[5]

This move toward monotheism was in response to the continual interactions with the empires of Mesopotamia, whose gods boasted lordship over the entirety of the empire.[6] Interactions with Assyria, Babylon, and Persia brought about a crisis. Judah's national God could not appear to have been beaten by the gods of the empire. So, as Judah suffered under empire and exile, Judah's God gained more and more power. With the example of imperial gods lording over foreign lands, a solution was clear.

Smith, *The Early History of God: Yahweh and the Other Deities in Ancient Israel*, 2nd ed. (Grand Rapids: Eerdmans, 2002). For the purpose of this discussion, the former volume will be more instructive. Smith differs with Jan Assmann's volume (*The Price of Monotheism*, trans. Robert Savage [Stanford, CA: Stanford University Press, 2009]), which suggests that the rise of monotheism within Israel was revolutionary. Smith's reconstruction is more convincing because it points to the uneven nature of the transition and the stages along the way.

3. Smith, *Memoirs of God*, 122–23.

4. Smith, *Origins of Biblical Monotheism*, 163.

5. Smith, *Memoirs of God*, 115–17. My attempt at summarizing the movement to monotheism, necessarily leaves out nuance and the tentative nature of some of these claims. Along with the focus on the individual rather than the family, and the interaction with empire, ancient Judah also experienced a significant catastrophe of kingship that should not be overlooked. The king as the divinity's national representative on earth linked the divine to a single location. In the absence of a monarch, Judah's God was no longer confined to one location. In addition, the movement to monotheism was likely not accepted across all strata of life in Yehud. Nevertheless, the ideology did catch on in scribal circles and in the circles of power that formed the biblical literature.

6. Smith, *Memoirs of God*, 115.

36 Anna Sieges-Beal

Judah's national God, YHWH, was the only god. Foreign gods were not more powerful; they simply did not exist.

The biblical narrative, as we have it, displays this new ideology. When Israel was allowed to return to their homeland under the edict of Cyrus, as both Ezra and Isaiah tell us, it was YHWH who stirred up his spirit to allow the return (Ezra 1:1–4; Isa 45:1–5). Cyrus, a foreign king, was YHWH's instrument. With this new way of understanding Judah's God on the books, the covenant people of the postexilic period had to reckon with how the only god would relate to the nations. For the purpose of this essay, our attention turns to prophetic circles and how the scribal prophecy of the postexilic period dealt with the dilemma of monotheism. As mentioned earlier, a spectrum of options from particularism to universalism emerged within prophetic literature. The three primarily emerged concerning foreigners' relationship to the one God.

The first option was to contend that YHWH would wipe out the nations through judgment. This particularistic mode promoted the idea that one people, the descendants of Abraham, could worship the one God to the exclusion of others. Another option was to assert that all nations would one day come to worship the one God in a singular place, Jerusalem. The descendants of Abraham happened to have singular ties to this singular place as it was located within the land the one God had given to the descendants of Abraham. Therefore, the second option maintained some links to the particularistic portion of the continuum while moving in the universalistic direction. A final prophetic view was that YHWH could be worshiped among the nations, apart from the temple in Jerusalem. The relationship between these three prophetic writings is complicated. This essay pairs the book of Jonah's universalistic point of view with both Joel (particularistic) and Isaiah (between universal and particular) to see how Jonah's unique voice challenges other prophetic concepts of YHWH's relationship to the nations. When Jonah and Joel are juxtaposed, the two show signs of intentional intertextual citations. They also share a scroll as both are part of the Book of the Twelve. Consequently, Jonah and Joel share a close textual relationship. The relationship between Jonah and postexilic Isaiah is more distant. Though Jonah does address the ideology of worship at the temple in Jerusalem, the two prophetic works do not share clear intertextual citations. Nevertheless, it is profitable to examine how Jonah relates to the ideology in both Joel and Isaiah.

2. Is YHWH the God of the Nations as Well? 37

2.3. Jonah and Joel

The book of Joel acts as an anchor for the entire Book of the Twelve.[7] It contains a conglomeration of the major themes that run throughout the corpus. Importantly, one of these themes is the divine name formula in Exod 34:6–7.[8] The divine name formula describes YHWH as a gracious and compassionate God but also a just God who punishes iniquity. Most commonly within the Twelve, the covenant people hope for God's mercy upon them and God's judgment against the nations.[9] Joel uses this formula to call the people of Judah to repentance by suggesting that YHWH might be compassionate and merciful if they do so (2:12–17). Joel also suggests that YHWH will judge the nations for their iniquity through mass slaughter (4:9–16) and that YHWH will rule in Jerusalem and "foreigners will never again pass through it" (4:17).[10]

---

7. James Nogalski, "Joel as 'Literary Anchor' for the Book of the Twelve," in *Reading and Hearing the Book of the Twelve*, ed. James Nogalski and Marvin A. Sweeney, SymS 15 (Atlanta: Society of Biblical Literature, 2000), 91–109.

8. E.g., one can find echoes of the divine name formula in Hosea, Joel, Amos, Obadiah, Jonah, Micah, Nahum, and Malachi; Jakob Wöhrle, *Der Abschluss des Zwölfprophetenbuches: Buchübergreifende Redaktionsprozesse in den späten Sammlungen*, BZAW 389 (Berlin: de Gruyter, 2008), 364; see also 365–99. See also Wöhrle, "A Prophetic Reflection on Divine Forgiveness: The Integration of the Book of Jonah into the Book of the Twelve," *JHebS* 9 (2010): 2–17, https://doi.org/10.5508/jhs.2009.v9.a7. Wöhrle is entering a discussion of the redactional layer associated with the grace formula from Exod 34:6–7 that is already in progress. Among the first to explore this option was Raymond Van Leeuwen. Van Leeuwen traced the use of Exod 34:6–7 through Hosea, Joel, Amos, Obadiah, Jonah, Micah, Nahum, and Malachi. For Van Leeuwen this layer was the "end-redaction" of the Twelve. It was concerned with questions of theodicy and those major events of 722 and 586. This final redaction of the Twelve corresponded to the final redaction of the Hebrew Bible and was carried out by scribal sages; see Van Leeuwen, "Scribal Wisdom and the Theodicy in the Book of the Twelve," in *In Search of Wisdom: Essays in Memory of John G. Gammie*, ed. Leo G. Perdue, Bernard Brandon Scott, and William Johnston Wiseman (Louisville: Westminster John Knox, 1993), 31–49.

9. Though, at times, this idea is flipped on its head, e.g., Amos 1:3–2:16. Nevertheless, most often, judgment is imagined for the nations (e.g., Obadiah and Nahum) and compassion (perhaps in the distant future) is hoped for God's covenant people.

10. Taken as a whole, the overwhelming message of Joel for the nations is that YHWH will destroy them. However, Joel 3:1 [MT] contains a prophecy in which YHWH pours out his spirit on "all flesh." "All flesh" refers to either a universal outpouring of YHWH's spirit or the outpouring on all flesh among the covenant people.

38   Anna Sieges-Beal

The book of Jonah contradicts Joel's claim concerning the possibility for YHWH's compassion for Judah but unmitigated judgment for the nations by concocting a repentance narrative for a foreign nation, the hated Assyrians. Jonah uses the divine name formula and other intertexts to show that the Ninevites are worthy of YHWH's mercy and that it is foolish to contend otherwise.

Within Jonah's account of the Ninevites' repentance, intertextual references to Joel and Exodus play an important role. Secondary literature has conceived of a variety of models for understanding the relationship between these intertexts (Exod 32:12 and 34:6, Joel 2:13b–14a and Jonah 3:9 and 4:2).[11] The most compelling argument, suggested by Aaron Schart, is that Jonah is a satire of the particularistic ideology found in Joel. Consequently, Schart argues that Jonah uses Joel as an intertextual referent.[12]

The latter option is more defensible because of the use of the second-person possessive that follows the pronouncement of the spirit's outpouring; see Leslie C. Allen, *The Books of Joel, Obadiah, Jonah, and Micah*, NICOT (Grand Rapids: Eerdmans, 1976), 98; Hans Walter Wolff, *Joel and Amos: A Commentary on the Books of the Prophets Joel and Amos*, trans. Samuel Dean McBride, Hermeneia (Philadelphia: Fortress, 1977), 67; James L. Crenshaw, *Joel: A New Translation with Introduction and Commentary*, AB 24C (New York: Doubleday, 1995), 165. Unless otherwise noted, all translations are mine.

11. John Strazicich argues that the Joel-compiler makes use of Jonah's midrashic complex for composition of Joel 2:12–14. Strazicich makes his case based on the syntactical similarities between Exod 34:6–7, 32:12b, and 14:12. He goes on to say that, though Joel relied on Jonah as an intertextual referent, he also went back to the account in Exodus to fill out his prophecy. However, why could Jonah not use Joel as his primary reference and also go back to the Exodus account to fill out his narrative? Strazicich, *Joel's Use of Scripture and the Scripture's Use of Joel: Appropriation and Resignification in Second Temple Judaism and Early Christianity*, BibInt 82 (Leiden: Brill, 2007), 149–61. Siegfried Bergler demonstrates strong lexical parallels between Exod 32:12, 14, 10; 14:12; 34:6 and Jonah 3:8b–10; 4:1–3. He shows far fewer lexical parallels between Joel 2:12–14 and the respective passages. However, Joel maintains similarity to Jonah in two instances in which there is no antecedent in Exodus (Jonah 3:8ba, 9aa // Joel 2:13ab, 14a; and Jonah 4:1ba // Joel 2:13ba). On the basis of these lexical data Bergler surmises that the author of Joel made use of Jonah to develop Joel's call to repentance. At the heart of this call was the understanding that if a pagan nation could enact such a turn surely the people of God could do the same (Bergler, *Joel als Schriftinterpret*, BEATAJ 16 [Berlin: Lang, 1988], 227–29). See also Wolff, *Joel and Amos*, 49–50.

12. See Schart, *Die Entstehung des Zwölfprophetenbuchs: Neubearbeitungen von Amos im Rahmen Schriftenübergreifender Redaktionsprozesse*, BZAW 260 (Berlin: de

2. Is YHWH the God of the Nations as Well?   39

This suggestion certainly makes the most sense rhetorically, as what follows will bear out.[13]

Exod 32:12 ba	=	Jonah 3:9b/~9aa	~	Joel 2:14ab (ישוב)
Exod 32:12 bb	=	Jonah 3:9ab // 10b/4:2bg	=	Joel 2:13bg/2:14ab (ונחם)
Exod 32:14	=	Jonah 3:10		
Exod 32:10ab	~	Jonah 4:1b		
Exod 14:12aa	=	Jonah 4:2aa		
Exod 34:6aa	~	Jonah 4:2ba	~	Joel 2:13ba (כי)
Exod 34:6ab	=	Jonah 4:2ba	=	Joel 2: 13ba
Exod 34:6b	=	Jonah 4:2bb	=	Joel 2: 13bb
Exod 14: 12	=	Jonah 4:3		

Gruyter, 1998), 287–89. Jonah's dependence on Joel is more rhetorically satisfying than Joel's reliance on Jonah. If one posits that Joel intertextually cites Jonah, the payoff is rhetorically unsatisfying. First, such a reading would require that Joel move the more universal ideology of Jonah to a particularistic ideology involving the nations only to bring about the repentance of Israel. Second, though it is entirely possible that Joel 2:13b–14a are intertextual citations of Jonah *and* Exod 32–34, it seems that the former dwarfs the latter (contra Thomas B. Dozeman, "Inner-Biblical Interpretation of Yahweh's Gracious and Compassionate Character," *JBL* 108 [1989]: 222–23). If we take Jonah as the intertextual citation first and Exod 32–34 only derivatively, it would appear that the plain sense of the message of Joel 2:12–17 is refracted inappropriately. Joel calls for repentance on the basis of an understanding that the God who showed mercy in the wilderness to an idolatrous people, sparing them certain annihilation, may be persuaded to do so again. The Joel passage instructs the priests to ask YHWH, "Why should the nations/Egyptians say?" in the same fashion as Moses in Exod 32:12. Here there is no need for a comparison to Nineveh's repentance, in fact, quite the opposite. In Joel, YHWH's mercy is a sign to the nations of his goodness and fidelity. The nations in view here are not those who have experienced God's mercy but those who observe God's mercy as it is dispensed to the people of God. Here Israel a sign to the nations not the nations a sign to Israel (contra Strazicich, *Joel's Use of Scripture*, 149–61; and Bergler, *Joel als Schriftinterpret*, 227–29).

13. In the table that follows, the = sign indicates strong correspondence of more than one word; ~ indicates weak correspondence.

40 Anna Sieges-Beal

When the repentance scene of Jonah 3:3–4:4 is read in light of Joel's call to repentance for the covenant people, one finds that the Ninevites, a despised foreign group, enact the repentance that Joel calls for.

The scribal prophets who composed Jonah used Joel's call to repentance in Joel 2:12–17 as a template for the repentance narrative in Jonah. Through a series of intertextual citations to Joel, Jonah shows how the Ninevites do precisely what Joel calls for (and more!). Paradigmatic in the entire narrative is the idea of YHWH's compassion based on the divine name formula in Exod 34:6. The prophetic speaker in Joel 2:13 calls the covenant people to repentance, because YHWH is "gracious and merciful, slow to anger, and abounding in steadfast love, and relents from punishing." Similarly, when YHWH shows the Ninevites compassion, the reluctant prophet, Jonah, accuses YHWH of being too merciful (Jonah 4:2): "That is why I fled to Tarshish at the beginning, for I knew that you are a *gracious God and merciful, slow to anger, and abounding in steadfast love, and ready to relent from punishing*" (emphasis added):

Exod 34:6: יהוה אל רחום וחנון ארך אפים ורב־חסד ואמת
Joel 2:13: חנון ורחום הוא ארך אפים ורב־חסד ונחם על־הרעה
Jonah 4:2: אתה אל־חנון ורחום ארך אפים ורב־חסד ונחם על־הרעה

Joel hopes for YHWH's compassion on the covenant people. The character of Jonah is displeased because YHWH has bestowed compassion on foreigners. In Jonah, foreigners receive the compassion that Joel reserves for the descendants of Abraham. In addition, Joel 1:14; 2:12; and 2:15 all suggest that the addressees declare a צום ("fast") as a demonstration of repentance. Jonah 3:5 answer's this call by remarking that the people of Nineveh declare a צום.[14] In addition to fasting, Joel calls the covenant people to put on שק ("sackcloth"; 1:13, 2).[15] Again, Jonah answers Joel's

---

14. Outside of these instances of the word, צום occurs in the Book of the Twelve only in Zech 7:5; 8:19 concerning the liturgical fasting of the Jewish calendar, not as an act of repentance.

15. It could be argued that this call to put on sackcloth is heightened in Joel 2:13, in which the addressees are told to rend their hearts and not their garments; i.e., this outward manifestation of repentance through change of attire should be brought to the heart level. In the Twelve, שק also occurs in Joel 1:8 and Amos 8:10. In both instances, the sackcloth is donned as an image of mourning because of severe tragedy and not because of a call to repentance.

2. Is YHWH the God of the Nations as Well?   41

call for sackcloth by outfitting everyone in Nineveh, even the livestock, in the clothing of repentance (Jonah 3:5, 6, 8).[16]

Accompanying fasting and sackcloth Joel also calls an assembly (1:14; 2:15). The assembly Joel designates is all-inclusive. All who live in the land (1:14) are to attend. The elders, children, those nursing, the bridegroom and bride, and the priests (2:16–17) are all called to this assembly of repentance. Jonah answers this call by showing every part of society (even the livestock) in a posture of repentance.[17] To top off this repentance scene, Jonah displays the wicked Ninevite king speaking the very words of Judah's prophet, Joel, "Who knows God may turn and be sorry," except that the foreign king does better. The king's words are, in fact, closer to Exod 32:12 than those of Joel.[18]

In Jonah, the repentance scene is exaggerated to the point of comedy. Even the animals put on sackcloth and fast. A hated foreign king speaks the words of Judah's prophet, Joel! The foil to this overblown repentance narrative is the sullen prophet Jonah who sulks because of YHWH's mercy to the Ninevites. The character of Jonah had hoped that YHWH's compassion and grace did not extend to his enemies among the nations, but who can argue with such an exemplary act of repentance that does even more than Joel required?

The prophet Jonah presents readers with a caricature of a certain kind of prophet.[19] Jonah explains his reticence to journey to Nineveh by citing

---

16. Only in Joel 1:13 and Jonah 3:5, 6 and 8 in the Twelve do we find the call to put on sackcloth and the answering of that call as an indicator of repentance.

17. It is likely that this strange account of livestock repenting is an allusion to Joel 1:18 in which even the cattle and sheep feel the effects of the day of the YHWH. Joel 1:18 mentions beasts, cattle, and sheep (צאן, בקר, בהמה) as those that will suffer on the day of YHWH. Jonah 3:7 contains the same list of animals (צאן, בקר, בהמה) as those who should fast as a sign of repentance. Though בהמה, בקר, and צאן are not lexically rare, the lists contain the same order and animals. The same progression (בקר, בהמה, צאן) occurs in Lev 1:2 and Neh 10:37 as well.

18. Bergler, *Joel als Schriftinterpret*, 235. Though Bergler sees the dependence in the opposite direction because he neglects the comedic and satirical nature of the piece.

19. Myriad approaches to the genre of Jonah have formed within the secondary literature. This study highlights the satirical nature of the writing that comes into stark focus when one considers the intertexts with Joel. Other approaches that are of use in understanding the writing can be found in Phyllis Trible, *Rhetorical Criticism: Context, Method, and the Book of Jonah*, Guides to Biblical Scholarship (Minneapolis: Fortress, 1994); Jonathan Magonet, *Form and Meaning: Studies in the Literary Techniques in the Book of Jonah*, BBET 2 (Bern: Lang, 1976).

42 Anna Sieges-Beal

the divine name formula, saying "O YHWH! Is not this what I said while I was still in my own country? That is why I fled to Tarshish at the beginning; for I knew that you are a gracious God and merciful, slow to anger, and abounding in steadfast love, and ready to relent from punishing" (Jonah 4:2). Jonah knew that YHWH's compassion might extend to the nations and was therefore reluctant to warn them of YHWH's judgment. Jonah is, in fact, so disappointed that YHWH has chosen to show mercy to the Ninevites that he wishes to die. In the closing scene, Jonah mourns the loss of a bush and YHWH calls the sullen prophet to account:

> Then the LORD said, "You are concerned about the bush, for which you did not labor and which you did not grow; it came into being in a night and perished in a night, and should I not be concerned about Nineveh, that great city, in which there are more than a hundred and twenty thousand persons who do not know their right hand from their left, and also many animals?" (Jonah 4:10–11)

In this way the voice of YHWH shames the sullen prophet and focuses on the importance of the foreigners. Notably, YHWH does not forget the repentance of the animals. This representation of the reluctant and miserable prophet, in agony over the extension of YHWH's compassion to the nations, satirizes prophetic voices such as Joel who relishes in the destruction of the foreigners (see Joel 4:12, 17).

In light of these observations, the book of Jonah stands against the particularistic ideology found in many prophetic books, which imply that YHWH's compassion to Israel demands YHWH's destruction of the nations. One might call to mind Nahum, Obadiah, or Jeremiah's oracles against the nations, among others. These prophetic ideologies are those at which the book of Jonah points a satirical barb. In light of the postexilic ideology of the oneness of God, the book of Jonah mocks other prophetic voices that might imagine that the one God's loyalty lies solely with the descendants of Abraham. The book of Jonah opens wide the arms of the one God to embrace all people, even the hated Assyrians.

2.4. Jonah and Isaiah

The Jonah narrative similarly challenges the notion that YHWH's mercy is available to the nations provided that they come to Jerusalem and worship YHWH at the temple. The perspective that God's compassion (or withholding of judgment) is available to foreigners who worship

2. Is YHWH the God of the Nations as Well?　　　　43

properly and in the proper place is most clearly seen in Isa 55–56.[20] Isaiah 55:7 employs portions of the divine name formula from Exod 34:6–7, repeating שוב, רחם, and the ideas of wickedness and pardon. All of this is in the context of an oracle concerning the nations: "See you shall call nations that you do not know, and nations that you do not know will run to you, because the Lord your God, the holy one of Israel has been glorified in you" (Isa 55:5). Isaiah 56:6–8 goes on to enumerate how this calling of the nations will play out: "The foreigners who join themselves to the Lord … these I will bring to my holy mountain, and make them joyful in my house of prayer; their burnt offerings and their sacrifices will be accepted on my altar; for my house shall be called a house of prayer for all peoples."[21]

---

20. Though some scholars divide Second and Third Isaiah between chapters 55 and 56, there is no need for this division. More recent work has taken seriously the idea that all of Isaiah was updated and edited over time. It is certainly likely that the postexilic community read and heard these two chapters together. See, e.g., Craig Broyles and Craig Evans, *Writing and Reading the Scroll of Isaiah: Studies of an Interpretive Tradition*, VTSup 70.2 (Leiden: Brill, 1997); and H. G. M. Williamson, *The Book Called Isaiah: Deutero-Isaiah's Role in Composition and Redaction* (Oxford: Clarendon, 1994). Isaiah 55 and 56 are also linked by their vision of foreigners coming to Jerusalem. Isaiah 56 is unique in that it imagines foreigners coming to the temple specifically. Therefore, most scholars contend that Isa 56 is later than 55 because it must have been composed at a time when there was a functioning temple. Isaiah 55 does not assume a functioning temple. For the purpose of this study, we can read the two together, because Jonah also assumes a functioning temple and therefore, the relationship that this essay explores between the two writings assumes that Isaiah tradents had already composed both Isa 55 and 56.

21. This kind of ideology that focuses on the importance of the temple and limits worship to the temple is prominent at different times in Israel's history. The importance of Jerusalem and worship at the temple is a prominent feature of the Deuteronomistic History. Similarly, after the construction of the temple in the postexilic period, one can discern a growing ideology that proper worship can only happen at the temple. In Jon Berquist's sociological reconstruction of Persian period Yehud, he effectively argues that the temple played a central role in defining social groups. The temple created a social boundary dividing the world into two categories: those who participated in the temple, the cult, and the ideology that surrounded it, and those who did not. Because of the content of temple life (e.g., worship, sacrifice, liturgy, prayer), the social boundary was extended. The boundary came to mean that those who were favored by God participated in the activity of the temple and those who were not favored by God did not. See Jon Berquist, *Judaism in Persia's Shadow: A Social and Historical Approach* (Eugene, OR: Wipf & Stock, 2003), 150.

44 Anna Sieges-Beal

Joel imagines proper worship and proper repentance as taking place in the temple as well. However, Joel holds out this opportunity only to the covenant people. Isaiah suggests that YHWH will gather foreigners to the temple to engage in proper worship and that YHWH's great compassion will be available to them there. This portion of Isaiah departs from the prevalent prophetic ideology (exemplified by Joel) that YHWH's compassion does not extend to the nations. Isaiah's vision, however, is not big enough for Jonah. Throughout the narrative, the book of Jonah shows that foreigners can worship YHWH properly, wherever they might be.

The book of Jonah opens with the prophet displaying similar thinking to that of Isaiah.[22] Initially, Jonah thinks that he can escape YHWH by fleeing to Tarshish. Perhaps YHWH is not in charge there. However, Jonah quickly discovers that YHWH's domain extends to the sea. When the storm begins and the foreign sailors are instructed to pray to their local gods, Jonah admits that he worships "YHWH, the God of heaven, who made the sea and the dry land." Jonah's admission that YHWH's dominion encompasses so many realms (including the sea upon which they sail) terrifies the foreign sailors "even more" (1:10).[23] Seemingly appalled, the sailors question Jonah. "What have you done?" they ask, as they learn that Jonah is fleeing from YHWH. It appears that even the foreign sailors understand YHWH's reach better than Israel's wayward prophet. Here we see a nod in the direction of the book of Jonah's unique universalistic monotheism. YHWH, far from being confined to Jerusalem and Judah, created all that there is and, therefore, controls all places, even the sea.

After the sailors agree to throw Jonah into the sea, the narrative informs the reader that the sailors "feared YHWH and they offered a sacrifice to

---

22. See Hans Walter Wolff, *Obadiah and Jonah: A Commentary*, trans. Margaret Kohl, CC (Minneapolis: Augsburg, 1987), 84.

23. Diana Edelman makes a distinction in her discussion of this passage between the national god of Judah, "Yahweh of Hosts," and a developing cult at the time of Jonah that honored "Yahweh God of the Heavens." According to Edelman "Yahweh God of the Heavens" was the god of all nations and all animal and plant life. This was the god to whom Jonah referred in conversation with the sailors. But, Jonah, himself holds onto the idea of the locally bound god even though he is able to articulate the correct attributes of the deity; he does not fully understand the domain of "Yahweh God of the Heavens"; see Edelman, "Jonah among the Twelve in the MT: The Triumph of Torah over Prophecy," in *The Production of Prophecy: Constructing Prophecy and Prophets in Yehud*, ed. Diana V. Edelman and Ehud Ben Zvi, Bible World (London: Equinox, 2009), 154–55.

2. Is YHWH the God of the Nations as Well? 45

YHWH and made vows to him." (1:16). The pagan sailors become worshipers of YHWH and offer a sacrifice to YHWH outside of the temple precincts. This vignette is in stark contrast to the form of worship described in Isa 56, not to mention the strict Deuteronomic code that prohibits sacrifice and YHWH worship apart from the temple.

As the foreign sailors worship, Jonah finds himself in the belly of a fish, and here he voices a prayer. The prayer, or psalm, was likely not original but was composed separately and was added later to the existing narrative.[24] Nevertheless, it functions within the story in a striking way. The psalm focuses on two realms, Sheol and the temple. The prophet hopes that YHWH will hear him from the bottom of the sea or the bottom of Sheol (2:3–7). Yet YHWH has just shown that he commands the sea and is present there. Jonah seems to have forgotten. The prophet closes his prayer by imagining that his words have somehow reached YHWH in his "holy temple" (2:7), therefore reinforcing the idea that YHWH's domain is there and not where the prophet is. Contrary to the prophet's suppositions, the narrative reinforces YHWH's presence in the sea, when YHWH speaks to the fish (not to Jonah), and the fish delivers Jonah to the dry land.

As the narrative continues, the sailors' act of foreign YHWH worship apart from the temple is paralleled in the Ninevite repentance scene of chapter 3.[25] The exuberant declaration of the king, "Who knows, God may yet relent" (Jonah 3:9) is an echo not only of Joel 2:14 but also Jonah 1:6 in which the foreign ship's captain implores Jonah to pray saying, "Perhaps he [Jonah's god] will take notice of us that we may not perish." Consequently, these two instances of foreigners worshiping YHWH appear to be related.[26]

---

24. It has long been noted that the Jonah of the psalm is remarkably different from the Jonah of the rest of the story. Gerhard von Rad notes "These pious words of humble thanksgiving simply do not fit the mulish Jonah" (von Rad, *God at Work in Israel* [Nashville: Abingdon, 1980], 68); see also Nogalski, *Redactional Processes in the Book of the Twelve*, BZAW 218 (Berlin: de Gruyter, 1993), 266–69.

25. See Wolff, *Obadiah and Jonah*, 153–54. Wolff also draws attention to the phrase נאבד ולא "that we may not perish" (1:6) that is repeated in 1:14 by the sailors, נאבדה אל־נא "do not let us perish," and attested again in 3:9 by the Ninevite king, ולא נאבד "that we may not perish." This observation draws these pagan groups together as those who seek salvation from YHWH but not in terms of the temple. Instead, they simply appeal to YHWH's mercy.

26. The lexical links coupled with the theme of correct worship among the nations outside of the temple make this case compelling.

These two narratives of foreign worship outside of the temple contrast nicely with the prophet Jonah's misconception of YHWH's presence outside of the bounds of Israel. The foolish prophet exhibits an ideology that would limit YHWH's compassionate activity to the temple in Jerusalem—a conception Isa 55–56 implicitly shares. The Jonah vignettes, however, burst open those boundaries, affirming that YHWH is available to be worshiped at sea, hears prayers from Sheol, and delights in repentance taking place in Nineveh. Thus, the book of Jonah holds that the one God is available to anyone, anywhere.

2.5. Conclusion

The book of Jonah takes on prophetic conceptions concerning the reach of YHWH's compassion as the one God for all people. Contrary to Joel, Jonah contends that divine compassion is available to the nations. Contrary to Isa 55–56, Jonah shows that YHWH is a God of all people and all places. The one God, according to the book of Jonah, is not confined to one people or one place, but offers compassion and mercy to foreigners, regardless of their location. In addition, the narrative satirizes prophetic voices such as those of Joel and Isaiah by creating the character of Jonah who misunderstands YHWH's dominion, accuses YHWH of being too merciful, and sulks over the loss of a shrub. Jonah's caricature of an Israelite prophet highlights the negative attributes of such prophetic ideologies.[27] The ideology presented in the book of Jonah is certainly a minority voice among the scribal prophets of the postexilic period. The only other hint at such ideology comes from Mal 1:11 in which YHWH indicates that his name will be great among the nations and that he will receive pure offerings from all places.[28] Malachi quickly moves on to other concerns but the book of Jonah is more singular in its treatment of the topic. The whole narrative appears to be aimed at this one goal of promoting YHWH as the God of all people and all places and parodying those who would suggest otherwise.

---

27. Wolff (*Obadiah and Jonah*, 83–88) sees Jonah as an allegorical "caricature of a typical Hebrew." Likewise, Nogalski (*Redactional Processes*, 267) holds that the final redactors of Jonah must have understood Jonah's character allegorically or metaphorically to represent Israel. See also Wöhrle, "Prophetic Reflection," 2–17.

28. Nogalski, *Redactional Processes*, 272. See also Jer 18:8 in which YHWH indicates that if a nation repents, he will have mercy on that nation.

Bibliography

Allen, Leslie C. *The Books of Joel, Obadiah, Jonah, and Micah*. NICOT. Grand Rapids: Eerdmans, 1976.

Assmann, Jan. *The Price of Monotheism*. Translated by Robert Savage. Stanford, CA: Stanford University Press, 2009.

Bergler, Siegfried. *Joel als Schriftinterpret*. BEATAJ 16. Berlin: Lang, 1988.

Berquist, Jon L. *Judaism in Persia's Shadow: A Social and Historical Approach*. Eugene, OR: Wipf & Stock, 2003.

Broyles, Craig, and Craig Evans. *Writing and Reading the Scroll of Isaiah: Studies of an Interpretive Tradition*. VTSup 70.2. Leiden: Brill, 1997.

Crenshaw, James L. *Joel: A New Translation with Introduction and Commentary*. AB 24C. New York: Doubleday, 1995.

Dozeman, Thomas B. "Inner-Biblical Interpretation of Yahweh's Gracious and Compassionate Character." *JBL* 108 (1989): 207–23.

Edelman, Diana V. "Jonah among the Twelve in the MT: The Triumph of Torah over Prophecy." Pages 150–67 in *The Production of Prophecy: Constructing Prophecy and Prophets in Yehud*. Edited by Diana V. Edelman and Ehud Ben Zvi. Bible World. London: Equinox, 2009.

Magonet, Jonathan. *Form and Meaning: Studies in the Literary Techniques in the Book of Jonah*. BBET 2. Bern: Lang, 1976.

Nogalski, James. "Joel as 'Literary Anchor' for the Book of the Twelve." Pages 91–109 in *Reading and Hearing the Book of the Twelve*. Edited by James Nogalski and Marvin A. Sweeney. SymS 15. Atlanta: Society of Biblical Literature, 2000.

———. *Redactional Processes in the Book of the Twelve*. BZAW 218. Berlin: de Gruyter, 1993.

Rad, Gerhard von. *God at Work in Israel*. Nashville: Abingdon, 1980.

Schart, Aaron. *Die Entstehung des Zwölfprophetenbuchs: Neubearbeitungen von Amos im Rahmen Schriftenübergreifender Redaktionsprozesse*. BZAW 260. Berlin: de Gruyter, 1998.

Smith, Mark S. *The Early History of God: Yahweh and the Other Deities in Ancient Israel*. 2nd ed. Grand Rapids: Eerdmans, 2002.

———. *The Memoirs of God: History, Memory, and the Experience of the Divine in Ancient Israel*. Minneapolis: Fortress, 2004.

———. *The Origins of Biblical Monotheism: Israel's Polytheistic Background and the Ugaritic Texts*. New ed. New York: Oxford University Press, 2003.

Strazicich, John. *Joel's Use of Scripture and the Scripture's Use of Joel: Appropriation and Resignification in Second Temple Judaism and Early Christianity.* BibInt. 82. Leiden: Brill, 2007.

Trible, Phyllis. *Rhetorical Criticism: Context, Method, and the Book of Jonah.* Guides to Biblical Scholarship. Minneapolis: Fortress, 1994.

Van Leeuwen, Raymond. "Scribal Wisdom and Theodicy in the Book of the Twelve." Pages 31–49 in *In Search of Wisdom: Essays in Memory of John G. Gammie.* Edited by Leo G. Perdue, Bernard Brandon Scott, and William Johnston Wiseman. Louisville: Westminster John Knox Press, 1993.

Williamson, H. G. M. *The Book Called Isaiah: Deutero-Isaiah's Role in Composition and Redaction.* Oxford: Clarendon, 1994.

Wöhrle, Jakob. *Der Abschluss des Zwölfprophetenbuches: Buchübergreifende Redaktionsprozesse in den späten Sammlungen.* BZAW 389. Berlin: de Gruyter, 2008.

———. "A Prophetic Reflection on Divine Forgiveness: The Integration of the Book of Jonah into the Book of the Twelve." *JHebS* 9 (2010). https://doi.org/10.5508/jhs.2009.v9.a7.

Wolff, Hans Walter. *Joel and Amos: A Commentary on the Books of the Prophets Joel and Amos.* Translated by Samuel Dean McBride. Hermeneia. Philadelphia: Fortress, 1977.

———. *Obadiah and Jonah: A Commentary.* Translated by Margaret Kohl. CC. Minneapolis: Augsburg, 1987.

Part 2

Unity and Oneness in the Classical World

3
The Politics of Oneness among the Greeks

Lynette Mitchell

3.1. Introduction

From at least the end of the sixth century, the Greeks thought of themselves as one community with a shared genealogy, a shared language and literary heritage, and shared sanctuaries. In fact, the ethos of the Greeks was community: contrary to its own apparent exclusionary rhetoric that divided the world into Greeks and barbarians, the politics of Greek identity—in creating a sense of unity and oneness—predominantly sought to include people rather than exclude them. In this chapter, we will look at the inclusive nature of Greek identity formation and the means by which it was expressed. We will begin by looking at cult as a means of creating and expressing a sense of one community, before turning to storytelling, with a particular emphasis on foundations stories that forged mythical connections between different parts of the Greek world. The study will then turn to the use of genealogies for binding the community together. A thread that will run through the discussion is the discursive nature of these locations and means of identity formation, and the almost playful awareness that the Greeks had of their inherent flexibility to stretch and reshape the boundaries of belonging. Although the focus of the discussion will mainly be on the period from the eighth to the fifth centuries BCE, as the time when the sense of community of the Hellenes crystalized, the chapter will begin by looking back to the Early Iron Age (roughly the twelfth to the ninth centuries BCE) and conclude by glancing forward to the world created by Alexander the Great in the fourth century BCE where the terms of belonging were not changed, but the membership of the community was transformed.

52   Lynette Mitchell

3.2. Collapse and Recovery

Toward the end of the second millennium BCE, many of the political communities of the eastern Mediterranean and Near East collapsed. The reasons for this widespread collapse at around the same time (ca. 1200 BCE) are unknown. There may have been no single cause, but there is evidence across the Near East and eastern Mediterranean of waves of upheaval and destruction across a number of generations, and a general change in the political and social structures from Greece to Mesopotamia. Although there were some continuities with what had gone before, the social and political landscape of 1050 BCE was very different from what it had been in 1250 BCE.[1]

In the Greek world, after the final collapse of the Mycenean palace economies in the mid-eleventh century BCE as part of this pattern of destruction, the devastated communities took time to recover. There were some continuities with their Bronze Age past; for example, the sacred character of some sanctuaries was remembered, even if the god honored was forgotten; some of the Mycenean palaces were reoccupied, but their spaces were used in different ways. However, much was lost. The art of writing disappeared, and connections with the outside world were broken. Communities in this period were small (often no more than one hundred people), impoverished, and unstable, and existence focused on survival. While there is evidence that these small communities were hierarchical and a number of them had what has been called "rulers' houses," it took time for these communities to recover enough to become interested again in the world outside, let alone take an interest in the possibility of belonging to a wider community with common features.[2]

However, fragile signs of recovery are evident by the tenth century, especially at Lefkandi on the island of Euboea where the so-called Tomb

---

1. For a useful summary of the transition from the twelfth-century collapse to recovery in these regions, see Marc Van de Mieroop, *A History of the Ancient Near East ca. 3000–323 BC*, 2nd ed., BHAW (Malden, MA: Blackwell, 2007), 190–206.

2. These were not only houses where a ruler appears to have lived, but were also centers of cult for the community, and include evidence of ritual dining; see Alexander Mazarakis Ainian, *From Rulers' Dwellings to Temples: Architecture, Religion and Society in Early Iron Age Greece (1100–700 BC)*, SIMA 21 (Jonsered: Åströms, 1997).

3. The Politics of Oneness among the Greeks 53

of the Hero (almost certainly a local ruler) has been excavated.[3] The hero is a warrior who was cremated and then interred in an antique bronze vase in a shaft grave with his weapons. In another shaft grave is the burial of a woman wearing gold jewelry, and another grave contains the bones of four horses. These three burials were discovered inside a building of large proportions, although it is unclear whether the building was erected to house the burials, or whether they were placed inside a preexisting building (perhaps his house?). In any case the scale of the building and the richness of the grave goods indicates that the warrior was a man of high social status, who also had access to prestige items.

There are other indications that communities were starting to regroup, and also that there were things that started to be held in common. Although the art of writing had been lost, in the Early Iron Age and Archaic period the weaving together of stories in a shared language (the same language used by the Myceneans) became not only a way of creating new bonds, but also of expressing them. Sanctuaries of individual gods were, at the beginning of the recovery, often very local in character. However, as communities became more stable, interest grew in the cult centers of what were now the most important deities (such as Zeus, by this point regarded as king of the gods) and sanctuaries became locations for both ritual activities and competitive (and often elite) displays of various kinds.[4]

It was in this period of reawakening and recovery that a new specifically Greek identity and sense of one community started to take shape. In discussions of Greek identity, it is often presumed that this sense of commonality was formed in opposition to the idea of the barbarian, essentially those who did not speak Greek, the βαρβαρόφωνοι, and it is certainly the case that the Greeks did, on one level, make a clear distinction between themselves and barbarians. The sense of contrast between those who were Greeks and those who were not probably emerged originally on the fringes of the Hellenic world, especially from the eighth century in colonial settings around the Mediterranean, but also among the Greek cities of Asia

---

3. Mervyn R. Popham, P. G. Calligas, and L. Hugh Sackett, eds., *Lefkandi II: The Protogeometric Building at Toumba: Part 2, The Excavation, Architecture and Finds* (Athens: British School at Athens, 1993).

4. Zeus was known as a storm god in the Mycenean era. Julia Kindt (*Rethinking Greek Religion* [Cambridge: Cambridge University Press, 2012], 13–14) credits Homeric epic and the poems of Hesiod for the unification and dissemination of this revised pantheon.

54 Lynette Mitchell

Minor, which from the seventh century BCE saw more than one phase of conquest and subjection and were integrated into the Persian Empire in the mid-sixth century. It also took stronger hold on the consciousness of the Greeks of the mainland after the unsuccessful invasions by the Persians at the beginning of the fifth century, although recent work has shown this apparent polarity was more complicated than it would first appear.[5]

However, the Greeks did not only think about their world as one divided between themselves and the rest and did not just derive their sense of unity and oneness from opposition, despite the continuing importance of this strand of thought. From a very early date, the Greeks (or those who came to think of themselves as Greeks) also had a vision of the world that was much more welcoming and receptive to those on the boundaries. This alternative worldview placed the Greeks as a people in a whole world context, even if the Hellenes were at the center of that world, as part of a unified vision of humanity, which included humanity's relation to the gods.[6] This vision of unity did not deny difference. Indeed, on many levels it embraced it.

An important element in, and a significant part of, the formation of a common community of Greeks was a strong sense of inclusiveness. In fact, while an enduring part of the Greek mentality was a wariness about outsiders and strangers (ξένοι), alongside these anxieties sat a similar concern that strangers should be protected, so that there were ritual means (for which Zeus was responsible as Zeus Xenios) for drawing the outsider into the community through ritualized friendships (ξενίαι) based on gift-exchange or through acts of supplication (ἱκετείαι) at sanctuaries.[7]

Further, to identify outsiders, one also had to know who it was that belonged. At the end of the fifth century Herodotus of Halicarnassus

---

5. See, e.g., Kostas Vlassopoulos, *Greeks and Barbarians* (Cambridge: Cambridge University Press, 2013).

6. The Hellenes was a name the Greeks adopted for themselves, as descendants of Hellen son of Deucalion (the Greek Noah), who by the sixth century at least had become their cultural hero. The origin of the Latin *Graeci* (our Greeks) is more obscure; Irad Malkin (*The Returns of Odysseus: Colonization and Ethnicity* [Berkeley: University of California Press, 1998], 146–50) argues that *Graikoi* is another early self-appellation that lost out at some point to Hellenes as the name the Greeks gave themselves.

7. On ritualized friendship (ξενία), see Gabriel Herman, *Ritualised Friendship and the Greek City* (Cambridge: Cambridge University Press, 1987); on supplication, see John Gould, "*Hiketaia*," *JHS* 93 (1973): 74–103.

3. The Politics of Oneness among the Greeks 55

wrote that τὸ Ἑλληνικόν, Greekness "is common blood, common language, common sanctuaries and sacrifices for the gods, and a common way of life" (*Hist.* 8.144.2).[8] We can more or less fix the crystallization of the idea of a "community of Hellenes" to the sixth century BCE, although the development of the individual strands—ties of kinship, a common religion, or at least a common religious landscape, and the idea of a common language—had varying and disparate trajectories.[9] However, as we will see in the rest of this chapter, identifying the boundaries of belonging of the unified community was an ongoing challenge, although the mechanisms for this identification also allowed for maximum flexibility, and ultimately gave the Hellenic community continued vibrancy and longevity.

3.3. Sanctuaries

The Early Iron Age recovery after the Bronze Age collapse is particularly evident at the sanctuaries. Sanctuaries were places where offerings and dedications were made to gods. But the Greeks as a people were fiercely competitive and placed great emphasis on honor and the pursuit of excellence. As a result, sanctuaries also became important for competitive display, not only in terms of dedications, but also other, particularly elite, pursuits, such as chariot racing.[10] Furthermore, at what were to become the two most important sanctuaries, Olympia and Delphi, which had slightly

---

8. Unless otherwise noted, all translations are mine.

9. See Lynette Mitchell, *Panhellenism and the Barbarian in Archaic and Classical Greece* (Swansea: Classical Press of Wales, 2007). There is an ongoing discussion about the unity of the Greek language because of the presence of diverse dialects; but for the abstracted sense of a Hellenic language, see, e.g., Anna Morpurgo Davies, "The Greek Notion of Dialect," *Verbum* 10 (1987): 7–27; Stephen Colvin, "Greek Dialects in the Archaic and Classical Ages," in *A Companion to the Ancient Greek Language*, ed. Edgar J. Bakker, BCAW (Chichester: Wiley-Blackwell, 2010), 200–212.

10. However, at Olympia the original competition at the games (founded in 776 BCE) was the footrace and chariot-racing was only added to the program in 680 BCE; see Paul Christesen, *Olympic Victor Lists and Ancient Greek History* (Cambridge: Cambridge University Press, 2007), 211–12. At Delphi (whose sanctuary had eighth-century origins), the games were first organized in 586 BCE; chariot-racing was introduced soon after. Unlike the Olympic games, the games at Delphi included musical competitions. See, generally, David G. Romano, "Athletic Festivals in the Northern Peloponnese and Central Greece," in *A Companion to Sport and Spectacle in Greek and Roman Antiquity*, ed. Paul Christesen and Donald G. Kyle, BCAW (Malden, MA: Wiley-Blackwell, 2014), 177–80.

56   Lynette Mitchell

different catchment areas, cities would also compete with each other in the lavishness of their building works, especially the treasuries that housed dedications made by the cities that built them.[11]

While the games at Olympia are traditionally dated from the early eighth century, the sanctuary itself was much older and the cult dates back to the eleventh century BCE.[12] It seems from the Olympic victor lists (although they are notoriously problematic), combined with archaeological and other evidence, that although originally a local festival the Olympic games started to attract participants from further afield by the seventh century.[13] It became explicitly Hellenic by at least the early fifth century; the officials, known as διαιτηταί in a late sixth-century inscription, were renamed Ἑλλανοδίχαι, "Hellenic judges," a change that must have happened at least by 476 BCE when the encomiastic poet Pindar refers to an Aetolian Ἑλλανοδίχης (*Ol.* 3.10–15).[14] An inscription from Olympia probably dating to roughly the same period gives the enforcing official the title Ἑλλανοζίχης (Buck no. 61).[15]

However, as Catherine Morgan has noted, a crucial moment for the formation of Hellenic identity came with the deliberate founding probably at the end of the sixth century of the περίοδος, or festival circuit of so-called crown games.[16] In a four-year cycle, the festivals at Olympia, Isthmia,

---

11. Michael Scott, *Delphi and Olympia: The Spatial Politics of Panhellenism in the Archaic and Classical Periods* (Cambridge: Cambridge University Press, 2010).

12. Brigitta Eder, "Continuity of Bronze Age Cult at Olympia? The Evidence of the Late Bronze Age and Early Iron Age Pottery," in *Potnia: Deities and Religion in the Aegean Bronze Age*, ed. Robert Laffineur and Robin Hägg, Aegaeum 22 (Liege: University of Liege, 2001), 201–9; Helmut Kyrieleis, *Anfänge und Frühzeit des Heiligtums von Olympia*, Olympische Forschungen 31 (Berlin: de Gruyter, 2006), 61–79.

13. See Christesen, *Olympic Victor Lists*, esp. 157–60.

14. For the διαιτητής, see Peter Siewert, "The Olympic Rules," in *Proceedings of an International Symposium on the Olympic Games, 5–9 September, 1988*, ed. William D. E. Coulson and Helmut Kyrieleis (Athens: Deutsches archäologisches Institut, 1992), 115; Thomas Heine Nielsen, *Olympia and the Classical Hellenic City-State-Culture* (Copenhagen: Royal Danish Academy of Science and Letters, 2007), 20–21.

15. For date of the Ἑλλανοζίχης of 475–450 BCE, see Lilian H. Jeffrey, *The Local Scripts of Archaic Greece*, rev. ed., Oxford Monographs on Classical Archaeology (Oxford: Oxford University Press, 1990), no. 15; the earlier date of "before 580 BC" is given by Carl Darling Buck, *The Greek Dialects* (Chicago: University of Chicago Press, 1955).

16. Morgan, *Athletes and Oracles: The Transformation of Olympia and Delphi in the Eighth Century*, Cambridge Classical Studies (Cambridge: Cambridge University

3. The Politics of Oneness among the Greeks   57

Delphi, and Nemea were billed as being "for Hellenes" (cf., e.g., Pindar, *Ol.* 1.116, frags. 52d.23, 118). For these festivals, Olympia and Delphi went some way toward defining who should participate in the games (and so in Greekness) by sending out sacred ambassadors to the cities to announce the festivals and the sacred truce, although the list of invitees was not pro-scriptive or exclusive in determining attendees.[17] Cities sent delegates as observers (θεωροί) to the festivals as well as athletes to the games, so that Irad Malkin has claimed that these ritual networks formed by the two-way traffic of sacred ambassadors and city delegates were both "formative and expressive" in the convergence of a Greek identity.[18]

These Panhellenic sanctuaries were also places where Greek iden-tity could be tested, with varying results. It was not uncommon for non-Greeks to make dedications at Greek sanctuaries (the most famous example is probably the dedications at Delphi and elsewhere made by the Lydian king, Croesus), but it was the general presumption that only Greeks were allowed to build treasuries at the Panhellenic centers or to take part in the games. Nevertheless, the Agyllaei of Etruria certainly consulted the Delphic oracle and also probably built a treasury (Herodo-tus, *Hist.* 1.167.1–2; Strabo, *Geogr.* 5.2.3), as did the Etruscans from Spina (Strabo, *Geogr.* 5.1.7, 9.3.8; Pliny, *Nat.* 3.120).[19] Herodotus thinks that

---

Press, 1990), 213. The Olympic games and the Pythian games at Delphi were quadren-nial, and the Pythian games took place in the third year of the Olympiad; the Nemean and Isthmian games were biennial in the second and third year of each Olympiad. These were the crown games, because the prizes in the games were crowns of olive (Olympia), laurel (Pythian games at Delphi), wild celery (Nemea), and pine (Isthmia), rather than valuable prizes awarded at other festivals.

17. The seminal work on the ἐπαγγελία, the announcement of the festivals and θεωροί (as sacred ambassadors), is still Paul Boesch, *ΘΕΩΡΟΣ: Untersuchung zur Epangelie griechischer Feste* (Göttingen: Mayer & Müller, 1908), although one should also note Paula Perlman, *City and Sanctuary in Ancient Greece: The Theorodokia in the Peloponnese*, Hypomnemata (Göttingen: Vandenhoeck & Ruprecht, 2000), 14–16.

18. Malkin, *A Small Greek World: Networks in the Mediterranean*, Greeks Overseas (New York: Oxford University Press, 2011), 20–21. On the θεωροί (as sacred delegates), see Ian Rutherford, *State Pilgrims and Sacred Observers in Ancient Greece: A Study of Theōriā and Theōroi* (Cambridge: Cambridge University Press, 2013). Confusingly, the term θεωροί could be used for the ambassadors who traveled from sanctuaries to cities, and the delegates who traveled from cities to sanctuaries as observers at the festivals.

19. For the Treasury of the Argyllaei, see Anne Jacquemin, *Offrandes monumen-tales à Delphes*, Bibliothèque des écoles françaises d' Athènes et de Rome (Paris: de Boccard, 1999), 72–74.

58   Lynette Mitchell

the Agyllaei were Etruscan, though Strabo thinks they were originally a Pelasgian (proto-Hellenic) foundation from Thessaly that was attacked by the Etruscans. Strabo also thinks that the city of Spina must have been a Greek foundation because they had a treasury, and Pliny says the city was founded by one of the Greek heroes of the Trojan wars, Diomedes (so that they were, in fact, Greek). There is also evidence that Etruscans made dedications at Olympia, and may have even participated in the games there.[20] One thing that these examples serve to demonstrate very clearly is how uncertain the boundaries of Greekness were and how uncertain the testing mechanisms were also, so that it was sometimes necessary, retrospectively, to understand groups of people as Greek in order to explain possible transgressions.

It is also often asserted that the Panhellenic games tested the exclusivity of Greekness in a more hard-nosed way, based on the fact that Herodotus tells a story of Alexander I of Macedon (an ancestor of Alexander the Great), who in the early fifth century was permitted to take part in the games at Olympia only because he was able to prove the Hellenic descent of the Macedonian kings (Herodotus, *Hist.* 5.22).[21] Herodotus is quite clear about his story: the other contestants complained that Alexander was not Greek, so Alexander provided an account of his descent from the Argive hero Temenus (which Herodotus also recounts; 8.137–139). Herodotus was not the only ancient author to accept the Greek descent of the Macedonian kings. Thucydides, another fifth-century historian, also thought that Alexander I was descended from Temenus (*P.W.* 2.99.3), though it is worth noting that even in the fourth century there were Greeks who considered the Macedonians barbarians.[22]

However, whether Alexander's Hellenicity was actually tested at the Olympic games is another matter, since his name does not appear in the victor lists, and there is good reason to think that this genealogy (and indeed the story about Alexander's participation at the games) may have been part of Macedonian propaganda to excuse themselves for the part

---

20. Giovannangelo Camporeale, "The Etruscans in the Mediterranean," in *The Etruscans outside Etruria*, ed. Giovannangelo Camporeale (Los Angeles: Getty Museum, 2004), 98–99.

21. E.g., Nielsen, *Olympia and the Classical Hellenic City-State-Culture*, 18–21.

22. On the varying views of ancient authors in the fifth and fourth centuries on Macedonian Hellenicity, see Mitchell, *Panhellenism and the Barbarian*, 204.

3. The Politics of Oneness among the Greeks 59

they played in the Persian Wars against the Greeks.[23] Yet what is more significant is that Alexander (allegedly) tested his Hellenic credentials simply by assuming that he was Greek, and it is this assumption that he would be included that is the real key to the story (though not often recognized), and that this claim was accepted because enough people believed the story. Herodotus says that the Eleans (who controlled the sanctuary at Olympus for a significant part of its history and so issued the invitation to possible attendees) told the Egyptians that the games were open to Eleans and to any of the Greeks "who wished to take part" (*Hist.* 2.160), οἱ βουλόμενοι. So there was not so much an exclusion clause as a self-defining inclusion principle that actually allowed a lot of flexibility around participation: the status of the father of Alexander the Great, Philip II of Macedon (whose Greekness was openly and often doubted), was not questioned when he took part in the Olympic games (he had an Olympic equestrian victory in 356 BCE [Plut. *Alex.* 3.5], and perhaps also 352 and 348) or when he organized the Pythian games [Delphi] in 349 BCE, or when Arrybas of Epirus (whose Greekness was even more ambivalent) had victories at Delphi and Olympia.[24]

This sense of belonging to a single community of cult by common participation in the rituals and competitions at these sacred centers was a powerful force. In the final turbulent years of the fifth century, the comic poet Aristophanes has the eponymous Lysistrata reproach the Greeks for destroying each other even though, like kinsmen, they sprinkle altars from one bowl at Olympia, Thermopylae, and Delphi (*Lysis.* 1128–1134). Born out of a need to compete, however, the sacred games did not create bonds that were strong enough to prevent the Greek cities from engaging in endemic warfare throughout the fifth and fourth centuries until in 338 BCE a Greek army was finally defeated by Philip II at the battle of Chaeronea. The Greek cities were forced to join his League of Corinth as part of his aim to undertake a war against Asia. Nevertheless, it was because of the

---

23. Eugene N. Borza, *In the Shadow of Olympus: The Emergence of Macedon* (Princeton: Princeton University Press, 1990), 80–84, 111–12.

24. For Philip II, see Eugene N. Borza, "Athenians, Macedonians, and the Origins of the Macedonian Royal House," in *Studies in Attic Epigraphy, History and Topography: Presented to Eugene Vanderpool*, Hesperia Supplement 19 (Princeton: American School of Classical Studies at Athens, 1982), 13; on Arrybas of Molossia, see Peter J. Rhodes and Robin Osborne, *Greek Historical Inscriptions 404–323 BC* (Oxford: Oxford University Press, 2003), 348–55.

60   Lynette Mitchell

constant warfare between the Greek cities, who constantly competed with each other for political preeminence, that strong stories of unity needed to be told.[25]

3.4. Storytelling and Foundation Stories

There has been much discussion on the formative years of Homeric epic, but it is generally agreed that the epic poems arose out of an oral tradition and were a fundamental part of the creation of a Hellenic identity. Homeric epic shows connections with the Bronze Age, although these connections are not simple, and have not always been easy to understand.[26] Homeric epic was only written down at some point after the eighth century (various dates have been suggested between the eighth and sixth centuries); although they obviously reflect some experiences from earlier periods (including the Bronze Age), it is now generally agreed that they mostly need to be contextualized in the Early Iron Age and Archaic period. It has been suggested that the *Odyssey* in particular, the story of Odysseus's return voyage from the siege of Troy, was a metaphoric reflection of the Greeks' own early travels as they started to sail in the Mediterranean again in the period around the tenth and ninth centuries.[27] It is also suggestive that one of the earliest examples of the new Greek alphabetic script (based on Phoenician syllabary) is a graffito on an eighth-century pot, the so-called Nestor's Cup from Pithecoussae (modern island of Ischia in southern Italy, which was a settlement of the Euboeans). Written at least partially in the epic dialect, it is often considered to be a joke on epic.[28]

---

25. See Lynette Mitchell, "The Community of the Hellenes," in *Federalism in Greek Antiquity*, ed. Hans Beck and Peter Funke (Cambridge: Cambridge University Press, 2015), 61–65.

26. For a fascinating summary of Homeric historiography, see John Bennet, "Linear B and Homer," in vol. 3 of *A Companion to Linear B: Mycenean Greek Texts and Their World*, ed. Yves Duhoux and Anna Morpogo Davies, BCILL 133 (Leuven: Peeters, 2014), 187–233.

27. See also Malkin, *Returns of Odysseus*. The Euboeans, in particular, as we can see from archaeological finds at Lefkandi, seem to have re-formed contacts with others in the Mediterranean, especially Cyprus, by the mid-tenth century BCE, or even earlier. For a useful summary of the material record, see Robin Lane Fox, *Travelling Heroes: Greeks and Their Myths in the Epic Age of Homer* (London: Penguin, 2008), 45–72.

28. See Russell Meiggs and David Lewis, eds., *Greek Historical Inscriptions to the End of the Fifth Century*, rev. ed. (Oxford: Oxford University Press, 1988), no. 1.

3. The Politics of Oneness among the Greeks   61

The use of the epic dialect (composed in dactylic hexameter that is probably related to the oral origins of the poems) itself was of significance. An artificial language form that was never used in conversation, it probably had connections to the syllabic Linear B language of the Bronze Age, and provided an early koine for the sharing of the Homeric and Hesiodic sagas, and so also the creation of a sense of a common community through language and story-telling.[29] These stories themselves not only brought together local narrative strands from around the Greek-speaking communities of the Mediterranean to create a story for the whole community; they also supported a generalized elite and heroic culture based on excellence in warfare.[30] In Hesiod's cosmogony, Zeus became king of the gods because of his victory over the Titans (Hesiod, *Theog.* 881–886, cf. *Op.* 668). In the *Iliad* it is the Lycian king Sarpedon (fighting on the Trojan side) who articulates most clearly the elite heroic code that underpins Homeric epic: "Our kings are not without fame [he says], who rule in Lycia, and they feast on fat sheep and choice honey-sweet wine, and their strength is noble, since they fight among the foremost Lycians" (Homer, *Il.* 12.310–321).[31] Rulers were warriors. There is continuing debate around whether the heroic burial at Lefkandi reflects the funerary rites of cremation and inhumation given to Patroclus in book 23 of the *Iliad*, or whether the rites awarded Patroclus reflect ritual practices at Lefkandi (and elsewhere). However it is clear that from the Early Iron Age there were new ways of honoring the heroic dead that differed significantly from the Bronze Age experience and that these new practices and the stories that were told by Greek speakers around the Mediterranean were tied to each other in profound and intimate ways.[32]

---

29. On the epic dialect, see, e.g., Martin L. West, "The Rise of the Greek Epic," *JHS* 108 (1988): 151–72; Michael Meier-Brüger, "The Rise and Descent of the Language of the Homeric Poems," in *Ancient Greece: From the Mycenean Palaces to the Age of Homer*, ed. Sigrid Deger-Jalkotzy and Irene S. Lemos, Edinburgh Leventis Studies 3 (Edinburgh: Edinburgh University Press, 2006), 417–26.

30. E.g., West, "Rise of the Greek Epic."

31. See esp. Hans van Wees, "Kings in Combat: Battles and Heroes in the *Iliad*," *ClQ* 38 (1988): 18–22. Sarpedon is Achilles's alter ego, as another son of Zeus, but on the Trojan side. Hera persuades Zeus that the noble Sarpedon has to die and he is killed (ironically) by Patroclus (Achilles's friend); Zeus then takes his revenge on Patroclus, which in turn makes the death of Achilles inevitable.

32. See Ian Morris, *Archaeology as Cultural History: Words and Things in Iron Age Greece*, Social Archaeology (Malden, MA: Blackwell, 2000), 218–38.

62 Lynette Mitchell

Another narrative means by which the Aegean communities tied themselves together was through foundation stories, which were intrinsically local. The Greeks told a large number of stories of migration, both of the Hellenes into the Greek mainland, and Greeks crossing the Aegean from the mainland to the coast of Anatolia. There are good reasons to doubt some of these; the so-called Dorian invasion, for example, is in all likelihood an invention of the fifth century BCE.[33] However, that there were periodic real migrations is also certain. The city of Miletus, which was to become such an important hub in Asia Minor in the archaic period, shows evidence of peoples from the south Aegean moving there in the Middle and Late Bronze Ages, probably principally from Crete, although there is also evidence of indigenous Carians among the early population group in the city.[34]

Nevertheless, these stories of migration not only created a link between the Greek mainland and the cities of Asia Minor but in fact created a center and periphery. Enduring bonds existed between Greek colonies and their mother cities, even if processes of foundation were rather more complicated than was once believed.[35] But stories about these ties could also be told in order to form a relationship between a putative colony and alleged mother city in the Greek mainland. A favorite way of telling stories about the relationship between the Greek mainland and the cities of Asia Minor was to talk about the Ionian migration, and the colonization of Asia Minor by the sons of Codrus, the mythical king of Athens.[36] Miletus at some point also embraced these stories of migration and foundation, and Neleus (one of the younger sons of Codrus) was claimed as the city's founder. There were also stories at Miletus of violence between the incoming colonists (cf. Herodotus, *Hist.* 1.146). However, there were numerous other stories about the foundation that did not involve conflict and named other founders. Indeed, one feature

---

33. Jonathan Hall, *Hellenicity: Between Ethnicity and Culture* (Chicago: University of Chicago Press, 2002), 73–82.

34. Vanessa B. Gorman, *Miletus, the Ornament of Ionia: A History of the City to 400 BCE* (Ann Arbor: University of Michigan Press, 2001), 14–31; Naoise Mac Sweeney, *Foundation Myths and Politics in Ionia*, Cambridge Classical Studies (Cambridge: Cambridge University Press, 2013), 65–67.

35. See esp. Irad Malkin, "Foundations," in *A Companion to Archaic Greece*, ed. Kurt A. Raaflaub and Hans van Wees, BCAW (Malden, MA: Wiley-Blackwell, 2009), 373–94.

36. On the Ionian migration, see generally, Mac Sweeney, *Foundation Myths*.

3. The Politics of Oneness among the Greeks   63

of these foundation stories more generally was that multiple and competing foundation stories were current for many cities at any one time.[37]

Yet it was not just Miletus that bought into (and in some sense came to need) the stories of foundation from the Greek mainland either through the sons of Codrus or the returning heroes of the Trojan Wars. Mimnermus (of Colophon or Smyrna in Asia Minor) also wrote in elegiac verse a *Smyrneis,* which was an account of the Smyrna's wars with Lydia (see *FGrHist* 578 F 5), although it probably also included material on the foundation of Smyrna as well as an account of the (mythical) foundation of Colophon in Asia Minor by the Homeric hero Andraemon of Pylos.[38] In the early fifth century, Panyassis of Harlicarnassus composed a poem about Codrus and Neleus and the colonization of Ionia (T1 Davies *EGF*), and Hellanicus thought that the people from Priene originated from Thebes (*FGrHist* 4 F 101). These stories may at some level reflect real migrations, as Irene Lemos has argued, as people left the mainland for safer places to live after the collapse of the Mycenean world, a migration that she argues is reflected in the archaeological record.[39] Jonathan Hall, on the other hand, has argued that the "Greeks" of Asia Minor invented migration myths in order to secure their interests with the mainland.[40] However, or whenever, these stories were invented (or "discovered") they served to forge links of kinship between Greek speakers on the Greek mainland with Greek speakers on the edges of the Greek world.

Although these stories of foundation from the Greek mainland were mythical, they nevertheless had real political power. In 499 BCE, Aristagoras of Miletus requested the Athenians' help in the revolt of the Ionians from the Persian Empire on the grounds that the Ionians were Athenian

---

37. Cf. Maurizio Giangiulio, "Constructing the Past: Colonial Traditions and the Writing of History; The Case of Cyrene," in *The Historian's Craft in the Age of Herodotus,* ed. Nino Luraghi (Oxford: Oxford University Press, 2001), 116–37.

38. For Smyrna, see Ewen L. Bowie, "Early Greek Elegy, Symposium and Public Festival," *JHS* 106 (1986): 29–30.

39. Lemos, *The Protogeometric Aegean: The Archaeology of the Late Eleventh and Tenth Centuries BC,* Oxford Monographs on Classical Archaeology (Oxford: Oxford University Press, 2002), 193.

40. While he does not rule out actual migrations from the Greek mainland to Asia Minor, Hall thinks that a self-conscious Ionian (and Aeolian) identity developed in the first instance among the communities of Asia Minor; see further Jonathan Hall, *Ethnic Identity in Greek Antiquity* (Cambridge: Cambridge University Press, 1997), 52; Hall, *Hellenicity,* 67–73.

64 Lynette Mitchell

colonists (Herodotus, *Hist.* 5.97). That the Athenians agreed to take part shows how powerful these stories were for creating and maintaining links between the Greeks of the mainland and those in Asia Minor. This also was to determine the course of the relationship between the Greeks and the Persians for the next 150 years.

3.5. Genealogies

Linked to (and often embedded within) these foundation stories were genealogies. Even in the Greek mainland, an important part of community building were the stories of common descent they told about themselves, the myth-histories.[41] In a process that Hall has called "aggregation," the Hellenic genealogy (so-called) is embedded in the sixth-century text the *Catalogue of Women*.[42] This text was structured as stories of heroines as a genealogy describing the common descent of local and regional ethnic groups from Dorus, Aeolus, and Ion, the sons of Hellen, the cultural hero of the Hellenes.[43] From this basic genealogical root, a complex tree was then able to grow as different peoples were grafted on.[44]

However, within a culture that was so essentially oral, genealogical (and so kinship) connections could readily be invented and so discovered. It was his genealogy as the descendant of the Argive Temenus that Alexander I of Macedon's story at the Olympic games (above) was said to have been justified through the myth-history of genealogy. Even if the story of the games itself is a later invention, the genealogy was simply an added extra. Genealogies, which were vehicles for explaining the present through the myth-histories of the past, could efficiently and effectively make anyone Greek as long as the genealogy was accepted. According to Herodotus (although this time he is obviously doubtful about the historicity of the whole story) before the Persian Wars the Persians sent an embassy to Argos claiming descent from Argive Perseus (*Hist.* 7.150; cf. 7.61), a story that does not seem to have taken hold. Likewise, there are

---

41. See esp. Catherine Morgan, *Early Greek States beyond the Polis* (London: Routledge, 2003), 46–47.

42. Hall, *Ethnic Identity* esp. 34–51; Hall, *Hellenicity*, 179–80.

43. Hall, *Ethnic Identity*, 40–51.

44. It is notable that the Inachids of Argos (which was to become a significant branch) are attached to the main stemma through the marriage of Dorus with the daughter of Phoroneus (see [Hesiod] frag. 10b Merkelbach and West).

3. The Politics of Oneness among the Greeks 65

also stories of Thracian kings who tried to claim kinship links with the Greeks and particularly the Athenians.[45]

Indeed, by the sixth century, the Greeks also used genealogies to locate themselves within the wider non-Greek world. That the earth was a limited space encircled by Ocean (probably developed and adapted from Near Eastern mythology) was an early idea suggested in Homeric epic.[46] On the other hand, genealogies created webs of interconnection as the Greeks mapped themselves genealogically onto this world space. For example, Egypt had long been a place of wonder for the Greeks, and the sixth-century *Catalogue of Women* had included Asiatic elements connecting Hellenes to Egypt and Asia (Aegyptus, Belus, and Arabus, e.g., [Hes.] frags. 127 and 137 Merkelbach and West) in the stemma of the descendants of the heroine Io (who herself was part of the Inachid stemma).[47] Io, who in the principal accounts of the story is the priestess at the Heraeum in Argos, is seduced by Zeus, turned into a heifer by Hera, and then, driven mad by a gad-fly, travels the known world, before ending up in Egypt, where, restored to human form, she gives birth to a son, Epaphus, on the banks of the Nile.[48] Epaphus, in turn, becomes the father not only of Libya, but also Danaus and Aegpytus, who each have

---

45. Mitchell, *Panhellenism and the Barbarian*, 203.

46. Geoffery S. Kirk, John E. Raven, and Malcolm Schofield, *The Presocratic Philosophers: A Critical History with a Selection of Texts*, 2nd ed. (Cambridge: Cambridge University Press, 1983), 10–17; James S. Romm, *The Edges of the Earth in Ancient Thought: Geography, Exploration and Fiction* (Princeton: Princeton University Press, 1992), 20–26. The sixth-century Anaximander of Miletus was the earliest Greek mapmaker, and like other Greek natural philosophers was interested in symmetry and opposites, but was the first to reflect on the shape of the earth, which he described as a round column suspended in the heavens; see Charles H. Kahn, *Anaximander and the Origins of Greek Cosmology* (New York: Columbia University Press, 1960), 76–84.

47. Martin L. West, *The Hesiodic Catalogue of Women: Its Nature, Structure and Origins* (Oxford: Oxford University Press, 1985), 76–78, cf. 132. In the *Iliad*, Egyptian Thebes is known for its wealth and its warriors (9.382–384), and in the *Odyssey* Helen administers a drug that was given to her by an Egyptian woman, a drug that takes away anger and pain, and brings forgetfulness of all terrible things (*Od.* 4.226–232). Menelaus says he visited Egypt (*Od.* 4.81–85), and Odysseus pretends that he does (*Od.* 14.257–286). The Greeks first settled in Egypt in the mid seventh century, as mercenaries for Psammetichus I (Herodotus, *Hist.* 2.152.4–154.3; cf. Meiggs and Lewis, *Greek Historical Inscriptions*, no. 7), who gave them land in return for helping him secure control of all Egypt.

48. Lynette Mitchell, "Euboean Io," *ClQ* 51 (2001): 339–52.

fifty daughters and fifty sons respectively. The sons of Aegyptus wanted forcibly to marry the daughters of Danaus, and, as a result of the Danaids' flight to Argos and their successful supplication in the city, Danaus was to become king of Argos; even more shockingly, Lynceus, the son of Aegyptus, who married Danaus's daughter Hypermnestra, was to succeed him as king (Pindar, *Nem.* 10.1, 13–14; Aeschylus, *Prom.* 867–869). Later, another Egyptian mytheme was also incorporated into the Io cycle, so that Epaphus's daughter, Libye, became the mother of Bousiris, the king of the Egyptians who sacrificed strangers that came to Egypt.[49]

Other non-Greeks were also incorporated into Greek genealogies. Of particular note is Pelops, the mythical king of Pisa in the Peloponnese and founder of the Olympic games, who was said to be either Lydian or Phrygian.[50] Cadmus, founding king of Thebes, and brother of Europa, at some stage in his mythical development, was given Phoenician descent.[51] By the late fifth century there was also a variant genealogy that made the Phoenicians descendants of Io, since the chorus of Euripides's *Phoenician Women*, claim that they are "of one family" with the children of Agenor, who was the father of Cadmus and Europe (cf. Herodotus, *Hist.* 4.147.4).[52]

These attempts to include non-Greeks in Greek genealogies were acts of genealogical imperialism, but they also reflect the Hellenes' interest in their place within the whole world space of the οἰκουμένη and as members of the world of humanity.[53] Even more, however, they also show the power of the Greek sense of inclusiveness, which sought to bring others, who might have been considered non-Greeks, into their genealogical orbit and

---

49. Bousiris's story is first known from narrative scenes on mainly Athenian pottery in the late sixth and early fifth centuries (see Margaret C. Miller, "The Myth of Bousiris: Ethnicity and Art," in *Not the Classical Ideal: Athens and the Construction of the Other in Greek Art*, ed. Beth Cohen [Leiden: Brill, 2000], 413–42), where Bousiris is represented as ethnically Egyptian (that is, as not Greek). However by the fourth century, Isocrates says that Bousiris father was Poseidon, but his mother was Libya daughter of Epaphus (10), thus making him another descendant of Io.

50. Mitchell, *Panhellenism and the Barbarian*, 181–82.

51. Mitchell, *Panhellenism and the Barbarian*, 182–84.

52. As we know from late traditions, Agenor is the son of Libya, daughter of Epaphus, and this story must have been known in the fifth century if not earlier since Euripides's chorus declares that Io as the mother of Epaphus is the προμάτωρ, and through her that the Phoenicians are kinsmen of the Cadmeians of Thebes.

53. For genealogical imperialism, see Mitchell, *Panhellenism and the Barbarian*, 179–84.

3. The Politics of Oneness among the Greeks 67

make them kin. As the perceptions of the edges of Greek world expanded, so did the perception of those who might belong to that world. Just as the Greeks insisted on the boundaries between Greeks and barbarians, because of their inclusive world view so they were also willing to test and blur those boundaries and even constantly to redefine them.

This testing of boundaries, and how contested the nature of oneness and belonging in the Greek world could be, is seen clearly through consideration of Aeschylus's play the *Suppliant Women* (*Supplices*), probably produced at Athens in the 460s. This play, at least on one level, explores the relationship between the Egyptian-born Danaids and their Greek "kinsmen" when they arrive in Argos as suppliants to seek protection from a forced marriage to their cousins, the Aegyptiads. Both the Aegyptiads and Danaids are descendants of Io, so both can claim kinship with the Argives.

Yet in the play the un-Greekness of both is also explored. On their arrival in Argos, the Danaids are afraid of their reception, since "everyone is ready to cast reproach on those who speak a different language [ἀλλόθροοι]" (Aeschylus, *Suppl.* 972–973). Both the Aegyptiads and Danaids are also described in the play as physically different, and as having a dark appearance. Although the sons of Aegyptus never themselves appear on stage (the herald arrives to drag the maidens away, probably accompanied by attendants), they are said to have "dark limbs" that show up against their white robes (*Suppl.* 719–20). Even more startlingly, the Danaids are described specifically as non-Greek (even un-Greek) and exotic. They also refer to their dark skin and "Nile-burned cheeks" (*Suppl.* 71) and call themselves a "sun-burned race" (*Suppl.* 155). When he first meets the Danaids, Pelasgus, the Argive king, also asks (*Suppl.* 234–237; cf. 120–121):

> From what country should we say this unhellenic company [ἀνελληνόστολος]
> has come luxuriating in barbarian robes [πέπλοι βάρβαροι]
> and wrappings? For it is not the clothing of Argive women
> nor even from the ways of Hellas.

Yet the Danaids have a positive right to supplicate the Argives because they are descendants of Io (*Suppl.* 16–19, 274–276, 291–324). Pelasgus, after hearing the whole story of their descent, believes it and accepts their ancient claims of kinship (*Suppl.* 325–326), as do the Argives (cf. *Suppl.* 632, 652). Furthermore, they do have Hellenic aspects: in particular, they are modest and, unlike the Egyptian herald, honor Greek gods and call

68 Lynette Mitchell

on Zeus, Apollo, Poseidon, and Hermes "'in his Hellenic form" (*Suppl.* 210–223).

The daughters of Danaus are therefore kin, but also strangers, and this dual role is fundamental to the play. Pelasgus sums up the ambiguity of their position when he calls them "citizen-strangers," ἀστοξένοι (*Suppl.* 354–358) . He also tells the Argive assembly that to reject the Danaids' claims would give rise to a two-fold pollution both of stranger (ξενικόν) and citizen (ἀστικόν; *Suppl.* 618–620). The Danaids are dark skinned and exotic, yet they are also ὅμαιμος, of the same blood, as the Argives.[54]

Nevertheless, the decision to include the Danaids within the community of the Argives is not uncomplicated. If the Danaids have a kinship link to the Argives, then so must the Aegyptiads. The relationship between the Aegyptiads and the Danaids is a significant relationship in the play, and they have an aversion to marriage with "self-same kin" (αὐτογενεῖ φυξανορίᾳ; *Suppl.* 8). But the Aegyptiads are violent, and their violence is one of the principal reasons the Danaids give for their flight from the hateful marriage. They describe their cousins as a "male-thronged, violent [ὑβριστής], Aegyptus-born swarm" (*Suppl.* 29–30) and pray that they may be saved by gods who respect justice and hate violence (*Suppl.* 78–82; cf. 104–105, 426–427). The violence of the Aegyptiads is borne out by the Egyptian herald's behavior in the final scenes of the play, when he threatens to drag the maidens forcibly from the altar. He (or perhaps his Egyptian henchmen) tells the Danaids to get on the ship or they will be pricked and poked, and, murderously and with much gore, have their heads cut off (*Suppl.* 836–841); he also threatens to drag them away by the hair (*Suppl.* 884, 909) and to tear their clothes (*Suppl.* 903–904). Not only are they violent, but also the Aegyptiads apparent distance from Greek values is accentuated by the herald's refusal to acknowledge Greek gods: 'I do not fear these gods. They did not rear me or bring me to full age by their care" (*Suppl.* 893–894; cf. 921–923). Even more, however, the union of a Danaid and an Aegyptiad through the marriage of Lynceus and Hypermnestra is to refound the Argive royal house: the removal of the Pelasgian house, and its replacement by the line of Danaus through Lynceus and Hypermnestra

---

54. It is of interest, and probably significance, that, although their non-Greekness is described in what could be regarded as barbarian terms, the word βάρβαρος is used only once in the play, and then to describe the Danaids's clothing (*Suppl.* 235); otherwise they are ἐπήλυδες, "incomers, strangers."

3. The Politics of Oneness among the Greeks 69

is already prefigured within the *Suppliant Women* when Danaus is voted a bodyguard (a normal mark of honor and protection for a ruler).[55]

The story of this Greek/non-Greek foundation was a challenging one to tell, but speaks to an awareness that the boundaries between Greeks and the rest of humanity were not sharply defined, that there was a realization that there were also different layers of belonging and community beyond that of the Hellenic community, and so there was a kind of unity within humankind beyond individual ethnicities. The testing of these boundaries, however, is itself significant not only for emphasizing the need for there to be boundaries, but also the explicit realization of their permeability and flexibility. There might be one community, but the boundaries of that community could expand (and contract), and this one community sat within another wider one that was itself unified in its place in the cosmos. The philosopher Heraclitus (at the end of the sixth century) had said "it is wise to agree all things are one" (DK22 B50).

3.6. Conclusion

Over a hundred years after the production of *Suppliant Women*, Alexander the Great of Macedon—whose Greekness was not questioned—led an army into Asia, probably with the intention of conquering the whole known world, and framed this campaign as a Homeric war against the barbarian (cf. Arrian, *Anab.* 1.12.1; 7.16.4). Geographical ideas at this time had become more sophisticated, but it was still the common view that the οἰκουμένη was limited, and that Alexander's plans for world conquest were achievable.[56] Although the idea that Alexander had a philosophical idea about the unity of mankind has long been dispelled, the practicalities of empire did mean that he had to find a way to bring together disparate peoples and cultures. To a large extent, the groundwork had already been laid, and the building blocks for this work were in place. Although Alexander himself died before his project was complete, in the Hellenistic Age that followed, the old strategies of inclusiveness

---

55. The story of Lynceus and Hypermnestra is known from later traditions, but was probably dealt with in one of the other two plays of this trilogy (*Aegyptioi, Supplices*, and *Danaïdes*); the order of the plays is unknown, and only *Suppliant Women* survives.

56. Klaus Geus, "Space and Geography," in *A Companion to the Hellenistic World*, ed. Andrew Erskine, BCAW (Malden, MA: Blackwell, 2003), 232–45.

70 Lynette Mitchell

proved remarkably effective in helping to reshape the world that Alexander had created. Magnesia on the Maeander established a new festival and sent sacred ambassadors to cities that they recognized as kin, now solidified through cult, as far afield as Antioch in Persis in the East and Sicily in the West (see *InvM* 18–87).[57] Indeed, in the Hellenistic Age claims of kinship proliferated. In the fifth century BCE, the city of Aspendus in Lycia was not a Greek city, although the Athenians demanded tribute from it (*IG* 1.71.2.156–157), but by the second quarter of the fourth century the Aspendians asked for and received Argive citizenship, and by the time Strabo was writing in the first century CE their founder was recognized as Mopsus on his return from the Trojan War with Amphilochus of Argos (*Geogr.* 14.4.2–3).[58] It was self-reinforcing stories of inclusion, oneness, and unity, told through cult and kinship, that allowed the Greek community to be continually remade.

Bibliography

Bennet, John. "Linear B and Homer." Pages 187–233 in vol. 3 of *A Companion to Linear B: Mycenean Greek Texts and Their World*. Edited by Yves Duhoux and Anna Morpogo Davies. BCILL 133. Leuven: Peeters, 2014.

Boesch, Paul. *ΘΕΩΡΟΣ: Untersuchung zur Epangelie griechischer Feste*. Göttingen: Mayer & Müller, 1908.

Borza, Eugen N. "Athenians, Macedonians, and the Origins of the Macedonian Royal House." Pages 7–13 in *Studies in Attic Epigraphy, History and Topography: Presented to Eugene Vanderpool*. Hesperia Supplement 19. Princeton: American School of Classical Studies at Athens, 1982.

———. *In the Shadow of Olympus: The Emergence of Macedon*. Princeton: Princeton University Press, 1990.

Bowie, Ewen L. "Early Greek Elegy, Symposium and Public Festival." *JHS* 106 (1986): 13–35.

Buck, Carl Darling. *The Greek Dialects*. Chicago: University of Chicago Press, 1955.

---

57. Kent J. Rigsby, *Asylia: Territorial Inviolability in the Hellenistic World*, HCS (Berkeley: University of California Press, 1996), 67–131; Rutherford, *State Pilgrims*, 271.

58. Olivier Curty, *Les Parenté legendaries entre cités grecque*, Hautes études du monde gréco-romain 20 (Geneva: Droz, 1995), no. 3.

3. The Politics of Oneness among the Greeks 71

Camporeale, Giovannangelo. "The Etruscans in the Mediterranean." Pages 78–101 in *The Etruscans outside Etruria*. Edited by Giovannangelo Camporeale. Los Angeles: Getty Museum, 2004.

Christesen, Paul. *Olympic Victor Lists and Ancient Greek History*. Cambridge: Cambridge University Press, 2007.

Colvin, Stephen. "Greek Dialects in the Archaic and Classical Ages." Pages 200–212 in *A Companion to the Ancient Greek Language*. Edited by Egbert J. Bakker. BCAW. Chichester: Wiley-Blackwell, 2010.

Curty, Olivier. *Les parentés légendaires entre cités grecque: Catalogue raisonné des inscriptions contenant le terme syngeneia et analyse critique*. Hautes études du monde gréco-romain 20. Geneva: Droz, 1995.

Eder, Brigitta. "Continuity of Bronze Age Cult at Olympia? The Evidence of the Late Bronze Age and Early Iron Age Pottery." Pages 201–9 in *Potnia: Deities and Religion in the Aegean Bronze Age*. Edited by Robert Laffineur and Robin Hägg. Aegaeum 22. Liege: University of Liege, 2001.

Geus, Klaus. "Space and Geography." Pages 232–45 in *A Companion to the Hellenistic World*. Edited by Andrew Erskine. BCAW. Malden, MA: Blackwell, 2003.

Giangiulio, Maurizio. "Constructing the Past: Colonial Traditions and the Writing of History; The Case of Cyrene." Pages 116–37 in *The Historian's Craft in the Age of Herodotus*. Edited by Nino Luraghi. Oxford: Oxford University Press, 2001.

Gorman, Vanessa B. *Miletus, the Ornament of Ionia: A History of the City to 400 B.C.E.* Ann Arbor: University of Michigan Press, 2001.

Gould, John. "*Hiketaia*." *JHS* 93 (1973): 74–103.

Hall, Jonathan. *Ethnic Identity in Greek Antiquity*. Cambridge: Cambridge University Press, 1997.

———. *Hellenicity: Between Ethnicity and Culture*. Chicago: University of Chicago Press, 2002.

Herman, Gabriel. *Ritualised Friendship and the Greek City*. Cambridge: Cambridge University Press, 1987.

Jacquemin, Anne. *Offrandes monumentales à Delphes*. Bibliothèque des écoles françaises d' Athènes et de Rome. Paris: de Boccard, 1999.

Jeffrey, Lilian H. *The Local Scripts of Archaic Greece*. Rev. ed. Oxford Monographs on Classical Archaeology. Oxford: Oxford University Press, 1990.

Kahn, Charles H. *Anaximander and the Origins of Greek Cosmology*. New York: Columbia University Press, 1960.

Kindt, Julia. *Rethinking Greek Religion*. Cambridge: Cambridge University Press, 2012.

Kirk, Geoffrey S., John E. Raven, and Malcolm Schofield. *The Presocratic Philosophers: A Critical History with a Selection of Texts*. 2nd ed. Cambridge: Cambridge University Press, 1983.

Kyrieleis, Helmut. *Anfänge und Frühzeit des Heiligtums von Olympia*. Olympische Forschungen 31. Berlin: de Gruyter, 2006.

Lane Fox, Robin. *Travelling Heroes: Greeks and Their Myths in the Epic Age of Homer*. London: Penguin, 2008.

Lemos, Irene. *The Protogeometric Aegean: The Archaeology of the Late Eleventh and Tenth Centuries BC*. Oxford Monographs on Classical Archaeology. Oxford: Oxford University Press, 2002.

Mac Sweeney, Naoise. *Foundation Myths and Politics in Ionia*. Cambridge Classical Studies. Cambridge: Cambridge University Press, 2013.

Malkin, Irad. "Foundations." Pages 373–94 in *A Companion to Archaic Greece*. Edited by Kurt A. Raaflaub and Hans van Wees. BCAW. Malden MA: Wiley-Blackwell, 2009.

——. *The Returns of Odysseus: Colonization and Ethnicity*. Berkeley: University of California Press, 1998.

——. *A Small Greek World: Networks in the Mediterranean*. Greeks Overseas. New York: Oxford University Press, 2011.

Mazarakis Ainian, Alexander. *From Rulers' Dwellings to Temples: Architecture, Religion and Society in Early Iron Age Greece (1100–700 BC)*. SIMA 121. Jonsered: Åströms, 1997.

Meier-Brüger, Michael. "The Rise and Descent of the Language of the Homeric Poems." Pages 417–26 in *Ancient Greece: From the Mycenaean Palaces to the Age of Homer*. Edited by Sigrid Deger-Jalkotzy and Irene S. Lemos. Edinburgh Leventis Studies 3. Edinburgh: Edinburgh University Press, 2006.

Meiggs, Russell, and David Lewis, eds. *Greek Historical Inscriptions to the End of the Fifth Century*. Rev. ed. Oxford: Oxford University Press, 1988.

Merkelbach, Reinhold, and Martin L. West, eds. *Fragmenta Hesiodea*. Oxford: Clarendon, 1967.

Miller, Margaret C. "The Myth of Bousiris: Ethnicity and Art." Pages 413–42 in *Not the Classical Ideal: Athens and the Construction of the Other in Greek Art*. Edited by Beth Cohen. Leiden: Brill, 2000.

3. The Politics of Oneness among the Greeks   73

Mitchell, Lynette. "The Community of the Hellenes." Pages 49–65 in *Federalism in Greek Antiquity*. Edited by Hans Beck and Peter Funke. Cambridge: Cambridge University Press, 2015.

———. "Euboean Io." *ClQ* 51 (2001): 339–52.

———. *Panhellenism and the Barbarian in Archaic and Classical Greece*. Swansea: Classical Press of Wales, 2007.

Morgan, Catherine. *Athletes and Oracles: The Transformation of Olympia and Delphi in the Eighth Century*. Cambridge Classical Studies. Cambridge: Cambridge University Press, 1990.

———. *Early Greek States beyond the Polis*. London: Routledge, 2003.

Morpurgo Davies, Anna. "The Greek Notion of Dialect." *Verbum* 10 (1987): 7–27.

Morris, Ian. *Archaeology as Cultural History: Words and Things in Iron Age Greece*. Social Archaeology. Malden, MA: Blackwell, 2000.

Nielsen, Thomas Heine. *Olympia and the Classical Hellenic City-State-Culture*. Copenhagen: Royal Danish Academy of Science and Letters, 2007.

Perlman, Paula. *City and Sanctuary in Ancient Greece: The Theorodokia in the Peloponnese*. Hypomnemata. Göttingen: Vandenhoeck & Ruprecht, 2000.

Popham, Mervyn R., P. G. Calligas, and L. Hugh Sackett, eds. *Lefkandi II: The Protogeometric Building at Toumba: Part 2, The Excavation, Architecture and Finds*. Athens: British School at Athens, 1993.

Rhodes, Peter J., and Robin Osborne. *Greek Historical Inscriptions 404–323 BC*. Oxford: Oxford University Press, 2003.

Rigsby, Kent J. *Asylia: Territorial Inviolability in the Hellenistic World*. HCS. Berkeley: University of California Press, 1996.

Romano, David G. "Athletic Festivals in the Northern Peloponnese and Central Greece." Pages 176–91 in *A Companion to Sport and Spectacle in Greek and Roman Antiquity*. Edited by Paul Christesen and Donald G. Kyle. BCAW. Malden, MA: Wiley-Blackwell, 2014.

Romm, James S. *The Edges of the Earth in Ancient Thought: Geography, Exploration and Fiction*. Princeton: Princeton University Press, 1992.

Rutherford, Ian. *State Pilgrims and Sacred Observers in Ancient Greece: A Study of Theōriā and Theōroi*. Cambridge: Cambridge University Press, 2013.

Siewert, Peter. "The Olympic Rules." Pages 111–17 in *Proceedings of an International Symposium on the Olympic Games, 5–9 September,*

1988. Edited by William D. E. Coulson and Helmut Kyrieleis. Athens: Deutsches archäologisches Institut, 1992.

Scott, Michael. *Delphi and Olympia: The Spatial Politics of Panhellenism in the Archaic and Classical Periods.* Cambridge: Cambridge University Press, 2010.

Van de Mieroop, Marc. *A History of the Ancient Near East ca. 3000–323 BC.* 2nd ed. BHAW. Malden, MA: Blackwell, 2007.

Vlassopoulos, Kostas. *Greeks and Barbarians.* Cambridge: Cambridge University Press, 2013.

Wees, Hans van. "Kings in Combat: Battles and Heroes in the *Iliad.*" *ClQ* 38 (1988): 1–24.

West, Martin L. *The Hesiodic Catalogue of Women: Its Nature, Structure and Origins.* Oxford: Oxford University Press, 1985.

———. "The Rise of the Greek Epic." *JHS* 108 (1988): 151–72.

4

The Politics of Oneness among the Romans

James R. Harrison

4.1. Scholarship on Roman Oneness

The question of Roman oneness is not a motif heavily trawled by classical scholars. Nevertheless, a steady stream of scholarship on the issue has agreed that Roman thinkers did envisage forms of political and cultural unity from the middle republic onward well into the Imperial age. Two approaches to the Roman expression of oneness have been undertaken. First, the oneness motif has been examined from the vantage point of its perceived terminological indicators: that is, (1) the reflections of Cicero and Sallust on *concordia* ("union," "harmony," "concord" [ὁμόνοια]);[1] (2) the establishment of οἰκουμένη ("the civilized world") by means of the Roman *imperium* ("dominion," "rule," "control");[2] and (3) Rome's military imposition of *pax* ("peace") throughout its empire.[3] At times, however, the polemical context

---

1. See Eiliv Skard, *Zwei religiös-politische Begriff Euergetes–Concordia* (Oslo: Dybwad, 1932); Walter F. Taylor, "The Unity of Mankind in Antiquity and in Paul" (PhD diss., Claremont Graduate School, 1981), 549–57; Mark A. Temelini, "Cicero's Concordia: The Promotion of a Political Concept in the Late Roman Republic" (PhD diss., McGill University, 2002); A. Keil McMatthew, "Concordia as an Historiographical Principle in Sallust and Augustine" (PhD diss., Fordham University, 2015).

2. Taylor, "Unity of Mankind," 519–30.

3. Taylor, "Unity of Mankind," 531–48. On Roman *pax*, see Gerardo Zampaglione, *The Idea of Peace in Antiquity* (Notre Dame: University of Notre Dame Press, 1973), 135–83; Klaus Wengst, *Pax Romana and the Peace of Jesus Christ* (Philadelphia: Fortress, 1987), 1–54; Andrew Crane, "Roman Attitudes to Peace in the Late Republican and Early Imperial Periods: From Greek Origins to Contemporary Evidence" (PhD diss., University of Kent, 2014); Hannah Cornwell, *Pax and the Politics of Peace: Republic to Principate* (Oxford: Oxford University Press, 2017).

76   James R. Harrison

of the rhetoric employed has been overlooked in this process, blunting to
some extent a full appreciation of its propagandist intent, and, consequently,
paying insufficient attention to the ambiguities characterizing the social
outworking of the various motifs. Furthermore, an exclusive concentration
on a particular strand of terminology can blind us to other examples of
unity terminology associated with the semantic domain.[4]

Second, at the level of ideology, E. A. Judge has argued that the idea
of the unity of humankind—announced by Alexander the Great during
his banquet of reconciliation at Opis—was adopted by the Romans
in a "piecemeal" policy of political assimilation, extending social recognition to outsiders by means of the allocation of "resident alien" or
"citizenship" status.[5]

---

4. The Senecan terminology of consensus (*consensus populi Romani, consensus
omnium bonorum, consensus universorum*) is often associated with *concordia*. As
Armand Pittet writes ("Le mot *consensus* chez Sénèque: ses acceptions philosopique
et politique," *MH* 12 [1955]: 41), "We see that *consensus*, a philosophical term in Stoic
doctrine, is a synonym of *concordia* and *unitas*. It designates the harmony established
in the soul by the mastery of reason over the senses." Seneca uses *consensus* to denote
the unity underpinning imperial rule (Pittet, "Le mot *consensus*," 43–46). By 31 BCE
Augustus could justifiably claim (Res gest. divi Aug. 34.1) that "by everyone's agreement I had power over everything" (*per consensum univorum [po]tens re[r]um om[n]
ium*). On the new restoration of Res gest. divi Aug. 34.1 and its significance for a reas-
sessment of the Augustan principate, see Alison E. Cooley, *Res Gestae Divi Augusti:
Text, Translation, and Commentary* (Cambridge: Cambridge University Press, 2009),
256–60; E. A. Judge, *The Failure of Augustus: Essays on the Interpretation of a Paradox*
(Cambridge: Cambridge Scholars, 2019), 181–84. The word *consensus* is also used of
the divine favor manifested toward the new *princeps* (Pittet, "Le mot *consensus*," 46).
Thus Tacitus presents Galba appealing to the power of divine and human consensus
(Tacitus, *Hist.* 15.1.2). On Velleius Paterculus's depiction of the unified political culture
of the early principate, see John Alexander Lobur, *Consensus, Concordia and the Formation of Roman Imperial Ideology*, Studies in Classics (New York: Routledge, 2008),
94–127. Translations of the ancient literature are from the Loeb Classical Library.

5. E. A. Judge, "Contemporary Political Models for the Interrelations of the New
Testament Churches," in *The First Roman Christians: Augustan and New Testament
Essays*, ed. James R. Harrison, WUNT 229 (Tübingen: Mohr Siebeck, 2008), 591–92.
On the banquet at Opis, see W. W. Tarn, *Alexander the Great and the Unity of Mankind*
(London: Milford, 1933); Henry M. de Mauriac, "Alexander the Great and the Politics
of 'Homonoia,'" *JHI* 10 (1949): 104–14; E. Badian, "Alexander the Great and the Unity
of Mankind," *Historia* 7 (1958): 425–44; G. G. Thomas, "Alexander and the Unity of
Mankind," *CJ* 63 (1968): 258–60; A. B. Bosworth, "Alexander and the Iranians," *JHS*
100 (1980): 1–21.

4. The Politics of Oneness among the Romans 77

Judge has also highlighted how the cosmopolitanism of Zeno, the founder of the Stoic school, became another important factor contributing to the motif of Roman unity. Zeno had famously proposed that "we should consider all men to be of one community and one polity, and that we should have a common life and an order common to us all" (Plutarch, *Alex. fort.* 6 [329b]). This "shadowy picture of a well-ordered and philosophic commonwealth," to quote Plutarch's distillation of Zeno's teaching (*Alex. fort.* 6 [329b]), evolved in later Roman Stoicism into the concept of two citizenships, that of one's city, and the other of the cosmos (Seneca, *On Leisure* 1). In the previous century, Cicero had outlined this perspective more extensively than Seneca (*Leg.* 1.22–39) and the viewpoint would also be later reaffirmed by Marcus Aurelius (*Med.* 6.44).[6]

In contrast to the approach enunciated above, Claudia Moatti has argued that Cicero established for the first time a "political universalism," espousing a radical community of all men (*civitas communis* [= *patria communis*]), who shared not only with one another but also with the gods in the Roman city.[7] This position prefigured the universalistic vision of Pliny the Elder, who spoke of *humanitas* being established "through a single fatherland of all the peoples" (*Nat.* 3.39–42; cf. 37.201).[8]

Finally, Jean Béranger has investigated the later Senecan body imagery, applied to Nero as the soul of the state and to the state as Nero's body (*Clem.* 1.5.1; 2.2.1), against the backdrop of the body imagery employed for the republican state.[9] The latter, Béranger argues, was derived from

---

6. Judge, "Contemporary Political Models," 593–94.

7. See Moatti, *The Birth of Critical Thinking in Republican Rome* (Cambridge: Cambridge University Press, 2015), 313–19.

8. Oscar E. Nybakken ("*Humanitas Romana*," *TPAPA* 70 [1939]: 411) notes regarding the unifying nature of *humanitas*: "Seneca quotes Terence's words, *homo sum, humani nihil a me alienum puto*, calls attention to the single and common source of the unity of humankind, and pleads for a universal sympathy and fellow-feeling among all men" (Seneca, *Ep.* 5.4; 95.52–53).

9. Béranger, *Recherches sur l'aspect idéologique du principat* (Basel: Reinhardt, 1953), 218–52. E.g., Livy, *Ab urbe cond.* 2.32.8–12; cf. 1.8.1; 26.16.9; Cicero, *Phil.* 8.15; *Mur.* 51; *Inv.* 2.168; *Cat.* 1.31; *Leg. Man.* 17; Dionysius of Halicarnassus, *Ant. rom.* 6.86.1. See Michelle V. Lee, *Paul, the Stoics, and the Body of Christ*, SNTSMS 137 (New York: Cambridge University Press, 2006), 29–39; Michael Squire, "Corpus Imperii: Verbal and Visual Figurations of the Roman 'Body Politic,'" *Word & Image* 31 (2015): 305–30.

Greek precedents.[10] This was later encapsulated in the terminological correspondence of the Latin and the Greek words *imperium* and ἡγεμονία.[11] Béranger has helpfully highlighted the contribution that the Greek philosophical heritage made to Roman thought about the state as a unified body. The mission and grandeur of the Roman conquest found a metaphysical justification that was confirmed scientifically by Greek philosophy.[12] The cosmic laws of universal harmony, articulated by the Pythagorean physicists and Plato, impinged upon the human order and the order of society. These laws inspired hopes of perfection and indivisibility in the ideal state.[13] But a genuine expression of perfection and divine justice would only be attained when the state "tried hard to form a balanced organism in which each (part) contributed to a common purpose."[14]

Despite the impressive pedigree of Roman thought about unity detected by the modern scholars above, a tantalizing question nevertheless remains. Why did the motif of oneness, with its Greek philosophical precedents well known to the Scipionic circle at Rome, take so long to be recognized in Roman political thought?[15]

The answer lies in the agonistic nature of republican politics. The leading men of the old noble houses competed furiously against each other for civic magistracies, military victories, and family clients in a relentless quest for ancestral glory, with a view to attaining the consulship in the *cursus honorum* by the age of forty-two. This aristocracy of esteem, replenished generation by generation, meant that unity was a social ideal far from the Roman nobleman's mind. Rather, by rivaling his elite contemporaries in the public arena, the Roman noble strove not only to equal but also to surpass by great deeds the glory of his ancestors. In this frenetic world of honor acquisition, little else mattered. The establishment of political unity by means of alliances between the great men was inevitably a fragile and

---

10. E.g. Plato, *Resp.* 5.464b; cf. 2.372e; 5.556e; Dinarchus, *Demosth.* 1.110.

11. Béranger, *Recherches sur l'aspect idéologique*, 247.

12. Béranger, *Recherches sur l'aspect idéologique*, 225.

13. Béranger, *Recherches sur l'aspect idéologique*, 225–26.

14. Béranger, *Recherches sur l'aspect idéologique*, 226. See also H. C. Baldry (*The Unity of Mankind in Greek Thought* [Cambridge: Cambridge University Press, 1965], 167–203) on how the Greek philosophical tradition had an impact on the Roman understanding of unity.

15. On the Scipionic circle and the Greek philosophical currents at Rome, see Skard, *Euergetes–Concordia*, 74–79; Baldry, *Unity of Mankind*, 172–73.

4. The Politics of Oneness among the Romans 79

short-lived construct, as the collapse of the First and Second Triumvirates (60–53, 43–33 BCE) amply demonstrated.[16]

As the crisis of the civil war continued to fracture the late republic, Cicero struggled to prevent disunity tearing apart the body politic, grappling first with the threat of the Catilinarian conspiracy, and then confronting the self-seeking careerists of the *populares* party. As a result, Cicero was progressively forced to reassess the nature of true glory and, concomitantly, to propose *concordia* between the senate and the *equites* in order to retrieve a desperate situation. However, it was only because of the triumph of the Julian house over its political opponents at Actium (31 BCE)—accompanied at that time by the emergence of a universal consensus regarding the providential rightness of Augustan power— that the propaganda about Roman oneness began to flourish, though in a rhetorical construct markedly different to W. W. Alexander Tarn's unity of humankind.[17]

Given the unpromising climate for the emergence of oneness in the late republic, what ideological legacy might Alexander's famous speech on the unity of humankind have generated in the Julio-Claudian era? This will be the primary focus of the essay, though brief attention will be given to the proposed terminological indicators of oneness, noted above, in a final section of the essay.

4.2. Did Alexander's Unity of Mankind Leave an Ideological Legacy for Rome?

Our ancient sources tell us that Alexander's banquet of reconciliation at Opis was staged in response to the mutiny of the Macedonian veterans,

---

16. On the quest for glory in Roman honorific culture, see Matthias Gelzer, *The Roman Nobility*, trans. Robin Seager, 2nd ed. (Oxford: Blackwell, 1975); J. E. Lendon, *Empire of Honour: The Art of Government in the Roman World* (Oxford: Clarendon, 1997); James R. Harrison, *Paul and the Imperial Authorities at Thessalonica and Rome: A Study in the Conflict of Ideology*, WUNT 273 (Tübingen, Mohr Siebeck, 2011), 205–32.

17. Tarn (*Alexander the Great and the Unity of Mankind*) depicts Alexander the Great as a dreamer who, on the basis of God's common fatherhood of humankind, believed that the various races of his empire could live in unity as brothers and become partners in the realm rather than its subjects. Tarn's construct misunderstands Alexander's intentions and is conceptually foreign to Augustus's subjugation of all races to Rome (Res gest. divi Aug. 25–33).

James R. Harrison

which had been provoked by their recent demobilization and by their jealousy over the favor Alexander was showing to the Persians in his army. The banquet is only reported by Arrian (*Anab.* 7.8–9, 11; cf. Plutarch, *Alex.* 71; Diodorus 17.109; Quintus Curtius 10.2.12–30). Arrian depicts the protocols as follows (*Anab.* 7.11):

> He sat down and so did everyone else, the Macedonians around him [ἀμφ᾽ αὐτόν], the Persians next to them, then any of the other peoples who enjoyed precedence for their reputation or some other quality. Then he and those around him [ἀμφ᾽ αὐτόν] drew wine from the same bowl and poured the same libations, beginning with the Greek seers and the Magi. He prayed for other blessings and for harmony and partnership in rule [ὁμόνοιαν καὶ κοινωνίαν τῆς ἀρχῆς] between Macedonians and Persians. It is said that there were 9,000 guests at the banquet, who poured the same libation and then sang the song of victory.

However, in response to Tarn's unity of humankind theory (see n. 17), E. Badian has argued that the Opis banquet was not "an international love feast."[18] Alexander's concentric circles of seating at the banquet make the ethnic divisions in the army even more explicit. Only the Macedonian veterans sit around Alexander and they alone drink from the same bowl. Around this inner Macedonian circle is the outer circle of the Persians. Outside of the second circle, only the *elite* representatives of the other nations are represented, as opposed to a socially inclusive representation from the nations. Not only do the concentric circles, radiating outward from Alexander, define the ever-diminishing ethnic status of the non-Macedonians in relation to the Macedonian king, but also the centrality of the Macedonian veterans is symbolically reaffirmed in their proximity of seating to Alexander and by their exclusive drinking rituals with him.[19] This is reinforced by Alexander calling his veterans "kinsmen" along with the Persian troops (Arrian, *Anab.* 7.11). Symbolically, the Persians and Macedonians are given kinsmen equality in rule of the empire by Alexander adopting the universal Persian protocol of kissing *both* groups in public greetings (Arrian, *Anab.* 7.11.1–2, 6; cf. Herodotus, *Hist.* 1.134; Diodorus, *Hist.* 16.50; Xenephon, *Cyr.* 1.4.27; 2.2.31), while he neverthe-

---

18. Badian, "Alexander the Great," 430.

19. Bosworth ("Alexander and the Iranians," 17) comments: "There is, then, no trace of a policy of a fusion. Once again the tendency seems to have been to keep the Iranians and Macedonians separate as a check and balance on the other."

4. The Politics of Oneness among the Romans 81

less accords priority of place to his Macedonian generals by preserving exclusive drinking rituals with them.[20]

Therefore, the critical phrase in Alexander's prayer, ὁμόνοιαν καὶ κοινωνίαν τῆς ἀρχῆς, is not a utopian request for concord and fellowship between the nations but rather a plea for a harmonious partnership between the Macedonian and Persian troops in ruling Alexander's empire. Undoubtedly, this included the combined Macedonian and Persian subjugation of the other nations excluded from this partnership.[21] The elites of nations could plausibly be co-opted, as required, to participate as subordinate officials in the administration of the satrapies by Alexander's Macedonian and Persian generals or governors, if this is a legitimate inference from the outer seating arrangement of the elites.[22] More likely, however, the elites of the other nations are merely present at the banquet as ambassadors of their conquered states. In other words, it is merely a conciliatory gesture of symbolic significance to the defeated. Once again, this arrangement does not represent the unity of humankind. Contextually, therefore, the word ὁμόνοια "is associated with community in empire." It denotes "the sharing in command of Alexander's empire," and does not point to a projected fusion of the races either in the present or in the future.[23]

Unsurprisingly, the same ideological ambiguities about unity are also expressed in Roman imperial sources touching on ethnic unity.[24] In contrast to Ovid's savage dismissal of the barbarian tribes among whom he was exiled, Pliny the Elder posits a positive role for Rome in bringing civilization

---

20. See Parivash Jamzadeh, *Alexander Histories and Iranian Reflections: Remnants of Propaganda and Resistance*, Studies in Persian Cultural History 3 (Leiden: Brill, 2012), 139–43.

21. Bosworth ("Alexander and the Iranians," 2) observes: "I cannot see how the Opis Prayer can imply anything other than that the Persians and Macedonians were to rule jointly over subject peoples." I would add, however, that Alexander nonetheless upholds the ethnic priority of the Macedonians over the Persians.

22. See Badian, "Alexander the Great," 428–32.

23. Bosworth, "Alexander and the Iranians," 2. Contra, Thomas ("Alexander and the Unity of Mankind," 260–61) argues the Alexander's ὁμόνοια was understood differently from the time of his successors to what Alexander originally intended, becoming philosophically "the Hellenistic concept of homonoia."

24. The following three paragraphs are adapted from James R. Harrison, "Paul's 'Indebtedness' to the Barbarian (Rom 1:14) in Latin West Perspective," *NovT* 55 (2013): 322–23.

82   James R. Harrison

to the barbarians.[25] Over against the triumphalism of the Augustan poets regarding the Roman Empire and the subjugated place of the barbarians, Pliny sets out his vision of the *humanitas* to be imposed upon the barbarian tribes. Italy, the "parent of all lands," was chosen by the gods[26]

> to gather together the scattered realms and to soften their customs and unite the discordant wild tongues of so many peoples into a common speech so that they might understand each other, and to give civilization to humankind [*humanitatem homini*], in short to become the homeland of every people in the entire world. (Pliny the Elder, *Nat.* 3.39)[27]

Given that many first-century Latin writers distinguished barbarians from Romans by virtue of their tribal *feritas* ("wildness," "savagery") and lack of *humanitas* ("civilization," "culture"), the universal civilizing mission of Rome articulated by Pliny the Elder is unexpected.[28] Pliny was probably influenced in this regard by the Stoic teaching on the unity of humankind and perhaps by Cicero's own reflections on *humanitas*.[29]

Nevertheless, Pliny adhered to the theories of the medical writers regarding the races of humankind.[30] He assigned cultural inferiority to the barbarians because of the impact of their geographical location upon their physique and disposition, whereas superiority in intellect and empire was accorded to the Romans because of their geographical position as "middle-of-the-earth" people (*Nat.* 2.80.190).[31] Nevertheless, although Pliny was a realist about the horrific customs and terrible living conditions of

---

25. For Ovid, see Harrison, "Paul's 'Indebtedness,'" 319–22.

26. Horace emphasizes Augustus's subjugation of the nations on behalf of Rome, including Gaul and Spain (*Carm.* 1.2.50–53; 1.12.33–60; 1.35.25–40; 1.37; 3.3.37–48; 3.5; 3.14; 4.2.33–36; 4.5.25–36; 4.14; 4.15; *Saec.* 54–60; *Epod.* 9; *Ep.* 2.1.250–257). See also Ovid, *Tr.* 2.225–236; 4.2.1–74; Propertius 2.10; 3.4; 4.6; Vergil, *Aen.* 6.851–853.

27. On the Roman assimilation of the Carthaginians, see Statius, *Silvae* 4.5.45–48.

28. Cicero, *Quint. fratr.* 1.1.34; Caesar, *Bell. gall* 1.1.3; Vitruvius, *De Arch.* 2.praef. 5; 9.praef. 2; Tacitus, *Agr.* 2.

29. See Andrew Fear ("The Roman's Burden," in *Pliny the Elder: Themes and Contexts*, ed. Roy K. Gordon and Ruth Morelleo, MnemosyneSup 329 [Leiden: Brill, 2011], 25) on how Pliny the Elder, in Stoic manner, establishes Roman unity amidst barbarian diversity (*Nat.* 27.2–3). On Cicero's *humanitas,* see Nybakken, "*Humanitas Romana*," passim.

30. On the medical writers, see Baldry, *Unity of Mankind*, 46–51.

31. See Davina C. Lopez, *Apostle to the Conquered: Reimagining Paul's Mission*, Paul in Critical Contexts (Minneapolis: Fortress, 2008), 101–3.

4. The Politics of Oneness among the Romans   83

the Gallic Druids (*Nat.* 30.12) and the Germanic Chauci (*Nat.* 16.3–4), he remained confident that the altruism of humankind and the eternal glory of Roman ancestral tradition (*Nat.* 2.18) would triumph over the barbarism of the nations.[32] As was the case with Alexander's Opis banquet, the unity of humankind would be a misnomer in describing Pliny the Elder's ethnic beliefs. Pliny believed in the enduring cultural superiority of the Romans in comparison to the other nations, in precisely the same manner that Alexander had maintained the ethnic priority of the Macedonians over against the Persians and all the other nations in reconciling his disaffected Macedonian veterans. True oneness of humanity is not subscribed to in each case.

Furthermore, it is worth pondering whether there was any indication in the Roman world of "the law of 'universal sympathy' governing the world," a dimension of the Greek philosophical tradition highlighted by Béranger above (see also n. 9, above). Iconography from Roman Gaul is instructive in this regard, but it poses similar ideological ambiguities to those we have already noted.[33]

An Augustan triumphal arch at Glanum (St Rémy, France), linked by Henri Rolland to one of Agrippa's visits (ca. 25 BCE onward), exhibits distinctive iconography on the northwest relief.[34] There we see a bound male captive on the right, but significantly the male togate figure on the left places his hand on the captive's shoulder.[35] James Bromwich interprets this gesture as "surely an appeal for reconciliation and assimilation."[36] The identity of this figure has been hotly debated. Anne Roth Congrès, for example, points to (in her view) the "Gallic coat draped in the Roman fashion" over the figure. From this she concludes that "perhaps he is the son of a warrior, or a Romanised native, who acquired the new culture and denounced the

---

32. See Fear, "Roman's Burden," 26–27.

33. The following three paragraphs are borrowed from James R. Harrison, "'More Than Conquerors' (Rom 8:37): Paul's Gospel and the Augustan Triumphal Arches of the Greek East and Latin West," *BurH* 47 (2011): 12–13.

34. Henri Rolland, *L'arc de Glanum* (Paris: Centre national de la recherche scientifique, 1977), 46; Rolland, *Saint-Rémy-de-Provence* (Bergerac: Générale, 1934), 79–89; Julien Bruchet, *Les antiques: L'arc et le mausolée de Glanum à Saint-Rémy-de-Provence* (Paris: Ophrys, 1969); Anne Roth Congrès, *Glanum: From Salluvian Oppidum to Roman City* (Paris: Éditions du patrimoine, 2010).

35. Rolland, *L'arc de Glanum*, 50–51, pl. 24.

36. Bromwich, *The Roman Remains of Southern France: A Guidebook* (London: Routledge, 1993), 217.

dream of independence and the consequences of rebellion."[37] By contrast, I. M. Ferris has suggested that the togate figure is Roma with her hand on the captive "in a proprietorial manner."[38]

Fig. 4.1. Northwest relief on arch at Glanum (St Rémy, France). Detail from a photograph of the arch by Andrea Schaffer, Creative Commons Licence Attribution 4.0 International (CC by 4.0).

Fig. 4.2. Silver denarius: Sydenham, *Coinage of the Roman Republic*, §926. Reverse shows the togate figure of L. Aemilius Paullus on the right touching the victory trophy, with King Perseus and his two sons as prisoners on the left. Obverse depicts the veiled and diademed head of Concordia ("Concord"). Author's photograph of his own coin.

---

37. Congrès, *Glanum*, 27.
38. Ferris, *Enemies of Rome: Barbarians through Roman Eye* (Stroud: Sutton, 2000), 45.

4. The Politics of Oneness among the Romans 85

In the view of Rolland, however, the figure is not a barbarian, but rather a togate Roman, who is a conqueror presenting his conquered enemy.[39] As proof, Rolland appeals to the coin of the famous republican general, Paullus Aemilius Lepidus "Macedonicus," who triumphed over Perseus, the Macedonian king, at Pydna in 168 BCE. On the denarius commemorating the victory, Lepidus places his hand on the trophy, not the captive, with Perseus standing nearby with his two sons.[40] Rolland argues that the same stance of the victor characterizes the iconography of both the denarius and the Glanum relief, so the republican allusion—and therefore its symbolic meaning—would have been obvious enough.[41] But there is no parallel in the Augustan arches for such an intimate gesture, especially since the stereotypical trophy of arms, ubiquitous in Gallic iconography and on the denarius of Lepidus, is removed from the scene at Glanum. Such a removal is unprecedented and therefore points in another interpretative direction.

In sum, Bromwich and Congrès are closer to the mark than Rolland in this case. While the suggestion of Roma remains, the fragmentary nature of the relief—missing the left half of its torso, left arm and head—makes certainty impossible. Alternatively, could this enigmatic figure represent a Romanized member of the Gallic provincial elite, a togate *amicus* of the Romans, who is urging reconciliation and assimilation? Indeed, relations of *amicitia* between the Romans and Alpine tribes were highlighted in the inscriptions and iconography of the Augustan arches at La Turbie (Monaco, France) and Susa (south of Turin, Italy).[42] Is this relief urging in its iconography a different approach on the part of the conquered Gallic tribes to their Roman overlords? This, in my opinion, remains the most likely interpretative option. The northwest relief, therefore, presents a social alternative to the eastern and western façade reliefs of humiliated captives on the Glanum arch. At the very best, we have here a striking gesture of reconciliation, but elsewhere the reliefs from the same monument on the eastern and western façades stereotypically dehumanize the subjugated barbarians. In conclusion, as soon as we move toward what might seem to be genuine expressions of sympathetic *humanitas* or oneness in

---

39. Rolland, *L'arc de Glanum*, 35.

40. Edwin Allen Sydenham, *The Coinage of the Roman Republic* (London: Spink, 1952), §926.

41. Rolland, *L'arc de Glanum*, 35.

42. See Harrison, '"More Than Conquerors,'" 7–9 (La Turbie) and 11 (Susa).

86 James R. Harrison

Roman ideology, ambiguities emerge and we are forced to back away from any definitive conclusion.

We turn now to Augustus's rendering of his conquest of the barbarian nations in his mausoleum inscription in the Campus Martius, the Res Gestae divi Augusti, which poses similar paradoxes.[43] In his self-eulogy, Augustus, among many other achievements, set out his *res gestae* (military "achievements") in Res gest. divi Aug. 25–33: the subjugation of the nations to Rome (25–27), the establishment of Roman colonies (28), the reversal of military disasters (29–30), and the achievement of diplomatic successes (31–33). In recounting his subjugation of the barbarian peoples, Augustus says that he spared only those foreign peoples "whom (he) could safely pardon" (32), either by subduing them militarily (29–30), or by extending *clementia* ("clemency") to their officials and kings in diplomatic contexts (31–33). Rhetorically, the narrative of these victories precedes his extended narrative of his beneficence (15–24) and prefaces his climactic delineation of his preeminence (34–35). In other words, the focus on the barbarian nations living beyond direct Roman rule (31–33) functions, somewhat surprisingly, as the rhetorical portal by which we enter the culmination of the Res Gestae divi Augusti, namely, Augustus's preeminence in merit (34.2). Alison Cooley rightly comments that readers of the Res Gestae divi Augusti would have been dazzled by the exotic names and the far-flung geographical locations of the barbarian kings, stretching from one side of the empire to the other.[44] So how does Augustus's depiction of the nations function rhetorically in the Res Gestae divi Augusti? Is he suggesting a unity among the client-king nations across his empire, fostered by his diplomacy as opposed to military conquest?

First, Augustus boasts about the result of his encounters with the barbarian peoples when his pardon was exercised (32.3): "And while I have been leader [*me principe*; ἐπ' ἐμοῦ ἡγενόνος] very many other peoples have

---

43. In what follows, I am not suggesting that Augustus divorced his public image from the exemplum of Alexander. The reverse is true. In terms of iconography, there were paintings of Alexander in the Forum Augustum (Pliny the Elder, *Nat.* 35.6.93–94), as well as a representation on a gem cameo of the Persian-garbed Alexander, symbolic of the world rulers, holding a globe before a reclining Augustus (Larry L. Kreitzer, *Striking New Images: Roman Imperial Coinage and the New Testament*, JSNTSup 134 [Sheffield: Sheffield Academic, 1996], 79 fig. 5). On Augustus emulating and surpassing Pompey and Alexander in the Res Gestae divi Augusti, see Cooley, *Res Gestae Divi Augusti*, 36–37.

44. Cooley, *Res Gestae Divi Augusti*, 249.

4. The Politics of Oneness among the Romans   87

experienced the good faith [*fidem*; πίστεως] of the Roman people." Edwin S. Ramage has discussed the interrelation of *fides* ("faith") and *iustitia* ("justice"), observing that Romans "viewed *fides* as the foundation of *iustitia*."[45] In the case of the international diplomacy in the Res Gestae divi Augusti, Ramage argues that "Augustus' sense of justice is triggering the *fides* (32.3) that attracts legations from the ends of the world."[46] Augustus's reputation for and commitment to justice had probably found its ideological precedent in the Roman general and statesman Camillus (446–365 BCE), who had been honored with the title "Second Founder of Rome." Both Livy and Cicero underscore in Camillus's case that "the good faith of the Romans [*fides Romana*] stems from the justice of the general [*iustitia imperatorus*]" (e.g. Cicero, *Off.* 1.35; Livy 5.27.11).[47] Augustus, also heralded as the "Second Founder of Rome," likewise sponsors justice for the nations that seek the benefits of Roman rule, as opposed to imposing unification upon them.[48] Moreover, this implicit emphasis upon Augustus's reputation for justice in Res gest. divi Aug. 31–33 leads rhetorically to the celebration of justice (*iustitia*; δικαιοσύνη) as one of Augustus's four cardinal virtues in Res gest. divi Aug. 34.2, each of which was inscribed on the golden shield of virtue (*clupeus virtutis*) in the Julian senate house.[49] Thus the rhetorical point is not focused on the unity of the nations under Augustan rule but rather centers upon the preeminent merit of Augustus as the just leader of the nations.

Second, in Res gest. divi Aug. 32.1, Augustus mentions four barbarian kings who sought his refuge as suppliants (*supplices*). The submission ritual is well known and highlights the role of Augustus as the dispenser of *clementia* ("clemency").[50] Once again, the rhetorical point of the vignette

---

45. Ramage, *The Nature and Purpose of Augustus' "Res Gestae*," Historia (Stuttgart: Steiner, 1987), 45–46, 89–90; quotation from 46.

46. Ramage, "*Res Gestae*," 46.

47. Ramage, "*Res Gestae*," 90.

48. See Harrison, *Paul and the Imperial Authorities*, s.v. index of subjects, "Augustus, as new Aeneas, as new Romulus."

49. Jan F. Gaertner ("Livy's Camillus and the Political Discourse of the Late Republic," *JRS* 98 [2008]: 52) has argued that Camillus's renown for *virtus, pietas*, and *iustitia* (35–39) may have been exploited by Augustus and his followers, especially in relation to the four virtues of his golden shield (Res gest. divi Aug.34.2: *virtutis clementiaeque et iustitiae et pietatis causa*), in order "to evoke the paradigm of Camillus and its prestige."

50. On the clemency of Augustus, see Melissa B. Dowling, *Clemency and Cruelty in the Roman World* (Ann Arbor: University of Michigan Press, 2006), 29–168.

88   James R. Harrison

is the preeminence of the Augustan virtues as opposed to any interest in the unity of the nations under Augustan rule.

Turning to Claudius's speech on the admission of Further Gaul citizens to the Senate, recorded on the Lyons tablet (*CIL* 13.1668; 48 CE), and Tacitus's rendering of the same address (*Ann.* 11.23–25), we see how the Roman version of unity was implemented among the barbarian nations.[51] The process is, as Judge observed, one of assimilation by the gradual Romanization of the barbarian tribes.[52] Consequently, Roman citizenship is extended to those barbarian tribes who had demonstrated loyalty to Rome—though Claudius implicitly concedes that an Italian senator is preferrable.[53] This allowed the admission of the provincial elites from the barbarian tribes to the Roman senate and, ultimately, in the case of the Spaniard Hadrian, accession to the rulership of Rome itself. The culmination of the process would be the extension of the Roman citizenship to all free men in the Roman Empire in 212 CE under Caracalla.

In conclusion, Tarn's overinterpretation of Alexander's banquet of reconciliation at Opis poses a similar danger for us in considering whether the legacy of Alexander's exemplum sponsored a desire for reconciliation or unity between people groups across the Roman Empire. Such an approach either misunderstands the intention of the rhetoric of the Roman sources in their context, or overlooks ambiguities inherent in the evidence, or is

---

51. For the translation of *CIL* 13.1668, see William Stearns Davis, ed., *Rome and the West*, vol. 2 of *Readings in Ancient History: Illustrative Extracts from the Sources*, 2 vols. (Boston: Allyn & Bacon, 1912–1913), 186–88; https://tinyurl.com/SBL03115a. For Tacitus's version, see Alexander Yakobson, "Us and Them: Empire, Memory and Identity in Claudius' Speech on Bringing Gauls into the Roman Senate," in *On Memory: An Interdisciplinary Approach*, ed. Doron Mendels (Bern: Lang, 2007), 19–36.

52. Judge, "Contemporary Political Models," 593. See Tacitus, *Ann.* 11.24: "new members have been brought into the Senate from Etruria and Lucania and the whole of Italy, that Italy itself was at last extended to the Alps, to the end that not only single persons but entire countries and tribes might be united under our name."

53. *CIL* 13.1668: "It will be objected that Gaul sustained a war against the divine Julius for ten years. But let there be opposed to this the memory of a hundred years of steadfast fidelity, and a loyalty put to the proof in many trying circumstances. My father, Drusus, was able to force Germany to submit, because behind him reigned a profound peace assured by the tranquility of the Gauls." [Interruption, seemingly by a senator]: "How now? Is not an Italian senator to be preferred to a provincial senator!?" Claudius: "I will soon explain this point to you, when I submit that part of my acts that I performed as censor, but I do not conceive it needful to repel even the provincials who can do honor to the Senate House."

4.3. Roman Ideals of Unity

4.3.1. Polybius, Οἰκουμένη, and the Julio-Claudian House

Taken as an Achaean hostage to Rome in 167 BCE, the general Polybius made close friendships with the Roman aristocratic circle of the Scipios and spent the remainder of his life writing his *Histories* about the hegemony of Rome over the Mediterranean from 220 to 168/167 BCE. In justifying the aims of his universal history, Polybius highlights οἰκουμένη: "For who of men is so indifferent or careless that he does not wish to know and by what sort of polity almost the whole inhabited world [οἰκουμένη], having been conquered, fell in less than fifty-three years to the one rule of the Romans—which is not found to have happened before" (Polybius, *Hist.* 1.1.5). To what extent should this early reference to οἰκουμένη by Polybius be seen as a precursor of an ideal of "unity" in the imperial world?

Although the origins of οἰκουμένη are uncertain, the word has a political, religious, philosophical, and geographical dimensions, differentiating the "inhabited earth" from the uninhabited parts of the world.[54] Over time οἰκουμένη came to designate a culturally unified world, placed under a common law that bound humanity together.[55] Thus the concept of οἰκουμένη became a tool of imperial propaganda in speaking about the worldwide and civilizing *imperium* of the Julio-Claudian house. The Latin word *imperium* was the ideological equivalent of οἰκουμένη (Cicero, *Mur.* 10.22; *Off.* 2.8.26–27), as the heading of the Res Gestae divi Augusti illustrates: "Below is a copy of the achievements of the deified Augustus, by which he made the world (*orbem terra[rum]*) subject to the rule [*imperio*] of the Roman people." Two examples demonstrate the positive impact of Julio-Claudian οἰκουμένη, but elements of ambiguity emerge regarding who receives the benefits of the so-called unity.

---

54. See Klaus Geus, "Oikoumene/Orbis Terrarum," *Oxford Classical Dictionary*, new ed. (Oxford: Oxford University Press, 2016), https://doi.org/10.1093/acrefore/9780199381135.013.8008.

55. Taylor, "Unity of Mankind," 520.

90   James R. Harrison

First, in a decree from the village of Bousris (Gizeh, Egypt) honoring the governor Tiberius Caludius Balbillus (ca. 55–59 CE), incorporated in an Egyptian-style relief, Nero is assimilated to the traditional Egyptian deity Agathos Daimôn and is effusively eulogized in the inscription:

> With good luck. Since [[Nero]] Claudius Caesar Augustus Germanicus Imperator, Agathos Daimôn of the inhabited world [τῆς οἰκουμένης], along with all the good deeds of his benefactions to Egypt has shown the most manifest foresight in sending to us Tiberius Claudius Babillus as governor, and because of this man's favors and benefactions Egypt is full of all good things, sees the gifts of the Nile growing greater year by year, and now enjoys even more the well-balanced rising of the god [i.e., the Nile]. (*OGIS* 666.2–7 [translation Robert K. Sherk, adapted])

This blend of Egyptian and Roman elements underscores the fact that the civilizing influence of Roman *imperium* not only embraced traditional Egyptian culture but also it blessed the province of Egypt through the beneficence of Nero and his governor.

Second, a carved sardonyx cameo, the *Gemma Augustea*, shows in its upper register the seminude Augustus, in the guise of Jupiter, being crowned by *Oikoumenê*. Before Augustus stands his adopted heir Tiberius, triumphant from his 9 CE victory over the Dalmatians, who are shown as bound captives in the lower register.[56] In this case, the unity of Julio-Claudian rule brings Jupiter-like blessings to the inhabited world, but, significantly, it comes at the expense of Rome's enemies at the boundaries of empire.

4.3.2. Cicero and *Concordia*: The Roman Equivalent of Ὁμόνοια

The Greek equivalent of *Concordia*, ὁμόνοια, was considered the greatest blessing to Hellenistic cities, in which senators and the best men were united and factions were dispelled (Xenephon, *Mem.* 4.4.16; Lysias 18.17).[57] Interstate rivalries were ameliorated by fostering ὁμόνοια ("political concord"), as the legends and iconography of coins from the cities of Asia Minor demonstrate.[58] The motif was employed

---

56. Kreitzer, *Striking New Images*, 77 fig. 4.

57. On the worship of Ὁμόνοια, see Gaétan Thériault, *Le Culte d'Homonoia dans les cités grecques* (Lyon: Maison de l'Orient et de la Méditerranée, 1996).

58. John P. Lotz, "The *Homonoia* Coins of Asia Minor and Ephesians 1:21," *TynBul* 50.2 (1999): 173–88.

4. The Politics of Oneness among the Romans 91

by historians (Polybius, Appian, Dionysios of Harlicarnassus) and orators (Antiphon, Dio Chrysostom).[59]

In the case of Rome, in 367 BCE Marcus Camillus erected a temple to Concordia in the forum to celebrate the accord between patricians and plebeians (Plutarch, *Cam.* 42–45). The temple was restored in 121 BCE to affirm the renewed harmony between the Senate and the *populares* after the social dislocation caused by Tiberius and Gaius Gracchus (Appian, *Bell. civ.* 1.26; Plutarch, *Ti. C. Gracch.* 17.6).[60] Intriguingly, Cicero shifts away from the traditional understanding of *Concordia* (the harmony of the republic) to new expressions of the ideal in the face of social disintegration and the threats posed to his own political career. In 63 BCE Cicero suggested the establishment of a *Concordia ordinum* (*Att.* 1.18.3)—an alliance between the senate and *equites*—with a view to maintaining the liberty and stability of the republic (*Clu.* 152; *Agr.* 3.4). Only concord between the senate and the *equites* could stave off the threats to traditional noble rule posed by the rebellion of Cataline (*Mur.* 1, 78; *Cat.* 4.15), the eventual split between the senate and the *equites* (*Att.* 1.17.8–10), and by the emergence of the antisenatorial First Triumvirate (60–53 BCE).

However, after Cicero's exile from Rome in 58 BCE, the orator abandoned the alliance between the senate and the *equites* for an alliance of all loyal citizens of any rank who would support the cause of the republic over against the *populares* (*Har. resp.* 60–61; *Rep.* 1.49; 2.69). Cicero sums up this consensus of all good men under "the more inclusive concept of *Concordia civium* or *Concordia civitatis.*"[61] Inevitably, this led Cicero to oppose Antony in 44 BCE, whom Cicero styled a threat to the republican "unanimity and harmony" (*consensum et concordium*; *Phil.* 4.14; cf. 8.8). Cicero paid the cost for his stance with his life the next year.

How did Cicero's innovative understanding of *Concordia* contribute to Julio-Claudian *concordia*? Cicero airs the conservative viewpoint that the *princeps* of the state creates its *concordia* (*Rep.* 2.42.69; *Leg.* 3.28; *Off.*

---

59. For details, see Laurence L. Welborn, "The Pursuit of Concord: A Political Ideal in Early Christianity" (PhD diss., Vanderbilt University, 1993), 5–6 n. 10. Note especially the orations on concord of Dio Chrysostom (*Or.* 38–41) and Aelius Aristides (*Or.* 23–25).

60. On the difficulty of identifying the temple site, see Arnaldo Momigliano, "Camillus and Concord," *ClQ* 36.3/4 (1942): 111–20.

61. Temelini, "Cicero's Concordia," 7.

92   James R. Harrison

2.22.27; *Cat.* 4.17.15).[62] The idea of a principate sets forth an important ideological strut that would undergird the self-conception of Augustus (Res gest. divi Aug. 13: "when I was leader"; *me princi[pe]*; cf. 30.1; 32.3; Horace, *Carm.* 1.2.50). The word *princeps* is conspicuously a "nonmagisterial term," emphasizing Augustus's preferred role of being a private citizen, whose influence (*auctoritas*) allowed him to excel everyone while only being a comagistrate in power (Res gest. divi Aug. 34.3).[63] Yet, simultaneously, the term resonated with its Ciceronian nuance of a leader who benefited the state.[64] *Concordia*, at the heart of Roman social and political relations, had found an unconventional champion in this new *princeps* who had united all its citizens, irrespective of their rank, in a new way of operating, based upon peace and universal consensus (Res gest. divi Aug. 12–13; 34.1). Consequently, Tiberius dedicated a temple to Concordia after the death of Augustus (*CIL* 1.231; Dio Cassius, *Hist. rom.* 55.8.9; 56.25; Suetonius, *Tib.* 20).

4.3.3. The Julio-Claudian Imposition of *Pax* upon the Roman Empire

The explosion of Roman interest in *pax* ("peace") began in the late republic when Rome was being ripped apart by civil war. Hopes for a final peace prematurely emerged during the Second Triumvirate. The treaty of Brundisium in 40 BCE had brokered a reconciliation between Octavian (the later Augustus) and Antony. At the time Vergil spoke rapturously about the birth of a portentous child with the advent of Saturn's new golden age: "he shall have the gift of divine life, shall see heroes mingled with gods, and shall himself be seen of them, and shall sway a world to which his father's virtues have brought peace" (*Ecl.* 4.15–17). However, the reconciliation between Octavian and Antony was ultimately doomed.

Peace did not become a reality until the triumph of Augustus over Antony and Cleopatra at the naval battle of Actium in 31 BCE. In 29 BCE the important phrase, "once peace had been achieved on land and [on sea]," concludes Augustus's victory monument at Nikopolis (*EJ* 12). Elsewhere Augustus asserts that he had brought peace (*pacavi*) to the Gallic, Spanish, and Germanic provinces (Res gest. divi Aug. 26.1). Authors such as Philo (*Legat.* 144–147), Velleius Parterculus (2.89.1–4) and Ovid

---

62. Welborn, "Pursuit of Concord," 7.

63. Judge, *Failure of Augustus*, 164.

64. Cooley, *Res Gestae Divi Augusti*, 161.

(*Metam.* 15.32–39; *Fast.* 1.709–22) also underscore the momentous nature of the Augustan peace. Also, Augustus emphasizes his establishment of peace through the striking vignette of the unprecedented closure of the doors of the Temple of Janus Quirinus three times during his principate, signifying that "peace had been achieved by victories on land and sea" (Res gest. divi Aug. 13).

Crucially, before the Augustan age, Pax was a minor deity without a temple.[65] But upon Augustus's dedication of the *ara Pacis Augustae* in the Campus Martius in 9 BCE (Res gest. divi Aug. 12–13), two annual sacrifices were offered each year to Pax on the altar on 30th January and 30th March (Ovid, *Fast.* 1.709–714; 3.881–882; cf. Res gest. divi Aug. 12.2). While the altar does not have any iconography of the goddess Pax, the patron goddess of harvests and fertility, Ceres, is depicted instead, symbolizing the prosperity of the Augustan golden age (Horace, *Saec.* 29–32).[66]

The motif of peace continues under Augustus's successors. Two examples will suffice. First, there is the Claudian numismatic evidence of a winged Pax holding a caduceus over a snake (*RIC* I² "Claudius" §§9, 27, 57).

Fig. 4.3. Silver denarius from the Claudian period, ca. 46–47 CE. Reverse legend is PACI AVGVSTAE ("to the Augustan peace"). The iconography shows Pax-Nemesis, winged and draped, with her left hand holding a winged caduceus, pointing downward at the snake, which glides away to the right. Image from London Coins, Auction 157 lot 1722, sold 04/06/2017; used by permission.

In the period of the Neronian quinquennium, too, the poet Calpurnius Siculus (*Ecl.* 1.42–48) presents the rule of Nero as a second Golden Age of justice and peace following hard upon the idyllic age of Augustus:

---

65. Cooley, *Res Gestae Divi Augusti*, 156.
66. See Orietta Rossini, *Ara Pacis*, new ed. (Rome: Electa, 2009), 36–45.

> Amid untroubled peace, the Golden Age springs to a second birth; at last kindly Themis, throwing off the gathered dust of her mourning returns to the earth; blissful ages attend the youthful prince who pleaded a successful case for the Iulii of the mother town (of Troy). While he, a very God, shall rule the nations, the unholy War-Goddess shall yield and have her vanquished hands bound behind her back, and, stripped of weapons, turn her furious teeth into her own entrails.

Finally, although some ancient writers point to the destructive nature of the peace established by Rome (e.g., Tacitus, *Agr.* 30; 4 Ezra 11:40–43; Petronius, *Sat.* 119.1–18, 27–36), peace was a powerful unifying element in the Julio-Claudian period, given the many decades of civil war in the late republic.

4.4. Conclusion

This essay has argued the unity of humankind sponsored by Alexander the Great was anything but universal and did not demonstrate any sense of oneness. Rather it enshrined the ethnic superiority of the Macedonian forces over against the Persians and, even more remotely, the rest of the marginalized nations. The same ambiguity existed in Roman relations with the barbarian nations. The occasional universalistic sentiments of Roman writers about the nations on the borders of empire stood at odds with the iconographic demeaning of the defeated nations on the Augustan victory arches and their assigned place of cultural and geographical inferiority in Roman thought. The only oneness that emerged out of the agonistic and status-obsessed Roman Republic was the triumph of the Julian house over the old noble houses, allowing a measure of consensus, peace, and concord to flourish under the providential auspices of the Benefactor of the world.

Bibliography

Badian, Ernst. "Alexander the Great and the Unity of Mankind." *Historia* 7 (1958): 425–44.

Baldry, H. C. *The Unity of Mankind in Greek Thought.* Cambridge: Cambridge University Press, 1965.

Béranger, Jean. *Recherches sur l'aspect idéologique du principat.* Basel: Reinhardt, 1953.

Bosworth, A. B. "Alexander and the Iranians." *JHS* 100 (1980): 1–21.

4. The Politics of Oneness among the Romans 95

Bromwich, James. *The Roman Remains of Southern France: A Guidebook.* London: Routledge, 1993.

Bruchet, Julien. *Les antiques: L'arc et le mausolée de Glanum à Saint-Rémy-de-Provence.* Paris: Ophrys, 1969.

Congrès, Anne Roth. *Glanum: From Salluvian Oppidum to Roman City.* New ed. Paris: Éditions du patrimoine, 2010.

Cooley, Alison E. *Res Gestae Divi Augusti: Text, Translation, and Commentary.* Cambridge: Cambridge University Press, 2009.

Cornwell, Hannah. *Pax and the Politics of Peace: Republic to Principate.* Oxford; Oxford University Press, 2017.

Crane, Andrew. "Roman Attitudes to Peace in the Late Republican and Early Imperial Periods: From Greek Origins to Contemporary Evidence." PhD diss., University of Kent, 2014.

Davis, William Stearns, ed. *Rome and the West.* Vol. 2 of *Readings in Ancient History: Illustrative Extracts from the Sources.* 2 vols. Boston: Allyn & Bacon, 1912–1913.

Dowling, Melissa B. *Clemency and Cruelty in the Roman World.* Ann Arbor: University of Michigan Press, 2006.

Fear, Andrew. "The Roman's Burden." Pages 21–34 in *Pliny the Elder: Themes and Contexts.* Edited by Roy K. Gordon and Ruth Morelleo. MnemosyneSup 329. Leiden: Brill, 2011.

Ferris, I. M. *Enemies of Rome: Barbarians through Roman Eyes.* Stroud: Sutton, 2000.

Gaertner, Jan Felix. "Livy's Camillus and the Political Discourse of the Late Republic." *JRS* 98 (2008): 27–52.

Gelzer, Matthias. *The Roman Nobility.* Translated by Robin Seager. 2nd ed. Oxford: Blackwell, 1975.

Geus, Klaus. "Oikoumene/Orbis Terrarum." *Oxford Classical Dictionary.* New ed. Oxford: Oxford University Press, 2016. https://doi.org/10.1093/acrefore/9780199381135.013.8008.

Harrison, James R. "'More Than Conquerors' (Rom 8:37): Paul's Gospel and the Augustan Triumphal Arches of the Greek East and Latin West." *BurH* 47 (2011): 3–20.

———. *Paul and the Imperial Authorities at Thessalonica and Rome: A Study in the Conflict of Ideology.* WUNT 273. Tübingen, Mohr Siebeck, 2011.

———. "Paul's 'Indebtedness' to the Barbarian (Rom 1:14) in Latin West Perspective." *NovT* 55 (2013): 311–48.

Jamzadeh, Parivash. *Alexander Histories and Iranian Reflections: Remnants of Propaganda and Resistance*. Studies in Persian Cultural History 3. Leiden: Brill, 2012.

Judge, E. A. "Contemporary Political Models for the Interrelations of the New Testament Churches." Pages 586–96 in *The First Roman Christians: Augustan and New Testament Essays*. Edited by James R. Harrison. WUNT 229. Tübingen: Mohr Siebeck, 2008.

———. *The Failure of Augustus: Essays on the Interpretation of a Paradox*. Cambridge: Cambridge Scholars, 2019.

Kreitzer, Larry L. *Striking New Images: Roman Imperial Coinage and the New Testament*. JSNTSup 134. Sheffield: Sheffield Academic, 1996.

Lee, Michelle V. *Paul, the Stoics, and the Body of Christ*. SNTSMS 137. New York: Cambridge University Press, 2006.

Lendon, J. E. *Empire of Honour: The Art of Government in the Roman World*. Oxford: Clarendon, 1997.

Lobur, John Alexander. *Consensus, Concordia and the Formation of Roman Imperial Ideology*. Studies in Classics. New York: Routledge, 2008.

Lopez, Davina C. *Apostle to the Conquered: Reimagining Paul's Mission*. Paul in Critical Contexts. Minneapolis: Fortress, 2008.

Lotz, John P. "The *Homonoia* Coins of Asia Minor and Ephesians 1:21." *TynBul* 50 (1999): 173–88.

Mauriac, Henry M. de. "Alexander the Great and the Politics of 'Homonoia.'" *JHI* 10 (1949): 104–14.

McMatthew, A. Keil. "Concordia as an Historiographical Principle in Sallust and Augustine." PhD diss., Fordham University, 2015.

Moatti, Claudia. *The Birth of Critical Thinking in Republican Rome*. Cambridge: Cambridge University Press, 2015.

Momigliano, Arnaldo. "Camillus and Concord." *ClQ* 36.3/4 (1942): 111–20.

Nybakken, Oscar E. "*Humanitas Romana*." *TPAPA* 70 (1939): 396–413.

Pittet, Armand. "Le mot *consensus* chez Sénèque: Ses acceptions philosophique et politique." *MH* 12 (1955): 35–46.

Ramage, Edwin S. *The Nature and Purpose of Augustus' "Res Gestae."* Historia. Stuttgart: Steiner, 1987.

Rolland, Henri. *L'arc de Glanum*. Gallia. Paris: Centre national de la recherche scientifique, 1977.

———. *Saint-Rémy-de-Provence*. Bergerac: Générale, 1934.

Rossini, Orietta. *Ara Pacis*. New ed. Rome: Electa, 2009.

Sherk, Robert K., ed. and trans. *The Roman Empire: Augustus to Hadrian.* Translated Documents of Greece and Rome 6. Cambridge: Cambridge University Press, 1988.

Skard, Eiliv. *Zwei religiös-politische Begriff Euergetes–Concordia.* Oslo: Dybwad, 1932.

Squire, Michael. "*Corpus Imperii*: Verbal and Visual Figurations of the Roman 'Body Politic.'" *Word & Image* 31 (2015): 305–30.

Sydenham, Edwin Allen. *The Coinage of the Roman Republic.* London: Spink, 1952.

Tarn, W. W. *Alexander the Great and the Unity of Mankind.* London: Milford, 1933.

Taylor, Walter F. "The Unity of Mankind in Antiquity and in Paul." 2 vols. PhD diss., Claremont Graduate School, 1981.

Temelini, Mark A. "Cicero's Concordia: The Promotion of a Political Concept in the Late Roman Republic." PhD diss., McGill University, 2002.

Thériault, Gaétan. *Le Culte d'Homonoia dans les cités grecques.* Lyon: Maison de l'Orient et de la Méditerranée, 1996.

Thomas, G. G. "Alexander and the Unity of Mankind." *CJ* 63 (1968): 258–60.

Welborn, Laurence L. "The Pursuit of Concord: A Political Ideal in Early Christianity." PhD diss., Vanderbilt University, 1993.

Wengst, Klaus. *Pax Romana and the Peace of Jesus Christ.* Philadelphia: Fortress, 1987.

Yakobson, Alexander. "Us and Them: Empire, Memory and Identity in Claudius' Speech on Bringing Gauls into the Roman Senate." Pages 19–36 in *On Memory: An Interdisciplinary Approach.* Edited by Doron Mendels. Bern: Lang, 2007.

Zampaglione, Gerardo. *The Idea of Peace in Antiquity.* Notre Dame: University of Notre Dame Press, 1973.

Part 3
Oneness and Unity in Early Judaism

5
The Qumran *yaḥad*:
Aspects of Oneness, Unity, and
Separation in the Dead Sea Scrolls

Carsten Claussen

The community behind the rule texts of Qumran called itself *yaḥad*. Although the precise meaning of the noun is not entirely clear, it certainly emphasized a sense of unity and oneness, of comm-*unity* and "that which is one." Throughout the history of research of the Dead Sea Scrolls the more or less sociological terminology of *sect* and *sectarian* has been used to describe the identity of the Qumran communities.[1] Making use of Bryan R. Wilson's sevenfold typology of sects the Qumranite groups were referred to as an "introversionist sect."[2] More recent studies have used the model of religious institutions and movements developed by Rodney Stark and William Sims Bainbridge.[3] Their approach defines elements that can

---

1. For a helpful overview, see Jutta M. Jokiranta, "Sociological Approaches to Qumran Sectarianism," in *The Oxford Handbook of the Dead Sea Scrolls*, ed. Timothy H. Lim and John J. Collins, Oxford Handbooks (Oxford: Oxford University Press, 2010), 200–231. See also her assessment in Jokiranta, *Social Identity and Sectarianism in the Qumran Movement*, STDJ 105 (Leiden: Brill, 2013), 17.

2. See the sevenfold typology of sects looking at their different responses to the world as developed by Bryan R. Wilson, *Magic and the Millennium: A Sociological Study of Religious Movements of Protest among Tribal and Third-World Peoples* (London: Heinemann, 1973), 22–26. Cf. Carsten Claussen, "John, Qumran, and the Question of Sectarianism," *PRSt* 37 (2010): 421–40; Eyal Regev, *Sectarianism in Qumran: A Cross-Cultural Perspective*, RelSoc 45 (Berlin: de Gruyter, 2007), 42–45; Jokiranta, *Social Identity*, 28–30.

3. Rodney Stark and William Sims Bainbridge, *The Future of Religion: Secularization, Revival and Cult Formation* (Berkeley: University of California Press, 1985);

102   Carsten Claussen

be used to measure such tension between a sect and the outside world.[4] These methodologies have proven themselves significantly helpful in constructing a sociological understanding of the Qumran movement. They may have also, however, led at times to a nontheological and thus reductionist perception of the Qumranite understanding of unity and especially the term *yaḥad*, which was then characterized as originally being "loaded with theological meaning, but [... which] eventually became a *terminus technicus* for the movement at large."[5] One may ask whether this gradual move from a theological to a sociological understanding may at times reveal more about the development of Qumran research than about the development of the Qumran movement. The following article takes a different angle, exploring how various characteristics of the *yaḥad* reflect aspects of one or probably more than one theological belief system of the Qumranites.[6]

This approach needs to take into account the development of the different Qumranite groups and their respective sources. The "Rule of the Community" (i.e., the Community Rule; 1QS) and the "Rule of the Congregation" (1Q28a [1QSa]) and also the "Damascus Document" (CD) probably refer to two (or more) different communities, the *yaḥad* of 1QS and 1Q28a and the "new covenant" or the "Community of the Renewed Covenant" of CD.[7] While some scholars argue in favor of the priority of 1QS, others have compared the two traditions and maintain the priority

---

Stark and Bainbridge, *A Theory of Religion*, Toronto Studies in Religion (New York: Lang, 1987); Stark and Bainbridge, *Religion, Deviance, and Social Control* (London: Routledge, 1996); see, e.g., Jutta M. Jokiranta, "'Sectarianism' of the Qumran 'Sect': Sociological Notes," *RevQ* 20 (2001): 223–39; Jokiranta, *Social Identity*, 30–33; Regev, *Sectarianism in Qumran*, 45.

4. Stark and Bainbridge, *Future of Religion*, 66: These elements are the "*difference* from the standards set by the majority or by powerful members of society, *antagonism* between the sect and society manifested in mutual rejection, and *separation* in social relations leading to the relative encapsulation of the sect" (emphasis original).

5. Alison Schofield, *From Qumran to the Yaḥad: A New Paradigm of Textual Development for the Community Rule*, STDJ 77 (Leiden: Brill, 2009), 141.

6. See James VanderKam and Peter Flint, *The Meaning of the Dead Sea Scrolls: Their Significance for Understanding the Bible, Judaism, Jesus, and Christianity* (New York: Harper Collins, 2002), 255–74; John J. Collins and Robert A. Kugler, eds., *Religion in the Dead Sea Scrolls*, SDSS (Grand Rapids: Eerdmans, 2000).

7. For two or more communities, see, e.g., Schofield, *Qumran*, 95. For new covenant, see בברית החדשה in CD A VIII, 21; cf., however, אנשי היחיד ("men of the *yaḥad*" or "men of the Unique One") in CD B XX, 32; cf. XX, 1, 14.

of the Damascus Rule.[8] Charlotte Hempel, for example, sees the communal legislation of CD as belonging to the "parent group of the *yaḥad*."[9] Although some more recent contributors have argued that CD and 1QS represent totally different congregations, a diachronic development seems more likely.[10]

Taking this development into account, the following study will consider the implications of the Qumranites' understanding of oneness by exploring these key areas: the *yaḥad* terminology, community organization, admission procedures, purity regulations, torah study and observance, treatment of communal property, meeting types, common meals, and the calendar system.

5.1. The Terminology of Self-Identification: A Theological Unity

The difficulties in identifying the people behind the Dead Sea Scrolls (and maybe the settlement) are reflected in the terminology used in Qumran research. The original identification as part of the Essene movement led to the name "Qumran Essenes." Other titles being used include "Qumran sect," "Qumran community," or simply the "Qumranites." More revealing for the identity of the Qumran community, however, is the terminology of self-designation and self-identification found in the scrolls. The Qumranites refer to themselves, for example, by the *termini technici* "sons of light" (בני אור)," "sons of truth" (בני אמת)," "sons of righteousness" (בני הצדוק)," or

---

8. For the priority of 1QS, see even more recently Regev, *Sectarianism in Qumran*, esp. 163–96. For very thorough research on the comparison between CD and 1QS see Charlotte Hempel, *The Laws of the Damascus Document: Sources, Traditions, and Redaction*, STDJ 29 (Leiden: Brill, 1998).

9. Hempel, *Laws*, 150.

10. For totally different communities, see, e.g., Regev, *Sectarianism in Qumran*, 45–50, 81–86, 163–96. For a diachronic development, see John J. Collins, "The Yaḥad and 'the Qumran Community,'" in *Biblical Traditions in Transmission: Essays in Honour of Michael A. Knibb*, ed. Charlotte Hempel and Judith M. Lieu, JSJSup 111 (Leiden: Brill: 2006), 81–96; cf. Michael A. Knibb, "Place of the Damascus Document," *Annals of the New York Academy of Sciences* 722 (1994): 149–62; Sarianna Metso, "The Relationship between the Damascus Document and the Community Rule," in *The Damascus Document: A Centennial of Discovery; Proceedings of the Third International Symposium of the Orion Center for the Study of the Dead Sea Scrolls and Associated Literature, 4–8 February, 1998*, ed. Joseph M. Baumgarten, Esther Chazon, and Avital Pinnick, STDJ 34 (Leiden: Brill: 1999), 85–93.

104 Carsten Claussen

simply "brothers" (אחי)."[11] Some probably more eminent members of the community are called "men of holiness" (אנשי הקודש; see 1QS V, 13). The movement behind the "Damascus Document" calls itself the "New Covenant in the Land of Damascus" (הברית החדשה בארץ דמשק) (CD A VI, 9; VIII, 21; CD B XX, 12). All of these terms carry positive connotations. In contrast to these, and as part of a dualistic terminology and worldview, all other people outside the community are termed "Sons of Darkness" (בני חושך) (see 1QM I, 1, 10, 16; 4Q496 III, 7).[12] More or less neutral or even positive designations for the whole community are either "the Many" (הרבים) (see 1QS VIII, 26), the "house of holiness" (בית קודש) (see 1QS VIII, 5), or most frequently "(the) *yaḥad*" (יחד or היחד).[13]

The term *yaḥad* (יחד or היחד), can be translated as "togetherness," "unity," "community," "oneness," or "that which is one."[14] It occurs more than fifty times in the Community Rule (e.g., 1QS I, 1, 12, 16; VI, 3, 7, 8), seven times in the Rule of the Congregation (1Q28a I, 26, 27; II, 2, 11, 17, 18, 21), and three times in the Scroll of Blessings (1Q28b [1QSb] IV, 26; V, 6, 21). Some scholars see a connection to three occurrences in the recension B of the Damascus Document: מורה היחיד (CD B XX, 1)

---

11. For "sons of light," see 1QS II, 16; III, 13, 24–25; 1QM I, 1, 3; 4Q280 2 1. For "sons of truth," see 1QS IV, 5–6; cf. בני אמתו in 4Q266 11 7. For "sons of righteousness," see 1QS IX, 14; 4Q259 III, 10; 4Q286 1 2, 7. For "brothers," see 1QS VI, 10, 22; 1Q28a I, 18; CD A VI, 20; VIII, 6; CD B XIX, 18; XX, 18; 1QM XIII, 1; XV, 4, 7.

12. For a substantial list of Qumran texts that exhibit dualistic ideology and terminology, see Jörg Frey, "Different Patterns of Dualism in the Qumran Library," in *Legal Texts and Legal Issues: Proceedings of the Second Meeting of the International Organization of Qumran Studies, Cambridge 1995; Published in Honor of J. M. Baumgarten*, ed. Moshe J. Bernstein, Florentino García Martínez, and John Kampen, STDJ 23 (Leiden: Brill, 1997), 275–335, esp. 277–78.

13. For a comprehensive overview, see Carsten Claussen and Michael Thomas Davis, "The Concept of Unity at Qumran," in *Qumran Studies: New Approaches, New Questions*, ed. Michael Thomas Davis and Brent A. Strawn (Grand Rapids: Eerdmans: 2007), 232–53, esp. 232–38.

14. For an overview, see Heinz-Josef Fabry, "יַחַד," *TDOT* 6:40–48, esp. 44, 47–48; Eyal Regev, "יַחַד *jaḥad*," *Theologisches Wörterbuch zu den Qumrantexten*, ed. Heinz-Josef Fabry and Ulrich Dahmen (Stuttgart: Kohlhammer, 2013), 2:121–30. Cf. the German neologism "Einung" in Leonhard Rost, "Der gegenwärtige Stand der Erforschung der in Palästina neu gefundenen hebräischen Handschriften: 11. Die Sektenrolle," *TLZ* 75 (1950): 341–44; Johann Maier, *Die Texte der Höhlen 1–3 und 5–11*, vol. 1 of *Die Qumran-Essener: Die Texte vom Toten Meer*, UTB 1862 (Munich: Reinhardt, 1995), 35, 37, 55 et passim.

5. The Qumran *yaḥad* 105

and יורה היחיד (CD B XX, 14) as designations of the teacher of righteousness or אנשי היחיד (CD B XX, 32) for "the men of the community."[15] The *nomen* rectum יחד is often used in phrases like "the rule of the *yaḥad*" (סרך היחד) (e.g., 1QS I, 1, 16), "the men of the *yaḥad*" (אנשי היחד) (e.g., 1QS V, 1; VI, 21; 4Q252 V, 5), "the council of the *yaḥad*" (עצת היחד) (4Q259 II, 9, 13) "precepts of the *yaḥad*" (משפטי היחד) (1QS VI, 15), "covenant of the *yaḥad*" (היחד ברית) (1QS VIII, 16–17; 1Q28b V, 21), "house of the *yaḥad* for Israel" (בית יחד לישראל) (1QS IX, 6), "table of the *yaḥad*" (שולחן יחד) (1Q28a II, 17), "the congregation of the *yaḥad*" (עדת היחד) (1Q28a II, 21), or the "teacher of the *yaḥad*" (מורה היחיד) (CD B XX, 1).[16] Maybe even more important for analyzing the Qumranites self-identification are phrases including *yaḥad* as *nomen regens* like "the *yaḥad* of truth" (יחד אמת) (1QS II, 24; cf. *yaḥad* of his [i.e., God's] truth, [י]חד אמתו), "the *yaḥad* of his [i.e., God's] council" (יחד עצתו) (1QS III, 6), "the *yaḥad* of holiness" (יחד קודש) (1QS IX, 2), and even "the *yaḥad* of God" (יחד אל) (1QS I, 12; II, 22). Altogether the root יחד appears 133 times in the scrolls: 6 times as a verb, 22 times as an adverb, with the noun appearing 101 times as יחד and 4 times as יחיד.[17]

Looking at the Old Testament, the occurrences of יחד in Deut 33:5 ("the community of the tribes of Israel" or "the tribes of Israel together") and in 1 Chron 12:18 ("I will have for you a heart for union") may help to clarify the semantic meaning.[18] However, the Israelites' response, when

---

15. Eduard Lohse, ed., *Die Texte aus Qumran: Mit masoretischer Punktation, Übersetzung, Einführung und Anmerkungen; Hebräisch und Deutsch*, 4th ed. (Darmstadt: Wissenschaftliche Buchgesellschaft, 1986), 105, 107; and Maier, *Die Qumran-Essener*, 1:35, 36, 37, suggest to read יחד instead of יחיד; Joseph M. Baumgarten and Daniel R. Schwartz, "Damascus Document (CD)," in *Damascus Document, War Scroll, and Related Documents*, vol. 2 of *The Dead Sea Scrolls: Hebrew, Aramaic, and Greek Texts with English Translations*, ed. James Charlesworth, PTSDSSP (Tübingen: Mohr Siebeck, 1995), 36, translate both מורה היחיד (CD B XX, 1) and יורה היחיד (CD B XX, 14): "the unique teacher," but אנשי היחיד (CD B XX, 32): "the men of the Community"; the translations of CD A and CD B follow this edition, unless otherwise noted.

16. For an overview of יחד, see Fabry, "יָחַד," 44.

17. Cf. Fabry, "יָחַד," 43.

18. For other instances of יחד that have been discussed (e.g., Ps 2:2; Ezek 4:3; Ezra 4:3), see Shemaryahu Talmon, "The Sectarian יחד: A Biblical Noun," *VT* 3 (1953): 133–40. For "the community of the tribes of Israel," cf. Stefan Beyerle, *Der Mosesegen im Deuteronomium: Eine text-, kompositions- und formkritische Studie zu Deuteronomium 33*, BZAW 250 (Berlin: de Gruyter, 1997), 295: "die Gemeinschaft der Stämme Israels"; another possible translation is "the unified tribes of Israel" (NRSV). For "the

106 Carsten Claussen

they receive the law at Sinai (Exod 19:8), may even be a bit closer to the Qumranites' understanding: "the people all answered as one" (ויענו כל־העם יחדו).[19] Richard Bauckham suggests that Mic 2:12, where God promises to "gather the survivors of Israel" (i.e., the exiles) and "set them together" (יַחַד) may have been read by the Qumranites as "God will gather the exiles 'as a community.'"[20] This is confirmed by the Qumran interpretation of 1Q14 (1QpMic) in terms of the fulfillment of Micah's prophecy in their own time.[21] It may well be that the *yaḥad* viewed itself as "the beginning of that regathering of Israel that was expected to take place in the last days."[22]

This biblical background may be part of the reason for the heavy usage of the term in the scrolls. It is obvious that *yaḥad* as a technical term stresses the Qumranites' understanding and belief of belonging together. While it has been quite common for a long time to identify the *yaḥad* with the one community that lived at Qumran, a heavily disputed passage in 1QS VI, 1c–9 seems to point in a different direction.[23] The passage clearly talks of a plurality of meeting places. The quorum of ten men being pre-

---

tribes of Israel together," see Yonder Moynihan Gillihan, *Civic Ideology, Organization, and Law in the Rule Scrolls: A Comparative Study of the Covenanters' Sect and Contemporary Voluntary Associations in Political Context*, STDJ 97 (Leiden: Brill, 2012), 292, who translates Deut 33:5 as "(God) was in Yeshurun king when were gathered the chiefs of the people, together, the tribes of Israel." See 1 Chr 12:18 (NRSV): "my heart will be knit to you."

19. For this suggestion, see James C. VanderKam, "Sinai Revisited" in *Biblical Interpretation at Qumran*, ed. Matthias Henze, SCSS (Grand Rapids: Eerdmans, 2005), 52.

20. Richard Bauckham, *Gospel of Glory: Major Themes in Johannine Theology* (Grand Rapids: Baker Academic, 2015), 27.

21. 1Q14 VIII mentions the "the council of the community" (עצת היחד). Cf. the quotation of Mic 2:6 in CD A IV, 20–21.

22. Bauckham, *Gospel of Glory*, 27.

23. For the community living at Qumran, see, e.g., James H. Charlesworth, "Community Organization: Community Organization in the Rule of the Community," in *The Encyclopedia of the Dead Sea Scrolls*, ed. Lawrence H. Schiffman and James C. VanderKam, 2 vols. (Oxford: Oxford University Press, 2000), 1:133–36; for the disputed passage, see Charlotte Hempel, *The Qumran Rule Texts in Context: Collected Studies*, TSAJ 154 (Tübingen: Mohr Siebeck, 2013), 80. The translation here (and also below where 1QS is quoted) is from Elisha Qimron and James H. Charlesworth, "Rule of the Community (1QS; cf. 4QS MSS A–J, 5Q11)," in *The Dead Sea Scrolls: Hebrew, Aramaic, and Greek Texts with English Translations; Rule of the Community and Related Documents*, ed. James H. Charlesworth, PTSDSSP (Tübingen: Mohr Siebeck, 1994), 1:27.

5. The Qumran *yaḥad*

sided over by a priest is reminiscent of similar meetings mentioned in the Damascus Rule (CD A XII, 22–XIII, 7). The text there (CD A XII, 22–23) is called "the rule for the settlers of the camps." There as well, for a group of ten men, a priest should also "not be absent."

From the above passage in 1QS VI, 1c–9 John J. Collins has concluded that "the 'rule for the assembly of the many' that begins in 1QS 6:8b seems to envision a large community, with multiple priests."[24] Thus the term יחד could refer to a larger organization, effectively an "umbrella organization," with the "men of the community" (אנשי היחד) (1QS V, 1; IX, 7) designating the entire *yaḥad*.[25] Collins also concludes that "the council of the *yaḥad* is simply the *yaḥad* itself."[26] Therefore, the term *yaḥad* must not be limited to the Qumranites who lived at the Qumran settlement but serves in a much broader sense to identify the unity and oneness of the whole community.[27] The oneness of the *yaḥad* is thus not limited to one or any of the settlements. The community at Khirbet Qumran was only one of many groups represented by the *yaḥad*. How was the *yaḥad* organized?

5.2. Communal Organization

As noted, the *yaḥad* was at its highest level most likely an umbrella organization of different communities in various places. Since the Damascus

---

24. John J. Collins, *Beyond the Qumran Community: The Sectarian Movement of the Dead Sea Scrolls* (Grand Rapids: Eerdmans, 2010), 67; Collins, "Yaḥad," 85–86.

25. For "umbrella organization," see, e.g., John J. Collins, "Forms of Community in the Dead Sea Scrolls," in *Emanuel: Studies in Hebrew Bible, Septuagint, and the Dead Sea Scrolls in Honor of Emanuel Tov*, ed. Shalom M. Paul et al., VTSup 94 (Leiden: Brill, 2003), 97–111, esp. 99; Collins, *Beyond the Qumran Community*, 67; cf. Regev, *Sectarianism in Qumran*; Jörg Frey, "Qumran: An Overview" in Jörg Frey, *Qumran, Early Judaism, and New Testament Interpretation: Kleine Schriften III*, ed. Jacob N. Cerone, WUNT 424 (Tübingen: Mohr Siebeck 2019), 79. For designating the entire *yaḥad*, see Collins, *Beyond the Qumran Community*, 71.

26. John J. Collins, "Beyond the Qumran Community: Social Organization in the Dead Sea Scrolls," *DSD* 16 (2009): 362.

27. However, at the same time it is also possible that the term *yaḥad* sometimes may simply refer to a group of people (like the "council") sitting together as in 11Q19 (11QTa) LVII, 12–13: "and twelve Levites, (13) who shall sit together with him for judgment [למשפט]" as Arie van der Kooij, "The *Yaḥad*: What Is in a Name?," *DSD* 18 (2011): 109–28, esp. 112, has argued. However, here the usage of יחד is most likely adverbial.

108   Carsten Claussen

Document and the Rule of the Community reveal different types of organizational structures, they deserve to be treated individually.[28]

The members of the "New Covenant in the Land of Damascus" lived in camps (מחנה) of men, women and children (CD A VII, 6–7).[29] A camp was constituted by a minimum of ten men, among them one priest. Then there were also larger organizational units of tens, fifties, hundreds, and thousands.[30] Every camp was led by some kind of local overseer, called a *mevaqer* (מבקר).[31] His authority pertained to basically all private and social issues of the members (cf. CD A XIII, 7–17) and he also led the meetings of the individual camps (CD A XII, 22b–XIV, 2). On a more global level there was a principal leader, called the "overseer of all the camps" (והמבקר אשר לכל המחנות) (CD A XIV, 8–9). He was responsible for leading the general meeting of all the camps (רבים) comprising priests, Levites, Israelites, and proselytes (CD A XIV, 3–6).[32] His responsibilities were more in the areas of administration, while the priests were the spiritual leaders of the community.[33] Broadly speaking and as has been noticed before, the Qumran community was organized very much like Israel in the Old Testament. The scroll 1QS II, 19–21 mentions priests, Levites, and then all the people while CD A XIV, 3–4 lists priests, Levites, Israelites, and proselytes. The "thousands and hundreds and fifties and tens" are reminiscent of Israel's army.[34]

------

28. Cf. Daniel Stökl Ben Ezra, *Qumran: Die Texte vom Toten Meer und das antike Judentum*, UTB 4681, Jüdische Studien 3 (Tübingen: Mohr Siebeck, 2016), 256–63.

29. Cf. the title "New Covenant in the Land of Damascus" (הברית החדשה בארץ דמשק) in CD A VI, 19; VIII, 21; CD B XX, 12. There are more than one hundred mentions of מחנה in various texts. See, e.g., CD A VII, 6–7; XIII, 4, 20; XIV, 3; cf. 1 Sam 2:15; 1QM III, IV. The terminology is reminiscent of exodus terminology, see, e.g., Exod 16:13; 19:16, 17; 29:14.

30. See CD A XII, 22b–XIII, 7a; 4Q266 (4QD^a) 9 II, 14–15; 4Q267 (4QD^b) 9 IV, 1–3; 4Q271 (4QD^f) 5 II, 20–21; for a description of the structure, see Charlotte Hempel, *The Damascus Texts*, Companions to the Qumran Scrolls (Sheffield: Sheffield Academic, 2000), 40; cf. Israel's organization in the wilderness according to Exod 18:21, 25.

31. See, e.g., CD A IX, 18, 19, 22; XIII, 6, 7, 13, 16.

32. For the leader being responsible for all camps, cf. CD A XIV, 3–18a; 4Q266 10 I, 1–11; 4Q267 9 V, 6–14; 4Q268 (4QD^c) II, 1–2; cf. Hempel, *Damascus Texts*, 40–41.

33. See Stökl, *Qumran*, 258.

34. 1QS II, 21–22; CD A XII, 23–XIII, 1; cf. C. T. R. Hayward, "'The Lord Is One': Reflections on the Theme of Unity in John's Gospel from a Jewish Perspective," in

A local group of the *yaḥad* as mentioned in the Community Rule consisted of at least ten males led by a priest (cf. 1QS III, 2). Here, too, general meetings were led by a *mevaqer* (מבקר) who was also responsible for the finances (1QS VI, 14–23).[35] Another officer mentioned is the *maskil* (משכיל), who may have been some kind of instructor (1QS III, 13–IV, 26; IX, 12–26, etc.). A council of twelve laymen and three priests may have been responsible for dealing with legal and social issues.[36] In contrast to the regulations of the Damascus Document there is no explicit mention of women and children in the Community Rule.[37] However, the Rule of the Congregation mentions the presence of women, children, and families within the congregation (1Q28a I, 4, 8–9). It is possible that women and children were members of the wider and earlier Qumran community but not of a more exclusive local group.

Overall, the organization described by the Community Rule seems to be a lot stricter compared to the Damascus Document. For both types of organization, one may say that strictness and hierarchy were used to stress oneness and unity. Such rigid strictness can also be seen when it comes to the admission procedure.

5.3. Admission Procedure

Jewish identity was, of course, a prerequisite for becoming a Qumranite. But in order to become admitted into the community it was also necessary to swear a special oath. The procedure is described in the Community Rule (1QS V, 7c–9a).[38] Since a similar procedure is mentioned in the earlier Damascus Document (CD A XVI, 2b–4a) it is very likely that

---

Early Jewish and Christian Monotheism, ed. Loren T. Stuckenbruck and Wendy E. S. North, JSNTSup 263 (London: T&T Clark, 2004), 146.

35. For the *mevaqer*, see 1QS VI, 12, 20; cf. CD A IX, 18, 19, 22; XIII, 6, 7, 13, 16; XIV, 8, 11, 13; XV, 8, 11, 14.

36. 1QS VIII, 1–5; cf. 1QS IX, 7: "The sons of Aaron alone shall rule over judgment and property."

37. Cf. Moshe J. Bernstein, "Women and Children in Legal and Liturgical Texts from Qumran," *DSD* 11 (2004): 191–211; Eyal Regev, "*Cherchez les femmes*: Were the Yahad Celibates?," *DSD* 15 (2008): 253–84, even challenges the notion that the Community Rule only refers to males. However, there is no explicit mention of women and children in 1QS. For discussion of Regev's position, see Joan E. Taylor, "Women, Children, and Celibate Men in the Serekh Texts," *HTR* 104 (2011): 171–90.

38. Translation from Qimron and Charlesworth, "Rule of the Community," 21, 23.

110   Carsten Claussen

this kind of oath stood at the very center of admission to all subgroups of the *yaḥad*.

An even more elaborate and multistage admission process is described in another passage of the Community Rule (1QS VI, 13b–23). Here the applicant was first subjected to an examination by "the Overseer at the head of the Many" (הפקיד ברוא הרבים) (1QS VI, 14). Later on, he was examined by the members of the community. At this stage during his first probationary year the applicant was still not allowed to touch the pure food of the community. After completing a second year and another examination, the applicant could then be accepted and registered, after which his belongings were finally merged into the property of the community. The institutionalization of this procedure is much more developed than the simple swearing of an oath as in the other two passages described above. It seems very likely that 1QS VI, 13b–23 reveals a later stage of development within the community.[39]

Finally, it is important to note that not everybody was welcome to enter the Qumran social domain. According to the Rule of the Congregation (1Q28a II, 3–9), the participation of lame, blind, or stuttering people in the assembly was forbidden, "for the angels of holiness are in their community."[40]

Why was such a strict admission procedure necessary? When one focuses on the oneness of the *yaḥad* it is crucial to realize that the admission process is only the first step in order to enter a system of extensive pressure and strict hierarchy. Qumran oneness is by no means to be equated with any kind of communal equality. Applicants and partial members strived for full membership. This involved giving up a large degree of individual identity and taking up the corporate identity of the *yaḥad*. On their way into the community people not only gave up their private belongings, but also "what might be called their intellectual property: their knowledge, counsel, and judgment."[41] This did not stop when one was finally admitted

---

39. See Hempel, *Qumran Rule Texts*, 29. In his description of the Essenes, Josephus describes a similar admission process (*B.J.* 2.137–138).

40. 1Q28a II, 8–9; cf. 4Q267 17 I, 6–9; CD A XV, 15–17; cf. the removal of disabled or unclean people from the assembly in Deut 23:15; Num 5, 3b.

41. Russell C. D. Arnold, *The Social Role of Liturgy in the Religion of the Qumran Community*, STDJ 60 (Leiden: Brill, 2006), 39; cf. Carol A. Newsom, *The Self as Symbolic Space: Constructing Identity and Community at Qumran*, STDJ 52 (Leiden: Brill, 2004), 73–75.

to full membership. During the annual covenant ceremony, the piety and behavior over the past year was examined. Thus members were ranked, inferior to some and superior to others. This ranking regulated the orders of seating at meals and speaking at meetings (1QS VI, 4–5, 8–13). By entering the community, the new members also left a world that was regarded morally and ritually impure and they entered the *yaḥad* as a sphere of maximal purity.

5.4. Purity

At the very heart of Qumranite self-identity was very likely a separation from the temple cult, since the Qumranites did not see the cultic and purity practices in Jerusalem in line with torah (e.g., 4QMMT).[42] The primary writers behind the Qumran rules were probably priests who, since they were unable to ensure the sanctity of the Jerusalem sanctuary, were hoping for the messianic era when they would regain control over the temple and its cult.[43] For the time in between they did everything in their power to organize their community to some degree as a provisional substitute for the temple, a "temple of men" (4Q174 I, 6: מקדש אדם).[44]

Francis Schmidt describes "the Assembly and the Council [... as the] inmost circle of the Community. A space of maximal holiness that is open only to the Many who submit to a maximal purification."[45] While the Jerusalem temple was seen as morally and ritually defiled, the Qumranites saw themselves as holy people. They probably thought that the divine presence

---

42. For more on the theme of purity at Qumran, see Lawrence H. Schiffman, *The Halakha at Qumran*, SJLA 16 (Leiden: Brill, 1975); Joseph M. Baumgarten, *Studies in Qumran Law*, SJLA 24 (Leiden: Brill, 1977); Jacob Neusner, *The Idea of Purity in Ancient Judaism*, SJLA 1 (Leiden: Brill, 1973); Jacob Milgrom, *Leviticus: A New Translation with Introduction and Commentary*, 3 vols., AB 3 (New York: Doubleday, 1991, 2000, 2001); Jonathan Klawans, *Impurity and Sin in Ancient Judaism* (Oxford: Oxford University Press, 2000), esp. 67–91; Klawans, *Purity, Sacrifice, and the Temple: Symbolism and Supersessionism in the Study of Ancient Judaism*, (Oxford: Oxford University Press, 2006), 145–74.

43. See Hannah K. Harrington, "Purity," in Schiffman and VanderKam, *Encyclopedia of the Dead Sea Scrolls*, 2:727.

44. Cf. Klawans, *Purity*, 166; cf. 173.

45. Francis Schmidt, *How the Temple Thinks: Identity and Social Cohesion in Ancient Judaism*, BibSem 78 (Sheffield: Sheffield Academic, 2001), 162. He refers to 1QS VIII, 5–6 in comparison to Exod 26:33.

112   Carsten Claussen

had left the temple but it is less clear to what degree they may have believed that God's presence dwelled in their midst. The emphasis on achieving maximum ritual and moral purity, however, was very important for the community (cf. 1QS V, 13), and may be confirmed by the numerous water installations of the archaeological site at Khirbet Qumran.[46] In contrast to the purity of the Qumranites, all others outside the *yaḥad* were not only seen as being impure, but any attempt on their part to attain purity was deemed to be futile (1QS II, 26–III, 6). The consequences of the *yaḥad* in offering and embodying a sense of highly exclusive purity can hardly be overestimated. It made contacts between the members of the *yaḥad* and other Jews and, of course, the Jerusalem temple difficult if not impossible. Already the early archaeologist at Khirbet Qumran, G. Lankester Harding, spoke of Qumran in terms of a "closed settlement."[47] This emphasis on exclusivistic purity surely strengthened the notion of elitist unity and oneness of the *yaḥad*.

5.5. Torah Study and Observance

The admission procedures of the Qumran community reveal not only its strict purity halakah but especially its rigid torah observance. This clearly separates the Qumranites from other Jews, who are called "the congregation of the men of deceit" (אנשי העול עדת) (1QS V, 2). Those Jews outside the *yaḥad* also knew the torah and were subject to it as well. Yet in the eyes of the Qumranites they did not study it properly, did not search for its hidden meaning, and knowingly transgressed the law (1QS V, 11–12). This was not the case within the *yaḥad*: "The Many shall spend the third part of every night of the year in unity, reading the Book, studying judgment" (1QS VI, 7). These are merely the common regulations for members of the community; there is also a special rule regarding some kind of representative for a small group: "And where there are ten (members) there must not be lacking there a man who studies the torah day and night" (1QS VI, 6). Among the texts read at Qumran, Deuteronomy featured heavily.[48] How-

---

46. Jodi Magness, *The Archaeology of Qumran and the Dead Sea Scrolls*, SDSS (Grand Rapids: Eerdmans, 2002), 134–62.

47. G. Lankester Harding, "Khirbet Qumrân and Wady Murabba'at: Fresh Light on the Dead Sea Scrolls and New Manuscript Discoveries," *PEQ* 84 (1952): 105.

48. Ulrich Dahmen, "Das Deuteronomium in Qumran als umgeschriebene Bibel," in *Das Deuteronomium*, ed. Georg Braulik, ÖBS 23 (Frankfurt: Lang, 2003),

5. The Qumran *yaḥad*

ever, the oneness of God in the Shema (Deut 6:4) is probably not linked to the idea of the *yaḥad*.[49]

Torah study emphasized the oneness of the *yaḥad* on different levels. It brought the members together in order to meet in small groups. This also gave structure to their daily routine. Of course, torah study also educated the members of the *yaḥad* how they could and should live in total obedience to the torah.

5.6. Communal Property

Regarding the practice of ownership, the Damascus Document and the Community Rule draw very different pictures.[50] The Damascus Document talks of personal items that were lost or stolen. When this happens "the owner shall cause to be pronounced an oath curse" (CD A IX, 11–12). The same passage also talks about property of which no owner was found (CD A IX, 10b–16a). The members were only expected to hand over the "wage of at least two days per month" to the *mevaqer*. This implies that private ownership of goods was allowed up to a certain degree.

In contrast to this the Community Rule indicates that the community finally owned all property (1QS I, 11–13; V, 2–3; VI, 2–3; IX, 8). As stipulated in 1QS, when a new member was admitted to the *yaḥad*, he had to hand over his whole property to the *mevaqer* at the end of the first probationary year. The property was merged with that of the community after a second year when he had finally been admitted to full membership.[51] Although the relationship of the Qumranites to the Essenes is not clear, it

---

269, has pointed out that among the about 220 Qumran manuscripts of biblical texts about 34 contain the book of Deuteronomy. Cf. Sidnie White Crawford, "Reading Deuteronomy in the Second Temple Period," in *Reading the Present in the Qumran Library: The Perception of the Contemporary by Means of Scriptural Interpretations*, ed. Kristin De Troyer and Armin Lange, SymS 30 (Atlanta: Society of Biblical Literature, 2005), 127–40.

49. Hayward, "'Lord Is One,'" 142–49, esp. 146, makes a case for a connection. However, Bauckham, *Gospel of Glory*, 24, has summarized the evidence in ancient Jewish literature and concluded that "for late Second Temple Judaism, 'God is one' means that there is only one God" and never that "God is unified rather than divided."

50. See James C. VanderKam, *The Dead Sea Scrolls Today*, 2nd ed. (Grand Rapids: Eerdmans, 2010), 108–11; Hempel, *Qumran Rule Texts*, 31–32; Stökl, *Qumran*, 261.

51. Hempel, *Qumran Rule Texts*, 31, mentions, that there are "a number of statements in the Community Rule that seem to allow for a certain amount of private

114 Carsten Claussen

is important to notice that both Josephus (*B.J.* 2.122–123) and Philo (*Prob.* 84, 91) know of the Essene practice of communal ownership.

The community of goods of the Qumran *yaḥad* had nothing to do with any ideal of poverty. If people have to surrender their private property to a community, they become highly dependent on the group, even as far as basic needs of food and clothing are concerned. Their dependency on the communal property and those who administered it therefore separated the Qumranites from their environs and made economic interaction with the outside world difficult. This situation was a sign of the Qumranites' unity and oneness but also for their strict separation from everything and everybody outside the community. Thus the community of goods may be seen as a strong indicator for the sectarian nature of the *yaḥad*.

5.7. Communal Meetings

The organization of the camps into "thousands and hundreds and fifties and tens" is documented in the Community Rule, the Rule of the Congregation, and also in the Damascus Document.[52] It implies that there must have been a number of meetings of rather different sizes. The largest meeting of the Qumranites must have been the meeting of all the camps. The rule for this may be found in CD A XIV, 3–4. It mentions priests, Levites, Israelites, and proselytes (CD A XIV, 3–6) as representing a fourfold community structure. The meeting was led by a priest, and all participants were assigned to a fixed position.

A similar description of rules for such meetings can be found in 1QS VI, 1b–10a. Here it is stressed that the members of the *yaḥad* "shall eat (in) unity [ויחד יואכלו] say benedictions (in) unity [ויחד יברכו], and give counsel (in) unity [ויחד יועצו]" (1QS VI, 2–3). This shall be done "wherever they are found [בכול מגוריהם]" (1QS VI, 2). Thus communal meals, communal prayers, and communal deliberations were the very essence of these meetings. They were led by a priest, and every participant sat on his assigned place according to his rank (1QS VI, 4).

In both documents the meeting is called מושב (CD A XIV, 3; 1QS VI, 8). Although the terminology is otherwise quite different, 1QS VI,

---

ownership" (cf. 1QS VII, 6–8, 24–25). However, this is far from certain; see Collins, *Beyond the Qumran Community*, 57–58.

52. 1QS II, 21–22; 1Q28a I, 14–15; I, 29–II, 1; CD A XIII, 2; cf. Num 31:14, 48, 52.

5. The Qumran *yaḥad* 115

8b–10a may be viewed as an adaptation of the earlier rule in CD A XIV, 3–6, 8b–12a.[53]

Other gatherings were held across the settlements in addition to these smaller and more regular meetings. An annual covenant renewal ceremony (1QS II, 19) was probably celebrated around the time of Shavuot. Its liturgy may have survived in four or five manuscripts, which are by convention called *Berakhot*.[54] They include legal material as well as curses on Belial and a reference to a census and to the half-shekel tax of the community and a number of hymns. Another rite, probably also performed at this annual general meeting, was for the initiation of new members and also repeated by the older members (4Q271 VII, 2 cf. 4Q275). It included a confession of sin (1QS I, 16–II, 18). This annual meeting was performed in a strictly hierarchical manner with the priests holding highest rank (1QS VI, 8–13) while an overseer (מבקר) presides (1QS VI, 12, 20). A similar type of annual general meeting of the "New Covenant" is reported in the Damascus Document (see CD A XIV, 8–17). The various meetings, whether small or large, whether on a daily basis or annually, certainly had a unifying effect on the community. These were the times when they prayed, performed rites and liturgies, organized their communal life and, of course, ate together.

5.8. Common Meals

A special type of meetings were the common meals held by the Qumranites. Eating and drinking are much more than just matters of physical sustenance—as Mary Douglas has put it, "food is not feed" and social eating can serve "as a system of communication."[55] In groups placing importance on the status of those deliberately present or absent and concerned with purity regulations that determine the types of food served and even the utensils used in serving, the practice of communal meals may tell a lot about the identity of those who are united at a table (or perhaps separated from others). In the Dead Sea Scrolls there are two texts, one

---

53. Cf. Hempel, *Qumran Rule Texts*, 33–34.

54. 4Q286–290, 4Q280 (?). Cf. James R. Davila, *Liturgical Works*, Eerdmans Commentaries on the Dead Sea Scrolls 6 (Grand Rapids: Eerdmans, 2000), 41–82.

55. Mary Douglas, "Introduction" in *The Anthropologist's Cookbook*, ed. Jessica Kuper (London: Routledge, 1977), 7; Douglas, *In the Active Voice* (London: Routledge, 1982), 85–86.

116   Carsten Claussen

from the Community Rule (1QS VI, 2, 4) and the other from the Rule of the Congregation (1Q28a II, 11–22), where the common meals of the Qumranites are briefly mentioned. These texts indicate that the members of the *yaḥad* took their meals as an eschatological and messianic banquet.[56]

New aspirants were not allowed to touch the pure food during the first year and until they had been examined (1QS VI, 16–17). They were at that point allowed to take bread, but it was only after further examination and not until completing a second year in the community (1QS VI, 20–21) that new members were permitted to "touch the drink of the Many" (1QS VI, 20). The strict regulations for permission to join in at the communal meals and to take bread and new wine were therefore a clear mark for the identity of the Qumranites. These regulations did not seem to pertain to a certain settlement, but were at the very heart of how identity was forged in all the dwelling places of the Qumranites. Wherever they lived they were obliged to hold communal meals, communal worship, and communal deliberation.

5.9. Calendar System

Calendars are at the very heart of the activities of any given society or social group.[57] Without an agreement on the numbering of days, weeks, and years as well as of special days for feasts and rituals, no group of people may be able to organize its social, political, economic, and religious life. In the Roman Empire, Jews followed a number of different calendrical systems.[58] Those in Greece, Macedonia, and Moesia used a lunar calendar. In Asia Minor, Syria, Libya, and Egypt (except for Alex-

---

56. Stökl, *Qumran*, 297.

57. For an overview of research on calendars, see Meret Strothmann, "Vertragen sich Sonne und Mond? Überlegungen zum Kalender als politisches Instrumentarium bei Römern und Juden," in *"Religio Licita?,"* ed. Görge K. Hasselhoff and Meret Strothmann, SJ 84 (Berlin: de Gruyter, 2017), 85–103.

58. For an overview of ancient calendars in general, see Jörg Rüpke, *The Roman Calendar from Numa to Constantine: Time, History, and the* Fasti, trans. D. M. B. Richardson (Chichester: Wiley-Blackwell, 2011); for ancient Jewish calendars see Roger T. Beckwith, *Calendar and Chronology, Jewish and Christian: Biblical, Intertestamental, and Patristic Studies*, AGJU 33 (Leiden: Brill, 1996); Sacha Stern, *Calendar and Community: A History of the Jewish Calendar, Second Century BCE to Tenth Century CE* (Oxford: Oxford University Press, 2001).

5. The Qumran *yaḥad*   117

andria), the Jewish synagogues adhered to the Julian solar calendar.[59] No other comparable reports about calendrical controversies in antiquity have been preserved apart from those concerning the Qumranites and their Jewish counterparts in the Jerusalem temple.[60] For the Qumran community, Shemaryahu Talmon has stressed the fundamental importance attached to the adherence to a calendar different from that used in Jerusalem.[61] The origins of the Qumran calendar probably go back to the very early stages of the movement. The large number of Qumran texts dealing with the calendar bears witness to the importance of the calendar for the Qumran community. For groups who live in the same geographic regions the use of different calendars reinforces their identity or separation. The Qumranites followed a 364-day calendar, which comes close to a 365.25-day solar calendar. Similar calendars of 360, 364, or even 365.25 days can also be found in the Astronomical Book of Enoch (1 En. 72–82), the Aramaic Levi Document, Jubilees, Slavonic Enoch, and the Temple Scroll.[62] Like Pesher Habakkuk, 1 Enoch and Jubilees also show polemics against the use of a solar calendar, while such criticism is absent from the Aramaic Levi Document.[63]

---

59. Cf. Philo, *QE* 1.1; *Her.* 149–150; for the Alexandrian calendar, see Chris Bennett, *Alexandria and the Moon: An Investigation into the Lunar Macedonian Calendar of Ptolemaic Egypt*, StHell 52 (Leuven: Peeters, 2011).

60. See Shemaryahu Talmon, "Anti-Lunar-Calendar Polemics in Covenanters' Writings," in *Das Ende der Tage und die Gegenwart des Heils: Begegnungen mit dem Neuen Testament und seiner Umwelt; Festschrift für Heinz-Wolfgang Kuhn zum 65. Geburtstag*, ed. Michael Becker and Wolfgang Fenske, AGJU 44 (Leiden: Brill, 1999), 29. However, e.g., the dating of the second Jewish revolt (132–136 CE) according to the "year of Bar-Kokhba" shows that other Jewish groups also distanced themselves by means of making up their own calendar system; see Yigael Yadin, Hannah Cotton, and Andrew Gross, eds., *The Documents from the Bar Kokhba Period in the Cave of Letters: Hebrew, Aramaic and Nabatean-Aramaic Papyri* (Jerusalem: Israel Exploration Society; Institute of Archaeology, Hebrew University; Shrine of the Book, Israel Museum, 2002), 45, 59, 66.

61. Shemaryahu Talmon, *The Calendar Reckoning of the Sect from the Judaean Desert*, ed. Chaim Rabin and Yigael Yadin, ScrHier 4 (Jerusalem: Magnes, 1965), 163–64.

62. 1 En. 74.12–13: 364-day calendar; 74.10–11; 75.1–2; 82.4–6: 360-day calendar. 1 En. 78.15–16 mentions a lunar calendar of 354 days. For allusions to various lunisolar cycles, see 1 En. 74.13–16. Jubilees 6.32 refers to a 364-day year. Cf. 4Q320–321; 4Q325. 2 En. 15:4 assumes a length of 365.25 days per year.

63. Cf. Jonas Greenfield, Michael E. Stone, and Esther Eshel, eds., *The Aramaic*

118 Carsten Claussen

While earlier research on Qumran presented the sole use of a solar calendar as a scholarly consensus, matters became more complicated after many of the texts from Cave 4 became available. It then became obvious that the Qumranites took into account not only a 364-day solar calendar and the corresponding date in the lunar calendar, but also the day of service for the priestly shift as documented in the *Mishmarot*-texts. It is not possible to go into greater detail in this essay.[64] But it is important to notice that the Qumran calendars differed from the 354-day lunar calendar followed in the Jerusalem temple. These discrepancies led to polemics against those who observed a different calendar system and it set the Qumranites apart from most of the outside ancient Jewish world.[65] At the same time it emphasized their sense of unity. However, the Qumran calendar was not only a matter of communal life. Most important, it also enabled the Qumranites to regulate their time and especially their festival calendar according to the divine will (1QS I, 14–15). The Damascus Document claims a special revelation about "hidden things in which all Israel had strayed: his holy Sabbaths, the glorious appointed times" (CD A III, 14). Calendar diversity is, of course, a serious threat to collective cohesion. Among other reasons (e.g., purity) it made joint worship between the "Community of the Renewed Covenant" and those Jews following the calendar of the temple in Jerusalem virtually impossible.[66] The observance of a special calendar strengthened the social cohesion on either side.

Levi Document: Edition, Translation, Commentary, SVTP 19 (Leiden: Brill, 2004), 20; Michael E. Stone, "Enoch, Aramaic Levi and Sectarian Origins," in *Selected Studies in Pseudepigrapha and Apocrypha: With Special Reference to the Armenian Tradition*, SVTP 9 (Leiden: Brill, 1991), 256.

64. See, however, the overview by Shemaryahu Talmon, "Calendars and Mishmarot," in Schiffman and VanderKam, *Encyclopedia of the Dead Sea Scrolls*, 1:108–17.

65. For polemics, cf. 1QpHab XI, 2–8; the text probably refers to a harassment of the "Wicked Priest," presumably the high priest in Jerusalem, by the early leader of the Qumran, called the "Teacher of Righteousness," on the very Day of Atonement. As mentioned above Jubilees and various Enochic and thus nonsectarian writings also used a similar calendar. Thus one should probably be careful not to talk of an exclusively "Qumran calendar."

66. Whether this, however, may be a strong enough argument in favor of Qumran sectarianism is in more recent research a matter of dispute. Cf. the overview of Sacha Stern, "Qumran Calendars and Sectarianism," in Lim and Collins, *Oxford Handbook of the Dead Sea Scrolls*, 232–53, esp. 247–50.

5. The Qumran *yaḥad* 119

5.10. Conclusion: Qumran Sectarianism—Between the Unity of the *yaḥad* and the Separation from Others

The two types of groups, behind the Damascus Document on the one hand and represented by the Rule of the Community and the Rule of the Congregation on the other hand, were in many ways quite different from their ancient Jewish context. They used a specific terminology. The organization of the priests, Levites, Israelites, and proselytes assigned a special rank for each of them within the community. The gradual admission procedure, especially in 1QS, was rather strict. The Qumranites had an exclusivistic view on purity, regarding all Jews outside the *yaḥad* as impure. The interpretation and observance of the torah was, according to their own view, quite specific and more rigorous than what other Jews practiced. Special emphasis on oneness and unity was exercised by their communal sharing of property. Various types of meetings and common meals were important for their understanding of living together. The Qumran calendars served not only to synchronize the festal calendar of the Qumranites with the heavenly world but also set them apart, bringing them into tension with other ancient Jewish communities of their time.

As has been shown above, not only the self-designation as *yaḥad*, but also the various above-mentioned characteristics reflect the religious and theological belief systems of the Qumran movement. As one scholar has rightly pointed out, "the idea of unity [… was] almost an obsession for the Jews who made up the group at Qumran."[67] Although the Qumranites read, among other texts, the same biblical scriptures as contemporary Jews their interpretation led to a rather different identity with an extreme emphasis on unity and oneness and a strict separation from the outside world.

Bibliography

Arnold, Russell C. D. *The Social Role of Liturgy in the Religion of the Qumran Community*. STDJ 60. Leiden: Brill, 2006.
Bauckham, Richard. *Gospel of Glory: Major Themes in Johannine Theology*. Grand Rapids: Baker Academic, 2015.

---

67. Hayward, "'Lord Is One,'" 142, see esp. 142–49, "Unity at Qumran."

120 Carsten Claussen

Baumgarten, Joseph M. *Studies in Qumran Law*. SJLA 24. Leiden: Brill, 1977.

Baumgarten, Joseph M., and Daniel R. Schwartz. "Damascus Document (CD)." Pages 4–57 in *Damascus Document, War Scroll, and Related Documents*. Vol. 2 of *The Dead Sea Scrolls: Hebrew, Aramaic, and Greek Texts with English Translations*. Edited by James Charlesworth. PTSDSSP. Tübingen: Mohr Siebeck, 1995.

Beckwith, Roger T. *Calendar and Chronology, Jewish and Christian: Biblical, Intertestamental, and Patristic Studies*. AGJU 33. Leiden: Brill, 1996.

Bennett, Chris. *Alexandria and the Moon: An Investigation into the Lunar Macedonian Calendar of Ptolemaic Egypt*. StHell 52. Leuven: Peeters, 2011.

Bernstein, Moshe J. "Women and Children in Legal and Liturgical Texts from Qumran." *DSD* 11 (2004): 191–211.

Beyerle, Stefan. *Der Mosesegen im Deuteronomium: Eine text-, kompositions- und formkritische Studie zu Deuteronomium 33*. BZAW 250. Berlin: de Gruyter, 1997.

Charlesworth, James H. "Community Organization: Community Organization in the Rule of the Community." Pages 133–36 in vol. 1 of *The Encyclopedia of the Dead Sea Scrolls*. Edited by Lawrence H. Schiffman and James C. VanderKam. 2 vols. Oxford: Oxford University Press, 2000.

Claussen, Carsten. "John, Qumran, and the Question of Sectarianism." *PRSt* 37 (2010): 421–40.

Claussen, Carsten, and Michael Thomas Davis. "The Concept of Unity at Qumran." Pages 232–53 in *Qumran Studies: New Approaches, New Questions*. Edited by Michael Thomas Davis and Brent A. Strawn. Grand Rapids: Eerdmans: 2007.

Collins, John J. *Beyond the Qumran Community: The Sectarian Movement of the Dead Sea Scrolls*. Grand Rapids: Eerdmans, 2010.

———. "Beyond the Qumran Community: Social Organization in the Dead Sea Scrolls." *DSD* 16 (2009): 351–69.

———. "Forms of Community in the Dead Sea Scrolls." Pages 97–111 in *Emanuel: Studies in Hebrew Bible, Septuagint, and the Dead Sea Scrolls in Honor of Emanuel Tov*. Edited by Shalom M. Paul, Robert A. Kraft, Lawrence H. Schiffman, and Weston W. Fields. VTSup 94. Leiden: Brill, 2003.

———. "The Yaḥad and 'the Qumran Community.'" Pages 81–96 in *Biblical Traditions in Transmission: Essays in Honour of Michael A. Knibb*.

5. The Qumran *yaḥad* 121

Edited by Charlotte Hempel and Judith M. Lieu. JSJSup 111. Leiden: Brill, 2006.

Collins, John J., and Robert A. Kugler, eds. *Religion in the Dead Sea Scrolls.* SDSS. Grand Rapids: Eerdmans, 2000.

Crawford, Sidnie White. "Reading Deuteronomy in the Second Temple Period." Pages 127–40 in *Reading the Present in the Qumran Library: The Perception of the Contemporary by Means of Scriptural Interpretations.* Edited by Kristin De Troyer and Armin Lange. SymS 30. Atlanta: Society of Biblical Literature, 2005.

Dahmen, Ulrich. "Das Deuteronomium in Qumran als umgeschriebene Bibel." Pages 269–309 in *Das Deuteronomium.* Edited by Georg Braulik. ÖBS 23. Frankfurt: Lang, 2003.

Davila, James R. *Liturgical Works.* Eerdmans Commentaries on the Dead Sea Scrolls 6. Grand Rapids: Eerdmans, 2000.

Douglas, Mary. *In the Active Voice.* London: Routledge, 1982.

———. "Introduction." Pages 1–7 in *The Anthropologist's Cookbook.* Edited by Jessica Kuper. London: Routledge, 1977.

Fabry, Heinz-Josef. "יַחַד." *TDOT* 6:40–48.

Frey, Jörg. "Different Patterns of Dualism in the Qumran Library." Pages 275–335 in *Legal Texts and Legal Issues: Proceedings of the Second Meeting of the International Organization of Qumran Studies, Cambridge 1995; Published in Honor of J. M. Baumgarten.* Edited by Moshe J. Bernstein, Florentino García Martínez, and John Kampen. STDJ 23. Leiden: Brill, 1997.

———. "Qumran: An Overview." Pages 45–81 in Jörg Frey, *Qumran, Early Judaism, and New Testament Interpetation: Kleine Schriften III.* Edited by Jacob N. Cerone. WUNT 424. Tübingen: Mohr Siebeck, 2019.

Gillihan, Yonder Moynihan. *Civic Ideology, Organization, and Law in the Rule Scrolls: A Comparative Study of the Covenanters' Sect and Contemporary Voluntary Associations in Political Context.* STDJ 97. Leiden: Brill, 2012.

Greenfield, Jonas, Michael E. Stone, and Esther Eshel, eds. *The Aramaic Levi Document: Edition, Translation, Commentary.* SVTP 19. Leiden: Brill, 2004.

Harding, G. Lankester. "Khirbet Qumrân and Wady Murabba'at: Fresh Light on the Dead Sea Scrolls and New Manuscript Discoveries." *PEQ* 84 (1952): 104–9.

Harrington, Hannah K. "Purity." Pages 724–28 in vol. 2 of *The Encyclo-*

pedia of the Dead Sea Scrolls. Edited by Lawrence H. Schiffman and James C. VanderKam. 2 vols. Oxford: Oxford University Press, 2000.

Hayward, C. T. R. "'The Lord Is One': Reflections on the Theme of Unity in John's Gospel from a Jewish Perspective." Pages 138–54 in *Early Jewish and Christian Monotheism.* Edited by Loren T. Stuckenbruck and Wendy E. S. North. JSNTSup 263. London: T&T Clark, 2004.

Hempel, Charlotte. *The Damascus Texts.* Companion to the Qumran Scrolls. Sheffield: Sheffield Academic, 2000.

———. *The Laws of the Damascus Document: Sources, Traditions, and Redaction.* STDJ 29. Leiden: Brill, 1998.

———. *The Qumran Rule Texts in Context: Collected Studies.* TSAJ 154. Tübingen: Mohr Siebeck, 2013.

Jokiranta, Jutta M. "'Sectarianism' of the Qumran 'Sect': Sociological Notes." *RevQ* 20 (2001): 223–39.

———. "Sociological Approaches to Qumran Sectarianism." Pages 200–231 in *The Oxford Handbook of the Dead Sea Scrolls.* Edited by Timothy H. Lim and John J. Collins. Oxford Handbooks. Oxford: Oxford University Press, 2010.

———. *Social Identity and Sectarianism in the Qumran Movement.* STDJ 105. Leiden: Brill, 2013.

Klawans, Jonathan. *Impurity and Sin in Ancient Judaism.* Oxford: Oxford University Press, 2000.

———. *Purity, Sacrifice, and the Temple: Symbolism and Supersessionism in the Study of Ancient Judaism.* Oxford: Oxford University Press, 2006.

Knibb, Michael A. "Place of the Damascus Document." *Annals of the New York Academy of Sciences* 722 (1994): 149–62.

Kooij, Arie van der. "The *Yaḥad*: What Is in a Name?" *DSD* 18 (2011): 109–28.

Lohse, Eduard, ed. *Die Texte aus Qumran: Mit masoretischer Punktation, Übersetzung, Einführung und Anmerkungen; Hebräisch und Deutsch.* 4th ed. Darmstadt: Wissenschaftliche Buchgesellschaft, 1986.

Magness, Jodi. *The Archaeology of Qumran and the Dead Sea Scrolls.* SDSS. Grand Rapids: Eerdmans, 2002.

Maier, Johann. *Die Texte der Höhlen 1–3 und 5–11.* Vol. 1 of *Die Qumran-Essener: Die Texte vom Toten Meer.* UTB 1862. Munich: Reinhardt, 1995.

Metso, Sarianna. "The Relationship between the Damascus Document and the Community Rule." Pages 85–93 in *The Damascus Document: A Centennial of Discovery; Proceedings of the Third International*

5. The Qumran *yaḥad*   123

Symposium of the Orion Center for the Study of the Dead Sea Scrolls and Associated Literature, 4–8 February, 1998. Edited by Joseph M. Baumgarten, Esther Chazon, and Avital Pinnick. STDJ 34. Leiden: Brill: 1999.

Milgrom, Jacob. *Leviticus: A New Translation with Introduction and Commentary.* 3 vols. AB 3. New York: Doubleday, 1991, 2000, 2001.

Neusner, Jacob. *The Idea of Purity in Ancient Judaism.* SJLA 1. Leiden: Brill, 1973.

Newsom, Carol A. *The Self as Symbolic Space: Constructing Identity and Community at Qumran.* STDJ 52. Leiden: Brill, 2004.

Qimron, Elisha, and James H. Charlesworth. "Rule of the Community (1QS; cf. 4QS MSS A–J, 5Q11)." Pages 1–52 in vol. 1 of *The Dead Sea Scrolls: Hebrew, Aramaic, and Greek Texts with English Translations; Rule of the Community and Related Documents.* Edited by James H. Charlesworth. PTSDSSP. Tübingen: Mohr Siebeck, 1994.

Regev, Eyal. "Cherchez les femmes: Were the yaḥad Celibates?" *DSD* 15 (2008): 253–84.

———. *Sectarianism in Qumran: A Cross-Cultural Perspective.* RelSoc 45. Berlin: de Gruyter, 2007.

———. "יחד, *jaḥad.*" Pages 121–30 in vol. 2 of *Theologisches Wörterbuch zu den Qumrantexten.* Edited by Heinz-Josef Fabry and Ulrich Dahmen. Stuttgart: Kohlhammer, 2013.

Rost, Leonhard. "Der gegenwärtige Stand der Erforschung der in Palästina neu gefundenen hebräischen Handschriften: 11. Die Sektenrolle." *TLZ* 75 (1950): 341–44.

Rüpke, Jörg. *The Roman Calendar from Numa to Constantine: Time, History, and the Fasti.* Translated by D. M. B. Richardson. Chichester: Wiley-Blackwell, 2011.

Schiffman, Lawrence H. *The Halakha at Qumran.* SJLA 16. Leiden: Brill, 1975.

Schmidt, Francis. *How the Temple Thinks: Identity and Social Cohesion in Ancient Judaism.* BibSem 78. Sheffield: Sheffield Academic, 2001.

Schofield, Alison. *From Qumran to the Yaḥad: A New Paradigm of Textual Development for the Community Rule.* STDJ 77. Leiden: Brill, 2009.

Stark, Rodney, and William Sims Bainbridge. *The Future of Religion: Secularization, Revival and Cult Formation.* Berkeley: University of California Press, 1985.

———. *Religion, Deviance, and Social Control.* London: Routledge, 1996.

———. *A Theory of Religion.* Toronto Studies in Religion. New York: Lang, 1987.

Stern, Sacha. *Calendar and Community: A History of the Jewish Calendar, Second Century BCE to Tenth Century CE.* Oxford: Oxford University Press, 2001.

———. "Qumran Calendars and Sectarianism." Pages 232–53 in *The Oxford Handbook of the Dead Sea Scrolls.* Edited by Timothy H. Lim and John J. Collins. Oxford Handbooks. Oxford: Oxford University Press, 2010.

Stökl Ben Ezra, Daniel. *Qumran: Die Texte vom Toten Meer und das antike Judentum.* UTB 4681. Jüdische Studien 3. Tübingen: Mohr Siebeck, 2016.

Stone, Michael E. "Enoch, Aramaic Levi and Sectarian Origins." Pages 247–58 in *Selected Studies in Pseudepigrapha and Apocrypha: With Special Reference to the Armenian Tradition.* SVTP 9. Leiden: Brill, 1991.

Strothmann, Meret. "Vertragen sich Sonne und Mond? Überlegungen zum Kalender als politisches Instrumentarium bei Römern und Juden." Pages 85–103 in *"Religio Licita?"* Edited by Görge K. Hasselhoff and Meret Strothmann. SJ 84. Berlin: de Gruyter, 2017.

Talmon, Shemaryahu. "Anti-Lunar-Calendar Polemics in Covenanters' Writings." Pages 29–40 in *Das Ende der Tage und die Gegenwart des Heils: Begegnungen mit dem Neuen Testament und seiner Umwelt; Festschrift für Heinz-Wolfgang Kuhn zum 65. Geburtstag.* Edited by Michael Becker and Wolfgang Fenske. AGJU 44. Leiden: Brill, 1999.

———. *The Calendar Reckoning of the Sect from the Judaean Desert.* Edited by Chaim Rabin and Yigael Yadin. ScrHier 4. Jerusalem: Magnes, 1965.

———. "Calendars and Mishmarot." Pages 108–17 in vol. 1 of *Encyclopedia of the Dead Sea Scrolls.* Edited by Lawrence H. Schiffman and James C. VanderKam. 2 vols. Oxford: Oxford University Press: 2000.

———. "The Sectarian יחד: A Biblical Noun." *VT* 3 (1953): 133–40.

Taylor, Joan E. "Women, Children, and Celibate Men in the Serekh Texts." *HTR* 104 (2011): 171–90.

VanderKam, James. *The Dead Sea Scrolls Today.* 2nd ed. Grand Rapids: Eerdmans, 2010.

———. "Sinai Revisited." Pages 44–60 in *Biblical Interpretation at Qumran.* Edited by Matthias Henze. SDSS. Grand Rapids: Eerdmans, 2005.

VanderKam, James, and Peter Flint. *The Meaning of the Dead Sea Scrolls: Their Significance for Understanding the Bible, Judaism, Jesus, and Christianity*. New York: Harper Collins, 2002.

Wilson, Bryan R. *Magic and the Millennium: A Sociological Study of Religious Movements of Protest among Tribal and Third-World Peoples*. London: Heinemann, 1973.

Yadin, Yigael, Hannah Cotton, and Andrew Gross, eds. *The Documents from the Bar Kokhba Period in the Cave of Letters: Hebrew, Aramaic and Nabatean-Aramaic Papyri*. Jerusalem: Israel Exploration Society; Institute of Archaeology, Hebrew University; Shrine of the Book, Israel Museum, 2002.

6

The Number One:
Oneness, Unity, and the One God in Philo of Alexandria

Jutta Leonhardt-Balzer

The number one and related terms occur more than eight hundred times in the writings of Philo of Alexandria. Despite this impressive tally the topic has largely been ignored in Philonic scholarship. There are discussions of Philo's monotheism and the role of the Logos in this context, but the issue of the number one and its role for Philo's thinking has not been at the center of scholarly attention. That the number one is not irrelevant for Philo can be seen from the fact that he calls God "the One." Starting with the first day of creation Philo attributes a special role to the number one. For him, it is related to the transcendent God, representing him as distant from the multiple forms of creation. To emphasize the role of God in the world, Philo uses detailed arithmological discussions of the number one. Because God is one there is only one temple and one torah. They represent God's singularity on earth. By representing him, however, they also communicate the one God to the world and allow the world to emulate and approach the one God. The concept of oneness as union, however, is rarely expressed using the term *one*.

6.1. The Concept of One

Philo's writings span more than 1,500 pages of texts. The number one, εἷς, is a very common word occurring 871 times.[1] The term μόνος, "alone"

---

1. Peder Borgen, Kåre Fuglseth, and Roald Skarsten, *The Philo Index: A Complete Greek Word Index to the Writings of Philo of Alexandria* (Leiden: Brill, 1999), 112–13.

128   Jutta Leonhardt-Balzer

or "only," occurs even more frequently at 1,593 times.[2] Related terms are rarer, although no less important.[3] The number one occurs in many of Philo's arithmological discussions, not only discussed by itself, but in its relationship to other numbers to explain their respective properties (cf. *Opif.* 47–49 on the number four). As a philosophical ideal, the number one or the idea of aloneness represents solitude and withdrawal from all aspects of mortal life (*Abr.* 30). Consequently, the idea of oneness in the sense of being solitary describes Philo's view of an ideal life, not the concept of being one with others. Thus, Noah is the example of the God-loving man who is the only one saved, the founder of a new generation (*Abr.* 46), and Moses learned his insights while being alone with God (*Mos.* 1.80). For Philo it is more important to be special, singular, than being united with others—unless the idea is union with God.

6.2. One and the Philosophy of Numbers

The number one is related to the incorporeal, already the number two and three exceed it and therefore miss the ideal (δυὰς μέντοι καὶ τριὰς ἐκβέβηκε τὴν κατὰ τὸ ἓν ἀσωματότητα, *Leg.* 1.3). The number one represents the creator, while anything more is related to matter, which consists of many parts, is divisible and changeable: "And, following the succession of nature, I will also say this, that the unit is the image of the first cause, the number two of matter, which is capable of emotion and division" (*Spec.* 3.180).[4] In this transcendence of the first principle and the relationship of the number one to creation Philo agrees with Eudorus, and this has been connected to an Alexandrian strand of Pythagoreanizing Platonism.[5]

---

2. Borgen, Fuglseth, and Skarsten, *Philo Index*, 228–29.

3. E.g., ἕνωσις, "unification," e.g., the union branch and stem in grafting of trees (*Agr.* 6), twenty-two times; ἑνόω, "to unify," as in the united limbs of a body (*Flacc.* 71) or the earth being held together by water like glue (*Opif.* 131), forty-one times (Borgen, Fuglseth, and Skarsten, *Philo Index*, 131–32); or μοναρχία, the rule of one alone, ten times; μονόω, "to single out," seven times; μόνωσις, "solitude," sixteen times (e.g., *Flacc.* 177); μονάς, the "unit," the "number one," eighty-one times; μοναστήριος, the hermit, twice; μόνιμος, five times; and μονή, fifteen times (Borgen, Fuglseth, and Skarsten, *Philo Index*, 228–29).

4. Ἑπόμενος δ᾽ ἀκολουθίᾳ φύσεως κἀκεῖνο λέξω, ὅτι μονὰς μέν ἐστιν εἰκὼν αἰτίου πρώτου, δυὰς δὲ παθητῆς καὶ διαιρετῆς ὕλης. All translations, unless otherwise noted, are mine.

5. On the relationship between Philo and Eudorus, see Mauro Bonazzi, "Towards

6. The Number One

The numbers one and seven are related (*Decal.* 102–103). They are equal: seven, "in power is superior to every other number, in nothing differing from the number one" (δυνάμει δὲ πρεσβυτάτη παντὸς ἀριθμοῦ, μηδὲν διαφέρουσα μονάδος, *Post.* 64–65), the virtues and God intertwined (*Deo* 11). There is an arithmological reason for this that lies in the theory of numbers. The number seven is not generated and does not generate, in this it resembles God (*Opif.* 100). It perfects all things (*Opif.* 102). The number one generates all the other numbers in order but is not generated by any other (*Opif.* 99).[6] The number seven is special because of the numbers under ten it alone repeats the unit seven times (*Opif.* 91), It can be derived from the unit using different arithmetic processes (*Opif.* 92–94). It consists of number one, two, and four, which have the most harmonious properties (*Opif.* 95). One represents the beginning, seven the end of all things (*Spec.* 1.188). The link between the one and the seven, the seven (as a prime number) is born only of the number one, thus the link between God and the Sabbath is a fundamental law (*Mos.* 2.209–211). Numbers shape the very fabric of creation.

6.3. One and Creation

God represents the above mentioned philosophical ideal in that he is not influenced by anyone or anything other than himself. Thus, he is only guided by his will when he creates (μόνος, *Opif.* 23). There are several principles about God and the world: He exists (*Opif.* 170), and "God is one" (θεὸς εἷς ἐστι, *Opfi.* 171), the world was created (171). Furthermore, "the world is also one, because the Creator is one, who made the work resemble him according to oneness" (εἷς ἐστιν ὁ κόσμος, ἐπειδὴ καὶ εἷς ὁ δημιουργὸς ὁ ἐξομοιώσας

Transcendence: Philo and the Renewal of Platonism in the Early Imperial Age," in *Philo of Alexandria and Post-Aristotelian Philosophy*, ed. Francesca Alesse, SPhA 5 (Leiden: Brill, 2008), 232–52. A slightly more Aristotelian influence has been surmised in the contrast between God's solitary perfection and the human aloneness by Francesca Calabi, "'It Would Not Be Good That the Man Should Be Alone': Philo's Interpretation of Gen 2:18 in *Legum Allegoriae*," SPhiloA 28 (2016): 255. On the particular Alexandrian mixture of Platonism and Pythagoreanism, see Luc Brisson, "Alexandrie, berceau du néoplatonisme: Eudore, Philon, Ammonios et l'école d'Alexandrie," in *Alexandrie la divine*, ed. Charles Méla and Frédéric Möri (Geneva: La Baconnière, 2014), 354–63.

6. τὸ μὲν οὖν ἓν γεννᾷ τοὺς ἑξῆς ἅπαντας ἀριθμοὺς ὑπ' οὐδενὸς γεννώμενον τὸ παράπαν.

αὐτῷ κατὰ τὴν μόνωσιν τὸ ἔργον, ὃς ἁπάσῃ κατεχρήσατο τῇ ὕλῃ εἰς τὴν τοῦ ὅλου γένεσιν), and finally that God cares for the world and continues to do so (*Opif.* 172).[7] This means God is unique, and he made the world unique. It does not mean, however, that the world is in any way similar to God.

The number one can be more influential than the many. Thus, Noah is an example of one thing or person being capable of demonstrating its opposite, even if that is much more numerous. One righteous person sheds light on the unrighteousness of many, or one light drives out darkness at creation (*Gig.* 2–3). The one can therefore outweigh the many. This can also be seen in the imbalance of night and day: for the day there is only one star, the sun, but for the night the multitude of moon and stars together (*Opif.* 57).

The nature of the number one as separate from the many is particularly dominant in Philo's account of the first day of creation:

> For each of the days he assigned a portion of the whole, but taking out the first one, which he does not even call "first," so that it may not be numbered among the others, instead he calls it "one," giving it the proper name, because he perceived in it the nature and representation of the oneness and ascribed it to it. (*Opif.* 15)[8]

Thus, one is not a number among others to count with (first, second, third day, etc.). One is independent of the other numbers, just as the first day is seen as separate from the other days because on the first day time itself and the capability to count is created.

> But when light came, darkness retreated and went away, and borders were set in the middle between them, namely evening and morning, straightaway, of necessity, the measure of time was perfected which the creator called

---

7. On arithmology and the role of different numbers in *De opificio mundi*, see Robert M. Berchman, "Arithmos and Kosmos: Arithmology as an Exegetical Tool in the *De Opificio Mundi* of Philo of Alexandria," in *Gnosticism, Platonism and the Late Antique World: Essays in Honour of John D. Turner*, ed. Kevin Corrigan and Tuomas Rasimus, Nag Hammadi and Manichaean Studies 82 (Leiden: Brill, 2013), 167–98.

8. Ἑκάστῃ δὲ τῶν ἡμερῶν ἀπένειμεν ἔνια τῶν τοῦ παντὸς τμημάτων τὴν πρώτην ὑπεξελόμενος, ἣν αὐτὸς οὐδὲ πρώτην, ἵνα μὴ ταῖς ἄλλαις συγκαταριθμῆται, καλεῖ, μίαν δ' ὀνομάσας ὀνόματι εὐθυβόλῳ προσαγορεύει, τὴν μονάδος φύσιν καὶ πρόσρησιν ἐνιδὼν τε καὶ ἐπιφημίσας αὐτῇ.

6. The Number One

"day," and not "the first," but "one," which is said on account of the oneness of the intelligible world, which has a single (monadic) nature. (*Opif.* 35)[9]

The imbalance between one and many can also be seen in the creation of humankind. Thus, God created all that is truly good and what is indifferent to virtue and vice. The ambivalent humans, however, who may lean toward either, were not created by God alone, for in Gen 1 it is said "let us make Man." Thus, God is the author of all blameless human actions, and his helpers that of vice (*Opif.* 74–75). This can even be seen in the development of humankind. Thus, while the first man was single, he was well. As soon as there was a second human being, things deteriorated. It was woman who brought vice into the world. Philo argues that love unites two animals in one in order to generate new, similar, life. Therefore, vice is built into the act of procreation itself and passed on through it (*Opif.* 151–153). On the other hand, humans are the only created beings capable of voluntary motion by virtue of the intellect, which makes human beings similar to God (*Deo* 46–48).

Philo argues that there is only one world (*Opif.* 170–172, *Aet.* 21). In *Aet.* 4 he identifies the concept as a Stoic idea. The idea also occurs in other books. According to *Spec.* 1.208 the whole world is one and all elements are equal. This also applies to humans. Philo describes that before the confusion of tongues, all humanity was united as one (*Conf.* 1). This unity, however, was not a good thing, but the cause of much evil and impiety toward God (*Conf.* 15). Thus, human oneness is not a positive ideal for Philo unless it is bound to God.

6.4. The Soul Is One

The ideal of oneness as singularity can be seen in Philo's idea of the soul: "as it is one, all the unspeakable impressions of everything, which is in the universe, are carried onto the soul" (ἐπὶ γὰρ μίαν οὖσαν τὴν ψυχὴν αἱ ἀμύθητοι τυπώσεις ἁπάντων τῶν ἐν τῷ παντὶ ἀναφέρονται, *Leg.* 1.61). The soul therefore can only carry one kind of impression: good or evil. However, as human beings are created in the above-mentioned sense and partici-

---

9. Ἐπεὶ δὲ φῶς μὲν ἐγένετο, σκότος δ' ὑπεξέστη καὶ ἀνεχώρησεν, ὅροι δ' ἐν τοῖς μεταξὺ διαστήμασιν ἐπάγησαν ἑσπέρα καὶ πρωΐα, κατὰ τἀναγκαῖον τοῦ χρόνου μέτρον ἀπετελεῖτο εὐθύς, ὃ καὶ ἡμέραν ὁ ποιῶν ἐκάλεσε, καὶ ἡμέραν οὐχὶ πρώτην, ἀλλὰ μίαν, ἣ λέλεκται διὰ τὴν τοῦ νοητοῦ κόσμου μόνωσιν μοναδικὴν ἔχοντος φύσιν.

pate in the plurality of creation, the soul, like the body, consists of different parts, united to a whole (*QG* 2.4). The potential plurality is explained when Philo interprets the two trees in the garden of Eden and comments on the soul. Like a seal, the soul can potentially receive multiple impressions. In reality, however, it only ever receives one impression until that is removed and replaced by another (*Leg.* 1.100). This explains why a soul can only be either good or evil.

Naturally, Philo expects the wise to be imprinted only by the good. This can be achieved by turning away from the multiple impressions of the world.[10] Philo also comments on the saying that man will leave his parents to be one with his wife that the soul that leaves wisdom unites with the object of its interest, the passions (*Leg.* 2.49). Those who serve the only wise, the one true God (τοῖς θεραπευταῖς τοῦ μόνου σοφοῦ γενησομένοις) leave all material things behind (*Ebr.* 69), and they receive "peace and priesthood" (εἰρήνη καὶ ἱερωσύνη) as reward (*Ebr.* 74, also 86–87). This person seeks everything from God (*Ebr.* 106–109). And the "worship of the only wise" (ἡ τοῦ μόνου θεραπεία σοφοῦ) is called "the surest freedom" (ἐλευθερία βεβαιοτάτη, *Conf.* 94). The focus on the one God leads to freedom from all passions and bad influences.

In order to turn to God, it is necessary to let the mind govern the senses and unite them just as God governs his creation (*Agr.* 49–50). If a soul is governed by God alone it does not lack anything (*Agr.* 54). Without such a governor the human being falls prey to the senses (*Plant.* 31). The wise rule not only over their own impulses, but they are also governors or shepherds of the men of irrational passions (*Plant.* 41). It is the governance of God that humans are not left without good governance, and the rule of the sound mind is parallel to that of a good king and to the rule of God who governs everything (*Plant.* 49–50), using the multitude of his powers (*Conf.* 170–175). Multiple rulers are not a good ideal. There is only one ruler of everything, and his rule is just and benevolent. Therefore all other forms of government (oligarchy, etc.) are banned (*Decal.* 155).

Man stands between the heavenly beings and the passions, represented by the female principle: The "angels as wholly bodiless souls" are linked to the number one, "completely intellectual, pure reasonings, they

---

10. On Philo's idea of mystical union with God, see Adam Afterman, "From Philo to Plotinus: The Emergence of Mystical Union," *JR* 93 (2013): 177–96; and Afterman, *"And They Shall Be One Flesh": On the Language of Mystical Union in Judaism*, Supplements to the Journal of Jewish Thought and Philosophy 26 (Leiden: Brill, 2016), 25–46.

6. The Number One 133

resemble the monad" (ἀγγέλους, ἀσωμάτους ψυχάς ... ὅλας δι᾽ ὅλων νοεράς, λογισμοὺς ἀκραιφνεῖς, μονάδι ὁμοιουμένας, *Spec.* 1.66). Conversely, within the human biology Philo distinguishes between the male and the female principle (πρὸς ἀνδρῶν, ἡ δὲ θήλεια καὶ πρὸς γυναικῶν), the masculine soul, which attaches itself to "God alone" (μόνῳ θεῷ), and the feminine soul, which seeks the multiple appearances of the many created things (*Spec.* 3.178).

There is only one instance in which a concept of "oneness" in the sense of different entities united by a common purpose occurs. Philo describes that it is possible that between humans there can also be a "union, of souls, joined together by goodwill" (ψυχῶν ἕνωσιν ἁρμοζομένων εὐνοίᾳ, *Her.* 40). However, this union again derives from a common focus on the only true, one God.

6.5. God Is One

The idea that God is one and the only God is axiomatic for Philo: "For God is his own place, and he himself is full of himself, and he is sufficient for himself, filling and surrounding everything else, which is deficient or deserted or empty, but himself he is not surrounded by anything else, for he is one and the universe" (*Leg.* 1.44).[11] God is one and the universe, but he is also different from matter, without beginning and end. Thus, Philo emphasizes: "He who thinks that God has a quality or that he is not one or that he is not uncreated and imperishable, does himself an injustice, not God" (*Leg.* 1.51).[12] Thus, "the One" is a name of God, used repeatedly by Philo (e.g., *Leg.* 3.48, 126).[13] Monotheism is the core and axis of Philo's theology.[14]

Although fundamentally different, it is possible for the human mind to approach the One (*Leg.* 3.126). To approach God the number one has a

---

11. Ἐπεὶ αὐτὸς ἑαυτοῦ τόπος καὶ αὐτὸς ἑαυτοῦ πλήρης καὶ ἱκανὸς αὐτὸς ἑαυτῷ ὁ θεός, τὰ μὲν ἄλλα ἐπιδεᾶ καὶ ἔρημα καὶ κενὰ ὄντα πληρῶν καὶ περιέχων, αὐτὸς δὲ ὑπ᾽ οὐδενὸς ἄλλου περιεχόμενος, ἅτε εἷς καὶ τὸ πᾶν αὐτὸς ὤν.

12. Ὁ γὰρ ἢ ποιότητα οἰόμενος ἔχειν τὸν θεὸν ἢ μὴ ἕνα εἶναι ἢ μὴ ἀγένητον καὶ ἄφθαρτον ἢ μὴ ἄτρεπτον ἑαυτὸν ἀδικεῖ, οὐ θεόν.

13. In using "the One" as a name Philo seems to prefigure Plotinus; see already René Arnou, *Le désir de Dieu dans la philosophie de Plotin*, 2nd ed. (Rome: Presses de l'Université grégorienne, 1967), 260–67.

14. Cf. Marta Alesso, "No es Bueno que el hombre esté solo," *Circe* 8 (2003): 17–30.

134 Jutta Leonhardt-Balzer

special importance. As there is one God, only one species is found worthy to worship him, and of humankind Moses comes to approach God alone, when he moves his mind toward God (*Gig.* 50–54). Thus, the firstborn and the first fruit are dedicated to God and offered in the temple, and the Levites are the first fruit of Israel (*Sacr.* 118, 134). God is the one being to be loved and honored (*Post.* 12). Ignorance of the one true God leads to the veneration of the many false deities that in truth do not exist at all (*Ebr.* 45).

God's existence independent of matter does not mean that he does not have anything to do with it. He is the only truly existent one and the only creator. As such he is the only true ruler over the world: "For he, who is the one who exists in truth, is also truly the Creator, because he brought that which did not exist into being. And he is also a king by nature, because no one can rule more justly over that which has been made than he who created them" (*Mos.* 2.100).[15] Philo can apply any available term for God as ruler. The "one God" is "monarch and leader of the universe" (ὁ τῷ ὄντι ἄρχων καὶ ἡγεμὼν εἷς ὁ θεός, *Cher.* 83). Similarly, "there is one lord and ruler of the universe" (κύριος εἷς ἁπάντων καὶ δεσπότης ἐστίν, *Cher.* 119). It is mad and impious to attribute the causes of things to others (*Spec.* 1.14) but the one "who is not only the God of gods, intelligible or perceptible by the senses, but also the creator of all" (ὃς οὐ μόνον θεὸς θεῶν ἐστι νοητῶν τε καὶ αἰσθητῶν ἀλλὰ καὶ πάντων δημιουργός, *Spec.* 1.20). Moses also teaches this truth (*Spec.* 1.30).

The correspondence between the philosophical principle and the scriptural teaching can also be seen in the *Legum allegoriae.* Based on Deut. 4:39 Philo emphasizes that God is the only one "in heaven and on earth below, and there is nobody else besides him" (*Leg.* 3.82).[16] The difference between the one and the many is also a Platonic principle, which Philo applies to ethics. "You see that there are several treasure houses of evil, but only one of good, because God is one" (*Leg.* 3.105).[17]

What applies to God does not apply to creation and vice versa, and thus oneness is a distinguishing principle between God and humankind.

---

15. Μόνος γὰρ πρὸς ἀλήθειαν ὢν καὶ ποιητής ἐστιν ἀψευδῶς, ἐπειδὴ τὰ μὴ ὄντα ἤγαγεν εἰς τὸ εἶναι, καὶ βασιλεὺς φύσει, διότι τῶν γεγονότων οὐδεὶς ἂν ἄρχοι δικαιότερον τοῦ πεποιηκότος.

16. Οὐχ ὅτι ἐστί τις ἄλλος οὐχ ὕψιστος ὁ γὰρ θεὸς εἷς ὢν "ἐν τῷ οὐρανῷ ἄνω ἐστὶ καὶ ἐπὶ τῆς γῆς κάτω, καὶ οὐκ ἔστιν ἔτι πλὴν αὐτοῦ.

17. Ὁρᾷς ὅτι κακῶν εἰσι θησαυροί· καὶ ὁ μὲν τῶν ἀγαθῶν εἷς ἐπεὶ γὰρ ὁ θεὸς εἷς.

6. The Number One

On Gen 2:18 Philo comments that God does not want the human being to be alone:

> Why is it not good, O prophet, that man is alone [οὐκ ἔστι καλὸν εἶναι μόνον]? Because, he says, it is good that he who is alone, should be alone [καλόν ἐστι τὸν μόνον εἶναι μόνον]. But God is alone and by himself one [μόνος δὲ καὶ καθ᾽ αὑτὸν εἷς ὢν ὁ θεός], and nothing else is like God [οὐδὲν δὲ ὅμοιον θεῷ], therefore it is not good that man is alone. For that God is alone can be understood in this way: that neither was there anything with God before the creation nor is anything placed in the same order to him after the creation of the world, for he does not need anything whatsoever. But this is the better understanding: God is alone and one [ὁ θεὸς μόνος ἐστὶ καὶ ἕν], not composite [οὐ σύγκριμα], a single nature [φύσις ἁπλῆ], but each of us and everything else that is created, is many things.... Therefore, God is set according to the one and the unit [τέτακται οὖν ὁ θεὸς κατὰ τὸ ἓν καὶ τὴν μονάδα], or rather the unit according to the one God [ἡ μονὰς κατὰ τὸν ἕνα θεόν]. For every number is younger than the world, as is time, but God is older than the world and its creator [ὁ δὲ θεὸς πρεσβύτερος κόσμου καὶ δημιουργός]. (*Leg.* 2.1–3)[18]

The difference between the singular and the many is not the only criterion for a distinction between God and creation. The unity in composition against the mixed also constitutes a difference: "And the divine is unmixed and undiluted, on account of which it makes a libation to the unmixed and undiluted and only God existing in unity" (*Her.* 183).[19] In order to communicate with creation God needs his powers as mediators.[20] Thus, his access to creation does not occur through the number one.

The access of creation to God, on the other hand, is possible by means of focus, focus on God alone and to turn away from creation. The one God is the only one worthy of trust (*Her.* 92–95). "Not to believe in creation, which is in all things untrustworthy, to only believe in God, the only truly

---

18. On the difference between the perfect solitary state of God and the composite state of humans, which is deficient if it is alone; see Calabi, "'It Would Not Be Good,'" 239–42.

19. Καὶ τὸ μὲν θεῖον ἀμιγὲς καὶ ἄκρατον, οὗ ἕνεκα τῷ ἀμιγεῖ καὶ ἀκράτῳ καὶ κατὰ τὴν μόνωσιν μονάδι ὄντι σπένδεται θεῷ.

20. "God, being attended by two heavenly powers, that of rule and of goodness, because he is one in the middle of them, presented a third image to the visual soul." (ὁ θεὸς δορυφορούμενος ὑπὸ δυεῖν τῶν ἀνωτάτω δυνάμεων ἀρχῆς τε αὖ καὶ ἀγαθότητος εἷς ὢν ὁ μέσος τριττὰς φαντασίας ἐνειργάζετο τῇ ὁρατικῇ ψυχῇ, *Sacr.* 59).

trustworthy, is the work of a great and heavenly mind, which is no longer entrapped by any of the things around itself" (*Her.* 93).[21]

God's connection with the number one can be found in Philo's arithmological musings: As God is the unmixed power, he is represented by the unit. The number two represents the mixed power (*Deo* 82–83). As God is one, it is fitting that the first commandment of the ten that represent the torah and structure the universe demands the worship of the highest being and creator of everything (*Decal.* 50–65). Yet God is not to be simply identified with the number one. Philo writes that it is necessary "to worship the existing one, who is greater than the good, more simple than the one, and more ancient than the unit" (*Contempl.* 2).[22]

The uniqueness of God is matched by the uniqueness of the temple: "since God is one [ἐπειδὴ εἷς ἐστιν ὁ θεός], there should be also only one temple [καὶ ἱερὸν ἓν εἶναι μόνον]" (*Spec.* 1.67). Further, only once a year the high priest is allowed to enter the holy of holies (*Legat.* 306–308). Yet not even the temple represents God. The core of the temple is invisible, like the deity itself, and even on the day when the high priest enters, he does not reveal what is in it (*Spec.* 1.72).

However, focus on God unites people, especially those people who speak in the name of God. They are united in mind and soul, and thus united they gather other people around them: "And when they [Moses and Aaron] thus arrived in Egypt with one mind and soul, they first of all collected together the elders of the nation in a secret place, and there they laid the commands of God before them" (*Mos.* 1.86).[23] Thus, even more than the one temple, the one people of God represents the One.

6.6. God's People Are One

Not only a single wise man, but the Jews as God's people participate in the supreme wisdom of Moses (*Deo* 148). The Jews are the only people who worship the uncreated and eternal one God, not the many gods, and

---

21. Ἀπιστῆσαι γενέσει τῇ πάντα ἐξ ἑαυτῆς ἀπίστῳ, μόνῳ δὲ πιστεῦσαι θεῷ τῷ καὶ πρὸς ἀλήθειαν μόνῳ πιστῷ μεγάλης καὶ ὀλυμπίου ἔργον διανοίας ἐστί, οὐκέτι πρὸς οὐδενὸς δελεαζομένης τῶν παρ' ἡμῖν.

22. Θεραπεύειν τὸ ὄν, ὃ καὶ ἀγαθοῦ κρεῖττόν ἐστι καὶ ἑνὸς εἰλικρινέστερον καὶ μονάδος ἀρχεγονώτερον.

23. Παραγενόμενοι δ' εἰς Αἴγυπτον γνώμῃ καὶ ψυχῇ μιᾷ τὸ μὲν πρῶτον τοὺς δημογέροντας τοῦ ἔθνους συναγαγόντες ἐν ἀπορρήτῳ μηνύουσι τοὺς χρησμούς.

their worship is representative of the whole creation (*Spec.* 2.165–167): "so that they offer prayers, festivals, and offerings for the common race of humans and worship the truly existing God for the sake of themselves and the others, who have run away from due worship" (*Spec.* 2.167).[24] This worship is focused on the temple, the only place that God permitted for sacrifices to him (*Somn.* 1.62–64). However, the principle of "one God, one temple, one nation" does not extend to "one land." No single country can hold all the Jews" (*Flacc.* 45).

The worship of the one God unifies his people: "There should only be one relationship and one sign of friendship, the desire for God and to say and do everything for the sake of piety" (*Spec.* 1.317).[25] This relationship supersedes all family ties (*Spec.* 1.17). The union of God's people therefore is not created by family ties and biological descent, but by a common focus on the one true God.

It is noteworthy, however, that Philo acknowledges the risk of sexual relationships to the union created by faith.

> Accordingly they [the Midianites] contrived all possible devices and made all possible attempts to turn them [Israel] away from honoring the One [τοῦ ἑνός], the truly Existent, and to change their religion to impiety.… They sent for the most beautiful among their women and said to them, "You see how unlimited is the number of the Hebrews, but their number is not so dangerous and menacing a weapon as their unanimity [ὁμόνοια] and mutual attachment [συμφωνία]. And the highest and greatest source of this unanimity [ὁμονοίας] is their creed [δόξα] of a single God [τοῦ ἑνὸς θεοῦ], through which, as from a fountain, they feel a love for each other, uniting [ἑνωτικῇ] them in an indissoluble bond." (*Virt.* 34–35)

The strategy of tempting Israelite males into idolatry by the seduction of women shows that the union of the nation can after all be threatened by sexual relationships, so it is not solely a matter of ideals. Philo's account, however, aims to show that the union of the nation by virtue of the ideals they hold in common is something that even the Jews' enemies acknowledge.

---

24. Ὡς τάς τε εὐχὰς καὶ ἑορτὰς καὶ ἀπαρχὰς ὑπὲρ τοῦ κοινοῦ γένους τῶν ἀνθρώπων ἐπιτελεῖν καὶ τὸν ὄντως ὄντα θεὸν θεραπεύειν ὑπέρ τε ἑαυτοῦ καὶ τῶν ἄλλων, οἳ τὰς ὀφειλομένας λατρείας ἀποδεδράκασι.

25. Ἔστω γὰρ ἡμῖν μία οἰκειότης καὶ φιλίας ἓν σύμβολον ἡ πρὸς θεὸν ἀρέσκεια καὶ τὸ πάντα λέγειν τε καὶ πράττειν ὑπὲρ εὐσεβείας.

138   Jutta Leonhardt-Balzer

The union of the Jews can be seen in the observance of the torah:

> For he [Moses] assumed with good reason that one who was their fellow-tribesman and fellow-kinsman related to them by the tie that brings the highest kinship, the kinship of having one citizenship [πολιτεία μία] and the same law and one God [εἷς θεός] who has taken all members of the nation for his portion, would never sin in the way just mentioned. (*Spec.* 4.159)

The union of the people of the one God also includes proselytes:

> Let them [i.e., proselytes] not be denied another citizenship or other ties of family and friendship, and let them find places of shelter standing ready for refugees to the camp of piety. For the most effectual love-charm, the chain that binds indissolubly the goodwill that makes us one [καὶ δεσμὸς ἄλυτος εὐνοίας ἐνωτικῆς] is to honor the one God [ἡ τοῦ ἑνὸς θεοῦ τιμή]. (*Spec.* 1.52–53)

This is a rare instance in Philo, in which the common veneration of the one God creates a bond between different ethnicities, not just between the Jews, but joining people from other nations to the people of God, thus creating a sense of unity, of oneness where there used to be none. The union of the people of God can include non-Jews, if they join in the common ideals. In this turn to social unity Philo differs from the general interest of Hellenistic philosophy in a theoretical basis for unity. Unlike these philosophical (and even his Jewish Hellenistic, such as Josephus and the Sibylline Oracles) counterparts, Philo is deeply aware of the social implications of proselytism for the people concerned.[26] He knows that the proselytes lose family, identity, and everything that defined them until then.

The Therapeutae demonstrate the social implications of oneness as it relates to virtue, the pursuit of which Philo envisages as the proper use of life. He emphasizes that the decalogue is addressed to individuals, because each individual who observes the divine law is valued equally to

---

26. Cf. Anthony J. Guerra, "The One God Topos in *Spec. Leg.* 1:52," in *Society of Biblical Literature 1990 Seminar Papers*, ed. David J. Lull, SBLSP 29 (Atlanta: Scholars Press, 1990), 148–57. For Philo, the Jewish people with their torah observance own privileged access to God, in which the proselytes participate. A detailed study on this can be found in Ellen Birnbaum, *The Place of Judaism in Philo's Thought: Israel, Jews, and Proselytes*, BJS 290, SPhiloM 2 (Atlanta: Scholars Press, 1996).

6. The Number One

a whole nation (*Decal.* 36–37). When Philo describes the Therapeutae he emphasizes that they spend their days in "solitary places," which is the only instance of his use of μοναστήριος. These sites he also calls holy places (*Contempl.* 25, 30). In the description of the great celebration of the Therapeutae Philo describes how the two choirs of the male and female singers first sing separately and then merge into one: "Then, when each of the choruses has feasted separately and by itself, like the people in the Bacchanals, drinking the unmixed wine of the love of God, they mingle and become one chorus from both [ἀναμίγνυνται καὶ γίνονται χορὸς εἷς ἐξ ἀμφοῖν], an imitation of the one that stood in ancient times at the Red Sea" (*Contempl.* 85). The union of the choirs mirrors the union of the love of God. While for Philo the Therapeutae are a particularly noble branch of the Jews, the principles they represent are shared by all, and they all participate in the blessings due to such a prominent representative of virtue.

As the people faithful to God the Jews are united and represented by the high priest:

> Thus also the high priest is the relation and nearest of kin to the whole people, presiding over and dispensing justice to all who dispute in accordance with the laws, and offering up prayers and sacrifices every day on behalf of the whole nation, and pleading for good things for them as for his own brethren, and parents, and children, that every age and every part of the nation, as if it were one body, may be united into one and the same community, devoted to peace and obedience to the law [ἵνα πᾶσα ἡλικία καὶ πάντα μέρη τοῦ ἔθνους ὡς ἑνὸς σώματος εἰς μίαν καὶ τὴν αὐτὴν ἁρμόζηται κοινωνίαν εἰρήνης καὶ εὐνομίας ἐφιέμενα]. (*Spec.* 3.131)[27]

The focus on the one God and the one temple makes the Jews vulnerable. Their worship and faithfulness to the one true God causes Gaius to attack the temple, their sole place of worship (*Legat.* 117–118). Unlike Gaius, who strove to be worshiped as a God, Augustus respected their tradition (*Legat.* 157–162). This is the difference between a monarch and a tyrant.[28] Philo emphasizes that the Jews would rather incur pains and torture than

---

27. On the worship of the high priest, see Jutta Leonhardt, *Jewish Worship in Philo of Alexandria*, TSAJ 84 (Tübingen: Mohr Siebeck, 2001), 128–29, 230–33.

28. This difference plays a major role in Philo's *De Iosepho*; see Friederike Oertelt, *Herrscherideal und Herrschaftskritik bei Philo von Alexandria: Eine Untersuchung am Beispiel seiner Josephsdarstellung in De Josepho und De Somniis II*, SPhA 8 (Leiden: Brill, 2014).

140   Jutta Leonhardt-Balzer

let a single commandment be interfered with (*Legat.* 209). This can be seen in the practical case of the embassy to Gaius: faced with the threat to the Jews posed by the emperor, the members of the embassy seek refuge in prayer to the one true God to keep the false god in check (*Legat.* 366).

Their special position as the people of the one God is not given to the Jewish people as such, but only in as much as they obey God. In *Spec.* 3.124–126, Philo describes the punishment that the Levites, in their zeal for God, inflict on the idolators among the people in the incident of the golden calf. Philo greatly emphasizes that they attack as one "as at a single signal [ὡς ἀφ' ἑνὸς συνθήματος]," starting with their own relatives, because they only regard those faithful to God as their family (126). The same combination of oneness as singularity and oneness as unity of purpose can be found in the parallel account in *Mos.* 2.170–173, where Philo emphasizes that the Levites alone are caught by the zeal for God, and that they act as a unit, refusing even family bonds to stay their hands. A similar principle is expressed in general terms when Philo points out that no wicked man can be the friend of a good person (*Spec.* 3.155). Not only the Levites serve as example of this principle—Philo describes the return of the scattered exiles as the return to the worship of the one God (*Praem.* 162), which unites the people who have strayed from virtue and are enslaved in foreign lands (*Praem.* 163–165). God guides them in one impulse (πρὸς ἕνα συντενοῦσιν, *Praem.* 165) back to him.

6.7. Conclusion: Oneness as a Social Concept

Thus, for Philo any concept of oneness is based on the focus on the one God. Union, unitedness, any feeling of belonging together can only derive from this focus on the common goal. The philosophical background to these ideas derives from different traditions, Platonic, Pythagorean, and Aristotelian.

Looking at political implications of this principle, it is clear that monarchical governments fit better than democratic structures. This not only fits well into the imperial structure of the Roman Empire, but it also corresponds to the political power of the high priest in the Jewish political constitution of the postexilic period.[29] The high priest was not only the

---

29. Cf. David Goodblatt, *The Monarchic Principle: Studies in Jewish Self-Government in Antiquity*, TSAJ 38 (Tübingen: Mohr, 1994).

6. The Number One   141

cultic but also a political focal point, even in Roman times. Even more important than the high priest is the concept that God is the supreme ruler of the universe and rules in a special way over the Jews through the torah, a concept that a generation later Josephus calls "theocracy" (*C. Ap.* 2.17).

The Jewish people have a special status in Philo's worldview. They are the people with the Mosaic torah, the laws of the one God, which mirror the structure of the universe perfectly.[30] Yet they do not have this position in themselves. It depends solely on their focus on the one God. Thus, unfaithful Jews are no better than pagans who do not care about the divine truth at all. On the other hand, pagans who convert to Judaism and thus focus on the one God are united with the faithful Jews. Philo is emphatic about their equal status within the family of the nation of God.[31] Philo would also allow for a philosophical access to the monotheistic God.

The union of the Jews is particularly shown in their zeal for the torah, especially when there is a threat to the monotheistic principle. This can be seen not only in the emphasis Philo places on the biblical story of the Levites' punishment of the idolatry of some Jews, but also in his account of his own contemporaries' willingness to die rather than let the emperor Gaius's statue defile the temple in Jerusalem. Again, the union of the nation depends on the common focus on the one God. On this note, Philo seems to be the first to emphasize the community and concord created by the common observance of the pilgrimage to the one temple in Jerusalem.[32]

---

30. The link between the torah and the structure of the created universe is the idea of the Logos. The Logos is a theological concept used to bridge universal ideas and historical objects or people in Second Temple Judaism. In this way he is used in Philo to argue for the universal relevance of the torah and in the Gospel of John to demonstrate the universal importance of Jesus; see Jutta Leonhardt-Balzer, "Der Logos und die Schöpfung: Streiflichter bei Philo (*Opif.* 20–25) und im Johannesprolog (Joh 1,1–18)," in *Kontexte des Johannesevangeliums: Das vierte Evangelium in religions- und traditionsgeschichtlicher Perspektive*, ed. Jörg Frey and Udo Schnelle, WUNT 1/175 (Tübingen: Mohr Siebeck, 2004), 295–319.

31. It is not quite clear, however, whether, for Philo, proselytism involved circumcision; cf. John J. Collins, "A Symbol of Otherness: Circumcision and Salvation in the First Century," in *"To See Ourselves as Others See Us": Christians, Jews, "Others" in Late Antiquity*, ed. Jacob Neusner and Ernest S. Frerichs, Studies in the Humanities (Chico, CA: Scholars Press, 1985), 163–86, esp. 170–76.

32. Cf. Ian Rutherford, "Concord and *Communitas*: Greek Elements in Philo's Account of Jewish Pilgrimage," in *Journeys in the Roman East: Imagined and Real*, ed. Maren R. Niehoff, Culture, Religion, and Politics in the Greco-Roman World 1 (Tübingen: Mohr Siebeck, 2017), 257–72.

142 Jutta Leonhardt-Balzer

Philo is thus an example of a strong focus on a particular tradition, combined with a universal openness to all.[33]

Bibliography

Afterman, Adam. *"And They Shall Be One Flesh": On the Language of Mystical Union in Judaism.* Supplements to the Journal of Jewish Thought and Philosophy 26. Leiden: Brill, 2016.

———. "From Philo to Plotinus: The Emergence of Mystical Union." *JR* 93 (2013): 177–96.

Alesso, Marta. "No es Bueno que el hombre esté solo." *Circe* 8 (2003): 17–30.

Arnou, René. *Le désir de Dieu dans la philosophie de Plotin.* 2nd ed. Rome: Presses de l'Université grégorienne, 1967.

Berchman, Robert M. "Arithmos and Kosmos: Arithmology as an Exegetical Tool in the *De Opificio Mundi* of Philo of Alexandria." Pages 167–98 in *Gnosticism, Platonism and the Late Antique World: Essays in Honour of John D. Turner.* Edited by Kevin Corrigan and Tuomas Rasimus. Nag Hammadi and Manichaean Studies 82. Leiden: Brill, 2013.

Birnbaum, Ellen. *The Place of Judaism in Philo's Thought: Israel, Jews, and Proselytes.* BJS 290. SPhiloM 2. Atlanta: Scholars Press, 1996.

Bonazzi, Mauro. "Towards Transcendence: Philo and the Renewal of Platonism in the Early Imperial Age." Pages 232–52 in *Philo of Alexandria and Post-Aristotelian Philosophy.* Edited by Francesca Alesse. SPhA 5. Leiden: Brill, 2008.

Borgen, Peder, Kåre Fuglseth, and Roald Skarsten. *The Philo Index: A Complete Greek Word Index to the Writings of Philo of Alexandria.* Leiden: Brill, 1999.

Brisson, Luc. "Alexandrie, berceau du néoplatonisme: Eudore, Philon, Ammonios et l'école d'Alexandrie." Pages 354–63 in *Alexandrie la divine.* Edited by Charles Méla and Frédéric Möri. Geneva: La Baconnière, 2014.

---

33. Cf. Jutta Leonhardt-Balzer, "Jewish Worship and Universal Identity in Philo of Alexandria," in *Jewish Identity in the Greco-Roman World—Jüdische Identität in der griechisch-römischen Welt*, ed. Jörg Frey, Daniel R. Schwartz, and Stephanie Gripentrog, AJEC 71 (Leiden: Brill, 2007), 29–53.

6. The Number One 143

Calabi, Francesca. "'It Would Not Be Good That the Man Should Be Alone': Philo's Interpretation of Gen 2:18 in *Legum Allegoriae*." *SPhiloA* 28 (2016): 239–56.

Collins, John J. "A Symbol of Otherness: Circumcision and Salvation in the First Century." Pages 163–86 in *"To See Ourselves as Others See Us": Christians, Jews, "Others" in Late Antiquity*. Edited by Jacob Neusner and Ernest S. Frerichs. Studies in the Humanities. Chico, CA: Scholars Press, 1985.

Goodblatt, David. *The Monarchic Principle: Studies in Jewish Self-Government in Antiquity*. TSAJ 38. Tübingen: Mohr, 1994.

Guerra, Anthony J. "The One God Topos in *Spec. Leg.* 1:52." Pages 148–57 in *Society of Biblical Literature 1990 Seminar Papers*. Edited by David J. Lull. SBLSP 29. Atlanta: Scholars Press, 1990.

Leonhardt, Jutta. *Jewish Worship in Philo of Alexandria*. TSAJ 84. Tübingen: Mohr Siebeck, 2001.

Leonhardt-Balzer, Jutta. "Der Logos und die Schöpfung: Streiflichter bei Philo (*Opif.* 20–25) und im Johannesprolog (Joh 1,1–18)." Pages 295–319 in *Kontexte des Johannesevangeliums: Das vierte Evangelium in religions- und traditionsgeschichtlicher Perspektive*. Edited by Jörg Frey and Udo Schnelle. WUNT 1/175. Tübingen: Mohr Siebeck, 2004.

———. "Jewish Worship and Universal Identity in Philo of Alexandria." Pages 29–53 in *Jewish Identity in the Greco-Roman World—Jüdische Identität in der griechisch-römischen Welt*. Edited by Jörg Frey, Daniel R. Schwartz, and Stephanie Gripentrog. AJEC 71. Leiden: Brill, 2007.

Oertelt, Friederike. *Herrscherideal und Herrschaftskritik bei Philo von Alexandria: Eine Untersuchung am Beispiel seiner Josephsdarstellung in De Josepho und De Somniis II*. SPhA 8. Leiden: Brill, 2014.

Rutherford, Ian. "Concord and *Communitas*: Greek Elements in Philo's Account of Jewish Pilgrimage." Pages 257–72 in *Journeys in the Roman East: Imagined and Real*. Edited by Maren R. Niehoff. Culture, Religion, and Politics in the Greco-Roman World 1. Tübingen: Mohr Siebeck, 2017.

7
Oneness, Unity, and Josephus's Theological Politics

Kylie Crabbe

For Josephus, unity is a virtue. But this essay argues it is a virtue that he deploys in characteristically pragmatic fashion, frequently serving a rhetorical purpose in his presentation of Jewish groups in the passages in which it appears. Unity is central to his positive portrayal of the Jewish people and their law in *Against Apion* and the *Jewish Antiquities*, arising from both the practice of the law and a similar oneness of both God and temple, whereas its absence is central to his explanation of defeat in the *Jewish War*. Similarly, concord features in his descriptions of the Jewish sects, as characteristic of the groups that attract Josephus's praise and lacking in those that he censures.

In addition to supporting his portrait of Jewish identity and practice, however, I suggest that Josephus's calls to unity also serve his political purposes throughout. They create an other to blame (the revolutionaries) and portray Jewish particularity in a way that allows for both a kind of hospitality to the other and Jewish superiority. After outlining the themes that emerge from key texts about unity, oneness, and disunity across Josephus's works, I discuss the continuity that emerges despite the differences across these texts. Josephus frequently invokes his portrait of harmony and unanimity in relation to features of his ostensibly conservative politics, in which the rule of the stronger indicates divine support of the reigning regime and revolt is not only impractical but sinful. In different ways, the passages feed into his consistent assertion that God is in control.

146   Kylie Crabbe

7.1. Unity as a Virtue of the Jewish People

Josephus leaves his reader in no doubt as to the merits of unity. In his final and most rhetorically sophisticated work, *Against Apion*, he elevates unity (in terms such as κοινωνία, συμφωνία, and ὁμόνοια) by featuring it among the list of virtues that exemplify the Jewish people.[1] Indeed, it is so significant a feature of Jewish life that other groups, Josephus claims, seek to emulate it (*C. Ap.* 2.280–286). Josephus follows an established Platonic-Aristotelian tradition by providing a list of virtues, but he also highlights particular virtues by altering the ordering and making his own additions.[2] In a section that begins toward the end of the second book of his apology, the virtue lists appear multiple times and with slight variations.

Josephus begins this larger unit (*C. Ap.* 2.145–296) by enumerating the virtues that he claims arise from the design of the Jewish law and constitution: "piety [εὐσέβειαν], fellowship with one another [κοινωνίαν τὴν μετ' ἀλλήλων], and universal benevolence [τὴν καθόλου φιλανθρωπίαν], as well as justice, endurance in labours, and contempt for death" (2.146).[3] Here he calls attention to piety by promoting it to first position and he adds κοινωνία, listing it second and before the standard virtues expected in such a list. When he returns to a further list of virtues a short time later, he presents εὐσέβεια as the key and overarching virtue to which the law leads. He makes a point of claiming that the Jewish legislator

---

1. Christine Gerber (*Ein Bild des Judentums für Nichtjuden von Flavius Josephus: Untersuchungen zu seiner Schrift Contra Apionem*, AGJU 40 [Leiden: Brill, 1997], 360–61) notes the interrelationship between the semantic fields of these terms and also recognizes the importance of the terms in wider Greco-Roman society.

2. Tessa Rajak, "The *Against Apion* and the Continuities in Josephus' Political Thought," in *The Jewish Dialogue with Greece and Rome: Studies in Cultural and Social Interaction*, AGJU 48 (Leiden: Brill, 2001), 204–6. Rajak suggests the virtues listed are at least partly in response to criticism of the Jewish people (204).

3. Josephus's phrasing here invites the reader to parallel κοινωνία with one another and benevolence to all; the κοινωνία, as will become clear, is a characteristic of Jewish particularity, but as is seen here, the unity at the core of Judaism also allows a certain hospitality to others. In relation to this list of virtues, see the description of the Essenes in *B.J.* 2.151–153. On the role of good philosophy in enabling one to face death well in Seneca and other Roman writers, see Steve Mason, ed. and trans., *Flavius Josephus: Judean War 2*, FJTC1b (Leiden: Brill, 2008), 86–87. Unless otherwise indicated, citations from Josephus are taken from the series Flavius Josephus: Translation and Commentary, edited by Steve Mason (Leiden: Brill, 1999–). Where the volume is not yet available, particularly *B.J.* 5–6, I have cited the LCL translation by Thackeray.

7. Oneness, Unity, and Josephus's Theological Politics 147

"did not make piety a part of virtue but recognised and established the others as parts of it" (2.170).[4] These other virtues that Josephus suggests are encompassed under piety are: "justice, moderation, endurance, and harmony among citizens in relation to one another in all matters [τὴν τῶν πολιτῶν πρὸς ἀλλήλους ἐν ἅπασι συμφωνίαν]" (2.170). Tessa Rajak describes this list as "the Platonic virtues in their Jewish adaptation" and she notes in particular in relation to συμφωνία, that this "intensely Josephan value squeezes out the expected Platonic and Aristotelian φρόνησις or practical wisdom."[5]

In each of the passages, these virtues are said to characterize the Jews, and when Josephus comes to list the traits that other groups seek to mimic, he repeats many of the same ideas. After claiming that Greek philosophers followed Moses in their understanding of God, frugality, and κοινωνία (*C. Ap.* 2.281), and that over time even the masses have copied Jewish piety, including in relation to sabbath rest, fasting, ritual lamp lighting, and food laws, he closes with a list of further virtues that others attempt to follow, with ὁμόνοια at the head. "They try to imitate also our concord [ἡμῶν ὁμόνοιαν] among ourselves, our distribution of possessions, our industriousness in crafts, and our endurance under torture on behalf of the laws" (2.283). In these ways Josephus characterizes Jewish values and lifestyle in a familiar literary device and with attributes that are highly valued by readers with Greek and Roman sensibilities. The addition of terms related to unity into such virtue lists underscores the value he places on this particular characteristic throughout his writing.

Josephus also discloses his priority for unity by presenting it as a virtue of his preferred Jewish sects. In his renowned philosophical school passages, he sets aside his narratives in order to instruct his reader about the sects into which the Jewish people are divided: Pharisees, Sadducees, and Essenes, and in the excursus in *A.J.* 18, a "fourth philosophy" that describes the Zealots (*B.J.* 2.119–166; *A.J.* 13.171–173; 18.12–22; cf. *Vita*

---

4. John Barclay notes that Plato talks about the "parts of virtue" (Plato, *Leg.*, 633a; though cf. *Prot.*, 329c); see Barclay, ed. and trans., *Flavius Josephus: Against Apion*, FJTC 10 (Leiden: Brill, 2006), 266.

5. Rajak, "Against Apion," 205; cf. John Barclay, "Matching Theory and Practice: Josephus's Constitutional Ideal and Paul's Strategy in Corinth," in *Paul beyond the Judaism/Hellenism Divide*, ed. Troels Engberg-Pedersen (Louisville: Westminster John Knox, 2001), 148–49.

148   Kylie Crabbe

10–12).[6] A key focus in the three main passages lies in differing ways the groups are said to attribute responsibility to fate (εἱμαρμένη), God (θεός), and human choices (ἀνθρώπων ἐκλογή) to act well or badly (cf. *B.J.* 2.162–165; *A.J.* 13.171–173; 18.13, 18), which are core beliefs that would distinguish between Stoics and Epicureans. This signals Josephus's presentation of Jewish groups as parallel to specific philosophical schools; in *Life* he makes the parallel even more explicit, describing: "the philosophical school of the Pharisees, which is rather like the one called Stoic among the Greeks" (*Vita* 12).[7] Attitudes toward fate and freewill loomed large in conflicts between proponents of Stoic and Epicurean philosophies.[8] By aligning the Jewish groups with these beliefs Josephus does more than relate the sects to different philosophies; he exploits the traditions in order to present a consistently positive portrait of some sects (Essenes, Pharisees) and a negative one of the other (Sadducees).[9] It is in this context that Josephus's broader attitude to unity is illuminated by the portrait of the groups that are said to exhibit it.

In each of the passages the Essenes are presented positively. Indeed, the vast bulk of the excursus in *B.J.* 2 is devoted to their merits (forty-three of the forty-seven sections).[10] Despite some notable differences between the different passages (e.g., the inclusion of Essenes who marry only in *B.J.* 2.160–161, whereas *A.J.* 18.21 asserts their singleness), their communal life is consistently characterized by their sharing, including an absolute

---

6. The passage in *Life* is offered in the context of Josephus's description of his own experience of sectarian training before he took a different vocational turn; it names but does not set out the features of each group in the same manner as the other passages.

7. As Steve Mason has noted ("Josephus's Pharisees: The Philosophy," in *In Quest of the Historical Pharisees*, ed. Jacob Neusner and Bruce D. Chilton [Waco, TX: Baylor University Press, 2007], 41–66), the ways in which these sects fit neatly onto the core claims of the different philosophical schools should give interpreters pause about attributing historicity to the descriptions of the groups.

8. Political considerations also arise from these claims about the roles of fortune or fate, and human action, with differing emphases on either the inflexibility of fate or capriciousness of fortune, giving a political valence to some comparisons of Stoicism and Epicureanism; see Lydia Matthews, "Roman Constructions of *Fortuna*" (DPhil diss., University of Oxford, 2012), 6; Kylie Crabbe, *Luke/Acts and the End of History*, BZNW 238 (Berlin: de Gruyter, 2019), 144–45, 151–54.

9. He also presents the fourth philosophy negatively in *A.J.* 18, in keeping with his negative treatment of revolt throughout.

10. Mason, *Judean War 2*, 84.

7. Oneness, Unity, and Josephus's Theological Politics 149

commitment to holding goods in common (*B.J.* 2.122–127; cf. *A.J.* 18.20).[11] Leaders are elected, and they are all "indivisible" (ἀδιαίρετος), seeking the good of all (*B.J.* 2.123). Steve Mason suggests that "concord" is "an Essene hallmark (*J. W.* 2.122–123, 134, 145)."[12] The direct comparison between the Pharisees and Sadducees in *B.J.* 2 gives an even clearer indication of the importance of unity, in the language of ὁμόνοια: "And whereas Pharisees are mutually affectionate and cultivate concord in relation to the community [τὴν εἰς τὸ κοινὸν ὁμόνοιαν ἀσκοῦντες], Sadducees have a rather harsh disposition even toward one another; encounters with their peers are as uncouth as those with outsiders" (2.166; cf. 2.119). The reader should be aware that, according to Josephus, the Pharisees (like Stoics) are positive examples in their religious belief and behavior, and the Sadducees (like their Epicurean rhetorical counterparts) are objects of disdain. Thus, the concord of the former and its lack in the latter confirms Josephus's overall emphasis on unity as a positive virtue.

7.2. The Basis for Jewish Unity

When he sets out the Jewish legal framework in each of *C. Ap.* 2 and *A.J.* 4, Josephus suggests that the sources of Jewish unity arise from the particular, concrete insights and practices that make the Jewish people superior.[13] Their unity is grounded in shared practices of the law, reflects an essential oneness at the heart of God and the temple, and relates to the Jewish social structure.

7.2.1. The Jewish Law and Its Practice

The broader passage in which the virtue lists discussed above appear in *Against Apion* is the last major section in the second (and final) book. Here Josephus continues his apologetic rebuttal of various criticisms leveled against the Jewish people, focusing in particular on Jewish law and practice (with Jewish piety and unity as frequent themes). After naming

---

11. The passage in *Jewish War* is also much longer and, of course, the earliest.

12. Mason, *Judean War 2*, 87.

13. Although his affirmation of the Jewish nation's unity does not claim an innate superiority, he does assert that "we were born for κοινωνία," and that divine favor comes from putting the interests of the community above the self (*C. Ap.* 2.196).

150 Kylie Crabbe

his interlocuters, Josephus sets out aspects of Jewish superiority.[14] As John Barclay notes, this section is both apology and encomium, praising Moses, the Jewish πολιτεία, and the law.[15]

In this passage, Moses is presented as the ideal legislator and teacher. The positive portrayal of the law is itself a significant element of Josephus's argument. In some Greek and Roman traditions, the introduction of law is considered evidence of a fall from utopia, with a legal framework the unsavory necessity prompted by human behaviors that require restriction. For instance, in an excursus on the development of legislation in his *Annals* (3.26–28), Tacitus describes an idyllic primeval time of harmony, in which there was no wrongdoing or law, following which human immorality developed: "when equality began to be outworn, and ambition and violence gained ground in place of modesty and self-effacement, there came a crop of despotisms, which with many nations has remained perennial" (Tacitus, *Ann.* 3.26 [LCL]). Thus legislation became, and continues to be, necessary. Such a narrative of decline suits Tacitus's "gloomy" mood in his moralizing historiography.[16] But there is no hint of such connotations in the introduction of the Jewish law for Josephus. His positive treatment suggests even a subtle subversion of Roman law, which by implication compares unfavorably to that Moses gave the Jewish people.[17]

Moses is the example who holds together word and deed, and whose lead the Jewish people then unanimously follow (*C. Ap.* 2.169).[18] These two facets of Moses's contribution in turn lie behind different kinds of unity to which Josephus refers: "social unity" (ὁμόνοια) and "unanim-

---

14. Here Josephus moves from responding to individual criticisms singly, as he had done earlier in the apology, to naming several criticisms and addressing them as a block together (Barclay, *Against Apion*, 242–43).

15. Barclay, *Against Apion*, 243; cf. *C. Ap.* 2.147, 287. Barclay notes the range of meanings for πολιτεία, from a formal sense of "form of government" to simply a "way of life"; he argues the former is more the focus in *Antiquities*, but that *Against Apion* moves more into the latter (Barclay, "Matching Theory and Practice," 140–41).

16. Miriam T. Griffin, "Tacitus as a Historian," in *The Cambridge Companion to Tacitus*, ed. A. J. Woodman, Cambridge Companions to Literature (Cambridge: Cambridge University Press, 2009), 171.

17. This is also supported by the description of Greek philosophers, through their core values, following Mosaic law (cf. *C. Ap.* 2.168, 256–257, 281).

18. Barclay takes this as a major theme in his comparison with Paul's response to the Corinthians (Barclay, "Matching Theory and Practice," 139–63).

7. Oneness, Unity, and Josephus's Theological Politics 151

ity of opinion" (συμφωνία).[19] An aspect of the genius of the Mosaic law, according to Josephus, lies in the practices that are embedded in it, leading to piety and effective teaching.[20] The tradition of hearing the law read ensures that "were anyone of us to be asked about the laws, they would recount them all more easily than their own name" (2.178).[21] Indeed, the law is as though "engraved on souls" (2.178; cf. *A.J.* 4.210). This is contrasted with other groups, who Josephus argues have had to appoint administrators to deal with their laws, rather than each person knowing the law themselves (*C. Ap.* 2.176–177).[22]

In this way, the law not only creates a community of common beliefs but brings about consistency in lifestyle and customs. Again, Josephus contrasts this with the lack of endurance of other groups who he suggests can simply sustain pious bursts in special festivals (2.189). He presents a positive portrait of his own harmonious community, claiming that nearly everyone always keeps the law: "it is rare to find a transgressor, and impossible to gain exemption from punishment" (2.178).

Unity is thus the result of the Jewish πολιτεία and law.[23] Josephus summarizes the effect of the shared practices that arise from this legislative framework, incorporating both social and creedal unity:

> It is this above all that has created our remarkable concord [τὴν θαυμαστὴν ὁμόνοιαν ἡμῖν ἐμπεποίηκεν]. For holding one and the same conception of God [τὸ γὰρ μίαν μὲν ἔχειν καὶ τὴν αὐτὴν δόξαν περὶ θεοῦ], and not differing at all in life-style or customs, produces a very beautiful harmony in [people's] characters [καλλίστην ἐν ἤθεσιν ἀνθρώπων συμφωνίαν ἀποτελεῖ]." (2.179; cf. 180–181)[24]

---

19. Rajak, "Against Apion," 203.

20. Rajak observes that this fits with "the standard Platonic-Aristotelian line, that a πολιτεία promotes the virtues through education" (Rajak, "Against Apion," 204).

21. Barclay's translation, modified for gender-inclusive language.

22. Barclay suggests that Josephus presents this as Moses's key innovation: making the legal framework accessible to the masses (Barclay, "Matching Theory and Practice," 143).

23. Barclay notes that this then "matches the traditional concern among constitutional theorists that the state not descend into discord or factionalism (στάσις)" (Barclay, "Matching Theory and Practice," 149).

24. Barclay observes that across 2.179–181 Josephus parallels "word/conception" (λόγος/δόξα) with "customs/habits" (ἔθη/ἐπιτηδεύματα), referring back also to 2.171–174 (Barclay, "Matching Theory and Practice," 271 n. 706), where Moses is presented as exemplifying coherence between word and deed. This is also in keeping with the

152 Kylie Crabbe

7.2.2. An Underlying Principle of Oneness

After initially establishing the connection between Jewish law and unity in *C. Ap.* 2, Josephus goes on to describe key laws.[25] When he opens his summary of those related to the temple and sacrifices, he delves further into the unity he finds at the heart of Jewish tradition, stating:

> One temple of the one God [εἷς ναὸς ἑνὸς θεοῦ][26]—for like is always attracted to like [φίλον γὰρ ἀεὶ παντὶ τὸ ὅμοιον]—common to all people as belonging to the common God of all [κοινὸς ἁπάντων κοινοῦ θεοῦ ἁπάντων]. (2.193)

Here Josephus grounds his claims about Jewish unity; it is not simply a form of social and creedal unity arising from shared practices of the law, but derives from a core oneness at the heart of that law (cf. 2.198), in its insights about the very nature of God and the shared participation in the single temple.[27] This oneness is necessarily reflected, by the principle of like being attracted to like, in all that flows from such a God. In this way, as Barclay observes, "Even the temple—single, particular, unambiguously Judean—can be affirmed as the proper correlate of this one, true God." Josephus manages to present the temple in this positive light even while incorporating "the very Athenian claim that it is 'common to all.'"[28]

---

ways that creedal and social unity derive from the law given by Moses, each reflecting a side of this dynamic.

25. Josephus divides the laws into those relating to "God and cult," the family and community relationships, and then foreigners and enemies (Barclay, *Against Apion*, 243).

26. Note the absence of the verb "to be," which is particularly interesting in light of the historical circumstances of the (destroyed) temple at the time of writing. I return to this below.

27. Josephus brings these ideas together also in his summary at the end of his description of the laws about God: "Such is our doctrine concerning God and his worship, and the law is one and the same" (2.198). Rajak describes this as a "principle of unity" (Rajak, "Against Apion," 203). Similarly, see also Andrew Byers, "The One Body of the Shema in 1 Corinthians: An Ecclesiology of Christological Monotheism," *NTS* 62 (2016): 519–24.

28. Barclay, *Against Apion*, 246. In rhetorical moves throughout this section of *Against Apion*, Josephus portrays Jewish tradition in terms that would be valued by a Roman audience; negative examples given for explicit comparisons are limited to Greek examples, such as the illustration of Greek mythology (246).

7. Oneness, Unity, and Josephus's Theological Politics 153

These themes are also present in Josephus's treatment of the Jewish constitution when relaying Deuteronomy in *A.J.* 4.196–301. In Moses's instructions he stresses the need to found "one holy city that is renowned for its excellence" and he stipulates, "let there be one Temple in it and one altar [νεὼς εἷς ἐν ταύτῃ ἔστω, καὶ βωμὸς εἷς]" (4.200).[29] After going into further detail about the altar's construction, he then draws in the oneness of God: "In another city let there be neither an altar nor a temple, for God is one [θεὸς γὰρ εἷς] and the stock of the Hebrews is one [τὸ Ἑβραίων γένος ἕν]" (4.201). Thus, this principle of unity shows that the oneness of the monotheistic deity undergirds each of the other elements, incorporating not only the stipulations around the single temple and altar, but reflecting an essential unity that is particular to the Hebrew γένος. Although this unity is not worked out further in this passage with terms like ὁμονοία and συμφωνία, as in *Against Apion*, an ethical element remains in Josephus's affirmation of the need for the Jews to be familiar with one another despite their wide-ranging geography, explaining that they should therefore converge on that one, holy city three times per year, exhorting: "coming together and taking a common meal, may they be dear to each other [συνιόντες ἀλλήλοις καὶ συνευωχούμενοι προσφιλεῖς ὦσι]" (4.203).

Two elements in both the *Against Apion* and *Antiquities* references warrant a further note: Josephus's approach to other temples and to other gods. In *Jewish War* he is clearly aware of the temple in Leontopolis, to which he refers without any apparent sense that its existence compromises something essential to the Jerusalem temple (*B.J.* 1.31–33; 7.431; cf. *A.J.* 13.70). Whether his view of oneness and the theological significance of the single temple in Jerusalem has developed between the earlier text and the later works, or the rhetorical purposes and audiences in the later works create a different need from that addressed by *Jewish War*'s historiographical account of recent events, it is evident that Josephus both is aware of other temples and also wishes to dismiss their claims.[30] Moreover, this emphasis on the single temple in Jerusalem in *Jewish War* and *Against*

---

29. Here Josephus does supply the verb "to be," in the present imperative (ἔστω), thus the translation "let there be." Although the reference in *A.J.* 4.200 has the hortatory sense of the third-person imperative and thus may seem to indicate an exhortation for the ongoing presence of the temple, some of its force may be moderated by its literary setting in Moses's past instruction. As noted above, there is no verb "to be" in the *Against Apion* reference.

30. As Louis H. Feldman notes (*Flavius Josephus: Judean Antiquities, Books 1–4*, FJTC

154 Kylie Crabbe

Apion exists independently of historical questions about the status of the destroyed Jerusalem temple at the time of his writing, a point to which I return below.

Josephus's emphasis on the one God may also be tempered with other points where he appears more pragmatically to recognize the piety other groups exhibit toward other gods.[31] In *Against Apion* he contrasts Judaism's singular God with the multiplicity of gods in Greek mythology, in an extremely negative critique of the latter (2.238–249). But the primary focus is on the immorality of the gods, rather than their multiplicity. In keeping with his rhetorical strategies throughout this section, where comparison is made with another tradition in order to show the Jewish tradition in a superior light, the parallel is Greek, whereas the positive portrait of the Jewish people conforms to the traditions and behavior that would be viewed positively in Roman tradition.[32] Nonetheless, here at least, Josephus presents monotheistic belief as capturing "the true nature of God," which was an insight, he suggests, beyond the grasp of Greek tradition, whose "great inconsistency and error concerning the deity" leads also to a legal failure: "because their legislators did not originally recognise the true nature of God, nor, when they had distinguished whatever accurate knowledge they were able to grasp, relate to this the rest of the structure of the constitution" (2.250).

Louis Feldman notes similarities between Josephus's phrasing in these passages and other relevant examples. When Philo discusses Moses's provision through the law in *On the Special Laws*, he likewise specifies that Moses "provided that there should not be temples built either in many places or many in the same place, for he judged that since God is one

---

3 [Leiden: Brill, 1999], 398–99 n. 581), Josephus now ignores or dismisses the claims of the Samaritans (with the temple on Mount Gerizim) and the Leontopolis temple.

31. E.g., Josephus says that "it is our tradition to observe our own and not to criticise others,'" claiming that Moses instructed the Jews not to "mock or slander the gods recognised by others, for the sake of the very name 'God'" (*C. Ap.* 2.237). These tolerant statements are the introduction to his detailed critique of Greek mythology, so on the one hand suggesting a legal framework of tolerance, and on the other attempting to demonstrate the inadequacy of others' views.

32. Barclay notes that this indicates the particularly sophisticated and complex nature of Josephus's apology and interaction with the traditions of the colonized power. It is also worth noting that the comparison to Greek mythology itself is not a fair portrait of Greek beliefs, where comparison to concepts in philosophical discourse would be more fitting (Barclay, *Against Apion*, 243–44).

7. Oneness, Unity, and Josephus's Theological Politics 155

[ἐπειδὴ εἷς ἐστιν ὁ θεός], there should be also only one temple [καὶ ἱερὸν ἓν εἶναι μόνον]" (*Spec. Laws* 1.67).[33] In 2 Baruch, Baruch offers a prayer in which the blessed position of Israel, which remains separate from the other nations, is safeguarded by the help of the law. Here the essential oneness is articulated by a connection between the singular God and the singular law: "we, who received one Law from the One" (2 Bar. 48:24; cf. *C. Ap.* 2.198).[34] The principle is further explicated in Midrash, with a comparison to other groups designed to demonstrate the superiority of Jewish approaches, somewhat akin to the approach Josephus takes in *Against Apion*. The rabbinic text asserts: "it is the way of the gentiles to have many religious observances and many priests and all of them are collected in one building, but we have only one God, one Torah, and one legal system, and one altar and one high priest" (Num. Rab. 18.7).[35] Whereas the one God is aligned by Philo with the one temple, and in 2 Baruch with the one law, this rabbinic text draws in further examples of oneness (including specifying the altar separately, as Josephus also does in *A.J.* 4.200), within an account of the superiority of the Jewish legal system. Thus, these other texts offer further examples of writers applying a principle of oneness derived from the divine into other domains, but it is Josephus who ties this to the unity of the people.

7.2.3. The Political Structure Arising from the Jewish Constitution

Finally, in *Against Apion* Josephus also presents the Jewish political structure as inherently related to this divine oneness. His portrait here appears to conflict with the way he has Moses set out the preferred structure in *A.J.* 4, that is, rule by the elite, alongside suggestions about how to ensure the best outcome from rule by monarchy, should the people make that compromise absolutely necessary. There he asserts:

> Now aristocracy and the life therein is best. Let not a longing for another government take hold of you, but be content with this. And having the

---

33. Cited by Feldman, *Judean Antiquities*, 399 n. 583.

34. Translation by A. F. J. Klijn, "(Syriac Apocalypse of) Baruch," in *The Old Testament Pseudepigrapha*, ed. James H. Charlesworth, ABRL (Garden City, NY: Doubleday, 1983).

35. Feldman cites this passage in relation to *A.J.* 4.200 (Feldman, *Judean Antiquities*, 399 n. 583).

156 Kylie Crabbe

laws as your masters do each thing according to them, for it is sufficient that God is your ruler. If, however, you should have a passion to have a king, let him be a compatriot, and let him always have a concern for justice and the other virtues. (*A.J.* 4.223)

Moses goes on to describe the attributes of a suitable king in these circumstances: conceding to laws and God (in that order), operating under the advice of the high priest and elders, and refraining from excess that he not become contemptuous of the laws (4.224).

But in *Against Apion* he rejects monarchy (rule by the one, μοναρχία), aristocracy, and democracy. Rather, he says:

Our legislator took no notice of any of these, but instituted the government as what one might call—to force an expression—a "theocracy" [θεοκρατίαν], ascribing to God the rule and power.... He represented him as single [ἕνα γοῦν αὐτὸν ἀπέφηνε] and uncreated and immutable through all eternity, more beautiful than any mortal form, known to us by his power, but as to what he is like in essence, unknown. (2.165–167)

Josephus here supplies the earliest surviving instance we have of the term *theocracy*, which again is linked to divine oneness.[36] Here the one God is the singular authority in a properly constructed society. Despite the different terminology, however, it is worth noting that even in *A.J.* 4 divine guidance is a significant factor and any king should take advice from the priests. In *Against Apion*, again, the singular divine authority is represented through priests who, as overseers and "judges in disputes," exact punishment on his behalf (2.185–187).

Thus, in the final section of his apology in *Against Apion* (2.145–296), Josephus emphasizes unity throughout. He claims that both social concord and creedal unanimity are derived from the practices of the law supplied by Moses. He argues that Moses's superior teaching model ensures that all know the law and persevere in its practices (providing examples for comparison). He gives a core place to unity through familiar rhetorical techniques, such as lists of virtues, and includes κοινωνία and ὁμόνοια among characteristics of the Jewish people that others actively seek to

---

36. Barclay rightly notes that, though some suggest the later reference to the priests' role in overseeing implementation of the law suggests he really means hierocracy, the key here is the singular authority and providence attributed to God (Barclay, "Matching Theory and Practice," 142–43).

7.3. Disunity as a Cause of the Jewish Defeat to Rome

emulate. Moreover, here, as in *A.J.* 4, he argues that such unity is entirely natural because it reflects at its heart the oneness of God and temple, taking the concept even further in claiming a Jewish political structure that gives singular authority to God. This serves his apologetic purpose in illustrating Jewish superiority. But with a perhaps surprising continuity with Josephus's earlier work, I suggest it also reflects a deeper purpose in Josephus's political approach to difference, political unrest, and divine control. This is a theme to which I return below.

7.3. Disunity as a Cause of the Jewish Defeat to Rome

Josephus's unstinting praise of unity in the Jewish community in *Against Apion* may come as something of a surprise to any of his audience who had chanced upon his earliest historiography. In his account of the conflict with Rome and the events that led up to it in *Jewish War*, Josephus identifies the Jewish *disunity* as one of the key causes of their military loss. Writing shortly after the war, Josephus's historiography presents a way of redirecting blame away from Rome and onto the Jewish revolutionaries, who in turn convinced the people as a whole to join them in civil strife (στάσις; cf. *B.J.* 2.352–355, 390–391; 6.249–253).[37]

On a practical level, Josephus recognizes a strategic necessity for unity in military campaigns. Thucydides describes the advantage enjoyed by an inexperienced army that is courageous and adheres uniformly to the directions of specifically charged generals, over a more experienced army hampered by too many generals and diverse orders, "combined with the disorder and insubordination of the troops" (Thucydides, *P.W.* 6.72).[38] Historians with a moralizing focus likewise affirm the need for unity. Diodorus Siculus suggests moral decline manifests in greed, complacency, and a lack of discipline, which leads to military defeat and regime change

---

37. Aspects of Josephus's apologetic stance in *Jewish War* suggest a double-edged audience: he wishes to excuse the revolt to Roman audiences, while also offering an explanation and way forward for Jewish audiences. On the complexity of Josephus's treatment of Rome, see Gregory E. Sterling, "Explaining Defeat: Polybius and Josephus on the Wars with Rome," in *Internationales Josephus-Kolloquium Aarhus 1999*, ed. J. U. Kalms, Münsteraner Judaistische Studien 6 (Münster: LIT, 2000), 135–51.

38. Similarly, military advice in *A.J.* 4.297 states that God should be "your supreme commander" and courage the key criterion for the earthly lieutenant selected, who should then be followed without division. Thackeray's LCL commentary draws the connection to Thucydides, *P.W.* 6.72 here.

158   Kylie Crabbe

(19.1.1–8; 37.1.1–6; 37.29.5–30.2).[39] Tacitus (who is full of nostalgia for earlier times, particularly the time of the republic) views military discipline as a virtue in itself and his criticism of Rome under imperial rule includes disunity as a sign of lack of discipline and emblematic of the decline he bemoans (*Hist.* 1.12, 28, 83–84).[40]

Josephus's account of the events that lead to defeat follows similar lines. Disunity is frequently the cause of difficulty (cf. *B.J.* 1.10, 25, 27; 3.496; 4.369).[41] There is a foolish and doomed fracture between the various groups who seek revolt, to the point that they waste their energies being at loggerheads with one another and fail to notice the impending threat of Rome's advance.[42] When they note developments in the Roman camp, this external impetus begins a process of the factions ("hitherto incessantly at strife," 5.71) working together through "a sorry alliance [κακῆς ὁμονοίας κατήρχοντο]" (72). A further insight leads them, though not without mistrust, to realize the need to work together:

> The rival factions shouted across to each other that they were doing all they could to assist the enemy, when they ought, even if God denied them lasting concord [εἰ καὶ μὴ διηνεκῆ δίδωσιν αὐτοῖς ὁμόνοιαν ὁ θεός], for the present at least to postpone their mutual strife [τὴν πρὸς ἀλλήλους φιλονεικίαν] and unite against the Romans [κατὰ Ῥωμαίων συνελθεῖν]. (5.278)

Here finally, Josephus suggests, a full union becomes possible: "The parties, consigning their hatred and private quarrels to oblivion, thus became one body [ἓν σῶμα γίνονται]" (279). But the pragmatic alliance comes too late.[43]

---

39. Kenneth S. Sacks, *Diodorus Siculus and the First Century* (Princeton: Princeton University Press, 1990), 43.

40. Ronald Syme, *Tacitus*, 2 vols. (Oxford: Clarendon, 1958), 1:175.

41. See discussion in Jonathan Klawans, "Josephus, the Rabbis, and Responses to Catastrophes Ancient and Modern," *JQR* 100 (2010): 290–95.

42. Josephus's own character offers another speech in book 6, in which he sets out the portents and signs that had always indicated when the temple would be destroyed; he asserts that the foretold destruction of Jerusalem aligned with the time when they would begin to "slaughter" their own compatriots (6.109).

43. As he reflects on the exploitative efforts of rivals Simon and John, Josephus evokes the language of unity in a way that simply calls attention to its absence: "As rivals for power they were divided, but in their crimes unanimous [ὁμόνια]" (5.441).

7. Oneness, Unity, and Josephus's Theological Politics   159

For Josephus, disunity also falls into theological categories: engaging in disunity and revolt is more than a failure to implement good military strategy; it is a sin. It also contributes to the Jewish people's failure to submit to the divine purpose. As the conflict accelerates toward disaster in book 5, Josephus presents his own character making an impassioned speech, agitatedly pacing along the city walls as he implores his compatriots to divert their course.[44] Here he recounts Israel's history, framed in such a way as to show that taking matters into one's own hands is always negative, offering the concluding summary: "in short, there is no instance of our forefathers having triumphed by arms or failed of success without them when they committed their cause to God: if they sat still they conquered, as it pleased their Judge, if they fought they were invariably defeated" (*B.J.* 5.390). Pausing between his account of biblical and more recent events, he declares:

> Why need I mention more? But, pray, who enlisted the Romans against our country? Was it not the impiety of its inhabitants? Whence did our servitude arise? Was it not from party strife [ἐκ στάσεως] among our forefathers, when the madness of Aristobulus and Hyrcanus and their mutual dissensions [ἀλλήλους ἔρις] brought Pompey against the city, and God subjected to the Romans those who were unworthy of liberty? (5.396)

Throughout this speech, Josephus presents the Jewish people as culpable and the Romans as surprisingly pious. The sin of disunity causes the divine punishment and Jewish servitude to Rome. The Romans are more respectful of the temple than the Jews themselves (5.402), who, by contrast, have contaminated the temple and even disown Hebrew tradition so that their actions are not held to the account of its law (5.443).[45] Moreover, Josephus affirms that by the "rule of the stronger" the people should already have realized that the Romans could not reign without divine support, and so any resistance to Rome constitutes fighting God (5.368, 377).[46] In a speech

---

44. Josephus is introduced as a character in his narrative at *B.J.* 2.568. He is portrayed as a respected military figure (3.142), full of ingenious strategies (3.171–175, 186–188, 271–275), and, from a key moment in book 3 onward, as being gifted with a prophetic insight about the reasons for the war (3.352–354; 4.623).

45. Eyal Regev, "Josephus, the Temple, and the Jewish War," in *Flavius Josephus: Interpretation and History*, ed. Jack Pastor, Pnina Stern, and Menahem Mor, JSJSup 146 (Leiden: Brill, 2011), 280–83.

46. For divine support for Roman rule, see *B.J.* 2.140, 360–361. On divine support for current leaders, whether political regimes or the holders of local offices, see Mason,

160   Kylie Crabbe

given by Agrippa in *B.J.* 2.345–401, where there are numerous parallels to
Josephus's speech in book 5, Agrippa emphasizes the arrogance of believing the Jewish people could oppose Rome, when more impressive regimes
had been unable to do so.[47] Josephus's speech reiterates and underscores
the arrogance of fighting God: it is both sinful, and inevitably unsuccessful. The appropriate response, therefore, according to Josephus, is to
repent—both to God (5.415–416) and to Rome (372–373).

Given the positive portrait of Rome, an authoritative and damning
assessment of the Jewish military decisions comes in the voice of Titus
later in book 6. The charge explicitly includes στάσις over ὁμόνοια. In the
face of the siege in the temple precinct and resulting famine, Josephus
observes that:

> Caesar declared himself innocent in this matter also in the sight of God,
> protesting that *he* had offered the Jews peace, independence, and an
> amnesty for all past offences, while *they*, preferring sedition to concord
> [τοὺς δὲ ἀντὶ μὲν ὁμονοίας στάσιν], war to peace, famine to plenty and
> prosperity, and having been the first to set fire with their own hands
> to that temple which he and his army were preserving for them, were
> indeed deserving even of such food as this. (6.215–216; cf. 1.10, 27)[48]

The mix of criticism of the Jewish people, with a key focus on disunity,
positive portrait of Roman rule, and affirmation of divine control, builds
to an important picture of how Josephus's use of unity reflects his politics.

7.4. The Effect of Calls to Unity: Josephus's Theological Politics

Josephus's presentation of the virtue of unity serves a political purpose
across his texts. While some have explained the differences between these
texts as the result of developments in Josephus's thinking about unity, or

---

Judean War 2, 113–14 n. 870. For further discussion, see Kylie Crabbe, "Being Found
Fighting against God: Luke's Gamaliel and Josephus on Human Responses to Divine
Providence," *ZNW* 106 (2015): 21–39.

47. See Tessa Rajak, "Friends, Romans, Subjects: Agrippa II's Speech in Josephus's
Jewish War," in *Images of Empire*, ed. Loveday Alexander, JSOTSup 122 (Sheffield:
JSOT Press, 1991), 122–34.

48. Thackeray's LCL translation, modified to correct an error; Thackeray has
Titus say here that the people prefer peace to war, but the Greek says the opposite, in
keeping with the meaning across this section.

7. Oneness, Unity, and Josephus's Theological Politics 161

the effects of the different genres, audiences, or purposes of his works, I suggest that the way Josephus's attitude to unity functions to support his underlying political claims reflects a striking *continuity* across his works.[49] Unity is a feature of his idealized portrait of the Jewish state. It reflects the oneness of the divine who enjoys a singular rule, and whose direction of the course of history confirms that those in power must have divine support. In this he grounds both his censure of revolt and his confidence in the ultimate superiority of the Jewish people's position.

When Josephus emphasizes piety and unity as core characteristics of the Jewish people in *Against Apion*, his account is explicitly idealized. He claims "theocracy" at a time when the Jews do not enjoy an independent state. Moreover, he grounds the Jewish unity in the core likeness of "the one temple of the one God" (*C. Ap.* 2.193; cf. *A.J.* 4.200), without any apparent hesitation about what this means in the wake of that one temple's destruction.[50] The one cursory nod to present realities comes when Josephus affirms that the law endures, observing that "even if we are deprived of wealth, cities, and other good things, at least the law endures for us immortal, and no Judean, however far they may go from their homeland, or however much they fear a cruel master, will not fear the law more than him" (*C. Ap.* 2.277).[51] While offering comparisons that portray Jewish practices and beliefs as superior, Josephus is thus free from the need to make allowances for real-life examples of any failure to meet these standards. The idealized structure also overrides real-life diversity among the Jewish people; and there is an implicit critique of other legal systems and political structures, as he addresses criticism

---

49. This is not to say that genre, purpose, audience, etc., are not important; they need to be taken into account as they will affect the meaning of particular texts. E.g., Rajak points out that an emphasis on theocracy might have been at risk of misinterpretation in *Jewish War*, where it might have been aligned with the beliefs and actions of the revolutionaries (Rajak, "Against Apion," 215); cf. similarities with the description of the fourth philosophy in *A.J.* 18.23.

50. Josephus's description of the cultic laws, part of the summary that he offers to demonstrate the superiority of Jewish law, is articulated in a mixture of present and future tense, but the future functions as a jussive, indicating the timelessness of the stipulations (Barclay, *Against Apion*, 279 n. 769; Gerber, *Ein Bild des Judentums*, 184–85). He also provides no indication of the current difficulties in implementing these stipulations in relation to sacrifice, given the lack of access to the altar.

51. Barclay's translation, modified for inclusive language; Rajak, "Against Apion," 206.

162 Kylie Crabbe

directed at the Jews to claim a compelling coherence at the heart of Jewish belief and practice.

In this way, Josephus's positive portrait of Jewish unity has wider implications for his attitude toward others. In *Against Apion*, unity stems from Jewish particularity.[52] It is absent from the religious framework of the Greeks (except in those shining examples of philosophers whose views on a monotheistic deity coincided, Josephus claims, with Moses's understanding; 2.168). As Christine Gerber notes, Josephus emphasizes the Jewish people's internal unity positively, rather than expressing the boundary between the community and others as a negative demarcation.[53] But the demarcation remains. What appears to be a benevolent hospitality to outsiders in this constitution reflects a call to join in the Jewish beliefs and practices: "to those who wish to come and live under the same laws as us he [Moses] gives a friendly welcome, reckoning that affinity [τὴν οἰκειότητα] is not only a matter of birth but also of choice in lifestyle" (2.210).[54] In this sense, what Josephus affirms is not harmony as an end necessarily in itself, achieved through consultation and negotiation, but as reflected in the unanimous practice of Jewish law (whose interpretation apparently leads to no differences of opinion).[55] When it comes to disagreement among different groups that all identify as Jewish elsewhere in Josephus's writings, he uses his calls to unity to make clear that harmony and unanimity should be achieved through agreement with his own perspective.

This is what Josephus explicitly exhorts in *Jewish War*, where his own character reveals his favored political position. Here, calling people to

---

52. Byers notes that Josephus's references to the one God, temple, altar, and Hebrew people "seems intended to emphasise an exclusive association," which makes the "social unity" of the people, as in the case of the other singular entities, "unique" (Byers, "One Body of the Shema," 521).

53. Gerber, *Ein Bild des Judentums*, 366; cf. 367–79.

54. The next line goes on to describe the deep sharing of the Jewish community as "our close company [συνηθείαι]" or "our intimate ways [συνηθείαις]" (2.210—on the textual variant see Barclay, who prefers the plural; *Against Apion*, 292 n. 848). Here Josephus is describing circumstances in which people would be excluded from the communion for seeking only a casual engagement.

55. Thompson observes: "The beauty of the law is seen in that harmony is maintained with foreigners without corrupting the law. The requirement, however, is that the foreigner must agree with the 'principles of conduct.'" Alan J. Thompson, *One Lord, One People: The Unity of the Church in Acts and Its Literary Setting*, LNTS 359 (London: T&T Clark, 2008), 54.

7. Oneness, Unity, and Josephus's Theological Politics 163

unity involves the historian in exerting a particular kind of power over others through his account, admonishing dissent and exhorting diverse voices to come together—by affirming *Josephus's* view on the best way forward. He uses the rhetoric of unity to confirm the blame for Jerusalem's destruction that he confers on the revolutionaries. The opposite of unity in *Jewish War* is the στάσις of the revolutionaries, and Josephus links the need to put this στάσις aside with a call to recognize the authority of Rome. This is core to the way he asserts both that throughout Israel's history God has supported those who do not take revolutionary action, and that rule comes from divine support, which is an even greater reason to refrain from opposing Rome.

Despite his positive treatment of Rome, however, Josephus's wider framing about divine control here, and throughout his works, ultimately relativizes Rome's position in the interests of Jewish priority. The Romans are instruments of the divine punishment of the Jewish people, whose circumstances will change. In the same speech in which his character affirms the rule of the stronger and divine punishment of the Jewish people for disunity and impiety (the *inverse* of their core traits in *Against Apion*), Josephus claims divine direction of the rotation through the empires: "Fortune [τὴν τύχην], indeed, had from all quarters passed over to them, and God [τὸν θεόν] who went the round of the nations, bringing to each in turn the rod of empire, now rested over Italy" (5.367).[56] Thus, at the same time as confirming the divine imperative of Rome's rule, Josephus emphasizes its time-limited nature; they enjoy rule "*now.*" In his later re-presentation of Daniel's prophecies in *A.J.* 10, Josephus will likewise situate Rome within the succession of empires, identifying its place as the penultimate empire in his discussion of Dan 8 (10.281), but resisting identifying the final events that Dan 2 prophesied would bring about the penultimate kingdom's end and install an unending divine reign (10.203–210).[57] Although anyone who is unclear on the implications arising from this coded reference is exhorted to consult the book of Daniel itself (10.210), Josephus praises Daniel for prophecy that is accurate in foretell-

---

56. Here he mirrors other texts that similarly view a succession of empires and the transition between empires being brought about by θεός or τύχη (see Crabbe, *Luke/ Acts and the End*, 57–134).

57. See discussion in Per Bilde, *Flavius Josephus, between Jerusalem and Rome: His Life, His Works, and Their Importance*, JSPSup 2 (Sheffield: JSOT Press, 1988), 187–88; Rajak, "Against Apion," 206.

ing not only events but also their timing (10.267), and seems to affirm this divine control of the transitions between empires unreservedly (cf. 10.277–280). While Rome does enjoy divine support "now," Josephus's readers should avoid στάσις and cooperate, knowing that the transition to divine reign will happen in God's own time.

Thus, although the claims about Jewish unity and disunity are different across Josephus's varied works, the purpose to which he puts these claims is strikingly similar. He presents a harmonious and unanimous ideal (from which his own community in *Jewish War* have clearly fallen short), which closes down diversity (either theoretically in *Against Apion* or as exhorted in *Jewish War*) at the same time as suggesting a way of coexisting with others (even if only until God takes decisive further action in the Jewish people's interest). The rhetoric about unity is related in different ways in both contexts to claims about divine control and to affirmations of Jewish priority.

7.5. Conclusion

Throughout his works Josephus gives attention to the virtue of unity in his mixed portraits of the Jewish people. In *Against Apion*, he describes unity as a virtue that is part of piety and core to Jewish belief and practice. It arises from shared practice of the law and reflects a principle of oneness at the heart of both God and temple (themes that he had already introduced in *A.J.* 4). The strong unity that holds together the Jewish community enables coexistence with others, as they are also inspired by Jewish concord and seek to emulate it. But in *Jewish War*, the Jewish people are instead characterized by both impiety and disunity. Josephus employs rhetoric about unity in order to demonstrate divine control over events; he blames the revolutionaries and exhorts his compatriots to turn away from στάσις through cooperation with Rome, recognizing their divine favor. Likewise, the underlying principle of unity from the singular God and temple in both *A.J.* 4 and *C. Ap.* 2 is distilled further in the latter into an affirmation of singular divine rule in theocracy, linking unity and oneness with divine oversight.

The connections between these ideas are made particularly clear in the closing section of *Against Apion*, where Josephus brings together concord, disdain for στάσις, and an assurance that those governed by the Jewish law may live amicably in their context knowing that, perhaps despite outward appearances, God is in charge. The description conflicts precisely with the

7. Oneness, Unity, and Josephus's Theological Politics   165

actual picture offered of the Jewish community in *Jewish War*, though it aligns with the behavior Josephus exhorts there.[58] It exemplifies Josephus's use of unity and its political effect:

> What could be more profitable than concord with one another [τί συμφορώτερον τοῦ πρὸς ἀλλήλους ὁμονοεῖν], and neither to fall out in adverse circumstances, nor in favourable ones to become violent and split into factions [μήτ᾽ ἐν συμφοραῖς διίστασθαι μήτ᾽ ἐν εὐτυχίαις στασιάζειν ἐξυβρίζοντας], but in war to despise death, and in peace to be diligent in crafts and agriculture, and to be convinced that God is in control, watching over everything everywhere? (2.294)

Bibliography

Barclay, John, ed. and trans. *Flavius Josephus: Against Apion*. FJTC 10. Leiden: Brill, 2006.

———. "Matching Theory and Practice: Josephus's Constitutional Ideal and Paul's Strategy in Corinth." Pages 139–63 in *Paul beyond the Judaism/Hellenism Divide*. Edited by Troels Engberg-Pedersen. Louisville: Westminster John Knox, 2001.

Bilde, Per. *Flavius Josephus, between Jerusalem and Rome: His Life, His Works, and Their Importance*. JSPSup 2. Sheffield: JSOT Press, 1988.

Byers, Andrew. "The One Body of the Shema in 1 Corinthians: An Ecclesiology of Christological Monotheism." *NTS* 62 (2016): 517–32.

Crabbe, Kylie. "Being Found Fighting against God: Luke's Gamaliel and Josephus on Human Responses to Divine Providence." *ZNW* 106 (2015): 21–39.

———. *Luke/Acts and the End of History*. BZNW 238. Berlin: de Gruyter, 2019.

Feldman, Louis H. *Flavius Josephus: Judean Antiquities, Books 1–4*. FJTC 3. Leiden: Brill, 1999.

Flavius Josephus. *Jewish War*. Translated by Henry St. John Thackeray. 3 vols. LCL. Cambridge: Harvard University Press, 1927–1928.

---

58. Barclay notes on this portrait of the Jewish people: "The claim to political unity is extraordinary. Falling out (διίστημι) and splitting into factions (στασιάζω) is precisely how Josephus describes the disintegration of the Judean nation before and during the Revolt; civic strife (στάσις) is a key theme in the narrative (e.g., *J.W.* 1.10, 25, 27). Here a political ideal overrides historical reality to a striking degree" (Barclay, *Against Apion*, 333 n. 1187).

Gerber, Christine. *Ein Bild des Judentums für Nichtjuden von Flavius Josephus: Untersuchungen zu seiner Schrift Contra Apionem*. AGJU 40. Leiden: Brill, 1997.

Griffin, Miraim T. "Tacitus as a Historian." Pages 168–83 in *The Cambridge Companion to Tacitus*. Edited by A. J. Woodman. Cambridge Companions to Literature. Cambridge: Cambridge University Press, 2009.

Klawans, Jonathan. "Josephus, the Rabbis, and Responses to Catastrophes Ancient and Modern." *JQR* 100 (2010): 278–309.

Klijn, A. F. J. "(Syriac Apocalypse of) Baruch." Pages 615–52 in *The Old Testament Pseudepigrapha*. Edited by James H. Charlesworth. 2 vols. ABRL. Garden City, NY: Doubleday, 1983.

Mason, Steve, ed. and trans. *Flavius Josephus: Judean War 2*. FJTC 1b. Leiden: Brill, 2008.

———. "Josephus's Pharisees: The Philosophy." Pages 41–66 in *In Quest of the Historical Pharisees*. Edited by Jacob Neusner and Bruce D. Chilton. Waco, TX: Baylor University Press, 2007.

Matthews, Lydia. "Roman Constructions of *Fortuna*." DPhil diss., University of Oxford, 2011.

Rajak, Tessa. "The *Against Apion* and the Continuities in Josephus' Political Thought." Pages 195–217 in *The Jewish Dialogue with Greece and Rome: Studies in Cultural and Social Interaction*. AGJU 48. Leiden: Brill, 2001.

———. "Friends, Romans, Subjects: Agrippa II's Speech in Josephus's Jewish War." Pages 122–34 in *Images of Empire*. Edited by Loveday Alexander. JSOTSup 122. Sheffield: JSOT Press, 1991.

Regev, Eyal. "Josephus, the Temple, and the Jewish War." Pages 279–93 in *Flavius Josephus: Interpretation and History*. Edited by Jack Pastor, Pnina Stern, and Menahem Mor. JSJSup 146. Leiden: Brill, 2011.

Sacks, Kenneth S. *Diodorus Siculus and the First Century*. Princeton: Princeton University Press, 1990.

Sterling, Gregory E. "Explaining Defeat: Polybius and Josephus on the Wars with Rome." Pages 135–51 in *Internationales Josephus-Kolloquium Aarhus 1999*. Edited by J. U. Kalms. Münsteraner Judaistische Studien 6. Münster: LIT, 2000.

Syme, Ronald. *Tacitus*. 2 vols. Oxford: Clarendon, 1958.

Tacitus. *Histories: Books 4–5; Annals; Books 1–3*. Translated by Clifford H. Moore and John Jackson. LCL. Cambridge: Cambridge University Press, 1931.

Thompson, Alan J. *One Lord, One People: The Unity of the Church in Acts and Its Literary Setting.* LNTS 359. London: T&T Clark, 2008.

Part 4
Oneness and Unity in the New Testament and Early Christianity

8

Jesus, the Shema, and Oneness in the Synoptic Gospels: The Formation of Early Christian Identity

Elizabeth E. Shively and Max Botner

The centrality of the Shema, the confession of God's oneness (Deut 6:4), is reflected in all three Synoptic Gospels.[1] The evangelists portray Jesus affirming the superlative place of the command to love God and love neighbor (Matt 22:36–38; Mark 12:29–30; Luke 10:27, 28). These portraits create common ground with Israel's tradition while also providing a foundation for the formation and maintenance of distinctly Christian piety and practice: the conviction that divine oneness entails the Lord God working through the Lord Christ. In what follows, we trace the ways in which the Synoptic evangelists intertwine a christological account of Israel's God with traditional expectations about covenantal piety (εὐσέβεια) and righteousness (διακιοσύνη), that is, devotion to the one God (Deut 6:4–5) and just behavior toward one's neighbor (Lev 19:18). Each evangelist adapts the Shema through the use of particular language, rhetoric, and narrative contexts. Attention to these adaptations shows how each writer, in his own way, recontextualizes and redefines the Shema and the command to love in light of the revelation of Jesus.

8.1. The Shema and the Ten Commandments: Piety and Justice in Early Judaism

Rabbinic literature attests to the identity-shaping function of the Shema. For example, the opening tractate of the Mishnah gives instructions

---

1. On the significance of the Shema in John's Gospel, see ch. 9 by Andrew Byers in the present volume.

-171-

about when to, how to, and who should recite the Shema in daily prayer (m. Ber. 1.1–4). Building on this tradition, the opening tractate of the Babylonian Talmud offers ways to recognize 'am ha-aretz (lit. "people of the land"), unobservant Jews, mainly by their failure to keep laws of purity and tithing; but also by their failure to follow a number of other observances such as wearing phylacteries, teaching their children the law, and reciting the Shema according to the prior instructions: "Our Rabbis taught, Who is an 'am ha-aretz? Anyone who does not recite the Shema evening and morning" (b. Ber. 47b). Conversely, then, we can assume that anyone who does recite the Shema evening and morning is recognized as a devout member of the community. Thus, from an early stage in rabbinic writings, recitation of the Shema, among other practices, functions to shape a certain identity.[2]

Religious practice in Second Temple Judaism would have provided an important antecedent for this later rabbinic teaching.[3] For example, Philo and Josephus mention twice-daily prayer in the context of injunctions to create *tephillin* and *mezuzot* (cf. Deut 6:8–9; Philo, *Spec.* 4.141–142; Josephus, *A.J.* 4.212–213); it seems plausible these prayers included the Shema. In addition, the Synoptic Gospels attest to the importance of the Shema and its identity-shaping function, which may presuppose its use in liturgical contexts.[4]

Most notably, Jesus combines Deut 6:4–5 with Lev 19:18 to place love of neighbor alongside love for God, grounded in God's oneness (Mark 12:29–32 and parr.). For the Markan Jesus, the Shema generates the identity-shaping practice of those who would enter God's reign. When the scribe affirms God's oneness and the indispensability of love for God

---

2. Sarit Kattan Gribetz, "The Shema in the Second Temple Period: A Reconsideration," *JAJ* 6 (2015): 84 n. 80.

3. This is the case, though the earliest literary evidence of the standardized use of the Shema in worship appears in Tannaitic sources; see Paul Foster, "Why Did Matthew Get the Shema Wrong? A Study of Matthew 22:37," *JBL* 122 (2003): 321–31; Gribetz, "Shema," 82–84. See also the nuanced discussion in David Instone-Brewer, *Prayer and Agriculture*, vol. 1 of *Traditions of the Rabbis from the Era of the New Testament* (Grand Rapids: Eerdmans, 2004).

4. E.g., Joel Marcus argues that the liturgical use of the Shema explains its placement in the controversy cycle in the temple; see Marcus, "Authority to Forgive Sins upon the Earth: The *Shema* in the Gospel of Mark," in *The Gospels and the Scriptures of Israel*, ed. Craig Evans and W. Richard Stegner, JSNTSup 104 (Sheffield: Sheffield Academic, 1994), 197. This may be the case, but it is impossible to verify.

8. Jesus, the Shema, and Oneness in the Synoptic Gospels 173

and neighbor, Jesus responds, "you are not far from the reign [βασιλεία] of God" (Mark 12:34).[5] We will address the nature and identity-shaping function of Jesus's words later. For now, it is crucial to note that Jesus's interlocutor understands his statement and repeats his words back to him with interpretation. This suggests that the fusion of Deut 6:4–5 and Lev 19:18 did not originate with the evangelists or Jesus.[6] Rather, such appears to have been a matter of self-evidence for at least some first-century Jews.

A look at contemporaneous literature substantiates this assessment.[7] Ample evidence shows that Jews of the late Second Temple period assumed the Ten Commandments summarized their covenantal obligations, which they divided into two sets of five, the two tablets of the law (cf. Deut 32:15; LAB 12.10): laws concerning "piety" (εὐσέβεια) or "holiness" (ὁσιότης) toward the Jewish God (Deut 6:5), and those concerning

---

5. Unless otherwise noted, all translations are ours.

6. Cf. Jub. 36.7–8: "Now I will make you swear with the great oath—because there is no oath which is greater than it, by the praiseworthy, illustrious, and great, splendid, marvelous, powerful, and great name which made the heavens and the earth and everything together—that you will continue to fear and worship him, as each loves his brother kindly and properly" (trans. James C. VanderKam, *The Book of Jubilees*, CSCO 511 [Leuven: Peeters, 1989], 238). While the writer is clearly interested in Lev 19:17–18 (cf. Jub. 7.20; 20.2; 36.4), it is not clear that Deut 6:4–5 is the source of the "great oath" or the injunction, "continue to fear and worship him"; see James C. VanderKam, *Jubilees 2: A Commentary on the Book of Jubilees Chapters 22–50*, Hermeneia (Minneapolis: Fortress, 2018), 960 n. 11. There are a number of texts in the Testaments of the Twelve Patriarchs that combine love for God and love for neighbor (cf. T. Iss. 5.2; 7.6; T. Dan. 5.3; T. Naph. 8.9–10; T. Benj. 3.3); on which see Marinus de Jonge, "The Two Great Commandments in the Testaments of the Twelve Patriarchs," *NovT* 44 (2002): 371–92. We cannot assume, however, that these fusions are pre-Christian, since the Testaments of the Twelve Patriarchs is demonstrably a Christian composition; see de Jonge, *The Testament of the Twelve Patriarchs: A Study of Their Text, Composition, and Origin*, Theologische Bibliotheek 25 (Assen: Van Gorcum, 1953); de Jonge, *Pseudepigrapha of the Old Testament as Part of Christian Literature: The Case of the Testaments of the Twelve Patriarchs and the Greek Life of Adam and Eve*, SVTP 18 (Leiden: Brill, 2003). On the methodological issues with treating texts such as the Testaments of the Twelve Patriarchs as Jewish with only minor Christian interpolations, see esp. James R. Davila, *The Provenance of the Pseudepigraph: Jewish, Christian, or Other?*, JSJSup 105 (Leiden: Brill, 2005).

7. See esp. Dale Allison, "Mark 12.28–31 and the Decalogue," in *The Gospels and the Scriptures of Israel*, ed. Craig Evans and W. Richard Stegner, JSNTSup 104 (Sheffield: Sheffield Academic, 1994), 270–78; Allison, *Resurrecting Jesus: The Earliest Christian Tradition and Its Interpreters* (London: T&T Clark, 2005), 149–65.

"justice/righteousness" (διαχιοσύνη) toward fellow citizens/neighbors (Lev 19:18).[8] Philo claims, for example, that the principal demands of the law of Moses, as articulated in the Ten Commandments, are "to God through piety and holiness [πρὸς θεὸν δἰ εὐσέβειας καὶ ὁσιότητος]" and "to humans through humanity and righteousness [πρὸς ἀνθρώπους διὰ φιλανθρωπίας καὶ διαχιοσύνης]" (*Spec.* 2.63; cf. *Prob.* 84; *Virt.* 51). Elsewhere, he concedes the possibility that someone might achieve the one without the other, thus, one can be either a lover of God (φιλόθεος) or a lover of humans (φιλάνθρωπος). Yet, in each case, "Both come but halfway in virtue [ἀρετή]." "They only have it whole," says Philo, "who win honor in both departments" (*Decal.* 110). This is, in fact, the norm: "for it belongs to the same character to be pious [εὐσεβής] and a lover of humans [φιλάνθρωπος]; and both these qualities, of holiness toward God and justice toward humans [ὁσιότης μὲν πρὸς θεόν, διαχιοσύνη δὲ πρὸς ἀνθρώπους], are commonly seen in the same individual" (*Abr.* 208). Thus, the expression of the full demands of the law necessarily combine love for God and love for neighbor.

Josephus, likewise, articulates Israel's *politeia* in terms of "piety" (εὐσέβεια) and "righteousness" (διαχιοσύνη). The historian notes that before someone could partake of the communal meal of the Essenes, for instance, the initiate must swear an oath: "first, that he will practice piety toward the deity [πρῶτον μὲν εὐσεβήσειν τὸ θεῖον], next, that he will observe righteousness toward humans [ἔπειτα τὰ πρὸς ἀνθρώπους δίκαια φυλάξειν]" (*B.J.* 2.139). John the Baptist apparently demanded the same from his initiates: to exercise "virtue" (ἀρετή) by acting "righteously toward one another [πρὸς ἀλλήλους δικαιοσύνῃ]" and "piously toward God [πρὸς τὸν θεὸν εὐσεβείᾳ]" (*A.J.* 18.117).

Though neither Philo nor Josephus employs Deut 6:4–5 and Lev 19:18 in their discussions of the Ten Commandments, each writer, not surprisingly, anchors Jewish piety in the Shema (cf. Philo, *Dec.* 65; Jose-

---

8. An array of texts evinces the general consensus that Lev 19:18 summarized the covenant command for communal righteousness (cf. Tob 4:15; Sir 17:14; 19:13–17; CD VII, 2–3; Matt 5:21–26, 43–48; Rom 13:9; Gal 5:14–15; Jas 2:8–13; Did. 1.2). The command to love one's neighbor is often interpreted with recourse to the immediate context; thus to "love" one's neighbor might be to "reprove" him/her (Lev 19:17) and/ or to avoid retaliation or bearing a grudge (19:18); see James L. Kugel, "On Hidden Hatred and Open Reproach: Early Exegesis of Leviticus 19:17," *HTR* 80 (1987): 43–61; Jacob Milgrom, *Leviticus 17–22: A New Translation with Introduction and Commentary*, AB 3A (New York: Doubleday, 2000), 1646–56.

8. Jesus, the Shema, and Oneness in the Synoptic Gospels

phus, *A.J.* 3.91). Yet their insistence that the virtuous end (ἀρετή) of the torah is the double command of εὐσέβεια and διαχιοσύνη appears to be an attempt to translate the vertical and horizontal demands of the torah into widely recognized categories (cf. Let. Aris. 228–235). The Synoptic Gospels recapitulate these demands by collocating Deut 6:4–5 and Lev 19:18: the former appositely articulates the basis of Jewish piety, that is, devotion to the one God, while the latter effectively safeguards communal justice, that is, love for one's neighbor.

8.2. Honoring the One God in the Gospel according to Mark

Mark is unique among the Synoptic evangelists in including the Shema (Deut 6:4) in his recitation of the double love command (Mark 12:29–30).[9] While it may go too far to suggest, as Joel Marcus does, that "the emphasis on the oneness of God is not as important [for Matthew and Luke] as it is for Mark," he is undoubtedly correct that this is a point of utmost concern for the evangelist.[10] Marcus points to two instances in the Second Gospel where the evangelist marks an exception clause (εἰ μή) followed by an allusion to the Shema (εἷς ὁ θεός): the first is placed on the lips of Jewish scribes (2:7), while the second is from the mouth of Jesus (10:18).[11] Taken together with 12:28–34, these three statements underscore the Markan conviction that the Shema—the confession that Israel's God is *one*—entails *two* Lords, the Lord God and the Lord Christ (cf. Mark 5:19–20).[12] We begin with the clearest articulation of the Shema of

---

9. In the interim between the submission this essay and the publication of the present volume, John J. R. Lee published a revised version of his 2011 PhD dissertation (*Christological Rereading of the Shema [Deut 6.4] in Mark's Gospel*, WUNT 2/533 [Tübingen: Mohr Siebeck, 2020]). We are in agreement with Lee that Mark's oneness language presses the audience to reimagine the identity of Israel's God in light of the revelation of Jesus. Ours, however, is a different research question: not Christology in isolation but the intersection of Christology and communal identity.

10. Marcus, "Authority," 197 n. 3.

11. Marcus, "Authority," 197.

12. On the significance of Ps 110 for early Christology, see Richard Bauckham, *Jesus and the God of Israel: God Crucified and Other Studies on the New Testament's Christology of Divine Identity* (Grand Rapids: Eerdmans, 2008), 173. On the Markan narrative construction of Jesus's identity as Lord, see Daniel Johansson, "*Kyrios* in the Gospel of Mark," *JSNT* 33 (2010): 101–24; and now esp. Jan Rüggemeier, *Poetik der markinischen Christologie: Eine kognitiv-narratologische Exegese*, WUNT 2/458 (Tübingen: Mohr Siebeck, 2017).

176 Elizabeth E. Shively and Max Botner

these three passages, 12:28–34, then ask what light it sheds on the earlier statements in 2:7 and 10:18.

The fusion in Mark 12:28–34 of God's oneness with the double love command is emphasized when the inquisitive scribe affirmingly repeats everything Jesus has said, even tacking on the additional comment that love of God and neighbor is "much more important than all whole burnt offerings and sacrifices" (12:33). But the scribe still lacks something: "You are not far from the kingdom of God," Jesus answers (12:34). That is to say, the scribe understands *what* the kingdom requires but he does not yet know *how* to enact these commandments that he knows are of first order. The *crux interpretum* lies in the adjacent pericope, the so-called *Davidssohnfrage* (12:35–37). Herein the Markan Jesus invites the audience to juxtapose the one Lord (κύριος εἷς ἐστιν) of the Shema (12:29) with the two Lords of Ps 110:1, "The Lord said to my Lord [εἶπεν κύριος τῷ κυρίῳ μου], 'Sit at my right hand until I put your enemies under your feet'" (12:36). The narrator's aside that the crowd "heard him [Jesus] with delight [ἤκουεν αὐτοῦ ἡδέως]" (12:37) echoes the imperative of the Shema, "Hear [ἄκουε], O Israel" (12:29), further reinforcing the connection between these two passages.[13] Thus the kingdom reality after which the scribe grasps is based on the recognition that the rule of the one God is manifest in a *second* Lord, the Messiah, who is not only a descendant of David but also the Son of God.[14]

Yet Mark's interest in the Shema is not only christological, but also ecclesiological. The evangelist is interested in how his account of the Shema bears upon the identity and practice of the Lord's community. A careful look at the language, grammar, and logic of Mark 12:28–34 bears this out. The scribe approaches Jesus and asks, "Which commandment is *first of all* [πρώτη πάντων]?" Presumably, the scribe is not asking for Jesus to name the first in order, but to name the first in importance.[15] The point is that

---

13. Lori Baron, "The Shema in Mark and John and the Parting of the Ways," in *The Ways That Often Parted: Essays in Honor of Joel Marcus*, ed. Lori Baron, Jill Hicks-Keeton, and Matthew Thiessen, ECL 24 (Atlanta: SBL Press, 2018), 191–92.

14. *Pace* Joel Marcus (*The Way of the Lord: Christological Exegesis of the Old Testament in the Gospel of Mark* [Louisville: Westminster John Knox, 1992], 139–45) we do not think Mark treats Davidic and divine sonship as a zero-sum competition; see Max Botner, *Jesus Christ as the Son of David in the Gospel of Mark*, SNTSMS 174 (Cambridge: Cambridge University Press, 2019).

15. This interpretation is supported by the observation that Matthew evidently interprets Mark this way in Matt 22:36, "which commandment of the law is the greatest

8. Jesus, the Shema, and Oneness in the Synoptic Gospels   177

the scribe wants Jesus to name the *one* command that is *greater* than all the rest. The Markan Jesus's expanded response, however, redefines what is πρώτη πάντων. He begins by stating that the *first* (πρώτη) commandment is the injunction to hear that God is one and to love the Lord your God with all your heart, soul, mind, and strength (Deut 6:4–5).[16] (The scribe's subsequent elaboration—"besides him there is no other" [12:33]—understands the Shema to be an affirmation of monotheism.) Then, Jesus groups with it the *second* (δευτέρα) command to love your neighbor as yourself (Lev 19:18). Finally, Jesus summarizes, "there is no other commandment greater *than these* [μείζων τούτων]" (12:31). In other words, it is not one commandment but *these two commandments together* that are first (that is, greatest) of all. The grammar and logic of the passage thus confirms what the collocation of Deut 6:4–5 and Lev 19:18 implies: acknowledgment of God's oneness is bound up with εὐσέβεια and διακιοσύνη; in other words, devotion to the one God and just behavior toward one's neighbor. On this point Jesus and the scribe agree. Yet Jesus concludes that the scribe still lacks what is needed to enact the double love commandment precisely because covenantal identity hinges on recognizing that Jesus is not merely a teacher (διδάσκαλος, 12:32) but the Lord Christ, the one in and through whom God's oneness is explained.

Additional observations strengthen this assertion. First, Mark alone includes the scribal response that love for God and neighbor "is more

---

[μεγάλη]." In this context, the term μεγάλη, "great," effectively means "greatest." Elsewhere, Matthew uses μεγάλη as opposite of ἐλάχιστος (5:19); see discussion in R. T. France, *The Gospel of Matthew,* NICNT (Grand Rapids: Eerdmans, 2007), 844–45.

16. The Markan version of Deut 6:5 is difficult to pin down. On the one hand, Mark's use of the preposition ἐκ shares an affinity with Deut 6:5 LXX, where the translator made the decision to render the Hebrew preposition ב as marking the *source* of love. On the other hand, Mark's list of *four* attributes (καρδία, ψυχή, διανοία, and ἰσχύς) goes against our best extant manuscripts, which attest to a threefold division in Deut 6:5. John William Wevers's reconstruction of the Old Greek (διανοία, ψυχή, and δύναμις) suggests the translator's *Vorlage* matched the threefold division in our MT: לבב, נפש, and מאד; see Wevers, *Deuteronomium,* SVTG 3.2 (Göttingen: Vandenhoeck & Ruprecht, 1977), 120. We should also note that the Greek manuscript tradition attests to the use of both διανοία (B Mᵐᵍ 963 108ᵐᵍ f¹²⁹ n⁴⁵⁸ 85ᵐᵍ-321 ′ᵐᵍ-344ᵐᵍ z¹⁸ ⁸³ 509 Tht Dtᵃᵖ Bo) and καρδία (א A Majority Text) as translation equivalents of לבב. Wevers opts for διανοία no doubt in part because it is "the much rarer rendering of לבב" (Wevers, *Notes on the Greek Texts of Deuteronomy,* SCS 39 [Atlanta: Scholars Press, 1995], 115).

178 Elizabeth E. Shively and Max Botner

important than all the whole burnt offerings and sacrifices" (12:33). While the scribe's response is itself unremarkable—What Jew or Greek thought a god would rejoice in a sacrifice from an unethical source?—it underscores the possibility that the central mandate of covenantal identity might continue even in the absence of a temple.[17] The Markan Jesus apparently commends this line of thinking (12:34). Second, the final scene in the temple does not concern Christology but justice. While the scribes claim to honor the one God, they use εὐσέβεια as a pretense to subvert the demands of διαχιοσύνη (12:38–40; cf. Mark 7:8–13); in fact, the temple itself, the dwelling place of the divine name and presence, has become the site of social and economic injustice (12:41–44; cf. 11:15–18). Thus, the one to whom God says, "Sit [κάθου] at my right hand" (12:36), now "sits" (καθίσας, 12:41) in judgment over the rich donors as well as those scribes who claim "the best seats" (πρωτοκαθεδρίαι, 12:39) in the synagogues.

Mark's previous allusions to the Shema (in 2:7 and 10:18) are equally, though more subtly, concerned with the conviction that acknowledging God's oneness in christological terms is bound up with devotion to the one God and just behavior toward one's neighbor. Mark 2:7 occurs in an episode that introduces a series of controversies over authority to forgive sins, table fellowship, and Sabbath law (2:1–3:6). In 2:1–12, Jesus addresses a man's need to be released not only from paralysis but also from sin, and the responding hardness of his opponent's hearts. The scribal deliberation that no one can forgive sins "except the one God" (εἰ μὴ εἷς ὁ θεός) is a clear indication of two things. First, the scribes recognize Jesus's claim to do what only Israel's God can do.[18] But second, they lack the requisite

---

17. The notion that the Jewish God rejoices in εὐσέβεια and διαχιοσύνη more than sacrifices is in keeping with the psalmists and prophets and is hardly antisacrificial; see esp. Jonathan Klawans, *Purity, Sacrifice, and the Temple: Symbolism and Supersessionism in the Study of Ancient Judaism* (Oxford: Oxford University Press, 2006), 75–100. Greeks were no different than Jews in presuming that a god's acceptance of a sacrificial gift was contingent upon the probity of the worshiper. See F. S. Naiden, *Smoke Signals for the Gods: Ancient Greek Sacrifice from the Archaic through Roman Periods* (Oxford: Oxford University Press, 2013), 154–55.

18. We agree with Marcus that Dan 7:13 informs the logic of the passage: the Son of Man has received all authority from the Ancient of Days and, therefore, has the *authority* to forgive sins *on earth* (2:10) (Marcus, "Authority," 201–5). In fact, the blasphemy charge in 2:7 forms an *inclusio* with the charge of blasphemy at Jesus's trial in 14:64, wherein he identifies himself as the Danielic figure who approaches the Ancient of Days. Certainly, the christological implications of this pericope are

8. Jesus, the Shema, and Oneness in the Synoptic Gospels 179

christological interpretation of the Shema that would allow them to identify Jesus's authority with that of the one God, which prevents them from rejoicing in the man's release from sin. Knowing their hearts, Jesus gives them a sign of his authority by healing the man, prefacing this healing with the words, "that you may know that the Son of Man has authority on earth to forgive sins" (2:10).

Mark does not say how the scribes respond to this particular healing; but he does narrate an ensuing series of controversy stories that culminate with Jesus's Sabbath healing of a man with a withered hand (3:1–6). Kurt Queller identifies this as a "chiastically parallel story" to ours in 2:1–12.[19] In 2:1–12, the controversy is over Jesus's authority to forgive sins; in 3:1–6, the controversy is about proper practice on the Sabbath. In both cases, Jesus's opponents maintain hard-hearted silence, to which he responds with knowledge and grief.[20] In the final controversy, Jesus's opponents wait to see if he will heal the man with the withered hand, and he responds, "Is it lawful on the Sabbath to do good or to do harm, to save a life or to kill?" Queller argues that with this answer, Jesus sharpens a covenantal choice between good and evil "into one between *doing* good and *doing* evil, and that between life and death into one between actively *saving* life and *killing*."[21] That is, "'killing' refers primarily to the choice *not* to extend the hand in active Sabbatarian release."[22] If this is so, then Jesus exposes a failure to act justly toward one's neighbor rooted in the failure to acknowledge Jesus's authority as Lord of the Sabbath. We suggest that the scribal protest in 2:7 stems from the same epistemic failure: a recalcitrance to the reality that the Lord God is at work through the Lord Jesus. This miscalculation disrupts the scribes' devotion to the one God and, precisely for that reason, incapacitates their ability to respond to their neighbor in love.

---

immense; though it appears the evangelist is up to something a bit more subtle than a straightforward identification of Jesus and God; *pace* Otfried Hofius, *Neutestamentliche Studien*, WUNT 132 (Tübingen: Mohr Siebeck, 2000) 38–56, 57–69. Matthew's redaction of his Markan source may be instructive: the point is that God has designated this authority τοῖς ἀνθρώποις, "to human beings" (Matt 9:8).

19. Queller, "'Stretch Out Your Hand': Echo and Metalepsis in Mark's Sabbath Healing," *JBL* 129 (2010): 737–58; see also Joanna Dewey's classic study, "The Literary Structure of the Controversy Stories in Mark 2:1–3:6," *JBL* 92 (1973): 394–401.

20. See also Queller, "'Stretch Out Your Hand,'" 752–53.

21. Queller, "'Stretch Out Your Hand,'" 752.

22. Queller, "'Stretch Out Your Hand,'" 752.

180 Elizabeth E. Shively and Max Botner

In the second case (10:17–22), a man approaches Jesus and asks the "good teacher" how he can inherit eternal life. Jesus responds, "Why do you call me good? No one is good except the one God [εἰ μὴ εἷς ὁ θεός]" (10:18). Marcus draws attention to the christological force of the allusion to the Shema in this verse:

> The Markan Jesus ... is challenging the man to attain a Christological insight, the realization that Jesus is good because God is good, and that Jesus as the Son of God, the earthly representative of the heavenly king, and the one indwelt by God's name, participates in the goodness of God's reign and manifests it eschatologically upon the earth. His goodness does not impugn the radicalized form of the *Shema* that attributes goodness only to God, because his goodness *is* God's goodness.[23]

Yet when the man addresses Jesus the second time, he drops the label "good" and instead addresses Jesus as "teacher" (διδάσκαλος, 10:20). Like the scribe in the temple, then, he lacks the christological interpretation of the Shema and so the requisite framework for maintaining εὐσέβεια and διακιοσύνη.

A closer look at the passage supports this point. The episode moves from a question about the nature of the one God (10:18) to the question of how the man is to follow the one God (10:19). Unsurprisingly, Jesus turns to the second table of the Ten Commandments, those concerning διακιοσύνη, which he later summarizes with the command, "love your neighbor as yourself" (Lev 19:18 in Mark 12:31). The young man's self-confidence, "all these I have guarded since my youth," is not struck down in ire but contested with love: Jesus looked at his misguided neighbor and *loved* him (ἠγάπησεν αὐτόν, 10:21). Like the scribe we meet later in the temple, this man appears to understand what is required for gaining eternal life, yet he still lacks something. Jesus might have said to this man, too, "You are not far from the kingdom of God." Instead, he exposes what the man lacks by challenging him to enact εὐσέβεια and διακιοσύνη by selling all he has, giving it to the poor, and *following him*. Mark mentions the man's wealth only at the very end of this account, and it is at this point that we feel the rhetorical impact of the comment, "he was shocked and went away grieving, for he had great possessions" (10:22). The man is unable to

---

23. Marcus, "Authority," 209–10, emphasis original. On the connection of the attribute of "goodness" to God alone, cf. Philo, *Leg.* 2:1.

8. Jesus, the Shema, and Oneness in the Synoptic Gospels   181

realize the extent to which Jesus is good and, therefore, chooses to keep the world and forfeit his soul (cf. 8:34–38). His response is illustrative of the reality that money and wealth provide an additional, and indeed almost insurmountable, obstacle in the path of those who would seek to guard covenantal righteousness.

Rather than treat Mark's interest in the Shema as an isolated issue of Christology, it seems more accurate to say that the evangelist envisages covenantal εὐσέβεια and διακιοσύνη intersecting in the person of Jesus. As διακιοσύνη flows from reimaging εὐσέβεια in light of the Christ event, so christological εὐσέβεια underscores and upholds the deep structure of διακιοσύνη. Mark would no doubt agree with Philo that "it belongs to the same character to be pious [ευσεβής] and a lover of humans [φιλάνθρωπος]" (*Abr.* 208). Indeed, failure to recognize the one God in and through the crucified Messiah receives the same Markan condemnation as failure to uphold the just requirements of the torah: one has chosen to reject the ways of God for the ways of human beings (7:8; 8:33).

8.3. Imitating the One God in the Gospel according to Matthew

The double love command appears in Matt 22:34–40, the parallel episode to Mark 12:28–34. There, a scribe representing a group of Pharisees comes to test Jesus (Matt 22:35).[24] He asks which commandment of the law is the great(est) (μεγάλη, 22:36), and Jesus immediately responds, "you shall love the Lord your God with all your heart, soul, and mind" (22:37; Deut 6:5). The Matthean Jesus omits the first part of the Shema (Deut 6:4), that which affirms the oneness of God.[25] Then, he summarizes that this one command to love God is the great(est) (μεγάλη) and first (πρώτη) command (22:38).

---

24. Matthew is unique in identifying Jesus's interlocutors as a group of Pharisees (cf. Mark 12:28; Luke 10:25) and in identifying the crowd to whom he poses the *Davidssohnfrage* as a gathering of Pharisees (cf. Mark 12:35; Luke 20:41). This paves the way for the Matthean invective against the Pharisees in Matt 23. See W. D. Davies and Dale C. Allison, Jr., *Commentary on Matthew XIX–XXVIII*, vol. 3 of *The Gospel according to Saint Matthew*, ICC (Edinburgh: T&T Clark, 1997), 266.

25. Foster compares the Synoptic versions and names the "the two most striking differences between the forms of the quotation" as the varying order and number of attributes and the varying use of prepositions (ἐx and/or ἐν, respectively). Yet he overlooks the fact that the most significant difference between Mark's version, on the one hand, and Matthew's and Luke's, on the other, is that the latter *omit* the first part of the Shema, Deut 6:4 (Foster, "Why Did Matthew Get the Shema Wrong?," 314).

182 Elizabeth E. Shively and Max Botner

Yet he adds that the second command, "you shall love your neighbor as yourself," is "like it" (ὁμοία αὐτῇ, 22:39).

The Matthean Jesus's language of likeness is reinforced by the parallel grammar and syntax of his commands:

| 10:37 | ἀγαπήσεις κύριον τὸν θεόν σου | love the Lord your God |
| 10:39 | ἀγαπήσεις τὸν πλησίον σου | love your neighbor |

Together, the language, grammar, and syntax strengthen the idea that the second command shares the importance and authority of the first. As a result, Jesus expands the scribe's viewpoint to embrace something more exhaustive and radical than he was likely expecting. That is, while the scribe had asked Jesus which *one commandment of the law* is the most important, Jesus replies that these *two commands to love God and neighbor* epitomize *all the law and the prophets* (22:40). Thus, even though Matthew excludes the explicit statement of God's oneness, he fuses the commands to love God and neighbor so as to retain and rework Mark's christological framework for maintaining εὐσέβεια and διακιοσύνη.

Unlike Mark, Matthew has no interest in painting a Pharisaic scribe in a positive light (cf. Mark 12:34). While Matthew no doubt agrees with his predecessor that piety and justice are superior to cultic sacrifice (cf. Matt 12:7), he sees no reason to praise the group he is about to lambast. In addition, Matthew's omission of the first part of the Shema undoes the Markan link between this pericope (Matt 22:34–40) and the *Davidssohnfrage* (22:41–46). Thus, while the Matthean audience still must reconcile the categories "son of David" and "lord of David" (the two are held together in the "son of God") they do not encounter what is perhaps Mark's greatest riddle: the one Lord of the Shema versus the two Lords of Ps 110.[26] This does not necessarily indicate that Matthew is less interested than Mark in a christological interpretation of God's oneness. In fact, Matthew is more than capable of showing that the one God is encountered in and through Jesus Christ (cf. 1:23).[27] Instead, the contrast suggests that Matthew's interest in the double love command differs from Mark's.

---

26. For the two being held together, see David M. Hay, *Glory at the Right Hand: Psalm 110 in Early Christianity*, SBLMS 18 (Atlanta: Scholars Press, 1989), 116–17.

27. See Richard B. Hays, *Echoes of Scripture in the Gospels* (Waco, TX: Baylor University Press, 2016), 162–75.

8. Jesus, the Shema, and Oneness in the Synoptic Gospels 183

The interpretive key, we suggest, is the Matthean Jesus's insistence that these two commandments, together, underpin *all the law and the prophets* (ὅλος ὁ νόμος κρέμαται καὶ οἱ προφῆται, 22:40).[28] In itself this position is not unique. Philo could summarize the law as love for God and for one's fellow human (*Spec.* 2.63), and the rabbis would use different verses, including Lev 19:18 (b. Shabb. 31a), as devices to articulate the *raison d'être* of the commandments. Yet, as Terence Donaldson notes, "the rabbis were interested in summary statements for pedagogical purposes, but Matthew has made this summary statement a norm and source for halakah."[29] Nowhere is this principle clearer than in the Sermon on the Mount (5:1–7:29).

Matthew places that lengthy discourse toward the beginning of Jesus's public ministry, emphasizing that Jesus is the authoritative teacher of God's torah for God's people. At the outset, Jesus frames his halakah with the declaration: "Do not think that I have come to abolish the law or the prophets; I have come not to abolish but to fulfill [them; οὐκ ἦλθον καταλῦσαι ἀλλὰ πληρῶσαι]" (5:17). The crux of the saying is the verb πληρόω, "fulfill," which has been interpreted in diverse ways.[30] We take it that the verb puts the emphasis on the person of Jesus as the hermeneutical center of scripture interpretation (cf. Matt 1:22; 2:15, 17, 23). Thus, Matthew's primary concern is to portray Jesus as he who reorients love for the one God around devotion to himself. The evangelist reinforces this concern through the antitheses that follow. Throughout, Jesus speaks with divine authority to interpret the law in light of the manifestation of the inbreaking of the kingdom of heaven. As Ulrich Luz comments, "God's will, as proclaimed in the Sermon on the Mount, is not simply an abstract command; it is the command of that same God who accompanies his people in the form of Jesus."[31]

What Mark had made explicit through the use of oneness language Matthew interprets implicitly for his purpose, which is to convey that to acknowledge the word of the Lord Christ is to acknowledge the word of

---

28. Terence L. Donaldson, "The Law That Hangs (Matthew 22:40): Rabbinic Formulation and Matthean Social World," *CBQ* 57 (1995): 689–709.

29. Donaldson, "Law That Hangs," 694.

30. See W. D. Davies and Dale C. Allison Jr., *Introduction and Commentary on Matthew I–VII*, vol. 1 of *The Gospel according to Saint Matthew*, ICC (Edinburgh: T&T Clark, 1988), 484–87.

31. Luz, *The Theology of the Gospel of Matthew*, New Testament Theology (Cambridge: Cambridge University Press, 1995), 48.

184 Elizabeth E. Shively and Max Botner

the Lord God. In some instances, this leads to halakic intensification of the law (5:21–26; 27–30); in others, it suggests that certain commandments have been abrogated (5:38–42).[32] Yet throughout, Matthew maintains that the authority of Jesus is the only means by which divine instruction of the old is brought to its *telos*. The kingdom of heaven is for those whose righteousness (δικαιοσύνη) surpasses that of the scribes and the Pharisees (5:20; cf. 23:3, 23). Such δικαιοσύνη is only available to those who refract the wisdom of the law through the life and teachings of Jesus.

This point is illustrated by Matthew's version of Jesus's encounter with the young man who inquires after eternal life (19:16–22). The Matthean Jesus demonstrates how the second table of the Ten Commandments, those concerned with covenantal δικαιοσύνη, are undergirded by Lev 19:18 (vv. 18–19).[33] The teachings themselves are not particularly novel. For example, the notion that harboring anger toward a brother or sister is a short step from retaliation (cf. Matt 5:22) is one of the chief concerns of ancient interpreters of Lev 19:18.[34] The Damascus Document includes an allusion to Lev 19:18 in a section that resonates with many of the themes of Matt 5:21–48:

> [The torah requires] to love each man his brother as himself [לאהוב איש את אחיהו כמהו], to support the poor, destitute, and proselyte, and to seek

---

32. James Crossley makes an important distinction between violent and nonviolent interpretations of the *lex talionis*; Crossley, "Matthew and the Torah: Jesus as Legal Interpreter," in *Matthew within Judaism: Israel and the Nations in the First Gospel*, ed. Anders Runesson and Daniel M. Gurtner, ECL 27 (Atlanta: SBL Press, 2020), 36–38. We agree that Matthew never presents Jesus in "flat contradiction *of the torah*" (given the nature of early Jewish halakah, one wonders whether such language is even helpful), but to say that this pericope "only makes judgment on the violent interpretation" (38) does not square with the language in 5:40–42.

33. Matthew more or less maintains Mark's story of the rich young ruler. Note, however, that Matthew adds the summary statement, "you shall love your neighbor as yourself" (19:19). This is another clear indication that the evangelist understands Lev 19:18 as a summary of the second table of the Ten Commandments.

34. In keeping with Lev 19:17–18, many interpreters conclude that "reproach" and "forgiveness" is an antidote to anger, hatred, or retaliation (cf. Sir 20:2; 28:1–7; 1QS V, 24–VI, 1; CD IX, 2–8; T. Gad 6.1–5; Sifra Lev. 19.17). Kugel notes similarities between the Qumranic interpretation of Lev 19:17–18 and the Matthean instructions for community discipline (Matt 18:15) (Kugel, "On Hidden Hatred," 55). We find it plausible that all of Matthew's commands concerning "forgiveness" (6:14–15; 18:21–22) and mercy (12:7; 23:3) reflect his particular interpretation of Lev 19:18.

8. Jesus, the Shema, and Oneness in the Synoptic Gospels   185

each man the peace of his brother [ולדרוש איש את שלום אחיהו]. And let
no man trespass with regard to his near kin; (rather, let him) stay away
from unchastity in accordance with the precept; let each man rebuke
his brother in accordance with the ordinance and not keep a grudge
from one day to the next. And let him separate himself from all impuri-
ties, according to their precepts; and let no man defile his holy spirit as
God distinguished them. All those who walk in these in perfect holiness
[בתמים קדש] (and) are governed according to all (these things), God's
covenant is an assurance to them. (CD VI, 20–VII, 5)[35]

The Matthean Jesus also wants his audience to be "perfect" (τέλειος) in
the arena of communal holiness. The injunction, "Be perfect, therefore, as
your heavenly Father is perfect [ἔσεσθε οὖν ὑμεῖς τέλειοι ὡς ὁ πατὴρ ὑμῶν
ὁ οὐράνιος τέλειός ἐστιν]" (5:48), may well be modeled on Lev 19:2, "You
shall be holy, for I the Lord your God am holy ['Άγιοι ἔσεσθε, ὅτι ἐγὼ ἅγιος
Κύριος ὁ θεὸς ὑμῶν]."[36] In contrast to the Damascus Document, though,
the Matthean Jesus does not restrict the mandate of Lev 19:18 to the category of "brother" (or even, by way of extension, "proselyte;" cf. Lev 19:34).
Rather, he insists that the command, "love your neighbor," is rooted in the
very nature of Israel's God, a God who refuses to turn away from anyone,
even the "enemy" (Matt 5:43–48). As a result, the practice of nonretaliation and reconciliation are not mere strategies to deescalate violence or
avoid "bearing" a neighbor's sin; they are, first and foremost, communal
ways of imitating God. As the sum of the law and the prophets, love for
God and neighbor thus becomes for Matthew the pedagogical mandate of
Christian discipleship: to teach "all the nations/gentiles" (πάντα τὰ ἔθνη) to
obey the ever-present Immanuel and his torah (Matt 28:19–20).[37]

---

35. English translation follows that of Joseph M. Baumgarten and Daniel R.
Schwartz, "Damascus Document (CD)," in *Damascus Document, War Scroll, and
Related Documents*, vol. 2 of *The Dead Sea Scrolls: Hebrew, Aramaic, and Greek Texts
with English Translations*, ed. James H. Charlesworth, PTSDSSP (Tübingen: Mohr Siebeck, 1995), 25.

36. Cf. Deut 18:13 LXX: "You shall be perfect [τέλειος] before the Lord your God"
(Hays, *Echoes*, 121).

37. There is significant debate over whether to translate πάντα τὰ ἔθνη as "all the
nations" or "all the gentiles." For an up-to-date discussion, see Terrence L. Donaldson,
"'Nations,' 'Non-Jewish Nations,' or 'Non-Jewish Individuals': Matthew 28:19 Revisited," in Runesson and Gurtner, *Matthew within Judaism*, 169–94. Matthias Konradt
argues persuasively that the mission to πάντα τὰ ἔθνη does not subvert the ongoing

186 Elizabeth E. Shively and Max Botner

8.4. Removing Boundaries around the
One God in the Gospel according to Luke

Luke builds Jesus's profile as Lord by joining his actions to those of the God of Israel and his Spirit. Luke speaks of the Lord God (κύριος ὁ θεός, 1:32) who is the savior in whom Mary rejoices ("in God my Savior," ἐπὶ τῷ θεῷ τῷ σωτῆρί μου, 1:47), and uses the same language to announce the birth of Jesus, the "Savior, who is Christ the Lord" (σωτὴρ ὅς ἐστιν χριστὸς κύριος, 2:11; cf. 2:26; 20:41–44).[38] The Lord Jesus begins his public ministry in tandem with the Lord God when he enters Galilee "in the power of the Spirit" (4:14). Jesus proclaims his Spirit-anointed ministry as the realization of the year of the Lord's favor to the poor, captives, blind, and oppressed (4:18–19, citing Isa 61:1–2; cf. Luke 7:22).[39] According to this proclamation, the Lord Jesus manifests the activity of the Lord God by bringing salvation to the marginalized.[40]

It is significant, then, that at the outset of the story of Jesus's healing of the paralytic, Luke uniquely states, "the power of the Lord [δύναμις κυρίου] was with him [Jesus] to heal" (Luke 5:17). This detail signals a development in the joint activity of the Lord God and the Lord Jesus to extend God's promised salvation. Luke follows Mark's account fairly closely, except that Luke replaces Mark's εἷς ὁ θεός with the phrase μόνος ὁ θεός (5:21). C. Kavin Rowe rightly points out that μόνος is not a mere modifier functioning to confirm God's unique prerogative to forgive sins; rather, the phrase μόνος ὁ θεός is an established Jewish declaration that the Lord God has no rival.[41] In fact, the Shema is set in a context

---

mission to "the lost sheep of the house of Israel." Konradt, *Israel, Kirche und die Völker im Mattäusevangelium*, WUNT 125 (Tübingen: Mohr Siebeck, 2007), 334–37.

38. See C. Kavin Rowe, *Early Narrative Christology: The Lord in the Gospel of Luke*, BZNW 139 (Berlin: de Gruyter, 2006), 49–55.

39. See Rowe's discussion of this passage; *Early Narrative Christology*, 78–82. For a discussion of Luke's text-form of Isa 61, see Bart J. Koet, "Isaiah in Luke-Acts," in *Isaiah in the New Testament*, ed. Steve Moyise and Maarten J. J. Menken (London: T&T Clark, 2005), 83–86.

40. The term "marginalized" is apropos for Luke, since as Joel B. Green (*The Gospel of Luke*, NICNT [Grand Rapids: Eerdmans, 1997], 211) notes, "although 'poor' is hardly devoid of economic significance, for Luke this wider meaning of diminished status honor is paramount."

41. Rowe, *Early Narrative Christology*, 102. Rowe does not, however, discuss why Luke would have chosen to replace εἷς ὁ θεός with μόνος ὁ θεός.

8. Jesus, the Shema, and Oneness in the Synoptic Gospels   187

that uses a conceptually equivalent phrase, in which the Lord is declared to be the unique God (אֵין עוֹד מִלְבַדּוֹ, οὐκ ἔστιν ἔτι πλὴν αὐτοῦ, Deut 4:35, 39).[42] The statements in Deut 4:35, 29 are integrally related with the Shema and the first commandment to affirm the uniqueness of YHWH. As Nathan MacDonald comments,

> Each statement ... functions in a different way. The statements in Deuteronomy 4 are the culmination of an argument based on the experience of Israel at Egypt and Sinai. They are a call to Israel to recognize and acknowledge that YHWH is unique, and thus the only god for them. The consequence of this recognition is that other gods should not be worshipped. In the first commandment this is expressed as an absolute prohibition. Finally, in the *Shema* YHWH's uniqueness for Israel is the basis of the command for whole-hearted devotion to YHWH (6:5), the theme of Deuteronomy 6–11.[43]

The phrase μόνος ὁ θεός expresses much the same as the statements in Deut 4 when it appears in Second Temple literature.[44] This phrase stresses that the Lord, and no other, is to be exalted and that the Lord, and no other, acts to save his people. (Perhaps this is why Luke uses the phrase in 5:21.) In Luke's account, it functions to buttress the scribes' and Pharisees' charge of blasphemy without dampening the christological import of the passage. On the lips of the scribes and Pharisees, this phrase reveals both their concern with piety and, ironically, their inability to see how the activity of the Lord Jesus reveals the power of the Lord God to enact righteousness by bringing salvation to a marginalized one who had to be lowered through the roof.

Luke's development of Jesus's activity and teaching heightens the relationship between εὐσέβεια and διακιοσύνη. The evangelist relocates the

---

42. Nathan MacDonald, *Deuteronomy and the Meaning of "Monotheism,"* 2nd ed., FAT 2/1 (Tübingen: Mohr Siebeck, 2012), 84. LXX translators use μόνος and πλήν to render a variety of Hebrew terms that formulate declarations about the uniqueness of Israel's God. See the use of μόνος in LXX Exod 22:20; Deut 32:12; 1 Sam 7:3–4; 2 Kings 5:17; 19:19; 2 Chr 6:30; 1 Esdr 8:25; Neh 9:6; Pss 4:8; 32:15; 71:18; 82:18; 85:10; 135:4, 7; 148:13; Sir 18:2; Isa 37:20; 44:24; Dan 3:45; and the use of πλήν in Exod 20:3; 22:20; Deut 4:35, 39; 32:39; 1 Sam 2:2; 1 Chr 17:20; Ps 17:31; Sir 33:5; Joel 2:27; Isa 44:8; 45:5, 6; 45:14; 45:21; 46:9; 64:4.

43. MacDonald, *Deuteronomy,* 85.

44. E.g., Exod 22:20; Pss 19:19; 85:10 [86:10 MT]; Isa 37:16, 20; 44:24; Dan 3:45; 2 Macc 7:37; Let. Aris. 132; Philo, *Conf.* 93; Jos, *A.J.* 8.13.5; John 5:44; Sib. Or. 3.760.

double love command from the temple of Jerusalem to the regions around the Sea of Galilee (Luke 10:25–28). At some unspecified time, a lawyer stands up to test Jesus by asking, "Teacher [διδάσκαλε], what shall I do to inherit eternal life [τί ποιήσας ζωὴν αἰώνιον κληρονομήσω]?" (10:25). Jesus responds by asking what is written in the law, and how he reads it (10:26). In response, the scribe recites a combination of Deut 6:5 and Lev 19:18, and Jesus affirms that he has answered rightly (10:28).[45]

The lawyer, however, wants to prove that he is in the right and that he has done what the law requires. So, he asks Jesus, "Who is my neighbor?" (10:29). In response, Jesus tells a parable in which a Samaritan pities and cares for a half-dead man on the side of the road, while a priest and a Levite ignore the man, likely out of concern for ritual purity (cf. Num 19:11–13).[46] Jesus asks the lawyer which of the three figures in the parable was a neighbor to the man, to which the lawyer replies, "the one who showed him mercy" (10:36–37). The parable provides a concrete illustration of what the scribe in Mark's account asserts, that to love God and neighbor is more important than all offerings and sacrifices (Mark 12:33), since it is the latter category of cultic commands that most concerns the priest and Levite in Luke's parable. Jesus addresses not only the question "Who is my neighbor?" (anyone) but also "How do I love my neighbor?" (the way the Samaritan does). The Samaritan becomes the exemplar of covenantal δικαιοσύνη because he loves his neighbor; the implication is that he (not priest nor the Levite) does what is necessary to gain eternal life. Thus, the parable functions radically not only to reform the nature of piety, but also to redefine the identity of the community that practices it.

Yet these observations only begin to scratch the surface of the parable's radical nature. Jesus's charge to the man, "Go and do likewise!" is first and foremost a call to reflection, before it is a call to action. It

---

45. This exchange suggests that the combination of "love God" and "love neighbor" does not originate with Jesus.

46. The remedy for corpse impurity is a seven-day period in which worshipers must wash themselves on the third and seventh days and ensure that they avoid contact with anything sacred. Failure to observe these stipulations, i.e., to guard the sancta from the corruption of human mortality, has the same defiling effects on the tabernacle as moral failures. See Jacob Milgrom's classic article, "The Priestly 'Picture of Dorian Gray,'" *RB* 83 (1976): 390–99. On competing understandings of ritual purity in the Second Temple period, see Jonathan Klawans, *Impurity and Sin in Ancient Judaism* (Oxford: Oxford University Press, 2000).

8. Jesus, the Shema, and Oneness in the Synoptic Gospels   189

is telling that this Jewish expert in the law cannot bear even to utter the word "Samaritan," but instead responds by whitewashing the man's ethnicity: this *Samaritan* is simply "the one who showed mercy." The lawyer is unprepared to embrace Jesus's definition of "neighbor" and so lacks the sine qua non of covenantal εὐσέβεια and διακιοσύνη. This is not simply a call to recognize that the one God is sovereign, but also to discern that in Jesus's ministry the hostility that existed between Jews and their geographical neighbors has been torn down (cf. Acts 8:14–17).

The cost of ethnic reconciliation is not something the Lukan Jesus takes lightly. Luke tells us that immediately after "he set his face to go to Jerusalem" (9:51), Jesus was rebuffed by a village of Samaritans precisely "*because* his face was set toward Jerusalem" (9:52). The sons of Zebedee inquire whether Jesus wants them to rain down fire from heaven upon the Samaritan village, but Jesus rebukes them (9:55). We then learn that widespread rejection of Jesus is not restricted to Samaritans but is the natural response of Galilean Jews as well (10:1–20). Thus, by the time the audience encounters the lawyer in 10:25, they have been conditioned to expect that proper response to Jesus is the result not of ancestry but of revelation (10:22). The Lukan Jesus's decision to cast a Samaritan as the protagonist of the parable is done with full hindsight: in his crucified body, the Messiah welcomes all who have rejected him.

Luke's interest in the double love command, then, is distinct from Mark's and Matthew's. The suggestion of the parable of the good Samaritan is not simply that covenantal obligations are realized in discipleship of Jesus (Mark). Nor is Luke's particular concern to show how the injunction to love one's neighbor leads to patterns of peace-making and nonretaliation rooted in the benevolent nature of the one God (Matthew). Rather, he seeks to inculcate a covenantal identity that sees outsiders and enemies as brothers and sisters.[47] This interest goes beyond the Matthean Jesus's call, "Love your enemies and pray for those who persecute you" (5:44). Perfection for the Lukan Jesus is not simply showing grace to your enemy; it is imagining a world in which this category is no longer appropriate or necessary. Luke's framework for maintaining εὐσέβεια and διακιοσύνη is at work as the Lord Jesus manifests the activ-

---

47. On the intersection of the terms "neighbor" and "brothers and sisters," see Mark A. Proctor, "'Who Is My Neighbor?' Recontextualizing Luke's Good Samaritan (Luke 10:25–37)," *JBL* 138 (2019): 217–18.

190 Elizabeth E. Shively and Max Botner

ity of the Lord God by bringing salvation to marginalized peoples. As such, "ethnic reasoning" becomes the means by which Luke explores the radical implications of the one God pouring out his Spirit on all flesh, liberally and without prejudice.[48]

8.5. Conclusion: Unity and Difference in Oneness

The Synoptic evangelists construct communal identity around the twin axioms of love for God and love for neighbor, which they argue intersect in the person of Jesus. This is not merely a witness to early Christology in the abstract, that is, to the concept that devotion to the Lord God entails devotion to the Lord Jesus. Rather, the evangelists suggest that christological devotion to the one God is always embodied in a particular people whose *raison d'être* is cruciform love for their neighbors. Breakdowns in εὐσέβεια necessarily adversely result in breakdowns of διαχιοσύνη, and vice versa. Just as a failure to recognize the Lord God at work in the Lord Jesus stifles justice, so any attempt to restrict the love of God manifest in the Lord Jesus undermines piety.

On the one hand, then, there is a clear sense in which the Synoptic account of God's oneness draws exclusionary boundaries. Christian communities cannot practice the double love commandment apart from their confession that Jesus is Lord, for it is only in Jesus that they discern the essence and shape of divine love. On the other hand, the divine love the Synoptic Gospels lay bare is a love that consistently breaks through the boundaries humans erect: the Markan Jesus reminds his audience that insiders are dense and often unable to discern the ways of God; the Matthean Jesus challenges his audience to respond to their enemies in love; and the Lukan Jesus goes so far as to make the despised other their

---

48. The term *ethnic reasoning* was coined by Denise Kimber Buell to describe the importance of ethnic and racial discourse in early Christian identity construction. See her *Why This New Race: Ethnic Reasoning in Early Christianity* (New York: Columbia University Press, 2005). Our use of the term is not intended to suggest that Luke presents the Jesus movement as a form of Christian nonethnic universalism over and against Jewish ethnic particularism. In fact, Luke presents Jews/Judeans as a multiethnic people *prior* to the outpouring of the Spirit at Pentecost; cf. Acts 2:5. See Cynthia M. Baker, "'From Every Nation under Heaven': Jewish Ethnicities in the Greco-Roman World," in *Prejudice and Christian Beginnings: Investigating Race, Gender, and Ethnicity in Early Christian Studies*, ed. Laura Nasrallah and Elisabeth Schüssler Fiorenza (Minneapolis: Fortress, 2009), 70–99.

debtor, the one to whom they should all aspire. The addressees the Synoptic Gospels envisage, therefore, do not have an exclusive claim to the one God. On the contrary, the identity-marker *one people* serves to designate the permeable boundaries of the community gathered around the Lord Jesus. This diverse, unified community bears witness to the one God whose very nature is marked by his intention to draw the other to himself.

Bibliography

Allison, Dale. "Mark 12.28–31 and the Decalogue." Pages 270–78 in *The Gospels and the Scriptures of Israel.* Edited by Craig Evans and W. Richard Stegner. JSNTSup 104. Sheffield: Sheffield Academic, 1994.

———. *Resurrecting Jesus: The Earliest Christian Tradition and Its Interpreters.* London: T&T Clark, 2005.

Baker, Cynthia M. "'From Every Nation under Heaven': Jewish Ethnicities in the Greco-Roman World." Pages 70–99 in *Prejudice and Christian Beginnings: Investigating Race, Gender, and Ethnicity in Early Christian Studies.* Edited by Laura Nasrallah and Elisabeth Schüssler Fiorenza. Minneapolis: Fortress, 2009.

Baron, Lori. "The Shema in Mark and John and the Parting of the Ways." Pages 187–210 in *The Ways That Often Parted: Essays in Honor of Joel Marcus.* Edited by Lori Baron, Jill Hicks-Keeton, and Matthew Thiessen. ECL 24. Atlanta: SBL Press, 2018.

Bauckham, Richard. *Jesus and the God of Israel: God Crucified and Other Studies on the New Testament's Christology of Divine Identity.* Grand Rapids: Eerdmans, 2008.

Baumgarten, Joseph M., and Daniel R. Schwartz. "Damascus Document (CD)." Pages 4–57 in *Damascus Document, War Scroll, and Related Documents.* Vol. 2 of *The Dead Sea Scrolls: Hebrew, Aramaic, and Greek Texts with English Translations.* Edited by James Charlesworth. PTSDSSP. Tübingen: Mohr Siebeck, 1995.

Botner, Max. *Jesus Christ as the Son of David in the Gospel of Mark.* SNTSMS 174. Cambridge: Cambridge University Press, 2019.

Buell, Denise Kimber. *Why This New Race: Ethnic Reasoning in Early Christianity.* New York: Columbia University Press, 2005.

Crossley, James. "Matthew and the Torah: Jesus as Legal Interpreter." Pages 29–52 in *Matthew within Judaism: Israel and the Nations in the First Gospel.* Edited by Anders Runesson and Daniel M. Gurtner. ECL 27. Atlanta: SBL Press, 2020.

Davies, W. D., and Dale C. Allison Jr. *Introduction and Commentary on Matthew I–VII*. Vol. 1 of *The Gospel according to Saint Matthew*. ICC. Edinburgh: T&T Clark, 1988.

———. *Commentary on Matthew XIX–XXVIII*. Vol. 3 of *The Gospel according to Saint Matthew*. ICC. Edinburgh: T&T Clark, 1997.

Davila, James R. *The Provenance of the Pseudepigraph: Jewish, Christian, or Other?* JSJSup 105. Leiden: Brill, 2005.

Dewey, Joanna. "The Literary Structure of the Controversy Stories in Mark 2:1–3:6." *JBL* 92 (1973): 394–401.

Donaldson, Terence L. "The Law That Hangs (Matthew 22:40): Rabbinic Formulation and Matthean Social World." *CBQ* 57 (1995): 689–709.

———. "'Nations,' 'Non-Jewish Nations,' or 'Non-Jewish Individuals': Matthew 28:19 Revisited." Pages 169–94 *Matthew within Judaism: Israel and the Nations in the First Gospel*. Edited by Anders Runesson and Daniel M. Gurtner. ECL 27. Atlanta: SBL Press, 2020.

Foster, Paul. "Why Did Matthew Get the Shema Wrong? A Study of Matthew 22:37." *JBL* 122 (2003): 309–33.

France, R. T. *The Gospel of Matthew*. NICNT. Grand Rapids: Eerdmans, 2007.

Green, Joel B. *The Gospel of Luke*. NICNT. Grand Rapids: Eerdmans, 1997.

Gribetz, Sarit Kattan. "The Shema in the Second Temple Period: A Reconsideration." *JAJ* 6 (2015): 58–84.

Hay, David M. *Glory at the Right Hand: Psalm 110 in Early Christianity*. SBLMS 18. Atlanta: Scholars Press, 1989.

Hays, Richard B. *Echoes of Scripture in the Gospels*. Waco, TX: Baylor University Press, 2016.

Hofius, Otfried. *Neutestamentliche Studien*. WUNT 132. Tübingen: Mohr Siebeck, 2000.

Instone-Brewer, David. *Prayer and Agriculture*. Vol. 1 of *Traditions of the Rabbis from the Era of the New Testament*. Grand Rapids: Eerdmans, 2004.

Johansson, Daniel. "*Kyrios* in the Gospel of Mark." *JSNT* 33 (2010): 101–24.

Jonge, Marinus de. *Pseudepigrapha of the Old Testament as Part of Christian Literature: The Case of the Testaments of the Twelve Patriarchs and the Greek Life of Adam and Eve*. SVTP 18. Leiden: Brill, 2003.

———. *The Testament of the Twelve Patriarchs: A Study of Their Text, Composition, and Origin*. Theologische Bibliotheek 25. Assen: Van Gorcum, 1953.

———. "The Two Great Commandments in the Testaments of the Twelve Patriarchs." *NovT* 44 (2002): 371–92.

Klawans, Jonathan. *Impurity and Sin in Ancient Judaism*. Oxford: Oxford University Press, 2000.

———. *Purity, Sacrifice, and the Temple: Symbolism and Supersessionism in the Study of Ancient Judaism*. Oxford: Oxford University Press, 2006.

Koet, Bart J. "Isaiah in Luke-Acts." Pages 79–100 in *Isaiah in the New Testament*. Edited by Steve Moyise and Maarten J. J. Menken. London: T&T Clark, 2005.

Konradt, Matthias. *Israel, Kirche und die Völker im Mattäusevangelium*. WUNT 215. Tübingen: Mohr Siebeck, 2007.

Kugel, James L. "On Hidden Hatred and Open Reproach: Early Exegesis of Leviticus 19:17." *HTR* 80 (1987): 43–61.

Lee, John J. R. *Christological Rereading of the Shema (Deut 6.4) in Mark's Gospel*. WUNT 2/533. Tübingen: Mohr Siebeck, 2020.

Luz, Ulrich. *The Theology of the Gospel of Matthew*. New Testament Theology. Cambridge: Cambridge University Press, 1995.

MacDonald, Nathan. *Deuteronomy and the Meaning of "Monotheism."* 2nd ed. FAT 2/1. Tübingen: Mohr Siebeck, 2012.

Marcus, Joel. "Authority to Forgive Sins upon the Earth: The *Shema* in the Gospel of Mark." Pages 196–211 in *The Gospels and the Scriptures of Israel*. Edited by Craig Evans and W. Richard Stegner. JSNTSup 104. Sheffield: Sheffield Academic, 1994.

———. *The Way of the Lord: Christological Exegesis of the Old Testament in the Gospel of Mark*. Louisville: Westminster John Knox, 1992.

Milgrom, Jacob. *Leviticus 17–22: A New Translation with Introduction and Commentary*. AB 3A. New York: Doubleday, 2000.

———. "The Priestly 'Picture of Dorian Gray.'" *RB* 83 (1976): 390–99.

Naiden, F. S. *Smoke Signals for the Gods: Ancient Greek Sacrifice from the Archaic through Roman Periods*. Oxford: Oxford University Press, 2013.

Proctor, Mark A. "'Who Is My Neighbor?' Recontextualizing Luke's Good Samaritan (Luke 10:25–37)." *JBL* 138 (2019): 203–19.

Queller, Kurt. "'Stretch Out Your Hand': Echo and Metalepsis in Mark's Sabbath Healing." *JBL* 129 (2010): 737–58.

Rowe, C. Kavin. *Early Narrative Christology: The Lord in the Gospel of Luke*. BZNW 139. Berlin: de Gruyter, 2006.

Rüggemeier, Jan. *Poetik der markinischen Christologie: Eine kognitiv-narratologische Exegese*. WUNT 2/458. Tübingen: Mohr Siebeck, 2017.

VanderKam, James C. *The Book of Jubilees*. CSCO 511. Leuven: Peeters, 1989.

———. *Jubilees 2: A Commentary on the Book of Jubilees Chapters 22–50*. Hermeneia. Minneapolis: Fortress, 2018.

Wevers, John William. *Deuteronomium*. SVTG 3.2. Göttingen: Vandenhoeck & Ruprecht, 1977.

———. *Notes on the Greek Texts of Deuteronomy*. SCS 39. Atlanta: Scholars Press, 1995.

9
One Flock, One Shepherd, One God: The Oneness Motif of John's Gospel

Andrew J. Byers

The prayer of Jesus in John 17 that his disciples may be one as he and the Father are one is widely understood by theologians and practicing Christians as a plea for ecclesial unity. Historians and biblical scholars have taken this petition for unity as a textual window through which the elusive Johannine context may be glimpsed, the ostensible appeal for harmony taken as the evangelist's response to a fractious community splitting at the social seams. The oneness motif in John is therefore understood in both churchly and historical-critical readings as a vision of *social harmony*.

This chapter on the Fourth Gospel's oneness language seeks to demonstrate that what Jesus actually prays for in John 17 is the consolidation of the divine social identity of the reconfigured people of God. This θεός is the God of Israel's Scriptures who is one, a theological appellation grounded in the Shema of Deut 6:4. Strikingly, this divine reference is shareable not only with Jesus, but also with the new human society emerging around him. To make such innovative christological and ecclesiological moves, the evangelist relies not only on Deut 6:4, but on the royal and nationalistic overtones of oneness found in Ezekiel. Social harmony is important, but it is an implication of the more foundational program of aligning those who believe in Jesus with the Shema's expression of theological oneness. After tracing the evangelist's narrative development of the term *one* in order to reach a more exegetically precise understanding of Jesus's prayer in John 17, I will present two concluding arguments, that one is the divine name believers are called to share with Jesus and the Father and that the Shema is a subtext thematically integrated into the entire gospel narrative.

196   Andrew J. Byers

9.1. John's Narrative Development of Oneness: An Overview

The term one appears beyond John 17, bearing thematic significance in 8:41; 10:16, 30; and 11:49–52. When Jesus prays that his disciples "may be one, as we are one," this deceptively simple term has been carefully freighted with multiple layers of meaning. I have written a more substantial description elsewhere of the fourth evangelist's cumulative development of oneness.[1] In what immediately follows, I offer brief summaries of those claims and venture fresh observations in interaction with recent contributions from other scholars.[2]

Oneness Text and Thematic Connotation	Shema (theology)	Shema (Christology)	Ezek 34/37 (Christology)	Ezek 34/37 (ecclesiology)
John 8:41 "one Father: God"	x			
John 10:16 "one flock, one shepherd"			x	x
John 10:30 "I and the Father are one"	x	x		
John 11:49–52 "One man" to die to gather God's people into "one"			x	x

---

1. Andrew J. Byers, *Ecclesiology and Theosis in John's Gospel*, SNTSMS 166 (Cambridge: Cambridge University Press, 2017), 103–52; and Byers, *John and the Others: Jewish Relations, Christian Origins, and the Sectarian Hermeneutic* (Waco, TX: Baylor University Press, 2021), 106–9.

2. Most notably, Lori Baron has recently published studies on John's use of the Shema: "The Shema in John's Gospel and Jewish Restoration Eschatology," in *John and Judaism: A Contested Relationship in Context*, ed. R. Alan Culpepper and Paul N. Anderson, RBS 87 (Atlanta: SBL Press, 2017), 165–73; Baron, "The Shema in Mark and John and the Parting of the Ways," in *The Ways That Often Parted: Essays in Honor of Joel Marcus*, ed. Lori Baron, Jill Hicks-Keeton, and Matthew Thiessen, ECL 24 (Atlanta: SBL Press, 2018), 187–210; see also Baron, *The Shema in John's Gospel*, WUNT 2/574 (Tübingen: Mohr Siebeck, 2022).

John 17:11, 21–23	x	x	x	x
"that they may be one, as we are one"				

As indicated in the table above, the Fourth Evangelist is not haphazard in his treatment of oneness. A strategically crafted pattern is at work in his creative exegesis of the Shema and two related oracles in Ezek 34 and 37. These scriptural oneness texts and their respective connotations alternate and then expand to accommodate one another. In the gospel's first instance of εἷς, the connotation is theological, drawn from Deut 6:4. In the next, the oneness language is drawn from Ezek 34 and 37 and the connotations are jointly christological and ecclesiological since those pretexts feature the one royal shepherd who will faithfully rule over the one people of God (as Judah and Israel are reunited into one nation). The semantic meaning of εἷς alternates back to theology in John 10:30. Here, since Jesus can share in the divine identity of the one, the Shema's theological frame is widened to include Christology. Soon afterward, Christology's pairing with ecclesiology returns as Ezekiel serves as the scriptural background for the oneness terminology in John 11. All three connotations (theological, christological, and ecclesiological) and both sets of biblical passages (Deut 6:4–9; Ezek 34 and 37) are then brought together and compressed into the words, "that they may be one, just as we are one" in John 17:22.[3] I will work through each of these iterations of Johannine oneness below.

9.1.1. John 8:41: "We Have One Father: God"

Paternity is the topic at hand in Jesus's most disturbing exchange with "the Jews."[4] At one level, Jesus is content to grant their claims to Abrahamic patrilineage. But they seem to confine Abraham's paternity merely to the sphere of biology: "I know that you are the seed of Abraham, *but…*" (8:37,

---

3. Unless noted otherwise, translations are mine.

4. By enclosing "the Jews" within so-called scare quotes I am acknowledging that there is a contextually grounded polemic at work in John beyond which his rhetorical use of οἱ Ἰουδαῖοι cannot be responsibly applied; see Ruth Sheridan, "Issues in the Translation of οἱ Ἰουδαῖοι in the Fourth Gospel," *JBL* 132 (2013): 671–95. For an alternative view, see Adele Reinhartz, "'Jews' and Jews in the Fourth Gospel," in *Anti-Judaism and the Fourth Gospel*, ed. Reimund Bieringer, Didier Pollefeyt, and Frederique Vandecasteele-Vanneuville (Louisville: Westminster John Knox, 2001), 227.

198   Andrew J. Byers

emphasis added). The conjunction ἀλλά indicates that their ties to Abraham are limited. Jesus grants that Abraham is their progenitor but not their father. "The Jews" may collectively be the σπέρμα of Abraham, but to be "the τέκνα of Abraham" they must do his works. Their alleged desire for Jesus's death aligns them with a different father. Though not directly identified as the devil until 8:44, "the Jews" may well be detecting that the conversation on paternity has shifted beyond genetics to a cosmic level because they reply with "we have one [ἕνα] Father: God" (8:41).

The theological significance of one here is often overlooked.[5] There are multiple fathers being discussed in this exchange, so one is not just a cardinal number here. It is employed, rather, as that unique modifier of Israel's God. Defending insinuations of illegitimacy, "the Jews" self-identify as children of the one God of the Shema, language that has biblical resonance with Mal 2:10: "Did not one God [θεὸς εἷς] create you? Is there not one Father [πατὴρ εἷς] over all of you?" (LXX).

"The Jews" have already heard Jesus use such Shema-related Deuteronomistic language in a previous discussion. In John 5, they were accused of failing to believe Moses (to whom Deuteronomy was attributed) as having "never heard" or seen the form of "the only God [τοῦ μόνου θεοῦ]" (5:44). John is establishing in chapter 5 covenantal negligence on behalf of the rightful heirs of Israel's monotheistic heritage: they have not heeded the words of the one and only God mediated through Moses.[6] In John 8, this

---

5. In his major study on Johannine oneness, Mark Appold acknowledges theological significance in 8:41 but claims that this instance "does not at all develop within the framework of Hebrew thought" (*The Oneness Motif in the Fourth Gospel: Motif Analysis and Exegetical Probe into the Theology of John* [Eugene, OR: Wipf & Stock, 2011], 174, see also 174–75, 162, 191–92, 243–45, 259–60). In addition to Baron's work cited above, scholars who do see some reference to the Shema in 8:41 include Richard Bauckham, *Jesus and the God of Israel: God Crucified and Other Studies on the New Testament's Christology of Divine Identity* (Grand Rapids: Eerdmans, 2008), 104; Bauckham, *Gospel of Glory: Major Themes in Johannine Theology* (Grand Rapids: Baker Academic, 2015), 21–41; Johannes Beutler, *A Commentary on the Gospel of John*, trans. Michael Tait (Grand Rapids; Eerdmans, 2017), 241–43; Andrew T. Lincoln, *The Gospel according to Saint John*, BNTC 4 (Peabody, MA: Hendrickson, 2005), 272; and Herman Ridderbos, *The Gospel of John: A Theological Commentary*, trans. John Vriend (Grand Rapids: Eerdmans, 1997), 313.

6. On the Shema in John 5, see Jörg Augenstein, *Das Liebesgebot im Johannesevangelium und in den Johannesbriefen*, BWANT 134 (Stuttgart: Kohlhammer, 1994), 60–61; Johannes Beutler, "Das Hauptgebot im Johannesevangelium," in *Das Gesetz im Neuen Testament*, ed. Karl Kertelge, QD 108 (Freiburg im Breisgau: Herder, 1986),

9. One Flock, One Shepherd, One God 199

theme of unfaithfulness is reasserted in terms of paternity and thus social identity as their filial relations to the one God are called into question. Though the christological logic of John's use of the Shema will become more explicit by the end of John 10, the implication is that a failure to hear and love Jesus, the emissary of the God who is one, is a breach of the monotheistic convictions of "the Jews" and thus a delegitimization of their membership within a Johannine construal of Israel.[7]

9.1.2. John 10:16: One Flock, One Shepherd

Though the Shema-like language appears throughout John 10, the formula of "one flock, one shepherd [μία ποίμνη, εἷς ποιμήν]" derives not from Deuteronomy but from Ezekiel.[8] As the good shepherd, Jesus speaks in the idiom of YHWH ("I am" [ἐγώ εἰμι]), yet directly presents himself in the first part of John 10 as the Davidic king of Ezek 34 and 37 who will gather and rescue the scattered people of God: "I will set up over them one [ἕνα/אחד] shepherd, my servant David"; "I will make them one [ἕν/אחד] nation in the land … and one [εἷς/אחד] king shall be king over them all"; "my servant David shall be king over them; and they shall all have one [εἷς/אחד] shepherd" (from 34:23; 37:22; and 37:24, NRSV). As a scriptural source supplemental to the Shema, the oracles from Ezekiel feature nationalistic and messianic oneness (becoming ecclesiological and christological, respectively, in their reappropriation). After centuries of division between Judah and Israel, God informed Ezekiel that he would send a singular ruler to govern a united nation, a union symbolized by the joining together of two rods. God declares he will "make them one [μίαν/אחד] stick, in order that they may be one [אחד] in my hand" (Ezek 37:19, NRSV). Jesus assumes for himself this Davidic vocation in the Shepherd Discourse (see also Num 27:12–23).[9] As in Ezekiel's day, so also in John's—the people of God are scattered and must be regathered into a singular unit.

226–29; Baron makes the case that the love commands in the Farewell Discourse are also tied to the Shema; Baron, "Shema in Mark and John," 200–202.

7. On John 10, see Brury Eko Saputra, *The Shema and John 10: The Importance of the Shema Framework in Understanding the Oneness Language in John 10* (Eugene, OR: Wipf & Stock, 2019).

8. Baron sees the Shema tied closely to the oneness language in Ezek 34/37; Baron, "Shema in John's Gospel," 166–70.

9. See also Gary T. Manning, *Echoes of a Prophet: The Use of Ezekiel in the Gospel*

9.1.3. John 10:30: "I and the Father are One"

The divine oneness Jesus claims to share with God in 10:30 is often seen as a functional unity of will, purpose, activity, or perhaps as an ontological union as construed in pagan mysticism.[10] The neuter singular use of one (ἕν) may well cloud the connection with the masculine singular use (εἷς) found in John 8:41 that is more directly identifiable with the LXX's version of the Shema. Yet as a theologically opportunistic writer, John exploits the lexical variability of *one* in the Greek to conduct his christological program. Jesus and God are coidentified with one another, but neither are allowed to collapse into the other, a dynamic that will eventually invite Trinitarian elaboration. God the Father is εἷς, so Jesus cannot also be εἷς. Yet together, they are ἕν—a plural unit. The neuter singular creates semantic space for their respective identities while retaining the theological force of the Shema.[11] Jesus is not just coaligned with the Father's will or merely an agent of divine activity. He actually participates in the identity of the one God of Israel's religious heritage, a claim "the Jews" seem convinced he has made since they respond by gathering stones to punish blasphemy.[12]

By pairing and correlating God and the Logos in his prologue, John positions himself in such a way that, as a Jewish writer, he is essentially unable to avoid a christological re-presentation of the Shema, which he takes up here, right at the gospel's center. Clearly, the evangelist is not content to assign to Jesus merely the oneness vocation of the Davidic shepherd; and his texts are serviceable for broader moves: in Ezek 34 and 37, God uses ἐγώ εἰμι four times in the relevant passages and affirms that he will also take on the role of shepherd. Though the oneness applied to Jesus in John 10:16 is messianic and most directly linked to Ezekiel, John fuses the divine and Davidic pastoral vocations and thus warrants a christological application in John 10:30 of the Shema.

---

of John and in Literature of the Second Temple Period, JSNTSup 270 (London: T&T Clark, 2004), 106–8; Richard B. Hays, *Echoes of Scripture in the Gospels* (Waco, TX: Baylor University Press, 2016), 320, 340–43.

10. See the brief discussion in Byers, *Ecclesiology and Theosis*, 139–40.

11. Byers, *Ecclesiology and Theosis*, 121–24.

12. For the language of divine identity, see Bauckham, *Jesus and the God of Israel*, 6–11.

9.1.4. John 11:50, 52: "One Man," "One People"

In keeping with his hermeneutical pattern, John's focal oneness text shifts again from the Shema to the Ezekiel oracles. The resurrection of Lazarus (perhaps narrated in light of Ezek 37:1–14) has precipitated concerns at the level of national leadership. In the minds of the Jewish leaders, populist attraction to Jesus may lead to a devastating Roman intervention (11:48). The solution presented is that one man should die for the sake of the people. It is clear that the Ezekiel oneness passages are in view because the consequence of this expedient death is the gathering into ἕν of the dispersed people of God. Parallel with the "one flock, one shepherd" formula of 10:16, John reinforces the developing theme that a christological fulfillment of David's role will entail the death of the Davidic (and divine) shepherd.

This scene at the end of John 11 also reveals more about the sort of ecclesial oneness John envisions. As in Ezekiel, John is concerned for God's scattered and dispersed people. Yet unlike Ezek 37, the union is not one of two nations or tribal confederations reestablished into a geographical domain. John relativizes the social designation of "nation [ἔθνος]" and places emphasis on the filial designation of "the children of God," which does not anticipate a centralized location (apart from the person of Jesus himself). Ezekiel's oracles envisage restoration to the physical Israel as a land and place. John, however, seems to be modifying this political (and eschatological) expectation. The oneness into which the dispersed children of God are gathered is not territorially defined and can only be elucidated when paired with the theological oneness of the Shema, the climactic move of the Johannine hermeneutics of one to which we now turn.

9.1.5. John 17: "That They May Be One, as We Are One"

In John 17, both sets of scriptural pretexts and all three connotations—theological, christological, and ecclesiological—are compressed in the prayer that they "may be one, as we are one." In standard readings, the oneness language of John 17 is roughly understood as two-dimensional, as a unity of social harmony with one another and also as joint solidarity in purpose with God and Jesus. But a reading of John 17 that eviscerates oneness of its prior narrative development is ultimately a *mis*reading. What happens when the complex narrative development of one is taken into account?

202 Andrew J. Byers

John has imbued one with the theological freight of the Shema and the christological and ecclesiological weight of the messianic restoration of the eschatological people of God. Confirmation that the Shema is in view is found in the reference to God as μόνος in 17:3 (see John 5:44); and the revelation that Jesus participated in the divine glory before the foundation of the world vindicates his own affiliation with his theological vision of oneness (17:5).

The Ezekiel texts are also at play as Jesus presents himself as the good shepherd who is concerned for his sheep.[13] His pastoral concerns are raised by the specific crisis at hand, described at the end of John 16. The hour of the shepherd's sacrificial death has come, and the immediate consequence will be the scattering of the flock (16:32). This dispersal is the imminent crisis addressed by ecclesial and christological oneness. True to his pastoral vocation, the pastoral and thus royal figure of Jesus is intent on gathering the scattered children of God into one (11:52). His prayer, therefore, addresses not internal factionalism, but (1) specifically, the external threats associated with his death, and (2) generally, the lamentable but long-standing status of God's people as dispersed and exiled throughout the world. The oneness motif in John 17 most urgently addresses *dispersal* not *disharmony*, the state of being *scattered* more than a state of *schism*.[14]

The prayer that oneness might be extended to those who will eventually believe in Jesus through the disciples' testimonies (17:20–21) accords with the agenda articulated in 10:16: "other sheep I have that are not out of this fold. I must bring those also, and they will hear my voice and become one flock, one shepherd." Jesus prays within the vocational mode of the one Davidic shepherd in Ezek 34 and 37. He longs for the restoration of the scattered people of God into one ecclesial identity.

But how do these connotations of oneness from Ezekiel function alongside the theological oneness of the Shema in this climactic prayer?

As a participant in preexistent divine glory, Jesus is one with the one God of the Shema in John 17. He is simultaneously the one shepherd over the disciples who are envisioned as the eschatological people of God (Ezek 34/37). For John, their eschatological mode of being is *divine*. They are a divinized people of God who share in the glory of Christ, a glory that is

---

13. J. Ramsey Michaels refers to John 17 as "the Shepherd's Prayer" (*The Gospel of John*, NICNT [Grand Rapids: Eerdmans, 2010], 857).

14. Byers, *Ecclesiology and Theosis*, 149.

more than mere fame or mortal grandeur. As established already in this prayer, this glory is the eternal glory of God himself (17:5, 22). Though liable to the charge of anachronism, deification language is serviceable for describing John's oneness ecclesiology.[15] The prologue has already established the divine standing of the children of God in the gospel's opening lines. They are born not by any mortal means, but ἐκ θεοῦ, out of God. This divine reorigination is affirmed in Jesus's explanation to Nicodemus that a believer must be born "from above." Though the children of God do not share in the divine *identity* as Jesus does, they do share in the divine *family* of the Father and the Son, a participation that requires some mode of regeneration as a divine being.[16]

In Ezekiel's context, the lost sheep of Israel had been scattered across a geographical domain. In John 17, the spatial realm in which the sheep find themselves vulnerable is not merely geographical but ultimately cosmic, hence Jesus's prayers about their relation to the "world" (17:15–16, 18). Though "world" can refer to a physical place, κόσμος is conceptually expanded in John and depicted as a realm onto which evil and the forces of darkness can be mapped. The one flock is gathered into a fold characterized not so much by a physical location, as in Ezekiel, but by a particular affiliation with one another, God, and Jesus (who is himself the new place of God's presence, as seen in 2:13–22). This affiliation is defined by shared bonds of divinity and filial love.

This reading of the prayer that they "may be one, as we are one," makes sense of an intra-Jewish conflict in which the Johannine Christians, predominantly Jews, find themselves accused of ditheistic heresy and thus the abrogation of their religious tradition.[17] On the contrary for the Fourth Evangelist: Johannine Christians are the true eschatological people, the one people of the one God who has sent his one shepherd to gather them.[18]

---

15. As acknowledged by Marianne Meye Thompson, *John: A Commentary*, NTL (Louisville: Westminster John Knox, 2015), 349. For a fuller treatment, see Byers, *Ecclesiology and Theosis*; and Michael J. Gorman, *Abide and Go: Missional Theosis in the Gospel of John*, Didsbury Lectures 2016 (Eugene, OR: Cascade, 2018).

16. John draws distinctions between the divine status of believers, God, and the Logos; see Byers, *Ecclesiology and Theosis*, 180–83.

17. Similarly, Baron, "Shema in John's Gospel," 167.

18. In early Judaism, the Shema's oneness could be extended and applied to God's people, as well as to other places, ideas, or objects; see, e.g., Josephus, *C. Ap.*, 2.193; *A.J.* 4.200–201; Philo, *Opif.*, 171–172; *Spec.* 1.52–53, 67; *Virt.* 34–35; 2 Bar. 48.24.

204   Andrew J. Byers

9.2. One: The Name of God, Jesus, and the Believers in John 17

Having provided an exegetical overview of John's oneness passages, I turn
now to the task of presenting two arguments based on these Johannine
hermeneutics of one. Before making the case that the Shema serves as a
major subtext interlaced throughout John's Gospel, I first show that one is
the divine name referred to in John 17.

Jesus declares in 17:6 that "I have manifested your name [ὄνομα] to
the people whom you gave to me." He then prays, "Holy Father, keep them
in your name [ὀνόματί], which you have given to me, in order that they
may be one [ἕν], as we are" (17:11). This name motif is revisited at the
prayer's end and presented in the context of love: "I made known to them
your name [ὄνομά] and I will make it known, in order that the love with
which you loved me may be in them and I in them" (17:26). Like the oneness theme, John's name motif in Jesus's prayer is preceded by narrative
development as the evangelist lays the conceptual groundwork for a Christology in which Jesus's sharing of the Father's divine name is plausible and
appropriate.[19] But what is this divine name in John 17?

Commentators rightly note that name in the ancient world is an
abbreviated representation of someone's honor, reputation, authority, and
character.[20] In this sense, by making known God's name to his disciples,
Jesus has simply revealed to them a fuller sense of who God is (as adum-
brated in 1:18). Though many commentaries quickly move on to the next
verses, some give space for questions about this name: could it be "I Am,"
YHWH/יהוה, or its equivalent in the LXX of "Lord"/κύριος?[21] Though he
takes time to address the questions, J. Ramsey Michaels reasons that these
are doubtful alternatives and he ends up supporting the more common

---

19. For a focused theological study on John's name motif, see Grant Macaskill,
"Name Christology, Divine Aseity, and the I Am Sayings in the Fourth Gospel," *JTI* 12
(2018): 217–41; esp. 230–35.

20. See, e.g., Jo-Ann Brant, *John*, Paideia (Grand Rapids: Baker Academic, 2011),
225; Bruce J. Malina and Richard L. Rohrbaugh, *Social-Science Commentary on the
Gospel of John* (Minneapolis: Fortress, 1998), 247–48.

21. For "I Am," see Raymond E. Brown, *The Gospel according to John (XII–XXI):
Introduction, Translation, and Notes*, AB 29A (Garden City, NY: Doubleday, 1966),
755–56. C. K. Barrett notes that YHWH/יהוה as reference to the divine name was
increasingly common in later Jewish texts; see Barrett, *The Gospel according to St John:
An Introduction with Commentary and Notes on the Greek Text*, 2nd ed. (London:
SPCK, 1978), 505. For "Lord"/κύριος, see Thompson, *John*, 352–53.

9. One Flock, One Shepherd, One God   205

view that the shared name is a trope meaning shared authority and honor.[22] Charles Gieschen has provided a more elaborate argument: the divine name was at times associated with the visible manifestation of YHWH in theophanic texts, and John is working within the apocalyptic traditions that have taken up this theme in early Jewish literature.[23]

Yet the term one is still regularly interpreted as social unity appropriate to the unity between Father and Son that their shared name represents. A direct connection between name and one is either overlooked, dismissed, or viewed as tertiary since the point of Jesus's prayer here is simply a caution against factionalism. Andrew Lincoln discerns a linkage between name and one, but it is indirect and ultimately in service to social harmony.[24] In his impressive study on John's name theology, Joshua Coutts notes connections between John's oneness language and the name motif, but the social implication of believers being kept in the name as one is interpreted as a safeguarding of internal social integrity.[25]

Though I largely agree here with Gieschen, Lincoln, and find Coutts arguments regarding Deutero-Isaiah important and largely compelling, I wish to extend their readings a bit further. In my view, the most logical interpretation of the name in John 17 is one, which works naturally in the flow of the text: "Holy Father, keep them in your name, which you have given to me, *in order that they may be one* [ἕν], *as we are*" (17:11; emphasis added). Of all the designations used thus far in John's Gospel for God, Jesus, and the disciples, none are common between them except one. Though more a circumlocution or condensed label, one can be directly linked to the divine name: "on that day the Lord [יהוה/κύριος] will be one [אחד/εἷς] and his name one [אחד/ἕν]" (Zech 14:9 NRSV).[26]

---

22. Michaels, *Gospel of John*, 867–68.

23. Gieschen, "The Divine Name That the Son Shares with the Father in the Gospel of John," in *Reading the Gospel of John's Christology as Jewish Messianism: Royal, Prophetic, and Divine Messiahs*, ed. Benjamin E. Reynolds and Gabriele Boccaccini, AJEC 106 (Leiden: Brill, 2018), 387–410.

24. Lincoln, *John*, 436–37. See also Beutler, *John*, 434.

25. Coutts, *The Divine Name in the Gospel of John: Significance and Impetus*, WUNT 2/447 (Tübingen: Mohr Siebeck, 2017), 130–31. Coutts makes the strong case that John's name theology derives primarily from Deutero-Isaiah where the concept is both eschatological and associative (with another—perhaps divine—figure; 2–3, 144, and throughout).

26. Baron also notes connection between the Johannine Shema and Zech 14:9; Baron, "Shema in Mark and John," 204. Zechariah's reference to the scattering of the

206 Andrew J. Byers

As Coutts convincingly demonstrates, John is drawn to the eschatological bearings and the associative qualities of the divine name. These
connotations are perhaps more strongly at play than many have acknowledged in John 17 because, in my reading, one designates not just a quality
of shared unity but an *actual name* for the Father, Son, and believers. Since
that very name is one, eschatology and inclusive association are more
explicitly reinforced.[27] The believers are not just called to a social harmony
that is vaguely reflective of the shared honor, authority, and character
of the Father and Son; in the crisis of reconfiguring their social identity
around a Christology many fellow Jews would have regarded as incompatible with their scriptural tradition, the believers are called to bear the
actual name of one that unequivocally associates them with the God of
Israel and his divine Son.[28] In bearing this name, Johannine believers are
not simply cautioned against disunity; they are imported into the divine
interrelation between the one God and the Son who belongs within the
overall frame of the Shema.

9.3. The (Re)narrativization of the Shema:
Deuteronomy 6:4–5 as Subtext for the Fourth Gospel

I turn now to the final argument of the study, that Deut 6:4–5 is a subtext
for John's entire narrative. The foregoing exegesis on the gospel's oneness

---

sheep at the striking of the shepherd (13:7) seems to be in view in John 16:32 (Mark
14:27), which is the crisis Jesus's prayer in John 17 seeks to address. Though he does
not make the connection between Zech 14:9 and the divine name in John 17, William
Randolph Bynum argues that the evangelist's citations of Zech 9:9 (John 12:15) and
12:10 (John 19:37) at the beginning and end of his passion narrative is deliberate in
which the content of Zech 9–12 is "synthesized and symbolized"; Bynum, "Quotations of Zechariah in the Fourth Gospel," in *Abiding Words: The Use of Scripture in
the Gospel of John*, ed. Alicia D. Myers and Bruce G. Schuchard, RBS 81 (Atlanta: SBL
Press, 2015), 49. Maarten J. J. Menken believes Zech 14:8 is alluded to in John 7:38;
see Menken, "The Minor Prophets in John's Gospel," in *The Minor Prophets in the New
Testament*, ed. Maarten J. J. Menken and Steve Moyise, LNTS 377 (London: T & T
Clark, 2009), 89–91.

27. Coutts notes the connection between YHWH and the Shema; *Name*, 149;
175–78; 188–89. Though he also recognizes resonance between the Shema and Zech
14:9 (189 n. 13), he does not seem to observe a direct link between the name and one
in John 17.

28. In making this argument, I envision myself not so much disagreeing with
Coutts as pressing his own logic and exegesis one step further.

9. One Flock, One Shepherd, One God   207

passages has, I hope, demonstrated that the Shema receives sustained and meticulous reflection throughout this ancient Jewish text. Having identified specific allusions to Deuteronomy's oneness theology, the claim is now more readily made that the Fourth Evangelist has so interwoven his composition with the central idea of the Shema (to love the one God by honoring his words) that his narrative portrays the creation of God's eschatological people on its terms.[29] This gospel, then, is a product of the Shema's theology renarrated around Jesus and in which the formation of God's children is grounded. As a Jewish writer, John seeks to accommodate the phenomenon of Jesus's divine identity within the Jewish Scriptures and the Jewish theology that have framed his sense of reality. If he is indeed determined to narrate the reconstitution of Israel around Jesus, he is almost forced to engage exegetically with Deut 6:4. Given the immense creedal significance of this scriptural text in John's early Jewish milieu, it would indeed be odd if he failed to offer some account of its impact on his work.[30]

The claim that the Shema is thematically foundational enough to be labeled a subtext in John is supported in part by the purpose and setting of Deut 6:4–9.[31] Though the Shema is normally understood as a text that is theological in content and meaning, its nationalistic and social ramifications in Deuteronomy are inestimable. The very idea of Israel is constituted by whole-hearted love for the God who is one. Stationed on the plains of Moab on the territorial cusp of the promised land, Deut 6:4–5 serves as Israel's foundational charge. Walter Moberly affirms that "the contextualization of these words [the Shema] within Deuteronomy means that they appear in the Old Testament's most systematic account of the relationship between YHWH and Israel" and serve as "the keynote

---

29. A similar observation is made by Stephen C. Barton, "Christian Community in the Gospel of John," in *Christology, Controversy and Community: New Testament Essays in Honour of David R. Catchpole*, ed. David G. Horrell and Christopher M. Tuckett, NovTSup 99 (Leiden: Brill, 2000), 290–94.

30. For a reflective discussion on the translation, meaning, context, and theology of the Shema, see R. W. L. Moberly, *Old Testament Theology: Reading the Hebrew Bible as Christian Scripture* (Grand Rapids: Baker Academic, 2015), 7–40; for its early Jewish significance, see Erik Waaler, *The Shema and the First Commandment in First Corinthians: An Intertextual Approach to Paul's Re-reading of Deuteronomy*, WUNT 2/253 (Tübingen: Mohr Siebeck, 2008), 123–205.

31. For a similar set of arguments, see Baron, "Shema in Mark and John," 195, 200–202.

208 Andrew J. Byers

of Moses's exposition of the covenant" between them.[32] Israel exists as a people anchored in the theology of divine oneness and characterized by love for this divine one.

Though his ecclesiological program is often dismissed or relegated to the christological sidelines, John is fundamentally concerned not only with Jesus, but with the new people of God that belief in Jesus brings into being.[33] The formation of the "children of God" (John 1:12–13) is premised on the reception of the Word who is eventually depicted as one with God, just as Israel's inception is premised on the reception of the words of the God who is one. That the evangelist intends a parallel between the formation of Israel through the law and the reconfiguration of Israel through the christological Logos is made clear in the final lines of the prologue: "The law was given through Moses; grace and truth came through Jesus Christ. No one has seen God at any time. It is God the only Son, who is in the bosom of the Father, who has made him known" (1:17–18).[34] As a narrative centered on this divine and royal figure about whom Moses wrote, who came to bring grace and truth, whose mission entails the re-formation of the people of God, John's account of Jesus is conducive to a robust appropriation of the christological and social implications of the Shema whose purpose and setting are eminently serviceable to Johannine ecclesiology.

Another basis for claiming that the Shema is a subtext for the Fourth Gospel is the evangelist's prolific references to love, words, and one, the key terms of Deut 6:4–5. John's use of Scripture is characterized less by direct citation and more by a sophisticated re-presentation of material through echoes and thematic allusions, at times signaled by verbal links.[35] C. K. Barrett has made the compelling case that John uses his scriptural source material the way he uses his synoptic material, incorporating it into

---

32. Moberly, *Old Testament Theology*, 8.

33. See Byers, *Ecclesiology and Theosis*, 25–71.

34. On the close conceptual ties between torah and John's Logos, see Craig Keener, *The Gospel of John: A Commentary*, 2 vols. (Peabody, MA: Hendrickson, 2003), 1:360–63.

35. For a helpful overview, see Alicia D. Myers, "Abiding Words: An Introduction to Perspectives on John's Use of Scripture," in Myers and Schuchard, *Abiding Words*, 1–20. Though Hays notes that John can offer direct verbal links to certain scriptural passages (e.g., "in the beginning" in John 1:1/Gen 1:1), he argues that the evangelist's primary mode of employing Scripture is through "evoking *images* and *figures*" from Israel's sacred texts; Hays, *Echoes*, 285 (emphasis original).

9. One Flock, One Shepherd, One God   209

"the thematic structure of the Gospel."[36] By way of example, the divine shepherd language from Ezekiel discussed above is not introduced by a citation formula; instead, John cues his scripturally informed readers and auditors to his source through key words, phrases, and verbal ideas, then artistically integrates the image of this pastoral figure into his narrative Christology.[37] Though the shepherd motif features most prominently in John 10, its thematic branches and scriptural roots cannot be disentangled from the gospel's whole. If the oneness language of Deut 6:4 is indeed being employed by John in 8:41; 10:30; and in John 17 as argued above, then the saturation throughout John of the terms love, words, and one (and relevant cognates) suggest a comprehensive integration of the Shema's theology into the broader narrative.[38]

As a vocational charge constitutive of Israel's corporate identity, the Shema beckons love for the one God expressed in faithfulness to God's words:

> Hear, O Israel: The Lord our God, the Lord is one [אחד/εἷς]. Love [אהבת/ἀγαπήσεις] the Lord your God with all your heart and with all your soul and with all your strength. These words [דברים/ῥήματα] that I give you today are to be on your hearts. (Deut 6:4–6a, NIV, modified)

In John's christological reworking of the Shema, Jesus is so fully included within the divine identity of the one that he himself is the worthy object of this love, a love expressed through faithfulness to divine words/commands:[39] "If you love me, you will keep my commandments" (14:15); "the one who has my commandments and keeps them—that is the one who loves me" (14:21); "if anyone loves me he will keep my word … the one not loving me does not keep my words" (14:23–24; see also 14:28 and 16:27). More

---

36. Barrett, "The Old Testament in the Fourth Gospel," *JTS* 48 (1947): 155–69. Barrett is drawing on Edwin Hoskyns's comments on John's use of the Synoptic Gospel material; Hoskyn, *The Fourth Gospel*, ed., Francis Noel Davey, 2nd ed. (London: Faber & Faber, 1947), 68–85.

37. See the discussion in Barrett, "Old Testament," 163–64.

38. For Barrett's discussion of the Shema in John, see "Old Testament," 161–62.

39. See Baron, "Shema in Mark and John," 200–202. "Nowhere in John does Jesus request that the disciples love God. John has replaced this with a request by Jesus that the disciples love him and his commandments" (Francis J. Moloney, *Love in the Gospel of John: An Exegetical, Theological, and Literary Study* [Grand Rapids: Baker Academic, 2013], 2).

210 Andrew J. Byers

broadly, the Johannine vision of discipleship articulated through the terminology of the Shema as group identity is anchored in the collective act of abiding in the words of Jesus (cf. 8:31), loving him (and one another), and participating in the divine oneness of the Father and Son.[40]

The evangelist at times constellates the Shema's terminology of love, words, and one (and sometimes hear), though semantic expansion occurs within its Johannine reconceptualization. In the acerbic exchange in John 8 discussed earlier, Jesus's fundamental critique of "the Jews" is expressed in terms of the Johannine Shema.[41] Jesus speaks "these words" [ταῦτα τὰ ῥήματα] (8:20), which he has *heard* from his father, while "the Jews" *hear* from a different father (ἀκούω appears six times throughout this discourse: 8:26, 38, 40, 43, 47). Those who continue in Jesus's word are the true disciples (8:31). Yet he must explain that his "word [λόγος] has no place" in them (8:37). Jesus rebuffs the claim that they have "one [ἕνα] father: God" with "if God was your Father, you would love [ἠγαπᾶτε] me, for I came from God" (8:42). The logic is Deuteronomistic: "the one who is from God hears the words of God [τὰ ῥήματα τοῦ θεοῦ ἀκούει]. For this reason you do not hear [ἀκούετε]: because you are not from God" (8:47; see also 8:51). In summary, the verbal actions associated with the Shema of loving God fully by hearing (Ἄκουε, Ἰσραηλ) and receiving his words are clustered around this instance of Johannine oneness.

Immediately after voicing the phrase "one flock, one shepherd" in John 10, Jesus speaks of love, though it is love directed not toward God but God's love directed toward himself (10:17).[42] The instant response is a schism among "the Jews" "on account of these words [τοὺς λόγους τούτους]"

---

40. The Shema's command to love God was often paired with the command to love others (Matt 22:37–39; Mark 12:30–31; Luke 10:26–28). This corollary is assumed by John and expressed in the emphasis on loving one another in both the gospel (John 13:34; 15:12, 17) and the epistles (1 John 2:10; 3:10–11, 14, 18, 23; 4:7, 11–12, 20–21; 2 John 5). See the preceding chapter in this volume by Elizabeth Shively and Max Botner; see also Augenstein, *Das Liebesgebot*, 61, 66, 183–85; Judith M. Lieu, *I, II, and III John: A Commentary*, NTL (Louisville: Westminster John Knox, 2008), 198–99.

41. The phrase "the Johannine Shema" is Baron's. See above.

42. C. T. R. Hayward also affirms the likelihood of a connection between the Shema and John's love commands; Hayward, "'The Lord Is One': Reflections on the Theme of Unity in John's Gospel from a Jewish Perspective," in *Early Jewish and Christian Monotheism*, ed. Loren T. Stuckenbruck and Wendy E. S. North, JSNTSup 263 (London: T&T Clark, 2004), 154.

9. One Flock, One Shepherd, One God 211

(10:19). In this scene, one is expanded to accommodate an ecclesial entity (as discussed earlier) and love is multidirectional.

The same clustering and semantic broadening of these Shema-terms occurs in the prayer of John 17:

> they have kept your word [λόγον] ... the words [ῥήματα⁴³] you gave to me I have given to them.... Holy Father, keep them in your name that you have given to me, in order that they may be one [ἕν], just as we are.... I have given to them your word [λόγον].... I do not ask concerning these only, but concerning those who believe in me through their word [λόγου], that they may be one [ἕν] ... that they may be one [ἕν] just as we are one [ἕν] ... in order that the world may know that you sent me and you loved [ἠγάπησας] them just as you loved [ἠγάπησας] me.... I have made known to them your name, and will make it known, that the love [ἀγάπη] with which you loved me might be in them. (17:8a, 11b, 14a, 20–21a, 22b, 23b, 26)

The multidirectional dynamics of love are once more broadened as the source and object are God and the disciples respectively. Divine oneness also opens up to include believers, and the words whose reception actualizes the people of God are God's, yet verbalized through multiple agents, those of Jesus and the disciples. The fluid and interchangeable semantics of the Shema's language observed in these passages from John 8, 10, and 17 find biblical precedence in Jer 32:37–41 (39:37–41 LXX). In this prophetic text, the terminology of one is drawn from Deut 6:4 but applied to Israel rather than God; and God is depicted as demonstrating his faithfulness toward Israel "with all my heart and all my soul."⁴⁴

If John is indeed drawing attention to the Shema in coordinating its terminology at key moments within his narrative (as argued in §9.1 above), then the Deuteronomistic weight of oneness cannot be dismissed or offloaded in our reading of the Fourth Gospel from its prologue to postscript. Because of the centrality of the Shema as a text generative of Israel, the Fourth Evangelist appropriates its formative power, broadens its meaning, and thematically integrates its reconfiguration into the entire narrative. If the evangelist has Philip declaring that "we have found him

---

43. In John, λόγος (forty times) and ῥῆμα (twelve times) are often interchangeable in meaning.

44. See J. Gerald Janzen, "An Echo of the Shema in Isaiah 51.1–3," *JSOT* 43 (1989): 69–82, esp. 77.

whom Moses wrote about in the law" (1:45) and if Jesus himself claims that Moses "wrote about me" (5:46), then we should be surprised *not* to find the Shema as a Johannine subtext.

9.4. Conclusion

The term one is the centerpiece of what may well be the Fourth Evangelist's most sophisticated program of thematic development. Oneness language gradually accrues polyvalence and serves as one of the gospel's strongest load-bearing terms. Though corporate unity is certainly an important implication of Johannine oneness, there are richer and more complex dynamics at work: Social harmony is a function of participation within a divine social identity. When the evangelist's core scriptural texts are recognized, it becomes clear that this gospel seeks to generate a new people around the divine Christ (20:30–31). Johannine oneness thus establishes Jesus as a participant in the Shema's articulation of divine identity and categorizes the collective children of God within Ezekiel's eschatological hopes. They are the one flock of the one shepherd who is one with God.

Bibliography

Appold, Mark L. *The Oneness Motif in the Fourth Gospel: Motif Analysis and Exegetical Probe into the Theology of John.* Eugene, OR: Wipf & Stock, 2011.

Augenstein, Jörg. *Das Liebesgebot im Johannesevangelium und in den Johannesbriefen.* BWANT 134. Stuttgart: Kohlhammer, 1993.

Baron, Lori. *The Shema in John's Gospel.* WUNT 2/574. Tübingen: Mohr Siebeck, 2022.

———. "The Shema in John's Gospel and Jewish Restoration Eschatology." Pages 165–73 in *John and Judaism: A Contested Relationship in Context.* Edited by R. Alan Culpepper and Paul N. Anderson. RBS 87. Atlanta: SBL Press, 2017.

———. "The Shema in Mark and John and the Parting of the Ways." Pages 187–210 in *The Ways That Often Parted: Essays in Honor of Joel Marcus.* Edited by Lori Baron, Jill Hicks-Keeton, and Matthew Thiessen. ECL 24. Atlanta: SBL Press, 2018.

Barrett, C. K. *The Gospel according to St John: An Introduction with Commentary and Notes on the Greek Text.* 2nd ed. London: SPCK, 1978.

9. One Flock, One Shepherd, One God

———. "The Old Testament in the Fourth Gospel." *JTS* 48 (1947): 155–69.

Barton, Stephen C. "Christian Community in the Gospel of John." Pages 279–301 in *Christology, Controversy and Community: New Testament Essays in Honour of David R. Catchpole*. Edited by David G. Horrell and Christopher M. Tuckett. NovTSup 99. Leiden: Brill, 2000.

Bauckham, Richard. *Gospel of Glory: Major Themes in Johannine Theology*. Grand Rapids: Baker Academic, 2015.

———. *Jesus and the God of Israel: God Crucified and Other Studies on the New Testament's Christology of Divine Identity*. Grand Rapids: Eerdmans, 2008.

Beutler, Johannes. *A Commentary on the Gospel of John*. Translated by Michael Tait. Grand Rapids: Eerdmans, 2017.

———. "Das Hauptgebot im Johannesevangelium." Pages 222–36 in *Das Gesetz im Neuen Testament*. Edited by Karl Kertelge. QD 108. Freiburg im Breisgau: Herder, 1986.

Brant, Jo-Ann. *John*. Paideia. Grand Rapids: Baker Academic, 2011.

Brown, Raymond E. *The Gospel according to John (XII–XXI): Introduction, Translation, and Notes*. AB 29A. Garden City, NY: Doubleday, 1966.

Byers, Andrew J. *Ecclesiology and Theosis in John's Gospel*. SNTSMS 166. Cambridge: Cambridge University Press, 2017.

———. *John and the Others: Jewish Relations, Christian Origins, and the Sectarian Hermeneutic*. Waco, TX: Baylor University Press, 2021.

Bynum, William Randolph. "Quotations of Zechariah in the Fourth Gospel." Pages 47–74 in *Abiding Words: The Use of Scripture in the Gospel of John*. Edited by Alicia D. Myers and Bruce G. Schuchard. RBS 81. Atlanta: SBL Press, 2015.

Coutts, Joshua. *The Divine Name in the Gospel of John: Significance and Impetus*. WUNT 2/447. Tübingen: Mohr Siebeck, 2017.

Gieschen, Charles A. "The Divine Name That the Son Shares with the Father in the Gospel of John." Pages 387–410 in *Reading the Gospel of John's Christology as Jewish Messianism: Royal, Prophetic, and Divine Messiahs*. Edited by Benjamin E. Reynolds and Gabriele Boccaccini. AJEC 106. Leiden: Brill, 2018.

Gorman, Michael J. *Abide and Go: Missional Theosis in the Gospel of John*. Didsbury Lectures 2016. Eugene, OR: Cascade, 2018.

Hays, Richard B. *Echoes of Scripture in the Gospels*. Waco, TX: Baylor University Press, 2016.

Hayward, C. T. R. "'The Lord Is One': Reflections on the Theme of Unity in John's Gospel from a Jewish Perspective." Pages 138–54 in *Early*

Jewish and Christian Monotheism. Edited by Loren T. Stuckenbruck and Wendy E. S. North. JSNTSup 263. London: T&T Clark, 2004.

Hoskyns, Edwyn C. *The Fourth Gospel.* Edited by Francis Noel Davey. 2nd ed. London: Faber & Faber, 1947.

Janzen, J. Gerald. "An Echo of the Shema in Isaiah 51.1–3." *JSOT* 13.43 (1989): 69–82.

Keener, Craig. *The Gospel of John: A Commentary.* 2 vols. Peabody, MA: Hendrickson, 2003.

Lieu, Judith M. *I, II, and III John: A Commentary.* NTL. Louisville: Westminster John Knox, 2008.

Lincoln, Andrew T. *The Gospel according to Saint John.* BNTC 4. Peabody, MA: Hendrickson, 2005.

Macaskill, Grant. "Name Christology, Divine Aseity, and the I Am Sayings in the Fourth Gospel." *JTI* 12 (2018): 217–41.

Malina, Bruce J., and Richard L. Rohrbaugh. *Social-Science Commentary on the Gospel of John.* Minneapolis: Fortress, 1998.

Manning, Gary T. *Echoes of a Prophet: The Use of Ezekiel in the Gospel of John and in Literature of the Second Temple Period.* JSNTSup 270. London: T&T Clark, 2004.

Menken, Maarten J. J. "The Minor Prophets in John's Gospel." Pages 79–96 in *The Minor Prophets in the New Testament.* Edited by Maarten J. J. Menken and Steve Moyise. LNTS 377. London: T&T Clark, 2009.

Michaels, J. Ramsey. *The Gospel of John.* NICNT. Grand Rapids: Eerdmans, 2010.

Moberly, R. W. L. *Old Testament Theology: Reading the Bible as Christian Scripture.* Grand Rapids: Baker Academic, 2015.

Moloney, Francis J. *Love in the Gospel of John: An Exegetical, Theological, and Literary Study.* Grand Rapids: Baker Academic, 2013.

Myers, Alicia D. "Abiding Words: An Introduction to Perspectives on John's Use of Scripture." Pages 1–20 in *Abiding Words: The Use of Scripture in the Gospel of John.* Edited by Alicia D. Myers and Bruce G. Schuchard. RBS 81. Atlanta: SBL Press, 2015.

Reinhartz, Adele. "'Jews' and Jews in the Fourth Gospel." Pages 213–27 in *Anti-Judaism and the Fourth Gospel.* Edited by Reimund Bieringer, Didier Pollefeyt, and Frederique Vandecasteele-Vanneuville. Louisville: Westminster John Knox, 2001.

Ridderbos, Herman. *The Gospel of John: A Theological Commentary.* Translated by John Vriend. Grand Rapids: Eerdmans, 1997.

Saputra, Brury Eko. *The Shema and John 10: The Importance of the Shema Framework in Understanding the Oneness Language in John 10*. Eugene, OR: Wipf & Stock, 2019.

Sheridan, Ruth. "Issues in the Translation of οἱ Ἰουδαῖοι in the Fourth Gospel." *JBL* 132 (2013): 671–95.

Thompson, Marianne Meye. *John: A Commentary*. NTL. Louisville: Westminster John Knox, 2015.

Waaler, Erik. *The Shema and the First Commandment in First Corinthians: An Intertextual Approach to Paul's Re-reading of Deuteronomy*. WUNT 2/253. Tübingen: Mohr Siebeck, 2008.

10

One Lord, One People: Kingship and Oneness in Acts

Alan J. Thompson

The theme of the unity of the church is widespread in Acts.[1] The oneness of the early Christian community (frequently using terminology such as ὁμοθυμαδόν, πᾶς, and ἐπὶ τὸ αὐτό) is seen in (among other things) their praying together (1:14; 2:42; 4:24), being together (1:15; 2:1, 44, 47; 5:12), holding everything in common (2:44), being of one heart and mind in agreement (4:32; 15:25), and sharing possessions (2:45; 4:32, 34).[2] Furthermore, disputes are resolved. The Ananias and Sapphira incident (5:1–11) is surrounded by summary passages that highlight the unity of the people of God and the continuing spread of the gospel (4:32–37; 5:12–16). Similarly, the complaint of the Hellenistic Jews against the Hebraic Jews (6:1–7) is resolved and surrounded by statements that highlight the continuing spread of the word (the proposal pleased the whole group [παντὸς τοῦ πλήθους], 6:5). Likewise, the Cornelius incident and subsequent criticism from the circumcised believers in Jerusalem is resolved (ἀκούσαντες δὲ ταῦτα ἡσύχασαν καὶ ἐδόξασαν τὸν θεόν, 11:18), as is the disagreement

---

1. For the purposes of this chapter I am assuming that the author of Luke and Acts is Luke, the occasional companion of Paul. See Craig S. Keener, *Acts: An Exegetical Commentary*, vol. 1 (Grand Rapids: Baker Academic, 2012), 221–57; Alan J. Thompson, *Luke*, EGGNT (Nashville: B&H Academic, 2016), 3–6. This chapter draws on and develops Thompson, *One Lord, One People: The Unity of the Church in Acts in Its Literary Setting*, LNTS 359 (London: T&T Clark, 2008).

2. Jacques Dupont, "L'union entre les premiers chrétiens dans les Actes des Apôtres," *NRTh* 91 (1969): 897–915, draws attention to Luke's use of κοινωνία, κοινός, ἅπαντα κοινά, and μία ψυχή.

218 Alan J. Thompson

recorded in chapter 15 (after the council there was unity between the apostles and elders and also "the whole church" [σὺν ὅλῃ τῇ ἐκκλησίᾳ], 15:22).[3]

This widely recognized emphasis on unity in Acts has generated a range of discussions about apparent idealization, similarities to ancient discussions of a "community of goods," Luke's apparently later smoothing out of earlier differences to suit a particular agenda such as a Pauline-Petrine unity, or perhaps his later and historically naïve look back at an earlier history that overlooks earlier differences. In light of the references to "united" *opposition* to believers (5:9; in 7:57; 18:12; 19:29 ὁμοθυμαδόν is also used) it is likely that Luke does not claim that simply unity in and of itself is the ideal. Unresolved disagreements among believers (15:36–41; 19:30–31; 21:12–13) indicate that Luke is not claiming that unity is the same as uniformity in all matters.[4]

In this chapter, I will connect the theme of unity in Acts to Luke's emphasis on the kingship of Jesus. For Luke, there is ultimately only one Lord, the Lord Jesus, and therefore one people of God.[5] In this sense, oneness in Acts is tied to a common adherence to the apostolic message of good news about the Lord Jesus. This unity of one people to one Lord is then worked out in activities such as prayer, meeting one another's needs, and seeking solutions to difficulties that arise. Before getting to kingship and oneness in Acts, however, some explanation for examining this combination is needed. The significance of this combination of one Lord and one people becomes clearer when the context of the combination of kingship and oneness claims for ancient rulers is remembered.

10.1. Roman Political Vision: One King, One People

Luke regularly reminds readers that he is locating his account of salvation history in the setting of Roman history, and Roman rulers in particular.[6] There are references to Caesar Augustus (Luke 2:1), Tiberius Caesar (3:1), the

---

3. Unless otherwise noted, Scripture translations are from the NIV.

4. For interaction with these suggestions, see Alan J. Thompson, "Unity in Acts: Idealization or Reality?," *JETS* 51 (2008): 523–42.

5. Richard Bauckham, *Gospel of Glory: Major Themes in Johannine Theology* (Grand Rapids: Baker Academic, 2015), 30: "The unitedness of the people is related to the uniqueness of their leader."

6. Kazuhiko Yamazaki-Ransom, *The Roman Empire in Luke's Narrative*, LNTS 404 (London: T&T Clark, 2010), 70–87; Craig A. Evans, "King Jesus and His Ambassadors: Empire and Luke-Acts," in *Empire in the New Testament*, ed. Stanley E. Porter and Cynthia Long Westfall (Eugene, OR: Pickwick, 2011), 120–39.

10. One Lord, One People: Kingship and Oneness in Acts 219

reign of Claudius (Acts 11:28; 18:2), and the proconsulship of Gallio in the Roman province of Achaia (18:12). Luke also twice records contrasts made between the kingship of Jesus and Caesar (Luke 23:2; Acts 17:7), provides detailed accounts of Paul's encounters with two Roman procurators (Porcius Festus and Antonius Felix), notes Paul's appeal to Caesar himself (25:11–12, 25; who is called κύριος in 25:26), describes a long journey to Rome under the care of Julius, a centurion of the cohort Augusta (27:1), and concludes with a statement of Paul's bold and unhindered proclamation of the reign of God and the Lord Jesus Christ in Rome itself, the heart of the empire (28:31).

This broad Roman context of Acts has also generated a range of discussions. Debate has often revolved around whether Luke is portraying Christianity favorably in an attempt to commend it to Roman authorities (i.e., as a law-abiding, legitimate, and not a dangerous religion), or whether Luke is portraying Roman authorities favorably in an attempt to commend them to his Christian readers (i.e., the empire has been beneficial to the spread of Christianity).[7] In both of these approaches the Roman Empire was essentially viewed in a positive light.[8] Richard Cassidy has highlighted problems with both positions, and in particular has drawn attention to the mixed portrayals of Roman officials in Acts.[9] In recent times, therefore, although there are difficulties in trying to relate Luke-Acts to specific aspects of the imperial cult in specific places or times, it is increasingly recognized that Luke's claims of universal authority for the risen King Jesus should be read in the context of widespread claims for the universal authority of the Roman emperor.[10] To cite just one specific

---

7. For Christianity as law-abiding, legitimate, and not dangerous, see, e.g., Hans Conzelmann, *The Theology of St. Luke*, trans. Geoffrey Buswell (New York: Harper & Row, 1960), 137–49; Ernst Haenchen, *The Acts of the Apostles: A Commentary* (Philadelphia: Westminster, 1971), 100–102. For seeing Luke as commending Roman authorities, see, e.g., Paul Walaskay, *"And So We Came to Rome": The Political Perspective of St. Luke*, SNTSMS 49 (Cambridge: Cambridge University Press, 1983), 63–67.

8. See the summary in Raymond Pickett, "Luke and Empire: An Introduction," in *Luke-Acts and Empire: Essays in Honor of Robert L. Brawley*, ed. David Rhodes, David Esterline, and Jae Won Lee, PTMS 151 (Eugene, OR: Pickwick, 2011), 5.

9. Cassidy, *Society and Politics in the Acts of the Apostles* (Maryknoll, NY: Orbis Books, 1987), 145–57; see also Cassidy, "Paul's Proclamation of Lord Jesus as a Chained Prisoner in Rome: Luke's Ending Is in His Beginning" in Rhodes, Esterline, and Lee, *Luke-Acts and Empire*, 142–53.

10. C. Kavin Rowe, "Luke-Acts and the Imperial Cult: A Way through the Conundrum?," *JSNT* 27 (2005): 279–88, succinctly highlights difficulties with reference to

220   Alan J. Thompson

example, the proclamation in Luke 2 of "good news … for all the people" (2:10), concerning the birth of a "savior" who is "Christ the Lord" (2:11), whose coming means "peace on earth" (2:14), compares with similar claims made by or about Augustus, who is himself explicitly mentioned in 2:1 (i.e., esp. the language of εὐαγγελίζω, σωτήρ, εἰρήνη, the universal claim for "all people," and the Roman census).[11]

This setting of Roman history and Roman rulers in Acts is also instructive for the theme of unity in Acts. Other chapters in this book have located the theme of unity in the broad setting of the Greco-Roman world so there is no need to rehearse those findings here.[12] For our purposes, I will provide a brief summary and sampling of some claims that combine kingship and unity to set the stage.[13] In general the frequent association of kingship and unity is seen in that: (1) descriptions of unity under a king's reign frequently characterize favorable accounts of that king's reign.[14] (2) Roman

---

particular claims in particular locations and times; in Rowe, *World Upside Down: Reading Acts in the Graeco-Roman Age* (Oxford: Oxford University Press, 2009), esp. 53–56, he notes the difficulty of swinging to the other extreme and viewing Acts as simply opposing Rome. Steve Walton, "The State They Were In: Luke's View of the Roman Empire," in *Rome in the Bible and the Early Church*, ed. Peter Oakes (Grand Rapids: Baker Academic, 2002), 1–41, summarizes a variety of approaches and critiques the view that Acts presents a proimperial viewpoint.

11. Further documentation for the inscriptions and decrees relevant to Luke 2 is found in Thompson, *One Lord, One People*, 61–63. On the census, see Joel Green, *The Gospel of Luke*, NICNT (Grand Rapids: Eerdmans, 1997), 126 (Josephus, *B.J.* 2.118, 433; *A.J.* 18.23). Seyoon Kim, *Christ and Caesar: The Gospel and the Roman Empire in the Writings of Paul and Luke* (Grand Rapids: Eerdmans, 2008), 80–81, agrees, though he is critical of many aspects of anti-imperial readings of Paul and Luke. Contra Richard Horsley, *The Liberation of Christmas: The Infancy Narratives in Social Context* (New York: Crossroad, 1989), 33, salvation in Lukan theology is within the framework of the fulfillment of Old Testament eschatological hopes (Luke 3:4–6; 4:18–19; 7:21–22; Acts 10:36, 43) rather than liberation from a particular political order; see Torsten Jantsch, *Jesus, der Retter: Die Soteriologie des lukanischen Doppelwerks*, WUNT 381 (Tübingen: Mohr Siebeck, 2017).

12. See esp. the chapters by Lynette Mitchell (ch. 3), James Harrison (ch. 4), and Kylie Crabbe (ch. 7).

13. See Thompson, *One Lord, One People*, 38 (summarizing 19–38).

14. Herodotus, *Hist.* 1.101, praises Deioces, and in 1.103 his grandson, Cyaxares; on Alexander the Great, see Plutarch, *Alex. fort.* 5–6 (329a–b); Diodorus, *Hist.* 18.4.4; 2 Bar. 73.1–74.4; Sib. Or. 3.350–80 (against Rome); 4 Ezra 13.12–13, 39 (also possibly against Rome).

10. One Lord, One People: Kingship and Oneness in Acts 221

emperors (and the empire) are particularly praised for bringing unity.[15] (3) Roman emperors may also be criticized for their failure to bring concord.[16] (4) Rule by one good ruler is said to bring unity, the greatest of blessings, and does not produce discord.[17] For example, Plutarch praises Alexander the Great for bringing together into one body (εἰς τὸ αὐτό) all people everywhere so that they would regard their lives as common (κοινάς) to all (*Alex. fort.* 5–6 [329a–b]). Diodorus praises Alexander's plan to bring the largest continents to common unity (εἰς κοινὴν ὁμόνοιαν, *Hist.* 18.4.4). Polybius praises the Roman Empire for the way the empire acts in concord and supports each other (συμφρονεῖν καὶ συνεργεῖν ἀλλήλοις) and cooperates both in public and in private (κοινῇ καὶ κατ' ἰδίαν) such that it is able to achieve whatever it sets out to do (*Hist.* 6.18.1–4). Aelius Aristides's *Or.* 24, *To the Rhodians: Concerning Concord*, argues for concord because "all the earth is united under one emperor with common laws for all" (οὐ κοινὴ μὲν ἅπασα γῆ, βασιλεὺς δὲ εἷς, νόμοι δὲ κοινοὶ πᾶσι, 24.31). First Maccabees 8:1–16 praises the good government and strength of the Romans because "they trust one man each year to rule over them and to control all their land; they all heed the one man, and there is no envy or jealousy among them." [18]

Lynette Mitchell and James Harrison have pointed out (see chs. 3 and 4, respectively) the darker side of kingship and unity exploited by Alexander the Great and Roman imperialism. The purpose here is to argue that the prominence of the theme of unity together with the theme of kingship—particularly *Roman* kingship—in ancient literature sheds further light on the Lukan emphasis on unity in Acts in the Roman setting that Luke regularly brings before readers.[19] The combination of the themes

---

15. Polybius, *Hist.* 6.11–18; Dionysius of Halicarnassus, *Ant. rom.* 2.2.2 (concerning Romulus); 1 Macc 8:16; Aelius Aristides, *Or.* 24.31; Vergil, *Ecl.* 4.4–17; *Georg.* 1.24–42; *Aen.* 1.257–296; 6.781–783, 788–796; 10.6–15; 12.189–194, 820–840; Horace, *Epod.* 16.63–66; Ovid, *Metam.* 1.198–201; 15.746–870 (esp. 15.820–831, 832–839), 877; Calpurnius Siculus, *Ecl.* 1.42, 46–47, 57, 64; 4.6, 99, 146; Einsiedeln Eclogues 2.22–24; Statius, *Silv.* 4.1.5–8; 4.2.1–2; 4.3.114–117.

16. See esp. Horace, *Ep.* 1.2.6–16; Lucan, *Civil War* (*Pharsalia*) 1.1–3; Statius, *Theb.* 1.214–247; see also Sib. Or. 3.350–380 (against Rome); 4 Ezra 13.12–13, 39.

17. Herodotus, *Hist.* 3.82 and Darius's criticism of oligarchy; 2 Macc 4:5–6.

18. The hope that a coming Davidic king would unite the people of God is also found in Ezek 34:11–13, 22–23; esp. 37:15–28. See Thompson, *One Lord, One People*, 33–35.

19. For similar arguments on the relation between unity and Greco-Roman kingship, see Julien Smith, ch. 13 in this volume.

222 Alan J. Thompson

of unity and kingship in Acts may further contribute to broader Lukan claims in Acts that Christ is the true king and that the Christian community is the true people of God. In order to demonstrate this, I will focus particularly on Acts 2 and 10–12 and the combination of the themes of kingship and oneness there.

10.2. Kingship and Community (Acts 2)

As many have noted, the Pentecost account and Peter's sermon in Acts 2 are programmatic for the rest of the narrative of Acts.[20] One of the main emphases of Peter's sermon is that the resurrection and exaltation of Jesus as Lord and Christ has brought about the eschatological promise of the Holy Spirit.[21] After stating that the promise to David concerning God's placement of "one of his descendants on his throne" (2:30) is speaking of the resurrection of the Christ (2:31–32), the crux of the sermon comes in 2:33 where the events of Pentecost are explained.[22] "Being therefore [οὖν] exalted at the right hand of God … he has poured out this that you both see and hear." Here it is spelled out that the coming of the Holy Spirit is a result of the exaltation of Christ.[23] Luke's use of the particle οὖν in verse 33 shows that the pouring out of the Holy Spirit on the day of Pentecost is evidence of the reign of the Lord Christ from the throne of David. This leads to the climax of the sermon in 2:34–36 where the conclusion of the argument (again with the use of οὖν) declares Jesus to be the Lord who sits at God's right hand whom God has made "both Lord and Messiah" (2:34–36).[24] In this context the terms κύριον … καὶ χριστόν point to Jesus's

---

20. E.g., Mark L. Strauss, *The Davidic Messiah in Luke-Acts: The Promise and Its Fulfillment in Lukan Christology*, JSNTSup 110 (Sheffield: Sheffield Academic, 1995), 131–32.

21. On the importance of the ascension for Luke, see David K. Bryan and David W. Pao, eds., *Ascent into Heaven in Luke-Acts: New Explorations of Luke's Narrative Hinge* (Minneapolis: Fortress, 2016).

22. Strauss, *Davidic Messiah*, 138–40; Darrell L. Bock, *Proclamation from Prophecy and Pattern: Lucan Old Testament Christology*, JSNTSup 12 (Sheffield: Sheffield Academic, 1987), 171–81.

23. Max B. Turner, *Power from on High: The Spirit in Israel's Restoration and Witness in Luke-Acts*, JPTSup 9 (Sheffield: Sheffield Academic, 1996), 295–96.

24. H. Douglas Buckwalter, *The Character and Purpose of Luke's Christology*, SNTSMS 89 (Cambridge: Cambridge University Press, 1996), 183–91. See also Max B. Turner, "The 'Spirit of Prophecy' as the Power of Israel's Restoration and Witness," in

10. One Lord, One People: Kingship and Oneness in Acts   223

status as the messianic king (the Davidic Messiah who rose from the dead, 2:25–33), who is now enthroned at God's right hand (the exalted Lord who reigns, 2:33–35).

In the wider context of Acts 1–2, the emphasis on Jesus's reign in 2:33–36 relates also to the narrative expectations for the kingdom of God that are raised in 1:1–11. Acts 1:3 states that during Jesus's forty days of instruction to his disciples he spoke about the kingdom of God. This is immediately followed by a reminder of the promise of the Holy Spirit with whom they will be baptized "in a few days" (1:5). This in turn prompts the question from the disciples concerning the restoration of the kingdom to Israel by Jesus (1:6). Then Jesus again directs the disciples' attention to the coming of the Holy Spirit and the program that will include "Jerusalem, all Judea and Samaria, and the ends of the earth." The allusions to Isa 32:15 (via Luke 24:49, ἐπελθόντος τοῦ ἁγίου πνεύματος ἐφ᾿ ὑμᾶς), Isa 43:10–12 (ἔσεσθέ μου μάρτυρες), and Isa 49:6 (ἕως ἐσχάτου τῆς γῆς)[25] indicate that Jesus's reference to the Holy Spirit in Acts 1:8 clarifies the means by which Jesus, through them, will bring God's reign.[26]

Thus, kingship has a vital role to play in Acts 1–2, which is the context of Acts 2:42–47. In moving beyond this observation to the theme of unity, the association of the theme of kingship with the theme of unity in Acts 1–2 is indicated by: (1) the integral relationship of Acts 2:42–47 to its preceding context; (2) the emphasis on the theme of unity in Acts 2:42–47; and (3) the summarizing phrase at the conclusion to this section in Acts 2:47.

First, we should note the vital connection between the account in Acts 1–2 and the description of the early Christian community in 2:42–47. There is a shift from the specific reference to "those who accepted his message" being added "that day" (i.e., "the day of Pentecost" 2:1) in 2:41 to the general summary of ongoing practices in 2:42–47. Nevertheless, the following suggests that it is best to treat 2:42–47 as a literary unit that is closely

---

Witness to the Gospel: The Theology of Acts, ed. I. Howard Marshall and David Peterson (Grand Rapids: Eerdmans, 1998), 333–34.

25. David W. Pao, *Acts and the Isaianic New Exodus*, WUNT 2/130 (Tübingen: Mohr Siebeck, 2000), 91–96.

26. Constantino A. Ziccardi, *The Relationship of Jesus and the Kingdom of God according to Luke-Acts* (Rome: Editrice Pontifica Università Gregoriana, 2008); Alan J. Thompson, *The Acts of the Risen Lord Jesus: Luke's Account of God's Unfolding Plan*, NSBT 27 (Downers Grove, IL: InterVarsity Press, 2011), 38–48, 103–8.

224   Alan J. Thompson

tied to the preceding events (see table 10.1 below): (1) The μέν ... δέ link
between verses 41 and 42 links the description of those who responded in
2:38–41 (i.e., who have all received the common gifts of forgiveness of sins
and the Holy Spirit) with the description of the community in 2:42–47; (2)
the use of προσκαρτερέω in 2:42 and προσκαρτεροῦντες ὁμοθυμαδόν in 2:46
recalls 1:14; (3) the use of προσευχή in 2:42 recalls 1:14; (4) the use of ἐπὶ
τὸ αὐτό in 2:44 and 2:47 recalls 2:1; (5) the use of προστίθημι in 2:41 and
2:47; and (6) the use of σῴζω in 2:40 and 2:47. The table below identifies the
links between 2:42–47 and the preceding narrative.

Preceding narrative	2:42–47
μέν ... (2:41)	... δέ (2:42)
προσκαρτεροῦντες ὁμοθυμαδόν (1:14)	προσκαρτερέω (2:42)
	προσκαρτεροῦντες ὁμοθυμαδόν (2:46)
προσευχή (1:14)	προσευχή (2:42)
ἐπὶ τὸ αὐτό (2:1)	ἐπὶ τὸ αὐτό (2:44 and 2:47)
προστίθημι (2:41)	προστίθημι (2:47)
σῴζω (2:40)	σῴζω (2:47)

Second, the emphasis in 2:42–47 on the unity of the Messiah's community
in common submission to him is indicated by their common devotion
to: (1) one body of teaching (τῇ διδαχῇ τῶν ἀποστόλων);[27] (2) common
meals (τῇ κλάσει τοῦ ἄρτου);[28] (3) prayer (ταῖς προσευχαῖς);[29] and (4) the

---

27. The "apostles' teaching" in this context picks up on the references already
made to the apostles as Jesus's chosen representatives (1:2, 24) and authentic witnesses
(1:3, 22). Continued devotion to apostolic teaching in this context then is an outworking of their common commitment to Jesus; see C. K. Barrett, *The Acts of the
Apostles: Preliminary Introduction and Commentary on Acts I–XIV*, ICC (Edinburgh:
T&T Clark, 1994), 163.

28. A reference to common meals in Acts 2:42 is more likely than merely the
Lord's Supper because: (1) the identical terminology in Luke 24:35 refers to a meal;
(2) the verbal form in Luke 24:30 and Acts 27:35 refers to a meal; (3) breaking bread
is probably clarified in Acts 2:46 as "sharing food" or "eating together"; and (4) the
opening act of a Jewish meal may be described as "breaking bread."

29. Common devotion to prayer (ταῖς προσευχαῖς) in this context expresses the
united dependence of the community on the Lord. So far in Acts, prayer has been
offered to the Lord Jesus (1:24), and the people of Israel have been exhorted to call
upon the name of the Lord (2:21). The wording here (ἦσαν προσκαρτεροῦντες) recalls

10. One Lord, One People: Kingship and Oneness in Acts   225

"community" (τῇ κοινωνίᾳ) that was demonstrated by having "all things in common" (εἶχον ἅπαντα κοινά). The expression of their "togetherness" (ἐπὶ τὸ αὐτό) in terms of selling and sharing possessions is further qualified in verses 45 and 46 by the distribution of possessions καθότι ἄν τις χρείαν εἶχεν (2:45; i.e., the sharing of goods was not total) and the κλῶντές τε κατ οἶκον ἄρτον (2:46; cf. also 12:12; i.e., they still had houses to meet in). The explanation given in 2:45–46 shows that the voluntary and occasional (i.e., specific acts to meet specific needs rather than a common pool) sharing of possessions was a concrete outworking of the commitment to unity referred to in 2:42 (προσκαρτεροῦντες ... τῇ κοινωνίᾳ) and highlighted in 2:44. Thus, the devotion of the early Christian community to τῇ κοινωνίᾳ is best understood as a commitment to the "common life of the community" rather than "a communal form of life."[30] This fellowship then is primarily a unity of those who together belong to one Lord as proclaimed by the apostles, and an expression of that unity in the sharing of possessions with those among them who were in need.[31]

Third, the inclusion of ἐπὶ τὸ αὐτό at the conclusion of this section (2:47) is also meant to highlight the integral connection between the exaltation of the Lord Jesus and the unity of his community. Acts 2:47b concludes the Pentecost account with the statement that ὁ δὲ κύριος προσετίθει τοὺς σῳζομένους καθ ἡμέραν ἐπὶ τὸ αὐτό. The Lord (ὁ κυριός) in the context of 2:34–36 is a reference to the Lord Jesus (cf. the use of κύριος in 1:6, 21, 24). He is not only saving people (the passive participle alludes to 2:21) and increasing the number of believers (as the use of προστίθημι indicates), he is also adding

---

the reference to their devotion to prayer in 1:14 where their unity in prayer is also highlighted (ὁμοθυμαδόν) and anticipates their practice in 4:24.

30. Contra Joseph Fitzmyer, *Acts of the Apostles: A New Translation with Introduction and Commentary*, AB 31 (New York: Doubleday, 1998), 270. See also David Seccombe, *Possessions and the Poor in Luke-Acts*, SNTSU (Linz: Fuchs, 1982), 204; Christopher M. Hays, *Luke's Wealth Ethics*, WUNT 2/275 (Tübingen: Mohr Siebeck, 2010), 191.

31. This simple observation is frequently neglected in discussions of this passage that focus on the "community of goods" or "friendship ideals." Although space prevents a full assessment of literary parallels to the summary passages, references to friendship do not appear in this context and the focus is not on a community of goods, but on meeting needs as an expression of the unity of the community in common allegiance to the Lord Jesus. Similar wording in Plato and Aristotle is found in discussions about the unity of the best governed community; see Thompson, *One Lord, One People*, 88–93.

226 Alan J. Thompson

them "to the community" or "together."[32] In the context of 2:1 and 2:44, the use of ἐπὶ τὸ αὐτό at the conclusion of the account in 2:47 highlights again the togetherness of the Lord's community.[33] More specifically, this concluding phrase in 2:47 claims that the togetherness or unity of the community in common allegiance to Christ (as emphasized in 2:42–47) is brought about by the reigning Lord himself (whose present reign has been emphasized in 1:1–2:41).

Thus, in its context, Acts 2:42–47 draws attention to the kingship of Jesus, the unity of his community, and even his role in uniting his people. In light of the frequent emphasis on descriptions of the unity and harmony brought about by kings in general and the Roman emperors in particular, it is possible that the combination of these themes in Acts 2 indicates that a claim is being made that Jesus is the true king in the context of contemporary claims for Roman rulers. This possibility is strengthened by Gary Gilbert's suggestion that the lists of nations frequently found in Roman political propaganda in the contexts of claims for worldwide rule provides a plausible context for the list of nations in Acts 2.[34] Gilbert notes the early interpretation of Tertullian who cites the list of nations from Acts 2 as part of his argument for

---

32. For increasing the number of believers, see NIV; Haenchen, *Acts of the Apostles*, 190, 193; Fitzmyer, *Acts*, 264, 273. For "to the community," see Luke Timothy Johnson, *The Acts of the Apostles*, SP 5 (Collegeville, MN: Liturgical Press, 1992), 56, 60; Barrett, *Acts of the Apostles*, 1.158. For "together," see Kirsopp Lake and Henry J. Cadbury, *The Beginnings of Christianity: Part I. The Acts of the Apostles*, ed. Frederick J. Foakes Jackson and Kirsopp Lake (London: Macmillan, 1920), 4:30.

33. The addition of (ἐν) τῇ ἐκκλησίᾳ in some manuscripts (e.g., 945, 1739, D) may be evidence of the tendency of copyists to further clarify or explain the text as a reference not just to numerical addition but addition to "the community" or to "the congregation." Note the parallel in 1 Cor 11:18 and 20. Note also the common rendering of *yaḥad* by ἐπὶ τὸ αὐτό in the LXX (cf. esp. Pss 2:2; 4:9; 18:10; 33:4; 36:38; 48:3, 11; 54:15; 70:10; 73:6, 8; 97:8; 101:23; 121:3; 132:1) and the use of *yaḥad* in 1QS I, 1; III, 7; V, 7 as a term for "the community"; see Thompson, *One Lord, One People*, 68.

34. For claims of worldwide rule, see Strabo, *Geogr.* 1.1.16–18; Polybius 1.1.5; Plutarch, *Ti. Gracch.* 9.6; and Agrippa's claim in Josephus, *B.J.* 2.380, 388; Ovid, *Fast.* 4.857–858. Lists of nations extolling the accomplishments of Roman emperors may be found in Pliny, *Nat.* 5.132–133; 7.98; Diodorus Siculus, *Hist.* 40.4; Virgil, *Aen.* 6.780–782; 8.714–728; Horace, *Carm.* 4.14; Josephus, *B.J.* 2.358–387; and Res gest. divi Aug. 25–33. Curtius Rufus (mid-first century CE) 6.3.2–3, lists fourteen nations of Alexander the Great's conquest, five of which are the same as Acts; see Gary Gilbert, "The List of Nations in Acts 2: Roman Propaganda and the Lukan Response," *JBL* 121 (2002): 497–529; Gilbert, "Luke-Acts and Negotiation of Authority and Identity in the Roman

10. One Lord, One People: Kingship and Oneness in Acts 227

the universal rule of Christ as the true king in the context of Roman and all other claims to lordship (Tertullian, *Adv. Jud.* 7; see also Tertullian, *Apol.* 34.1). Although the focus in Acts 2 is on Israel (in fulfilment of Acts 1:6–8), the description of the crowd gathered at Pentecost anticipates developments to follow in the narrative of Acts.[35] The claim of universal authority is indicated here with the reference to Jews "from every nation *under heaven*" (2:5, emphasis added) that picks up on the earlier reference to "heaven" in 2:2 and reminds readers of Jesus's exalted position in heaven over all (1:10–11).

In highlighting the kingship of Jesus and the unity of those under his reign, Luke is touching on a widely recognized theme. Thus, the plausibility that Luke is interacting with contemporary claims for authority in Acts 2 is indicated by (1) the repeated emphasis on the claims of ancient literature for the unity brought about by rulers, in particular the emphasis on the unity brought by the Roman rulers; (2) the emphasis on both the exaltation of Jesus as Lord and ruling (Davidic) Messiah as well as the associated emphasis on the unity of his people; and (3) the universalistic emphasis expressed in the list of nations in Acts 2 in the context of the universal authority claimed by Roman rulers expressed in lists of nations. In contrast to the brutality and force of the Roman conquest, however, the authority of the reigning Lord Jesus results in the forgiveness of sins and the gift of the Holy Spirit for those who belong to him.[36] This claim for universal authority will again be made as Jesus is declared to be "Lord of all" (10:36) in a context that includes "even the Gentiles" (11:18).

10.3. Jew and Gentile:
One Lord, One People, One Holy Spirit (Acts 10–11)

Kavin Rowe highlights the significance of the Roman context of Peter's statement in Acts 10 that "*this one* [Jesus] is Lord of all" (οὗτός ἐστιν πάντων

World," in *The Multivalence of Biblical Texts and Theological Meanings*, ed. Christine Helmer, SymS 37 (Atlanta: Society of Biblical Literature, 2006), 83–104.

35. I.e., "Jews" (2:5); "Jews and converts" (2:11); "all Israel" (2:36; cf. 2:14, 22); in keeping with allusions to Ezek 37 and the list in Isa 11:11 (both in the context of the themes of kingship and unity); as well as "from every nation" (2:5); "all people" (2:17); "everyone" (2:21); "all who are far off" (2:39; an allusion to gentiles, also Isa 57:19; Acts 22:21); see Pao, *Isaianic*, 230–32.

36. H. Douglas Buckwalter, "The Divine Savior," in Marshall and Peterson, *Witness to the Gospel*, 107–23. For the brutality of Rome, see Tacitus, *Agr.* 30: "They rob, butcher, plunder, and call it 'empire'; and where they make a desolation, they call it 'peace.'"

228   Alan J. Thompson

κύριος, 10:36, emphasis added).[37] Peter declares this before the Roman Centurion, Cornelius (and his household), in Caesarea, a city whose very name recalls the emperor Augustus.[38] Furthermore, the language of "Lord of all" evokes the claims for the universal lordship of the Roman emperor, especially given the use of the term κύριος for the emperor in 25:26.[39] In addition to this obvious and direct claim for the universal lordship of Christ, readers of Luke-Acts may note the more subtle link between the description of Jesus in 10:38 and the "kings of the Gentiles" in Luke 22:24–26. The description of Jesus's earthly ministry as "doing good [εὐεργετῶν] and healing all who were under the power of the devil" (10:38) recalls Jesus's warnings to the apostles in Luke 22:24–26 about "those in authority over them (who) are called benefactors [εὐεργέται]."[40] Jesus warned the apostles that their leadership in his kingdom is not to be like "the kings of the Gentiles" who "lord it over them [κυριεύουσιν αὐτῶν]." The universal claims for Jesus continue in Acts 10. It is the Lord Jesus who is the judge of all ("the living and the dead"), and "everyone" must believe in him to receive forgiveness of sins (10:42–43).

In the context of these claims for universal authority, however, one of the main emphases of this passage is the unity of those who belong to this one Lord. Similar to Acts 2, though now with a focus on Jew and gentile, the people of God are united together under the one Lord Jesus through the promise of forgiveness of sins and the gift of the Holy Spirit. This unity of Jew and gentile believer is particularly emphasized with parallels to Pentecost. Thus, (1) everyone who believes in the name of Jesus receives the forgiveness of sins (10:43; cf. 2.38); (2) the gentile believers speak "in tongues and praise [μεγαλυνόντων] God" (10:46; cf. 2:11); (3) the Holy

---

37. Rowe, "Luke-Acts and the Imperial Cult," 279–300. Rowe notes the demonstrative pronoun here.

38. See Benjamin R. Wilson, "Jew-Gentile Relations and the Geographic Movement of Acts 10:1–11:18," *CBQ* 80 (2018): 81–96, for the Roman setting of Caesarea.

39. E.g., Epictetus *Diatr.* 4.1.12 (ὁ πάντῶν κύριος καῖσαρ) cited by Rowe, "Luke-Acts and the Imperial Cult," 292; see also Justin R. Howell, "The Imperial Authority and Benefaction of Centurions and Acts 10.34–43: A Response to C. Kavin Rowe," *JSNT* 31 (2008): 25–51.

40. NRSV. See also Evans, "King Jesus and His Ambassadors," 131. For the translation here, see Thompson, *Luke*, 345. These are the only occurrences of εὐεργετέω and εὐεργέτης in the New Testament. Evans notes (132) that "the Lukan Peter does not say 'oppressed by Rome' or 'oppressed by Rome's client rulers.' King Jesus, humanity's true 'Benefactor,' is not at war with the kings of the earth."

10. One Lord, One People: Kingship and Oneness in Acts 229

Spirit is God's "gift" (δωρεά, 10:45; 11:17; cf. 2:38); and (4) recollection of "what the Lord had said" refers to Jesus's promise to baptize with the Holy Spirit (11:16; cf. 1:5). Furthermore, Peter states that "they have received the Holy Spirit *just as we have*" (ὡς καὶ ἡμεῖς, 10:47, emphasis added), the Holy Spirit came on them "as he had come on us" (ὥσπερ καὶ ἐφ ἡμᾶς, 11:15), and God has given them "the same gift he gave us" (τὴν ἴσην δωρεὰν ... ὡς καὶ ἡμῖν, 11:17).

In this same context the resolution of another conflict and potential division frames the repetition of the account of Cornelius's conversion in Acts 11:1–18. This frame (11:1–2, 18) indicates that the purpose for repeating the account is not merely to reinforce the points made in Acts 10 but also to draw attention to the ongoing theme of unity. The significance of the following account is seen in the all-inclusive reference to "the apostles and the believers throughout Judea" in 11:1 (i.e., the Christian community as a whole). The dispute with Peter arises from "the circumcised believers" (οἱ ἐκ περιτομῆς, 11:2; i.e., Jewish believers, cf. 10:45).[41] The effect of the recognition that the gentiles had received "the same gift" (11:17) from the ascended Lord (11:16; cf. 10:36) was that the dispute with the circumcised believers that began in 11:1 was settled. Their objections ceased "when they heard this" (ἀκούσαντες δὲ ταῦτα ἡσύχασαν, 11:18).[42]

Thus, the declaration that the Lord Jesus is "Lord of all" before a Roman Centurion in Caesarea has rightly been recognized as a claim for the Lord Jesus that should be understood in the context of other claims for universal lordship. In this same context, however, the unity of those under this Lord is particularly emphasized. This unity is a soteriological unity between Jew and gentile in common belief in the Lord Jesus that results in the common reception of forgiveness of sins and the gift of the Holy Spirit. This unity is then the basis for relational unity expressed in the resolution of conflict over table fellowship. Acts 11:1–3 records a threat to the outworking of this unity as the dispute between the circumcised believers and Peter highlights the potential for ongoing division between Jew and gentile. This potential dispute between circumcised and uncircumcised believers was overcome when there was common submission to "what the Lord had said" (11:16) and common recognition that "the same

---

41. That they were believers is evident from Peter's speech (cf. esp. 11:15, 17) and their response in 11:18b.

42. Lit. "silenced" (though since they then "glorified God" it is their objections that were silenced/ceased).

230 Alan J. Thompson

gift" of the Holy Spirit had been received through belief in the same Lord Jesus (11:17).[43]

10.4. A Counterexample in Caesarea:
King Herod and Those Who Suffer under His Rule (Acts 12)

In this section of Acts the summary statements of Acts 9:31 and 12:24 frame the focus on Peter. In a broad sense, the account of Peter's encounter with Cornelius in Caesarea introduces this section and the account of Peter's encounter with Herod concludes the section. Whereas Acts 10 indicates that a combination of the themes of Jesus's lordship and the unity of those under his reign contributes to Lukan christological claims in Caesarea, a counterexample may be found in the description of King Herod and those under his reign at the dramatic conclusion to Acts 12, also in Caesarea.[44] Agrippa, a grandson of Herod the Great raised in Rome, was on good terms with members of the Roman imperial family. His title "king" was bestowed on him by the emperor Gaius, and his realm included Galilee, Perea, and later, under the reign of Claudius, Judea.[45] At this time, Agrippa had conferred upon him "the whole of his grandfather's kingdom."[46] Although the purpose of the account in Acts 12 has been much debated, the impotence of Herod as king in his opposition to the Christian community is certainly prominent.[47] In spite of the great lengths King Herod goes to in securing Peter in prison in Jerusalem (12:4), "the Lord" ([ὁ] κύριος) sent his angel to rescue Peter (12:11; cf. 12:7) so that Peter declares that it is ultimately "the

---

43. In the process of the reconciliation of the dispute in Acts 15 (στάσεως καὶ ζητήσεως οὐκ ὀλίγης, 15:2), Peter refers back to the Cornelius episode and reinforces the emphasis found there on the soteriological unity of Jews and gentiles ("God ... showed that he accepted them [i.e., the gentiles] by giving the Holy Spirit to them, *just as he did to us. He made no distinction between us and them*." 15:8–9, emphasis added).

44. See Kazuhiko Yamazaki-Ransom, "Paul, Agrippa I, and Antiochus IV: Two Persecutors in Acts in Light of 2 Maccabees 9," in Rhodes, Easterline, and Lee, *Luke-Acts and Empire*, 109, for a succinct summary of the Roman significance of this account in the context of Caesarea, "the Roman provincial capital" of Israel.

45. See Josephus, *A.J.* 19.292, 351–52; *B.J.* 2.215–217. See also Daniel R. Schwartz, *Agrippa I: The Last King of Judaea*, TSAJ 23 (Tübingen: Mohr, 1990).

46. Josephus, *B.J.* 2.215 (τῇ πατρῴα βασιλείᾳ πάσῃ).

47. See O. Wesley Allen Jr., *The Death of Herod: The Narrative and Theological Function of Retribution in Luke-Acts*, SBLDS 158 (Atlanta: Scholars Press, 1997), 5–24, 93–98.

10. One Lord, One People: Kingship and Oneness in Acts   231

Lord" (ὁ κύριος) who brought him out of Herod's prison (12:17). At the conclusion of the chapter "an angel of the Lord" strikes again as Herod is struck down and dies, in Caesarea (12:23). Thus despite the efforts of King Herod, the tyrant who opposed and persecuted the believers, the chapter concludes with the summary statement: "the word of God continued to increase and spread" (12:24).[48]

After the dramatic rescue of Peter, however, Herod is described as a ruler unable to maintain harmony (12:18–23). Within three verses the language of disunity *and* unity is used to describe those under his rule. In 12:18–19 the rescue of Peter (highlighting the impotence of Herod's rule) is followed by "no small commotion [τάραχος] among the soldiers" under Herod's rule and Herod's order for their execution. Then after Herod's move to Caesarea, he is described as "very angry" (NLT, θυμομαχέω) with the people of Tyre and Sidon who in turn are described as united (ὁμοθυμαδόν) in their appeal for peace (εἰρήνη) because of their dependence on the king's country for their food supply (12:20). In light of Luke's positive use of the term ὁμοθυμαδόν to describe the unity of those who believe in the Lord Jesus (1:14; 2:46; 4:24; 5:12; 15:25), the themes of unity and disunity as seen in the description of a disturbance among those under Herod's rule, Herod's opposition to people under his rule, and a "united" appeal to him for "peace," must be seen as contributing to Luke's portrait of the downfall of this enemy of the word.[49]

Furthermore, the whole account is framed with references to the kingship of Herod.[50] Although the account opens in 12:1 by calling him "King Herod" (Ηρῳδης ὁ βασιλεύς), it is not until the description of the appeal for peace (εἰρήνη) from the people of Tyre and Sidon that Herod's kingship is again emphasized, in the context of his return to Caesarea (12:19–21).

---

48. Pao, *Isaianic*, 152. See also Scott Cunningham, *"Through Many Tribulations": The Theology of Persecution in Luke-Acts*, JSNTSup 142 (Sheffield: Sheffield Academic, 1997), 241–42.

49. Allen, *Death of Herod*, 87, observes that "the king is consistently and solely presented in terms of the conflicts in which he is engaged." Although ὁμοθυμαδόν can sometimes simply refer to being together, in this context this is togetherness in action, a united appeal to Herod; see Steve Walton, " Ομοθυμαδόν in Acts: Co-location, Common Action or 'Of One Heart and Mind'?," in *The New Testament in Its First Century Setting: Essays on Context and Background in Honour of B. W. Winter on His Sixty-fifth Birthday*, ed. Peter J. Williams et al. (Grand Rapids: Eerdmans, 2004), 100.

50. Walter Schmithals, *Die Apostelgeschichte des Lukas*, ZBK (Zurich: TVZ, 1982), 115, cited in Barrett, *Acts of the Apostles*, 572.

232   Alan J. Thompson

Blastus is the chamberlain of "the king" (τοῦ βασιλέως); the people of Tyre and Sidon are dependent on "the king's" country (ἀπὸ τῆς βασιλικῆς) for food; then, following this description of conditions under Herod's rule (in the narrative the dispute remains unresolved) he is said to be wearing "royal robes" (ἐσθῆτα βασιλικήν) and sitting on his "throne" (καθίσας ἐπὶ τοῦ βήματος) when he is struck down and dies, in Caesarea.

Thus, the references to turmoil, absence of peace, and his opposition to unity in the portrait of Herod's rule together with the emphasis on Herod as king add to the contrast here with the Lord Jesus in the context of Acts 10–12. A king such as Herod with such close associations with Rome does not have peace in his realm and the only unity found under his reign is a united despair under his tyrannical rule.[51] The "Lord" (ὁ κύριος) who brought his servant Peter out of Herod's prison (12:17) and whose angel brings judgment upon Herod in Caesarea (12:23) is the one who is "Lord of all" (πάντων κύριος), brings true peace to those who belong to him (10:36), and unites Jew and gentile into one people, also in Caesarea.[52] All of the people who belong to this Lord Jesus together receive forgiveness of sins and "the same" Holy Spirit.

10.5. Conclusion

In summary, the audience of Acts would recognize the context for the claims made for the universal lordship of the Lord Jesus in Acts, especially in Acts 2 and 10–12, as one that included other claims for universal authority, not least those made by and for Roman rulers. In this same broad historical context claims made for the validity of rulers and kings were often associated with claims for the unity of those under their rule. This broader historical context provides a plausible context for the juxtaposition of the themes of the kingship of the Lord Jesus and the unity of those under his reign in Acts. In Acts 2, Jesus is the Lord who reigns from the right hand of God and those who have together received the same gifts

---

51. Hans-Josef Klauck, *Magic and Paganism in Early Christianity: The World of the Acts of the Apostles*, trans. Brian McNeil (Minneapolis: Fortress, 2003), 43–44, highlights the claims made about Nero's "divine voice" in Tacitus, *Ann.* 14.15.8; 16.22.1; and Dio Cassius, *Hist. rom.* 62.20.4–6. Cf. Howell, "Imperial Authority," 44, in response to Rowe, "Luke-Acts and the Imperial Cult," 282–83.

52. On the references to discord in the cities of the Roman Empire in Acts, see Thompson, *One Lord, One People*, 117–20, 125–32, 143–70.

10. One Lord, One People: Kingship and Oneness in Acts   233

of forgiveness and the Holy Spirit from him devote themselves to apostolic teaching about the Lord Jesus and express their unity in meeting one another's needs. In Acts 10–11 the Lord Jesus is declared to be "Lord of all" in Caesarea and the gulf between Jew and gentile is bridged through common belief in him and (again) the common gifts of forgiveness and the Holy Spirit. This unity on the basis of "what the Lord had said" (11:16) is the basis for the experience of that unity in the resolution of their dispute. In the broader context of Acts 10–12, Acts 12:18–24 again places the themes of kingship and unity together in Caesarea. In this instance, however, King Herod is shown to be a tyrannical ruler and those under his reign suffer under his harsh treatment such that the only unity that is found among those under his reign is a unity of those seeking peace and sustenance. Thus, in Acts, those who together receive from the Lord Jesus the gifts of forgiveness and the Holy Spirit are one people under the reign of the one true Lord. This claim in a historical context in which concord contributed to claims for kingship, contributes to the Lukan claim that Jesus is Lord of all.

Bibliography

Allen, O. Wesley, Jr. *The Death of Herod: The Narrative and Theological Function of Retribution in Luke-Acts*. SBLDS 158. Atlanta: Scholars Press, 1997.

Barrett, C. K. *The Acts of the Apostles: Preliminary Introduction and Commentary on Acts I–XIV*. ICC. Edinburgh: T&T Clark, 1994.

Bauckham, Richard. *Gospel of Glory: Major Themes in Johannine Theology*. Grand Rapids: Baker Academic, 2015.

Bock, Darrell L. *Proclamation from Prophecy and Pattern: Lucan Old Testament Christology*. JSNTSup 12. Sheffield: Sheffield Academic, 1987.

Bryan, David K., and David W. Pao, eds. *Ascent into Heaven in Luke-Acts: New Explorations of Luke's Narrative Hinge*. Minneapolis: Fortress, 2016.

Buckwalter, H. Douglas. *The Character and Purpose of Luke's Christology*. SNTSMS 89. Cambridge: Cambridge University Press, 1996.

———. "The Divine Savior." Pages 107–23 in *Witness to the Gospel: The Theology of Acts*. Edited by I. Howard Marshall and David Peterson. Grand Rapids: Eerdmans, 1998.

Cassidy, Richard J. "Paul's Proclamation of *Lord* Jesus as a Chained Prisoner in Rome: Luke's Ending Is in His Beginning." Pages 142–53 in

Luke-Acts and Empire: Essays in Honor of Robert L. Brawley. Edited by David Rhodes, David Esterline, and Jae Won Lee. PTMS 151. Eugene, OR: Pickwick, 2011.

———. *Society and Politics in the Acts of the Apostles.* Maryknoll, NY: Orbis Books, 1987.

Conzelmann, Hans. *The Theology of St. Luke.* Translated by Geoffrey Buswell. New York: Harper & Row, 1960.

Cunningham, Scott. *"Through Many Tribulations": The Theology of Persecution in Luke-Acts.* JSNTSup 142. Sheffield: Sheffield Academic, 1997.

Dupont, Jacques. "L'union entre les premiers chrétiens dans les Actes des Apôtres." *NRTh* 91 (1969): 897–915.

Evans, Craig A. "King Jesus and His Ambassadors: Empire and Luke-Acts." Pages 120–39 in *Empire in the New Testament.* Edited by Stanley E. Porter and Cynthia Long Westfall. Eugene, OR: Pickwick, 2011.

Fitzmyer, Joseph A. *Acts of the Apostles: A New Translation with Introduction and Commentary.* AB 31. New York: Doubleday, 1998.

Gilbert, Gary. "The List of Nations in Acts 2: Roman Propaganda and the Lukan Response." *JBL* 121 (2002): 497–529.

———. "Luke-Acts and Negotiation of Authority and Identity in the Roman World." Pages 83–104 in *The Multivalence of Biblical Texts and Theological Meanings.* Edited by Christine Helmer. SymS 37. Atlanta: Society of Biblical Literature, 2006.

Green, Joel B. *The Gospel of Luke.* NICNT. Grand Rapids: Eerdmans, 1997.

Haenchen, Ernst. *The Acts of the Apostles: A Commentary.* Philadelphia: Westminster, 1971.

Hays, Christopher M. *Luke's Wealth Ethics.* WUNT 2/275. Tübingen: Mohr Siebeck, 2010.

Horsley, Richard. *The Liberation of Christmas: The Infancy Narratives in Social Context.* New York: Crossroad, 1989.

Howell, Justin R. "The Imperial Authority and Benefaction of Centurions and Acts 10.34–43: A Response to C. Kavin Rowe." *JSNT* 31 (2008): 25–51.

Jantsch, Torsten. *Jesus, der Retter: Die Soteriologie des lukanischen Doppelwerks.* WUNT 381. Tübingen: Mohr Siebeck, 2017.

Johnson, Luke Timothy. *The Acts of the Apostles.* SP 5. Collegeville, MN: Liturgical Press, 1992.

Keener, Craig S. *Acts: An Exegetical Commentary.* Vol. 1. Grand Rapids: Baker Academic, 2012.

Kim, Seyoon. *Christ and Caesar: The Gospel and the Roman Empire in the Writings of Paul and Luke*. Grand Rapids: Eerdmans, 2008.

Klauck, Hans-Josef. *Magic and Paganism in Early Christianity: The World of the Acts of the Apostles*. Translated by Brian McNeil. Minneapolis: Fortress, 2003.

Lake, Kirsopp, and Henry J. Cadbury. *The Beginnings of Christianity: Part I. The Acts of the Apostles*. Edited by Frederick J. Foakes Jackson and Kirsopp Lake. 5 vols. London: Macmillan, 1920–1933.

Pao, David W. *Acts and the Isaianic New Exodus*. WUNT 2/130. Tübingen: Mohr Siebeck, 2000.

Pickett, Raymond. "Luke and Empire: An Introduction." Pages 1–22 in *Luke-Acts and Empire: Essays in Honor of Robert L. Brawley*. Edited by David Rhodes, David Esterline, and Jae Won Lee. PTMS 151. Eugene, OR: Pickwick, 2011.

Rowe, C. Kavin. "Luke-Acts and the Imperial Cult: A Way through the Conundrum?" *JSNT* 27 (2005): 279–300.

———. *World Upside Down: Reading Acts in the Graeco-Roman Age*. Oxford: Oxford University Press, 2009.

Schmithals, Walter. *Die Apostelgeschichte des Lukas*. ZBK. Zurich: TVZ, 1982.

Schwartz, Daniel R. *Agrippa I: The Last King of Judaea*. TSAJ 23. Tübingen: Mohr, 1990.

Seccombe, David. *Possessions and the Poor in Luke-Acts*. SNTSU. Linz: Fuchs, 1982.

Strauss, Mark L. *The Davidic Messiah in Luke-Acts: The Promise and Its Fulfillment in Lukan Christology*. JSNTSup 110. Sheffield: Sheffield Academic, 1995.

Thompson, Alan J. *The Acts of the Risen Lord Jesus: Luke's Account of God's Unfolding Plan*. NSBT 27. Downers Grove, IL: InterVarsity Press, 2011.

———. *Luke*. EGGNT. Nashville: B&H Academic, 2016.

———. *One Lord, One People: The Unity of the Church in Acts in Its Literary Setting*. LNTS 359. London: T&T Clark, 2008.

———. "Unity in Acts: Idealization or Reality?" *JETS* 51 (2008): 523–42.

Turner, Max B. *Power from on High: The Spirit in Israel's Restoration and Witness in Luke-Acts*. JPTSup 9. Sheffield: Sheffield Academic, 1996.

———. "The 'Spirit of Prophecy' as the Power of Israel's Restoration and Witness." Pages 327–48 in *Witness to the Gospel: The Theology of Acts*. Edited by I. Howard Marshall and David Peterson. Grand Rapids: Eerdmans, 1998.

Walaskay, Paul. *"And So We Came to Rome": The Political Perspective of St. Luke.* SNTSMS 49. Cambridge: Cambridge University Press, 1983.

Walton, Steve. "'Ὁμοθυμαδόν in Acts: Co-location, Common Action or 'Of One Heart and Mind'?" Pages 89–105 in *The New Testament in Its First Century Setting: Essays on Context and Background in Honour of B. W. Winter on His Sixty-Fifth Birthday.* Edited by Peter J. Williams, Andrew D. Clarke, Peter M. Head, and David Instone-Brewer. Grand Rapids: Eerdmans, 2004.

———. "The State They Were In: Luke's View of the Roman Empire." Pages 1–41 in *Rome in the Bible and the Early Church.* Edited by Peter Oakes. Grand Rapids: Baker Academic, 2002.

Wilson, Benjamin R. "Jew-Gentile Relations and the Geographic Movement of Acts 10:1–11:18." *CBQ* 80 (2018): 81–96.

Yamazaki-Ransom, Kazuhiko. "Paul, Agrippa I, and Antiochus IV: Two Persecutors in Acts in Light of 2 Maccabees 9." Pages 107–21 in *Luke-Acts and Empire: Essays in Honor of Robert L. Brawley.* Edited by David Rhodes, David Esterline, and Jae Won Lee. PTMS 151. Eugene, OR: Pickwick, 2011.

———. *The Roman Empire in Luke's Narrative.* LNTS 404. London: T&T Clark, 2010.

Ziccardi, Constantino A. *The Relationship of Jesus and the Kingdom of God according to Luke-Acts.* Rome: Editrice Pontifica Università Gregoriana, 2008.

11

Paul on Oneness and Unity in 1 Corinthians

Stephen C. Barton

First Corinthians is a source of perennial fascination to the historian of earliest Christianity as also to the Christian theologian.[1] Unlike almost any other New Testament text, it reveals with particular clarity the beliefs and behaviors of a first-generation association of Christ-followers. Related to this, it offers a window into the complexities and tensions created by adherence to Christ and participation in the Christ cult for residents of a significant multicultural, religiously plural, Mediterranean city. Yet further, it displays the efforts of one of the most significant of early Christian leaders and teachers, the apostle Paul, to nurture his children in the faith toward a deeper appreciation of the implications of their baptism and calling for their mundane existence both individual and corporate. More specifically, 1 Corinthians is a study in one leader's attempt to build up a Christian community in the face of pressures threatening division and disunity. Put otherwise, it is a study in *unity in the making*.

In what follows, I trace first evidence in the letter showing that oneness and unity are by no means peripheral concerns. Then follows an identification of the cultural dynamics and forces threatening disunity and the subversion of the Christ-followers' common life. Finally, I offer an account of how Paul responds, focusing particularly on his summons to move more fully from an anthropocentric existence to an eschatological existence grounded in God, Christ, and the Spirit.

---

1. For their comments on this essay, I would like to thank especially James Harrison, David Horrell, Michael Lakey, and Andrew Lincoln. Unless indicated otherwise, English translations are from the NRSV.

-237-

238   Stephen C. Barton

11.1. Prima Facie Evidence of an Interest in
Oneness and Unity in 1 Corinthians

A striking feature of Paul's language in 1 Corinthians is his multiple uses of the number one (εἷς) along with the terminology of oneness, unity, or commonality:[2]

1. Forms of εἷς occur, remarkably, some thirty times.[3] More significant than its frequency, however, is its strategic deployment. For example, several occurrences appear in the pastorally critical context of the divisive impact of the behavior of members who retain multiple cultic allegiances, in contradiction of their creedal confession of the oneness of God and the one lordship of Christ (cf. 1 Cor 8:6) and of their eucharistic partaking of the "one bread [εἷς ἄρτος]" (10:17), on which more below.

2. As well as the language of ones, the expression "the same" (τὸ αὐτό) is used with particular intensity at a number of points to designate something or someone shared or to refer to things practiced in common. Most notable is its threefold occurrence in the crucial, agenda-setting appeal Paul makes at the beginning of the letter: "Now I appeal to you, brothers and sisters ... that all of you be in agreement [ἵνα τὸ αὐτὸ λέγητε πάντες] and ... that you be united in the same mind and the same purpose [ἐν τῷ αὐτῷ νοΐ καὶ ἐν τῇ αὐτῇ γνώμῃ]" (1:10).[4]

3. Then there is the use of σύν-compounds implying cooperation, sharing, or togetherness. Paul and Apollos are συνεργοί ("coworkers") (3:9): others, including Stephanas, are designated similarly (16:16). Paul claims to be advising the Corinthians for their "benefit" (σύμφορον; 7:35; cf. 1:33). Meetings of the church are constituted by group members "coming together," where the verb συνέρχομαι is used (11:17, 18, 20, 33, 34; 14:23, 26); a core practice is "eating together" (συνεσθίειν; 5:11; cf. 11:33); and church members are exhorted to "suffer together" (συμπάσχω) and "rejoice together" (συγχαίρω, 12:26).

---

2. See further, Margaret M. Mitchell, *Paul and the Rhetoric of Reconciliation: An Exegetical Investigation of the Language and Composition of 1 Corinthians* (Louisville: Westminster John Knox, 1992), ch. 3, esp. 180–81.

3. See 3:8; 4:6; 6:16 (twice), 17; 8:4, 6 (twice); 9:24; 10:8, 17 (thrice); 11:5; 12:9, 11, 12 (twice), 13 (thrice), 14, 18, 19, 20, 26 (twice); 14:27, 31; 16:2.

4. Cf. also 1 Cor 7:5; 10:3, 4; 11:20; 12:4, 5, 6, 8, 9, 11, 25. Noteworthy in 12:11 is its conjunction of "one" and "the same" (τὸ ἓν καὶ τὸ αὐτό) with reference to the Spirit.

11. Paul on Oneness and Unity in 1 Corinthians

4. The use of forms of πᾶς ("all") to convey ideas of solidarity and inclusion is all-pervasive, sometimes used in combination with εἷς. Exemplary are the following: "together with all those ... in every place" (σὺν πᾶσιν ... ἐν παντὶ τόπῳ) (1:2); "all things are yours ... all belong to you" (πάντα γὰρ ὑμῶν ἐστιν ... πάντα ὑμῶν) (3:21–22); "all [πάντες] partake of one bread [ἑνὸς ἄρτου]" (10:17); "For in the one Spirit [ἐν ἑνὶ πνεύματι] we were all [πάντες] baptized into one body [εἰς ἓν σῶμα] ... and were all [πάντες] made to drink of one Spirit [ἓν πνεῦμα]" (12:13); and in the words of farewell with which the letter ends, "My love be with all of you" (μετὰ πάντων ὑμῶν) (16:24).

5. The metaphors Paul uses include metaphors of unity. Most important in this respect is the metaphor of the body, often deployed in combination with the number one, as in "we who are many are one body [ἓν σῶμα]" (10:17; cf. 12:12, 13, 20). Given less prominence, but also expressive of oneness, this organic metaphor is complemented by an agricultural metaphor ("you are God's field," 3:9) and by architectural metaphors ("you are God's building ... God's temple," 3:9, 16).

Taking these five sets of data together, the presence of a motif of oneness in 1 Corinthians cannot be doubted. Important, as we shall see, is the fact that the oneness spoken of or implied is not an abstract matter of a mathematical kind but *a personal and social matter* of singularity, sociality, and solidarity linking heaven and earth.

11.2. The Problem of Disunity in Corinth and Its Manifestations

If we ask after the *motivation* behind Paul's language of oneness, the presenting factor appears to be the news that has reached him (1:11; 5:1; 11:18; 16:17) of threats to the unity of the Christian κοινωνία. The underlying problem, from Paul's point of view, appears to be that the Corinthian Christ-followers—especially the gentile converts—are importing into the Christian association the habits, practices, and values integral to their prior and ongoing life in the wider society, including their participation in voluntary associations of various kinds.[5] In consequence, their calling to a new life of holiness as saints under the lordship of Christ (1:2) is being compromised, the holiness of the church as God's temple (3:16,

---

5. John S. Kloppenborg, *Christ's Associations: Connecting and Belonging in the Ancient City* (New Haven: Yale University Press, 2019).

17) is being polluted, and the glory of God (6:20; 10:31) is being dishonored. Put otherwise, the conversion and consequent resocialization of the Corinthian Christ-followers is incomplete.

That the oneness of the church is at risk, articulated in ways remarkably evocative of the political and social dynamics of the wider culture, is evident, as Lawrence Welborn, Margaret Mitchell, and James Harrison (among others) have demonstrated so comprehensively.[6] Indicative is the following:

1. Adopting language common to ancient Greek and Roman political and constitutional discourse, Paul accuses the Corinthians of engaging in behavior disruptive of ecclesial harmony. According to 1:10–12, there are "divisions" (σχίσματα) and "quarrels" (ἔριδες); and these find expression in competitive clamor in favor of one authority figure over another: "I belong to Paul," or "I belong to Apollos," or "I belong to Cephas, or "I belong to Christ" (cf. 3:3–4, 21a).[7] Given the attention in 1:18–4:21 to "wisdom" (σοφία) and its close corollary, eloquent speech (λόγος)—virtues carrying massive cultural cachet—it appears that divisions are taking place over who among the visiting apostles and teachers speaks with greatest persuasive power and personal appeal. Just as, in the wider world, attachment to a gifted sophist, perhaps as a wealthy benefactor, will augment the reputation and status of a household head, his family, friends, and clients, so, in the church, attachment to one apostolic figure over another for personal advantage will have been a natural instinct. In short, it appears that the Christian association has become one more site, within a wide range of cultural and political locations, for accruing prestige and social capital.

2. Contributing to the tensions is the culturally approved practice of "boasting" (καύχησις), itself a form of aggressive self-promotion. In the wider culture, victory in what is an unashamedly competitive contest (ἀγών) between men of influence brings an increase in personal glory, honor, and power in every area of life, including the household, voluntary associations, religious cults, the courts, and civic administration at

---

6. Welborn, "On the Discord in Corinth: 1 Corinthians 1–4 and Ancient Politics," *JBL* 106 (1987): 83–113; Mitchell, *Paul*; Harrison, *Paul and the Ancient Celebrity Circuit: The Cross and Moral Transformation*, WUNT 430 (Tübingen: Mohr Siebeck, 2019).

7. On the way such slogans reflect the fact that "personal adherence is the basic relationship from which party identification developed" in ancient politics, see Welborn, "Discord," 90–93, quotation from 90.

11. Paul on Oneness and Unity in 1 Corinthians 241

all levels. A significant asset in the contest is attachment to a person of eminence. This is reflected in Paul's anxieties concerning "boasting," as in 3:21–22: "Let no one boast about human leaders ... whether Paul or Apollos or Cephas" (cf. 1:29, 31 [citing Jer 9:24]; 4:7). It is reflected also in his implied criticism of people who are "puffed up" (φυσιόω) on account of their allegiance to one leader over another, as in 4:6: "I have applied all this to Apollos and myself for your benefit, brothers and sisters ...so that none of you will be puffed up [φυσιοῦσθε] in favor of one against another" (where competitive attachment to either a "Paul party" or an "Apollos party" is in view; cf. also 4:18, 19; 5:2; 8:1; 13:4).

3. Among specific aggravations of the church's oneness, and exemplary of the threat posed by persons who are "puffed up" or "arrogant" (5:2 NRSV), is that expression of wisdom or freedom that takes embodied form in sexual license, what Paul, shaped by the moral traditions of the Scriptures and Hellenistic Judaism, terms πορνεία. The cases in point are multiple. (1) First Corinthians 5 speaks to a situation of incest perpetuated by a man apparently so dominant in the church that his behavior is tolerated, even for some a cause for boasting (5:6). (2) First Corinthians 6:12–20 speaks to the practice of male members of the fellowship having recourse to prostitutes and forming, in consequence, what Paul regards as a sexual oneness contradictory of their oneness of spirit with the risen Lord (6:16–17). (3) First Corinthians 7 speaks to the issue of marriage and sex rules where Paul's concern is for behaviors that counter marital discord by promoting mutuality and harmony: the body that is "one's own" (τοῦ ἰδίου σώματος) belongs (remarkably) to the other partner (7:4); abstention from sexual congress is allowed only "by agreement" (ἐκ συμφώνου) (7:5); and lack of self-control is avoided by "coming together [ἐπὶ τὸ αὐτό] again" (7:5).

4. If in 5:1–7:40 Paul addresses the disruptive effects of being "puffed up" (5:2) in respect of sex and marriage; in 8:1–11:1 he addresses the disruptive effects of being "puffed up" (cf. 8:1a) in respect of food and commensality. A clear logic underpins the sequence. Both have to do with the use of the body, where the body symbolizes the body politic, either its unity or discord.[8] Both are spheres of consumption where power can be exercised with a view to an enhanced personal reputation. Both are arenas of and for coming together with the potential for either domination

---

8. Dale B. Martin, *The Corinthian Body* (New Haven: Yale University Press, 1995).

242   Stephen C. Barton

and disharmony or mutual acceptance and conviviality. Both are aspects
of daily life whose capacity to generate social enmity makes them the focus
of instruction among the moral philosophers.

Given the continuities between these two potent (because bodily)
realms of social intercourse, it is not surprising that divisive arrogance
finds expression again, this time in relation to table matters and manners
(cf. also 11:17–34). Some, probably from among the (likely more cos-
mopolitan) converts from paganism, are making display of their γνῶσις
("knowledge") that "no idols in the world really exists" (8:4) by eating in
temple rooms food sacrificed to the gods, thereby maintaining customs
and contacts native to them from their preconversion days. It appears,
however, that such expressions of individual liberty (ἐξουσία) are being
exercised at the cost of ecclesial solidarity. Commensalism of this kind is
a "stumbling-block" (πρόσκομμα) to the "weak" (8:9), presumably Jewish-
Christian brothers and sisters whose consciences on matters of idol-food
are so conditioned by torah-observance as to be highly sensitive (8:10–12),
and therefore a potential cause of communal fracture.

5. The succeeding section of Paul's letter (11:2–14:40) offers evidence
of yet further threats to unity, now focused more on divisions that surface when church members come together. It is as if, having strengthened
the disciplinary lines running *around* the church in order to reinforce the
Corinthians' rather underdeveloped sense of distinctive identity as one,
Paul now seeks to strengthen the disciplinary lines running *through* the
church to reinforce the order and unity of the Corinthians' common life,
hence, the interim conclusion, "all things should be done decently and in
order" (14:40). In this, Paul is doing what is expected of authority figures
at every level of Greco-Roman society, of which rules governing behavior
in voluntary associations offer a good analogy.[9]

Thus, there is innovation in the hierarchy of genders in the practice
of the Christian cult that is generating discord on account of the threat it
poses to conventional patterns of patriarchal, household-based social order
(11:2–16).[10] It appears that women prophets are exercising their authority
as members of the eschatological new creation, where, as Paul says elsewhere, there is "no male and female" (cf. Gal 3:28; diff. 1 Cor 12:13!), by

---

9. See further Harrison, *Ancient Celebrity Circuit*, 297–329, on "Paul's House-
Churches and the Cultic Associations."

10. Michael J. Lakey, *Image and Glory of God: 1 Corinthians 11:2–16 as a Case
Study in Bible, Gender and Hermeneutics*, LNTS 418 (London: T&T Clark, 2010).

11. Paul on Oneness and Unity in 1 Corinthians 243

praying and prophesying with their heads "uncovered": they are letting their hair down and/or removing their veils (11:5–6). Interestingly, as with matters to do with sex and food, the appropriate *deportment of the body* is at issue as contributing to either the stability or instability of the group. In this case, because the head is a symbolic location of authority, and head covering is emblematic of honor, social propriety, and the natural order (cf. 11:14), such innovation is causing contention (φιλονεικία, cf. 11:16). Using another σύν-compound to invoke consensus, Paul moves decisively to impose a measure of cultural conformity: "we have no such custom [συνήθειαν], nor do the churches of God" (11:16b).

6. Table matters and manners recur as a cause of disunity in 11:17–34. Previously, table-fellowship with *outsiders* in the precincts of pagan temples is the issue; here, the contentious issue is table-fellowship *within* the Christian fellowship itself (noting forms of συνέρχομαι ["come together"] in 11:17, 18, 20, 33, 34). Says Paul, in emotion-charged language shot through with terminology from the world of factional politics and the ideology of personal domination:

> I hear that there are divisions [σχίσματα] among you.... Indeed, there have to be factions [αἱρέσεις] among you, for only so will it become clear who among you are genuine.... For when the time comes to eat, each of you goes ahead with your own supper [τὸ ἴδιον δεῖπνον], and one goes hungry and another is drunk. What, do you not have homes to eat and drink in? Or do you show contempt [καταφρονεῖτε] for the church of God and humiliate [καταισχύνετε] those who have nothing? (11:18–22)

Clearly, disparities of wealth and status between members are being dramatized every time they come together to eat. What should be a ritual of incorporation and group solidarity, with members sharing their food and drink in acts of reciprocal hospitality, has become a ritual of rivalry and competitive display in the quest for personal honor threatening to split the fellowship.[11]

7. Yet another cause of disunity when the Corinthian believers come together is the matter headlined as "Concerning spiritual things" (Περὶ

---

11. See Gerd Theissen's seminal essay, "Social Integration and Sacramental Activity: An Analysis of 1 Cor 11:17–34," in *The Social Setting of Pauline Christianity: Studies of the New Testament and Its World*, ed. Gerd Theissen (Edinburgh: T&T Clark, 1982), 145–74.

δὲ τῶν πνευματικῶν; 12:1–14:40). What gradually emerges is that certain forms of inspired speech—glossolalia in particular—are being exalted in ways that are detrimental to the stability and edification of the church as a whole. Interestingly, in 12:1–4 there is a hint of a phenomenon that we have noted previously, that practices (in this case, of ecstatic utterance) learned in pagan cults are being imported into church meetings. Overall, what Paul calls χαρίσματα ("gifts") are being exercised in ways destructive of church unity. Indicative of his concerns is 12:24b–25: "But God has so arranged the body, giving the greater honor to the inferior member, that there may be no dissension [σχίσμα] within the body, but the members may have the same [τὸ αὐτό] care for one another" (cf. 14:33). As to what kinds of behavior are threatening disorder, it appears that Paul is countering several destructive tendencies: the tendency to exalt one kind of contribution over others and to apportion honor and shame accordingly, and the tendency to (as we might say) weaponize such contributions in the cause of individual self-aggrandizement (cf. 13:4–5!) at the cost of the building up of the fellowship (noting occurrences of forms of οἰκοδομή in 14:3, 4, 5, 12, 17, and 26).

8. We know from Jewish (cf. Josephus, *B.J.* 2.119–158, 162–166) and early Christian sources that differences of belief concerning the fate of the dead are identity-defining, even creating enmity between one group and another. According to the testimony of Acts, for example, when Paul, standing before the Sanhedrin, declares himself to belong to the party that believes in the resurrection of the dead, "a dissension [στάσις] began between the Pharisees and the Sadducees, and the assembly was divided [ἐσχίσθη] … and a great clamor [κραυγὴ μεγάλη] arose…. And when the dissension became violent [Πολλῆς δὲ γινομένης στάσεως] … [the tribune intervened to protect Paul from a lynching]" (Acts 23:6–10). Against such a background, with its evocation of the intensity of feeling generated by differences of belief, we can be sure that when Paul turns to the matter of resurrection belief at the letter's climax (15:1–58), he is addressing another matter conducive of discord among church members (cf. 15:12, 35). In the face of θάνατος ("death"), the ultimate source of personal, social, and cosmic chaos and dissolution—in comparison with which party politics and human striving pale into insignificance—what Paul urges is the unifying power of hope in God (cf. 13:13) and of sharing in the victory that really matters, the one made possible "through our Lord Jesus Christ" (15:54–57).

9. Although the main argument of the letter ends at 15:58, with a final reminder of the qualities of personal and social character required

11. Paul on Oneness and Unity in 1 Corinthians

for the ongoing stability of the church, hints of other potential sources of discord emerge in Paul's final instructions and farewell.[12] One such is money matters. Given that the church membership includes both rich and poor (1:26) and that money is a mark of status, a means of exercising influence as a benefactor, and a prerequisite for building a personal following, not to mention an opportunity for profiteering, it is not surprising that Paul's instructions regarding the collection for Jerusalem are a model of circumspection.

11.3. Paul's Response to Disunity in Corinth

With the self-proclaimed authority of a father in relation to his children (4:14–15), Paul writes to confront the Corinthians with their failings in solidarity and to persuade them to embrace more fully their shared baptismal identity as the eschatological Israel (10:1–11) and the body of Christ (12:12–13). Of course, as indicated already, Paul's response utilizes a whole lexicon of words and ideas from Greco-Roman society and politics that will have been familiar to citizens of Roman Corinth.[13] No doubt, he does so because central to the concerns of Greco-Roman utopian ideals and constitutional thought is the establishment and maintenance of unity, peace, and order. But what is significant and novel is the way Paul engages a theological, christological, and pneumatological hermeneutic—a wisdom quite at odds with that of the sophists—to challenge the Corinthians' ingrained cultural reflexes and to open them up to transformed ways of thinking and acting, including a reimagining of what it means to be *constituted as one*. Richard Hays expresses well this aspect of Paul's response: "The brilliance of Paul's letter lies in his ability to diagnose the situation in theological terms and to raise the inchoate theological issues into the light of conscious reflection in light

---

12. On the overall shape of the argument as one of (what the ancient rhetoricians would have identified as) deliberative rhetoric, see Mitchell, *Paul*, 20–64.

13. Striking, however, is the fact that the political term perhaps closest to Paul's concern with the unity of the church, ὁμόνοια ("oneness of mind," "concord"), is completely absent, not only from 1 Corinthians, but from the entire Pauline and post-Pauline corpus. On this conundrum, see James R. Harrison, "Honouring the Concord of the Ephesian Demos," in *Ephesus*, vol. 11 of *New Documents Illustrating the History of Early Christianity*, ed. James R. Harrison and Bradley J. Bitner (Grand Rapids: Eerdmans, forthcoming).

246   Stephen C. Barton

of the gospel."[14] Among the most important aspects of Paul's response are the following.

11.3.1. Christ

In the face of their disastrous habit of seeing and doing things in human terms (cf. κατὰ σάρκα in 1:26; σαρκικοί in 3:3) with its manifestation in self-aggrandizement, boasting, rivalry, and division, Paul seeks to move the Corinthians from an anthropocentric frame of reference to a theocentric, and specifically Christocentric, frame of reference. In brief, what Paul does is to redirect the Corinthians' attention *upward and forward, to Christ*— and therefore also to God and the Spirit. As Roy Ciampa and Brian Rosner put it: "If Corinthian problems can be attributed to their cultural background, Paul's various responses may be ascribed to his understanding of Christ and the significance of his lordship; in almost every case Paul pits Christ against the prevailing culture."[15] It is as if, in focusing relentlessly on Christ, Paul is offering, not an alternative faction leader, but a heavenly Κύριος ("Lord") who by virtue of his death, resurrection, exaltation to universal rulership, and imminent return is able to trump all factions and to unite all humanity in a kingdom of universal concord. It is no exaggeration to say that Paul is inviting the Corinthians to a conversion of the imagination according to which space, time, persons, and values are transformed in relation to Christ.[16]

That Paul's reference point is Christ, and that Christ as one—unique in relation to God and humankind—is a focus of unity is evident throughout the letter. (1) As regards the contested matter of identity and authority: Paul self-identifies as an "apostle of Christ Jesus" (cf. 1:1; 9:1–2; 15:9) who, as the appointed agent of a divine being, is indebted to no human authority, is above party politics (cf. 4:15b), is able to rule in disciplinary matters in the name of the Lord Jesus (cf. 5:3–5), and is able to give authoritative instruction "received from the Lord" in matters of

---

14. Hays, *First Corinthians*, IBC (Louisville: Westminster John Knox, 1997), 8.

15. Ciampa and Rosner, "The Structure and Argument of 1 Corinthians: A Biblical/Jewish Approach," *NTS* 52 (2006): 215. As they point out, indicative of the letter's Christocentrism is that "Christ" is used sixty-four times, "Lord" sixty-six times, and "Jesus" twenty-six times.

16. Richard B. Hays, "The Conversion of the Imagination: Scripture and Eschatology in 1 Corinthians," *NTS* 45 (1999): 391–412.

11. Paul on Oneness and Unity in 1 Corinthians 247

both belief and practice (cf. 11:23; 14:37; 15:1–2). (2) Regarding the complex, multiple identities of the believers in Corinth: from the outset, they are brought under the one rubric of "those who are sanctified in Christ Jesus" and who belong to a universal association of "all who in every place call on the name of the Lord Jesus Christ, both their Lord and ours" (1:2). (3) Regarding the novel, culturally mixed (Jew-gentile) fellowship into which they have been called: it is the κοινωνία of no less a benefactor-figure and savior than "[God's] Son, Jesus Christ our Lord" (1:9), a fellowship that renders disunity absurd, as if Christ can be "divided" (1:13)! When a building metaphor is invoked, the unique foundation upon which the temple of believers is being built is Jesus Christ (3:11). (4) Regarding sexual discipline: the arrogant behavior of the incestuous man is condemned as a defilement of a community made pure by the sacrifice of Christ the paschal lamb (5:7). In respect of a related matter, the maxim, "All things are lawful for me" (6:12) provides no justification for sex with a πόρνη because the universal sovereignty of the risen Christ means that the body belongs to the Lord (6:13). Even more, becoming one body with a prostitute is a contradiction of being united in one spirit with the Lord (6:15–17). (5) Regarding the morality of meals—what is eaten, where, and with whom—a self-denying ordinance is in order so as not to scandalize the weaker brother or sister, since they are ones "for whom Christ died" (8:11). Indeed, to wound their conscience is to "sin against Christ" (8:12). (6) Regarding the practice of Christian freedom: If torah is no longer definitive, what *is* definitive is being ἔννομος Χριστοῦ (lit. "in-lawed to Christ"; 9:21). As regards models for imitation in the moral life, says Paul: "Be imitators of me, *as I am of Christ*" (11:1, emphasis added). (7) Regarding the exercise of gifts, the controlling metaphor for the relation of individual contributions to the edification of the group is "the [one!] body of Christ (12:27). (8) Regarding life in the face of death: resurrection faith, and its implications for the moral life are grounded uncompromisingly in the death and resurrection of Christ (15:3–9, 12–19, 20–28), identified also as the eschatological Adam (15:45), the man of heaven (15:49), the divine agent of victory over death (15:57), and the one because of whom the labor of believers in this life is "not in vain" (15:58). (9) The farewell greeting Paul writes with his own hand is a final reminder, if one were needed, of the allegiance to Christ that is Paul's own and that is his desire for the church, expressed, notably, in the language of love (ἀγάπη): "My love be with all of you *in Christ Jesus*" (16:22–24, emphasis added).

248   Stephen C. Barton

11.3.2. God

The main reason why Paul responds to Corinthian disunity by seeking to redirect their gaze upward and forward to Christ is because it is Christ crucified, risen, and coming who is the wisdom and power *of God*, the one who reveals the glory *of God*.[17] Paul's theology, rooted as it is in his biblical and Jewish heritage, is thoroughly theocentric. Symptomatic is the doxology at the climax of his account of the eschatological mystery of the resurrection: "But *thanks be to God*, who gives us the victory through our Lord Jesus Christ" (15:57, emphasis added). How (what we have come to think of as) Paul's christological monotheism contributes to his attempt to counter pagan values and transform the believers' divisive patterns of sociality is evident in the ways he seeks to *renarrate* the Corinthians' worldview and self-understanding in terms of a scripture-informed, cruciform apocalyptic theology. Among important aspects of this culture-critical theology are the following.

1. The attention that Paul gives to wisdom, that measure of personal worth and social status so highly valued by the elite among the Corinthian Christ-followers, is striking. This is the focus of Paul's theological culture critique in chapters 1–4. In the background are deeply rooted Jewish and Greco-Roman cultural values that associate wisdom with formal education, persuasive speech, masculinity, wealth, power, glory, and mastery of the world. In such a culture, a claim to possess wisdom constitutes a claim to *distinction*, setting its owner apart and warranting a place of social pre-eminence: "Already you have … become kings [ἐβασιλεύσατε]!" (4:8). It is something about which to boast.

But for Paul, this is a kind of *idolatry of the self*, the product of an agonistic social order infiltrating the church with divisive consequences. His response is to offer a disruptive, apocalyptic wisdom, characterized by sharp paradoxes expressive of *the difference God makes in God's sovereign freedom and holiness*. Here, true wisdom is what the world regards as "foolishness" (μωρία): and over against skill in persuasive eloquence (ἐν σοφίᾳ λόγου) is set a message (λόγος) so shocking as to be revelatory and transformative—what Paul calls, "the word of the cross" as nothing less than the "power of God" (1:18). At the heart of this word is the revelation of a mystery previously hidden (2:7; cf. 4:1; 14:2; 15:51): of God's Christ

---

17. See also Ciampa and Rosner, "Structure and Argument," 212–18.

11. Paul on Oneness and Unity in 1 Corinthians 249

crucified and risen as the end of human vainglory, the defeat of death, and the inauguration of a new creation, participation in which is the privilege of a people called to bring glory to God.

Just taking 1:18–31, the theocentricity of Paul's reworking of wisdom is emphatic. He quotes (from Isa 29:14) God's word of judgment on "the wisdom of the wise" (1:19); attributes to God's (hidden) wisdom the failure of the world to know God through wisdom (1:21a); attributes also to God the decision to save those who believe through the foolishness of preaching (1:21b); speaks of Christ crucified as "the power of God and the wisdom of God" (1:24); focuses emphatically on the divine election of "the foolish to shame the wise" (1:27–28); reminds the Corinthians that "[God] is the source of your life in Christ Jesus, who became for us wisdom from God" (1:30); and climaxes with a second scriptural quotation (Jer 9:23–24), "Let the one who boasts, boast in the Lord" (1:31). In brief, what this represents is a *decentering* of conventional wisdom as a core value and lifestyle, and a *recentering* on God and on Christ as the wisdom of God, recognition of which provides a transcendental basis for a human solidarity in which hierarchies of identity, status, and worth are transformed.

2. Fundamental to Paul's critique of a wisdom that reinforces social distinctions is the idea of *God as one, the unique universal sovereign in the one kingdom of God* acting out of grace to disrupt the power of Satan, sin, and death in creation and human affairs by the revelation of a deliverer, Jesus, the Christ, Lord, Son of God, and the calling into being through him of a holy oneness, eschatological Israel, set apart for God's glory.[18] Importantly, to speak of God in terms of universal sovereignty is to invoke *constitutional* language profoundly reminiscent of the constitution of Israel in biblical and Jewish thought and in the teaching of Jesus.[19] Here, the oneness of the people is understood as *the corollary on earth* of the oneness of the God who rules from heaven. It is the divine calling of the people, by their oneness in obedience to God's holy law and worship in God's house, to glorify a God jealous for God's name. What Josephus writes is symptomatic. Speaking specifically of

---

18. The relative infrequency of references to the kingdom of God (4:20; 6:9–10; 15:50) by no means reduces its significance for Paul.

19. William Horbury, "Constitutional Aspects of the Kingdom of God," in *The Kingdom of God and Human Society: Essays by Members of the Scripture, Theology and Society Group*, ed. Robin S. Barbour (Edinburgh: T&T Clark, 1993), 60–79.

250 Stephen C. Barton

the constitution bequeathed by Moses for founding a city, Josephus has Moses say:

> Let there be one holy city [ἱερὰ πόλις ἔστω μία] in that place in the land of Canaan that is fairest and most famous for its excellence, a city which God shall choose for himself, by prophetic oracle. And let there be one temple [νεὼς εἷς] therein, and one altar [βωμὸς εἷς].... In no other city let there be either altar or temple; for God is one and the Hebrew race is one [θεὸς γὰρ εἷς καὶ τὸ Ἑβραίων γένος ἕν]. (A.J. 4.200–201 [LCL])

Here, God's oneness takes expression as a marking out—a making of distinctions, a drawing of lines of separation—for which the key terms and symbols have to do with *holiness*: one holy city chosen by God, one temple, one altar, one people, in one place only. Furthermore, in so far as separation has *inclusion* as its flipside, oneness as a human and divine-human solidarity is implied also: the places are also spaces for a people to inhabit as one.

A comparable biblical-Jewish conception, reworked christologically and eschatologically, underlies Paul's response to Corinthian disunity.[20] What he offers, in effect, is a renarration of who they are, to whom they belong, and how they are to live. Reconstituted as one body through the ritual of baptism (12:13), the Corinthians are to see themselves as part of a universal people, diverse ("Jews or Greeks, slaves or free"), yet one and singular, under the sovereignty of the one God who rules through the divine agency of both the Lord Jesus and the Spirit and the earthly agency of authorized members of the community (12:28).

3. Exemplifying this is the critical attention Paul gives to the threat of spiritual and communal chaos posed by divisions related to "food sacrificed to idols" (εἰδωλόθυτα; 8:1–11:1). From Paul's argument here, what emerges is a judgment that eating dedicated idol-food in the temple of an idol is an affront to God. It is so because it constitutes a catastrophic *blurring of lines of loyalty to God as one* in God's uniqueness and sovereignty, as also of loyalty to the Lord, Jesus Christ, who is one in his uniqueness as mediator of the divine life. In an unprecedented and therefore highly significant

---

20. John M. G. Barclay, "Matching Theory and Practice: Josephus's Constitutional Ideal and Paul's Strategy in Corinth," in *Paul beyond the Judaism/Hellenism Divide*, ed. Troels Engberg-Pedersen (Louisville: Westminster John Knox Press, 2001), 139–63; esp. 149–63.

11. Paul on Oneness and Unity in 1 Corinthians 251

reformulation of the Shema (Deut 6:4)—Israel's central acknowledgment of covenant loyalty to the Lord alone confessed daily in prayer—marking out a clear line of connection and obligation, Paul says:[21]

> Indeed, even though there may be so-called gods in heaven or on earth—as in fact there are many gods and many lords—yet *for us* there is one God [εἷς θεός], the Father, from whom are all things and *for whom we exist*, and one Lord [εἷς κύριος], Jesus Christ, through whom are all things and *through whom we exist.* (8:5–6, emphasis added)

That the distinction of God in God's oneness, elaborated christologically, implies separation becomes clear in the follow-up in chapter 10. Here, the Corinthians are inscribed into the scriptural narrative of the exodus interpreted eschatologically as a narrative warning of the judgment of God on God's people when they engage in idolatry (10:1–13, esp. v. 11). The point is: God in God's oneness—singularity, uniqueness, jealousy (10:22a)—*brooks no rivals.* Hence, "Flee from the worship of idols!" (10:14). And, in bringing the paraenesis to a climax, attention is drawn to what should be the true *telos* of the believer's life: "so, whether you eat or drink, or whatever you do, do everything for the glory of God" (10:31; cf. 6:20). Here, the horizon of mundane life, dominated by competitive consumption in the quest for individual advantage and social esteem, is raised heavenwards toward God, as well as being expanded outward toward "Jews … Greeks … [and] the church of God" (10:32).

11.3.3. Spirit

Paul's response to disunity in the church is also pneumatological, which is to say that it has to do with an appeal to the *felt reality* of God's transformative presence as indwelling Spirit. How such an appeal provides a basis for beliefs, values, and practices that are unitive rather than divisive includes the following.

1. As an experience of revelation and empowerment, experience of the Spirit represents an opening into epistemological and social *innovation* unbound by, or transformative of, traditional ways of seeing and doing.

---

21. On the allusion to the Shema, see Erik Waaler's brilliant monograph, *The Shema and the First Commandment in First Corinthians: An Intertextual Approach to Paul's Re-reading of Deuteronomy*, WUNT 2/253 (Tübingen: Mohr Siebeck, 2008).

252 Stephen C. Barton

This includes sophistic wisdom and its associated social hierarchies and discriminations. Paul himself, testifying to a personal experience likely to have nullified potential rivalry with Apollos, says: "My speech and my proclamation were not with plausible words of wisdom, but with a demonstration of the Spirit and of power [πνεύματος καὶ δυνάμεως], so that your faith might rest not on human wisdom but on the power of God" (2:4–5). What such testimony implies is a dismantling of culturally dominant patterns of communication under the impact of communication claiming the authority of the Spirit. Intriguingly, while this opens the way for the coming into being of a sociality somewhat novel in its social mix and status-leveling (1:26–29), it also opens the way for a hierarchy of a different kind, where what counts is maturity in the Spirit (2:6–13).

2. Because the experience of the Spirit is an experience of *reception and indwelling* (12:13), it is an experience of divine gratuity, of an economy of grace and gift. Such an economy is inimical to competition and boasting since the benefactor is God's free and sovereign Spirit and the gifts are given in ways incongruous with, and therefore disruptive of, conventional culturally approved patterns of worth and obligation.[22] As Paul says: "What do you have that you did not receive? And if you received it, why do you boast [τί καυχᾶσαι] as if it were not a gift?" (4:7).

But as well as being disruptive, such an economy is also *constructive*. Paul seeks, not only to wean the Corinthians from their divisive ways and prior attachments, but even more to establish a new kind of constitution according to which power, authority, worth, and obligation are ordered *charismatically*, that is, according to the free movement of the gift-giving Spirit.

Paul lays this out in 1 Cor 12–14. Salient points include the following: (1) Given that, when they "come together" (11:17), they are to share table-fellowship in ways that unite rather than divide, so too, they are to engage in the Christ cult, not for their own glory, but "for the common good [πρὸς τὸ συμφέρον]" (12:7; cf. συμφέρω in 6:12; 10:23) and mutual "upbuilding" (cf. οἰκοδομή in 14:3, 5, 12, 26). (2) That Paul makes a terminological shift from πνευματικά to χαρίσματα (12:4; cf. vv. 9, 28, 30, 31) is significant. This represents a shift from understanding spiritual power as the property of the one exercising it, and therefore something to boast

---

22. On the idea of the incongruous gift in Paul, see John M. G. Barclay, *Paul and the Gift* (Grand Rapids: Eerdmans, 2015), 72–73 and passim.

11. Paul on Oneness and Unity in 1 Corinthians   253

about, to understanding spiritual power as a gift (χάρισμα) of divine grace (χάρις), and therefore something for which to thank God and to use in the service of Christ and the church. (3) The authorizing and empowering source of the various "gifts," "services," and "activities" is emphatically divine, not human (12:4): so again, no ground for boasting. What is more, because these gifts, services, and activities are Spirit-inspired and God-given, the implication is that the Christ cult is a present participation in the eschatological life of heaven.[23] As such, any worldly beliefs or behaviors that represent the divisive patterns from which the Corinthians have been called have no place. (4) The gifts most prized for their cultural caché, such as wisdom and knowledge, are (for want of a better word) democratized. They are no one's presumptive right, and their reception is mediated by no human agent, but by the Spirit: "To one is given through the Spirit the utterance of wisdom, and to another the utterance of knowledge according to the same Spirit.... All these are activated by one and the same Spirit, *who allots to each one individually just as the Spirit chooses*" (12:8, 11, emphasis added). (5) Against any tendency to exalt one gift at the expense of others (along with the associated distribution of honor and shame), Paul insists on recognition of the diversity of gifts (12:4–6, 12, 14, etc.). Significantly, when Paul offers a representative list, the gift that seems to have been a cause of boasting and display—speaking in "various kinds of tongues"—is placed last (12:10, 28, 30). (6) To drive home the point that there is a diversity of gifts whose purpose is to unify the fellowship, Paul appeals to the metaphor of the body (τὸ σῶμα) and the necessary *interdependence* of its various members (12:12–26). This is a common trope in the ancient political rhetoric of concord.[24] What is striking here, and contrary to conventional usage, is that the metaphor is applied in a way that contradicts presumptive orderings of power and social distinction:[25] "But God has so arranged the body, giving the greater honor to the inferior member, that there may be no dissention [σχίσμα] within the body, but the members may have the same [τὸ αὐτό] care for one another" (12:24b–25).

---

23. Note the reference to speaking in the "tongues of angels," in 13:1; also, the implied presence of angels in 11:10b.

24. See Mitchell, *Paul*, 157–64; also, David G. Horrell, "Σῶμα as a Basis for Ethics in Paul," in *Ethische Normen des frühen Christentums: Gut—Leben—Leib—Tugend*, ed. Friedrich W. Horn, Ulrich Volp, and Ruben Zimmermann WUNT 313 (Tübingen: Mohr Siebeck, 2013), 351–63.

25. Martin, *Corinthian Body*, 94–96.

254 Stephen C. Barton

3. Integrally related to the social impact, both disruptive and constructive, of the freedom of the Spirit and the incongruity of the gift is the impact on *personal identity*. There is a sense in which, because the gift is incongruous, *the recipient becomes incongruous also*, both to him/herself and to the wider culture. Spirit-possessed Christ-followers no longer fit in ways they previously took for granted. In particular, honor and worth are found now, not in self-advancement at the expense of the other, but in *self-abnegation for the sake of the other*, where the other is one's fellow-believer both locally and translocally and, above all, God in God's oneness and glory.

Symptomatic are the following: (1) There is the example of Paul himself. Especially revealing are two autobiographical digressions. In 1 Cor 9, Paul shows what it means to place obligation to the other, "for the sake of the gospel" (9:23), over one's personal freedom; and in 1 Cor 13, he elaborates that virtue of sacrificial care for the other (ἀγάπη) that is the eschatological measure and goal both of his own χαρίσματα and, by extension, of Christian existence as a whole. (2) Then there is Paul's lexicon of terms and images whose application to the Corinthians constitutes an invitation to see themselves as bound to their fellow-believers, not in relations of rivalry and enmity, but in relations transformed by the cruciform gospel and inspired by the Spirit. The language of *kinship* (especially siblingship) among those who constitute eschatological Israel is one example.[26] Indeed, the term ἀδελφός ("brother") is one of the most common among Paul's terms of address (1:10, 11, 26; 2:1; 3:1; 4:6; 5:11; etc.), and it clearly implies mutual belonging and loyalty. So, in the case of dealing with grievances, Paul stresses how shameful it is for brothers to take a case before the public courts (6:5–8), and in the matter of the divisive effect of eating idol food, he says: "Therefore, if food is a cause of *my brother's* falling, I will never eat meat, lest I cause *my brother* to fall" (8:13, RSV, emphasis added). (3) Remarkable, finally, is the symbolic erasure of significant markers of personal distinction and differentiation that is the work of the Spirit in baptism (12:13). As the individual body is reconstituted by the Spirit in baptism, so s/he becomes a member of an eschatological body, the "body of Christ [σῶμα Χριστοῦ]" (12:27). The mark of *this* body is solidarity: "If one member suffers, all suffer together [συμπάσχει πάντα] with it; if one member is honored, all rejoice together [συγχαίρει πάντα] with it" (12:26).

---

26. Cf. Reidar Aasgaard, *"My Beloved Brothers and Sisters!" Christian Siblingship in Paul*, JSNTSup 265 (London: T&T Clark, 2004).

11.4. Conclusion

"For in the one Spirit we were all baptized into one body—*Jews or Greeks, slaves or free*—and we were all made to drink of one Spirit" (12:13, emphasis added). At a two millennia distance, it is difficult to appreciate fully the social novelty of regular gatherings in spaces private and public of peoples of different cultures and ethnicities (Jews and Greeks) and diverse locations in the socio-political order (slaves and free). Equally difficult to appreciate are, not only the effervescence and creativity to which such gatherings gave opportunity, but also the tensions and rivalries to which such gatherings were vulnerable given the intense competitiveness in the quest for personal glory characteristic of the wider cultural ethos.

Against this backdrop, 1 Corinthians is fascinating for the window it opens onto Paul's efforts, in his pedagogical role as a father-figure, to counter forces subversive of the community and to build up its common life. What is clear, as we have seen, is the imperative Paul places on believing and doing what unites the community. What is clear also is that he places this imperative on theological, christological, and pneumatological foundations, themselves shaped by predominantly Jewish traditions interpreted eschatologically in the light of Christ. Interestingly, while Paul displays significant concerns about boundary maintenance for the preservation of unity—unity in holiness—his focus is at least as much on the constitution of a new kind of solidarity, what we might call a *charismatic*, one Spirit, solidarity whose vocation is to glorify God (10:31), and within which ethnic identities, culturally ingrained habits, and distinctions of birth, status, and gender are relativized. Here, what Paul makes normative is that self-abnegation for the sake of the other, and in solidarity with the other, which is the "more excellent way" of love (12:31b–14:1a). But because "now we see in a mirror, dimly" (13:12a), there is a sense that unity is a future goal, as well as a present practice. It is an eschatological reality, grounded in the oneness whose source is God, Christ, and the Spirit. As such, its realization in the present is always partial, always a matter of prophecy and discernment, and always in the making.

Bibliography

Aasgaard, Reidar. *"My Beloved Brothers and Sisters!" Christian Siblingship in Paul.* JSNTSup 265. London: T&T Clark, 2004.

Barclay, John M. G. "Matching Theory and Practice: Josephus's Constitutional Ideal and Paul's Strategy in Corinth." Pages 139–63 in *Paul beyond the Judaism/Hellenism Divide*. Edited by Troels Engberg-Pedersen. Louisville: Westminster John Knox, 2001.

———. *Paul and the Gift*. Grand Rapids: Eerdmans, 2015.

Ciampa, Roy E., and Brian S. Rosner. "The Structure and Argument of 1 Corinthians: A Biblical/Jewish Approach." *NTS* 52 (2006): 205–18.

Harrison, James R. "Honouring the Concord of the Ephesian Demos." In *Ephesus*. Vol. 11 of *New Documents Illustrating the History of Early Christianity*. Edited by James R. Harrison and Bradley J. Bitner. Grand Rapids: Eerdmans, forthcoming.

———. *Paul and the Ancient Celebrity Circuit: The Cross and Moral Transformation*. WUNT 430. Tübingen: Mohr Siebeck, 2019.

Hays, Richard B. "The Conversion of the Imagination: Scripture and Eschatology in 1 Corinthians." *NTS* 45 (1999): 391–412.

———. *First Corinthians*. IBC. Louisville: Westminster John Knox, 1997.

Horbury, William. "Constitutional Aspects of the Kingdom of God." Pages 60–79 in *The Kingdom of God and Human Society: Essays by Members of the Scripture, Theology and Society Group*. Edited by Robin S. Barbour. Edinburgh: T&T Clark, 1993.

Horrell, David G. "Σῶμα as a Basis for Ethics in Paul." Pages 351–63 in *Ethische Normen des frühen Christentums: Gut—Leben—Leib—Tugend*. Edited by Friedrich W. Horn, Ulrich Volp, and Ruben Zimmermann. WUNT 313. Tübingen: Mohr Siebeck, 2013.

Kloppenborg, John S. *Christ's Associations: Connecting and Belonging in the Ancient City*. New Haven: Yale University Press, 2019.

Lakey, Michael J. *Image and Glory of God: 1 Corinthians 11:2–16 as a Case Study in Bible, Gender and Hermeneutics*. LNTS 418. London: T&T Clark, 2010.

Martin, Dale B. *The Corinthian Body*. New Haven: Yale University Press, 1995.

Mitchell, Margaret M. *Paul and the Rhetoric of Reconciliation: An Exegetical Investigation of the Language and Composition of 1 Corinthians*. Louisville: Westminster John Knox Press, 1992.

Theissen, Gerd. "Social Integration and Sacramental Activity: An Analysis of 1 Cor 11:17–34." Pages 145–74 in *The Social Setting of Pauline Christianity: Studies of the New Testament and Its World*. Edited by Gerd Theissen. Edinburgh: T&T Clark, 1982.

Waaler, Erik. *The* Shema *and the First Commandment in First Corinthians: An Intertextual Approach to Paul's Re-reading of Deuteronomy.* WUNT 2/253. Tübingen: Mohr Siebeck, 2008.

Welborn, L. L. "On the Discord in Corinth: 1 Corinthians 1–4 and Ancient Politics." *JBL* 106 (1987): 83–111.

12
One Seed and One God:
Divine Oneness and Ecclesial Unity in
Galatians and Romans

Robbie Griggs

Since E. P. Sanders revised prevailing views of ancient Jewish theology over forty years ago, scholars have struggled to understand Paul's theological coherence.[1] For example, though there is now recognition of the singular character of Paul's gospel in Galatians and agreement on the literary unity of the letter, there is no consensus on theology that undergirds these.[2] Specifically, the problem of Paul's antithetical logic is again troubling scholars: *Why*, precisely, if Christ, then *not* torah (Gal 5:2–4)?[3] Moreover, Paul's confession "God is one" occupies a prominent place in the development of this antithesis since he confesses divine oneness in Gal 3:20 in *contrast* to

---

1. See now John M. G. Barclay, *Paul and the Gift* (Grand Rapids: Eerdmans, 2015), 151–65.

2. For the singular character of Galatians, see, e.g., John H. Schütz, *Paul and the Anatomy of Apostolic Authority*, NTL (Louisville: Westminster John Knox, 2007), 123; Beverly Roberts Gaventa, "The Singularity of the Gospel: A Reading of Galatians," in *Thessalonians, Philippians, Galatians, Philemon*, vol. 1 of *Pauline Theology*, ed. Jouette M. Bassler (Minneapolis: Fortress, 1991), 147–59; Gaventa, "The Singularity of the Gospel Revisited," in *Galatians and Christian Theology: Justification, the Gospel, and Ethics in Paul's Letter*, ed. Mark W. Elliott et al. (Grand Rapids: Baker Academic, 2014), 187–99. For the unity of the letter, see Susanne Schewe, *Die Galater zurückgewinnen: Paulinische Strategien in Galater 5 und 6*, FRLANT 208 (Göttingen: Vandenhoeck & Ruprecht, 2005), 16–59.

3. John M. G. Barclay, "Paul, the Gift and the Battle over Gentile Circumcision: Revisiting the Logic of Galatians," *ABR* 58 (2010): 36–56.

260 Robbie Griggs

the angelic deliverance and Mosaic mediation of the torah at Sinai (3:19).[4] It is important to recognize that this confession occurs within the development of a broader oneness motif in this theologically sophisticated epistle: Paul asserts the singularity of the one and only saving gospel (Gal 1:6, 7); locates the prepreaching of that singular gospel in the Abrahamic promise (Gal 3:8, 18; cf. Gen 12:2, 3) that concerns its "one" seed (Gal 3:16); names Jew and Greek, slave and free, male and female "one in Christ Jesus" (Gal 3:28); and identifies the "one word" of neighbor-love as the fulfilment of the torah (Gal 5:14; cf. Lev 19:18).

We will trace the development of this oneness motif in Galatians in three parts, concluding with a comparison to Paul's explicit appeal to divine oneness in Rom 3:30. The argument is that Paul's antithetical theological logic depends on his particular construal of divine oneness in christological terms. The antithesis between Christ and torah is neither merely a result of human inability or Israel's general failure to obey the torah, nor does it arise from a dogmatic preference for the Christ event or an apocalyptic change in redemptive-history.[5] Rather, Paul argues "if Christ, not torah-piety," because, *by divine design and action*, only in Christ does the church fulfill the aims of torah-virtue.[6] He envisions both a singular divine saving action in Christ to which the torah is integrally related yet ultimately subordinated (Gal 3:21, 22) and a unified, ethnically diverse church

---

4. For the likely dependence of the confession on Deut 6:4, see Christopher R. Bruno, *"God Is One": The Function of "Eis Ho Theos" as a Ground for Gentile Inclusion in Paul's Letters*, LNTS 497 (London: T&T Clark, 2013), 1–23.

5. For human inability, see, e.g., R. Barry Matlock, "Helping Paul's Argument Work? The Curse of Galatians 3.10–14," in *Torah in the New Testament: Papers Delivered at the Manchester-Lausanne Seminar of June 2008*, ed. Peter Oakes and Michael Tait, LNTS 401 (London: T&T Clark, 2009), 154–79. For Israel's general failure, see Richard B. Hays, "The Letter to the Galatians," *NIB* 11:258–59: those who are "of the works of the law" are under a curse "not because obedience is theoretically impossible, but because Israel historically has failed and has in fact incurred the judgment of which Deuteronomy solemnly warns." For the Christ event, see E. P. Sanders, *Paul, the Law, and the Jewish People* (Philadelphia: Fortress, 1983), 21–27. On the paradigmatic significance of the question, "What time is it?," see J. Louis Martyn, *Galatians: A New Translation with Introduction and Commentary*, AB 33A (New York: Doubleday, 1997), 23; similarly, Martinus de Boer, *Galatians: A Commentary*, NTL (Louisville: Westminster John Knox, 2011), 201–2.

6. By *torah-piety*, I mean the practices characteristic of Jewish life (e.g., circumcision); by *torah-virtue*, I mean the love that is, for Paul, both a disposition produced by the Spirit (5:22, 23) and the aim of the torah (5:14; cf. Lev 19:18).

12. One Seed and One God

in Christ in which the one word of torah-virtue is fulfilled (5:14). As we shall see, this Pauline construal of divine oneness in Christ both forecloses any *Sonderweg* and renders torah-piety a matter of communal indifference *of necessity.*[7] Likewise, such a christological oneness, with its own ecclesial and ethical order, constitutes a sort of Pauline grammar of divine oneness and communal unity, a "truth of the gospel," that is serviceable even in different circumstances in the church of Rome.

12.1. Oneness and Unity in Paul's Story (Gal 1–2): The Truth of the Gospel as Unconditioned Reciprocity

In Gal 1–2, Paul reframes the views of his opponents through a theologically loaded retelling of his apostolic autobiography. Against those Jewish Christians who would present obedience to torah norms as a natural consequence of gentile commitment to the Messiah Jesus, Paul tells stories of the donation and reception of the singular Christ-gift. With the insistence on *one* gospel that necessarily excludes torah norms for communal unity, Paul both drives a wedge between himself and his opponents and introduces a *leitmotif* of singularity that drives his argument forward.

12.1.1. Galatians 1: The Singular Gospel and the Gift

Paul begins his appeal to the Galatians by contrasting recent events in their churches with his own life. His initial point is that there is only one message that corresponds to God's saving gift. This message distinguishes Paul from his opponents and, thereby, forces a choice on the Galatians.[8] His enemies are those "who seek to distort the gospel of Christ" (1:7) and their message is a "different gospel" (1:6).[9] The present deliberations in Galatia are, for Paul, a rapid-onset abandonment of "the one who called [them] in the gift of Christ" (ταχέως μετατίθεσθε ἀπὸ τοῦ καλέσαντος ὑμᾶς ἐν χάριτι [Χριστοῦ]). Paul then raises the stakes, pronouncing a double-anathema on any agent, whether of heaven or earth, who preaches another gospel (1:8, 9). The problem is the singular character of the gospel. There is no

---

7. See, e.g., Matthew Thiessen, *Paul and the Gentile Problem* (Oxford: Oxford University Press, 2016), 105–60.

8. For Paul as an example of "the working of the gospel," see Beverly Roberts Gaventa, "Galatians 1 and 2: Autobiography as Paradigm," *NovT* 28 (1986): 313.

9. Translations are my own unless noted otherwise.

262 Robbie Griggs

possibility of reconciling the views of his opponents with the good news he preaches, the Christ-gift it offers, or the God who saves through it. This Pauline rhetoric of singularity produces a dilemma for the Galatians, but it also requires elaboration and defense.

The defense of this singular gospel starts with Paul's story of how he became an apostle. Anticipating the charge of pragmatism, Paul asserts that "if [he] were still pleasing human beings, then [he] would not be a slave of Christ" (εἰ ἔτι ἀνθρώποις ἤρεσκον, Χριστοῦ δοῦλος οὐκ ἂν ἤμην) (1:10). The implication is that he *used* to be a people-pleasing preacher of circumcision (cf. Gal 5:11), but now, unlike his *compromised opponents*, he is rightly devoted to God. This devotion Paul traces to God's action. His message has a divine—not human—origin and character, coming to Paul "through a revelation of Jesus Christ" (δι᾽ ἀποκαλύψεως Ἰησοῦ Χριστοῦ) (1:11, 12). That revelation set Paul's life on a trajectory that was antithetical both to his "former life in Judaism" (τὴν ἐμὴν ἀναστροφήν ποτε ἐν τῷ Ἰουδαϊσμῷ) (1:13) and, thus, to the present practice of his opponents.[10] So, Paul's pivot from devotee of his ancestral traditions and church enemy to apostle to the gentiles is *from God*. He, like the Galatians, was "called [by God] through [God's] gift" (καλέσας διὰ τῆς χάριτος αὐτοῦ) (1:15). Moreover, just as they were recipients of an unconditioned and incongruous gift as *gentiles*, he is such a recipient as a *Jew* who was marked out for this gift from birth (1:15) and despite being a persecutor of the church (1:13).[11] And lest the Galatians get the wrong idea, his subsequent interactions with the apostles in Jerusalem were both limited and relatively inconsequential for his preaching ministry (1:16–22). The only news worth reporting from Jerusalem at that time was of the astonished praise offered to God for Paul's about-face (1:23). In short, for Paul, the question about devotion to God is the correct one, but this query ought to lead the Galatians

---

10. Given Paul's characterization of himself as intent on persuading God only (1:10) and his subsequent opposition to the imposition of torah-piety *simpliciter* in the church, the religiopolitical term *Judaism* and not the politicogeographic term *Judeanism* is the better translation of his use of Ἰουδαϊσμός. For an overview of the debate over Paul's use of Ἰουδαῖος and Ἰουδαϊσμός, see Matthew V. Novenson, "Paul's Former Occupation in *Ioudaismos*," in Elliott et al., *Galatians and Christian Theology*, 24–39.

11. For the Christ-gift as unconditioned (given without regard to prior conditions) and incongruous (given despite the unworthiness of the recipient) in Gal 1, see, e.g., Barclay, *Paul and the Gift*, 351–87; Orrey McFarland, "'The One Who Calls in Grace': Paul's Rhetorical and Theological Identification with the Galatians," *HBT* 35 (2013): 151–65.

12. One Seed and One God

to his way of viewing things! They both, he, a Jew, and they, gentiles, were called by means of God's unconditioned and incongruous gift in Christ, and this benefaction has implications for the status of torah observance in the church's life.

12.1.2. Galatians 2: The Gift and the Unconditioned Unity of the Church

Paul's next two stories specify the implications of the one gospel for a church of Jews and gentiles. In short, the saving Christ-gift should be received in the church without respect to torah observance, that is, just as it is *given* by God.[12] While this entailment is being debated in Galatia, it had already been enacted in Paul's second trip to Jerusalem. Despite pressure from "false brothers" to have his Greek companion Titus circumcised (2:3, 4), Paul and his team resisted "so that the truth of the gospel might be preserved for [the Galatians]" (2:5). Paul narrates the response of his peers to specify the content of this truth. Rather than adding further Jewish stipulations to his mission, the leaders in Jerusalem (James, John, and Peter) "gave [Paul] and Barnabas the right hand of fellowship" (2:9). Paul attributes this unconditioned welcome to the Jerusalem leaders' right perception of God's benefaction: they "recognized the gift given [to Paul by God]" (2:9). Since they perceived that God was doing the same work in Paul's gentile mission and in Peter's mission to the Jews (2:7, 8), they returned unconditioned fellowship to Paul's mixed team.[13] Ironically, the situation in Galatia had been previewed in Jerusalem, and the leaders then saw the divine intention for unconditioned communal unity in the Christ-gift and so sided with God/Paul!

Paul's account of the controversy in Antioch serves both as a contrast to this unconditioned fellowship in Jerusalem and as a final frame through which to view the situation in Galatia. While the truth of the gospel was preserved in Jerusalem, it is threatened by the division of community along the lines of torah-piety in Antioch. The Jerusalem leaders rightly recognized God's work in Paul's apostleship, extending unconditioned fellowship; Peter and others later behaved at odds with the gospel's truth (οὐκ

---

12. On the logic of "balanced reciprocity," wherein a gift entails "returning the same kind of gifts, or gifts of equal value for those received," see Stephan Joubert, *Paul as Benefactor: Reciprocity, Strategy and Theological Reflection in Paul's Collection*, WUNT 2/124 (Tübingen: Mohr Siebeck, 2000), 22.

13. Barclay, *Paul and the Gift*, 363–64.

ὀρθοποδοῦσιν πρὸς τὴν ἀλήθειαν τοῦ εὐαγγελίου, 2:14) by separating themselves from the gentiles in Antioch. In that case, Paul considered a public confrontation over the duplicity (ὑπόκρισις, 2:13) of Peter (and the Jewish Christians) essential for restoring the unconditioned unity of the church: "If you, though a Jew, live as a gentile and not a Jew, how is it that you are compelling gentiles to live as Jews [ἰουδαΐζειν]?" (2:14)[14] This is a rather stark rhetorical climax to the story Paul has been telling since anticipating the charge of people-pleasing in Gal 1:10. If anyone has been guilty of disingenuous compromise, it was Peter at Antioch. Likewise, if the Galatians doubt the seriousness of Paul's anathemas on his opponents, they need only consider that he alone was willing to publicly recognize the divine verdict of condemnation on Peter's divisive behavior.

Paul ends his theologically freighted autobiographical stories with a summary of his position. His contention, which he will explain and defend throughout the remainder of Galatians, is that the torah-piety his opponents recommend is a matter of indifference from the perspective of true righteousness. As with those gentile "sinners" (2:15), even the Jewish Christians themselves recognize that faith in Christ is the evidence of God's justifying verdict, not the works of the law (2:16).[15] The question that arises next brings Paul to a basic issue: If the "truth" that Paul sees in the singular gospel is correct, that is, that God's unconditioned and incongruous gift entails the unified community of Jews and gentiles without regard to torah observance, does that not make Christ himself an advocate for sin (διάκονος ἁμαρτίας, 2:17)? Paul rejects the inference for two interrelated reasons. First, to reestablish torah-piety *after having lived in violation of it* would be to admit that his manner of life as an apostle was in violation of God's will (2:18).[16] This he cannot do because, second, it was through his obedience to the torah that his life ordered by torah-piety came to an

---

14. Though the meaning of ἰουδαΐζειν here is unclear, the context indicates a significant violation and, after Peter's reversal, subsequent imposition of Jewish commensality norms. See E. P. Sanders, "Jewish Association with Gentiles and Galatians 2:1–14," in *The Conversation Continues: Studies in Paul and John in Honor of J. Louis Martyn*, ed. Robert T. Fortna and Beverly Roberts Gaventa (Nashville: Abingdon, 1990), 170–88.

15. With Barclay, "What Paul is discussing in 2:16 are not complete soteriological systems, but the evidential basis on which God can consider someone 'righteous' (or worthy) in his sight" (Barclay, *Paul and the Gift*, 380).

16. John M. G. Barclay, *Obeying the Truth: A Study of Paul's Ethics in Galatians*, SNTW (Edinburgh: T&T Clark, 1988), 80.

12. One Seed and One God 265

end, in order for a life ordered to God's will to commence (2:19).[17] That is, it was his life in Judaism that brought him to oppose God's church *before* having his life rearranged by God's gift. It is the self-offering of the Messiah in which this old agency of Paul's is ended ("I have been crucified with Christ. It is no longer I who live, but Christ lives in me") and a new agency and orientation are begun ("And the life I now live in the flesh, I live by faith in the Son of God," 2:20).[18] It is this new and newly ordered life resulting from "the gift of God" that Paul will not reject by acquiescing to Jewish Christian pressure to live as though righteousness comes through the torah (2:21). The end of his life under the torah was not a pragmatic concession to his role as apostle to the gentiles; it was constitutive of his life toward God. Moreover, as was recognized in Jerusalem and, in Paul's view, threatened in Antioch, this life toward God was to be lived necessarily without respect to the norms of torah-piety in the church.

12.2. The Singular Saving Intention (Gal 3–4): One God and One Church in Christ

As with the autobiographical section, Gal 3–4 begins with a pointed evaluation of the Galatian situation (i.e., someone has "bewitched" [βασκαίνω] them, 3:1). Yet, the focus widens from an appeal to particular stories to a consideration of redemptive-history. This wider lens matches a key development in Paul's oneness motif, as he argues that God acted in the same way in both the lives of the Galatians and of the patriarch Abraham. Just as the Galatians experienced manifestations of the Spirit's power not "by works of the law" but "by hearing with faith," so "Abraham 'believed God, and it was credited to him as righteousness'" (3:5, 6). By linking the Galatians' experiences of God's action with Abraham's experience, Paul begins to argue for a deeper redemptive-historical design. Namely, having reframed the views of his opponents in the autobiography, he turns to argue against those views by reading the history of Israel and the Galatian church as the plan of the One God. As we will argue, a closer examination

---

17. Barclay captures the force of Paul's statement: "[Paul's] break with the torah, he says, is *in order to live (in faithfulness) to God* (ἵνα θεῷ ζήσω). The capacity to make such a statement signals a profound dislocation: like all Jews, he desires to 'live to God,' but the Torah no longer defines what this entails" (Barclay, *Paul and the Gift*, 386, emphasis original).

18. Barclay, *Paul and the Gift*, 386.

266   Robbie Griggs

of Paul's appeal to divine oneness exposes the shortcomings of traditional and recent revisionist accounts of his antithetical theological logic. Specifically, traditional accounts do not explain why the torah should not order the church's life *after Christ*, dogmatic accounts misunderstand the evidential requirements of Paul's situation, and redemptive-historical explanations misconstrue the appeal to necessity in his reasoning. Thus, a reconsideration of Paul's argument is required.

12.2.1. Galatians 3:8–18: The Prepreached Gospel and the One Seed

Paul reads redemptive-history as the plan of the One God first by identifying a specific saving intention in the Abrahamic promise. In Gal 3:8 Paul asserts that the promise of blessing to the nations is recorded in scripture *in anticipation* (προοράω) of the fact that "God justifies the gentiles by faith" (ἐκ πίστεως δικαιοῖ τὰ ἔθνη ὁ θεός). Thus, Paul interprets this scriptural promise as a "prepreaching of the gospel" (προευαγγελίζομαι). The Abrahamic promise, for Paul, is *by divine design* and *in nuce* materially identical to the singular, unconditioned gospel he has been defending. To support this identification of the Galatians' experience with Abraham's (3:5–7), Paul begins tracing the divine saving action from the promise to Abraham, through the curse of the law, to the curse-bearer, and thus finally to blessing (Gal 3:8–14). Since Martin Luther, however, interpreters have had to contend with the problem of Paul's inferential logic.[19] In Gal 3:10, Paul asserts that those who are "of the works of the law" are under a curse, while the scriptural support he adduces from Deut 27:26 announces a curse on those who "*do not do all that is written in the book of this law.*" To bridge this gap between categorical and contingent curses, scholars have typically posited an unstated premise regarding human inability, whereby, for Paul, the recipients of the law cannot fulfill its demands.[20] Those who might rely on the "works of the law" for divine approbation were (proudly) attempting the impossible. On this reading, both Jews and gentiles are recipients of the unconditioned Christ-gift as an *incongruous* gift, that is, by virtue of their shared sinful humanity.

Following Sanders and rejecting traditional conceptions of Jewish theology as legalistic in character, recent scholars have opted for two basic

---

19. Luther, *Weimarer Ausgabe* 40.I.2:396.

20. See, e.g., Ernest. DeWitt Burton, *A Critical and Exegetical Commentary on the Epistle to the Galatians*, ICC (Edinburgh: T&T Clark, 1921), 164.

alternative explanations of Paul's inferential logic. Adopting Sanders's own dogmatic explanation, some scholars have argued that Paul's experience of the Christ event renders his appeals to scripture in Gal 3:8, 10 as a kind of brute proof-texting.[21] The basic error of a dogmatic construal, though, is the failure to reckon with the fact that the Christ event was a shared experience for Paul *and his Jewish-Christian opponents*. Paul owes his interlocutors reasons for his inferences, because they see the implications of the Christ event differently. Others, adapting the arguments of scholars like James Scott and N. T. Wright, have claimed that Paul's inferential reasoning was Deuteronomic or redemptive-historical.[22] That is, Paul is neither implying inability nor dogmatically proof-texting, but rather he is appealing to the fact of Israel's corporate failure.[23] As Richard Hays puts it, Paul is seeking to prevent the Galatians from "joining a losing team."[24] Construing Paul's inferential logic as an appeal to fact does not, however, account for the element of *necessity* in his reasoning. Unlike the autobiographical section, Paul is no longer appealing to the *fact* of the singular gospel and its recognition but rather he is explaining why redemptive-history *inevitably produces this pattern* of promise, curse, curse-bearer, and blessing (Gal 3:8–14).[25] His answer is that this pattern is, in part, attributable to the plan of the One God *evident already in the delivery of the promise itself.* Dogmatic accounts ignore the evidential requirements of Paul's situation, while redemptive-historical readings underplay the element of necessity in his reasoning. What is needed still is an account of Paul's inferential logic that explains the relation between categorical curse and contingent scriptural support.

---

21. Martyn, *Galatians*, 311; de Boer, *Galatians*, 200–201.

22. See N. T. Wright, *The Climax of the Covenant: Christ and the Law in Pauline Theology* (Edinburgh: T&T Clark, 1991), 137–56; James Scott, "'For as Many as Are of Works of the Law Are Under a Curse' (Galatians 3:10)," in *Paul and the Scriptures of Israel*, ed. Craig A. Evans and James A. Sanders, JSNTSup 83 (Sheffield: Sheffield Academic, 1993), 187–221.

23. Francis Watson has argued, e.g., that Paul's perception of the cursed state of the people arises, in part, from his reading of the end of Deuteronomy itself, which implies that the curse will inevitably spread to the whole nation (*Paul and the Hermeneutics of Faith*, 2nd ed. [London: T&T Clark, 2015], 394–96).

24. Hays, "Galatians," 259.

25. *Pace* Barclay (*Paul and the Gift*, 405–6 n. 39), who suggests that Paul's reasoning reflects "simply a sense that Israel's history proved her collective and persistent incapacity to be obedient."

268   Robbie Griggs

In this connection, Paul provides an important clue in his next construal of redemptive-history as the intention of the One God. For after reading the Abrahamic promise as the gospel prepreached, he specifies Christ as the envisioned recipient of the Abrahamic inheritance itself. As the justification of the gentiles was envisioned in Gen 12:3, so Christ was intended in the "seed" promise in Gen 22:18 as the means of that justification.[26] He argues, "It does not say, 'And to offsprings,' as to many, but as to one, 'And to your offspring,' who is Christ" (Gal 3:16). The key point, for our purposes, is that Paul is asserting a divinely determined relation between the Abrahamic promise(s) and Christ, the one heir, which, given his basic schema, necessitates the law's cursing function. The Abrahamic inheritance comes properly *only* through and to the one seed who bears the curse. On this view, the divine words recorded in scripture reflect a fixed intention that God is bringing about in the singular gospel Paul preaches. The law was given 430 years after the promise, which means that it cannot overturn God's prior commitment (3:17). Further, the law cannot overturn the initial promissory character of God's covenant: "For if the inheritance comes by the law, it no longer comes by promise; but God gave it to Abraham by a promise" (3:18). An appeal to the *fact* of Israel's cursed state will not explain the logic of necessity in what, for Paul, is a divinely determined redemptive-historical pattern. Rather, what Paul sees in the varied events and scriptural utterances is one determinative divine saving intention, whereby the promissory inheritance must be delivered to believing heirs in the Christ event alone.[27] Thus, Paul's first substantive argumentative move in support of his account of the singular gospel depends on a particular reading of the promise as the intention of the One God. If one wants to know why heirs are identified by faith and not by works of the law, then Paul contends that one must attend to God's singular and specifically promissory commitment *and its fulfillment*. There is one gospel prepreached in anticipation of the one seed and those whom God will justify by faith in him. Thus, the unconditioned and incongruous gospel Paul preaches is a matter of God's specific intention and agency from the

---

26. For the argument that Gen 22:18 is Paul's source in Gal 3:16, see C. John Collins, "Galatians 3:16: What Kind of Exegete Was Paul?," *TynBul* 54 (2003): 75–86.

27. Paul's personifications of γραφή, then, serve to identify how God's varied utterances relate to what he is doing now; cf. Watson, *Hermeneutics*, 40.

12. One Seed and One God

beginning of Israel's history.[28] Still, what are we to make of Paul's appeal to the contingent curse of Deut 27:26?

12.2.2. Galatians 3:19–29: The Torah, Divine Oneness, and Church Unity

This essay contends that a compelling interpretation of Paul's inferential logic depends, in part, on a careful consideration of his appeal to divine oneness in Gal 3:20. While scholars have focused on whether Paul's view of the law is positive or negative, or continuous or discontinuous with the Christ event, in general, the following reading argues that he considers the torah itself as a particular feature of the intention of the One God. In short, Paul reads the law's curse as added ultimately *by God* with a singular saving intention in mind: to confine all humanity under sin in anticipation of the Christ event. Likewise, having served its confining purpose, the law itself is, for Paul, confined by God to a cosmos conditioned by sin, rendering its differentiating practices a matter of indifference to the community that is "one in Christ Jesus" (3:28). There are several exegetical observations in support of this reading of the torah as *by divine design* subordinate yet integral to the singular gospel. First, Paul adopts the same teleological mode of reading the torah as he did with the promise. When he asks "Why then the law?" (3:19), he answers in relation to the coming Christ event. The law "was added [to the promise] for the sake of transgressions, until the seed might come to whom the promise had been made" (τῶν παραβάσεων χάριν προσετέθη, ἄχρις οὗ ἔλθῃ τὸ σπέρμα ᾧ ἐπήγγελται) (3:19).[29] Like the promise, the deliverance of the torah has the one seed as its trajectory and goal. Yet, when Paul turns to the circumstances of the law's delivery, he poses a potential problem. Unlike the promise, the law was *not* put in place directly by the One God.[30] Instead, the observation that the law "was

---

28. *Pace* Preston M. Sprinkle, *Law and Life: The Interpretation of Leviticus 18:5 in Early Judaism and in Paul*, WUNT 2/241 (Tübingen: Mohr Siebeck, 2007), 133–64, who reduces Paul's logic to a general antithesis between divine and human agency.

29. On the correlation of the Abrahamic "seed" and the Davidic "seed" in ancient Judaism, Gal 3:16 and 3:19, see J. Thomas Hewitt, "Ancient Messiah Discourse and Paul's Expression Ἄχρις οὗ Ἔλθῃ τό Σπέρμα in Galatians 3.19," *NTS* 65 (2019): 398–411.

30. With Charles H. Giblin, "Three Monotheistic Texts in Paul," *CBQ* 37 (1975): 541, "Paul is characterizing Moses's role precisely in reference to the proximate, multiple source (angels) of that which Moses transmitted."

administered by angels by the hand of a mediator" (διαταγεὶς δι᾽ ἀγγέλων ἐν χειρὶ μεσίτου) (3:19), gives rise to Paul's appeal to divine oneness: "The mediator is not of one, but God is one" (ὁ δὲ μεσίτης ἑνὸς οὐκ ἔστιν, ὁ δὲ θεὸς εἷς ἐστιν) (3:20).

This distinction between Moses and God leads us to the second feature of Paul's reading of the torah as integral to the One God's intention. As with the promise, Paul reads the circumstances of the torah's delivery as indicative of God's purpose for the law. The torah's mediated character is an indication of the law's subordination *by God* to the divine saving intention in the Christ event.[31] We see this in how Paul evaluates two possible interpretations of his appeal to divine oneness. Since he has insisted that God gave the promise not to "many" but to "one" offspring (3:16), Paul's distinction between God and the varied agents in the torah's delivery raises the possibility that "the law is against the promises of God" (3:19). Ironically, some scholars have read Paul as implying a cleavage between the law and the promise, whereby the angels are anti-God powers who have co-opted the law for their own cursing purposes.[32] Yet Paul's own hypothetical imagines a situation in which the law would "make-alive" such that "righteousness really would be from the law" (3:21). That is, the law would be contrary to the promises if it represented a *Sonderweg*, an alternative to the saving Christ-gift (cf. Gal 2:19–21).[33] In Paul's view, then, his opponents' position ironically denies God's intention in both the promise *and the torah*. Again, this is indicated by Paul's reading of "the scripture": Genesis 12:3 prepreached the gospel, and Deut 27:26 serves that same gospel.[34] Rather than presenting a *Sonderweg* (ἀλλά), the scripture itself (ἡ

---

31. For the argument that Paul might be distancing God from the law, given parallels with Philo's argument that, in creating human beings, God used assistants to distance himself from human sin (cf. *Opif.* 69–75; *Conf.* 168–183; *Fug.* 68–72; *Mut.* 30–32), see Stefan Nordgaard, "Paul and the Provenance of the Law: The Case of Galatians 3,19–20," *ZNW* 105 (2014): 64–79; Barclay, *Paul and the Gift*, 403–4.

32. J. Louis Martyn, "God's Way of Making Things Right," in *Theological Issues in the Letters of Paul* (Edinburgh: T&T Clark, 2005), 152. Cf. de Boer, *Galatians*, 228–31.

33. Paul is contending with the soteriological implications of his opponents' position; see Frederich Avemarie, "Paul and the Claim of the Law according to the Scripture: Leviticus 18:5 in Galatians 3:12 and Romans 10:5," in *The Beginnings of Christianity: A Collection of Articles*, ed. Jack Pastor and Menachem Mor (Jerusalem: Yad Ben-Zvi, 2005), 140–41.

34. The parallel personification of γραφή here with Gal 3:8 suggests that Paul has the curse of Deut 27:26 in mind; see Watson, *Hermeneutics*, 475.

γραφή) encloses "all things under sin [τὰ πάντα ὑπὸ ἁμαρτίαν]," precisely, "so that the promise by faith in Jesus Christ might be given to those who believe [ἵνα ἡ ἐπαγγελία ἐκ πίστεως Ἰησοῦ Χριστοῦ δοθῇ τοῖς πιστεύουσιν]" (3:22). For Paul, Deut 27:26 *as scripture* serves as a cosmic moral jailor, such that to be enslaved to sin, under a curse, and dead are conceptually synonymous. This dead reality enslaved to sin is what *God intends* in the torah, precisely with the singular, unconditioned, and incongruous gospel in view. If his opponents are correct that torah *practice per se* identifies divine heirs, then the promise is contradicted by the torah in both its initial promissory character and its fulfillment as divine life-giving gift in Christ. Put positively, the singular plan of the One God does not admit a *Sonderweg*, but rather the confining curse of torah has, by divine design from the outset of its delivery, the saving Christ-gift in view for believing Jew and gentile alike. To confess One God, for Paul, is therefore to confess a subordinate but integral role for the torah in the singular gospel.

Finally, Paul reads the torah as integral yet subordinate to the One God's intention by arguing for the prearranged obsolescence of the works of the law. As with the promise, Paul considers the torah in relation to the singular divine plan for an unconditioned community in Christ. But to do so, he argues that, in addition to its confining role, the law itself is confined and fitted by God to the time prior and the world opposed to Christ's advent.[35] The key issue for our purposes is how Paul's oneness language relates to his conception of ecclesial unity. Notably, both the word "one" (εἷς) and the singular "seed" (σπέρμα) play a key role. Paul's much debated statement that "there is neither Jew nor Greek, slave nor free, male nor female" depends on the Galatians' oneness with Christ: "for you are all one [εἷς] in Christ Jesus" (3:28). Likewise, this same oneness with Christ is the ground for their identification as Abraham's children: "for if you are of Christ, then you are Abraham's seed [σπέρμα], heirs according to promise" (3:29). Crucially, Paul's use of the language of sonship with this account of ecclesial oneness enables an explanation of the law's necessary yet necessar-

---

35. If τὰ στοιχεῖα τοῦ κόσμου (Gal 4:3, 9) refers to the four elements of ancient cosmology, then Paul's identification of Jewish and pagan worship practices (4:9, 10) may indicate that torah-piety is not only confined to the time but also fitted to the cosmos. I.e., in following the cycle of life and death, the Jewish calendar belongs to "the present evil age" and its world. On the debate over τὰ στοιχεῖα τοῦ κόσμου, see Martinus C. de Boer, "The Meaning of the Phrase τὰ Στοιχεῖα τοῦ Κόσμου in Galatians," *NTS* 53 (2007): 204–24.

272 Robbie Griggs

ily limited role in redemptive-history. For if the law is like a child-minder (παιδαγωγός) put in place by God, then the law's role is itself confined to the period of his children's immaturity.[36] As Paul writes, "we are no longer under a child-minder, for you are all sons of God through faith in Jesus Christ" (3:25b–26). In other words, for Paul, the school of the law had justification by faith as its ultimate lesson (3:24), and with the advent of that faith in Christ, humanity has graduated from the law's tutelage.

When Paul turns from narrating stories that illustrate "the truth of the gospel" to argue for this singular gospel, he reads both the Abrahamic promise and the Mosaic torah as expressions of the One God's saving intention. There is one gospel prepreached to Abraham in anticipation both of the one seed and those whom God will justify by faith in him. God's intention for the torah was to enclose all things under sin in anticipation of this liberating Christ event. This reading of the torah's purpose resolves, in part, the problem of Paul's inferential logic by indicating that the assumption of human inability does bridge the gap between the contingent and categorical curses in Gal 3:10—and *by divine design*. This does not in itself resolve the problem of Paul's antithetical logic. For it does not explain why *once that inability* is removed in the Christ event the torah itself might not order the life of the church.[37] At this point, Paul's argument for unconditioned ecclesial unity is funded by his appeal to christological and divine oneness. With the advent of God's Son (4:4), the sons of God "through faith in Christ Jesus" (3:26) are all one in him (3:28) and thus correctly identified as Abraham's singular seed (3:29). By contrast, torah-piety is confined by God to the age of humanity's immaturity and is thus a matter of indifference in the church. In Paul's view, God's intention in the promise *and* the torah was one community of Jews and gentiles—unconditioned by the distinctions of worth that might be implied by ethnicity, liberty, and sexual difference—in the one seed, the son of God, Jesus Christ.

---

36. On the παιδαγωγός metaphor, see N. H. Young, "*Paidagogos*: The Social Setting of a Pauline Metaphor," *NovT* 29 (1987): 150–76.

37. There is nothing exclusionary about the practice of torah per se. The question at issue is not if the gentiles will be included in the church in Galatia but if the unity of the church's life will be characterized by torah-piety. For an analysis of the specious assumptions underwriting the common antithesis between a particular and exclusionary ancient Judaism and a universal and inclusive early Christianity, see David G. Horrell, "Paul, Inclusion and Whiteness: Particularizing Interpretation," *JSNT* 40 (2017): 123–47.

12. One Seed and One God   273

12.3. The One Word of Ecclesial Unity and
Divine Evaluation (Gal 5)

In the letter's closing, Paul shifts from an argument against the relevance of torah norms to a positive account of the church's communal order. Scholars have long focused on the role of this ethical section in the letter, as it is not altogether clear how the theology Paul has developed to this point coheres with the implications he draws from it for life in Galatia.[38] In contrast, my aim here is to show two ways that the theological argument advances in Gal 5, situate these developments within Paul's appeal to christological oneness and ecclesial unity, and suggest how they resolve the problem of his inferential logic.

12.3.1. Galatians 5:1–15: The One Word of Love and Obeying the Truth

Paul begins the letter's closing by emphasizing the dire effects of adopting circumcision in the Galatian churches. By effectively seeking divine vindication in torah-piety they are courting disaster: "Christ [will be] of no advantage to you" (5:2), "You have been released from Christ" (5:4), and "you have fallen from the gift"(5:4). Moral "freedom," Paul contends, is found not in returning to a "yoke of slavery" (5:1), but by recognizing that it is "through the Spirit by faith" that the church awaits eschatological vindication, "the hope that pertains to righteousness" (5:5). And it is from this eschatological vantage "in Christ Jesus" that the bankruptcy of moral capital built on distinctions between circumcision and uncircumcision— the distinction "counts for nothing" (τι ἰσχύει)— is disclosed in light of the principle of "faith working through love" (5:6).[39] With this assertion that "faith working through love" is what counts, Paul turns to his positive account of God's vision for the church. Most generally, that vision is antithetical. Rather than indulging the "passions of the flesh," the Galatians should "through love enslave themselves to one another" (5:13). The antithesis is not with the law per se. For it is in the one word of neighbor-love in Lev 19:18 that "the whole law is fulfilled" (5:14). This appeal to Lev 19:18 is not surprising.[40] For with the phrase "one word," Paul reads the law's love command, like its curse, in relation to the singular Christ

---

38. See Schewe, *Die Galater zurückgewinnen.*
39. On the metaphorical phrase τι ἰσχύει, see Barclay, *Paul and the Gift,* 392–93.
40. *Pace* de Boer, *Galatians,* 325.

274 Robbie Griggs

event and its good news. The "one word" spoken by God envisions the "one seed": Christ and the church of Jews and gentiles in him.

This identification of what counts eschatologically with the law's own moral aim creates a strong undercurrent of irony. Paul has chastised the Galatians for not "obeying the truth," warned them that the leaven of his opponents' teaching is not from God, and expressed an exasperated wish that these teachers would emasculate themselves (Gal 5:7–12). Now, he opposes circumcision precisely because the Galatians are called to freedom (Ὑμεῖς γὰρ ἐπ᾽ ἐλευθερίᾳ ἐκλήθητε, 5:13) from torah-piety for the sake of resisting the flesh and meeting God's aim as expressed in the torah itself (5:14; Lev 19:18). The implication is shocking: if the Galatians order their lives according to torah-piety, they will succumb to the flesh and risk the unthinking, bestial destruction of their community (5:15; cf. 5:26)—violating the torah's one word. This oneness reading of the law marks a significant advance in Paul's theological argument. It further undermines the case for adopting torah-piety, because not only is circumcision a matter of indifference, but ironically its practice tends not toward the fulfillment but the contravention of the law's singular moral vision. Thus, for Paul, Gen 12:3; Deut 27:26; and Lev 19:18 relate to a singular divine intention, a truth that must be received and obeyed. This "truth of the gospel" results in a new unified community of Jews and gentiles in which the torah's moral aim is fulfilled, all arising only from the Christ-gift received by faith.

12.3.2. Galatians 5:16–26: The Spirit's Singular Fruit or Life under the Law

Paul's explanation of the means by which this community might resist the flesh and find unity in love provides the solution to the problem of his inferential logic. In short, the antithesis between the flesh and the Spirit indicates that the torah's curse is applicable to all humanity because all are enslaved to their own evil desires. As is widely recognized, Paul's vice and virtue lists are concerned with different things: his "works of the flesh" are a series of actions, while his "fruit of the Spirit" is the singular disposition of love in its manifold expressions.[41] This difference in focus serves Paul's rhetorical and theological aim. Though the precise force of Gal 5:17 is uncertain, Paul clearly personifies the "Flesh" and the Spirit as agents

---

41. See, e.g., Troels Engberg-Pedersen, *Paul and the Stoics* (Louisville: Westminster John Knox, 2000), 164.

12. One Seed and One God   275

involved, in some sense, with the production of human desires and their corresponding actions. The desires of the flesh and Spirit are "opposed to each other, to keep you from doing the things you want to do" (Gal 5:17d). In light of this desire-action nexus, Paul's appeals to the Galatians to act according to the disposition the Spirit provides indicate that this relational dynamic is the only means of avoiding fleshly activities and fulfilling the torah's aim. For Paul's metaphors frame the required actions as enduring and deliberate alignment with the Spirit: they are "through love" to "enslave themselves to one-another" (5:13), to "walk by the Spirit" (5:16), to be "led by the Spirit" (5:18), and so on. Crucially, Paul's final exhortation is grounded in a sort of death and life reality: "Those who are of Christ Jesus have crucified the flesh with its passions and desires. If we exist by the Spirit, let us order our lives by the Spirit" (5:24, 25). Thus, in a fashion similar to the death-life pattern of Gal 2:19, 20, the death to one evil set of desires corresponds to, in some sense, a new existence by the Spirit.[42] The appropriate response for these new agents is, then, to live out that new life. Interestingly, there is no corresponding relational account of the flesh and the old agency. This has led some scholars to posit the absence of agency under the flesh, perhaps with the flesh signifying a tyrannical cosmic power.[43] However, Paul clearly has an anthropological reality in view, for in the warning about the consequences of one's dispositions and actions, the contrast is between "one who sows to his own flesh" (τὴν σάρκα ἑαυτοῦ) and "one who sows to the Spirit" (6:8).[44] Recognition of this anthropological and relational frame matters because it helps us explain Paul's antithetical theological logic, while also accounting for his apparent ambivalence regarding the torah itself. The problem is neither that the torah has been co-opted by anti-God powers, nor that torah-piety is simply obsolete given the advent of Christ and the Spirit. Rather, the torah was given ultimately *by God* to a dead humanity, enslaved to evil desires and thus bound to misuse it. That is why, for Paul, the contingent curse of Deut 27:26 becomes a categorical reality

---

42. Rightly, John W. Yates, *The Spirit and Creation in Paul*, WUNT 2/251 (Tübingen: Mohr Siebeck, 2008), 172: "The spirit has not simply indwelt in order to empower. The spirit has indwelt so as to give new life."

43. For absence of agency, see, e.g., Oliver O'Donovan, "Flesh and Spirit," in Elliott et al., *Galatians and Christian Theology*, 277. For the Flesh as a cosmic power, see Martyn, *Galatians*, 501 n. 88.

44. The individual stakes are high. Those who indulge the flesh and practice its community-dividing actions "will not inherit the kingdom of God" (5:21; cf. 6:5, 8).

276 Robbie Griggs

for all who are of the works of the law (Gal 3:10). Yet, God's own aim of love expressed in the torah anticipated a new humanity and unified community of Jews and gentiles awaiting a new cosmos in Christ. It is in this sense, then, that those who are "led by the Spirit" are not "under the law" (5:18): they are free from its curse and piety, paradoxically and precisely, in order to fulfill the law's moral vision.

12.4. Romans: A Pauline Grammar of Oneness and Unity?

Can we speak more broadly of a Pauline grammar of divine oneness and ecclesial unity, a christological conception of oneness that entails a community unconditioned by torah-piety yet ordered by love? At first glance, Paul's appeal to divine oneness in Rom 3:30 is rather different to that in Gal 3:20.

> For we hold that a person is justified by faith apart from works prescribed by the law. Or is God the God of Jews only? Is he not the God of gentiles also? Yes, of gentiles also, since God is one [εἷς ὁ θεός]; and he will justify the circumcised on the ground of faith and the uncircumcised through that same faith. Do we then overthrow the law by this faith? By no means! On the contrary, we uphold the law. (Rom 3:28–31, NRSV)

Here, Paul's confession links the prior assertion that God is the God of both Jews and gentiles (3:29) with his subsequent contention that the divine justification of the circumcised and uncircumcised will be by faith (3:30b). The implication is that God's oneness as disclosed in the Christ event reveals a universal jurisdiction over all classes of humans. The key point for our purposes is the flexibility and relative portability of Paul's appeal to divine oneness in christological terms. In both Gal 3:20 and Rom 3:30, Paul's appeal to divine oneness supports his identification of a singular and unconditioned divine saving action in Christ. Yet, in Rom 3:30 he stresses not a singular saving intention underlying varied Scriptural witnesses, as in Galatians, but a universal jurisdiction that necessitates the justification of Jews and gentiles alike by faith in Christ.[45] Nonetheless, in both cases appeal to the oneness of God supports Paul's contention that

---

45. With Gilbin, "Monotheistic Texts," 542. Contra Bruno, who pays insufficient attention to the scriptural mode of argumentation in Galatians and ends up blunting the specific thrust of Gal 3:20 vis-à-vis Rom 3:30 (Bruno, *"God Is One,"* 175–94).

12. One Seed and One God 277

justification is unconditioned—enacted through faith in the Christ-gift and not according to the works of the law.

While the focus of Paul's appeals to divine oneness varies, the entailments he adduces for communal unity are similar in both letters. First, the unconditioned character of the Christ-gift corresponds to a unified human condition. In Gal 5 the Spirit-Flesh antithesis locates the problem of human inability in the evil desires characteristic of those outside of and in opposition to the Spirit's creative and life-ordering agency. While in Rom 7 we find a similar moral psychology, whereby to be "of the flesh, sold under sin" (7:14) is to experience "sinful passions [τὰ παθήματα τῶν ἁμαρτιῶν]" (7:5) as a slave master that renders humans "captive to the law of sin" (7:23), in Rom 1 we learn that this predicament is attributable to divine judgment that handed humans as a class over to "the desires of their hearts [ταῖς ἐπιθυμίαις τῶν καρδιῶν αὐτῶν" (1:24; cf. 8:5–8).[46] Moreover, with the most extensive use of oneness language in Romans, Paul reads Adam, his sin, and the resulting reign of death teleologically in relation to Christ's "one righteous act" that brought "to all human beings the righteousness which is life [εἰς πάντας ἀνθρώπους εἰς δικαίωσιν ζωῆς]" (5:18).[47] Thus, the unified human condition in Romans is attributed to divine action vis-à-vis (sinful) human agency generally, while in Galatians this condition is viewed particularly through the specific curse effected by God for all "under the law" (5:18; cf. 3:22). Second, though Paul is explicit about the goodness of torah only in Romans (7:7, 12, 14), in both texts Paul specifies the love of neighbor as the law's ultimate aim. Further, he identifies the Spirit-guided church as the only community that fulfills this aim. Thus, in specifying faith as the manner by which the One God will justify Jews and gentiles, in Rom 3:31 Paul denies that he and others overturn the law; rather, they uphold the law "through faith" (διὰ τῆς πίστεως).[48] In this respect, "the righteous requirement of the law is fulfilled" in those

---

46. On the relation between these two chapters, see Simon J. Gathercole, "Sin in God's Economy: Agencies in Romans 1 and 7," in *Divine and Human Agency in Paul and His Cultural Environment*, ed. John M. G. Barclay and Simon J. Gathercole, LNTS (London, 2006), 158–72.

47. There are twelve uses of εἷς in Rom 5:12–19.

48. The denial and affirmation are related to Paul's immediately preceding exclusion of any Jewish boast in the works of the law (3:27, 28). Thus, as in Galatians, while torah-piety is a matter of indifference in the church (cf. Rom 14:14–21), torah-virtue is not.

who walk "not according to the Flesh but according to the Spirit" (8:4). Likewise, as in Galatians, this righteousness has to do with love, as the "[commandments] are summed up in this word" of Lev 19:18 (Rom 13:9) and "the one who loves another has fulfilled the law" (Rom 13:8).

12.5. Conclusion

Paul confesses divine oneness at a key moment in the argument of Galatians. Since God is one, for Paul, there can be no ultimate contradiction between the divine intention in the promise, its fulfillment in the Christ event, and the torah. Rather, the torah's curse is integral to the good news because it confines all things under sin in anticipation of the life-giving Christ-gift. Likewise, the church created by this gift is necessarily unconditioned by the torah, because God has fitted and confined torah-piety to the age and world of humanity's immaturity. Rather, as those who are one in Abraham's seed, the church of Jews and gentiles fulfills the torah's moral vision by obeying its one word of neighbor-love. In this way, the varied divine speech acts of scripture express a unified divine intention culminating in the singular "truth of the gospel," a truth that must be received and obeyed. As we saw in both Galatians and Romans, this truth constitutes a Pauline grammar of christological oneness. In these letters, divine oneness grounds the communal unity of Jews and gentiles, as they share a common human plight, a singular means of unconditioned divine salvation in the Christ-gift, and a unified life of love by means of the Spirit.

Bibliography

Avemarie, Frederich. "Paul and the Claim of the Law according to the Scripture: Leviticus 18:5 in Galatians 3:12 and Romans 10:5." Pages 125–48 in *The Beginnings of Christianity: A Collection of Articles.* Edited by Jack Pastor and Menachem Mor. Jerusalem: Yad Ben-Zvi, 2005.

Barclay, John M. G. *Obeying the Truth: A Study of Paul's Ethics in Galatians.* SNTW. Edinburgh: T&T Clark, 1988.

———. *Paul and the Gift.* Grand Rapids: Eerdmans, 2015.

———. "Paul, the Gift and the Battle over Gentile Circumcision: Revisiting the Logic of Galatians." *ABR* 58 (2010): 36–56.

Boer, Martinus C. de. *Galatians: A Commentary.* NTL. Louisville: Westminster John Knox, 2011.

12. One Seed and One God 279

———. "The Meaning of the Phrase τὰ Στοιχεῖα τοῦ Κόσμου in Galatians." *NTS* 53 (2007): 204–24.

Bruno, Christopher R. *"God Is One": The Function of "Eis Ho Theos" as a Ground for Gentile Inclusion in Paul's Letters*. LNTS 497. London: T&T Clark, 2013.

Burton, Ernest DeWitt. *A Critical and Exegetical Commentary on the Epistle to the Galatians*. ICC. Edinburgh: T&T Clark, 1921.

Collins, C. John "Galatians 3:16: What Kind of Exegete Was Paul?" *TynBul* 54 (2003): 75–86.

Engberg-Pedersen, Troels. *Paul and the Stoics*. Louisville: Westminster John Knox, 2000.

Gathercole, Simon J. "Sin in God's Economy: Agencies in Romans 1 and 7." Pages 158–72 in *Divine and Human Agency in Paul and His Cultural Environment*. Edited by John M. G. Barclay and Simon J. Gathercole. LNTS. London: T&T Clark, 2006.

Gaventa, Beverly Roberts. "Galatians 1 and 2: Autobiography as Paradigm." *NovT* 28 (1986): 309–26.

———. "The Singularity of the Gospel: A Reading of Galatians." Pages 147–59 in *Thessalonians, Philippians, Galatians, Philemon*. Volume 1 of *Pauline Theology*. Edited by Jouette M. Bassler. Minneapolis: Fortress, 1991.

———. "The Singularity of the Gospel Revisited." Pages 187–99 in *Galatians and Christian Theology: Justification, the Gospel, and Ethics in Paul's Letter*. Edited by Mark W. Elliott, Scott J. Hafemann, N. T. Wright, and John Frederick. Grand Rapids: Baker Academic, 2014.

Giblin, Charles H. "Three Monotheistic Texts in Paul." *CBQ* 37 (1975): 527–47.

Hays, Richard B. "The Letter to the Galatians." *NIB* 11:181–348.

Hewitt, J. Thomas. "Ancient Messiah Discourse and Paul's Expression Ἄχρις οὗ Ἔλθῃ τό Σπέρμα in Galatians 3.19." *NTS* 65 (2019): 398–411.

Horrell, David G. "Paul, Inclusion and Whiteness: Particularizing Interpretation." *JSNT* 40 (2017): 123–47.

Joubert, Stephan. *Paul as Benefactor: Reciprocity, Strategy and Theological Reflection in Paul's Collection*. WUNT 2/124. Tübingen: Mohr Siebeck, 2000.

Martyn, J. Louis. *Galatians: A New Translation with Introduction and Commentary*. AB 33A. New York: Doubleday, 1997.

———. "God's Way of Making Things Right." Pages 141–56 in *Theological Issues in the Letters of Paul*. Edinburgh: T&T Clark, 2005.

Matlock, R. Barry. "Helping Paul's Argument Work? The Curse of Galatians 3.10–14." Pages 154–79 in *Torah in the New Testament: Papers Delivered at the Manchester-Lausanne Seminar of June 2008.* Edited by Peter Oakes and Michael Tait. LNTS 401. London: T&T Clark, 2009.

McFarland, Orrey. "'The One Who Calls in Grace': Paul's Rhetorical and Theological Identification with the Galatians." *HBT* 35 (2013): 151–65.

Nordgaard, Stefan. "Paul and the Provenance of the Law: The Case of Galatians 3,19–20." *ZNW* 105 (2014): 64–79.

Novenson, Matthew V. "Paul's Former Occupation in *Ioudaismos*." Pages 24–39 in *Galatians and Christian Theology: Justification, the Gospel, and Ethics in Paul's Letter.* Edited by Mark W. Elliott, Scott J. Hafemann, N. T. Wright, and John Frederick. Grand Rapids: Baker Academic, 2014.

O'Donovan, Oliver. "Flesh and Spirit." Pages 271–84 in *Galatians and Christian Theology: Justification, the Gospel, and Ethics in Paul's Letter.* Edited by Mark W. Elliott, Scott J. Hafemann, N. T. Wright, and John Frederick. Grand Rapids: Baker Academic, 2014.

Sanders, E. P. "Jewish Association with Gentiles and Galatians 2:11–14." Pages 170–88 in *The Conversation Continues: Studies in Paul and John in Honor of J. Louis Martyn.* Edited by Robert T. Fortna and Beverly Roberts Gaventa. Nashville: Abingdon, 1990.

———. *Paul, the Law, and the Jewish People.* Philadelphia: Fortress, 1983.

Schewe, Susanne. *Die Galater zurückgewinnen: Paulinische Strategien in Galater 5 und 6.* FRLANT 208. Göttingen: Vandenhoeck & Ruprecht, 2005.

Schütz, John H. *Paul and the Anatomy of Apostolic Authority.* NTL. Louisville: Westminster John Knox, 2007.

Scott, James M. "'For as Many as Are of Works of the Law Are under a Curse' (Galatians 3:10)." Pages 187–221 in *Paul and the Scriptures of Israel.* Edited by Craig A. Evans and James A. Sanders. JSNTSup 83. Sheffield: Sheffield Academic, 1993.

Sprinkle, Preston M. *Law and Life: The Interpretation of Leviticus 18:5 in Early Judaism and in Paul.* WUNT 2/241. Tübingen: Mohr Siebeck, 2007.

Thiessen, Matthew. *Paul and the Gentile Problem.* Oxford: Oxford University Press, 2016.

Watson, Francis. *Paul and the Hermeneutics of Faith.* 2nd ed. London: T&T Clark, 2015.

Wright, N. T. *The Climax of the Covenant: Christ and the Law in Pauline Theology*. Edinburgh: T&T Clark, 1991.

Yates, John W. *The Spirit and Creation in Paul*. WUNT 2/251. Tübingen: Mohr Siebeck, 2008.

Young, N. H. "*Paidagogos*: The Social Setting of a Pauline Metaphor." *NovT* 29 (1987): 150–76.

13
Unity in Christ:
Virtue and the Reign of the Good King in Ephesians and Colossians

Julien C. H. Smith

13.1. The Puzzle of Unity: Divine Achievement or Human Effort?

The author of Ephesians and Colossians, referred to below as Paul, presents the audiences of these two letters with a puzzle concerning the realization of unity within the church.[1] This puzzle can be illustrated most clearly in Ephesians, in which the death, resurrection, and heavenly enthronement of Christ has cosmic consequences. Gentiles have been welcomed into God's covenant family, the commonwealth of Israel; thus Jews and gentiles, previously alienated from each other, now constitute in Christ "one new humanity in place of the two" (Eph 2:15).[2] On this account, unity in the church has been achieved by divine fiat. Yet later in the letter, Paul enjoins his audience to make "every effort to maintain the unity of the

---

1. The question of authorship of these two letters, no less than the relationship between them, continues to be debated. Arguments for deutero-Pauline authorship can be found in Andrew T. Lincoln, *Ephesians*, WBC 42 (Dallas: Word, 1990), lix–lxxiii; for Pauline authorship, Harold W. Hoehner, *Ephesians: An Exegetical Commentary* (Grand Rapids: Baker Academic, 2002), 2–61. I have come to regard Pauline authorship as likely, yet by no means certain. Of greater significance for the present argument is the setting and purpose of both letters. With Charles H. Talbert, *Ephesians and Colossians*, Paideia (Grand Rapids: Baker Academic, 2007), 12–15, I read both letters as "efforts to shape Christian identity formation and growth within the context of the general cultural ethos of the early imperial period" (15).

2. Biblical quotations, unless otherwise noted, are from the NRSV.

-283-

Spirit in the bond of peace" (Eph 4:3). Here, it would appear, unity in the church is achieved, or at the least maintained, through the church's effort.

The same puzzle appears in Colossians, more obscurely, yet with greater urgency. In this letter, Paul again highlights Christ's cosmic significance, declaring that in Christ "God was pleased to reconcile to himself all things, whether on earth or in heaven, by making peace through the blood of his cross" (Col 1:20). The church is exhorted to clothe itself with the new self, renewed in the image of its creator, in which "there is no longer Greek and Jew, circumcised and uncircumcised, barbarian, Scythian, slave and free" (Col 3:11). Yet it can be inferred that disunity persists in the church, revealed in Paul's admonitions not to fall prey to "philosophy and empty deceit" (Col 2:8) and to "bear with one another and … forgive each other" (Col 3:13).[3] The puzzle is this: Is unity in the church a divine or human achievement? Has God in Christ already established unity in the church, or must the church by its own effort work to establish unity? Or is unity in the church the product of divine and human cooperation? And if so, can one say with clarity precisely what God has done and what remains for the church?

One could, of course, resolve this tension by discounting as merely hyperbolic Paul's declaration of peace as God's achievement in Christ. Or taking Paul at his word, one could explain the tension as the paradox of Paul's inaugurated eschatology. Paul believes that the resurrection of Jesus has inaugurated "the ends of the ages" (1 Cor 10:11), yet he also describes his current reality as "the present evil age" (Gal 1:4). Christ's cosmic reign has been inaugurated, yet not consummated; Paul can thus speak of Christ ruling in the heavenly places "not only in this age but also in the age to come" (Eph 1:21). One might, in other words, attribute the paradoxical achievement of unity in the church to the already-but-not-yet quality of Christ's reign. This comes closer to Paul's meaning, but I think one may go even further in solving this puzzle by noting the ways in which Paul's portrayal of Christ in these letters reflects the portrait of the ideal king

---

3. Identifying the opponents behind the so-called Colossian heresy has been notoriously difficult. Yet if one cannot confidently know much about it, one can at least say that some members of the congregation were persuaded by it. Note that Paul uses the present tense in 2:20: "Why do you live…. Why do you submit?" This would indicate that some have been persuaded by this heresy and have changed their behavior. It seems reasonable to assume that this has resulted in some level of disunity.

13. Unity in Christ 285

in Jewish and Greco-Roman antiquity.[4] Paul's argument with respect to unity in the church can best be understood by attending to three integrally related functions attributed to the ideal king in Mediterranean antiquity: the establishment of unity, the transmission of divine benefactions, and the inculcation of virtue. In order for unity to be achieved within the πόλις, virtue must first be inculcated within the citizenry, and both unity and virtue were considered the consequence of the good king's benefaction. These functions of the ideal king shed light on the relationship in Ephesians and Colossians between the moral effort required by the church in order to maintain unity within itself, and the divine benefaction that enables this effort.[5] For the sake of space, the following argument will largely trace the train of thought in Ephesians, noting points of resonance with Colossians.

13.2. Christ as Peacemaker

The primary theme uniting the argument of Ephesians is God's plan to reconcile the fractured cosmos through God's appointed agent, Jesus the Christ (Eph 1:10). As part of the plan to reconcile the fractured cosmos, God has welcomed gentiles into the commonwealth of Israel, thus in effect reconciling the human family: "But now in Christ Jesus you who once were far off have been brought near by the blood of Christ. For he is our peace; in his flesh he has made both groups into one and has broken down the dividing wall, that is, the hostility between us" (Eph 2:13–14). We hear of a similar claim in Colossians, of a humanity renewed in the image of Christ, in which "there is no longer Greek and Jew, circumcised

---

4. See my earlier monograph, Julien C. H. Smith, *Christ the Ideal King: Cultural Context, Rhetorical Strategy, and the Power of Divine Monarchy in Ephesians*, WUNT 2/313 (Tübingen: Mohr Siebeck, 2011), in which I argue that Paul's portrayal of the Christ in Ephesians as a type of ideal king unites many of that letter's central themes and sharpens its rhetorical strategy. A number of recent studies have also presented persuasive arguments that Paul, throughout his undisputed corpus, regards Jesus as a royal figure: Matthew V. Novenson, *Christ among the Messiahs: Christ Language in Paul and Messiah Language in Ancient Judaism* (New York: Oxford University Press, 2012); N. T. Wright, *Paul and the Faithfulness of God*, Christian Origins and the Question of God 4 (Minneapolis: Fortress, 2013); Joshua W. Jipp, *Christ Is King: Paul's Royal Ideology* (Minneapolis: Fortress, 2015).

5. See Alan Thompson, ch. 10 in this volume, in which he argues for a similar connection between unity and Christ's kingship in Acts.

286   Julien C. H. Smith

and uncircumcised, barbarian, Scythian, slave and free; but Christ is all and in all" (Col 3:11).[6] Such claims would have resonated loudly with both the Jewish and Greco-Roman portrayal of the good king as a peacemaker, one who establishes on earth the divine unity that exists in the heavens.

Across a wide array of texts drawn from biblical tradition as well as postbiblical Jewish thought, the reign of the ideal king was associated with the establishment of peace, harmony, and concord.[7] In Israel's prophetic tradition, the righteous king was hailed as the "prince of peace," under whose reign "there shall be endless peace for the throne of David and his kingdom" (Isa 9:6–7; cf. Isa 11:1–9). In similar fashion, the psalmist prayed for the reign of the just king: "In his days may righteousness flourish and peace abound, until the moon is no more" (Ps 72:7). The Sibylline Oracles envisioned an eschatological kingdom characterized by the peaceful reign of prophet-kings who "take away the sword for they themselves are judges of men and righteous kings" (3.781–782).[8] Steeped in the Hellenistic traditions of kingship, the Letter of Aristeas placed on the lips of a Jewish elder the conviction that "the most important feature in a kingdom" is "to establish the subjects continually at peace" (291–292 [Shutt]). Philo praised Augustus as "the guardian of peace ... the first and the greatest and the common benefactor" (*Legat.* 147, 149). The biblical character Joseph, while not technically a king, ruled as pharaoh's vicegerent and was, in Philo's view, the quintessential statesman. Joseph's royal virtue was displayed in his ability to create "order in disorder and concord where all was naturally discordant" (*Ios.* 269).

In Greco-Roman thought, the portrayal of the good king as one who establishes and maintains harmony within the πόλις stretches back at least as far as Classical Greece. Isocrates believed that kings, out of the abundance of devotion to humanity (φιλανθρωπία) "must try to preserve

---

6. Paul writes in Col 3:10 of the "image of its creator" but it is clear from 1:15 that this image can also be identified with Christ; so Jerry L. Sumney, *Colossians: A Commentary*, NTL (Louisville: Westminster John Knox, 2008), 202.

7. The following summary borrows from chs. 2 and 3 of my earlier work, Smith, *Christ the Ideal King*; see the summaries on 86–89, 170–73.

8. John J. Collins, *The Sibylline Oracles of Egyptian Judaism*, SBLDS 13 (Missoula, MT: Scholars Press, 1974), 35, describes the perspective of book three of the Sibylline Oracles as "royal eschatology—the expectation of radical and decisive change to be brought about by a king or kingdom." English translations of Jewish pseudepigrapha are from James H. Charlesworth, ed., *The Old Testament Pseudepigrapha*, 2 vols., ABRL (Garden City, NY: Doubleday, 1983–1985).

13. Unity in Christ 287

harmony, not only in the states over which they hold dominion, but also in their own households" (*Nic.* 41 [Norlin]).[9] In the Hellenistic era, Neopythagorean political philosophers conceived of this harmony not merely as political in nature, but cosmic. The ideal king, the "living law" by which the πόλις was preserved in a state of justice and harmony, reflected and in some measure embodied divinity:[10]

> Now the king bears the same relation to the state as God to the world; and the state is in the same ratio to the world as the king is to God. For the state, made as it is by a harmonizing together of many different elements, is an imitation of the order and harmony of the world, while the king who has an absolute rulership, and is himself Animate Law [νόμος ἔμψυχος], has been metamorphosed into a deity among men. (Archytas, *On Law and Justice* 4.7.61)[11]

In the Roman period, the Stoic philosopher Musonius Rufus employed the concept of the living law to capture the ideal king's god-like ability to effect harmony:

> In general it is of the greatest importance for the good king to be faultless and perfect in word and action, if, indeed, he is to be a "living law" [νόμον ἔμψυχον] as he seemed to the ancients, effecting good government and harmony, suppressing lawlessness and dissension, a true imitator of Zeus and, like him, a father of his people. (*That Kings Should Also Study Philosophy* 64.10–15)[12]

---

9. Unless otherwise noted, English translations of Greek and Roman texts are from the Loeb Classical Library.

10. The understanding of a king as living law was widespread: For Philo, the philosopher-king par excellence was Moses, who reigned by virtue of the "living law" (νόμος ἔμψυχος) within him (*Mos.* 1.162; 2.4). Plutarch used similar terms to describe the good king's ability to rule as originating from "reason endowed with life within him [ἔμψυχος ὤν ἐν αὐτῷ λόγος]" (*Princ. iner.* 3 [780d] [Babbitt et al.]).

11. English translations of the Neopythagorean philosophers are taken from Kenneth Sylvan Guthrie, trans., *The Pythagorean Sourcebook and Library: An Anthology of Ancient Writings Which Relate to Pythagoras and Pythagorean Philosophy*, ed. David R. Fideler (Grand Rapids: Phanes, 1987). For helpful discussion along with translation of selected Neopythagorean kingship treatises, see Erwin R. Goodenough, "The Political Philosophy of Hellenistic Kingship," *YCS* 1 (1928): 55–102.

12. English translation from Cora E. Lutz, "M. Rufus, 'The Roman Socrates,'" *YCS* 10 (1947): 65.

288   Julien C. H. Smith

Plutarch also believed that harmony and concord were the prerogatives of the good king, as seen in his encomiastic tribute to the virtues of Alexander the Great. Although ultimately unsuccessful, Alexander sought to bring together "into one body all men everywhere, uniting and mixing in one great loving-cup, as it were, men's lives, their characters, their marriages, their very habits of life" (*Alex. fort.* 6 [329c] [Babbitt et al.]). Augustus even praised himself for having established peace (Res gest. divi Aug. 13), as did his numerous admirers.[13] Panegyricists lauded any number of Roman emperors for having established a golden age of peace.[14] The notion that the ideal king creates peace and harmony was so widespread in both Jewish and Greco-Roman literature that one may safely assume the authorial audiences of Ephesians and Colossians would have been familiar with it.[15]

How do the arguments of these letters resonate with this particular aspect of the audience's cultural repertoire? In the opening *berakah* of Ephesians, God is praised for his plan to gather, or sum up ($\dot{\alpha}\nu\alpha\kappa\epsilon\phi\alpha\lambda\alpha\iota\dot{o}\omega$), all things in heaven and on earth *through* the Christ (Eph 1:10).[16] Reconciliation between humanity and God (Eph 2:1–10) and within humanity itself (Eph 2:11–22), both effected through the agency of Christ, is understood as the working out of God's wider plan to restore a fractured cosmos. Acting thus as God's vicegerent to establish harmony, Christ fulfills the function of the ideal king in Mediterranean antiquity.[17] Looking closer, the political implications of Christ's peacemaking emerge. Gentiles, previously aliens from the commonwealth ($\pi o\lambda\iota\tau\epsilon\dot{\iota}\alpha$) of Israel, have now been included within God's covenant family, again through Christ (Eph 2:12–13).[18]

---

13. Vergil, *Aen.* 1.286–294; 6.791–797; Seneca, *Apoc.* 10; cf. *Clem.* 2.1.3–2.2 on his hope for a golden age to be ushered in by Nero.

14. Martial, *Epig.* 5.19.1–2, 6; Statius, *Silv.* 1.6.39–50; Pliny, *Pan.* 94.2; Suetonius, *Aug.* 22; cf. *Tib.* 37.

15. The term "authorial audience" refers to a hypothetical audience sharing the same broad cultural competence as the author that enables it to understand the author's communication; see Peter J. Rabinowitz, "Truth in Fiction: A Reexamination of Audiences," *Critical Inquiry* 4 (1977): 121–41.

16. The dative phrase $\dot{\epsilon}\nu$ $\tau\tilde{\omega}$ $X\rho\iota\sigma\tau\tilde{\omega}$ is understood to have instrumental force here and in many instances throughout the letter; see John A. Allan, "The 'In Christ' Formula in Ephesians," *NTS* 5 (1958): 54–61.

17. Smith, *Christ the Ideal King*, 88, 171, 206–7.

18. Taking $\dot{\epsilon}\nu$ $\tau\tilde{\omega}$ $\alpha\ddot{\iota}\mu\alpha\tau\iota$ $\tau o\tilde{\upsilon}$ $X\rho\iota\sigma\tau o\tilde{\upsilon}$ instrumentally.

13. Unity in Christ

But the fact that the cosmic and political unity achieved through Christ resonated with the putative achievement of countless kings and emperors also creates a problem for the audience. Talk is cheap, and political talk is possibly the cheapest on the market. The imperial propaganda boasting of a golden age of peace, the *pax Romana* as *pax deorum*, was as ubiquitous as it was false. The *pax Romana* was an era of prosperity and concord for the élites within the Roman Empire, but not for those subjugated by Rome's military might. For conquered nations, the peace of Rome often meant severely limited freedom and even servitude.[19] Thus, what confidence could Paul's audience place in his claim that in fact Christ had actually achieved the unity of which many others had falsely boasted? After all, even in the church, it could hardly be claimed that distinctions of ethnic identity, gender, and status no longer divided. Could Paul's audience have understood God's reconciliation of the human family through Christ as more than empty propaganda? To address this question, one must begin by recognizing that some modes of peacemaking are more effective than others. The Roman policy of peace won at the tip of the spear may have, for a time, achieved the cessation of hostility but did nothing to address its root causes. Indeed, it merely exacerbated them. Alexander the Great's dream of ethnic fusion through intermarriage at least recognized that peace depended upon social bonds such as those fostered within kinship groups. Alexander's dream, of course, was never realized.[20] What, then, can one say about the way in which Christ is understood to have achieved peace as well as the nature of the unity thereby established?

To begin with, the cost of peacemaking was borne by Christ himself. Whereas the Roman peace was achieved by the blood of slain enemies, the peace of the Christ is achieved through his own blood. Christ's own death is the means by which strangers and aliens have been brought near the commonwealth from which they were previously estranged (Eph 2:13; cf. Col 1:21–22).[21] Proximity, however, is not the same as membership. Thus,

---

19. Klaus Wengst, *Pax Romana and the Peace of Jesus Christ*, trans. John Bowden (Philadelphia: Fortress, 1987), 7–13, 21–24.

20. Diodorus of Sicily records Alexander as having left instructions to Craterus to unite Europe and Asia through intermarriage (*Hist.* 18.4.4). This policy of ethnic fusion, though admired by his successors, was never implemented (*Hist.* 18.4.6).

21. The passage in Colossians is actually referring to reconciliation with God, which Paul discusses in Eph 2:1–10. Reconciliation of humanity to God and within humanity itself are both aspects of God's plan to reconcile the cosmos. This can be

290   Julien C. H. Smith

second, in order actually to incorporate gentiles into the commonwealth of
Israel, Christ abolished the source of enmity between gentiles and Jews by
destroying the "dividing wall of partition" (τὸ μεσότοιχον τοῦ φραγμοῦ, Eph
2:14). The wall here, I take it, refers to the partition in the temple separating the court of the gentiles from the court of Israel, referred to by Josephus
(*A.J.* 15.417; *B.J.* 5.194; cf. Acts 21:26–31). Metaphorically, the destruction
of this wall denotes, as the next verse explains, Christ's abolition of the
Mosaic law, with its commandments and ordinances, an act that removes
the hostility between Jews and gentiles and so welcomes outsiders into God's
covenant family (Eph 2:13–15). I understand Paul to be talking here about
torah observance not merely as a practice that culturally distinguishes Jews
from gentiles, but more importantly as an important symbol of exclusion,
and hence, a source of hostility.[22] Christ's removal of this symbol is not, in
Paul's view, merely an empty gesture, but rather a profound and decisive act
that genuinely contributes to peace. Gentiles qua gentiles have now been
welcomed into the commonwealth of Israel. In sum, the mode of Christ's
peacemaking is conducive to genuine unity both because it is noncoercive
and because it addresses the way in which cultural difference functions as
a source of hostility between Jews and gentiles. Yet there is still something
incomplete about the peace established through Christ.

   Although Christ's death has removed the source of hostility between
Jew and gentile (Eph 2:14) and put to death the hostility between humanity
and God (Eph 2:16), one might well imagine that Jews and gentiles would
find it difficult to live peacefully with one another in view of the long history of cultural difference and hostility.[23] (Indeed, this difficulty can well
be imagined *within* a cultural group as well as between different cultural
groups.) The daily task of living together in peace requires effort: if a wall
has been torn down, another structure—a holy temple, a dwelling place
for God—is in the process of being built up (Eph 2:21–22). The distinction
between the peace achieved through Christ and the present task of learning to live in peace is reflected by the shift in verb tense in Eph 2:11–22.

---

seen in the parallelism in Eph 2:15b and 2:16a; see Gerhard Sellin, *Der Brief an die
Epheser*, 9th ed., KEK 8 (Göttingen: Vandenhoeck & Ruprecht, 2008), 217.

   22. It does not follow, however, that Paul is abolishing torah observance for Jewish
Christians. The argument in this letter is directed toward a gentile audience.

   23. Miriam Pucci Ben Zeev, "Jews among Greeks and Romans," in *The Eerdmans
Dictionary of Early Judaism*, ed. John J. Collins and Daniel C. Harlow (Grand Rapids:
Eerdmans, 2010), 237–55.

13. Unity in Christ

The verbs and participles used to describe Christ's actions in 2:11–17 are largely perfects, imperfects, and aorists; 2:18–19 use present tense verbs to describe the current state of affairs resulting from Christ's actions; 2:20 can be seen as a transition, using an aorist passive participle to indicate that this new humanity has been established on the apostles and prophets; and 2:21–22 use present tense verbs to indicate the present and ongoing work of growing and being built into a dwelling for God.[24]

To better grasp the ongoing need for maintaining the peace of Christ in the church, one must consider more closely the metaphor of the wall of hostility that Christ is understood to have broken down. Effective as symbols of division and as instruments of physical separation, walls can both symbolize and foster hostility. Several contemporary examples may serve to illustrate the point. The Berlin Wall was effective both in separating East and West Berlin and as a potent symbol of the broader animosity between East and West during the Cold War. More recently, consider the border wall proposed by former President Trump: as yet unbuilt, the mere idea of the wall became a divisive political symbol. Even closer to the topic at hand, the present-day security wall that encloses the West Bank has proven effective both symbolically and physically, in separating Palestinians from the State of Israel. While the removal of a physical wall can be accomplished in the span of days or weeks, the lingering effects of the hostility engendered by the wall last considerably longer. Returning to Paul's metaphor, removing the "wall" of torah observance for gentiles creates the "space" for gentiles within the commonwealth of Israel, providing them with the same "access in one Spirit to the Father" as God's covenant people Israel (Eph 2:18). Yet the removal of the wall by itself does not excuse both old and new "members of the household of God" from the task of learning to live in harmony together. The church is equipped for this task by means of Christ's benefaction, a function of the good king in antiquity.

13.3. Christ as Benefactor of Divine Virtue

In fulfillment of God's plan to restore the fractured cosmos, Christ has united humanity into one body, and yet this body must make "every

---

24. ἦτε, ἀπηλλοτριωμένοι (2:12); ἐγενήθητε (2:13); ποιήσας, λύσας (2:14); καταργήσας, κτίσῃ (2:15); ἀποκαταλλάξῃ, ἀποκτείνας (2:16); ἐλθών, εὐηγγελίσατο (2:17); ἔχομεν (2:18); ἐστέ (2:19, twice); ἐποικοδομηθέντες (2:20); συναρμολογουμένη, αὔξει (2:21); συνοικοδομεῖσθε (2:22).

292 Julien C. H. Smith

effort to maintain the unity of the Spirit in the bond of peace" (Eph 4:3). The means by which the church does so is through the benefaction of Christ: "each of us was given grace according to the measure of Christ's gift" (Eph 4:7). Paul lends emphasis to the portrayal of Christ as benefactor through a *midrash* of Ps 67:19 LXX: in the original, God *received* gifts, but in Paul's reshaping, Christ "*gave* gifts to his people" (Eph 4:8). Christ's activity resonates with the well-known function of the good king as benefactor in antiquity. In both Jewish and Greco-Roman antiquity, the understanding of the good king as benefactor is rooted in the activity of the divine benefactor(s). The king imitates the benefactions of the god(s), thereby *transmitting* these divinely bestowed benefits upon the people. Thus, in the Letter of Aristeas, the Jewish elders address the king, "'As God showers blessings [εὖ ἐργάζεται] upon all, you too in imitation of him are a benefactor [εὐεργέτεῖς] to your subjects'" (281 [Shutt]).[25] The same sentiment is echoed by the Neopythagorean political philosopher, Diotogenes:

> A good king must extend assistance to those in need of it and be beneficent. Good kings, indeed, have dispositions similar to the Gods, especially resembling Zeus, the universal ruler, who is venerable and honorable through the magnanimous preeminence of virtue. He is benign because he is beneficent [εὐεργετικός] and the giver of good. (*On Kingship* 4.7.62)

The king's benefaction obligated his subjects in a relationship of reciprocity: "his friends he made subject to himself by his benefactions, the rest by his magnanimity he enslaved" (Isocrates, *Evag.* 45 [Norlin]).[26] The actual benefits bestowed by the king varied widely, from the material— gifts of grain, reductions of taxes, financing of entertainments, patronage of temples—to the spiritual. In the latter category, the king was praised for bestowing upon the people the gift of his divine virtue.

The tradition of the good king's reign as integral to the acquisition of virtue has its roots in the political philosophy of Classical Greece. Preeminence in virtue was the requirement for rule, and the king's art, or τέχνη,

---

25. The psalmist chides an ungrateful Israel for forgetting the benefactions (εὐεργεσιῶν) of the LORD (Ps 77:11; cf. Ps 12:6; Wis 16:11 LXX).

26. See the discussion of reciprocity characteristic of the Greco-Roman culture of benefaction in John M. G. Barclay, *Paul and the Gift* (Grand Rapids: Eerdmans, 2015), 24–51; Talbert, *Ephesians and Colossians*, 20–25.

13. Unity in Christ   293

was the making of virtuous people.[27] These theoretical musings found currency in the era of Hellenistic monarchies among the Neopythagorean philosophers. Ecphantus, for example, extols the good king, whose benefaction inculcates virtue within his subjects through the divine λόγος within him:

> [He] will beneficently endeavor to assimilate all his subjects to himself.... For without benevolence, no assimilation is possible.... The king alone is capable of putting this good into human nature so that by imitation of him, their Better, they will follow in the way they should go. But his logos, if it is accepted ... restores what has been lost by sin. (*On Kingship* 4.7.65)

These ideas became more widespread in the Roman era, as autocratic rule expanded its horizon beyond the πόλις to the world. Plutarch recounts that the subjects of Rome's legendary King Numa were enabled to live virtuously and in harmony by merely beholding their king:

> When they see with their own eyes a conspicuous and shining example of virtue in the life of their ruler, they will of their own accord walk in wisdom's ways, and unite with him in conforming themselves to a blameless life of friendship and mutual concord, attended by righteousness and temperance. (*Numa* 20.8)[28]

Christ's function as benefactor conforms to the portrait of the good king in antiquity. In the opening *berakah* of the letter, Paul writes that God "has blessed us in Christ [ἐν τῷ Χριστῷ] with every spiritual blessing in the heavenly places" (Eph 1:3). If we take the force of the prepositional phrase ἐν τῷ instrumentally, Christ is the means by which God's blessing is transmitted to the church.[29] The church's reciprocal response to Christ's

---

27. Plato believed that the ideal king should be a philosopher in order to attain virtue (*Resp.* 5.473d). Plato's student, Aristotle, similarly believed that the goal of the state should be to inculcate virtue in its citizenry (*Eth. nic.* 1179b–1181b). Although Aristotle primarily looked to laws to train people in the habits of virtue, he conceded that this task could be accomplished by a person supreme in virtue, who would indeed be a god among men (*Pol.* 1284a.3–11).

28. Philo's writings suggest that these ideas were known among first century Jews as well (*Ios.* 86–87, 157, 174; cf. 164; *Mos.* 2.4, 36, 43, 189).

29. Smith, *Christ the Ideal King*, 186; Allan, "'In Christ,'" 57–58.

294 Julien C. H. Smith

benefaction is "to lead a life worthy of the calling" to which they have been called (Eph 4:1).[30] Yet this response is itself enabled by the benefaction, the goal of which is the inculcation of Christ's character. Christ gave gifts, Paul continues, "for the building up of the body of Christ, until all of us come to ... maturity, to the measure of the full stature of Christ" (Eph 4:12–13). The church has thus "learned Christ" (Eph 4:20), that is, become transformed into the character of Christ.[31] The same idea is conveyed in Colossians through the metaphor of clothing oneself with the new self, which is being renewed in the image of Christ (Col 3:10). Being transformed into the image of Christ entails the inculcation of virtue: this is seen in the parallelism in the way the Colossian believers are to clothe themselves with virtue as they clothe themselves with the new self, renewed in Christ's image (Col 3:12, 14). In light of Christ's having made peace (Col 1:20) and identification *as* "our peace" (Eph 2:14), it seems likely that these imperatives would have been interpreted as exhortations for the church to put on Christ's peacemaking, peaceful character. This possibility becomes even more likely when one considers two integrally related functions of the ideal king in antiquity: benefaction and the inculcation of virtue.

Finally, it is important to note that Christ's transformative benefaction is distributed through the gift of apostles, prophets, evangelists, pastors, and teachers to the church (Eph 4:11). The divine benefaction is conveyed, it would appear, through human agency. Why might this be the case? One possibility is suggested by the importance of imitation in the process of human growth: "'we become like' what we imitate."[32] Becoming a mature person, attaining "the full stature of Christ," is an inescapably

---

30. Talbert, *Ephesians and Colossians*, 23–24, claims that Paul's language here, "I ... beg you [Παρακαλῶ]," reflects the technical terminology used to call forth the reciprocal response to benefaction.

31. Of course at this point in the argument, Paul is warning his audience against living "as the gentiles live" (4:17), *as though* they had not learned Christ. For the argument that "learning Christ" functions as a metaphor for character transformation, see Smith, *Christ the Ideal King*, 226–31.

32. Susan Grove Eastman, *Paul and the Person: Reframing Paul's Anthropology* (Grand Rapids: Eerdmans, 2017), 141. Here, Eastman is commenting upon the insight of Plato, *Phaedr.* 253a–b on participating in God by becoming like God, and *Theaet.* 176e, 177a on becoming like what we imitate. Earlier in the book, drawing upon work in the philosophy of mind and developmental psychology, she observes that "mimetic interaction" is fundamental for human development. Imitation, or rather *being* imitated, is crucial for intimacy (65–68).

13. Unity in Christ 295

social process in which intention and effort is required to imitate human exemplars. The argument thus far has claimed that Christ has established peace within the church and given to the church the gifts required to maintain its unity. Both actions correspond with functions of the ideal king in antiquity. But now another question emerges: Why should the inculcation of virtue be a necessary condition for unity?

13.4. Clothed with Christ: Taking Off Vice, Putting On Virtue

To understand the role of virtue in "maintain[ing] the unity of the Spirit in the bond of peace" (Eph 4:3), one must first understand the relationship between virtue and vice. Paul's argument in both Ephesians and Colossians reflects the belief in antiquity that the abolition of vice was the necessary precursor to unity.[33] Abolishing vice is, of course, the corollary of inculcating virtue. Both were the prerogative of the ideal king in antiquity. Vergil implies that it is the *scelus* ("wickedness," an offense meriting divine wrath) of the Roman people that is the root of civil war (*Georg.* 1.463–468). Augustus must therefore wipe out every trace of *scelus* when he ushers in the golden age (*Ecl.* 4.11–14).[34] The role of the good king in abolishing vice among the people can be seen in the writings of Seneca, Dio Chrysostom, and Suetonius, as well as in Jewish texts such as the Psalms of Solomon and the Testaments of the Twelve Patriarchs.[35] The eradication of vice was not, however, an end in itself, but rather the means to a greater good, the establishment of harmony, another prerogative of the ideal king, as demonstrated above. This is implied perhaps already in Vergil, but comes to expression most potently with Dio Chrysostom. He is emphatic that "only by getting rid of the vices" that plague civic life within the πόλις, "only so … is it possible ever to breathe the breath of harmony" (*Or.* 34.19). For Dio, then, the abolition of vice is a necessary precursor to the establishment of harmony.

The structure of Paul's argument in Ephesians would seem to bear out Dio's intuition. In Eph 4:1–16, Christ bestows gifts upon the church that

---

33. The following summation of ancient textual evidence is borrowed from Smith, *Christ the Ideal King*, 234.

34. Andrew Wallace-Hadrill, "The Golden Age and Sin in Augustan Ideology," *Past and Present* 95 (1982): 24.

35. Seneca, *Clem.* 1.1.1; 1.6.3; 1.22.2–3; 2.1.3–2.2; Dio Chrysostom, *Or.* 2.55–56, 77; 34.19; Suetonius, *Vesp.* 11; Ps. Sol. 17.27; T. Lev. 18.9c.

296   Julien C. H. Smith

contribute to its unity. Paul picks up the topic of unity again in Eph 5:22–6:9, in which he argues for a traditional ordering of the household, albeit one in which the reciprocal relationships between husbands and wives, fathers and children, and masters and slaves have been reconfigured "in Christ" (cf. Col 3:18–4:1). In between these two sections of the letter one finds an extensive exhortation to cast off vice and put on virtue (Eph 4:17–5:21; cf. Col 3:5–17).[36] Paul's moral instruction at this point in the letter might appear to be a digression until one considers Dio's remarks. If Paul, like Dio, regards putting off vice and putting on virtue as instrumental to unity, then his exhortations here, although formally a digression, appear rather as a vital plank in his larger argument. If Christ is to create unity in the church and in the household, this will only happen as the church puts on Christ's character, thereby acquiring a new bodily *habitus*.[37] When one looks more carefully at the vices and virtues that Paul discusses, one sees that unity is indeed in the forefront of his concerns. The discussion below will focus on the more concise treatment found in Col 3:5–17.

At first glance, the vices that are to be put to death seem to have little to do with the unity of the church as a whole but concern sexual sin, which, from the perspective of western individualism, one might consider to be of a private nature: "fornication, impurity, passion, evil desire, and greed (which is idolatry)" (Col 3:5; cf. Eph 4:19, 22; 5:3, 5, 12). Yet surely the unrestrained, greedy, and idolatrous pursuit of sexual gratification erodes the trust that is foundational to community life.[38] The next set of vices, "anger, wrath, malice, slander, and abusive language from your mouth," describe a discourse of violence that not only is inimical to the flourishing of the community, but also can serve to justify and normalize the first set

---

36. In both letters, Paul employs the traditional two ways form of moral exhortation. On the background, form, and function of this type of ethical paraenesis, see Smith, *Christ the Ideal King*, 221–26.

37. The discussion below of putting off vice and putting on virtue runs parallel to the argument in Barclay, *Paul and the Gift*, 493–519. In Rom 5–8 and 12–15, Paul is concerned with the replacement of a "deeply inculcated *habitus* of sin" by a new embodied Christian *habitus*. Virtues, like the "perceptions, goals, dispositions, and values" that comprise a *habitus* (516), must be practiced and are embodied.

38. Brian J. Walsh and Sylvia C. Keesmaat, *Colossians Remixed: Subverting the Empire* (Downers Grove, IL: IVP Academic, 2004), 160–62. On the importance of sexual love to community life, and the community's sacred duty to protect it against the predation of the industrial economy, see Wendell Berry, *Sex, Economy, Freedom and Community: Eight Essays* (New York: Pantheon, 1993), 117–73, esp. 133–34.

of community-destroying vices (Col 3:8; cf. Eph 4:25, 26, 29, 31).[39] These vices, which constitute the "old self" are to be stripped off, replaced with the virtues constitutive of the "new self" renewed in the image of Christ: "compassion, kindness, humility, meekness, and patience," forgiveness, and above all, love (Col 3:12–14; cf. Eph 4:24, 32; 5:1–2). These virtues are political, in that they envision a renewed πόλις, an alternative commonwealth to the surrounding Roman Empire.[40] The result, Paul insists, is that the peace of Christ will rule in their hearts (Col 3:15). The heart here does not indicate mere interiority, as though Paul envisioned simply a sense of mental or spiritual peacefulness. The heart is understood rather as the will, the locus of executive function.[41] The reigning of Christ's peace in the heart describes a community of individuals so transformed into Christ's peacemaking and peaceable character that their decisions habitually reflect this. Thus, the community that clothes itself with Christ's character, putting off vices and putting on virtues, will find that it is also the community in which the peace of Christ is established.

13.5. Spatialized Eschatology and the Hidden Realm of Divine Activity

If the church, through the benefaction of Christ, puts on the peacemaking character of Christ and so maintains unity within the church, to what extent does the church influence the larger world? How much does the unity within the church contribute to the unity of humankind outside the church? At first blush, the answer would seem, "not much." Both Ephesians and Colossians display a markedly sectarian ethic, keen to preserve the character of the community against the threat of outside influence. Yet, this is not the whole picture. In thinking about the church's relationship to outsiders, it is instructive to reflect upon the spatialized eschatological perspective that frames the arguments of Ephesians and Colossians. In Ephesians, for example, the church is understood to be enthroned with Christ in the heavenly places (Eph 2:6). Similarly, in Colossians, the church must see its life as hidden with Christ, who is seated with God above (Col 3:1–3). The hidden quality of the church's life in Christ expresses spatially the eschatological reserve that Paul more commonly

---

39. Walsh and Keesmaat, *Colossians Remixed*, 164–68.
40. Walsh and Keesmaat, *Colossians Remixed*, 172–83.
41. See Johannes Behm, "καρδία," *TDNT* 3:605–14, esp. D.2.c.

298   Julien C. H. Smith

expresses temporally.[42] The future has invaded the present. Heaven has been brought to earth. The dimension of God's rule (heaven) has been brought into the sphere of human dominion (earth) but it is hidden from human perception. The church, however, can both see this reality, since baptism brings one into the realm of God's reign on earth (Eph 4:5; Col 2:12, 20; 3:1) and by its life together makes it visible.

This task, to be sure, is fraught with tension. Paul largely endorses the hierarchical organization of the household economy that prevailed within Greco-Roman society (Col 3:18–4:1; Eph 5:21–6:9). This acceptance of cultural norms, however, is framed by Paul's audacious claim that the distinctions between social groups no longer exist as a result of the renewal inaugurated by Christ's reign (Col 3:11). Paul would thus seem to question the way in which divisions within the human family have been reified so as to appear part of the fabric of reality.[43] In pursuing unity across the lines of cultural difference and hostility, the church exposes these divisions as merely cultural products and points to the hidden truth that God through Christ has reconciled humanity to God and to itself. The task of the church with respect to outsiders is thus to interpret this hidden reality, to put flesh on the new humanity by putting on the character of Christ.[44]

To draw together the threads of the argument, I return to my original question: Is unity in the church in these two letters understood as a divine or human achievement? To say that it is a divine achievement that both enables and requires human effort may sound like nonsense unless this claim is framed within the cultural context of the reign of the ideal king. Such a figure was seen both to establish peace and through his benefaction to inculcate virtue, the latter being the necessary condition for the former. So when the church is enjoined to moral activity that results in

---

42. It is often claimed that the spatialized eschatology in these two letters is at odds with the Jewish temporal eschatology one sees in Paul's undisputed letters. The temporal element, however, is not absent, e.g., the age to come, Eph 1:21; the coming of God's wrath, Col 3:6. See Lincoln, *Ephesians*, 65, 261, 422–24, 446; Sumney, *Colossians*, 192.

43. Walsh and Keesmaat, *Colossians Remixed*, 173, argue that Paul is "denaturalizing these reified societal structures and unveiling them as the cultural lies they are."

44. In this task of interpretation, the congregation functions as the "hermeneutic of the gospel"; Lesslie Newbigin, *The Gospel in a Pluralist Society* (Grand Rapids: Eerdmans, 1989), 222–33.

13. Unity in Christ

299

unity—putting on the character of Christ—both activity and result must be understood as enabled by the reign of Christ.[45]

Bibliography

Allan, John A. "The 'In Christ' Formula in Ephesians." *NTS* 5 (1958): 54–62.

Barclay, John M. G. *Paul and the Gift*. Grand Rapids: Eerdmans, 2015.

Behm, Johannes. "καρδία." *TDNT* 3:605–14.

Ben Zeev, Miriam Pucci. "Jews among Greeks and Romans." Pages 237–55 in *The Eerdmans Dictionary of Early Judaism*. Edited by John J. Collins and Daniel C. Harlow. Grand Rapids: Eerdmans, 2010.

Berry, Wendell. *Sex, Economy, Freedom and Community: Eight Essays*. New York: Pantheon, 1993.

Collins, John J. *The Sibylline Oracles of Egyptian Judaism*. SBLDS 13. Missoula, MT: Scholars Press, 1974.

Eastman, Susan Grove. *Paul and the Person: Reframing Paul's Anthropology*. Grand Rapids: Eerdmans, 2017.

Goodenough, Erwin R. "The Political Philosophy of Hellenistic Kingship." *YCS* 1 (1928): 55–102.

Guthrie, Kenneth Sylvan, trans. *The Pythagorean Sourcebook and Library: An Anthology of Ancient Writings Which Relate to Pythagoras and Pythagorean Philosophy*. Edited by David R. Fideler. Grand Rapids: Phanes, 1987.

Hoehner, Harold W. *Ephesians: An Exegetical Commentary*. Grand Rapids: Baker Academic, 2002.

Isocrates. *To Demonicus; To Nicocles; Nicocles or the Cyprians; Panegyricus;. To Philip; Archidamus*. Translated by George Norlin. LCL. Cambridge: Harvard University Press, 1928.

Jipp, Joshua W. *Christ Is King: Paul's Royal Ideology*. Minneapolis: Fortress, 2015.

Lincoln, Andrew T. *Ephesians*. WBC 42. Dallas: Word, 1990.

Newbigin, Lesslie. *The Gospel in a Pluralist Society*. Grand Rapids: Eerdmans, 1989.

---

45. Here I am in substantial agreement with Barclay, *Paul and the Gift*, 518, commenting on Romans: "Because the life of the believer is thus *derived* from Christ, Paul does not have to play the agency of the believer off against the agency of Christ/the Spirit; he does not need to insist that the *real* agent is the Spirit" (emphasis original).

Novenson, Matthew V. *Christ among the Messiahs: Christ Language in Paul and Messiah Language in Ancient Judaism.* New York: Oxford University Press, 2012.

Plutarch. *Moralia.* Translated by Frank Cole Babbitt et al. 16 vols. LCL. Harvard: Harvard University Press, 1927–1969.

Lutz, Cora E. "M. Rufus, 'The Roman Socrates.'" *YCS* 10 (1947): 3–147.

Rabinowitz, Peter J. "Truth in Fiction: A Reexamination of Audiences." *Critical Inquiry* 4 (1977): 121–41.

Sellin, Gerhard. *Der Brief an die Epheser.* 9th ed. KEK 8. Göttingen: Vandenhoeck & Ruprecht, 2008.

Smith, Julien C. H. *Christ the Ideal King: Cultural Context, Rhetorical Strategy, and the Power of Divine Monarchy in Ephesians.* WUNT 2/313. Tübingen: Mohr Siebeck, 2011.

Sumney, Jerry L. *Colossians: A Commentary.* NTL. Louisville: Westminster John Knox, 2008.

Talbert, Charles H. *Ephesians and Colossians.* Paideia. Grand Rapids: Baker Academic, 2007.

Wallace-Hadrill, Andrew. "The Golden Age and Sin in Augustan Ideology." *Past and Present* 95 (1982): 19–36.

Walsh, Brian J., and Sylvia C. Keesmaat. *Colossians Remixed: Subverting the Empire.* Downers Grove, IL: IVP Academic, 2004.

Wengst, Klaus. *Pax Romana and the Peace of Jesus Christ.* Translated by John Bowden. Philadelphia: Fortress, 1987.

Wright, N. T. *Paul and the Faithfulness of God.* Christian Origins and the Question of God 4. Minneapolis: Fortress, 2013.

14

Oneness and the Once for All in the
Catholic Epistles and Hebrews

Nicholas J. Moore

14.1. Introduction

The Catholic Epistles and Hebrews share several concerns bearing on questions of oneness and unity with other early Christian and ancient texts: disunity and strife, community life and cohesion, relationship to outsiders, persecution, and perseverance. This essay argues that the oneness of God in James and the Johannine Epistles underlies appeals to ethical and social cohesion; this is a familiar correlation, seen in many other early Christian texts. I also make the case that the *singularity of divinely initiated event* in Jude, 1 Peter, and most extensively in Hebrews (expressed primarily with the term "once for all") fulfills similar social and ethical functions to the *singularity of divine being*. That is to say, alongside the oneness motif, we can also discern a onceness motif in early Christian literature. This essay will demonstrate that these notions play analogous roles, and thus that divine on(c)eness is fundamentally constitutive of Christian social identity.

It is useful at the outset to identify three themes in these letters[1] that will help us to trace the oneness motif: social cohesion, group distinctiveness, and ethical consistency. "Social cohesion" refers to the degree to which a group, in this case a Christian church or community, exhibits internal harmony and unitedness as opposed to factions, schism, or disputes. "Group distinctiveness" denotes the identity of the group as one and

---

1. I use this conventional label for convenience, while recognizing that the genre of several of these texts (esp. Hebrews, James, 1 John) is not necessarily epistolary.

302   Nicholas J. Moore

recognizable, over against society more generally or the group's detractors or persecutors more specifically.[2] By "ethical consistency" I mean both the coherence of an individual's moral behavior and the moral comportment of the group as a whole. Of course, these three are not mutually exclusive or discrete: Ethical consistency may well promote social cohesion, which in turn makes a group more distinct, just as a group's distinctiveness and internal social cohesion can affect each other. The interaction between these three aspects is significant but is also neither unidirectional nor symmetrical. All three of these themes will come into play in various ways as we examine the texts.

This chapter is divided into two parts: the first focuses on oneness as it derives from the Shema (Deut 6:4–5), explicitly in James and, as I shall argue, implicitly in the Johannine Epistles. The second part turns to the more esoteric concept of temporal *once*ness (ἅπαξ) as found in 1 Peter, Jude, and Hebrews; as I shall demonstrate, this motif has extensive theological import, which gives rise to ethical and social implications.

14.2. Oneness

14.2.1. James: Wholeheartedness Because God Is One

It is something of a commonplace in scholarship on the Epistle of James to note the hypothesis that it is fragmented, lacking structure or coherence— exemplified most notably by Dibelius's commentary—and then to reject this view.[3] At the same time, the consensus that James does have coherence and a central theme is not matched by a clear consensus as to what

---

2. Social cohesion takes place through what David Horrell describes as "assimilation" (minimizing difference within a category) and group distinctiveness through "accentuation" (exaggerating differences between categories). See Horrell, "'Becoming Christian': Solidifying Christian Identity and Content," in *Handbook of Early Christianity: Social Science Approaches*, ed. Anthony J. Blasi, Paul-André Turcotte, and Jean Duhaime (Walnut Creek, CA: AltaMira, 2002), 312–13. For arguments that use of the Shema promotes group distinctiveness (and that this is more fundamental than its use to promote social cohesion), see Andrew J. Byers, "The One Body of the Shema in 1 Corinthians: An Ecclesiology of Christological Monotheism," *NTS* 62 (2016): 517–32; Byer, *Ecclesiology and Theosis in the Gospel of John*, SNTSMS 166 (Cambridge: Cambridge University Press, 2017), 129–52.

3. Martin Dibelius, *James: A Commentary on the Epistle of James*, trans. Michael A. William, Hermeneia (Philadelphia: Fortress, 1976).

14. Oneness and the Once for All 303

that key theme might be.[4] Without claiming that divine oneness and the corresponding human response of ethical wholeheartedness represent *the key* to James, then, I nevertheless wish to argue that they have a sufficient degree of prominence to be important to the letter as a whole.[5] One's view of the overall coherence of James, and the dominant theme (if any) within it, will of course affect any assessment of just *how* important this theme is.

We begin with the Shema, which is clearly evoked in Jas 2:19: "You believe that God is one [εἷς ἐστιν ὁ θεός]; you do well. Even the demons believe—and shudder."[6] It is striking that this reference to the Shema is brief and incidental: the author is looking for an uncontroversial point of doctrine that will command universal assent, as part of his wider argument about the relationship of faith to works. Although the Shema in itself is not important to the argument of Jas 2 (any other widely accepted creedal statement might have served just as well), this apparently casual reference shows that the author assumes it to be basic. Its importance for the letter gains greater plausibility in the combination of 2:19 with 4:12, which states that there is *one* lawgiver and judge (εἷς ἐστιν ὁ νομοθέτης καὶ κριτής). A further significant reference is 1:17, where "Father of lights" evokes language used in Jewish morning prayers; the Shema was quite probably recited in daily prayers in the first century CE, and in this light language of "no variation or shadow due to change" evokes God's oneness all the more.[7]

Language of changelessness is not used in relation to humans, but conceptual similarities abound. The "double-souled" (δίψυχοι, usually translated "double-minded," 1:8; 4:8) who doubt (διακρίνομαι, 1:7) should not expect to receive anything from God.[8] James's terminology is closely linked to that of the Shema: Where it exhorts the Israelites to love the one God with the whole of their ψυχή ("soul," Deut 6:5 LXX), James states

---

4. For this point, and discussion of the possible contenders, see Todd C. Penner, "The Epistle of James in Current Research," *CRBS* 7 (1999): 272–75.

5. Penner reckons the various proposals are variations on one or two fundamental themes (Penner, "James in Current Research," 275). Certainly themes such as "perfection" and "singleness/sincerity" would have significant overlap with "wholeheartedness."

6. Bible quotations are from the NRSV unless otherwise stated.

7. Donald J. Verseput, "James 1:17 and the Jewish Morning Prayers," *NovT* 39 (1997): 177–91 esp. 178–86.

8. On δίψυχος see Stanley E. Porter, "Is *Dipsuchos* (James 1,8; 4,8) a 'Christian' Word?," *Bib* 71 (1990): 469–98 and the literature cited there, esp. 477.

304 Nicholas J. Moore

that the δίψυχος, the "double-souled" person, should not expect to receive anything from God. It is not unreasonable to infer that this relates to such a person's failure to obey the Shema. In a sharp contrast to divine singularity, the sinful human posture is one of *doubling* (the δι of δίψυχος from δίς, "twice") or *division* (the particle δια- carrying "the fundamental idea [of] separation").[9]

Stated positively, believers are to strive to be mature and complete (τέλειοι καὶ ὁλόκληροι, 1:4), to fulfill the royal law of neighbor-love (τελέω, 2:8) and display the consistently pure speech that characterizes the "perfect man" (τέλειος ἀνήρ, 3:2; cf. 3:9–12; 5:12), which emerges from a purified heart (4:8). Such perfection reflects God himself, who gives perfect gifts and a perfect law (1:17, 25).[10] All told, this amounts to a significant thematic interest in wholeheartedness or single(minded)ness: believers are to be single in their devotion to God, not double, precisely because God is one.[11]

This ethical consistency is not simply an individual concern, moreover: it also bears on social cohesion. The condemnation of favoritism in 2:1–13 can be construed as an appeal to consistent treatment of others irrespective of wealth or status. The recipients are described as having "made distinctions [διεκρίθητε] among yourselves" (2:4). While the passive of διακρίνω here does not bear the same sense of "doubting" as the middle form διακρίνομαι in 1:7, the use of the same verb invites a comparison. Double-minded doubters are more likely to be swayed into making distinctions among persons, or vice versa, as Elliott notes: "ethnic, economic, and social differences had led to social division; and division, to personal doubt." Elliott goes on to suggest that James's addressees were undergoing "an erosion of integrity and cohesion at both the personal and the social levels."[12] Social cohesion will also express itself in mutual forbearance and prayer for one another (5:9, 16).

---

9. BDAG, s.v. "διά," 223.

10. On perfection in James see Martin Klein, *"Ein vollkommenes Werk": Vollkommenheit, Gesetz und Gericht als theologische Themen des Jakobusbriefes*, BWANT 139 (Stuttgart: Kohlhammer, 1995).

11. Douglas J. Moo, *The Letter of James*, PNTC (Grand Rapids: Eerdmans, 2000), 46, identifies the "central concern" as spiritual wholeness; Hubert Frankemölle, "Zum Thema des Jakobusbriefes im Kontext der Rezeption von Sir 2,1–18 und 15,11–20," *BN* 48 (1989): 21–49, opts for singleness/sincerity.

12. John H. Elliott, "The Epistle of James in Rhetorical and Social Scientific Perspective: Holiness-Wholeness and Patterns of Replication," *BTB* 23 (1993): 75.

14. Oneness and the Once for All 305

Two further motifs, purity and wisdom, are pertinent here: James 1:27 defines "pure and undefiled" religion in terms of care for orphans and widows, and remaining "unstained by the world." "To be holy, according to James, is to be whole—with respect to personal integrity, communal solidarity, and religious commitment."[13] Here (as also in 2:5 and 4:4) a concern for group distinctiveness from the world surfaces. In 4:4 a clear dichotomy is stated, in which friendship with God and with the world are mutually exclusive: the group must decide on its allegiance.[14] More significantly, the appeal to purity (καθαρός, ἀμίαντος, 1:27) in the practice of religion reflects the pure (ἀγνός) divine wisdom that is without hypocrisy (ἀνυπόκριτος, 3:17); such wisdom will overcome earthly wisdom, resulting in peace, because—unlike the behavior condemned in Jas 2—it is impartial (ἀδιάκριτος, 3:17). Again, the play with a cognate of διακρίνω is at least suggestive of a thematic connection. This same connection between divine wisdom and wholeheartedness is found in 1:5–8: wisdom comes from God who gives "generously" (NRSV) or "simply," "with sincerity" (ἁπλῶς);[15] it must be sought with faith (ἐν πίστει) rather than doubt (διακρινόμενος) or double-mindedness (δίψυχος), because these are incompatible with receptivity to divine wisdom.

The Epistle of James displays recurrent interest in God's oneness, simplicity, and constancy. This divine oneness corresponds to the repeated ethical injunction to be pure, wise, and wholehearted or, to state it negatively, not to be double-minded or to doubt (various instances or cognates of διακρίνω). This consistency of speech, of action with stated belief, and of treatment of others irrespective of socio-economic status, has consequences for social cohesion within the synagogue, and for group distinction from the world.

14.2.2. The Johannine Epistles: Love as Enacted Oneness

In the Johannine Epistles, in contrast to James, terms such as "one" and "unity" are absent. These letters nevertheless display significant concern for oneness. In this section I shall argue that they do so by evoking the

---

13. Elliott, "Epistle of James," 78.

14. Moo describes 4:4 as "arguably the thematic center of the letter" (Moo, *Letter of James*, 24).

15. So Scot McKnight, *The Letter of James*, NICNT (Grand Rapids: Eerdmans, 2011), 87–88; Moo, *Letter of James*, 58–59.

306 Nicholas J. Moore

Shema, and then briefly outline the various social and ethical implications they draw from this.

The Johannine Epistles display an overriding concern for love between God and his people, and among believers (1 John 2:10; 3:10–18, 23; 4:7–12, 16–21; 2 John 5).[16] This dual emphasis on love of God and love of neighbor reflects the pairing of Deut 6:4–5 and Lev 19:18 in the synoptic tradition (Matt 22:36–40 // Mark 12:28–33 // Luke 10:25–28) and in the Testaments of the Twelve Patriarchs (T. Iss. 5:1–2; T. Dan 5:3).[17] While these passages are not explicitly cited in the letters, nevertheless "the Johannine love command ... resonates with the combination of loving God and loving neighbor that was a ubiquitous summary of the Torah in Jewish works of the period."[18]

In this, the letters mirror the Fourth Gospel, and in particular Jesus's farewell discourse in John 13–17, with its recurrent love theme. This discourse is, moreover, bookended by allusions to these two love commands. In John 13:34 the instruction to love one another echoes Lev 19:18; its "newness" relates not to the command per se but rather to Jesus's focus on his own enacted love as an exemplar ("*just as* I have loved you").[19] In John 17 the oneness motif surfaces explicitly in the petition that God's people might be one as Jesus and the Father are one (17:11, 21–23); a strong case can be made for the underlying importance of the Shema for this passage (as also for John's Gospel more widely).[20] At the least this should leave us

---

16. "The love of God" (ἡ ἀγάπη τοῦ θεοῦ, 1 John 2:5; cf. 2:15; 3:1, 16–17; 4:7–12, 16; 5:3; 2 John 6) certainly includes God's love for humans, which is a prominent and recurrent Johannine emphasis, especially in 1 John. There is, however, little agreement among commentators as to whether the genitive also functions objectively, i.e., denoting believers' love for God; see Raymond E. Brown, *The Epistles of John*, AB 30 (New York: Doubleday, 1982), 255–57. I take it to incorporate love *for* God as well as from God, because of the equivalence of obeying God's commands with loving him, and the presupposition of human love for God implicit in, e.g., 1 John 4:20–5:2. Note Stephen Smalley's comments on 2 John 6: "the 'love' in view is undefined, but both divine and human love are implied. The two kinds of love are inseparable" (*1, 2, 3 John*, WBC 51 [Waco, TX: Word, 1984], 326).

17. On the pairing of these love commandments in the Synoptic Gospels, see ch. 8 in this volume by Elizabeth Shively and Max Botner.

18. Alicia D. Myers, "Remember the Greatest: Remaining in Love and Casting out Fear in 1 John," *RevExp* 115 (2018): 51.

19. On καθώς see Brown, *Epistles of John*, 262–63.

20. On this see the essay by Andrew Byers, ch. 9 in this volume; also Byers, *Ecclesiology and Theosis*, 103–52; Lori Baron, *The Shema in the Gospel of John*, WUNT 2/574 (Tübingen: Mohr Siebeck, 2022).

open to the possibility of a similar dynamic of the Shema's influence in the Johannine Epistles as well.

In this connection, the noun κοινωνία, "fellowship," occurs four times in 1 John (1:3 [twice], 6, 7; cf. κοινωνέω in 2 John 11). Although the term is absent from John's Gospel, it has been argued that it bears a similar conceptual sense to the widespread Johannine language of "being" or "remaining in" (εἶναι/μενεῖν ἐν).[21] It may additionally carry financial and social associations in its application to human relations.[22] In 1 John it clearly encompasses both relationship with God (1:3, Father and Son; 1:6, God) and relationship with the community (1:3, us; 1:7, one another): that is to say, it is another way in which the Johannine letters convey ideas expressed elsewhere using the Deut 6 and Lev 19 pairing.

There are two key passages that bear further examination, 1 John 2:7 and 2 John 6, both of which exhort believers to continue in love. The primary referent of these verses is Jesus's new commandment in John 13:34, to love one another, and therefore the dominant Old Testament influence is Lev 19:18.[23] Hearing this commandment "from the beginning" echoes the fact that it stems from Jesus's own ministry and the believers' own conversion. Nevertheless, there are significant verbal parallels to Deut 6:4–6 as well, as can be seen from the words highlighted below (double underline = match; single underline = cognate).

Ἀγαπητοί, οὐκ ἐντολὴν καινὴν γράφω ὑμῖν ἀλλ᾽ ἐντολὴν παλαιὰν ἣν εἴχετε ἀπ᾽ ἀρχῆς· ἡ ἐντολὴ ἡ παλαιά ἐστιν ὁ λόγος[24] ὃν ἠκούσατε. (1 John 2:7)
Beloved, I am writing you no new commandment, but an old commandment that you have had from the beginning; the old commandment is the word that you have heard.

---

21. Rudolf Schnackenburg, *Die Johannesbriefe*, 4th ed., HTKNT 13 (Freiburg im Breisgau: Herder, 1970), 66–72; Brown, *Epistles of John*, 186, 232; for a contrasting view see John Painter, "The 'Opponents' in I John," *NTS* 32 (1986): 54–55.

22. Pheme Perkins ("Koinōnia in 1 John 1:3–7: The Social Context of Division in the Johannine Letters," *CBQ* 45 [1983]: 631–41, esp. 633–35) connects κοινωνία with the Roman concept of *societas* and with Paul's usage, esp. in Philippians.

23. In 1 John 2:7–8 this is described as both "new" and "old." For the Lev 19:18 influence, see Smalley, *1, 2, 3 John*, 54–55; Myers, "Remember the Greatest," 54–57.

24. "Word" and "commandment" are interchangeable (Brown, *Epistles of John*, 251–52).

308   Nicholas J. Moore

καὶ αὕτη ἐστὶν ἡ <u>ἀγάπη</u>, ἵνα περιπατῶμεν κατὰ τὰς <u>ἐντολὰς</u> αὐτοῦ· αὕτη ἡ <u>ἐντολή</u> ἐστιν, καθὼς <u>ἠκούσατε</u> ἀπ᾽ ἀρχῆς, ἵνα ἐν αὐτῇ περιπατῆτε. (2 John 6)
And this is <u>love</u>, that we walk according to his <u>commandments</u>; this is the <u>commandment</u> just as you have <u>heard</u> it from the beginning—you must walk in it.

<u>ἄκουε</u> Ισραηλ κύριος ὁ θεὸς ἡμῶν κύριος εἷς ἐστιν καὶ <u>ἀγαπήσεις</u> κύριον τὸν θεόν σου ἐξ ὅλης τῆς καρδίας σου καὶ ἐξ ὅλης τῆς ψυχῆς σου καὶ ἐξ ὅλης τῆς δυνάμεώς σου καὶ ἔσται τὰ <u>ῥήματα</u> ταῦτα ὅσα ἐγὼ <u>ἐντέλλομαί</u> σοι σήμερον ἐν τῇ καρδίᾳ σου καὶ ἐν τῇ ψυχῇ σου (Deut 6:4–6)
<u>Hear</u>, O Israel: The Lord is our God, the Lord alone. <u>You shall love</u> the Lord your God with all your heart, and with all your soul, and with all your might. Keep these <u>words</u> that I am <u>commanding</u> you today in your heart.

A further connection is between walking (περιπατέω) in/according to God's commands (2 John 6, cf. 4; 1 John 2:6) and the instruction to discuss them when walking along the way (πορευόμενος ἐν ὁδῷ, Deut 6:7; the MT has the *qal* infinitive construct of הלך, "to walk"). Beyond these two key verses, the Johannine letters emphasize the importance of hearing God's word and obeying it (e.g., 1 John 3:22–24; 2 John 4–6; 3 John 3–4); this emphasis is less ubiquitous than love but is still extensive. Indeed, obedience to commands and love are at points equated. If an allusion to the Shema is discerned here, this might also add depth to the phrase "from the beginning" (ἀπ᾽ ἀρχῆς). This already carries significant Johannine freight, referring to the Word's presence with God before creation (ἐν ἀρχῇ, John 1:1; cf. 1 John 1:1), and it is thus plausible that it could bear a time reference earlier than the believers' conversion or Jesus's giving of the commandment. An "old commandment" that God's people "have heard" might, by way of a reactualization of Israel's past—of a similar kind to the reactualization that is already at work in the book of Deuteronomy itself—evoke the Shema in addition to the "old/new" commandment to love one another.[25]

The dual directing of love and fellowship toward God and one another, the similarities with John 13–17, and the parallels with Deut 6, together

---

25. Brown suggests "the epistolary author is implicitly equating the commandment of Jesus with the Decalogue," which parallels and complements my argument, although he does not mention the Shema (Brown, *Epistles of John*, 265, cf. 280–81, 286).

14. Oneness and the Once for All

strongly suggest that the Shema and the theme of God's oneness undergird the Johannine Epistles' ethical vision. It remains only to outline briefly the social implications of this oneness. These can be seen quite clearly in the immediate context of the two verses highlighted above. Obedience to commandments is equated with knowledge of and love for God (1 John 2:3–6; 2 John 5–6): the presbyter urges his addressees to continue to walk in a way that is ethically consistent with Jesus's example and command. Social cohesion is implied in the content of the command to love one another, which as we have seen derives from Lev 19:18 as well as Jesus's teaching in John 13:34, and this is mentioned explicitly in 2 John 5 and spelled out at greater length in 1 John 2:9–11. Finally, the distinctiveness of the group is expressed in terms of a contrast between love for the world and the love of the Father (1 John 2:15–17), and between not sharing with (κοινωνέω) the "deceiver" but rather abiding (μένω) in Christ's teaching (2 John 7–11). The oneness of God undergirds a corresponding totality of devotion toward him with inescapable communal entailments.

14.3. Onceness

14.3.1. Jude and 1 Peter: Onceness in Salvation History as a Basis for Group Identity

In this second half of the chapter our focus turns to the other Catholic Epistles and Hebrews, and to the lexical term ἅπαξ (and its more emphatic cognate ἐφάπαξ). This term, often translated "once," can have a quantitative or numerical sense ("one time"), a subcategory of which is an indefinite temporal sense ("formerly," overlapping with ποτέ), or it can have a qualitative sense ("completely").[26]

῞Απαξ occurs twice in the short letter of Jude, in verses 3 and 5:

ἀνάγκην ἔσχον γράψαι ὑμῖν παρακαλῶν ἐπαγωνίζεσθαι τῇ ἅπαξ παραδοθείσῃ τοῖς ἁγίοις πίστει (Jude 3, NA28)
I find it necessary to write and appeal to you to contend for the faith that was once for all entrusted to the saints.

---

26. BDAG, s.vv. "ἅπαξ"; "ἐφάπαξ"; and Horst Balz, s.v. "ἅπαξ," *EDNT* 1:115–16, distinguish qualitative/quantitative. Gustav Stählin, "ἅπαξ, ἐφάπαξ," *TDNT* 1:381–84 additionally recognizes the "indefinite concept of time" as a subcategory of quantitative.

310 Nicholas J. Moore

The numerical sense of ἅπαξ may be in play in Jude 3, but the emphatic and urgent tone, heightened by the apparent change of course in the middle of the verse ("while [*or* although] eagerly preparing to write … I find it necessary to write and appeal"), suggests that the qualitative sense is more prominent.[27] The revelation or entrusting of faith to the saints happened not just at a certain point in the past, but in a whole and complete manner.[28] The addressees need to "contend for" this faith in the context of a threat to group identity by "certain intruders" (v. 4). Although participating in the group (e.g., by sharing in love feasts, v. 12), they are ungodly (v. 15) and divisive (v. 19). In response to these threats to the group's unity and ethics, the letter underlines the importance of contending for and being built up in the one faith, once delivered (vv. 3, 20).[29]

The second occurrence of ἅπαξ in Jude 5 is subject to much greater textual variation. I lay out here two recent critical editions, and my translations reflecting three possible interpretations:

(a) Ὑπομνῆσαι δὲ ὑμᾶς βούλομαι, εἰδότας ὑμᾶς πάντα ὅτι [ὁ] κύριος ἅπαξ λαὸν ἐκ γῆς Αἰγύπτου σώσας τὸ δεύτερον τοὺς μὴ πιστεύσαντας ἀπώλεσεν (NA27)
(i) I want to remind you, although you know this fully, that the Lord, who once for all saved a people from the land of Egypt, later destroyed those who did not believe (cf. NRSV)
(ii) I want to remind you, although you know this fully, that the Lord, who *formerly* [*first*] saved a people from the land of Egypt, *later* [*second*] destroyed those who did not believe

(b) Ὑπομνῆσαι δὲ ὑμᾶς βούλομαι, εἰδότας ὑμᾶς ἅπαξ πάντα ὅτι Ἰησοῦς λαὸν ἐκ γῆς Αἰγύπτου σώσας τὸ δεύτερον τοὺς μὴ πιστεύσαντας ἀπώλεσεν (NA28)
(iii) I want to remind you, although you know this once for all, that Jesus, who saved a people from Egypt, later destroyed those who did not believe (cf. RSV)

---

27. Herbert Bateman, *Jude*, Evangelical Exegetical Commentary (Bellingham, WA: Lexham, 2017), 124–26; Anton Vögtle, *Der Judasbrief/Der 2. Petrusbrief*, study ed., EKKNT 22 (Ostfildern: Patmos, 2016), 23–24; Richard Bauckham, *Jude, 2 Peter*, WBC 50 (Waco, TX: Word, 1983), 29–30.

28. Like many commentators, Vögtle connects this with the "once for all" tradition we explore below; Vögtle, *Der Judasbrief*, 24.

29. Bauckham notes Jude's concern is the gospel's *moral* more than its doctrinal implications; Bauckham, *Jude, 2 Peter*, 34.

14. Oneness and the Once for All   311

The NA28, whose text of the Catholic Epistles is based on the Editio Critica Maior, reads Ἰησοῦς in place of κύριος and places ἅπαξ with the audience's action of knowing instead of the Lord's/Jesus's action of saving. The location of ἅπαξ is of greater concern to us here.[30] Both positions for ἅπαξ have substantial external support.[31] Reading (b) has generally been seen as harder because of the redundancy of ἅπαξ alongside πάντα, but reading (a) is arguably as difficult if not more so because ἅπαξ does not normally contrast with (τὸ) δεύτερον, and there is no obvious referent for God's "once-for-all" salvation. In practice internal evidence points in both directions, and internal considerations that support each position can be taken either as indications of original coherence, or as factors prompting scribes to make a change.[32] As the variants are so finely balanced, there is not space here to make a case for one over the other, and I will instead explore the implications of both positions.

These two possibilities are open to three interpretations, as laid out above, since the presence of τὸ δεύτερον ("secondly") could imply that ἅπαξ indicates a temporal contrast (meaning "first, formerly"), as in (ii). In fact, however, given the presence of the term just two verses earlier in a theologically freighted context it seems likely to carry a qualitative and theological sense here (i.e., ruling out [ii] but leaving open [i] and [iii]).[33]

The sense reflected in (iii) connects with Jude 3 in assigning a theological sufficiency to the revelation of salvation, although here relating to the present addressees' knowledge, rather than to the imparting of "the faith"

---

30. Scott Hafemann ("Salvation in Jude 5 and the Argument of 2 Peter 1:3–11," in *The Catholic Epistles and Apostolic Traditions: A New Perspective on James to Jude*, ed. Karl-Wilhelm Niebuhr and Robert W. Wall [Waco, TX: Baylor University Press, 2009], 331) describes this as an "even more important, though more nuanced problem" than the Jesus/Lord variants.

31. With εἰδότας note: A B C² P72; with σώσας: ℵ Ψ 88 442 1243 1611. See Bateman, *Jude*, 162–65 for a thorough treatment of the textual evidence. Hafemann argues that there is slightly stronger external support for the NA27 reading; "Salvation in Jude 5," 332.

32. Reading (b) would parallel Jude 3; on (a) ἅπαξ would function like ποτέ or τὸ πρῶτον in conjunction with τὸ δεύτερον. In support of (a), see Bateman, *Jude*; for (b), see Bauckham, *Jude, 2 Peter*, 42–43.

33. Hafemann ("Salvation in Jude 5," 335–37) supports option (i), proposing a connection to the exodus sequence, which also integrates the "first/second" contrast: God saves definitively ("once for all") after the (first) rebellion in the golden calf episode, but at the "second" rebellion at Kadesh Barnea destroys the unfaithful.

312   Nicholas J. Moore

more generally. This would reinforce the appeal to contend for the faith as they have received it, with memory of God's past salvation/judgment contributing to their group identity.[34] Reading (i) on the other hand would underscore the once-for-all nature of divine saving activity, complementing a foundational revelation (Jude 3) with a foundational salvific event that grounds the group's identity in the action of God.[35] In either case, we find *a singular divine event* (whether revelation or salvation) representing definitiveness and totality: a onenesss that is sufficiently theologically developed to be able to ground an appeal for persistence in faith, godly living, and perseverance with the group in the face of an emerging threat.[36]

Turning to 1 Peter, in exhorting its addressees to persist in doing good rather than evil in the face of suffering, the author sets up Christ as an example: "For Christ also suffered for sins once for all [ἅπαξ περὶ ἁμαρτιῶν ἔπαθεν]" (3:18).[37] In 1 Peter, Christ's suffering is both paradigmatic and salvific. As a foundational event, much like Noah's ark and baptism (3:20–21), Christ's suffering saves his followers. Yet this singular historical event also sets the tone for the whole of the Christian life, as the author is at pains to spell out. First Peter views the once-for-all Christ event as both the means of salvation for its audience and as a model of Christian living in the face of suffering. If the immediate context for this mention of Christ's once-for-all death is an appeal to suffer for doing good, the wider context is an appeal to ethical living for the sake of both social harmony (3:8–9)

---

34. On communal memory and identity in Jude, see Ruth Anne Reese, "Remember 'Jesus Saved a People out of Egypt,'" in *Muted Voices of the New Testament: Readings in the Catholic Epistles and Hebrews*, ed. Katherine M. Hockey, Madison N. Pierce, and Francis Watson, LNTS 565 (London: T&T Clark, 2017), 87–100.

35. In line with Rom 6:10; 1 Pet 3:18; Hebrews passim (see below). This reading gains in plausibility if the variant "Jesus" is preferred to "Lord," on which, in addition to the ECM, see Philipp F. Bartholomä, "Did Jesus Save the People out of Egypt? A Reexamination of a Textual Problem in Jude 5," *NovT* 50 (2008): 143–58.

36. Second Peter is a helpful point of contrast, in that its author omits material from Jude 3–5 (in part because of these verses' occasional nature). Arguably the divine gift of "all things for life and godliness" in 2 Pet 1:3 offers a parallel concept of singular divine event inspiring ethical consistency.

37. The variant ἅπαξ ἐδέχετο occurs in some late manuscripts of 1 Pet 3:20, though this is likely a misreading of ἀπεξεδέχετο, influenced by ἅπαξ (3:18) and ποτέ, ὅτε (immediately preceding). The *once-for-all* aspect of Christ's death fits less well with the surrounding appeal to go on enduring suffering, leading many commentators to see 3:18–19 as traditional material; e.g., Paul J. Achtemeier, *1 Peter: A Commentary on First Peter*, Hermeneia (Minneapolis: Fortress, 1996), 241–42, 246–47.

14. Oneness and the Once for All 313

and group distinctiveness (3:9, 13–17).[38] Here, in contrast to Jude and 1–3 John, this distinctive identity is conceived on an attractional rather than hostile basis: winning over through conduct (3:1) or words (ἀπολογία, 3:15). Even when the other is not won over, the intended outcome is shaming rather than retaliation (3:9, 16). The once-for-all historical event of Christ's suffering and death has become theologically weighted, definitive both for the salvation Peter's audience have experienced and for the distinctive life they are to go on living in the face of opposition.

Both Jude and 1 Peter, then, make reference to a theme of oneness, related to a foundational initial event, experience, or catechesis, which forms a basis for appeals to their audiences to continue in the face of intruders or persecution. In both cases, oneness can fulfil a similar creedal function to oneness as found, for example, in Eph 4. We now turn to the fullest development of the theological potential of oneness in early Christianity, the Epistle to the Hebrews.

14.3.2. Hebrews: Oneness in the Christ-Event, Conversion, and Apostasy

Hebrews uses the term (ἐφ)άπαξ with theological import more frequently than the rest of the New Testament combined.[39] The word occurs primarily in the context of the letter's extensive cultic imagery: Christ offered himself "once for all" (7:27), "entered once and for all into the most holy place" (9:12, my translation), "has appeared once for all at the end of the age to remove sin by the sacrifice of himself" (9:26). In conjunction with the theme of "perfection" (τελείωσις, τελειόω, e.g., 7:28) and the motif of Christ's heavenly session or enthronement (on the basis of Ps 110:1; e.g., Heb 8:1), Hebrews' emphasis on the "once for all" is imbued with a strong theological note of completeness and all-sufficiency. The salvation achieved by Christ in offering his body and sitting at God's right hand

---

38. On social identity in 1 Peter, see David G. Horrell, *Becoming Christian: Essays on 1 Peter and the Making of Christian Identity*, LNTS 394 (London: T&T Clark, 2013).

39. Leaving aside stock phrases such as καὶ ἅπαξ καὶ δίς. The occurrences in Hebrews are 6:4; 7:27; 9:7, 12, 26–28 (thrice); 10:2, 10 (cf. the use of μία to continue the same point in 10:12, 14); 12:26–27 (twice). For studies of this theme in Hebrews, see Aloysius Winter, *Die überzeitliche Einmaligkeit des Heils im "Heute": Zur Theologie des Hebräerbriefes* (Neuried: Ars Una, 2002); James W. Thompson, "EPHAPAX: The One and the Many in Hebrews," *NTS* 53 (2007): 566–81; Nicholas J. Moore, *Repetition in Hebrews: Plurality and Singularity in the Letter to the Hebrews, Its Ancient Context, and the Early Church*, WUNT 2/388 (Tübingen: Mohr Siebeck, 2015).

314   Nicholas J. Moore

(10:10–14) is total, finished, and eternally valid, and there is no longer any sin offering (10:18).

The background of this notion is twofold: first, it comes from the early Christian tradition associated with Jesus's death and resurrection. We observed this in 1 Pet 3 above, and I suggested that it might be echoed in Jude 5; it is also found in Rom 6:10 as part of an exhortation to stop sinning and live in newness of life, since "the death [Christ] died, he died to sin, once for all." Romans, 1 Peter, and Hebrews all have a connection to Rome (see Rom 1:7; 1 Pet 5:13; Heb 13:24), suggesting this tradition may have a particular Roman or western association. The other source for this theme as it is developed in Hebrews is the Jewish Day of Atonement, Yom Kippur. Of the various annual festivals, this one alone is described as "once a year" in the Old Testament (אחת בשנה/ ἅπαξ τοῦ ἐνιαυτοῦ; Exod 30:10 [twice]; Lev 16:34).[40] The importance of Yom Kippur for Hebrews' cultic construal of Christ's death is widely recognized: The letter refers to high priestly activity, entry behind the curtain, and entry into the most holy place or inner sanctuary. Moreover, Hebrews explicitly uses the high priest's entry "once a year" (ἅπαξ τοῦ ἐνιαυτοῦ, Heb 9:7) on Yom Kippur as a model for the "once for all" entrance of Christ into heaven (ἐφάπαξ, 9:12).

In combining early Christian crucifixion traditions with tabernacle cult traditions, Hebrews marks a minor but significant shift from Rom 6 and 1 Pet 3. It is not Christ's death in and of itself that is once for all, but rather his entrance into heaven as the culmination of the ritual process that sees him as priest offer himself as sacrificial victim to God, after which he is enthroned at his right hand.[41] This can be seen most clearly in the following verses:

> when Christ came as high priest ... he entered once and for all [ἐφάπαξ] into the most holy place by his own blood, thus obtaining eternal redemption. (Heb 9:11–12, my translation)

---

40. The qualification "once a year" is extended to other festivals in Second Temple literature, e.g., Jub. 6.17; 49.7; Philo, *Spec.* 2.146; see Moore, *Repetition in Hebrews*, 42; more broadly on backgrounds to this motif, see 38–66.

41. The fullest recent articulation of this view is David M. Moffitt, *Atonement and the Logic of Resurrection in the Epistle to the Hebrews*, NovTSup 141 (Leiden: Brill, 2011).

14. Oneness and the Once for All

[Christ] has appeared once for all [ἅπαξ] at the end of the age to remove sin by the sacrifice of himself. (Heb 9:26)

In Heb 9:12 it is the entrance into heaven, here construed as the inner chamber of the tabernacle, that results in redemption. In Heb 9:26 Christ appears in heaven (cf. 9:24, "he entered heaven itself") once for all to remove sin by his sacrifice. This does not mean Christ's death is unimportant, but it does represent a different emphasis and perspective in which resurrection, ascension, and heavenly session are incorporated into the oneness of the Christ event.[42]

Hebrews, then, takes an idea that is already present in Christian thought and heightens its theological significance by connecting it with the high point of the Old Testament liturgical calendar. A historically singular event has become a theologically singular event and is thus even more suited to undergird social implications. One occurrence of ἅπαξ, in Heb 6, alerts us to these implications.[43] This infamous passage describes "those who have once [ἅπαξ] been enlightened, have tasted the heavenly gift and become sharers in holy spirit, and have tasted the good word of God and the powers of the coming age" (6:4–6, my translation) and states that if they subsequently fall away it is impossible to restore them to repentance. The description of those in danger of apostasy does not directly evoke baptism, although early interpreters readily took it that way.[44] Yet a number of features suggest a reference to initiatory experience: the catechetical summary in 6:1–2;[45] the aorist participles; use of ἅπαξ; language of "enlightenment" (cf. 10:32; Justin, *1 Apol.* 61.12). There is, moreover, a

---

42. This extension of oneness is nevertheless decisively complete at Christ's enthronement and does not continue in or alongside his heavenly intercession. See Nicholas J. Moore, "Sacrifice, Session, and Intercession: The End of Christ's Offering in Hebrews," *JSNT* 42 (2020): 521–41. On the function of Christ's death in Hebrews on this model, see R. B. Jamieson, *Jesus' Death and Heavenly Offering in Hebrews,* SNTSMS 172 (Cambridge: Cambridge University Press, 2018), esp. 190 on "once for all" in Hebrews and Paul.

43. The literature on Heb 6 is too voluminous to cite here; alongside interpretation of the passage itself, most commentaries offer excursuses on "falling away" or the warning passages, with bibliography.

44. See Philip Edgcumbe Hughes, "Hebrews 6:4–6 and the Peril of Apostasy," *WTJ* 35 (1973): 137–55.

45. The word for "baptisms" here is βαπτισμός, used of Jewish ritual washings, not βάπτισμα, the more usual term for John's/Christian baptism.

316   Nicholas J. Moore

clear connection to the Christ event in the reasons given for the irrevo-
cable nature of apostasy: it is to "recrucify" (ἀνασταυροῦντες) the Son of
God and "hold him up to shame" (παραδειγματίζοντες, 6:6), both of which
evoke Christ's death. Those who are "once enlightened" are those who
have identified with and benefited from the "once for all" Christ event;[46] to
spurn and profane this saving event through grave sin (see 10:26, 29) and
then seek readmittance to the group is equivalent to seeking a repetition
of Christ's saving work.

This pastoral exhortation connects with our limited knowledge of
Hebrews' setting. Hebrews shows no interest in Jew-Gentile relationships,
and operates in a framework largely set by the Old Testament; its audience
is therefore likely to be Jewish Christian, or just possibly wholly Gentile,
but is highly unlikely to be mixed.[47] Social harmony among different
ethnic-religious groups within the church, of the kind promoted by, for
example, Eph 2, is therefore not a concern. Hebrews is, however, aware of
pressures facing its audience, both internal (sluggishness and immaturity,
e.g., 5:11–13) and external (persecution, e.g., 10:32–34). Persevering with
Jesus and with his followers in the face of these pressures, "adhesion" rather
than "cohesion," is a core and recurrent concern of the letter. In Heb 6 we
glimpse the connection of the author's emphasis on theological oneness
with his concern for his audience's continuing adhesion to the group: the
oneness of enlightenment or conversion is so closely allied to the onceness of the Christ event that to go back on one is to go back on the other.
Conversely, the author's goal is for the community to persevere with the
singular people of God on the basis of the singular act of God in Christ.

14.4. Conclusion

This chapter has explored themes of oneness and unity in the Catholic
Epistles and Hebrews. I argued that the foundational Jewish confession

---

46. On translating ἀνασταυρόω "recrucify," not "crucify," see Moore, *Repetition
in Hebrews*, 130–37. Hermut Löhr, *Umkehr und Sünde im Hebräerbrief*, BZNW 73
(Berlin: de Gruyter, 1994), 242–49, resists close identification of Christ's sacrifice once
with the one opportunity to repent; I address these concerns in Moore, *Repetition in
Hebrews*, 139–43.

47. On identity in Hebrews, exploring the tension between oldness and newness,
continuity and discontinuity, see Ole Jakob Filtvedt, *The Identity of God's People and
the Paradox of Hebrews*, WUNT 2/400 (Tübingen: Mohr Siebeck, 2015).

of God's oneness in the Shema (Deut 6:4–5) holds importance for James's vision of wholehearted human living, both individually and corporately, which avoids doubt, double-mindedness, and partiality. The Johannine Epistles, despite an absence of terminology of "oneness," display strong thematic interests in a love ethic toward God and others within the community; this is closely allied to the pairing of the love commands of Deut 6 and Lev 19, and reflects comparable use of these traditions in John's Gospel.

Turning to vocabulary of "once for all," I argued that onceness in Jude and 1 Peter pertains to the Christian revelation and to decisive moments in salvation history and is deployed to encourage ongoing commitment to group identity. The christological and soteriological import of onceness receives fullest treatment in Hebrews, where it describes the Christ event's all-sufficiency on the model of Yom Kippur combined with the early Christian tradition regarding Jesus's once-for-all death. In this, we have seen that onceness—especially in relation to the Christ event and the associated reception of revelation or salvation at conversion—has a significant impact on social cohesion, group distinctiveness, and ethical behavior.

In sum, we can conclude that onceness plays a role not dissimilar from that of oneness as derived from the Shema in James and the Johannine Epistles, and in other early Christian texts. To treat themes of on(c)eness together is not to override the differences in deployment and signification of these distinct terms—"one" relates more naturally to numerical singularity and unity, "once" to temporal singularity and completeness—but it is to emphasize the similar theological potentiality that both terms carry, a potentiality that early Christian writers readily exploited. On(c)eness does not simply convey sustained reflection on the nature of God, revelation, or salvation; it also bears wide-ranging implications for the lived reality of these fledgling Christian communities.

Bibliography

Achtemeier, Paul J. *1 Peter: A Commentary on First Peter*. Hermeneia. Minneapolis: Fortress, 1996.

Baron, Lori. *The Shema in John's Gospel*. WUNT 2/574. Tübingen: Mohr Siebeck, 2022.

Bartholomä, Philipp F. "Did Jesus Save the People out of Egypt? A Reexamination of a Textual Problem in Jude 5." *NovT* 50 (2008): 143–58.

Bateman, Herbert. *Jude*. Evangelical Exegetical Commentary. Bellingham, WA: Lexham, 2017.

Bauckham, Richard. *Jude, 2 Peter*. WBC 50. Waco, TX: Word, 1983.

Brown, Raymond E. *The Epistles of John*. AB 30. New York: Doubleday, 1982.

Byers, Andrew J. *Ecclesiology and Theosis in the Gospel of John*. SNTSMS 166. Cambridge: Cambridge University Press, 2017.

———. "The One Body of the Shema in 1 Corinthians: An Ecclesiology of Christological Monotheism." *NTS* 62 (2016): 517–32.

Dibelius, Martin. *James: A Commentary on the Epistle of James*. Translated by Michael A. Williams. Hermeneia. Philadelphia: Fortress, 1976.

Elliott, John H. "The Epistle of James in Rhetorical and Social Scientific Perspective: Holiness-Wholeness and Patterns of Replication." *BTB* 23 (1993): 71–81.

Filtvedt, Jakob. *The Identity of God's People and the Paradox of Hebrews*. WUNT 2/400. Tübingen: Mohr Siebeck, 2015.

Frankemölle, Hubert. "Zum Thema des Jakobusbriefes im Kontext der Rezeption von Sir 2,1–18 und 15,11–20." *BN* 48 (1989): 21–49.

Hafemann, Scott. "Salvation in Jude 5 and the Argument of 2 Peter 1:3–11." Pages 331–42 in *The Catholic Epistles and Apostolic Traditions: A New Perspective on James to Jude*. Edited by Karl-Wilhelm Niebuhr and Robert W. Wall. Waco, TX: Baylor University Press, 2009.

Horrell, David G. *Becoming Christian: Essays on 1 Peter and the Making of Christian Identity*. LNTS 394. London: T&T Clark, 2013.

———. "'Becoming Christian': Solidifying Christian Identity and Content." Pages 309–35 in *Handbook of Early Christianity: Social Science Approaches*. Edited by Anthony J. Blasi, Paul-André Turcotte, and Jean Duhaime. Walnut Creek, CA: AltaMira, 2002.

Hughes, Philip Edgcumbe. "Hebrews 6:4–6 and the Peril of Apostasy." *WTJ* 35 (1973): 137–55.

Jamieson, R. B. *Jesus' Death and Heavenly Offering in Hebrews*. SNTSMS 172. Cambridge: Cambridge University Press, 2018.

Klein, Martin. *"Ein vollkommenes Werk": Vollkommenheit, Gesetz und Gericht als theologische Themen des Jakobusbriefes*. BWANT 139. Stuttgart: Kohlhammer, 1995.

Löhr, Hermut. *Umkehr und Sünde im Hebräerbrief*. BZNW 73. Berlin: de Gruyter, 1994.

McKnight, Scot. *The Letter of James*. NICNT. Grand Rapids: Eerdmans, 2011.

Moffitt, David M. *Atonement and the Logic of Resurrection in the Epistle to the Hebrews*. NovTSup 141. Leiden: Brill, 2011.

Moo, Douglas J. *The Letter of James*. PNTC. Grand Rapids: Eerdmans, 2000.

Moore, Nicholas J. *Repetition in Hebrews: Plurality and Singularity in the Letter to the Hebrews, Its Ancient Context, and the Early Church*. WUNT 2/388. Tübingen: Mohr Siebeck, 2015.

———. "Sacrifice, Session, and Intercession: The End of Christ's Offering in Hebrews." *JSNT* 42 (2020): 521–41.

Myers, Alicia D. "Remember the Greatest: Remaining in Love and Casting out Fear in 1 John." *RevExp* 115 (2018): 50–61.

Painter, John. "The 'Opponents' in I John." *NTS* 32 (1986): 48–71.

Penner, Todd C. "The Epistle of James in Current Research." *CRBS* 7 (1999): 257–308.

Perkins, Pheme. "Koinōnia in 1 John 1:3–7: The Social Context of Division in the Johannine Letters." *CBQ* 45 (1983): 631–41.

Porter, Stanley E. "Is *Dipsuchos* (James 1,8; 4,8) a 'Christian' Word?" *Bib* 71 (1990): 469–98.

Reese, Ruth Anne. "Remember 'Jesus Saved a People out of Egypt.'" Pages 87–100 in *Muted Voices of the New Testament: Readings in the Catholic Epistles and Hebrews*. Edited by Katherine M. Hockey, Madison N. Pierce, and Francis Watson. LNTS 565. London: T&T Clark, 2017.

Schnackenburg, Rudolf. *Die Johannesbriefe*. 4th ed. HTKNT 13. Freiburg im Breisgau: Herder, 1970.

Smalley, Stephen S. *1, 2, 3 John*. WBC 51. Waco, TX: Word, 1984.

Stählin, Gustav. "ἅπαξ, ἐφάπαξ." *TDNT* 1:381–84.

Thompson, James W. "EPHAPAX: The One and the Many in Hebrews." *NTS* 53 (2007): 566–81.

Verseput, Donald J. "James 1:17 and the Jewish Morning Prayers." *NovT* 39 (1997): 177–91.

Vögtle, Anton. *Der Judasbrief/Der 2. Petrusbrief*. Study ed. EKKNT 22. Ostfildern: Patmos, 2016.

Winter, Aloysius. *Die überzeitliche Einmaligkeit des Heils im "Heute": Zur Theologie des Hebräerbriefes*. Neuried: Ars Una, 2002.

15
Social Surds and the Crisis of
Ecclesial Oneness in 1 Clement

T. J. Lang

The lengthy letter known as 1 Clement is written from the Christian assembly in Rome, identified at the outset as "sojourning as an exile" (ἡ παροικοῦσα), to its ecclesial counterpart in Corinth, which inhabits the same transitory condition (τῇ παροικούσῃ, 1.1).[1] As in Paul's original correspondence with Corinthian believers, the primary concern in 1 Clement is again a matter of intraecclesial "strife" (ἔρις; 1 Cor 1:11; 3:3; 2 Cor 12:20).[2] The vocabulary of conflict pervades this letter. The crisis in Corinth is a "defiled and unholy sedition [στάσις]" (1.1); it is a "schism" (σχίσμα); "war" (πόλεμος); "anarchy" (ἀκαταστασία); "dissension" (διχοστασία); "tumult" (θυμός); "oppression" (διωγμός); "captivity" (αἰχμαλωσία); and it somehow involves a situation of a generational discord and divisive "personal favoritism" (πρόσκλισις).[3] The only antidote to such discord is, of course,

---

1. I translate παροικέω with the specific terminology of exile in anticipation of the important function of voluntary exile in the ultimate solution to the discord in Corinth (see esp. 1 Clem. 54). The word often applies to strangers in a foreign land (cf. Luke 24:18). The identity of the author (or authors) is unknown. I refer to whoever is responsible for the composition of the letter as "the author," despite the fact it is written in the first-person plural. By the second century, the author is identified as "Clement"; see Irenaeus, *Haer.* 3.3.3; Clement of Alexandria, *Strom.* 1.38.8; 4.105; 4.111.1; 6.65.3; Eusebius, *Hist. eccl.* 4.22.1 (Hegesippus); 4.23.11 (Dionysius of Corinth). The identity of the "Clement" mentioned in Shepherd of Hermas is uncertain (Herm. Vis. 2.4.3). Unless otherwise noted, all translations are mine.

2. 1 Clem. 3.2; 5.5; 6.4; 9.1; 14.2; 35.5; 44.1; 46.5; 54.2.

3. For στάσις: 2.6; 3.2; 14.2; 46.9; 51.1; 54.2; 57.1; 63.1; for στασιάζω: 4.12; 43.2; 46.7; 47.6; 49.5; 51.3; 55.1; for σχίσμα: 2.6; 46.5; 46.9; 49.5; 54.2; for πόλεμος: 3.2; 46.5;

-321-

322   T. J. Lang

concord: the reestablishment of "peace" (εἰρήνη); "harmony" (ὁμόνοια); "sibling love" (φιλαδελφία); and a concern for "the common good of all" (τὸ κοινωφελὲς πᾶσιν).[4] The proposed path to such concord is, however, not via the peaceful reunification of all involved but rather a noble act of voluntary exile by those charged with sedition (54–55). In other words, oneness restored by division, diplomatically arranged.

I approach the malady of ecclesial unrest in 1 Clement in light of a phenomenon I refer to as the "social surd."[5] This phrase identifies circumstances where individuals in tightly knit communities disrupt (or otherwise exceed) the tidy binary of insider/outsider. Social surds, like irrational numbers, unsettle attempts at clear-cut sociological fractioning and call into question the intelligibility of a community's collective oneness. For various reasons, surd individuals cannot be cast as categorical outsiders, but they are also not sufficient as insiders. Social surds *are* what ought not *be*. Surd individuals thereby problematize accounts of communal cohesion and prompt new forms of social management. In the case of 1 Clement, this is manifest in the recommendation of noble self-banishment for those accused of sedition, an offer sweetened by assurances of dignity and ongoing ecclesial protection (54.1–3)—and all this despite the

---

56; for διχοστασία: 3.2; 14.1; 43.6; for διχοοτασία: 46.5; 51.1; for θυμός: 46.5; for διωγμός: 3.2; for αἰχμαλωσία: 3.2. For the generational discord, see 3.3. For the problem of πρόσκλισις, see 21.7; 47.3; 47.4; 50.2. In 47.3–4 the letter refers to the prior issue of πρόσκλισις addressed by Paul at the outset of 1 Corinthians. The word only occurs in the Pauline corpus in 1 Tim 5:21.

4. For εἰρήνη: 1.1; 2.2; 3.4; 15.1; 16.5; 19.2; 20.1, 9, 10, 11; 22.5; 60.3, 4; 61.1, 2; 62.2; 63.2; 64.1; 65.1; for εἰρηνεύω: 15.1; 54.2; 56.12, 13; 63.4; for ὁμόνοια: 9.4; 11.2; 20.3, 10, 11; 21.1; 30.3; 34.7; 49.5; 50.5; 60.4; 61.1; 63.2; 65.1; for ὁμονοέω: 62.2; for φιλαδελφία: 47.5; 48.1; for τὸ κοινωφελὲς πᾶσιν: 48.6.

5. The word *surd*, etymologically from the Latin *surdus*, is used in mathematics for irrational numbers. The word is extended figuratively to irrational circumstances and facts that defy neat resolution or rationalization. In theology, it is often evoked in discussions of natural evil. I have discovered I am not the first to use the phrase *social surd*, though I did not know others had formulated it when I put these two words together. Bernard Lonergan, e.g., does different things with the category of the social surd in his works, but my usage is similar to his description of the "false fact," which he defines as "the actual existence of what should not be." See Lonergan, *Understanding and Being: The Halifax Lectures on Insight*, vol. 5 of *Collected Works of Bernard Lonergan*, ed. Elizabeth A. Morelli and Mark D. Morelli (Toronto: University of Toronto Press, 1990), 236.

15. Social Surds and the Crisis of Ecclesial Oneness in 1 Clement 323

severity of the misdeeds. This is precisely the sort of creative social policy that materializes in response to a surd reality.

The chapter ensues as follows: (1) It surveys in greater detail the depiction in 1 Clement of disorder in Corinth and then the letter's recommendation of an honorable, self-imposed exile for the accused agitator(s). (2) It briefly explores various others forms of social control and exclusion exhibited in early Christianity (e.g., Matt 18:15–17; 1 Cor 5:1–8 [cf. 1 Tim 1:20]; 2 Cor 2:5–11; Rom 16:17; Titus 3:10; 2 John; 3 John). (3) It next discusses an earlier instance of the social surd phenomenon in Corinth, namely, the case of the Ἄπιστοι ("unbelievers" in modern translations) in 1 and 2 Corinthians.[6] (4) It considers the politics of exile in antiquity and 1 Clement's particular application of it. (5) Finally, it returns to the treatment of ecclesial discord in 1 Clement in order to rethink the challenges of ecclesial oneness in a more general sense.

15.1. The Crisis in Corinth

Many details about the disturbance in Corinth are uncertain and unknown, but the reason for the letter is announced in general terms at the outset. There has been a "defiled and unholy rebellion [στάσις]" in the Corinthian assembly roused by "a few rash and arrogant individuals" (1.1). The letter intends to provide counsel regarding this purported coup.[7] Little

---

6. T. J. Lang, "Trouble with Insiders: The Social Profile of the Ἄπιστοι in Paul's Corinthian Correspondence," *JBL* 137 (2018): 981–1001.

7. *Counsel* is an important word here. The Roman church is not presenting itself as dictating what the Corinthian assembly must do, however much soft or hard power they might actually have. To command would be contrary to the genre of the letter, which ancient rhetorical handbooks define as συμβουλευτικόν, or "deliberative rhetoric." (Such works were often conventionally titled Περὶ Ὁμονοίας ["On Concord"], which is a key theme for our author.) The aim of such rhetoric is to urge and persuade an audience toward a particular action or path; it does not command. See esp. W. C. van Unnik, "Studies on the So-called First Epistle of Clement," in *Encounters with Hellenism: Studies on the First Letter of Clement*, ed. Cilliers Breytenbach and Laurence L. Welborn, AGJU 53 (Leiden: Brill, 2004), 115–81; Barbara E. Bowe, *A Church in Crisis: Ecclesiology and Paraenesis in Clement of Rome*, HDR 23 (Minneapolis: Fortress, 1988). For detailed analysis of Paul's prior exercise in deliberative rhetoric vis-à-vis the Corinthian church (with much detail about this genre that is helpful for appreciating the rhetorical dynamics at work in 1 Clement), see Margaret M. Mitchell, *Paul and the Rhetoric of Reconciliation: An Exegetical Investigation of the Language and Composition of 1 Corinthians* (Louisville: Westminster John Knox, 1992), 20–64. I concur

324   T. J. Lang

else can be inferred about this intraecclesial στάσις until much later in the letter, when it emerges that there has been a crisis of leadership (chs. 42–44, 47). Apparently, a small faction within the community—"one or two people" (47.6)—have managed to unseat presbyters who had been duly appointed. But it is not just the small faction who are to blame. The letter indicts the entire church. The whole congregation is exhorted to repent and restore harmony, which must involve the reinstatement of the deposed leaders (57.1).

Before examining in detail the Roman church's propositions for restoring ecclesial oneness, which is only presented near the end of the letter, it is important first to survey the letter's total terrain and the various ways it encourages resolution to the crisis in Corinth and ecclesial concord more broadly.

After a formulaic greeting, the letter begins by acknowledging that the church in Rome had recently endured its own troubling ordeals (1.1), which delayed the sending of the letter. (Whether or not the Corinthians officially solicited the advice of the Roman community is not indicated.)[8] Immediately after referring to the sedition in Corinth, which is the stated reason for the letter, it turns to the Corinthian church's otherwise famed reputation (1.1–2.8). Theirs is an assembly "venerable and famous and worthy of love by all people" (1.1). Most importantly, the letter recalls how formerly the Corinthian assembly enjoyed a "rich and abundant peace" (2.2) wherein "all rebellion [πᾶσα στάσις] and all schism [πᾶν σχίσμα] was detestable" (2.6). Following these words of acclamation, the letter then returns again to the trouble in Corinth, offering additional hints about the social dynamic of the crisis. The sedition is characterized as a matter of stark opposition (3.3), with vocabulary drawn from

---

with Mitchell's judgment that, as important as the work of the above authors unquestionably is, "they are perhaps too quick to give the credit for the initial application of Greco-Roman political ideals to the Christian church to [the author of 1 Clement], instead of Paul, whose 1 Cor perhaps provided both the impetus and the paradigm for that later work" (17 n. 58).

8. Questions about the possible priority, power, or authority ascribed to (or claimed by) the church in Rome at this point must be set aside, though an ecclesially centralized priority is highly unlikely. The church in Rome at this time was itself highly fractionalized. Indispensable for the early history of the Roman church, its fractionalization, and the place of 1 Clement in all this, is Peter Lampe, *From Paul to Valentinus: Christians at Rome in the First Two Centuries*, ed. Marshall D. Johnson, trans. Michael Steinhauser (Minneapolis: Fortress, 2003).

15. Social Surds and the Crisis of Ecclesial Oneness in 1 Clement 325

1 Cor 4:10. Those "without honor" (οἱ ἄτιμοι) are pitted against those "with honor" (τοὺς ἐντίμους), the "disreputable" (οἱ ἄδοξοι) against the "esteemed" (τοὺς ἐνδόξους), the "senseless" (οἱ ἄφρονες) against the "wise" (τοὺς φρονίμους), and, perhaps most importantly, the "young" (οἱ νέοι) against the "old" (τοὺς πρεσβυτέρους), or, indeed, quite literally, the "presbytery." Certainty about the social configuration of the conflict is not possible, but some sort of generational discord is surely implied in this final oppositional pairing.[9] It seems likely that a few younger members of the congregation have risen up and somehow deposed aging presbyters. Other members of the church may very well have abetted such a rebellion. Whatever the case, from the perspective of Rome, "justice and peace have been abandoned" (3.4) and the authority of the original presbyters must be restored.

After these introductory chapters, the bulk of the letter meanders through a series of examples (ὑπόδειγμα), elicited mostly from Jewish writings, that the author uses in various ways to recommend the reestablishment of peace in Corinth, or to warn of the potential consequences of its absence. The first and most numerous examples all relate to the problem of jealousy and its devastating effects. Hence the stories of Cain and Abel (4.1–7), or Jacob and Esau (4.8), or Joseph and his brothers (4.9), as well as a number of others (see 4.10–13; 5.4; 5.5–7; 6.1–2). The message in all these is that interpersonal "jealousy" (ζῆλος) has grievous social outcomes. These models, then, are negative and cautionary, and the focus on jealously perhaps insinuates what the Roman church thinks is at the root of what has gone wrong. After these initial warnings about what jealousy begets, the author turns to examples that encourage positive dispositions that apply to the circumstance in Corinth. First is repentance. Acknowledging wrongdoings is, in Rome's eyes, the foundation for repairing social order. The letter thus reminds its audience that "the grace of repentance" is for all the world (7.4) and that "in generation after generation the Master has given a place for repentance to those who turn to him" (7.5). The stories of Noah and Jonah offer examples (7.6–7). These stories are then supplemented by exhortations to repentance in Ezekiel (33:11–17) and Isaiah (1:16–20; 1 Clem. 8.1–5). Whether or not the various personages in Corinth thought they needed to repent, the letter clearly insists that this is where they ought to begin.

---

9. See esp. Laurence L. Welborn, *The Young against the Old: Generational Conflict in First Clement* (Lanham, MA: Lexington/Fortress Academic, 2018).

326 T. J. Lang

Having established the foundation of repentance, the letter proceeds to lay out a series of positive virtues that have been exemplified in various individuals. The first examples, Enoch and Noah, are presented as models of obedience. The author also notes how, in the case of the ark, the rescued animals entered it "in harmony" (ἐν ὁμονοίᾳ) (9.4), which is likewise a model for what is needed in Corinth: social order. Next, the obedience of Abraham is outlined at some length (10.1–7). There is also mention of Abraham's hospitality (φιλοξενία; 10.7).[10] Hospitality is likewise emphasized in the examples of Lot (11.1) and Rahab (12.1–8). These examples of sociability are no doubt purposely highlighted given the particular social ills afflicting the Corinthian community. The examples of hospitality also anticipate the ultimate solution presented in chapter 54, which is the agitators' voluntary exile, but with the assurance they will be hospitably welcomed by Christian assemblies everywhere. Beginning in chapter 13, the author turns to the theme of humility and humble mindedness (ταπεινοφρονέω). This is illustrated in numerous examples, including Christ (16.1–17), Elijah and Elisha (17.1), Ezekiel (17.1), Abraham (17.3), Job (17.3–4), Moses (17.5–6), David (18.1–17), and Jacob (31.4). There are also, in all this, continued warnings about the errors of "strife and sedition" (14.2) and exhortations to peacefulness (15.1; 19.1–3; 22.5). One particularly important digression in the letter comes in 20.1–12, where the author explores a series of examples from nature that demonstrate order and accord in the cosmos. The sun, moon, and stars run their courses "in harmony" (ἐν ὁμονοίᾳ) and do not deviate from them (20.3). The earth brings forth food "without discord" (μὴ διχοστατοῦσα) (20.4). The seasons yield their place to one another "in peace" (ἐν εἰρήνῃ) (20.9). So also the smallest of animals gather together "in harmony and peace" (ἐν ὁμονοίᾳ καὶ εἰρήνῃ; 20.10). All aspects of the universe were ordained by its creator to be "in peace and harmony" (ἐν εἰρήνῃ καὶ ὁμονοίᾳ; 20.11). The message is clear: discord does not belong to the ordained order of creation.

Much more could be said about these early and middle sections of the letter, but the above is sufficient for appreciating the tactical reasoning of the letter and its general approach to conflict resolution. I turn now to the more specific policy recommendation of noble

---

10. The Corinthian church's reputation for hospitality is praised in 1.2.

15. Social Surds and the Crisis of Ecclesial Oneness in 1 Clement 327

exile described in 54.1–4. After addressing (and sometimes read-dressing) an array of virtues and themes from chapter 21 onward, the letter begins to shift toward the specific crisis of leadership in Corinth in chapter 42. Here the author reinforces the importance of ecclesial organization under "bishops and deacons" (42.4–5). This is, the letter maintains, in accord with God's will and rooted in apostolic authority. In chapter 44 the letter notes that the apostles themselves anticipated that "there will be strife for the title bishop [ἔρις ἔσται ἐπὶ τοῦ ὀνόματος τῆς ἐπισκοπῆς]" (44.1). They therefore established the procedure where bishops are only to be replaced upon death (44.2). Hence it is unjust to remove a current bishop (44.3). The letter states: "Our sin is not small if we expel from the episcopate [τῆς ἐπισκοπῆς ἀποβάλωμεν] those who have blamelessly and devoutly offered its gifts" (44.4). The Corinthian church has allegedly done just this (44.6). The letter goes on to explain how it is characteristic of the righteous to suffer and be rejected (45.1–8), thereby placing the deposed bishops on the side of justice and the rest of the congregation on its opposite, and the author again laments the consequences of their coup: "Why are there strife and anger and divisions and schisms and war among you?" (46.5). In chapter 47, the letter returns to Paul's own prior dealings with conflict in Corinth, referring to the situation described by Paul in 1 Cor 1:10–13. The author notes that the shameful situation appears to involve only one or two persons who have "revolted against the presbyters" (στασιάζειν πρὸς τοὺς πρεσβυτέρους) (47.6). However many people are involved, the whole church appears to be in crisis. Is there a solution?

The obvious answer is the restoration of peace, harmony, and communal love, which in a variety of ways (and with particular emphasis on forgiveness) is what the letter calls for in chapters 48–53. Love, in particular, is praised in chapters 49–50 in lyrical language reminiscent of 1 Cor 13, but with the reminder that "love does not involve schism; love does not lead rebellion; love does all things in harmony" (ἀγάπη σχίσμα οὐκ ἔχει ἀγάπη οὐ στασιάζει ἀγάπη πάντα ποιεῖ ἐν ὁμονοίᾳ) (49.5). As the carrot of love is here countered with the stick censure, the "leaders of the rebellion and division" (ἀρχηγοὶ στάσεως καὶ διχοστασίας) are exhorted to "consider the common hope" (τὸ κοινὸν τῆς ἐλπίδος σκοπεῖν) of the community (51.1). This is all predictable advice given the circumstances. In situations of conflict, the prudent mediator urges peace in order to reconcile warring factions.

328 T. J. Lang

But this is precisely what makes the ultimate solution to the schism in Corinth so perplexing. In 54.1–4 the author finally appeals directly to the Corinthian congregants, and the agitators in particular.[11]

> Who then among you is noble? Who is compassionate? Who is full of love? Let that person declare: "If sedition, strife, and schism are on account of me, I will depart; I will go away, wherever you wish, and I will obey the rulings of the congregation; only allow the flock of Christ to be at peace with the presbyters appointed to lead it." The person who does this will acquire great fame in Christ, and every place will receive him, for "the earth is the Lord's and the fulness of it."[12] Those who live as citizens, without regret, in the commonwealth of God have done and will do such things.

For a letter so dominated by the themes of peace and harmony, this recommendation of honorable self-exile is all the more surprising.[13] This solution is, in fact, not one of ultimate unity, with all sides reconciled in harmony. It is a restoration of unity by local banishment.[14] The conditions of the offer are likewise baffling. These individuals who have allegedly incited ecclesial anarchy and slandered the community's reputation (1.1; 47.6–7) are offered fame and nobility, even something of a hero's welcome wherever they should choose to reside, so long as this is not among the assembly in Corinth. Put in more general terms: They will remain insiders in the larger city of God just as they make themselves exiles of the particular flock of Christ in Corinth.

Before scrutinizing this solution in more detail and considering what it means for the theme of oneness, it is important first to consider some

---

11. The critical importance of this chapter for the letter is widely acknowledged. To cite two major commentators, see Andreas Lindemann, *Die Clemensbriefe*, HNT 17 (Tübingen: Mohr Siebeck, 1992), 16–17; Horacio E. Lona, *Der erste Clemensbrief*, KAV 2 (Göttingen: Vandenhoeck & Ruprecht, 1998), 552–53.

12. Psalm 24:1. Cf. 1 Cor 10:26, where this verse is applied to consuming meat from the marketplace.

13. For the political context of voluntary exile, see the excellent work of Laurence L. Welborn, "Voluntary Exile as the Solution to Discord in *1 Clement*," *ZAC* 18 (2003): 6–21.

14. *Local* is key. The insurgents are assured they will be received by other congregations, so it is in no way an absolute exclusion or excommunication from the faith. In practical terms, it is not clear how such an exile would be negotiated or what form it would take, but at the very least banishment from the city seems likely (cf. 55.1).

15.2. Social Control and Exclusion in Early Christianity

other forms of boundary maintenance and mechanisms for social exclusion in early Christianity.

15.2. Social Control and Exclusion in Early Christianity

To speak in sociological terms: a community has form, and its boundaries—the limits that distinguish "us" from "them," "inside" from "outside"—define the contour of that form. Particularly in the case of small or vulnerable groups, a strong group self-consciousness is reinforced by strongly enforced borders. Unity is thus fortified by processes of differentiation and exclusion. A sense of social oneness requires otherness, and, in the case of in-group deviance, the reinforcement of oneness often necessitates social marginalization and exclusion. This is true of every tribe of three or more. For relevant precursors to Christian expressions of social control, there are important Jewish precedents for internal disciplinary procedures involving punishment and social exclusion. Examples from Israel's political history range from prescriptions of capital punishment for various offenses (see, e.g., the cases described in Exod 21–22; Lev 20; Deut 17–22), to the eviction of lepers or various deviant individuals (Lev 13:44–45; Num 5:2–3; 15:30–31), to the banishment of returned exiles who failed to return to Jerusalem within a stipulated time (Ezra 10:7–8). In all these cases, societal integrity (or safety), and in-group identity, are maintained and reinforced through exclusion. This is how societies maintain identities. The early Christian assemblies were no exception.

Although early Christian social management largely avoided capital punishment (but see Acts 5:1–11), New Testament material does exhibit evidence of exclusionary practices. The evidence is varied, but the concern for boundary maintenance and group identity is prevalent (and sociologically unsurprising).[15] In Matt 16:19, the authority given to Peter "to bind and to loose" likely relates to some responsibility for communal management, including exclusionary measures. This is corroborated by the recurrence of "binding and loosing" language in the more developed procedure for internal discipline outlined in Matt 18:15–18. According to this

---

15. On diverse approaches to the insider/outsider boundary in New Testament material, see Nathan Eubank, "Damned Disciples: The Permeability of the Boundary between Insiders and Outsiders in Matthew and Paul," in *Perceiving the Other in Ancient Judaism and Early Christianity*, ed. Michal Bar-Asher Siegal, Wolfgang Grünstäudl, and Matthew Thiessen, WUNT 394 (Tübingen: Mohr Siebeck, 2017), 33–47.

330   T. J. Lang

passage, if someone sins against another member of the community, they are first to be confronted personally by the aggrieved party. If still uncompliant, one or two additional witnesses should intervene and confirm the situation (cf. Deut 19:15). If the matter is still not settled, then the whole assembly (ἐκκλησία) is called upon to resolve the dispute. If again unsuccessful, the accused party should be expelled.[16] In 2 John, the importance of exclusion is related to individuals who are depicted as deviant claimants of Christ who represent false teachings. Such individuals are not to be received as insiders even though they might seem to be so. Because of their false views about Christ, the readers are ordered not to receive them in their homes or welcome them in any way (2 John 10): "to welcome is to participate in the evil doings of such a person" (2 John 11). A different scenario is at work in 3 John, but it is again one involving inner-group ostracism. This case involves the author of the letter and one Diotrephes, who has refused relations with both the author and those associated with him, even expelling the author's envoy from his church (ἐκ τῆς ἐκκλησίας ἐκβάλλει; 3 John 10).[17] The reason for the rejection is unclear, but it would seem to be another case of inner-group factionalism and a repudiation of oneness.

Now to the Pauline evidence. The most explicit terminology for exclusion is the word anathema (ἀνάθεμα), which communicates a formal divine curse. In Gal 1:6–9, Paul laments the fact that many in Galatia seem (in his eyes) to have defected from his gospel by turning to a rival version of it. He twice declares that anyone who proclaims an alternative gospel should be anathema (1:8–9), which is his way of summoning the curse of God. Similar ἀνάθεμα formulas appear in 1 Cor 12:3 and 16:22. In Rom 9:3, Paul testifies that he would offer himself to be ἀνάθεμα on behalf of his people. He further defines anathema as separation from Christ, and so clearly marking exclusion. But Paul also recommends exclusion or names deviance in other ways besides the ἀνάθεμα formula. In Rom 16:17, the

---

16. Given Matthew's compositional location (whatever it is) and the use of ἐκκλησία, it is unclear how much this disciplinary procedure reflects Palestinian synagogue policy or something the historical Jesus actually prescribed, or imposes on his character subsequent ecclesial developments, or involves some complicated conflation of all these possibilities and other unknowns.

17. The social dynamic here is often skewed (or potentially so) by overdetermined translations; see esp. Margaret M. Mitchell, "'Diotrephes Does Not Receive Us': The Lexicographical and Social Context of 3 John 9–10," *JBL* 117 (1998): 299–320.

15. Social Surds and the Crisis of Ecclesial Oneness in 1 Clement   331

readers are instructed to watch out for individuals who "cause dissension and offense" (τὰς διχοστασίας καὶ τὰ σκάνδαλα) and oppose the instruction they received from Paul. He gives them the stern imperative: "Shun them" (ἐκκλίνετε ἀπ' αὐτῶν). The word here for "dissension" (διχοστασία) is also used to describe the sedition in 1 Clem. 46.5 and 51.1, but its author does not apply Paul's advice in Rom 16:17. If he knows it, this Roman author has either not recalled or not regarded Paul's imperative for dealing with διχοστασία. A similar concern with "factious individuals" (αἱρετικὸν ἄνθρωπον) who cause "dissentions" (ἔρεις) and "wars" (μάχας) is discussed in Titus 3:9–11. The Pauline advice here is again that believers should "reject" or "shun" (παραιτοῦ) any who are responsible for such discord. Again, whether or not the author of 1 Clement knew this Pauline advice about how to respond to seditious individuals, he has not applied it.

Most relevant for comparison with 1 Clement are Paul's dealings with questions of social exclusion in his original correspondence with Corinth, which similarly deals with the ills of "factionalism" (σχίσμα) and communal "strife" (ἔρις) in the Corinthian church (1 Cor 1:10–11).[18] Paul's aim is to urge unity, which he commends at the outset (1:10).[19] But on the issue of πορνεία in 1 Cor 5:1–13, he views oneness as impossible and exclusion obligatory. He has been informed that a certain man belonging to the Corinthian assembly is having immoral sexual relations (πορνεία) with his stepmother (5:1). Paul is outraged the community has permitted such an affair—perhaps even celebrated it ("and you are arrogant!")—when they should have perfunctorily excluded the man from their communion: "you should remove the man committing this act from your midst" (ἀρθῇ ἐκ μέσου ὑμῶν ὁ τὸ ἔργον τοῦτο πράξας) (5:2). As for Paul, he has made his ruling on the matter (5:3). The church's responsibility is now to hand this man over to Satan, with hope that in the eschaton his spirit may be saved (5:5).[20] Paul's ardent concern is for the *internal* purity of the Corinthian body.[21] Those guilty of sexual immorality are a pollutant that must be cleansed (5:6–8). As he goes on to clarify,

---

18. The definitive work on this subject is Mitchell, *Paul*.

19. As Mitchell notes: "1 Corinthians is throughout an argument for ecclesial unity, as centered in the πρόθεσις, or thesis statement of the argument, in 1:10" (*Paul*, 1).

20. For "handing over to Satan," see 1 Tim 1:20. This is another Pauline text that recommends excluding deviant insiders.

21. Echoing the important work of Dale B. Martin, *The Corinthian Body* (New Haven: Yale University Press, 1995), esp. 168–70 on the issues at play in 1 Cor 5.

332   T. J. Lang

however, this strong commitment to internal purity does not entail sectarian retreat from worldly realities and interactions (5:9–13). His concern is limited to circumstances wherein immorality, including socially disruptive behavior such as avarice (πλεονέκτης), abuse (λοίδορος), and greed (ἅρπαξ; 5:11), is within the community's midst. Note that according to Paul even social transgressions may necessitate ecclesial exclusion.

15.3. Social Surds and Ecclesial Oneness

The author of 1 Clement knows Paul's first letter to the Corinthians and is particularly familiar with its intervention in matters of local factionalism (47.1–4). It is not immoderate to suppose that the author, writing from Rome, also knows Paul's letter to the Romans. Both missives authorize exclusionary practices in Pauline assemblies, and Romans in particular sanctions exclusion in the case of internal "dissension" (διχοστασία; 16:17; 1 Clem. 46.5 and 51.1). If the error of the Corinthian agitators was as egregious as 1 Clement intimates, why then does Rome not recommend some form of ecclesial excommunication? Why does it offer the sweetened deal of noble self-exile? The Pauline texts surveyed above do not help answer this question. Although Paul's ruling in 1 Cor 5 and the arrangement offered to the Corinthian insurgents in 1 Clem. 54 are aligned in the ultimate outcome, namely, the local exclusion of problematic individuals, they differ sharply in the way exclusion is applied. To provide a plausible sociological solution to the situation in 1 Clement, I explore the social phenomenon I have termed the social surd. I have argued this phenomenon was familiar to the earliest Corinthian believers and required Paul's own politic social control.[22] To return to my definition: Social surds are individuals whose social status defies the clean insider/outsider binary. In always complicated but exceptionally severe ways, surd individuals are simultaneously inside and outside communal identity. While forms of an insider/outsider experience may be felt by all members of a community insofar as they all belong to other nonoverlapping social worlds, surd individuals push questions of belonging to a point of crisis. Their existence manifests an impossibility, or an urgent transgression of an ideal. When it comes to communal management, and especially in matters of boundary maintenance, social surds thus require imaginative social regulation.

---

22. Lang, "Trouble with Insiders."

15. Social Surds and the Crisis of Ecclesial Oneness in 1 Clement 333

I have argued that the social surd phenomenon is what best accounts for a curious group of deviant individuals of some prominence in the earliest Corinthian community: the Ἄπιστοι, conventionally translated "unbelievers." This translation renders them as though they were generic outsiders, or all non-Christ believing humanity, but the actual evidence in the Corinthian letters suggests otherwise. The Ἄπιστοι are in fact surprisingly prominent in the life of the community. They have been called upon to intervene in internal legal disputes (1 Cor 6:6); they maintain marriage relations with believers, and this despite severe social risks (1 Cor 7:12–15); they maintain social ties with the believers by sharing meals, again with potential social risks in ritually sensitive contexts (1 Cor 10:27); they gather with the believers in worship with enough frequency that Paul offers liturgical advice on how best to accommodate them (1 Cor 14:21–5); they also have apparently tempted some of the believers into joining them in what Paul views as illicit ritual partnerships (2 Cor 6:14–15).[23] I do not question that the Ἄπιστοι referred to in these passages are outsiders. But whoever they are and however they relate to Christ-devotion, they are also insiders in the most socially significant ways.

If Paul is to bend the Corinthians into the social formation he would have them be—but with the Ἄπιστοι tightly entwined in their lives—delicate social control is needed. To give just one example of such social tact, take Paul's reasoning on marriage relations in 1 Cor 7:12–16. As discussed above, Paul has already reiterated to the Corinthian assembly that his concern is not with their casual interaction with the worldly immorality of the marketplace but rather with the immorality that occurs within the community's ranks (1 Cor 5:9–13). This is what pollutes the community. This is why prostitution must not be condoned. It is a contagion that infects the entire ecclesial body (1 Cor 6:15–20). Paul's instruction is therefore crystal clear: "Shun immorality" (φεύγετε τὴν πορνείαν) (1 Cor 6:18). But, most curiously, this reasoning does not apply to relations between believers and the Ἄπιστοι. Not only does Paul endorse marital bonds with them, he even sanctions ongoing sexual relations, upending the idea that the Ἄπιστοι, like prostitutes, might become a contagion. In fact, rather than pollute believers, the believers purify the Ἄπιστοι (1 Cor 7:14), and so they can trust their children will be "clean" (1 Cor 7:15). Notice: Through some movement of reason no longer obvious to interpreters, both the direction of the

---

23. The authenticity of this last passage is disputed.

334 T. J. Lang

transfer and the nature of what is transmitted have been inverted.[24] I am not suggesting Paul is an unprincipled community organizer. Rather what I see here is the type of rationalizing that is required to deal discerningly with surd realities. Since social surds are both insiders of the community in the most serious of ways and outsiders in other serious ways, neither blunt exclusion nor laissez-faire inclusion are adequate to deal with them. To well-ordered social fractioning, surds are irrational. And for irrational circumstances, nimble minds are needed.[25]

15.4. The Politics of Exile

Immediately after advocating for the magnanimous voluntary exile of those affiliated with the mutiny (54.1–4), the author incentivizes this offering by referring to other examples of magnanimous self-sacrifice. He refers to "kings and rulers" who gave their lives in times of pestilence so as to save their citizens "through their own blood" (55.1). He affirms many other gallant figures who left cities to avert sedition (55.1), which is precisely what is advised for Corinth. He also recalls various Christians who delivered themselves to slavery in order to ransom others from it (55.2). Finally, he recalls women who risked themselves to save their people, focusing specifically on the heroic deeds of Judith and Esther (55.3–6).[26]

---

24. There may actually be some halakic ideas stimulating Paul's thinking here; see Benjamin D. Gordon, "On the Sanctity of Mixtures and Branches: Two Halakic Sayings in Romans 11:16–24," *JBL* 135 (2016): 355–68, esp. 364; Yonder Moynihan Gillihan, "Jewish Laws on Illicit Marriage, the Defilement of Offspring, and the Holiness of the Temple: A New Halakic Interpretation of 1 Corinthians 7:14," *JBL* 121 (2002): 711–44.

25. It is worth recalling: Paul's creative handling of the Ἄπιστοι in Corinth is one thing—a highly sensitive social dynamic. But the entire gentile mission with the new inclusion of pagans within Jewish identity is, in sociological terms, a surd situation of a much larger scale. It seems to me that gentile Messiah-followers also fit the profile of the social surd. In Paul's eyes, they are insiders indeed. But in the sociological sense, they are still outsiders in serious ways, particularly in matters of torah observance. Paul's word for the surd situation of gentiles within the people of Israel's God is "unnatural": "For if you have been cut from what is by nature a wild olive tree and grafted, *contrary to nature* [παρὰ φύσιν], into a cultivated olive tree, how much more will these natural branches be grafted back into their own olive tree" (Rom 11:24, emphasis added).

26. This perhaps raises intriguing, if unanswerable, questions about the role of women in the sedition.

The rhetorical aim in this is unsubtle. It is to coax the Corinthian usurpers into claiming a similar fame through their own self-imposed exile. Despite what the Roman church views as the perversity of their misdeeds, the seditious faction is offered one last inducement.

As a program for social oneness, this proposed path is in reality one of disunion. Although the author still exhorts those who "laid the foundation of the sedition" to submit again to the original presbyters (57.1), division is still required. But this separation is not one of absolute exclusion. Although the author had Pauline precedent for strong exclusionary measures, these are not invoked, and instead the creative resolution of voluntary exile is recommended. The specific events leading to this recommendation are certainly too complex to reconstruct, but in general terms the matter is straightforward: The crisis in Corinth is a surd reality. It is a situation where *ought* and *is* prove irreconcilable, and so it compels creative social policy. Rome has determined that unification via division is the best way to reestablish social oneness and harmony. Further, if this is accepted, the agitators still save face.

The idea of voluntary exile is not our author's own invention. This procedure is well-established in the "discourse of displacement" in Greco-Roman political thought.[27] The author is thus applying culturally available political resources rather than any known Pauline or early Christian precedent. Much of 1 Clement also, in retrospect, can be viewed as building toward this particular political solution. It is no accident that in the very first lines both the Roman and Corinthian assemblies are characterized as "sojourning as an exile," as I suggest translating ἡ παροικοῦσα.[28] The rehearsal of the exilic stories of Abraham (10.2) and Jacob (31.4) are likewise, in retrospect, newly suggestive. Abraham "went out" (ἐξέρχομαι) from home and kindred and, in turn, "inherited the promises of God."

---

27. See esp. Jan Felix Gaertner, "The Discourse of Displacement in Greco-Roman Antiquity," in *Writing Exile: The Discourse of Displacement in Greco-Roman Antiquity and Beyond*, ed. Jan Felix Gaertner, MnemosyneSup 283 (Leiden: Brill, 2007), 1–20. For the relation of this material to 1 Clement (with reference to the prior scholarship on this connection) see Welborn, "Voluntary Exile." Subsequent Christians would also evoke pagan traditions of self-sacrifice or exile as comparanda for Christ's own self-offering; see, e.g., Origen, *Comm. Jo.*, 6.279, which seems to refer to 1 Clem. 55.1.

28. See n. 1. Welborn also writes: "This outcome [voluntary exile] has been carefully prepared from the first sentence of the letter" ("Voluntary Exile," 7). I also think he is correct in viewing this introduction as suggesting that "exile is to be understood as the permanent condition of all Christians" (8).

336   T. J. Lang

So also Jacob "left his own land" (ἐκχωρέω) and, in turn, was granted the scepter of the twelve tribes. The call to voluntary exile in 1 Clement seems to involve a similar reward schema with its offer of great glory (54.3). Also relevant to this call to exilic existence is the author's recounting of Paul, whose journeys are depicted as something of an exilic reality with the verb φυγαδεύω (5.6), which can be translated along the lines of "live in exile or banishment." So also Paul received, in turn, "illustrious fame on account of his faith" (τὸ γενναῖον τῆς πίστεως αὐτοῦ κλέος). It is worth pointing out that so many of the other figures paraded before the readers of 1 Clement faced significant episodes of departure from home and exilic-like wanderings, even if this is not what the letter specifically highlights about them: Noah (9.4), Lot (11.1–2), Joseph (4.9), Moses (4.10; 17.5–6; 43.1–6; 53.2–5), David (4.13; 18.1–17; 52.1–4), Daniel (45.6–7), Ezekiel (17.1), Jonah (7.7), among others.

15.5. Conclusion: One and Not-One

To return to the theme of oneness. The human brain is inclined to view the world, including social worlds, in terms of clearly delineated structures.[29] The insider/outsider binary is one such tidy construct for cleanly ordering relations of the one to the not-one. This binary is, without question, a necessary one. In terms of current employees of the University of Saint Andrews, I am (as I write these words) an insider, and so correctly counted among that lot. In terms of membership in the National Rifle Association, I am not. It is important to stress that vast topographies of social life would be unintelligible without the insider/outsider divide. But it is also often too blunt an instrument for sorting the more complex dynamics at work inside social worlds, and especially small communities with complicated or ambiguous boundaries. As one ancient social theorist remarked to a community he founded: "There must be divisions among you so that those who are genuine among you should be recognized" (1 Cor 11:19). The notion of "divisions among you" is the critical observation. Even on the inside of a community there are additional insider/outsider relations alongside other hierarchies and divisions of identity and responsibility. This is all vital for appreciating how complicated, fragile, and contested

---

29. Much could be cited here. For an entry into the relevant psychological literature, see Jacob Feldman, "The Simplicity Principle in Perception and Cognition," *Wiley Interdisciplinary Reviews: Cognitive Science* 7 (2016): 330–40.

15. Social Surds and the Crisis of Ecclesial Oneness in 1 Clement   337

matters of communal oneness can be. The situation behind 1 Clement is a banner example.

In the last few decades there have been significant advances in the conceptual frameworks within which historians view early Christian history and developments in early Christian theology and self-understanding. The essentialism reified in Walter Bauer's binary of "orthodoxy" and "heresy" is inadequate.[30] So also the "trajectories" model of James Robinson and Helmut Koester is insufficient to address the actual evidence, which is in fact far more multifaceted than orderly trajectories allow.[31] More recent work has come to acknowledge this complexity and the variegated interplay of theological and liturgical diversity within wider spheres of shared identity.[32] With respect to the Rome of 1 Clement, Peter Lampe's *Die stadtrömischen Christen in den ersten beiden Jahrhunderten* has significantly advanced scholarly understanding of the plurality of Christ-devotion and institutional structures in urban Rome in the first two centuries.[33] He speaks of the "fractionation" of various ecclesial "islands" across the city. This fractionation promoted a "breath-taking theological diversity" and a pluralism that itself was sustained by a high degree of shared tolerance:[34] "Scattered throughout the city, different groups could exist next to each

---

30. Bauer, *Rechtgläubigkeit und Ketzerei im ältesten Christentum* (Tübingen: Mohr, 1934). More influential than the German original is its 1971 English translation: *Orthodoxy and Heresy in Earliest Christianity*, ed. and trans. Robert A. Kraft and Gerhard Krodel (Philadelphia: Fortress, 1971). For a recent and robust critique of Bauer, highlighting in particular the coincidence of Bauer's central thesis with liberal Protestant ideals, see Christoph Markschies, *Christian Theology and Its Institutions: Prolegomena to a History of Early Christian Theology*, trans. Wayne Coppins, BMSEC (Waco, TX: Baylor University Press, 2015), 303–31.

31. Robinson and Koester, *Trajectories through Early Christianity* (Philadelphia: Fortress, 1971). See esp. the critique of Larry Hurtado, "Interactive Diversity: A Proposed Model of Christian Origins," *JTS* 64 (2013): 445–62.

32. Besides the work of Markschies and Hurtado cited above, also representative of this trend is the older but still excellent essay by Rowan Williams, "Does It Make Sense to Speak of Pre-Nicene Orthodoxy?," in *The Making of Orthodoxy: Essays in Honour of Henry Chadwick*, ed. Rowan Williams (Cambridge: Cambridge University Press, 1989), 1–23.

33. Lampe, *Die stadtrömischen Christen in den ersten beiden Jahrhunderten: Untersuchungen zur Sozialgeschichte*, 2nd ed., WUNT 2/18 (Tübingen: Mohr, 1989 [1987]). This second edition is the basis of the 2003 English translation, which is also revised. See n. 8.

34. Lampe, *From Paul to Valentinus*, 381, esp. 381–412.

338 T. J. Lang

other and let each other go their own way without it immediately coming to an 'explosion' between them."[35]

As Lampe has so thoroughly demonstrated, the Rome of 1 Clement was a world of theological plurality and tolerance that would be unimaginable in later centuries. In the mid-second century, Rome was a city where Justin, Tatian, Hermas, Marcion, Valentinus, Ptolemaeus, Cerdo, Carpocratians, Quartodecimans, Jewish Christians, and the author of 1 Clement could have crossed paths without killing one another.[36] These figures and groups certainly polemicized, but that they identified each other as people with whom to argue is significant; as is the fact that, in many cases, deep differences seem to have been maintained even within shared ecclesial space.[37]

The culture of Christianity in 1 Clement's Rome was largely not one of exclusionary procedures, at the very least because there were not yet robust centralized mechanisms to enforce anything like this. New ideas and structures of authority could be sustained so long as there were communities and institutional structures available to sustain them. Difference and disagreement were widespread, and the toleration of difference (whether happy or not) was an important entailment of this. It seems to me the creative compromise 1 Clement forges for the Corinthian schismatics is another outworking of the "extensive tolerance" characteristic of this particular window in early Christian history.[38] Rome thus recommends the Corinthian assembly apply the established political policy of volunteer exile, severing the agitators from the local community but not from the larger flock of Christ, as opposed to something like outright excommunication. Oneness is to be restored by division, but a division diplomatically tendered with restored honor for all involved. As in Paul's prior engagement with the Ἄπιστοι in Corinth, the solution to ecclesial oneness in 1 Clement is another instance of *Realpolitik* responding to a surd reality. As

---

35. Lampe, *From Paul to Valentinus*, 396 n. 29.

36. Lampe, *From Paul to Valentinus*, 381–84.

37. Lampe, *From Paul to Valentinus*, 385–96. Marcion is perhaps the most significant exception to this, though even his story in Rome is a complicated one, and Lampe suggests that, had he held his zeal in check, "Marcion in all probability would have been able to remain in eucharistic fellowship with the other house communities of the city" (393).

38. Lampe, *From Paul to Valentinus*, 396. Lampe defines *tolerance* in very modest terms as "letting alone those who teach other doctrines" (395 n. 28).

15. Social Surds and the Crisis of Ecclesial Oneness in 1 Clement   339

a vision for social oneness, concord via disunion is certainly not ideal. But it is a reminder that some social realities are more intractable than our ideals admit.

Bibliography

Bauer, Walter. *Orthodoxy and Heresy in Earliest Christianity*. Edited and translated by Robert A. Kraft and Gerhard Krodel. Philadelphia: Fortress, 1971.

———. *Rechtgläubigkeit und Ketzerei im ältesten Christentum*. BHT. Tübingen: Mohr, 1934.

Bowe, Barbara E. *A Church in Crisis: Ecclesiology and Paraenesis in Clement of Rome*. HDR 23. Minneapolis: Fortress, 1988.

Eubank, Nathan. "Damned Disciples: The Permeability of the Boundary between Insiders and Outsiders in Matthew and Paul." Pages 33–47 in *Perceiving the Other in Ancient Judaism and Early Christianity*. Edited by Michal Bar-Asher Siegal, Wolfgang Grünstäudl, and Matthew Thiessen. WUNT 394. Tübingen: Mohr Siebeck, 2017.

Feldman, Jacob. "The Simplicity Principle in Perception and Cognition." *Wiley Interdisciplinary Reviews: Cognitive Science* 7 (2016): 330–40.

Gaertner, Jan Felix. "The Discourse of Displacement in Greco-Roman Antiquity." Pages 1–20 in *Writing Exile: The Discourse of Displacement in Greco-Roman Antiquity and Beyond*. Edited by Jan Felix Gaertner. MnemosyneSup 283. Leiden: Brill, 2007.

Gillihan, Yonder Moynihan. "Jewish Laws on Illicit Marriage, the Defilement of Offspring, and the Holiness of the Temple: A New Halakic Interpretation of 1 Corinthians 7:14." *JBL* 121 (2002): 711–44.

Gordon, Benjamin D. "On the Sanctity of Mixtures and Branches: Two Halakic Sayings in Romans 11:16–24." *JBL* 135 (2016): 355–68.

Hurtado, Larry. "Interactive Diversity: A Proposed Model of Christian Origins." *JTS* 64 (2013): 445–62.

Lampe, Peter. *From Paul to Valentinus: Christians at Rome in the First Two Centuries*. Edited by Marshall D. Johnson. Translated by Michael Steinhauser. Minneapolis: Fortress, 2003.

———. *Die stadtrömischen Christen in den ersten beiden Jahrhunderten: Untersuchungen zur Sozialgeschichte*. 2nd ed. WUNT 2/18. Tübingen: Mohr, 1989.

Lang, T. J. "Trouble with Insiders: The Social Profile of the Ἄπιστοι in Paul's Corinthian Correspondence." *JBL* 137 (2018): 981–1001.

Lindemann, Andreas. *Die Clemensbriefe*. HNT 17. Tübingen: Mohr Siebeck, 1992.

Lona, Horacio E. *Der erste Clemensbrief*. KAV 2. Göttingen: Vandenhoeck & Ruprecht, 1998.

Lonergan, Bernard. *Understanding and Being: The Halifax Lectures on Insight*. Vol. 5 of *Collected Works of Bernard Lonergan*. Edited by Elizabeth A. Morelli and Mark D. Morelli. Toronto: University of Toronto Press, 1990.

Markschies, Christoph. *Christian Theology and Its Institutions: Prolegomena to a History of Early Christian Theology*. Translated by Wayne Coppins. BMSEC. Waco, TX: Baylor University Press, 2015.

Martin, Dale B. *The Corinthian Body*. New Haven: Yale University Press, 1995.

Mitchell, Margaret M. "'Diotrephes Does Not Receive Us': The Lexicographical and Social Context of 3 John 9–10." *JBL* 117 (1998): 299–320.

———. *Paul and the Rhetoric of Reconciliation: An Exegetical Investigation of the Language and Composition of 1 Corinthians*. Louisville: Westminster John Knox Press, 1992.

Robinson, James M., and Helmut Koester. *Trajectories through Early Christianity*. Philadelphia: Fortress, 1971.

Unnik, W. C. van. "Studies on the So-called First Epistle of Clement." Pages 115–81 in *Encounters with Hellenism: Studies on the First Letter of Clement*. Edited by Cilliers Breytenbach and Laurence L. Welborn. AGJU 53. Leiden: Brill, 2004.

Welborn, Laurence L. "Voluntary Exile as the Solution to Discord in *1 Clement*." *ZAC* 18 (2014): 6–21.

———. *The Young against the Old: Generational Conflict in First Clement*. Lanham, MA: Lexington/Fortress Academic, 2018.

Williams, Rowan. "Does It Make Sense to Speak of Pre-Nicene Orthodoxy?" Pages 1–23 in *The Making of Orthodoxy: Essays in Honour of Henry Chadwick*. Edited by Rowan Williams. Cambridge: Cambridge University Press, 1989.

16

"I Was Doing My Part, Therefore, as a Man Set on Unity": Ignatius of Antioch and Unity and Concord in the Church

John-Paul Lotz

16.1. Ὁμόνοια and ἕνωσις: Ignatius's Quest for Unity in the Church

As the preceding chapters in part 4 of this volume have attested, the quest for unity in the early church was an essential feature of its communal identity (see, e.g., Acts 2:1). The sort of unity envisioned and called for was experienced across the barriers of language, class, and ethnicity, mediated through the common experience of the inspiration of the Holy Spirit at baptism, and expressed through faith in Jesus as the Messiah in their common worship. Much of the New Testament is concerned with the themes of unity and harmony, along with the related ideas of forgiveness and reconciliation (John 17:22–23; Acts 5:12; Eph 4:32; 2 Cor 5:18). In later Johannine correspondence, the presence of division in the church is described in the harshest of terms and its fomenters are rejected as those who have left the faith (1 John 2:18–19). Moreover, the idea of one church—consisting of Jews and gentiles, built on the one foundation of the apostles and prophets, and bound together in a divine unity—is one of the enduring visions of the Pauline letter to the Ephesians:

> But now in Christ Jesus you who once were far off have been brought near by the blood of Christ.... For through him we both have access in one Spirit to the Father. So then you are no longer strangers and aliens, but you are fellow citizens with the saints and members of the household of God, built on the foundation of the apostles and prophets, Christ

342 John-Paul Lotz

Jesus himself being the cornerstone, in whom the whole structure, being joined together, grows into a holy temple in the Lord. (Eph 2:13, 18–21)[1]

The New Testament speaks of unity in combination with a variety of other important theological modifiers. Followers of the new way have a unity of spirit (Eph 4:3), a unity of mind (1 Pet 3:8), a unity between followers (John 10:16), a unity of the body of the church (Rom 12:4), a eucharistic union with Christ (John 6:51–57), a unity with the Father (John 14:20), and a unity of faith (Eph 4:13). The majority of these uses, however, simply employ the Greek term for "one" (εἷς, μία, ἕν) and its cognates, and these occur over 345 times in the New Testament. The noun ἑνότης, however, is relatively rare, occurring only twice in Eph 4, while the verb ἑνόω is missing entirely from the New Testament, as well as the noun ἕνωσις.

On the other hand, these missing terms appear only a generation later rather conspicuously in the letters of Ignatius of Antioch, with a much wider frame of reference, and in combination with a new and important concept for second century Christianity that Clement of Rome may have popularized with his language of ὁμόνοια.[2] In fact, Ignatius himself was an energetic preacher of unity, as his letters bear witness. In *Phld.* 8:1, he declares himself to be "a man set on unity" (ἄνθρωπος εἰς ἕνωσιν κατηρτισμένος) who was doing his part, though a prisoner, to unify the churches he encountered along his journey to martyrdom in Rome. Variations of ἕνωσις and ἑνότης occur nine and eleven times respectively. The verb ἑνόω ("to unite") occurs six times, mostly in participial form. Added to these references to various types of unity, Ignatius uses and invents a variety of words with the συν-prefix for "with" or "together" and employs these liberally in his Asianic rhetorical style of proclamation.[3] Finally, Ignatius makes much of ὁμόνοια, a current political slogan for public unanimity. He employs this term with layered political connotations to address the pressing issues of ecclesial unity, while applying ἕνωσις and ἑνότης in a more theological sense, as Gregory Vall helpfully illumines in

---

1. All biblical quotoations are from the ESV 2016 edition.

2. 1 Clem. 9.4; 11.2; 20.3; 34.7; 60.4; 63.2; 65.1

3. For a comprehensive discussion on Ignatius's use of the idea of unity, the best modern resource is the monograph by Gregory Vall, *Learning Christ: Ignatius of Antioch and the Mystery of Redemption* (Washington, DC: Catholic University of America Press, 2013), 88–199.

16. "I Was Doing My Part, Therefore, as a Man Set on Unity" 343

his study on Ignatius.[4] Vall parses Ignatius's care for unity well when he affirms Pope Benedict XVI's honorific title for the Syrian bishop: "*Doctor Unitatis.*"[5] Yet, there is another chord that Ignatius strikes, not quite as deep as the mysticism of union with the Father and the Son, but still urgent for the times: a unity and harmony with the bishop. In his address to the church in Magnesia, he makes the appeal that they "be eager to do everything in godly harmony [ἐν ὁμονοίᾳ θεοῦ], the bishop presiding in the place of God"(*Magn.* 6.1). Perhaps he might also be called a "prisoner for harmony," writing to the church in Tralles that "my chains ... exhort you: persevere in your concord [διαμένετε ἐν τῇ ὁμονοίᾳ ὑμῶν]" (*Trall.* 12.1).

Ignatius ambulates between the two concepts of unity and concord in the spiritual realm and in the earthly church with such fluidity and imagination that unity and concord become extensions of each other. In Ignatius's letters, divine ἔνωσις and communal ὁμόνοια are redefined rhetorically in his admonitions so that they often resemble each other. Vall sees this fluidity exemplified for unity in particular in Ignatius's letter to the Magnesians in which he prays that there will be in them "a union [ἔνωσιν] of flesh and spirit of Jesus Christ, our everlasting life, of faith and love ... and of Jesus and the Father" (*Magn.* 1.2–3).[6] However, Ignatius can say that Satan's very powers are nullified by the concord of their faith (*Eph.* 13.1), and he often describes this harmony as a divine concord (*Magn.* 13.2) or as a triad with faith and love (*Phld.* 15.2).

In this chapter I direct my attention to the neglected sociopolitical concept of ὁμόνοια in part because Ignatius used this term in ways that consciously evoked the practical side of political unity, and may have been deemed an appropriate concept by the Syrian bishop to employ in ways that could not be misunderstood as docetic or protognostic as might be the case with ἔνωσις. For an authoritative look at the uses of this term in Ignatius, Vall's landmark study remains the clearest articulation. His understanding of a three-fold unity that is interpenetrating: between the Father and the Son, between the flesh and Spirit of the Son, and in the faith and love of believers, is a convincing synopsis of Ignatius's understanding of unity through the lens of ἔνωσις.[7] While Ignatius's mystical

---

4. Gregory Vall, *Learning Christ*, 91.

5. Vall, *Learning Christ*, 88; Benedict XVI, *Church Fathers: From Clement of Rome to Augustine* (San Francisco: Ignatius Press, 2008), 16.

6. Vall, *Learning Christ*, 91.

7. See Vall, *Learning Christ*, 88–199.

344   John-Paul Lotz

theology may well have been more profound than he has been credited
for in the past, the pragmatic side of his episcopal responsibility of fostering harmony in the church is also an important dimension reflecting
how postapostolic Christians interpreted the need for, and the purpose of,
unity in the church.

A helpful entrée into this uncommon concept in early Christianity
might be a comparison with a contemporary orator who traversed some of
the same territory as Ignatius did on his own journey through Asia Minor
en route to his Roman execution. Dio Chrysostom was a celebrated orator
during the literary revival in the second century known as the Second
Sophistic.[8] His overlap with Ignatius in time and geography makes him a
helpful comparative figure as a cosufferer under the regimes of Domitian
and Nerva, and his flowering under Trajan may coincide with some early
datings of Ignatius's period of activity as well.

16.2. Ὁμόνοια, Dio Chrysostom, and Ignatius of Antioch

16.2.1. The Use of ὁμόνοια in Antiquity

The first literary appearance of ὁμόνοια occurs in Thucydides's *Peloponnesian Wars* (8.75.2; 8.93.3), though we do find cognates as early as
Aristophanes and Herodotus.[9] The fact that ὁμόνοια appears at the end of
the upheavals of the late fifth century in Greece may indicate a fatigue with
conflict that led many to hope for a return to civic harmony. Decades of
war had undermined the Greek sense of political and civic harmony, and
the violent proliferation of στάσις ("discord") had equally eroded other
terms for social unity such as εὐνομία and ἰσονομία.[10] The unchecked esca-
lation of internal and intercity discord during the Peloponnesian Wars was
estimated by Hans-Joachim Gehrke to have been close to 283 recorded
instances, a stunning two to five civil wars per annum.[11] This large-scale

---

8. See also Allen Brent, *Ignatius of Antioch and the Second Sophistic: A Study of Early
Christian Transformation of Pagan Culture*, STAC 36 (Tübingen: Mohr Siebeck, 2006).

9. Gaétan Thériault, *Le Culte d'Homonoia: Dans les cites grecques* (Quebec:
Sphinx, 1996), 7.

10. Athanasius Moulakis, *Homonoia: Eintracht und Entwicklung eines politischen
Bewusstseins*, Schriftenreihe zur Politik und Geschichte 10 (Leipzig: List, 1973), 21–22.

11. Gehrke, *Stasis: Untersuchungen zu den inneren Kriegen in den griechischen
Staaten des 5. und 4. Jahrhunderts v. Chr*, Vestigia 35 (Munich: Beck, 1985), 258–59.

16. "I Was Doing My Part, Therefore, as a Man Set on Unity"   345

demise in the internal peace of Achaea and the Peloponnese left the entire region decimated economically and politically, and changed the power-configurations of the Aegean permanently. In the end, it provided the kind of opportunity that Philip of Macedon had been waiting for: the subjugation of the Greek cities.

By the fourth century the term ὁμόνοια had been a part of political discourse for over a generation. Isocrates lauded the military discipline of the Spartans, and he attributed this to their internal ὁμόνοια (*Panath.* 217). On other occasions Isocrates might urge the ideal of a panhellenic ὁμόνοια among the Greek cities with the goal of eventually invading the Persians in Asia Minor (*Panath.* 13). In his mind, there was no more noble discourse a politician or an orator might give at that time, than calling the Greeks to "oneness of mind" (ὁμονοία) and to war against their enemy the Persians (*Antid.* 77). He sensed that at the level of local politics, and even in intercity diplomacy, the idea of ὁμόνοια might only be practicable through the unifying exigencies of an external war against the "barbarians," led by Phillip of Macedon (*Paneg.* 141). Other writers were less visionary in their appreciation of the value of ὁμόνοια, but no less intentional: Aristotle described it as the first sign of reconciliation between parties in a city (*Ath. pol.* 40.3), but a quote from the laws of Athens cited by Demosthenes illumines just how fragile ὁμόνοια could be when he cites a civic resolution of the council and assembly to send ambassadors to encourage Phillip to "preserve his agreement [ὁμονοίαν] and compact with us" (*Cor.* 164).

From the end of the classical period until the beginning of the principate, the written record is unhelpful in filling out a sense of the development of the concept of ὁμόνοια. The epigraphic record is our most reliable source in reconstructing to some degree the religious nature of ὁμόνοια in the process of divinization that occurred in its use in the Greek cities during the Hellenistic period.[12] For example, there is an inscription

---

12. There is a considerable body of inscriptional evidence from the entire Mediterranean world, many of which have been cataloged and commented on by Theriault, *Le Culte d'Homonoia*. As a sampling, the following may be consulted: SEG 30.1119 is an inscription from Nakone in Sicily from the third century that records an annual sacrifice on an altar to the goddess Homonoia; *GIBM* 3.443 is an inscription from Iasos in Caria that seems to reflect a reconciliation after the return of exiles; SEG 42.1012 is an inscription from Mylasa and Priene that records the first instance of a priest of Homonoia in the Hellenistic era; *GIBM* 3.600 is an inscription from the reign of Commodus that attests to the presence of priests of Homonoia in the city of Ephesus.

346   John-Paul Lotz

on an altar from Plataea dated from the fourth century BCE that indicates the degree to which ὁμόνοια evolved to express religious ideals, while retaining its fundamental political meaning. It is a memorial altar to the cult of ὁμόνοια of the Hellenes and of Zeus Eleutherios at Plataea. In his analysis of this cult, William C. West thinks that the combination ὁμόνοια of the Hellenes with Zeus Eleutherios might suggest an early date for the divinization of ὁμόνοια, perhaps as early as Phillip II, or a little later, under Alexander the Great.[13] Phillip urged ὁμόνοια among the Greeks joining the League of Corinth, and Alexander may have demanded the same in regard to the Chians and the inhabitants of Priene.[14] The associate of Plataea with the Persian wars of the fifth century, along with several traditions, link the rebuilding of the city to Alexander the Great. The familiar political slogans of ὁμόνοια and ἐλευθερία may well have been personified in a cult there to commemorate the city's refounding.[15]

Throughout the fourth century BCE, the cult of ὁμόνοια is attested in Achaea, as attested by inscriptions on altars at Olympia and Athens.[16] There are also inscriptions on statue bases in Asia Minor bearing the language of ὁμόνοια, although it is not always easy to know whether these inscriptions refer to a divinization of ὁμόνοια, or whether they reflect the political brokering of restored relations between cities, which seems to have been more common.[17] While the fundamental meaning of ὁμόνοια in the fifth and fourth centuries was associated with harmony at the local level between political factions *within* a city, both Lysias and Isocrates make the innovative allusion to ὁμόνοια existing *between* cities as a theme in their arguments for a common war against the Persians.

In her comprehensive study of the ὁμόνοια-coins of Asia Minor, Ursula Kampmann shows how the large corpus of coins that date from the first and second centuries CE for the cities of Pergamon, Ephesus, and Smyrna reflect the internecine rivalry between the cities over the honorific title πρώτη ἀσίας.[18] The ὁμόνοια-coin issues sought to reflect changes in how

---

13. West, "Hellenic Homonoia and the New Decree from Plataea," *GRBS* 18 (1977): 307–19.

14. West, "Hellenic Homonoia," 318.

15. West, "Hellenic Homonoia," 316–17.

16. Alan Shapiro, "Homonoia," *LIMC* 5:477.

17. Shapiro, "Homonoia," 477.

18. Kampmann, *Die Homonoia-Verbindungen der Stadt Pergamon oder der Versuch einer kleinasiatischen Stadt unter römischer Herrschaft eigenständige Politik zu*

16. "I Was Doing My Part, Therefore, as a Man Set on Unity"   347

these cities were ranked in the provincial koinon and the attempt at negotiating any potential advances or changes in status peaceably. In fact, many of the coins minted between Ephesus, Smyrna, and Pergamon seem to represent such very attempts at the dissolution of conflict between those cities over which one had the right to primacy.[19] At an official meeting of the delegates of the cities at the provincial councils, where a common sacrifice at the altar of the imperial cult was dedicated, the status of each city was projected for all to see at the entrance parade to the festivals that accompanied the assize.[20] Nevertheless, it was harmony that was often the first virtue to be sacrificed at such festivals as the civic representatives jockeyed for position over the status of primacy.[21] Even smaller cities might issue ὁμόνοια-coins, but these do not usually reflect the ending of disputes, rather they seem to reflect a change in the status of the smaller city in relation to a more prominent city or metropolis.[22] The numismatic record shows us that by the first century CE ὁμόνοια had evolved to express both political and religious overtones, and could be associated by the Romans more specifically with the symbolic language of the imperial cult.[23]

16.2.2. Dio Chrysostom and the Politics of Concord

Dio Chrysostom, a contemporary of Ignatius and a resident of the province of Bithynia-Pontus, leaves us perhaps the most comprehensive discussion of ὁμόνοια as a political virtue from the Imperial age.[24] Dio often gave orations on the nature of ὁμόνοια, and found himself solicited on several occasions to broker concord between Nicomedia and Nicaea (the leading civic rivals of Bythinia-Pontus), as well as between his own hometown of Prusa and Apamaea, a Roman colony and rival neighbor (see *Or.* 38; 40). Dio's *Ora-*

---

betreiben, Saarbrücker Studien zur Arhäologie und alten Geschichte 9 (Saarbrücker: Saarbrücker Druckerei und Verlag, 1996), 375–76.

19. Kampmann, *Die Homonoia-Verbindungen*, 385.

20. Kampmann, *Die Homonoia-Verbindungen*, 383.

21. S. R. F. Price, *Rituals and Power: The Roman Imperial Cult in Asia Minor* (Cambridge: Cambridge University Press, 1984), 130.

22. Kampmann, *Die Homonoia-Verbindungen*, 386.

23. For more on the numismatic background of ὁμόνοια, see John-Paul Lotz, *Ignatius and Concord: The Background and Use of the Language of Concord in the Letters of Ignatius of Antioch*, Patristic Studies (New York: Lang, 2007), 46–51.

24. Christopher Price Jones, *The Roman World of Dio Chrysostom*, Loeb Classical Monographs (Cambridge: Harvard University Press: 1978), 94.

348   John-Paul Lotz

tions describe both the civil and domestic conflicts within a city, as well as the rivalries and enmities that raged between them. Strife and discord were exposed as the greatest evils a city could experience, and these were set in apposition to ὁμόνοια and peace as the greatest blessing. On numerous occasions, Dio cites examples of how the two affected the welfare of both citizens of the cities in conflict, and their urban neighbors (*Or.* 39.2–4).

But Dio is not the only witness to the virtues of ὁμόνοια in the principate; Plutarch his contemporary also uses ὁμόνοια in his political treatises (*Praec. ger. rei publ.* 10 [805e] and 19 [816a]). Within a generation, the orator Aelius Aristides would advocate ὁμόνοια among the leading cities of Asia with a flourishing brand of sophistic deference to the ruling powers of Rome that became a common feature of the imperial ὁμόνοια speeches (*Or.* 23.3). Dio's own personal involvement in the rivalries of cities he advised and advocated for puts him in proximity to the civic issues of the day and makes him a useful personality to evaluate more closely. He understood civil discord as an insider, whether for his own city or for others, and the primary audiences for his orations were equally well schooled in the contemporary problem of civic discord.[25] In Dio's thirty-eighth oration we have a valuable window into the world of Greek politicians and moralists of the first and second centuries and in particular, how they used ὁμόνοια as a way of describing healthy civic relations. Dio's use of ὁμόνοια in the context of rivalry among the leading cities of Bythinia-Pontus helps us observe the manner in which Greek citizens and politicians interacted with each another when it came to civil discord within their cities and with those cities regarded as rivals.[26]

---

25. On Dio generally, see Heinrich von Arnim, *Leben und Werke des Dio von Prusa: Mit einer Einleitung; Sophistik, Rhetorik, Philosophie in ihrem Kampf um die Jugendbildung* (Berlin: Wiedeman, 1898); Paolo Desideri, *Dione di Prusa: Un intellettuale greco nell'Impero romano*, Biblioteca di cultura contemporanea 135 (Messina: d'Anna, 1978); and Jones, *Roman World of Dio Chrysostom.* For Dio and civil discord, see Jones, *Roman World of Dio Chrysostom,* 95–104; for his relationship with other cities, see Simon Swain, *Hellenism and Empire: Language, Classicism, and Power in the Greek World, AD 50–250* (Oxford: Clarendon, 1996), 225–41; with Alexandria, William D. Barry, "Aristocrats, Orators, and the 'Mob': Dio Chrysostom and the World of the Alexandrians," *Historia* 42 (1993): 82–103; Bruce W. Winter, *Philo and Paul among the Sophists,* SNTSMS 96 (Cambridge: Cambridge University Press, 1997), 40–59; with Tarsus, A. A. R. Sheppard, "A Dissident in Tarsus? (Dio Chrysostom, *Or.* 66)," *LCM* 7 (1982): 149–50; and J. L. Moles, "Dio Chrysostom: Exile, Tarsus, Nero and Domitian," *LMC* 8 (1983): 130–34.

26. Lotz, *Ignatius and Concord,* 73–79.

16. "I Was Doing My Part, Therefore, as a Man Set on Unity"   349

In this oration, we come to understand more clearly how those who were in positions of influence in the cities of the Greek East sought to quell the turmoil of civil discord and restore the ordered hierarchy in which their social privileges and status were secured. Thanking the Nicomedians for their gift of citizenship, along with the attendant responsibilities required by such civic privileges, Dio offers to reciprocate not as a benefactor or a flatterer, but as an advisor to the city on matters of the greatest importance (38.2). He introduces his theme (ὁμόνοια with the Nicaeans), and offers his plan of address (38.8). Like a physician dealing with a sick patient (the two cities, collectively), Dio will diagnose the ailment and offer remedies for its resolution. Nicomedia and Nicaea had reached such a pitch of discord that few could have conceived of ὁμόνοια as something the Nicomedians might ever achieve with the Nicaeans (38.6). Dio's encomium to ὁμόνοια, which follows his introduction, tells us a lot about his own anthropology and cosmology, and especially the influence of Stoicism in his view of the world.[27] Ὁμόνοια, Dio proclaims, has its source in the "greatest of divine things" and is analogous to friendship, reconciliation, and kinship (38.11). Ὁμόνοια unifies the elements, is the very blessedness that the gods share in common, and is that great virtue that mortals consistently fail to achieve because of their preference for its opposite, discord (στάσις). Dio compares ὁμόνοια with the harmony that characterizes both family and social relationships, firmly embedding the term within the basic institutions of the Greek *polis* (38.15).[28] This expresses something about how Dio perceived the ordered social relationships that made up his world. Dio stands very near the top with the other aristocrats of the Greek world, followed by the citizens, commoners, and slaves, and finally by the barbarians and beasts of the world. Those who engage in wars and conflict are, therefore, socially and morally nothing more than "wild beasts" (38.17). What is worse, those who vainly battle for titles and glory are mere fools, who, unlike the educated man, misunderstand the difference between false and genuine glory (38.29). To the well-flattered ears of Greeks under Roman rule, Dio appeals to their philosophic past, and offers the Nicomedians, true heirs of the tradition of the Stoa, a means of being more noble than their (Roman)

27. See Brunt's evaluation of the philosophical influences on Dio's writings; Peter A. Brunt, "Aspects of the Social Thought of Dio Chrysostom and of the Stoics," *Proceedings of the Cambridge Philosophical Society* 19.2 (1973): 19.

28. Swain, *Hellenism and Empire*, 220.

superiors.[29] Dio's celebration of ὁμόνοια is also united with the idea of peace (εἰρήνη) and general human welfare, an idyllic picture of order and civic harmony resembling a festival (38.43). Dio's scheme is revealing. Setting ὁμόνοια among the fundamental building blocks of the cosmos (38.11), he situates it in the very fabric of family and human relationships (38.16) and its absence is manifested in wars and conflicts (38.17), as well as natural calamities, which Dio sees as the gods' warnings to humans to live in harmony with one another (38.18). Dio moves intentionally from the basic components of life, through family and social relationships, empire, and finally to the divine, where ὁμόνοια finds its consummate sanction.

By attempting to recover the primacy from Nicaea, the Nicomedians have merely exposed their real lack of power and the hollowness of their ambitions (38.27–28). Nicomedia will receive no tribute from the Nicaeans (as the cities of the Delian League paid to Athens), nor will they rob Nicaea of their status as an assize district, or (even less likely!) garrison Nicaea.[30] Neither will the "tithes" of Bithynia accrue to them for in reality, Nicomedia's power in the province can only be elevated by Rome, and no dissension with Nicaea can win them these privileges (38.26).[31] Dio marvels that they merely wish to be "inscribed" or "registered" (ἐπιγραφῶμέν) as "first," even if it has no substantial value. In Dio's appeal, unless it is actually true, then the title is only a source of vanity (38.29–30). Real power, under the present conditions involves greater leadership than the struggle for inscriptions: As the *metropolis*, Nicomedia has a role to play in the provincial council that its quest for symbolic

---

29. On philosophers and concord: 38.5; on those who engage in warfare: 38.20; on true primacy: 38.35. Dio's implications are obviously veiled, but his resistance to Roman hegemony as a Greek was duly tempered by his status as a Greco-Roman aristocrat. Bruce F. Harris quotes A. N. Sherwin-White as proposing that Dio was working for a "reconciliation of the Hellenistic and Roman worlds" as a way of preparing the way for the later ideal of the *communis patria* of the later empire; see Harris, "Dio of Prusa: A Survey of Recent Works," *ANRW* 33.5:3869; Sherwin-White, *The Roman Citizenship*, 2nd ed. (Oxford: Clarendon, 1973), 261.

30. In fact, during Pliny's tenure as proconsul of Bithynia, Nicomedia itself was garrisoned with a mounted cohort; see David Magie, *Roman Rule in Asia Minor to the End of the Third Century after Christ*, 2 vols. (Princeton: Princeton University Press, 1950), 2:603.

31. See discussion of tithes in Jones, *Roman World of Dio Chrysostom*, 87. Tithes were possibly a rent or tribute collected by Roman officials resident in Nicaea, or it might be a reference to the tax-farmers who were formerly headquartered in Nicaea.

16. "I Was Doing My Part, Therefore, as a Man Set on Unity" 351

primacy could threaten.[32] Rather than antagonizing Nicaea through this vain battle over titles, Nicomedia ought to present itself as a model of fair dealing (38.31). In fact, there would be more to gain in joining forces with Nicaea, and exerting greater influence over all the cities of Bithynia (through the provincial council) and thereby present a united front as a more legitimate deterrent against unscrupulous provincial governors who may "wish to commit a wrong" (38.34).[33]

Regrettably, this is not the present state of things between the two cities, and their rivalry, far from investing one or the other with more power, is actually undermining them both and debasing what little autonomy they might actually have (38.34). As it is, in their struggle with each another, they must abase themselves by courting the alliances and loyalty of the other, lesser cities in the province (38.35). In such a state, how can they ever hope to resolve their present situation with the governor?[34] With Bithynia's two most powerful cities cut up into rivalry, the governor's strategy of divide and conquer allows him to commit all kinds of indignities against the province as a whole simply by courting this city or that city against the others (38.36). The governors seize the properties of private citizens, commit every kind of injustice, and in the end, brazenly celebrate their indignities and crimes by awarding the empty title of primacy (πρώτους) to one city, and treating them all as if they were "the very last [ἐσχάτοις]!" Furthermore, these titles "excite laughter" in Rome and are humiliatingly called "Greek failings" (Ἑλληνικὰ ἁμαρτήματα) among them (38.38). Once upon a time, Athenians and Spartans fought for empire, but the present contest between Nicomedia and Nicaea is a fool's errand, contending for the humiliating right to lead the procession at festivals and imperial cult ceremonies (38.38), that in the most public of ways displayed their subservience to their true masters.[35]

---

32. Dio's mention of Nicomedia's special function as metropolis seems to indicate that this title was presently not shared with Nicaea, that it was in fact theirs alone (38.31; see also 38.39).

33. See Swain, *Hellenism and Empire*, 239 n. 189, on the disadvantages of a divided provincial council and the prosecution of governors.

34. It is unclear what this might be, although it is conceivably a provincial suit against a governor; Jones, *Roman World of Dio Chrysostom*, 88.

35. For a full assessment of imperial cult processions, see Guy M. Rogers, *The Sacred Identity of Ephesos: Foundation Myths of a Roman City* (London: Routledge, 1991); see also Price, *Rituals and Power*, 122–32.

352   John-Paul Lotz

Dio's intentions seem clear. He is interested in quelling the rivalry between the two cities in order to secure what power they do have, and of protecting them from abdicating more control to Rome through their mutual animosity. For Dio, ὁμόνοια was a tool for quelling the civil discord that robbed the cities and the provincial council of their clout in the face of Roman governors. While the aristocratic elite of the Greek East were often on friendly terms with the emperors, the governors were not always welcomed or respected.[36] What may have been at the back of Dio's mind was how to secure his privileged status in the power configurations of the Greco-Roman world, and the appeal to ὁμόνοια was one way to facilitate greater provincial and civic distance from Roman intervention, and so the opportunity for the ruling elite to carry on with their agendas secured by the status quo.[37] Ὁμόνοια was not simply a ploy for Dio in his participation in the power struggles among the aristocrats of his province, but it was certainly not only a philanthropic ideal that he was hoping to inculcate into the Bithynians.[38] For Dio, ὁμόνοια was a means of negotiating the delicate balance between compliance and resistance that characterized provincial relations with Rome at this time.

16.2.3. Ignatius and the Struggle for Unity

Contemporary with Dio Chrysostom and the politics of the Roman East, postapostolic Christianity was involved in its own struggles as it faced a growing heterodoxy in the churches the apostles had left behind. A significant amount of diversity existed within Christianity by the beginning of the second century, and Ignatius was very much involved with this battle for the success of the "true faith." Especially in Asia Minor, heretical movements like the Nicolaitans (Rev 2:15), Montanists, Marcionites, gnostics, docetists, and a variety of Jewish-Christian groups contended for their places in the newly emerging Christian religion.[39]

---

36. Swain, *Hellenism and Empire*, 221–22.

37. See Sheppard, "Dissident in Tarsus," 242–52.

38. Swain, *Hellenism and Empire*, 225.

39. For Marcionites, see Walter Bauer, *Orthodoxy and Heresy in Earliest Christianity*, ed. and trans. Robert A. Kraft and Gerhard Krodel (Philadelphia: Fortress, 1971), 82. For Jewish-Christian groups, see William R. Schoedel, *Ignatius of Antioch: A Commentary on the Letters of Ignatius of Antioch*, Hermeneia (Philadelphia: Fortress, 1985), 16–17. For the situation more generally, see J. B. Lightfoot, *The Apostolic*

16. "I Was Doing My Part, Therefore, as a Man Set on Unity"   353

In the seven letters that we have from him, Ignatius is primarily concerned with combating a docetic gnosticism and Jewish Christianity in its various forms, perhaps even a synthesis of both.[40] His method of critique is polemical and sharp; even if at times humble and self-effacing, Ignatius tolerates no deviance from the true gospel (*Eph.* 16.2; *Magn.* 10.3; *Trall.* 7.1; 9.1). In turn, he exhorts the churches to unity and concord (ὁμόνοια) under the authority and in submission to the bishop, the presbyters, and the deacons of each of the churches to which he writes.[41] Outside of Clement's letter to the Corinthians, this is the first occurrence of the word ὁμόνοια in the literature of early Christianity.[42] Though absent from the New Testament, as noted earlier, the term does occur in several places within the Septuagint (Lev 20:5, Pss 54:55; 82:5). Josephus and Philo both use the word, but not with its developed political import as in the literature of the second century. It is perhaps a possibility that ὁμόνοια's association with the political propaganda emerging from Domitian's expansion of the imperial cult in Asia Minor during the early 90s propelled the term into popular discourse, whether through the coinage, inscriptions, or in the speeches of the orators.[43] Ignatius employs the term in the context of his exhortations for unity in the churches and in this sense seems very much to be situated within the genre of the "ὁμόνοια-speech."[44]

Ignatius's letters represent his Syrian and Antiochean background much more than they do the situation in Asia Minor.[45] In fact, his language

---

Fathers, vol. 2.1, (Peabody, MA: Hendrickson, 1989). The fact that Ignatius does not mention the Quartodeciman debates, Montanism, Basilides, Saturninus, Marcion or Valentinian, all of which were heretical movements or personages that he would have known of, tends to indicate an early dating for the epistles. For further argumentation, see Lightfoot, *Apostolic Fathers*, 355–73.

40. Lightfoot, *Apostolic Fathers*, 378; Paul J. Donahue, "Jewish Christianity in the Letters of Ignatius of Antioch," *VC* 32 (1978): 81–93.

41. Schoedel, *Ignatius of Antioch*, 12.

42. 1 Clem. 9.4; 11.2; 20.3, 10; 34.7; 30.3; 49.5; 50.5; 60.4; 61.1; 63.2; 65.1.

43. Johannes Weiss and Rudolf Knopf, *The History of Primitive Christianity*, trans. Frederick C. Grant et al., 2 vols. (London: Macmillan, 1937), 2:806–7; Peter R. Franke, "Zu den Homonoia-Münzen Kleinasiens," in *Stuttgarter Kolloquium zur historischen Geographie des Altertums*, Geographica historica 4 (Bonn: Habelt, 1987), 94; *GIBM* 4.894; 1.2–13; Dio Chrysostom, *Or.* 38.

44. Dale B. Martin, *The Corinthian Body*, (New Haven: Yale University Press, 1995), 38–39.

45. Hans Lietzmann, *A History of the Early Church*, trans. B. L. Woolf, 2 vols. (New York: Meridian Books, 1961), 1:237.

354 John-Paul Lotz

is characteristic of Asianism with its use of multiple adjectives and compound verb forms, as well as its bombastic style.[46] The epistolary structure of his letters reflect contemporary Hellenistic genres, comparable to the diplomatic royal letters of the east, and are similar to Paul's letters, though "notoriously passionate and formless."[47] This may have had something to do with his rather exuberant temperament, but also with the circumstances under which he was writing: he was being detained by ruthless soldiers and was on his way to be martyred in the arena at Rome (*Rom.* 5.1).[48] Ignatius's theology and ecclesiology are unwavering in their defense of the "threefold ministry" of bishop, presbyters, and deacons, and his letters are addressed to those who belong to them.[49] He makes a concerted reference to the members of the churches whom he collectively "sees" in the person of their bishop in each of his letters, thereby identifying himself with them and shunning all those outside of the bishop's authority (Ignatius, *Eph.* 1.3; *Magn.* 2.1; *Trall.* 7.1, 7.2).

In this veritable "last will and testament," Ignatius writes to consolidate the unity of the churches he is leaving behind, and the soundness of their doctrine against the threat of heresy (*Eph.* 6.2; *Smyrn.* 4.1). In doing so, he appeals to the authority of the bishops, and exhorts the believers in each of the churches to maintain unity and concord (ὁμόνοια). A look at Ignatius's letter to the Magnesians may help reveal whether he was using the term ὁμόνοια in a fashion similar to Dio Chrysostom (politically), which may shed some light on how Ignatius's ecclesiology was influenced by the familiar structures of power that dominated the Roman world at that time, or whether like Paul, his theological predecessor, he was engaged in the process of reifying the language of contemporary society for use in the imagery of Christianity (theologically).[50]

Ignatius addresses the Magnesians in a standard epistolary format, which some have called the *parakalo*-type, referring to the hortatory

---

46. William R. Schoedel, "Epistles of Ignatius," *ABD* 3:385.

47. Schoedel, *Ignatius of Antioch*, 7. For similarities to royal letters of the east, see Herman J. Sieben, "Die Ignatianen als Briefe," *VC* 32 (1978): 1–18.

48. Leslie W. Barnard, "The Background of St. Ignatius of Antioch," *VC* 17 (1963): 193.

49. Lightfoot, *Apostolic Fathers*, 39.

50. See in particular on the Pauline side of this question, Margaret M. Mitchell, *Paul and the Rhetoric of Reconciliation: An Exegetical Investigation of the Language and Composition of 1 Corinthians* (Louisville: Westminster John Knox, 1992).

16. "I Was Doing My Part, Therefore, as a Man Set on Unity"

nature of the argumentation. Ignatius is not writing to petition for something, or simply to inform; he is specifically writing to warn and instruct the churches, though not as an "apostle" but as a "fellow slave" (*Trall.* 3.3; *Eph.* 3.1).[51] Ignatius first of all praises the Magnesians for the orderliness (πολυεύτακτος) of their love toward God, and takes it upon himself to offer (to sing!) prayers for them that there might be a union (ἔνωσις) in them of the flesh and spirit of Christ, a union of faith and love, and a union of Jesus and the Father (*Magn.* 1.1). This introductory laudation sets the tenor for the rest of the letter. Ignatius is concerned with unity of doctrine as well as unity in the churches, and he expresses this with ἔνωσις, which generally refers to a type of communal unity, as opposed to a metaphysical unity.[52] Ignatius frames the letter with these three injunctions to unity, which are found again in paragraph 13 before the closing section of the letter. The union in the believers of the flesh and spirit of Christ foreshadows Ignatius's exhortation to unity within the church under the submission and leadership of the bishop, as Christ was obedient to the Father (7.1). The union of faith and love is not expressly developed in the letter to the Magnesians, but it draws on a concept that Ignatius elaborates on in his letter to the Ephesians, where faith and love are the "beginning and end of life," and the union of the two is equated with God himself (*Eph.* 14.1–2). In the preceding paragraph Ignatius maintains that the very powers of Satan are destroyed by the ὁμόνοια of their faith, and this is certainly the gist of his warnings against being "led astray by strange doctrines," ἑτεροδοξία, in *Magn.* 8.1. Finally, the union of Jesus and the Father seems to foreshadow Ignatius's warnings regarding the practice and belief of Jewish ideas, which denied the divinity of Jesus, as well as his birth, death, and resurrection (8.2; 11.1).

Before Ignatius moves into his defense of their bishop, he very systematically acknowledges that it was in their Bishop Damas, their presbyters Bassus and Apollonius, and their deacon Zotion that he "saw" the entire congregation (2.1). The complimentary words Ignatius lays to Zotion's account are informative: he is "subject to the bishop as to the grace of God,

---

51. Sieben, "Die Ignatianen als Briefe," 10.

52. This term is attested from the time of the Pre-Socratics, and appears in Aristotle (*Phys.* 222a, 20) all the way down to Philo (*Leg.* 1, 8) with the general sense of union or unity; Schoedel, *Ignatius of Antioch*, 105; the term ἔνωσις is not nuanced in the same way as ὁμόνοια is in contemporary writers, and does not refer to any particular type of union.

356   John-Paul Lotz

and to the presbytery as to the law of Jesus Christ" (2.1). Zotion, perhaps, stands figuratively for those who are truly being saved.[53] Ignatius is in fact limiting his validation to those members whom he can "see," who are associated with and in submission to Damas, their bishop. Ignatius proceeds to affirm Damas's authority as a bishop, and vouches for him, though his outward appearance is youthful (3.1). He further praises the presbyters since they defer to the bishop as to God, the father of Jesus. But yielding outwardly is not enough, and Ignatius continues by warning those who would feign submission to the bishop, but "disregard him in all their actions" (4.1). Their disregard for the bishop in fact amounts to holding separate meetings, which Ignatius is quick to remind are not valid according to the commandment (4.1), and which he denounces elsewhere (*Trall.* 7.2). Here we see Ignatius's overriding concern with unity, and his distaste for any kind of independence from the unity and authority of the bishop.[54]

Prior to his encomium on unity and concord (ὁμόνοια), Ignatius interjects a warning in the striking metaphorical image of two coinages (5.2). Ignatius seems to have in mind those members of the church in Magnesia who do not offer genuine deference to the bishop and reminds them of the judgment to come and the choice between two things (τὰ δύο). This language evokes similar teachings in Judaism and Christianity at the time regarding the two ways that are familiar from Barnabas (18–20), the Didache (1–6), and Qumran (1QS 3:13–4:26), with their eschatological orientation toward the end of the age.[55] For Ignatius, it is clear: one belongs either to Christ or to this world (5.2).

The use of coinage as a metaphor has Christian precedents in Jesus's own words with the Pharisees in their debate over what belonged to God, and what belonged to Caesar (Matt. 22:19). But in Ignatius's letter, a sharper focus is brought to bear on the relevance of the minting of coins and episcopal authority.[56] Each coin (νομίσματα) is impressed (ἐπικείμενον) with a particular stamp (χαρακτήρ) upon it (5.2), the one with the stamp of God's character, the other with character of the world. In the context of the times, could this coinage metaphor be referring to

---

53. *Zotion* is also found in papyri and inscriptions as *Sotion*, which is not too far removed from allusions to *soterian*, "deliverance" or "salvation."

54. Lightfoot, *Apostolic Fathers*, 2:103.

55. Schoedel, *Ignatius of Antioch*, 110.

56. Aristophanes, *Ran.* 717; Plutarch, *Adul. amic.* 2 (49e); and later Clement of Alexandria., *Exc.* 86.

16. "I Was Doing My Part, Therefore, as a Man Set on Unity"   357

the popular and prolific ὁμόνοια-coins of Asia Minor? Coins from the reign of Caracalla testify to the minting of ὁμόνοια-coins in Magnesia, and its close proximity to Ephesus (about fourteen miles) makes it likely that citizens from Magnesia would have been aware of these ὁμόνοια-issues between Ephesus, Smyrna, and Pergamon from at least the time of Domitian's reign.[57] As Peter Franke observed, the cities of Asia Minor may have produced as many as 24 million such coins during the reigns of Augustus through Gallianus, originating from more than 150 cities.[58] The coins generally had an image of the emperor on the obverse, with the city gods and the inscription ὁμόνοια on the reverse.[59] These issues were not ceremonial gratuities, but were bronze issues appropriate for the commerce of everyday life, and cities like Smyrna, Ephesus, Pergamon, Nicomedia, and Nicaea minted large issues of such bronze asses (obols).[60] There is also evidence that ceremonial silver Cistophoroi were minted in the cities of Asia Minor at festivals where the imperial cult was celebrated.[61] By employing the popular image of ὁμόνοια-coins, Ignatius may have been preparing his hearers for an exhortation to maintain unity and concord in their churches.

This, in fact, is Ignatius's exhortation (6.1): that they be eager (σπουδάζετε) to do everything in the concord of God (ἐν ὁμόνοια θεοῦ). For Ignatius, this means respecting and submitting to the structures of authority established in the churches, with the bishop representing God, the presbyters, the council of the apostles, and the deacons with the ministry of Jesus Christ. Union with God is dependent on being united with their bishop, and by avoiding divisions and respecting those who preside (προκαθημένοις) over them, they will be an "example and lesson of immortality" (6.2). Ignatius argues that the parallel of Christ's submission to the Father must be expressed in the congregation's submission to the bishop and presbyters, in which scenario

---

57. Ephesus, Magnesia (Maender): *BMC* Ionia 174, no.106 (Mionnet *Suppl.* 6:242, no. 1059); Smyrna, Ephesus: *BMC* Ionia 111, no. 407; Smyrna, Ephesus, Pergamum: Mionnet *Suppl.* 6:134, no. 370.

58. Franke, "Homonoia-Münzen," 89.

59. Franke, "Homonoia-Münzen," 90–91.

60. These were roughly equivalent to Roman dupondii; see Kenneth W. Harl, *Coinage and the Roman Economy, 300 B.C. to A.D. 700* (Baltimore: Johns Hopkins University Press, 1996), 109–11.

61. Harl, *Coinage*, 100.

358 John-Paul Lotz

there is no room for heterodoxy or heteropraxis, but all things are done in common and in unity (7.1). The encomium to unity continues in a style and language reminiscent of the Pauline Epistle to the Ephesians 4:1–6 characterized by the repetition of ἓις, μία, and ἓν. There, the author exhorted (παρακαλῶ) the members of the churches to "be eager" (σπουδάζοντες) to maintain unity and oneness. In *Magnesians*, Ignatius's final image is one of the entire congregation hurrying to one altar and one temple where they worship the same Jesus Christ who comes from and returns to one Father (7.2), possibly evoking the idea of worship at the imperial cult temple.[62] If so, there are clear parallels with the language of ὁμόνοια and the rhetoric of imperial unity that orators in the Second Sophistic admonished their hearers to conceive as mediated through the emperor. The famous decree by the koinon of Asia in 9 BCE that Augustus had ushered in a golden age of peace, where the virtues of Pax and Concordia (εἰρήνη and ὁμόνοια) were associated with his person, is an earlier, albeit notable example.[63]

Ignatius proceeds to warn the Magnesians against a kind of docetic-Judaism (8–10), common to Asia Minor after the destruction of the temple in Jerusalem, but probably also present in Antioch in Syria where Ignatius ministered.[64] He has no patience with those who want to worship Jesus Christ and follow Judaism, and chastises the Magnesians to recall the orthodox faith of Jesus's incarnation, passion, and resurrection (11.1). The union of Christ with the Father is essential for Ignatius's affirmation of Jesus's divinity, and he sums up the letter in his conclusion by once more exhorting them to a unity of the flesh and spirit, faith and love, and of the Son and the Father (with the Spirit; 13.1). This complex union is realized by submitting to the bishop and presbyters as Christ did to the Father, and as the apostles did to Jesus and the Father. Ignatius sends greetings from the Ephesians and the Smyrneans who are with him, as well as all the other churches, as if reminding those who are entertaining disunity with the bishop that they are excluded from fellowship with these congregations who affirm their unity with Damas and the Magnesians. Farewell is offered in the concord of God (ὁμόνοια θεοῦ), which he char-

---

62. Allen Brent, "Ignatius of Antioch and the Imperial Cult" *VC* 52 (1998): 30–58.

63. Allen Brent, *The Imperial Cult and the Development of Church Order: Concepts and Images of Authority in Paganism and Early Christianity before the Age of Cyprian*, VCSup 45 (Leiden: Brill, 1999), 70, 71.

64. Bauer, *Heresy*, 87–89.

16. "I Was Doing My Part, Therefore, as a Man Set on Unity"   359

acterizes as a spirit that knows no division, which is Jesus Christ, as if to offer one final picture of what it means to be united in right doctrine and true unity in the church.[65]

16.3. Conclusions

How does Ignatius's use of the social and political vocabulary of *concordia et pax* employed by the Roman imperial propagandists among their eastern subjects inform our understanding of the kind of unity in the churches that Ignatius was seeking to foster? What does his use of ὁμόνοια tell us about his understanding of ἕνωσις in the context of bishops, congregations, and competitive communal expressions of Christianity (Χριστιανισμός) among the churches he sought to lead as "a man set on unity"? Vall has made a strong case for the importance of ἕνωσις as the theological centerpiece to Ignatius's theology. Unity between the Father and the Son made manifest in the incarnation as a unity of the flesh and spirit of Christ Jesus himself, becomes the spiritual pathway to God as his followers move from faith to love.[66] Added to Vall's robust discussion of Ignatian theological categories, I have tried to show how the less prominent, but perhaps more practical, extension of ecclesial unity via the socio-political terminology of ὁμόνοια features as an important interpretation for the way in which political unity was brokered and maintained in the churches Ignatius wrote to. As Dio Chrysostom sought to admonish the warring cities of Asia to abandon αἵρεσις and στάσις and seek ὁμόνοια, in order to avoid the retributive force of Rome's disfavor, Ignatius of Antioch may well have reified the popular and well-known political ideal and applied it to the necessity of unity in the church under the authority of the bishop. For it is only the church that has "found mercy" and is "firmly established" that has preserved a godly concord (ὁμόνοια; *Phld.*, inscr.). Such a church must share together with the bishop "one mind," and only in their concord can they sing praises worthy of the Father (*Eph.* 4.1, 2). Their frequent gatherings under the one altar of the bishop who breaks the one bread is a medicine of immortality (20.2), and in the concord of their faith, Satan's works are destroyed (13.1).

Ignatius use of ὁμόνοια in the early part of the second century offers us a picture of the church buffeted not only by competing interpretations of

---

65. Kirsopp Lake, trans., *The Apostolic Fathers*, vol. 1, LCL (Cambridge: Cambridge University Press, 1912), 211.

66. Vall, *Learning Christ*, 91–96.

the faith (αἵρεσις), but also a good deal of human competition for power and control (στάσις). The theological solution for these challenges was a profound understanding and experience of divine ἕνωσις as believers gathered together with the bishop to celebrate the body and blood of Christ, truly born of Mary, and of God, and in whose body there was a unity of flesh and spirit that brought into visible reality the even more profound unity that always existed between the Father and the Son. But at the daily and practical level of human communal contingencies, the less theological but very familiar public morality of ὁμόνοια was reinterpreted by Ignatius as a solution to the question of power and control. To be in harmony with the mind of God, one needed to be in harmony with the mind of the bishop, and to sing praises worthy of the Father, one needed to do so in a concord that was not only a profession of faith, but a practice of submission. Though ἕνωσις was certainly the more sublime of the two terms, ὁμόνοια may have corresponded with Ignatius's talents as a statesman more effectively in his quest to ward off the forces of demonic division and protect the young churches under their not always charismatic bishops.

Bibliography

Arnim, Heinrich von. *Leben und Werke des Dio von Prusa: Mit einer Einleitung; Sophistik, Rhetorik, Philosophie in ihrem Kampf um die Jugendbildung*. Berlin: Wiedeman, 1898.

Barnard, Leslie W. "The Background of St. Ignatius of Antioch." *VC* 17 (1963): 193–206.

Barry, William D. "Aristocrats, Orators, and the 'Mob': Dio Chrysostom and the World of the Alexandrians." *Historia* 42 (1993): 82–103.

Bauer, Walter. *Orthodoxy and Heresy in Earliest Christianity*. Edited and translated by Robert A. Kraft and Gerhard Krodel. Philadelphia: Fortress, 1971.

Benedict XVI. *Church Fathers: From Clement of Rome to Augustine*. San Francisco: Ignatius Press, 2008.

Brent, Allen. "Ignatius of Antioch and the Imperial Cult." *VC* 52 (1998): 30–58.

———. *Ignatius of Antioch and the Second Sophistic: A Study of Early Christian Transformation of Pagan Culture*. STAC 36. Tübingen: Mohr Siebeck, 2006.

———. *The Imperial Cult and the Development of Church Order: Concepts* and *Images of Authority in Paganism and Early Christianity before the Age of Cyprian.* VCSup 45. Leiden: Brill, 1999.

Brunt, Peter A. "Aspects of the Social Thought of Dio Chrysostom and of the Stoics." *Proceedings of the Cambridge Philosophical Society* 19.2 (1973): 9–34.

Desideri, Paolo. *Dione di Prusa: Un intellettuale greco nell'Impero romano.* Biblioteca di cultura contemporanea 135. Messina: d'Anna, 1978.

Donahue, Paul J. "Jewish Christianity in the Letters of Ignatius of Antioch." *VC* 32 (1978): 81–93.

Franke, Peter R. "Zu den Homonoia-Münzen Kleinasiens." Pages 81–102 in *Stuttgarter Kolloquium zur historischen Geographie des Altertums.* Edited by Eckhart Olshausen. Geographica historica 4. Bonn: Habelt, 1987.

Gehrke, Hans-Joachim. *Stasis: Untersuchungen zu den inneren Kriegen in den griechischen Staaten des 5. und 4. Jahrhunderts v. Chr.* Vestigia 35. Munich: Beck, 1985.

Harl, Kenneth W. *Coinage and the Roman Economy, 300 B.C. to A.D. 700.* Baltimore: Johns Hopkins University Press, 1996.

Harris, Bruce F. "Dio of Prusa: A Survey of Recent Works." *ANRW* 33.5:3853–81.

Jones, Christopher Price. *The Roman World of Dio Chrysostom.* Loeb Classical Monographs. Cambridge: Harvard University Press: 1978.

Kampmann, Ursula. *Die Homonoia-Verbindungen der Stadt Pergamon oder der Versuch einer kleinasiatischen Stadt unter römischer Herrschaft eigenständige Politik zu betreiben.* Saarbrücker Studien zur Arhäologie und alten Geschichte 9. Saarbrücker: Saarbrücker Druckerei und Verlag, 1996.

Lake, Kirsopp, trans. *The Apostolic Fathers.* Vol. 1. LCL. Cambridge: Cambridge University Press, 1912.

Lightfoot, J. B. *The Apostolic Fathers.* 2nd ed. 5 vols. Peabody, MA: Hendrickson, 1989.

Lietzmann, Hans. *A History of the Early Church.* Translated by B. L. Woolf. New York: Meridian Books, 1961.

Lotz, John-Paul. *Ignatius and Concord: The Background and Use of the Language of Concord in the Letters of Ignatius of Antioch.* Patristic Studies. New York: Lang, 2007.

Magie, David. *Roman Rule in Asia Minor to the End of the Third Century after Christ.* 2 vols. Princeton: Princeton University Press, 1950.

Martin, Dale B. *The Corinthian Body*. New Haven: Yale University Press, 1995.

Mitchell, Margaret M. *Paul and the Rhetoric of Reconciliation: An Exegetical Investigation of the Language and Composition of 1 Corinthians*. Louisville: Westminster John Knox Press, 1992.

Moles, J. L. "Dio Chrysostom: Exile, Tarsus, Nero and Domitian." *LMC* 8 (1983): 130–34.

Moulakis, Athanasius. *Homonoia: Eintracht und Entwicklung eines politischen Bewusstseins*. Schriftenreihe zur Politik und Geschichte 10. Leipzig: List, 1973.

Price, S. R. F. *Rituals and Power: The Roman Imperial Cult in Asia Minor*. Cambridge: Cambridge University Press, 1984.

Rogers, Guy M. *The Sacred Identity of Ephesos: Foundation Myths of a Roman City*. London: Routledge, 1991.

Schoedel, William R. "Ignatius, Epistles of." *ABD* 3:384–87.

———. *Ignatius of Antioch: A Commentary on the Letters of Ignatius of Antioch*. Hermeneia. Philadelphia: Fortress, 1985.

Shapiro, Alan. "Homonoia." *LIMC* 5:476–79.

Sheppard, A. A. R. "A Dissident in Tarsus? (Dio Chrysostom, *Or.* 66)." *LCM* 7 (1982): 149–50.

Sherwin-White, A. N. *The Roman Citizenship*. 2nd ed. Oxford: Clarendon, 1973.

Sieben, Herman J. "Die Ignatianen als Briefe." *VC* 32 (1978): 1–18.

Swain, Simon. *Hellenism and Empire: Language, Classicism, and Power in the Greek World, AD 50–250*. Oxford: Clarendon, 1996.

Thériault, Gaétan. *Le Culte d'Homonoia: Dans les cites grecques*. Quebec: Sphinx, 1996.

Vall, Gregory. *Learning Christ: Ignatius of Antioch and the Mystery of Redemption*. Washington, DC: Catholic University of America Press, 2013.

Weiss, Johannes, and Rudolf Knopf. *The History of Primitive Christianity*. Translated by Frederick C. Grant et al. 2 vols. London: Macmillan, 1937.

West, William C. "Hellenic Homonoia and the New Decree from Plataea." *GRBS* 18 (1977): 307–19.

Winter, Bruce W. *Philo and Paul among the Sophists*. SNTSMS 96. Cambridge: Cambridge University Press, 1997.

Contributors

Rev. Dr. Stephen C. Barton, Honorary Fellow, Department of Theology and Religion, Durham University and Honorary Research Fellow, Department of Religions and Theology, University of Manchester

Dr. Anna Sieges-Beal, Assistant Professor of Religious Studies, Gardner-Webb University

Dr. Max Botner, Associate Professor of Biblical Studies at William Jessup University (Rocklin, California) and Director of the Center for Bible Study

Rev. Dr. Andrew J. Byers, Tutor in New Testament, Ridley Hall, Cambridge

Prof. Dr. Carsten Claussen, Professor of New Testament, Theologische Hochschule Elstal

Rev. Dr. Kylie Crabbe, Senior Research Fellow, Institute for Religion and Critical Inquiry, Australian Catholic University

Rev. Dr. Robbie Griggs, Associate Professor of Systematic Theology, Covenant Theology Seminary, St. Louis, Missouri

Prof. James R. Harrison, Professor of Biblical Studies and Research Director, Sydney College of Divinity

Rev. Dr. Walter J. Houston, Emeritus Fellow of Mansfield College Oxford, and Honorary Research Fellow in the Department of Religions and Theology, University of Manchester

Dr. T. J. Lang, Senior Lecturer in New Testament Studies, University of Saint Andrews

364   Contributors

Dr. Jutta Leonhardt-Balzer, Honorary Senior Lecturer, School of Divinity, History and Philosophy, University of Aberdeen

Dr. John-Paul Lotz, Associate Professor of Church History and Historical Theology, School of Divinity, Regent University

Prof. Lynette Mitchell, Professor of Greek History and Politics, University of Exeter

Rev. Dr. Nicholas J. Moore, Academic Dean and Lecturer in New Testament, Cranmer Hall, Saint John's College, Durham University

Dr. Elizabeth E. Shively, Professor of Christian Scriptures, Baylor University's George W. Truett Seminary

Dr. Julien C. H. Smith, Associate Professor of Humanities and Theology, Valparaiso University

Dr. Alan J. Thompson, Senior Lecturer in New Testament Studies, Sydney Missionary and Bible College

Ancient Sources Index

Old Testament

Genesis	
1:1	15, 208
1:28–30	23
2:18	135
3:5	14–15
3:22	14
6:4	35
6:13–21	23
9:8–16	30
12–50	19
12:2	260
12:3	260, 268, 270, 274
14:18	30
14:18–20	19
15:12–16	22
17:7	23
18	20
21:33	19
22:18	268
29:31–30:24	28
32:22–32	20
32:26–29	26
33:20	19
35:2–4	19
35:7	19
35:16–20	28
46:8–27	28
49:1–28	28
49:25	35
Exodus	
1:1–5	28
1:7	28
3:1–15	22
6:2–3	23
6:7	23
12:40–42	29
14:12	38–39
16:13	108
19–24	18
19:8	106
19:16	108
19:17	108
20:3	187
21–22	329
22:20	187
24	18
24:7	26
29:14	108
29:45–46	23
30:10	314
32–34	18, 39
32:10	38, 39
32:12	38, 39, 41
32:14	38, 39
32:26	18
34:6	38–40
34:6–7	37–38, 43
Leviticus	
1:2	41
13:44–45	329
16:34	314
19	307, 317
19:2	185
19:17	174
19:17–18	173, 184

-365-

Leviticus (cont.)

19:18   171–75, 177, 180, 183–85, 188, 260, 273–74, 278, 306–7, 309
19:34   185
20   329
20:5   353

Numbers

1:5–16   29
1:20–42   29
1:47–48   29
5:2–3   329
5:3   110
15:30–31   329
16:46–50   26
19:11–13   188
26   29
27:12–23   199
28:8–9   26
32   29
34   29

Deuteronomy

4   187
4:29   187
4:32   18
4:32–40   18
4:34   17
4:35   17, 187
4:39   17, 134, 187
6   307, 317
6–11   17, 187
6:4   3, 6, 8, 15–16, 113, 171–73, 175, 181, 195–97, 206–12, 251, 260
6:4–5   174–75, 177, 181, 206–12, 302, 306, 317
6:4–6   209, 307
6:4–9   197, 207
6:5   16, 173, 177, 187–88, 303
6:7   308
6:8–9   172
7:1–6   17
7:9   17
12   29
12:14   29

17–22   329
18:13   185
19:15   330
23:15   110
27   30
27:4   30
27:13   30
27:13–14   30
27:26   265, 269–71, 274–75
28   26
30   26
30:15–20   26
32   15
32:8   15
32:8–9   35
32:12   187
32:15   173
32:39   187
33:5   105

1 Samuel

2:2   187
2:15   108
7:3–4   187

2 Kings

5:17   187
17   28
17:24–34   28
19:19

1 Chronicles

12:18   105–6
17:20   187

2 Chronicles

6:30   187

Ezra

1:1–4   36
4:1–2   28
4:2   25
4:3   105
9:1–2   25
10   25

Ancient Sources Index

10:7–8	329	148:13	187
Nehemiah		**Song of Songs**	
9:6	187	6:9	16
10:37	41		
13:28	27	**Isaiah**	
		1:16–20	325
Psalms		9:6–7	286
2:2	105, 226	11:1–9	286
4:8	187	11:11	227
4:9	226	13–23	33
12:6	292	29:14	249
17:31	187	32:15	223
18:10	226	37:16	187
19:19	187	37:20	187
24:1	328	41:21–24	14
32:15	187	43:10–12	223
33:4	226	44:8	187
36:38	226	44:24	187
48:3	226	45:1–5	36
48:11	226	45:5–6	187
54:15	226	45:14	187
54:55	353	45:21	187
68:18	292	46:9	187
70:10	226	49:6	223
71:18	187	55	43
72:7	286	55–56	43, 46
73:6	226	55:5	43
73:8	226	55:7	43
77:11	292	56	43
78:68	30	56:6–8	43
82	35	57:19	227
82:5	353	61:1–2	186
82:18	187	64:4	187
86:10	187	66:18–24	34
96	15		
97	15	**Jeremiah**	
97:8	226	4:17	34
101:23	226	9:23–24	249
110	175, 182	9:24	241
110:1	176, 313	18:8	46
121:3	226	32:37–47	211
132:1	226	46–51	33–34
135:4	187		
135:7	187		

368 Ancient Sources Index

Ezekiel	
4:3	105
11:14–21	24
11:17	25
11:18	24
11:20	24
25–32	34
28:3–4	14
28:9	14–15
33:11–17	325
33:21	24
33:23–29	24
33:24	24
33:25–26	24
33:27–29	24
34	6, 196–97, 199, 200, 202
34:11–13	221
34:22–23	221
34:23	199
36–37	25
37	6, 196–97, 199–202, 227
37:1–14	201
37:15–28	221
37:19	199
37:22	199
37:24	199

Daniel	
2	163
3:45	187
7:13	178
8	163

Hosea	
12	21
12:12–13	21

Joel	
1:2	40
1:3	41
1:13	40
1:14	40–41
1:18	41
2:12	40
2:12–14	38

2:12–17	37, 39–40
2:13	38–40
2:13–14	38
2:14	39, 45
2:15	40
2:16–17	41
2:27	187
2:28	37
4:9–16	37
4:17	37

Amos	
1:3–2:16	37

Jonah	
1:6	45
1:10	44
1:14	45
1:16	45
2:3–7	45
2:7	45
3	45
3:3–4:4	40
3:5	40–41
3:6	41
3:7	41
3:8	38, 41
3:8–10	38
3:9	38–39, 45
3:10	39
4:1	38
4:1–3	38
4:2	38–40, 42
4:3	39
4:10–11	42
4:12	42
4:17	42

Micah	
2:6	106
2:12	106
4	34

Zechariah	
7:5	40

Ancient Sources Index

8	34
8:19	40
9–12	206
9:1–8	34
9:9	206
13:7	206
14:8	206
14:9	205–6

Malachi

1:11	45
2:10	198

Deuterocanonical Books

Tobit

4:15	174

Wisdom

16:11	292

Sirach

17:14	174
18:2	187
19:13–17	174
20:2	184
28:1–7	184
33:5	187
50:25–26	28

1 Maccabees

8:1–16	221
8:16	221

2 Maccabees

4:5–6	221
7:37	187

1 Esdras

8:25	187

Pseudepigrapha

2 Baruch

48.24	155, 203

73.1–74.4	220

1 Enoch

72–82	117
74.10–11	117
74.12–13	117
74.13–16	117
75.1–2	117
78.15–16	117
82.4–6	117

2 Enoch

15.4	117

4 Ezra

11.40–42	94
13.12–13	220–21
13.39	220–21

Jubilees

6.17	314
6.32	117
7.20	173
20.2	173
36.4	173
36.7–8	173
49.7	314

Letter of Aristeas

132	187
228–235	175
281	292
291–292	286

Liber antiquitatum biblicarum

12.10	173

Psalms of Solomon

17.27	295

Sibylline Oracles

3.350–380	220–21
3.760	187
3.781–782	286

Ancient Sources Index

Testament of Benjamin

    3.3 — 173

Testament of Dan

    5.3 — 173, 306

Testament of Gad

    6.1–5 — 184

Testament of Issachar

    5.1–2 — 306

    5.2 — 173

    7.6 — 173

Testament of Levi

    18.9 — 295

Testament of Naphtali

    8.9–10 — 173

Dead Sea Scrolls

CD — 102–3

    III, 14 — 118

    IV, 20–21 — 106

    VI, 9 — 104

    VI, 19 — 108

    VI, 20 — 104

    VI, 20–VII, 5 — 185

    VII, 2–3 — 174

    VII, 6–7 — 108

    VIII, 4 — 108

    VIII, 6 — 104, 108

    VIII, 7 — 108

    VIII, 13 — 108

    VIII, 16 — 108

    VIII, 20 — 108

    VIII, 21 — 102, 104, 108

    IX, 2–8 — 184

    IX, 10–13 — 113

    IX, 11–12 — 113

    IX, 18 — 108, 109

    IX, 19 — 108, 109

    IX, 22 — 108, 109

    XII, 22–23 — 107

    XII, 22–XIII, 2 — 108

    XII, 22–XIII, 7 — 107–8

    XII, 23–XIII, 1 — 108

    XIII, 6 — 108

    XIII, 7 — 108

    XIII, 7–17 — 108

    XIII, 13 — 108

    XIII, 16 — 109

    XIV, 3 — 108, 114

    XIV, 3–4 — 108, 114

    XIV, 3–6 — 108, 114–15

    XIV, 3–18 — 108

    XIV, 8 — 109

    XIV, 8–9 — 108

    XIV, 8–12 — 115

    XIV, 8–17 — 115

    XIV, 11 — 109

    XIV, 13 — 109

    XV, 14 — 109

    XV, 15–17 — 110

    XVI, 2–4 — 109

    XIX, 18 — 104

    XX, 1 — 102, 104–5

    XX, 12 — 104, 108

    XX, 14 — 102, 105

    XX, 18 — 104

    XX, 32 — 102, 104–5

1QM

    I, 1 — 104

    I, 3 — 104

    I, 10 — 104

    I, 16 — 104

    III, 4 — 108

    XIII, 3 — 104

    XV, 4 — 104

    XV, 7 — 104

1QpHab

    XI, 2–8 — 118

1QS — 102, 103

    I, 1 — 104–5, 226

    I, 11–13 — 113

    I, 12 — 104–5

Ancient Sources Index

I, 14–15	118	VI, 21	105
I, 16	104–5	VI, 22	104
I, 16–II, 19	115	VIII, 1–5	109
II, 19	115	VIII, 5	104
II, 19–21	108	VIII, 16–17	105
II, 21–22	108	VIII, 26	104
II, 22	105	IX, 6	105
II, 24	105	IX, 7	107, 109
II, 26–III, 6	112	IX, 8	113
III, 2	109	IX, 12–26	109
III, 6	105		
III, 7	226	1Q14	106
III, 13	104		
III, 13–IV, 26	109, 356	1Q28a	102
III, 24–25	104	I, 4	109
IV, 5–6	104	I, 8–9	109
V, 1	105, 107	I, 18	104
V, 2	112	I, 26	104
V, 2–3	113	I, 27	104
V, 7	226	II, 1	105
V, 7–9	109	II, 2	104
V, 13	104, 112	II, 3–9	110
V, 24–VI, 1	184	II, 8–9	110
VI, 1–9	106, 107	II, 11	104
VI, 1–10	114	II, 11–22	116
VI, 2	114, 116	II, 17	104–5
VI, 2–3	113, 114	II, 18	104
VI, 3	104	II, 21	104–5
VI, 4	114, 116		
VI, 4–5	111	1Q28b	
VI, 6	112	IV, 26	104
VI, 7	104, 112	V, 6	104
VI, 8	104, 107, 114	V, 21	104–5
VI, 8–10	114–15		
VI, 8–13	111, 115	4Q37	15
VI, 10	104		
VI, 12	115	4Q174	111
VI, 12–20	109		
VI, 13–23	110	4Q252	105
VI, 14	110		
VI, 14–23	109	4Q259	104–5
VI, 15	105		
VI, 16–17	116	4Q266	108
VI, 20–21	116		
VI, 20	115–16	4Q267	108, 110

372 Ancient Sources Index

4Q268	108	15.417	290
		18.12–22	147
4Q271	108, 115	18.13	148
		18.18	148
4Q275	115	18.20	149
		18.21	148
4Q286	104	18.23	161, 220
		18.117	174
4Q280	104		
		Josephus, *Bellum judaicum*	
4Q320–321	117	1.10	158, 160
		1.25	158
4Q325	117	1.27	158, 160
		1.31–33	153
4Q394 (4QMMT)	111	2	148
		2.118	220
4Q496	104	2.119	149
		2.119–158	244
11Q19		2.119–166	147
LVII, 12–13	107	2.122–123	114
		2.122–127	149
Ancient Jewish Writers		2.123	149
		2.134	149
Josephus, *Antiquitates judaicae*		2.139	174
3.91	174–75	2.140	159
4	149, 155–57, 164	2.145	149
4.196–301	153	2.151–153	146
4.200	153, 155, 161	2.160–161	148
4.200–201	203, 250	2.162–165	148
4.201	153	2.162–166	244
4.203	153	2.166	149
4.210	151	2.215	230
4.212–213	172	2.294	165
4.223	156	2.345–401	160
4.224	156	2.352–355	157
4.297	157	2.358–387	226
8.13.5	187	2.360–361	159
10	163	2.380	226
10.203–210	163	2.388	226
10.210	163	2.390–391	157
10.267	164	2.433	220
10.277–280	164	2.568	159
10.281	163	3.142	159
13.70	153	3.171–175	159
13.171–173	147–48	3.186–188	159

Ancient Sources Index

3.271–275	159
3.352–354	159
3.496	158
4.369	158
4.623	159
5.71–72	158
5.194	290
5.278–279	158
5.367	163
5.368	159
5.372–373	160
5.377	159
5.390	159
5.396	159
5.402	159
5.415–416	160
5.441	158
5.443	159
6.109	158
6.215–216	160
6.249–253	157
7.431	153

Josephus, *Contra Apionem*

2	149, 152, 164
2.17	141
2.145–196	146
2.145–296	156
2.146	146
2.147	150
2.165–167	156
2.168	150, 162
2.169	150
2.170	147
2.171–174	151
2.176–177	151
2.178	151
2.179	151
2.180–181	151
2.185–187	156
2.189	151, 161
2.193	152, 203
2.196	149
2.198	152, 155
2.210	162

2.277	161
2.237	154
2.238–249	154
2.250	154
2.256–257	150
2.280–286	146
2.281	147, 150
2.283	147
2.287	150

Josephus, *Vita*

10–12	147–48
12	148

Philo, *De Abrahamo*

30	128
46	128
208	174, 181

Philo, *De aeternitate mundi*

21	131

Philo, *De agricultura*

54	132
49–50	132

Philo, *De cherubim*

83	134
119	134

Philo, *De confusione linguarum*

1	131
15	131
93	187
94	132
170–175	132
168–183	270

Philo, *De decalogo*

36–37	139
50–65	136
65	174
102–103	129
110	174
155	132

Ancient Sources Index

Philo, *De Deo*

11	129
46–48	131
82–83	136
148	136

Philo, *De ebrietate*

45	134
69	132
74	132
86–87	132
106–109	132

Philo, *De fuga et inventione*

68–72	270

Philo, *De gigantibus*

2–3	130
50–54	134

Philo, *De Iosepho*

86–87	293
157	293
164	293
174	293
269	286

Philo, *De mutatione nominum*

30–32	270

Philo, *De opificio mundi*

15	130
23	129
35	131
47–49	128
57	130
69–75	270
74–75	131
91	129
92–94	129
95	129
99	129
100	129
102	129
131	128

151–153	131
170	129
170–172	131
171	129
171–172	203
172	130

Philo, *De plantatione*

31	132
41	132
49–50	132

Philo, *De posteritate Caini*

12	134
64–65	129

Philo, *De praemiis et poenis*

162	140
163–165	140
165	140

Philo, *De sacrificiis Abelis et Caini*

59	135
118	134
134	134

Philo, *De somniis*

1.62–64	137

Philo, *De specialibus legibus*

1.14	134
1.17	137
1.20	134
1.30	134
1.52–53	138, 203
1.66	133
1.67	136, 155, 203
1.72	136
1.188	129
1.208	131
1.317	137
2.63	174, 183
2.146	314
2.165–167	137
2.167	137

Ancient Sources Index

375

3.124–126	140	Philo, *Quastiones et solutiones in Exodum*	
3.126	140	1.1	117
3.131	139		
3.155	140	Philo, *Quastiones et solutiones in Genesis*	
3.178	133	2.4	132
3.180	128		
4.141–142	172	Philo, *Legum allegoriae*	
4.159	138	1	355
		1.3	128
Philo, *De virtutibus*		1.44	133
34–35	137, 203	1.51	133
51	174	1.61	131
		1.100	132
Philo, *De vita contemplativa*		2.1	180
2	136	2.1–3	135
25	139	2.49	132
30	139	3.48	133
85	139	3.82	134
		3.105	134
Philo, *De vita Mosis*		3.126	133
1.80	128		
1.86	136	Philo, *Quis rerum divinarum heres sit*	
1.162	287	40	133
2.4	287, 293	92–95	135
2.36	293	93	136
2.43	293	149–150	117
2.189	293	183	135
2.100	134		
2.170–173	140	Philo, *Quod omnis probus liber sit*	
2.209–211	129	84	114, 174
		91	114
Philo, *In Flaccum*			
45	137	New Testament	
Philo, *Legatio ad Gaium*		Matthew	
117–118	139	1:22	183
144–147	92	1:23	182
147	286	2:15	183
149	286	2:17	183
157–162	139	2:23	183
209	139	5:1–7:29	183
306–308	136	5:17	183
366	139	5:20	184
		5:21–26	174, 184
		5:21–48	184

376 Ancient Sources Index

Matthew (*cont.*)

5:22	184
5:27–30	184
5:38–42	184
5:40–42	184
5:43–48	174, 185
5:44	189
5:48	185
6:14–15	184
10:37	182
10:39	182
12:7	182, 184
16:19	329
18:15	184
18:15–17	323
18:15–18	329
18:21–22	184
19:16–22	184
19:18–19	184
19:19	184
22:19	356
22:34–40	181–82
22:35	181
22:36	176, 181
22:36–38	171
22:36–40	306
22:37	181
22:37–39	210
22:38	181
22:39	182
22:40	182–83
22:41–46	182
23:3	184
23:23	184
28:19–20	185

Mark

2:1–12	178–79
2:1–3:6	178
2:7	175–76, 178–79
2:10	178–79
3:1–6	179
5:19–20	175
7:8	181
7:8–13	178

8:33	181
8:34–38	181
10:17–22	180
10:18	175–76, 178, 180
10:19	180
10:20	180
10:21	180
10:22	180
11:15–18	178
12:28	181
12:28–34	175–76, 181, 306
12:29	176
12:29–30	171, 175
12:29–32	172
12:30–31	210
12:31	177, 180
12:32	177
12:33	176–78, 188
12:34	173, 176, 178, 182
12:35	181
12:35–37	176
12:36	176, 178
12:37	176
12:38–40	178
12:39	178
12:41	178
12:41–44	178
14:27	206
14:64	178

Luke

1:32	186
1:47	186
2:1	218, 220
2:10	220
2:11	186, 220
2:14	220
2:26	186
3:1	218
3:4–6	220
4:14	186
4:18–19	186, 220
5:17	186
5:21	186–87
7:21–22	220

Ancient Sources Index

7:22	186	8:44	198
9:51	189	8:47	210
9:52	189	8:51	210
9:55	189	10	199, 211
10:1–20	189	10:16	196, 199–202, 342
10:22	189	10:17	210
10:25	181, 188–89	10:19	211
10:25–28	188, 306	10:30	3, 196–97, 200, 209
10:26	188	10:36	220
10:26–28	210	10:43	220
10:27–28	171	11	197, 201
10:28	188	11:16	233
10:29	188	11:48	201
10:36–37	188	11:49–52	196
20:41	181	11:52	202
20:41–44	186	12:10	206
22:24–26	228	12:15	206
23:2	219	12:18–24	233
24:18	321	13–17	306, 308
24:30	224	13:34	210, 306–7, 309
24:35	224	14:15	209
24:49	223	14:20	342
		14:21	209
John		14:23–24	209
1:1	308	14:28	209
1:12–13	208	15:12	210
1:17–18	208	15:17	210
1:18	204	16:27	209
1:45	212	16:32	202, 206
2:13–22	203	17	6, 195, 201–4, 206, 209, 211
5	198	17:3	202
5:44	187, 198, 202	17:5	202, 203
5:46	212	17:6	204
6:51–57	342	17:8	211
7:38	206	17:11	197, 204–5, 211, 306
8	198, 211	17:15–16	203
8:20	210	17:18	203
8:26	210	17:20–21	202
8:31	210	17:21–23	197, 211, 306
8:37	197	17:22	197, 203
8:38	210	17:22–23	341
8:40	210	17:26	204, 211
8:41	196–99, 200, 209	19:37	206
8:42	210	20:30–31	212
8:43	210		

Ancient Sources Index

Acts

1–2	223
1:1–11	223
1:1–2:41	226
1:2	224
1:3	223
1:5	223, 229
1:6	223, 225
1:6–8	227
1:8	223
1:10–11	227
1:14	217, 224–25, 231
1:15	217
1:21	225
1:24	224–25
2	222–27
2:1	217, 226, 341
2:2	227
2:5	227
2:11	227, 228
2:14	227
2:17	227
2:21	224–25, 227
2:22	227
2:25–33	223
2:30	222
2:31–32	222
2:33	222
2:33–35	223
2:33–36	223
2:34–36	222, 225
2:36	227
2:38	228, 229
2:38–41	224
2:39	227
2:40	224
2:41	223–24
2:42	217, 224–25
2:42–47	223–24, 226
2:44	217, 224–26
2:45	217, 225
2:46	224–25, 231
2:47	217, 223–26
4:24	217, 225, 231
4:32	217

4:32–37	217
4:34	217
5:1–11	217, 329
5:9	218
5:12	217, 231, 341
5:12–16	217
6:1–7	217
6:5	217
7:57	218
8:14–17	189
9:31	230
10–11	227–30
10:36	227–29, 232
10:38	228
10:42–43	228
10:43	228
10:45	229
10:46	228
11:1	229
11:1–2	229
11:1–3	229
11:1–18	229
11:15	229
11:16	229
11:17	229, 230
11:18	217, 227, 229
11:28	219
12	230–32
12:1	231
12:4	230
12:7	230
12:11	230
12:12	225
12:17	231–32
12:18–19	231
12:18–23	231
12:19–21	231
12:20	231
12:23	231–32
12:24	230–31
15	218, 230
15:2	230
15:22	218
15:25	217, 231
15:36–41	218

Ancient Sources Index

17:7	219	1 Corinthians	
17:26	30	1:1	246
18:2	219	1:2	239, 247
18:12	218–19	1:9	247
19:29	218	1:10	238, 254, 331
19:30–31	218	1:10–11	331
21:12–13	218	1:10–12	240
21:26–31	290	1:10–13	327
22:21	227	1:11	239, 254, 321
23:6–10	244	1:13	247
25:11–12	219	1:18	248
25:25	219	1:18–31	249
25:26	219, 228	1:18–4:21	240
27:1	219	1:19	249
27:35	224	1:21	249
28:31	219	1:24	249
		1:26	245–46, 254
Romans		1:26–29	252
1:7	314	1:27–28	249
1:24	277	1:29	241
3:27	277	1:30	249
3:28	277	1:31	241, 249
3:28–31	276	1:33	238
3:29	276	2:4–5	252
3:30	260, 276	2:6–13	252
3:31	277	2:7	248
5–8	296	3:1	254
5:12–19	277	3:3	246, 321
5:18	277	3:3–4	240
6:10	312	3:8	238
7:5	277	3:9	238–39
7:7	277	3:11	247
7:12	277	3:16	239
7:14	277	3:21	240
7:23	277	3:21–22	239, 241
8:4	278	4:1	248
8:5–8	277	4:6	238, 241, 254
9:3	330	4:7	241, 252
11:24	334	4:8	248
12–15	296	4:10	325
12:4	342	4:14–15	245
13:8	278	4:15	246
13:9	174, 278	4:18	241
14:14–21	277	4:19	241
16:17	323, 330–31	4:20	249

380 Ancient Sources Index

1 Corinthians (cont.)

5	332
5:1	239, 331
5:1–8	323
5:1–13	331
5:1–7:40	241
5:2	241, 331
5:3	331
5:3–5	246
5:5	331
5:6	241
5:6–8	331
5:7	247
5:9–13	332–33
5:11	238, 254, 332
6:5–8	254
6:6	333
6:9–10	249
6:12	247, 252
6:12–20	241
6:13	247
6:15–17	247
6:15–20	333
6:16	238
6:16–17	241
6:17	238
6:18	333
6:20	240, 251
7:4	241
7:5	238, 241
7:12–15	333
7:12–16	333
7:14	333
7:15	333
7:35	238
8:1	241
8:1–11:1	241, 250
8:4	238, 242
8:5–6	251
8:6	3, 238
8:9	242
8:10–12	242
8:11	247
8:12	247
8:13	254

9	254
9:1–2	246
9:21	247
9:23	254
9:24	238
10:1–11	245
10:1–13	251
10:3	238
10:4	238
10:8	238
10:11	284
10:14	251
10:17	238–39
10:22	251
10:23	252
10:26	328
10:27	333
10:31	240, 251, 255
10:32	251
11:1	247
11:2–16	242
11:2–14:40	242
11:5	238
11:5–6	243
11:10	253
11:14	243
11:16	243
11:17	238, 243, 252
11:17–34	242–43
11:18	226, 238–39, 243
11:18–22	243
11:19	336
11:20	226, 238, 243
11:23	247
11:33	238, 243
11:34	238, 243
12:1–4	244
12:1–14:40	244, 252
12:3	330
12:4	238, 252–53
12:4–6	253
12:5	238
12:6	238
12:7	252
12:8	238, 253

Ancient Sources Index

12:9	238, 252	15:20–28	247
12:10	253	15:35	244
12:11	238, 253	15:45	247
12:12	238–39, 253	15:49	247
12:12–13	245	15:50	249
12:12–26	253	15:51	248
12:13	238–39, 242, 250, 252, 254–55	15:54–57	244
12:14	238, 253	15:57	247–48
12:18	238	15:58	244, 247
12:19	238	16:2	238
12:20	238–39	16:16	238
12:24–25	244, 253	16:17	239
12:25	238	16:22	330
12:26	238, 254	16:22–24	247
12:27	247, 254	16:24	239
12:28	250, 252–53		
12:30	252–53	2 Corinthians	
12:31	252	2:5–11	323
12:31–14:1	255	5:18	341
13	254, 327	6:14–15	333
13:1	253	12:20	321
13:4	241		
13:4–5	244	Galatians	
13:12	255	1–2	261–63
13:13	244	1:4	284
14:2	248	1:6	260–61
14:3	244, 252	1:6–9	330
14:4	244	1:7	260–61
14:5	244, 252	1:8	261
14:12	244, 252	1:8–9	330
14:17	244	1:9	261
14:21–25	333	1:10	262, 264
14:23	238	1:11	262
14:26	238, 244, 252	1:12	262
14:27	238	1:13	262
14:31	238	1:15	262
14:33	244	1:16–22	262
14:37	247	1:23	262
14:40	242	2	263–65
15:1–2	247	2:3	263
15:1–58	244	2:4	263
15:3–9	247	2:5	263
15:9	246	2:7	263
15:12	244	2:8	263
15:12–19	247	2:9	263

Ancient Sources Index

Galatians (*cont.*)

2:13	264
2:14	264
2:15	264
2:16	264
2:17	264
2:18	264
2:19	265, 275
2:19–21	270
2:20	265, 275
2:21	265
3–4	265–72
3:1	265
3:5	265
3:5–7	265
3:6	265
3:8	260, 265, 267, 270
3:8–14	265, 267
3:8–18	265
3:10	265, 267, 272, 276
3:16	260, 268–70
3:17	268
3:18	268
3:19	260, 269–70
3:19–29	269
3:20	259, 269–70, 276
3:21	260, 270
3:22	260, 271, 277
3:24	272
3:25–26	272
3:26	272
3:28	242, 260, 269, 271, 272
3:29	271–72
4:3	271
4:4	272
4:9	271
4:10	271
5	273–76, 277
5:1	273
5:1–15	273–74
5:2	273
5:2–4	259
5:4	273
5:5	273
5:6	273

5:7–12	274
5:11	262
5:13	273–75
5:14	260–61, 273–74
5:14–15	174
5:15	274
5:16	275
5:16–26	274–76
5:17	274–75
5:18	275–77
5:21	275
5:22	260
5:23	260
5:24	275
5:25	275
5:26	274
6:5	275
6:8	275

Ephesians

1:3	293
1:10	285, 288
1:21	284, 298
2	316
2:1–10	288–89
2:6	297
2:11–17	291
2:11–22	288, 291
2:12	291
2:12–13	288
2:13	289, 291, 341–42
2:13–14	285
2:13–15	290
2:14	290–91, 294
2:15	283, 290–91
2:16	290–91
2:17	291
2:18	291–91
2:18–19	291
2:18–21	341–42
2:20	291
2:21	291
2:21–22	290–91
2:22	291
4	313

Ancient Sources Index

4:1	294	3:18–4:1	296, 298
4:1–6	358		
4:1–16	295–96	1 Timothy	
4:3	284, 292, 295, 342	1:20	323, 331
4:5	298	5:21	322
4:7	292		
4:8	292	Titus	
4:11	294	3:10	323
4:12–13	294		
4:13	342	Hebrews	
4:17–5:21	296	5:11–13	316
4:19	296	6	315
4:20	294	6:1–2	315
4:22	296	6:4	313
4:24	297	6:4–6	315
4:25	297	7:27	313
4:26	297	7:28	313
4:29	297	8:1	313
4:31	297	9:7	313–14
4:32	297, 341	9:11–12	314
5:1–2	297	9:12	313–15
5:3	296	9:24	315
5:5	296	9:26	313, 315
5:12	296	9:26–28	313
5:21–6:9	296, 298	10:2	313
		10:10	313
Colossians		10:10–14	314
1:20	284, 294	10:18	314
1:21–22	289	10:26	316
2:8	284	10:29	316
2:12	298	10:32	315
2:20	284, 298	10:32–34	316
3:1	298	12:26–27	313
3:1–3	297	13:24	314
3:5	296		
3:5–17	296	James	
3:6	298	1:4	304
3:8	297	1:5–8	305
3:10	294	1:7	303–4
3:11	284, 286, 298	1:8	303
3:12	294, 297	1:17	303–4
3:12–14	297	1:25	304
3:13	284	1:27	305
3:14	294	2	303, 305
3:15	297	2:1–13	304

384   Ancient Sources Index

James (cont.)		2:15–17	309
2:4	304	2:18–19	341
2:5	305	3:1	306
2:8	304	3:10–11	210
2:8–13	174	3:10–18	306
2:19	303	3:14	210
3:2	304	3:16–17	306
3:9–12	304	3:18	210
3:17	305	3:22–24	308
4:4	305	3:23	210, 306
4:8	303	4:7	210
4:12	303	4:7–12	306
5:9	304	4:11–12	210
5:12	304	4:16	306
5:16	304	4:16–21	306
		4:20–21	210
1 Peter		4:20–5:2	306
3	314	5:3	306
3:1	313		
3:8	342	2 John	
3:8–9	312	4	308
3:9	313	4–6	308
3:13–17	313	5	210, 306
3:15	313	5–6	309
3:16	313	6	306–8
3:18	312	7–11	309
3:20	312	10	330
3:20–21	312	11	307, 330
5:13	314		
		3 John	
2 Peter		3–4	308
1:3	312	10	330
1 John		Jude	
1:1	308	3	309–12
1:3	307	3–5	312
1:6	307	4	310
1:7	307	5	309–10, 314
2:3–6	309	12	310
2:5	306	15	310
2:7	307	19	310
2:7–8	307	20	310
2:9–11	309		
2:10	210, 306	Revelation	
2:15	306	2:15	352

Ancient Sources Index

Rabbinic Works

b. Shabbat
31a	183

m. Berakot
1.1–4	172
47	172

Numbers Rabbah
18.7	155

Early Christian Writings

1 Clement
1.1	321, 323–24, 328
1.1–2.8	324
1.2	326
2.2	322, 324
2.6	321, 324
3.2	321–22
3.3	322, 324
3.4	322, 325
4.1–7	325
4.9	325, 336
4.10	336
4.10–13	325
4.12	321
4.13	336
5.4	325
5.5	321
5.5–7	325
6.1–2	325
6.4	321
7.4	325
7.5	325
7.6–7	325
7.7	336
8.1–5	325
9.1	321
9.4	322, 326, 336, 342, 353
10.1–7	326
10.2	335
10.7	326
11.1	326
11.1–2	336
11.2	322, 342, 353
12.1–8	326
13	326
14.1	322
14.2	321, 326
15.1	322, 326
16.1–17	326
16.17	332
17.1	326, 336
17.3	326
17.3–4	326
17.5–6	326, 336
18.1–17	326, 336
19.1–3	326
20.1–12	326
20.3	322, 326, 342, 353
20.4	326
20.9	326
20.10	322, 326, 353
20.11	322, 326
21.1	322
21.7	322
22.5	326
30.3	322, 353
31.4	326, 335
34.7	322, 342, 353
35.5	321
42	327
42–44	324
42.4–5	327
43.1–6	336
43.2	321
43.6	322
44.1	321, 327
44.2	327
44.3	327
44.4	327
44.6	327
45.1–8	327
45.6–7	336
46.5	321–22, 327, 331–32
46.7	321
46.9	321
47	324

Ancient Sources Index

1 Clement (cont.)

47.1–4	332
47.3	322
47.3–4	322
47.4	322
47.5	322
47.6	321, 324, 327
47.6–7	328
48–53	327
48.1	322
48.6	322
49–50	327
49.5	321–22, 327, 353
50.2	322
50.5	322, 353
51.1	321–22, 327, 331–32
51.3	321
52.1–4	336
53.2–5	336
54	321, 326, 332
54–55	322
54.1	321
54.1–3	322
54.1–4	327–28, 334
54.2	321, 322
54.3	336
55.1	321, 334–35
55.2	334
55.3–6	334
56	322
56.12	322
56.13	322
57.1	321, 324, 335
60.4	322, 342, 353
61.1	322, 353
62.2	322
63.1	321
63.2	322, 342, 353
63.4	322
65.1	322, 342, 353

Augustine, De civitate Dei

5.24	2

Barnabas

18–20	356

Clement of Alexandria, *Excerpta ex Theodoto*

86	356

Clement of Alexandria, *Stromateis*

1.38.8	321
4.105	321
4.111.1	321
6.65.3	321

Didache

1–6	356
1.2	174

Eusebius, *Historia ecclesiastica*

4.22.1	321
4.23.11	321

Ignatius, *To the Ephesians*

1.3	354
3.1	355
4.1	359
4.2	359
6.2	354
13.1	343, 359
14.1–2	355
16.2	353
20.2	359

Ignatius, *To the Magnesians*

1.1	355
1.2–3	343
2.1	354–56
3.1	356
4.1	356
5.2	356
6.1	343, 357
6.2	357
7.1	355, 358
7.2	358
8–10	358
8.1	355

Ancient Sources Index

387

8.2	355	Aeschylus, *Prometheus vinctus*	
10.3	353	867–869	66
11.1	355, 358		
13.1	358	Aeschylus, *Supplices*	
13.2	343	8	68
		16–19	67
Ignatius, *To the Philadelphians*		29–30	68
inscr.	359	71	67
15.2	343	78–82	68
		104–105	68
Ignatius, *To the Romans*		120–121	67
5.1	354	155	67
		210–223	68
Ignatius, *To the Trallians*		234–237	67
3.3	355	235	68
7.1	353, 354	274–276	67
7.2	354, 356	291–324	67
9.1	353	325–326	67
12.1	343	354–358	68
		426–427	68
Ignatius, *To the Smyrnaeans*		618–620	68
4.1	354	632	67
		652	67
Irenaeus, *Adversus haereses*		719–720	67
3.3.3	321	836–841	68
		884	68
Justin, *Apologia i*		893–894	68
61.12	315	903–904	68
		909	68
Origin, *Commentarii in evangelium Joan-*		921–923	68
nis		972–973	67
6.279	335		
		Appian, *Bella civilia*	
Tertullian, *Adversus Judaeos*		1.26	91
7	227		
		Archytas, *On Law and Justice*	
Tertullian, *Apologeticus*		4.7.61	287
34.1	227		
		Aristophanes, *Lysistrata*	
Greco-Roman Literature		1128–1134	59
Aelius Aristides, *Orationes*		Aristophanes, *Ranae*	
23–25	91	717	356
24	221		
24.31	221		

388 Ancient Sources Index

Aristotle, *Athēnaīn politeia*
40.3 — 345

Aristotle, *Ethica nicomachea*
1179–1181 — 293

Aristotle, *Physica*
20 — 355
222a — 355

Aristotle, *Politica*
1284a.3–11 — 293

Arrian, *Anabasis*
1.12.1 — 69
7.8–9 — 80
7.11 — 80
7.11.1–2, 6 — 80
7.16.4 — 69

Caesar, *Bellum gallicum*
1.1.3 — 82

Calpurnius Siculus, *Eclogue*
1.42 — 221
1.42–48 — 93
1.46–47 — 221
1.57 — 221
1.64 — 221
4.6 — 221
4.99 — 221
4.146 — 221

Cicero, *De haruspicum responso*
60–61 — 91

Cicero, *De inventione rhetorica*
2.168 — 77

Cicero, *De Lege agraria*
3.4 — 91

Cicero, *De legibus*
1.22–39 — 77
3.28 — 91

Cicero, *De officiis*
1.35 — 87
2.22.27 — 91–92
2.8.26–27 — 89

Cicero, *De republica*
1.49 — 91
2.42.69 — 91
2.69 — 91

Cicero, *Epistulae ad Atticum*
1.17.8–10 — 91
1.18.3 — 91

Cicero, *In Catalinam*
1.31 — 77
4.15 — 91
4.17.15 — 92

Cicero, *Orationes philippicae*
4.14 — 91
8.15 — 77
8.8 — 91

Cicero, *Pro Cluentio*
152 — 91

Cicero, *Pro Lege manilia*
17 — 77

Cicero, *Pro Murena*
1 — 91
10.22 — 89
51 — 77
78 — 91

Cicero, *Epistulae ad Quintum fratrem*
1.1.34 — 82

Demosthenes, *De corona*
164 — 345

Dinarchus, *In Demosthenem*
1.110 — 78

Ancient Sources Index

Dio Cassius, *Historiae romanae*

55.8.9	92
56.25	92
62.20.4–6	232

Dio Chrysostom, *Orationes*

2.55–56	295
2.77	295
23.3	348
34.19	295
38	347, 353
38–41	91
38.2	349
38.5	350
38.6	349
38.8	349
38.11	349–50
38.15	349
38.16	350
38.17	349–50
38.18	350
38.26	350
38.27–28	350
38.29	349
38.29–30	350
38.31	351
38.34	351
38.35	350–51
38.36	351
38.38	351
38.39	351
38.43	350
39.2–4	348
40	347

Diodorus Siculus, *Historiae*

16.50	80
17.109	80
18.4.4	220–21, 289
18.4.6	289
19.1.1–8	158
37.1.1–6	158
37.29.5–30.2	158
40.4	226

Dionysius of Halicarnassus, *Antiquitates romanae*

2.2.2	221

Diotogenes, *On Kingship*

4.7.62	292

Ecphantus, *On Kingship*

4.7.65	293

Einsiedeln Eclogues

2.22–24	221

Epictetus, *Diatribai (Dissertationes)*

4.1.12	228

Hellanicus of Lesbos, (*FGrHist* 4)

F101	63

Heraclitus, DK22

B50	69

Herodotus, *Historiae*

1.101	220
1.103	220
1.134	80
1.146	62
1.167.1–2	57
2.152.4–154.3	65
2.160	59
3.82	212
4.147.4	66
5.22	58
5.97	64
7.150	64
7.61	64
8.137–139	58
8.144.2	55

Hesiod, *Theogonia*

881–886	61

Hesiod, Fragments

frag. 127	65
frag. 137	65

Ancient Sources Index

Hesiod, *Opera et dies*
668   61

Homer, *Iliad*
3   61
9.382–384   65
12.310–321   61

Homer, *Odyssey*
4.81–85   65
4.226–232   65
14.257–286   65

Horace, *Carmina*
1.2.50   92
1.2.50–53   82
1.12.33–60   82
1.35.25–40   82
1.37   82
3.3.37–48   82
3.5   82
3.14   82
4.2.33–36   82
4.14   82, 226
4.15   82

Horace, *Epistulae*
1.2.6–16   221
2.1.250–257   82

Horace, *Epodi*
9   82
16.63–66   221

Horace, *Carmen saeculare*
29–32   93
54–60   82

Isocrates, *Antidosis*
77   345

Isocrates, *Evagoras*
45   292

Isocrates, *Nicocles*
41   286–87

Isocrates, *Panathenaicus*
13   345
217   345

Isocrates, *Panegyricus*
141   345

Livy, *Ab urbe condita*
1.8.1   77
2.32.8–12   77
5.27.11   87
26.16.9   77

Lucan, *De Bello Civile (Pharsalia)*
1.1–3   221

Lysias, *Orationes*
18.17   90

Marcus Aurelius, *Meditations*
6.44   77

Martial, *Epigramata*
5.19.1–2   288
5.19.6   288

Mimnermus, (*FGrHist* 578)
F5   63

Musonius Rufus, *Dissertationes*
64.10–15   287

Ovid, *Fasti*
1.709–714   93
1.709–722   93
3.881–882   93
4.857–858   226

Ovid, *Metamorphoses*
1.198–201   221
15.746–870   221
15.877   221

Ancient Sources Index

15.32–30	93	Pliny, *Panegyricus*	
		94.2	288
Ovid, *Tristia*			
2.225–36	82	Plutarch, *Ad principem ineruditum*	
4.2.1–74	82	3 (780d)	287
Petronius, *Satyrica*		Plutarch, *Alexander*	
119.1–18	94	3.5	59
119.27–36	94	30.12	83
		71	80
Pindar, *Nemeonikai*			
10.1, 13–14	66	Plutarch, *Camillus*	42–45
Pindar, *Olympionikai*		Plutarch, *De Alexandri magni fortuna aut*	
Frags. 52d.23	57	*virtute*	
1.116	57	5–6 (329a–b)	220–21
1.118	57	6 (329c)	288
3.10–15	56	6 (329e)	77
Plato, *Phaedrus*		Plutarch, *Quomodo adulator ab amico*	
253	294	*internoscatur*	
		2 [49e]	356
Plato, *Respublica*			
2.372e	78	Plutarch, *Lycurgus*	2
5.464b	78		
5.473d	293	Plutarch, *Numa*	
5.556e	78	20.8	293
Plato, *Theaetetus*		Plutarch, *Praecepta gerendae rei publicae*	
176	294	10 (805e)	348
177	294	19 (816a)	348
Pliny, *Naturalis historia*		Plutarch, *Solon*	2
2.18	83		
2.80.190	82	Plutarch, *Tiberius et Caius Gracchus*	
3.39	82	17.6	91
3.39–42	77	9.6	226
3.120	57		
5.132–133	226	Polybius, *Historiae*	89
7.98	226	1.1.5	89, 226
16.3–4	83	6.11–18	221
27.2–3	82	6.18.1–4	221
30.12	83		
35.6.93–94	86	Propertius, *Elegiae*	
37.201	77	2.10	82

392 Ancient Sources Index

Propertius, Elegiae (cont.)

3.4	82
4.6	82

Quintus Curtius Rufus, *Historiae Alexandri Magni*

6.3.2–3	226
10.2.12–30	80

Res gestae divi Augusti

12–13	92–93
12.2	93
13	92–93, 288
15–24	86
25–27	86
25–33	79, 86, 226
26.1	92
28	86
29–30	86
30.1	92
31–33	86–87
32	86
32.1	87
32.3	86–87, 92
34–35	86
34.1	92
34.2	86–87
34.3	92

Seneca, *Apocalyntosis Claudii*

10	288

Seneca, *De clementia*

1.1.1	295
1.5.1	77
1.6.3	295
1.22.2–3	95
2.1.3–2.2	287, 295
2.2.1	77

Seneca, *De Otio*

1	77

Statius, *Silvae*

1.6.39–50	288

4.1.5–8	221
4.2.1–2	221
4.3.114–117	221
4.5.45–48	83

Statius, *Thebais*

1.214–247	221

Strabo, *Geographica*

1.1.16–18	226
5.1.7	57
5.2.3	57
9.3.8	57
14.4.2–3	70

Suetonius, *Augustus*

22	288

Suetonius, *Tiberius*

20	92
37	288

Suetonius, *Vespasianus*

11	295

Tacitus, *Agricola*

2	82
30	94, 227

Tacitus, *Annales*

3.26	150
3.26–28	150
11.23–25	88
11.24	88
14.15.8	232
16.22.1	232

Tacitus, *Historiae*

1.12	158
1.28	158
1.83–84	158
15.1.2	76

Thucydides, *Peloponnesian War*

2.99.3	58

Ancient Sources Index

6.72	157	*CIL*	
8.75.2	344	1.231	92
8.93.3	344	13.1668	88

Velleius Parterculus, *Historiae Romanae* · *EGF*

2.89.1–4	92	T1 Davies	63

Vergil, *Aeneid* · *GIBM*

1.257–296	221	3.443	345
1.286–294	288	3.600	345
6.780–782	226	4.894	353
6.781–783	221		
6.788–796	221	*IG*	
6.791–797	288	1.71.2.156–157	70
6.851–853	82		
8.714–858	226	*InvM*	
10.6–15	221	18–87	70
12.189–194	221		
12.820–840	221	*OGIS*	
		666.2–7	90

Vergil, *Eclogae*

4.4–7	221	SEG	
4.11–14	295	30.1119	345
4.15–17	92	42.1012	345

Vergil, *Georgica*

1.24–42	221
1.463–468	295

Vitruvius, *De architectura*

2.praef. 5	82
9.praef. 2	82

Xenophon, *Cyropaedia*

1.4.27	80
2.2.31	80

Xenophon, *Memorabilia*

4.4.16	90

Greco-Roman Inscriptions

BMC

Ionia 111, 407	357
Ionia 174, 106	357

Modern Authors Index

Aasgaard, Reidar 254
Achtemeier, Paul J. 312
Afterman, Adam 132
Alesso, Marta 133
Allan, John A. 288, 293
Allen, Leslie C. 38
Allen, O. Wesley, Jr. 230–31
Allison, Dale C. 173, 181, 183
Andersen, Francis I. 16
Appold, Mark L. 3, 198
Arnim, Heinrich von 348
Arnold, Russell C. D. 110
Arnou, René 133
Assmann, Jan 35
Augenstein, Jörg 198, 228
Avemarie, Frederich 270
Badian, Ernst 76, 80–81
Bainbridge, William Sims 101–2
Baker, Cynthia M. 190
Baldry, H. C. 78, 82
Barclay, John 147, 150–52, 154, 156, 161–62, 250, 252, 259, 262–65, 267, 270, 273, 277, 292, 296
Barnard, Leslie W. 354
Baron, Lori 176, 196, 198–99, 203, 205, 207, 209, 210, 306
Barrett, C. K. 204, 208–09, 224, 226, 231
Barry, William D. 348
Bartholomä, Philipp F. 312
Barton, Stephen C. 196, 207
Bateman, Herbert 310–11
Bauckham, Richard 106, 113, 175, 198, 200, 218, 310–11
Baumgarten, Joseph M. 103–5, 111, 185
Bauer, Walter 337, 352, 358

Beckwith, Roger T. 116
Behm, Johannes 297
Ben Zeev, Miriam Pucci 290
Benedict XVI 343
Bennett, Chris 117
Bennet, John 60
Béranger, Jean 77–78, 83
Berchman, Robert M. 130
Bergler, Siegfried 38–39, 41
Bernstein, Moshe J. 104, 109
Berquist, Jon L. 43
Berry, Wendell 296
Beutler, Johannes 3, 198, 205
Beyerle, Stefan 105
Bilde, Per 163
Birnbaum, Ellen 138
Bock, Darrell L. 222
Boer, Martinus C. de 260, 267, 270–71, 273
Boesch, Paul 57
Bonazzi, Mauro 128
Borgen, Peder 127–28
Borza, Eugen N. 59
Bosworth, A. B. 76, 80–81
Bowe, Barbara E. 323
Bowie, Ewen L. 63
Brant, Jo-Ann 204
Brent, Allen 344, 358
Brisson, Luc 129
Bromwich, James 83, 85
Brown, Raymond E. 204, 306–8
Broyles, Craig 47
Bruchet, Julien 83
Bruno, Christopher R. 3, 260, 276
Brunt, Peter A. 349

Modern Authors Index

Buckwalter, H. Douglas   222, 227
Buck, Carl Darling   70
Buell, Denise Kimber   190
Burton, Ernest DeWitt   266
Byers, Andrew J.   152, 162, 196, 200, 202–3, 208, 302, 306
Bynum, William Randolph   206
Cadbury, Henry J.   226
Calabi, Francesca   129, 135
Calligas, P. G.   53
Camporeale, Giovannangelo   58
Carr, David M.   20–21
Cassidy, Richard J.   219
Charlesworth, James H.   105–6, 109, 155, 185, 286
Christesen, Paul   55–56
Ciampa, Roy E.   246, 248
Claussen, Carsten   104
Collins, C. John   268
Collins, John J.   101–3, 107, 114, 118, 141, 286, 290
Colvin, Stephen   55
Congrès, Anne Roth   83–85
Conzelmann, Hans   219
Cooley, Alison E.   76, 86, 92–93
Cornwell, Hannah   75
Cotton, Hannah   117
Coutts, Joshua   205–6
Crabbe, Kylie   148, 160, 163
Crane, Andrew   75
Crawford, Sidnie White   113
Crenshaw, James L.   38
Crossley, James   184
Cunningham, Scott   231
Curty, Olivier   70
Dahmen, Ulrich   104, 112
Davies, Philip R.   27
Davies, W. D   181, 183
Davis, William Stearns   88
Davila, James R.   115, 173
Desideri, Paolo   348
Dewey, Joanna   179
Dibelius, Martin   302
Donahue, Paul J.   353
Donaldson, Terence L.   183, 185

Dor, Yonina   25
Douglas, Mary   115
Dowling, Melissa B.   87
Dozeman, Thomas B.   21, 39
Dupont, Jacques   217
Eastman, Susan Grove,   294
Edelman, Diana V.   44
Eder, Brigitta   56
Elliott, John H.   304–5
Elliott, Mark W.   259, 262, 275
Engberg-Pedersen, Troels   147, 250, 274
Eshel, Esther   117
Eubank, Nathan   329
Evans, Craig A.   3, 43, 172–73, 218, 228, 267
Fabry, Heinz-Josef   104–5
Faust, Avraham   27
Fear, Andrew   82–83
Feldman, Jacob   336
Feldman, Louis H.   153–55
Ferris, I. M.   84
Filtvedt, Jakob   316
Finkelstein, Israel   27
Fitzmyer, Joseph A.   225–26
Flint, Peter   102
Foster, Paul   172, 181
France, R. T.   177
Franke, Peter R.   353, 357
Frankemölle, Hubert   304
Frey, Jörg   104, 107, 141–42
Fuglseth, Kåre   127–28
Gaertner, Jan Felix   87, 335
Gathercole, Simon J.   227
Gaventa, Beverly Roberts   259, 261, 264
Gehrke, Hans-Joachim   344
Gelzer, Matthias   79
Gerber, Christine   146, 161–62
Gerhardsson, Birger   3
Gericke, Jaco   14–15
Geus, Klaus   69, 89
Giangiulio, Maurizio   63
Giblin, Charles H.   269
Gieschen, Charles A.   205
Gilbert, Gary   226
Gillihan, Yonder Moynihan   106, 334

Modern Authors Index

Goodblatt, David	140	Jacquemin, Anne	57
Goodenough, Erwin R.	287	Jamieson, R. B.	315
Gordon, Benjamin D.	334	Jamzadeh, Parivash	81
Gorman, Michael J.	203	Jantsch, Torsten	220
Gorman, Vanessa B.	62	Janzen, J. Gerald	211
Grabbe, Lester L.	25, 54	Jeffrey, Lilian H.	56
Green, Joel B.	186, 220	Jipp, Joshua W.	285
Greenfield, Jonas	117	Johansson, Daniel	175
Gribetz, Sarit Kattan	172	Johnson, Luke Timothy	226
Griffin, Miraim T.	150	Jokiranta, Jutta M.	101–2
Gould, John	54	Jones, Christopher Price	347–48,
Gross, Andrew	117	350–51	
Guerra, Anthony J.	138	Jonge, Marinus de	173
Guthrie, Kenneth Sylvan	287	Joubert, Stephan	263
Haenchen, Ernst	219, 226	Judge, E. A.	76–77, 88, 92
Hafemann, Scott	311	Kahn, Charles H.	65
Hall, Jonathan	62–64	Kampmann, Ursula	346–47
Harding, G. Lankester	112	Keener, Craig S.	208, 217
Harl, Kenneth W.	357	Keesmaat, Sylvia C.	296–98
Harrington, Hannah K.	111	Kim, Seyoon	220
Harris, Bruce F.	350	Kindt, Julia	53
Harrison, James R.	76, 79, 81–83, 85,	Kirk, Geoffrey S.	65
87, 240, 242, 245		Klauck, Hans-Josef	232
Hay, David M.	182	Klawans, Jonathan	111, 158, 178, 188
Hays, Christopher M.	225	Klein, Martin	304
Hays, Richard B.	182–85, 200, 208,	Klijn, A. F. J.	155
245–46, 260, 267		Kloppenborg, John S.	239
Hayward, C. T. R.	108, 113, 119, 210	Knibb, Michael A.	103
Hempel, Charlotte	103, 106, 108, 110,	Knopf, Rudolf	353
113, 115		Knoppers, Gary	25, 27–29, 30
Herman, Gabriel	54	Koester, Helmut	337
Hensel, Benedikt	25, 27–28	Koet, Bart J.	186
Hewitt, J. Thomas	269	Konradt, Matthias	185–86
Hoehner, Harold W.	283	Kooij, Arie van der	107
Hofius, Otfried	179	Kreitzer, Larry L.	86, 90
Horbury, William	249	Kugel, James L.	174, 184
Horrell, David G.	207, 237, 253, 272,	Kugler, Robert A.	102
302, 313		Kyrieleis, Helmut	56
Horsley, Richard	220	Lake, Kirsopp	226, 359
Hoskyns, Edwyn C.	209	Lakey, Michael J.	237, 242
Houston, Walter J.	19, 22, 28	Lampe, Peter	324, 337–38
Howell, Justin R.	228, 232	Lane Fox, Robin	60
Hughes, Philip Edgcumbe	315	Lang, Bernhard	18
Hurtado, Larry	337	Lang, T. J.	323, 332
Instone-Brewer, David	172	Lee, John J. R.	3, 175

Modern Authors Index

Lee, Michelle V. 77
Lemos, Irene 61, 63
Lendon, J. E. 79
Leonhardt-Balzer, Jutta 139, 141–42
Lewis, David 60, 65
Lietzmann, Hans 353
Lieu, Judith M. 103, 210
Lincoln, Andrew T. 205, 237, 283, 298
Lindemann, Andreas 328
Lobur, John Alexander 76
Löhr, Hermut 316
Lohse, Eduard 105
Lona, Horacio E. 328
Lonergan, Bernard 322
Lopez, Davina C. 82
Lotz, John Paul 90, 347–48
Lutz, Cora E. 287
Luz, Ulrich 183
Mac Sweeney, Naoise 62
Macaskill, Grant 204
MacDonald, Nathan 13, 15–17, 187
Macintosh, A. A. 32
Magie, David 350
Magness, Jodi 112
Magonet, Jonathan 41
Maier, Johann 104–5
Malina, Bruce J. 204
Malkin, Irad 54, 57, 60, 62
Manning, Gary T. 199
Marcus, Joel 3, 172, 175–76, 178, 180, 196
Markschies, Christoph 337
Martin, Dale B. 241, 253, 331, 353
Martyn, J. Louis 260, 264, 267, 270, 275
Mason, Steve 146, 148–49, 159–60
Matlock, R. Barry 260
Matthews, Lydia 148
Mauriac, Henry M. de 76
Mazarakis Ainian, Alexander 52
McCullough, David 2
McFarland, Orrey 262
McKnight, Scot 205
McMatthew, A. Keil 75
Meier-Brüger, Michael 61
Meiggs, Russell 60, 65

Menken, Maarten J. J. 186, 206
Merkelbach, Reinhold 64–65
Metso, Sarianna 103
Michaels, J. Ramsey 202, 204–5
Milgrom, Jacob 111, 174, 188
Miller, Margaret C. 66
Mitchell, Lynette 55, 58, 60, 65–66, 221
Mitchell, Margaret M. 238, 240, 245, 253, 323–24, 330–31, 354
Moatti, Claudia 77
Moberly, R. W. L. 16, 19–20, 207–8
Moffitt, David M. 314
Moles, J. L. 348
Moloney, Francis J. 209
Momigliano, Arnaldo 91
Moo, Douglas J. 304–05
Moore, Nicholas J. 313–16
Morgan, Catherine 56, 64
Morpurgo Davies, Anna 55
Morris, Ian 61
Moulakis, Athanasius 344
Myers, Alicia D. 206, 208, 306–7
Naiden, F. S. 178
Nielsen, Thomas Heine 56, 58
Newbigin, Lesslie 298
Newsom, Carol A. 110
Neusner, Jacob 111, 141, 148
Nogalski, James 37, 45–46
Nordgaard, Stefan 270
Novenson, Matthew V. 262, 285
Nybakken, Oscar E. 77, 82
O'Donovan, Oliver 275
Oertelt, Friederike 139
Osborne, Robin 73
Painter, John 307
Pao, David W. 222–23, 227, 231
Penner, Todd C. 303
Perkins, Pheme 307
Perlman, Paula 57
Peterson, Erik 3
Pickett, Raymond 219
Pittet, Armand 76
Popham, Mervyn R. 53
Porter, Stanley E. 3, 218, 303
Price, S. R. F. 347, 351

398 Modern Authors Index

Proctor, Mark A. 189
Pury, Albert de 21–22
Queller, Kurt 179
Qimron, Elisha 106, 109
Rabinowitz, Peter J. 306
Rad, Gerhard von 14, 45
Rajak, Tessa 146–47, 151–52, 160–61, 163
Ramage, Edwin S. 87
Raven, John E. 65
Regev, Eyal 101–4, 107, 109, 159
Reinhartz, Adele 197
Reese, Ruth Anne 312
Rhodes, Peter J. 59
Ridderbos, Herman 198
Rigsby, Kent J. 70
Robinson, James M. 337
Rogers, Guy M. 351
Rohrbaugh, Richard L. 204
Rolland, Henri 83, 85
Romano, David G. 55
Romm, James S. 65
Rosner, Brian S. 246, 248
Rossini, Orietta 93
Rost, Leonhard 104
Rowe, C. Kavin 186, 219–20, 227–28, 232
Rüggemeier, Jan 175
Rüpke, Jörg 116
Rutherford, Ian 75, 70, 141
Sackett, L. Hugh 53
Sacks, Kenneth S. 158
Sanders, E. P. 259–60, 264–67
Saputra, Brury Eko 199
Schart, Aaron 38
Schiffman, Lawrence H. 106, 111, 118
Schmid, Konrad 20–22
Schmidt, Francis 111
Schmithals, Walter 231
Schoedel, William R. 352–56
Schofield, Alison 102
Schofield, Malcolm 65
Schütz, John H. 277
Schwartz, Daniel R. 105, 142, 185, 230
Schewe, Susanne 259, 273

Schnackenburg, Rudolf 307
Scott, James M. 267
Scott, Michael 56
Seccombe, David 225
Sellin, Gerhard 290
Shapiro, Alan 346
Sheppard, A. A. R. 348, 352
Sheridan, Ruth 197
Sherk, Robert K. 90
Sherwin-White, A. N. 350
Sieben, Herman J. 354–55
Siewert, Peter 56
Silberman, Neal Asher 27
Skard, Eiliv 75, 78
Skarsten, Roald 127–28
Smalley, Stephen 306–7
Smith, Julien C. H. 285–86, 188, 293–96
Smith, Mark S. 34–35
Smith, Morton 18
Sprinkle, Preston M. 269
Squire, Michael 77
Stark, Rodney 101–2
Sterling, Gregory E. 157
Stern, Sacha 116, 118
Stökl Ben Ezra, Daniel 108, 113, 116
Stone, Michael E. 117–18
Strauss, Mark L. 222
Strazicich, John 38–39
Strothmann, Meret 116
Sumney, Jerry L. 286, 298
Swain, Simon 348–49, 351–52
Sydenham, Edwin Allen 84–85
Syme, Ronald 158
Talbert, Charles H. 283, 292, 294
Tan, Kim Huat 3
Talmon, Shemaryahu 105, 117–18
Tarn, W. W. 76, 79–80, 88
Taylor, Joan E. 109
Taylor, Walter F. 75, 89
Temelini, Mark A. 75, 91
Thériault, Gaétan 90, 344
Theissen, Gerd 243
Thiessen, Matthew 176, 196, 261, 329
Thomas, G. G. 76, 81

Modern Authors Index

Thompson, Alan J. 162, 217–18, 220–21, 223, 225–26, 228, 232
Thompson, James W. 313
Thompson, Marianne Meye 203–4
Trible, Phyllis 41
Turner, Max B. 222
Unnik, W. C. van 323
Vall, Gregory 342–43, 359
Van de Mieroop, Marc 52
Van Leeuwen, Raymond 37
Van Seters, John 19
VanderKam, James 102, 106, 111, 113, 118, 173
Veijola, Timo 18
Verseput, Donald J. 303
Vlassopoulos, Kostas 54
Vögtle, Anton 310
Waaler, Erik 3, 207, 251
Walaskay, Paul 219
Wallace-Hadrill, Andrew 295
Walsh, Brian J. 296–98
Walton, Steve 220, 231
Watson, Francis 267–68, 270, 312
Wees, Hans van 61–62
Weinfeld, Moshe 16
Weiss, Johannes 353
Welborn, Laurence L. 91–92, 240, 323, 325, 328, 335
Wengst, Klaus 75, 289
West, Martin L. 61, 64–65
West, William C. 346
Westermann, Claus 20
Westfall, Cynthia Long 218
Wevers, John William 177
Williams, Rowan 337
Williamson, H. G. M. 25, 43
Wilson, Benjamin R. 228
Wilson, Bryan R. 101
Winter, Aloysius 313
Winter, Bruce W. 231, 348
Wöhrle, Jakob 37
Wolff, Hans Walter 38, 44–46
Wright, N. T. 3, 267, 285
Yadin, Yigael 117
Yakobson, Alexander 88

Yamazaki-Ransom, Kazuhiko 218, 230
Yates, John W. 275
Young, N. H. 272
Zampaglione, Gerardo 75
Ziccardi, Constantino A. 223

Printed in the USA
CPSIA information can be obtained
at www.ICGtesting.com
CBHW031428090624
9757CB00004B/67